# Marriages

of

# Orange County

# Virginia

## 1757-1880

Therese A. Fisher, A.G.

HERITAGE BOOKS
2020

# HERITAGE BOOKS
## AN IMPRINT OF HERITAGE BOOKS, INC.


**Books, CDs, and more—Worldwide**

For our listing of thousands of titles see our website
at
www.HeritageBooks.com


Published 2020 by
HERITAGE BOOKS, INC.
Publishing Division
5810 Ruatan Street
Berwyn Heights, Md. 20740

International Standard Book Number
Paperbound: 978-0-7884-3843-1

Orange County, Virginia was created from the western part of Spotsylvania County in January 1734/35. Orange's original western boundary was the Mississippi River. Augusta, (1738) Frederick (1738) Culpeper (1749) and Greene (1838) were all formed from Orange County. Germanna, created in 1714 by Governor Spotswood to mine his iron deposits was the first settlement in Orange, although many of the original German settlers of that county spread into other Virginia counties by 1726.

Orange County records are remarkably intact with the earliest marriages recorded in 1757. While saying the records are intact, that does not mean that every marriage ever performed in Orange County was recorded in the bonds, ministers returns and marriage licenses in the county courthouse. Fee books and deed books recorded some early marriages not recorded in the bonds and marriage register, but that is probably more of an indication of records that may exist among private papers that were never recorded in any county book. In its earliest days, Baptists were prevalent in the county but the ministers were often jailed and church members who allowed preaching by the Baptists in their homes brought into court for violating the policy of a state religion (the Episcopal). My suspicion is that numbers of marriages performed by the Baptist ministers were never recorded in the courthouse to protect the congregation members from persecution.

Researchers who do not find their known Orange County ancestors among the marriages recorded at the courthouse should check adjoining counties for that marriage. Until the 1990's, marriages were recorded in the county of the bride's residence. County boundaries have never been a deterrent to love or family alliances.

Abbreviations used most frequently in this book are;

OB      Orange County Marriage Bond
OM      Orange County Minister's Return or Marriage Register
OMB     Orange County Marriage Bond
OML     Orange County Marriage License
OMR     Orange County Marriage Register
POB     Place of Birth
POC     Person of Color
POM     Place of Marriage
POR     Place of Residence

dec'd   deceased
s       single (does not mean never married)
w       widowed
d/o     daughter of
s/o     son of

| r.r. | railroad (such as in r.r. hand or worker) |
|------|-------------------------------------------|
| Co   | County                                    |
| Co.  | County                                    |

Anything in brackets [ ] indicates that it was not in the original record but was added from other sources based on my research. Most frequent sources were the death records in the Orange County courthouse and data from the *William and Mary Quarterly* 1st and 2nd Series. All places are understood to be in Virginia unless otherwise specified.

If the researcher makes a comparison of the information in this marriage book with other books on the Orange County marriages, they are certain to note some differences. This is due more to poor transcription of the original creators of the Marriage Register than the people who transcribed the marriage register for publication. When the marriage register that was microfilmed and is currently in use at the Library of Virginia and the Family History Centers was created, whoever made the record was not as careful transcribing the information from the original marriage bonds, licenses and returns as we would expect and hope for in a transcriber. While the handwriting is beautiful, many errors and omissions occurred in names and dates, which was one of the main reasons I decided to create this book. In compiling the marriages, I utilized the original courthouse bonds, licenses and ministers' returns. Ulysses Joyner, the circuit court clerk at the time that I began this project, not only allowed me access to the records in his care, but specifically invited me to include the later marriage records in the book. Through his kindness and interest, I was able to compile a more complete and accurate record of the Orange County marriages than previously compiled. As a matter of fact, Mr. Joyner asked me to go well into the twentieth century with the marriages. However, I became so overwhelmed by the number of records, both later and that I missed in my previous books, that I had to stop in 1880, more from exhaustion than from lack of material.

While Mr. Joyner has now retired as the Orange County Clerk of the Circuit Court, his legacy of preservation and interest in the records will benefit Orange County and those who trace their ancestry back into Orange County for many years to come. I wish to state my gratitude to him and dedicate this book to him.


Therese Fisher A.G.


iv

# MINISTERS WHO LABORED IN ORANGE COUNTY
## AND THEIR RELIGIONS (when determined)

ABELL, Ephraim
ANDERSON, John - Presbyterian
ATKINSON, William R. - Presbyterian
AUGUST, R.F.
BARNETT, John _ Episcopalian
BARNETT, W.J. - Baptist
BEDINGER, Everett W. - Presbyterian
BENNETT, Bartlett - Baptist
BETTERMAN, S.M.
BILLINGSLEY, John A.
BINGHAM, George
BLAIR, H.
BLEDSOE, Aaron
BOGGS, Hugh - Episcopalian
BOOTEN, Ambrose C. - Baptist
BRIGGS, W.S.
BROADDASS, William F. - Baptist
BROWN, Daniel
BRUCE, Silas - Baptist
CALHOUN, William - Presbyterian
CAMPBELL, W.H.
CAMPER, W.H. - Baptist
CARPENTER, William Jr. - Lutheran
CARSON, Theo M.
CAVE, Robert C.
CHANCELLOR, Melzi S. - Baptist
CHANDLER, Jeremiah
CLEGHORN, Elisha B. - Presbyterian
COLE, John
COLEMAN, R.L.
CONNER, Lewis - Baptist
CONWAY, D.T.
COOK, J.B. - Baptist
CRAIG, Elijah - Baptist
CRAIG, John - Presbyterian
CRAWFORD, P.
CREEL, Benjamin - Baptist (pastor of Liberty Church)
CURRY, Albert B. - Presbyterian
CUTLER, L.A.

DABNEY, Robert L. - Presbyterian
DINWIDDIE, John C. - Presbyterian
DOHERTY, John - Catholic
DOUGLASS, William - Methodist
EARNEST, J. - Episcopalian
EVE, George - Baptist
EWING, Daniel B. - Presbyterian
FISHER, David
FRAZER, Herndon
FRENCH, J. A.
GARNETT, James - Baptist
GARRETT, John - Baptist
GEORGE, Cumberland - Baptist
GIBERNE, William - Episcopalian
GILLUM, Calmon
GIPSON, F.L.
GOING, Samuel - Baptist
GOODWIN, Hugh - Baptist
GORDON, John C.
GOSS, Hamilton - Baptist
GOSS, James
GOSS, John - Baptist
HAMPER, W.H.
HANDY, Isaac W. K. - Presbyterian
HANSBROUGH, J.S.
HATCHER, H.E. - Baptist
HAWKINS, E.P.
HAWKINS, Thomas R.
HAWLEY, William - Episcopalian
HERNDON, R.D.
HILL, William A. - Presbyterian
HITER, William G.
HOKE, Herbert M. - Methodist
HOPE, H.M.
HOUSTON, William W. - Presbyterian
HUGHES, Robert - Zion Hill Church
HULLUM, Duke W.
HUNSBURGER, Jacob - Baptist
JAMES, Daniel - Baptist
JOHNSON, C.T. - Baptist
JOHNSON, Lewis B. - Presbyterian
JOHNSON, Philip - Baptist
JONES, Robert - Baptist

JONES, William G.H. - Episcopalian
KABLER, Frederick - Lutheran
KENNEDY, Leroy (also listed as CANADY) - Baptist
LEE, William B.
LELAND, John
LINNEY, H.M.
LOCHNER, Lewis
MANSFIELD, John
MANSFIELD, Joseph .A. - Baptist
MARSHALL, Herbert - Episcopalian
MARSHALL, Mungo - Episcopalian
MARTIN, George
MARTIN, Thomas - Episcopalian
MARYE, James Jr. - Episcopalian
MASON, Sanders
MASON, William - Baptist
MAURY, Matthew - Episcopalian
MCCOWEN, J.W.
MCCUE, John - Presbyterian
MCGILL, John
MCGUIRE, Edward C. - Episcopal
MILLER, Alexander - Presbyterian
MOFFETT, Anderson - Baptist
MORRIS, George - possibly Baptist
NALLEY, George - Baptist
NEWMAN, George - Baptist
NICHOLS, Frank
O'NEIL, Charles - Episcopalian
PAINTER, Joseph C. - Presbyterian
PARKER, Dabney
PERRY, Elijah Richard - Evangelistic Christian
POLLOCK, Abraham D. - Presbyterian
PRESSLEY, J.H. - Baptist
PRICE, John
QUARLES, Charles
RAWLINGS, James M. - Presbyterian
RHOADES, P.S.
ROBERTS, James D.
ROBERTSON, John H.
ROBERTSON, W.E. - Baptist
ROBINSON, Willis - Baptist
SANDERS, Nathaniel - Baptist
SCOTT, C.R.

SEE, Charles S.M. - Presbyterian
SHIP, Edward G. - Baptist
SIMS, George - Baptist
SMITH, Benjamin M. - Presbyterian
SMITH, George A. - Episcopalian
SPERRY, Peter - Baptist
STEPHENS, Richard
STRICKLER, Givens B. - Presbyterian
STRIDER, John P. - Presbyterian
TATUM, Isham
TIBBS, Franklin - Baptist
TWIMAN, George - Baptist
VAUGHN, C.T. - Baptist
WADDELL, James - Presbyterian
WALKER, Thomas
WATTS, Jacob
WELCH, Oliver - Baptist
WHITE, Jacob
WILEY, Allen - Baptist
WILLIS, John C.
WILLIS, M.C.
WILLSON, James C. - Presbyterian
WINGATE, John - Episcopalian
WITHERS, James - Baptist
WOODSON, Robert R.

**ABEL**, Alexander & **ABEL**, Polly d/o Caleb ABEL POR Orange 3 Oct 1811 Joseph HILMAN surety (OB)

**ABEL**, John & **TINDER**, Margaret; 5 Oct 1777 by banns , both of St. Thomas Parish (OB)

**ABELL**, Alexander & **ABELL**, Polly d/o Caleb ABELL 3 Oct 1811 surety Joseph HILMAN (OB)

**ABELL**, John S. & **KING**, Sally; 30 Jul 1805 surety Caleb ABELL (OB)

**ABELL**, Richard S. & **HILMAN**, Sarah A. d/o Uriel HILMAN who is also surety 28 Apr 1817 (OB) 30 Apr 1817 by J.C. GORDON (OM)

**ABRAHAM**, Francis & **MALLORY**, Jestin 20 Nov 1804 surety Thomas PROCTOR (OB)

**ACRE**, James & **ACRE**, Elizabeth 21 Dec 1798 surety John MORRIS (OB)

**ACREE**, William & **MORRIS**, Rebecca 25 Dec 1804 by Hamilton GOSS (Misc Min Ret)

**ACREE**, William over 21 & **MORRIS**, Rebecca d/o John MORRIS also surety 24 Dec 1804 (OB)

**ADAMS**, Thomas B. Jr. s/o Thomas ADAMS & **TALIAFERRO**, Mary M. George G. TALIAFERRO guardian who is also surety 2 Oct 1833 (OB)

**ADAMS**, Benjamin of St. Thomas Parish & **COLEMAN**, Milly of St. Thomas Parish 7 April 1780 (OM) surety Lawrence EGBERT (OB)

**ADAMS**, Elisha & **SMITH**, Delia d/o James SMITH 22 Dec 1795 surety John ADAMS (OB)

**ADAMS**, Festus S. s/o Robert ADAMS and Mildred MASON age 19 s farmer POB POR Orange & **CHILDRESS**, Virginia C. d/o Giles R.CHILDRESS and Sarah PATTON age 18 s POB Spotsylvania POR Orange; POM Orange 6 Mar 1866 (OMR) 26 Feb 1866 (OML)

**ADAMS**, Jacob POC age 30 s POB POR Orange s/o John ADAMS and Matilda BURTON farm laborer & **HACKETT**, Lucy Mary POC age 18 s POB Madison Co POR Orange d/o Reuben HACKETT and Lucy GEE (?) 23 Dec 1869 POM Orange by Philip JOHNSON (OMR)

**ADAMS**, James & **HARPER**, Patsey 17 May 1810 surety Ellick HAWKINS (OB)

**ADAMS**, James POR St. Thomas Parish & **CHAMBERS**, Mary d/o Thomas CHAMBERS POR St. Thomas Parish 16 May 1782 surety George BLEDSOE (OB)

**ADAMS**, James POR St. Thomas Parish & **WELCH**, Eley POR St. Thomas Parish 3 May 1773 (OM)

**ADAMS**, John Albert POC age 32 s labourer POB POR Orange s/o John Albert and Matilda ADAMS & **JOHNSON**, Amy POC age 45 w POB POR Orange POM Little Zion, Orange 2 Oct 1878 by Willis ROBINSON (OMR)

1

**ADAMS**, John Q. s/o Robert ADAMS and Mildred MASON age 22 s farmer POB POR Orange & **BROOKING**, Lucy J. d/o Charles R.BROOKING and Susan SANDERS age 20 s POB POR Orange; POM Orange 15 Feb 1866 (OMR) 13 Feb 1866 (OML)

**ADAMS**, Robert & **MASON**, Mildred d/o George MASON 30 Jul 1833 surety Thomas TINDER (OB)

**ADAMS**, Thomas B. & **BURNLEY**, Judith d/o Frances BURNLEY 20 Jun 1807 surety William B. TAYLOR by Robert JONES (OB)(OM)

**ADAMS**, Thomas B. Jr. s/o Thomas B. ADAMS & **TALIAFERRO**, Mary M. ward of George G. TALIAFERRO who is also surety 2 Oct 1833 (OB)

**ADAMS**, Thomas J. & **OWENS**, Martha Ann 25 Sep 1847 surety Albert KENNEDY (OB)

**ADAMS**, Thompson & **BURRUS**, Martha Ann d/o Joseph BURRUS who is also surety 7 Mar 1839 surety Julius MUNDAY (OB)

**AERY**, George & **SHIFLETT**, Elizabeth; 17 Nov 1808 by George BINGHAM (OM)

**AERY**, William & **DAWSON**, Amandy d/o William H. DAWSON 7 Mar 1839 surety Leroy DAWSON (OB)

**AHART**, Abram Jr. s/o Abram AHART Sr. & **KIRK**, Judith 25 Mar 1793 surety George MCDANIEL (OB)

**AHART**, Jacob of St. Thomas Parish & **BRUCE**, Mary; of St. Thomas Parish 21 Sep 1777 by banns (OM)

**AHART**, John & **PEARSON**, Peggy d/o Robert PEARSON 12 Dec 1783 surety Galin WHITE (OB)

**AIRY**, William & **STOWERS**, Mary 16 Aug 1788 surety Lewis STOWERS (OB)

**ALCOCK**, Robert & **BELL**, Mary w 13 Jan 1786 surety James TAYLOR (OB)

**ALCOCK**, William & **BELL**, Catey 15 Mar 1785 surety James TAYLOR (OB)

**ALEXANDER**, Henry & **IRVIN**, Elizabeth 13 Oct 1828 surety William COLE (OB)

**ALEXANDER**, James & **AHART**, Franky; 14 Jun 1792 by George EVE (OM)

**ALEXANDER**, James H. POC age 35 w laborer POB Henrico POR New York City s/o James ALEXANDER and Hannah CLAYTON & **JONES**, Annie E. age 22 s POB POR Orange d/o Walter G. JONES and Catharine BROOKS POM Baptist Church, Orange 2 Nov 1876 by W.J. BARNETT (OMR)

**ALEXANDER**, James of St. Thomas Parish & **TOWNSEND**, Jerusa of St. Thomas Parish; 10 Apr 1776 by banns (OB)

**ALEXANDER**, James P. age 34 s POB Mifflin, PA POR Culpeper s/o James and Celia ALEXANDER farmer & **HALSEY**, Annie A. age 22 s POB POR Orange d/o Joseph J. HALSEY and Millie J. MORTON 4 Feb 1874 POM Orange (OMR)

**ALEXANDER**, Robert & **GRAY**, Mary Page 7 Jan 1846 surety Phillip MALLORY (OB)

**ALEXANDER**, Samuel D. & **BURRUS**, Anna 22 Dec 1816 by J. GOSS (OM)

**ALLEN**, Councel POC age 39 w POB Louisa Co POR Orange s/o George ALLEN and Patsy CARTER laborer & **PATRICK**, Tabby POC age 40 w POB POR Orange d/o George TIBBS and Lucy WALKER 6 Jan 1872 POM Orange by Frank TIBBS (OMR)

**ALLEN**, David W. s/o James ALLEN and Alexandria LONG age 36 s farmer POB Botetout Co POR Augusta Co & **WALLACE**, Martha A. d/o Jesse D.WALLACE and Ellen COCHRAN age 36 s POB Rockingham Co POR Orange; POM Orange C.H. 4 Sep 1863 (OMR) (OML)

**ALLEN**, Isreal POC age 23 s POB POR Orange s/o Julius ALLEN and Fanny _____ laborer & **BROWN**, Susan POC age 22 s POB POR Orange d/o George BROWN and Esther _____ 27 Dec 1872 POM Orange by F.L. GIPSON (OMR)

**ALLEN**, James & **WOOLFOLK**, Patsy; 23 Sep 1787 surety Thomas WOOLFOLK Jr. (OB)

**ALLEN**, James s/o J. Tanner ALLEN and Anna ALLEN age 25 s servant POB POR Orange POC & **BRAMHAM**, Laura d/o Giles BRAMHAM age 22 s POB POR Orange POC; POM Orange 2 Nov 1867 (OMR) 1 Nov 1867 (OML)

**ALLEN**, John & **HEAD**, Sarah; 22 Dec 1808 by Jacob WATTS (OM)

**ALLEN**, John F. s/o John and Almira ALLEN age 33 s teacher POB Sandisfield, Mass POR Henry Co, Alabama & **ATKINS**, Eliza F. d/o Joseph and Mary ATKINS age 25 s POB POR Orange; POM Orange 20 Aug 1857 (OMR) (OML)

**ALLEN**, Pounce POC age 35 s POB Louisa Co POR Orange s/o George ALLEN and Patty CARTER laborer & **TAYLOR**, Betsey age 27 w POB POR Orange d/o Tom JOHNSON and Mary JACKSON DOM 22 Aug 1869 POM Orange by Frank TIBBS (OMR)

**ALLEN**, Thomas POC age 25 s labourer POB POR Orange s/o John T. ALLEN and Amanda SAMUAL & **WALKER**, Eliza Ann POC age 24 s POB POR Orange d/o Michael WALKER and Sarah GRYMES POM Orange 9 May 1878 by John S. HANSBROUGH (OMR)

**ALLEN**, William & **TURNER**, Ann M. 20 Nov 1848 surety David HUME (OB) 21 Nov 1848 by J. EARNEST (OM)

**ALLEN**, William & **TURNER**, Ann M. 20 Nov 1848 surety David HUME (OB)

**ALLEN**, William & **TURNER**, Anna M. 21 Nov 1848 by J. ERNEST (OM)

**ALLEN**, William & **WALLACE**, Elizabeth d/o James WALLACE who is also surety 12 Aug 1801 (OB) 13 Aug 1801 (OM)

**ALLEN**, William POC age 23 s labourer POB POR Orange s/o Julius and Fanny ALLEN & **RANDOLPH**, Margaret POC age 21 s POB POR Orange d/o James RANDOLPH and Nelly HERNDON POM Nazareth Baptist Church, Orange 27 Dec 1878 by Willis ROBINSON (OMR)

**ALLEN**, William POC age 35 s farm laborer POB Henrico POR Orange s/o Anderson ALLEN and Adeline ROBINSON & **FRAZER**, Judy POC age 30 w POB Gloucester POR Orange POM Orange Mar 1876 (OMR)

**ALLISON**, John William s/o Robert and Maria Allison age 20 s spinning POB Culpeper POR Orange & **SMITH**, Jane d/o Harris and Susan SMITH age 21 s POB Stafford POR Orange; POM Orange 17 Aug 1854 (OMR)

**ALMOND**, John F. & **ROBINSON**, Mary Ann permission by Thomas ROBINSON 20 Jan 1834 surety Hansford T. SANDERS (OB)

**ALMOND**, Lewis & **JONES**, Susan C. d/o James JONES 8 Nov 1847 surety James MASON (OB)

**ALSOP**, William P. & **HAMILTON**, Margaret D. d/o James HAMILTON who is also surety 19 Sep 1843 (OB) 22 Sep 1843 by L.L. FOX (OM)

**ALVIS**, Henry & **ARMSTRONG**, Agnes; 19 Oct 1798 by George BINGHAM (OM)

**AMFIELD**, John & **FRANKLIN**, Martha R. POB Sumner Co., TN d/o John and Eliz. FRANKLIN 16 Nov 1834 surety James G. BLAKEY (OB)

**AMOS**, Charles & **MITCHELL**, Elisabeth d/o William MITCHELL 30 Dec 1833 surety Martin BREEDLOVE (OB)

**AMOS**, Jackson s/o Estes AMOS and Mary DARNELL age 35 s miller POB POR Madison Co & **DARNELL**, Frances d/o Fielding DARNELL age 34 w POB Madison Co POR Orange; POM Orange 23 Jul 1865 (OMR) 14 Jul 1865 (OML)

**AMOS**, Joseph & **MARR**, Ann; 18 Apr 1798 surety Alexander MARR (OB)

**AMOS**, William M. & **DANIEL**, Tempy 31 Dec 1824 surety William ACRE (OB) 4 Jan 1825 by J. GOSS (OM)

**AMOS**, Wirter & **DARNELL**, Mary 26 Dec 1831 surety Rice DARNELL (OB) 27 Dec 1831 by J. GOSS (OM)

4

**AMUS**, Benjamin & **ACRE**, Nancy; 26 Feb 1796 surety William ACRE (OB)

**ANCELL**, Henry & **BEAZLEY**, Nancy 28 Dec 1801 surety Richard WILLIAMS (OB) 31 Dec 1801 by Hamilton GOSS (OM)

**ANCELL**, James & **ESTIS**, Frances 31 Dec 1815 surety Edmund ESTIS by George BINGHAM (OB) (OM)

**ANCELL**, Michael & **WILIAMS**, Nancy d/o Joseph WILLIAMS who is also surety 23 Dec 1816 (OB)

**ANCELL**, Robert & **PERESON**, Frances 6 Sep 1804 by George BINGHAM (Misc Min Ret)

**ANCELL**, Robert over 21 & **PERESON**, Frances over 21; 27 Aug 1804 surety Thomas COX (OB)

**ANDERSON**, Augustine s/o Obediah ANDERSON & **ANDERSON**, Margaret d/o Joel ANDERSON 15 Dec 1827 surety Yancey POWELL (OB)

**ANDERSON**, Benjamin over 21 & **MILLER**, Mary d/o John MILLER who is also surety 14 Oct 1807 by George BINGHAM (OM) (OB)

**ANDERSON**, Charles W. age 23 s blacksmith POB POR Nelson s/o John W. ANDERSON and Sarah J. RHOADES & **COOPER**, Bettie W. age 22 s POB POR Orange d/o William J. COOPER and Sarah BROOKMAN POM Orange 26 Aug 1879 by Charles P. SCOTT (OMR)

**ANDERSON**, George age 32 s POB Albemarle Co POR Orange s/o Jack ANDERSON and Frances _____ laborer & **BARBOUR**, C. Ella age 17 s POB POR Orange d/o Phil BARBOUR and Nancy ROSE 15 Aug 1869 POM Orange by Philip JOHNSON (OMR)

**ANDERSON**, Jacob POC age 22 s farm labourer POB POR Orange s/o Billy HENDERSON and Bettie HENDERSON & **PORTER**, Rose POC age 18 s POB POR Orange d/o Moses PORTER and Pallas TRIBLINGS POM Mt. Pleasant Church, Orange 24 Aug 1878 by C.T. JOHNSON (OMR)

**ANDERSON**, James B. age 21 s POB Madison POR Alexandria s/o John T. ANDERSON and Molisie WAYMAN railroading & **BRADLEY**, Jennie M. age 18 s POB Alexandria POR Orange d/o John H. BRADLEY and Jane W. SMILLET 30 Nov 1880 POM Gordonsville, Orange by P. DONOHOE (OMR)

**ANDERSON**, James M. & **SOUTHERLAND**, Eliza d/o John SOUTHERLAND ward of Richard RICHARDS 30 Oct 1848 surety James SOUTHERLAND (OB)

**ANDERSON**, James W. s/o Henry ANDERSON and Martha GAINES age 26 s printer POB Franklin Co. GA POR Covington, GA & **BICKERS**, Henrietta S. d/o William H.BICKERS and Elizabeth HAWKINS age 23

s POB POR Orange; POM Orange 21 Jan 1866 (OMR) 19 Jan 1866
(OML)

ANDERSON, Joel & **REDDISH**, Lucy; 30 May 1805 by George
BINGHAM (OM)

ANDERSON, John & **LOWER**, Nancy 28 Nov 1815 by George
BINGHAM (OMR)

ANDERSON, John s/o Jacob ANDERSON & **LOWER**, Nancy d/o
Michael LOWER 27 Nov 1815 surety Thomas TERRILL (OB)

ANDERSON, Joseph s/o Obediah ANDERSON & **ANDERSON**,
Elizabeth d/o Joel ANDERSON 11 Apr 1826 surety Peter MARSH
(OB)

ANDERSON, Nathan D. & **BELL**, Milley; 24 Oct 1798 surety Thomas
BELL (OB)

ANDERSON, Washington POC age 21 s POB Albemarle Co POR Orange
s/o Jack ANDERSON and Frances _____ steam mill hand &
**WINSTON**, Catherine POC age 21 w POB Greene Co POR Orange
d/o Prudence _____ 27 Dec 1872 POM Orange by Frank TIBBS
(OMR)

ANDERSON, William & **HAWKINS**, Lucy 25 May 1809 by Jeremiah
CHANDLER (OM)

ANDERSON, William & **HAWKINS**, Lucy d/o Reubin HAWKINS 22
May 1809 surety Benjamin SANDERS (OB)

ANDERSON, William POC age 23 s POB POR Orange s/o Nelson TATE
and Malvina TATE laborer & **JACKSON**, Eliza POC age 18 s POB
POR Orange d/o Nathaniel JACKSON and Sarah JACKSON 10 Apr
1870 POM Orange by Frank TIBBS (OMR)

APPERSON, Alfred & **JONES**, Melinda d/o James JONES who is also
surety 3 Sep 1836 (OB)

APPERSON, Cincinnatus age 28 s POB Orange POR Georgia s/o Alfred
APPERSON and Malinda JONES tanner & **TINSLEY**, Susan A. s
POB POR Orange d/o Edward TINSLEY and Lucy Ann ROACH 29
Dec 1869 POM Orange by Melzi S. CHANCELLOR (OMR)

APPERSON, Jos. age 58 w POB Spotsylvania Co POR Orange s/o Peter
APPERSON and Frances LOBB (or LABB) farmer & **TINDER**,
Margaret age 42 w POB Culpeper Co POR Orange d/o John
BLEDSOE and Peggy PERRY 24 Jun 1869 POM Orange by Sanders
MASON (OMR)

APPERSON, Joseph permission by Alfred APPERSON who is also surety
& **PERRY**, Lucinda 13 Jan 1834 (OB)

APPERSON, Thomas & **PALMER**, Eliney 30 Nov 1830 surety Willis
OVERTON (OB)

APPISON, Richard & **FISHER**, Susan d/o James FISHER who is also
surety 14 Nov 1831 (OB)

**ARHART**, Jacob & **BALLARD**, Nanny; 21 Dec 1773 both of St. Thomas Parish (OB)

**ARMISTEAD**, Lewis age 21 s POB POR Orange s/o Samuel ARMISTEAD and Hannah ARMISTEAD farm laborer & **DADE**, Agnes age 22 s POB POR Orange d/o Patsy DADE 11 Dec 1869 POM Orange by I.W.K. HANDY (OMR)

**ARNALL**, William B. & **MARTIN**, Jane d/o William H. MARTIN who is also surety 9 Sept 1809 (OB) 10 Sept 1809 (OM)

**ARNOLD**, James & **ATKINS**, Elizabeth 8 Feb 1790 surety James ATKINS (OB)

**ARNOLD**, Thomas & **SANFORD**, Peggy 28 Jan 1802 POM Orange by Robert JONES (Misc Min Ret)

**ARNOLD**, Thomas & **SANFORD**, Peggy; 27 Jan 1802 surety Pierce SANFORD (OB)

**ARNOLD**, William B. & **MARTIN**, Jane 9 Sep 1809 surety William H. MARTIN (OB)10 Sep 1809 by Robert JONES (OMR)

**ARNOLD**, Willis & **GOLDEN**, Margaret over 21; 23 Jul 1804 surety Julien KING (OB)

**ASHTON**, Henry age 25 s POB West Indies POR Culpeper s/o Henry ASHTON and Grace BELL farmer & **PARKER**, Annie E. age 25 s POB POR Orange d/o William PARKER & Mary ROLLINS 22 Nov 1871 POM Orange by H.E. HATCHER (OMR)

**ATKINS**, Achilles & **GROOM**, Elizabeth 6 Apr 1826 surety Solomon GROOM (OB)

**ATKINS**, B.F. age 21 s POB POR Orange s/o Henry C. ATKINS and Maria L. LAYTON hewer & **NEWMAN**, Mildred E. age 22 s POB POR Orange d/o Reuben NEWMAN and Mary J. CLARK 24 Aug 1870 POM Orange by Thomas R. HAWKINS (OMR)

**ATKINS**, Charles D. & **EVANS**, Mary d/o John W. EVANS 23 Jun 1845 Andrew GAINES surety (OB)26 Jun 1845 by Joseph S. JACKSON (OMR)

**ATKINS**, Davis & **MALLORY**, Alice 27 May 1822 surety Joseph EDWARDS (OB)

**ATKINS**, Dickinson s/o Gentry ATKINS who is also surety & **ATKINS**, Margaret 28 Oct 1823 (OB)

**ATKINS**, Edward & **WISDOM** Frankie; 25 Jan 1780 of St. Thomas Parish surety Joseph ATKINS (OB)

**ATKINS**, Gentry & **CHILES**, Frankey; 24 Dec 1801 surety Wisdon ATKINS (OM)

**ATKINS**, Henry C. age 56 s POB POR Orange s/o Gentry ATKINS and Fanny CHILDS farmer & **LAYTON**, Maria L. age 50 POB POR Orange by Thos. R. HAWKINS (OMR)

**ATKINS**, Hezekiah & **CHILES**, Sally; 23 Nov 1788 surety James CHILES (OB)

**ATKINS**, Hezekiah & **HORD**, Polly d/o Daniel HORD who is also surety 14 Oct 1828 (OB)

**ATKINS**, James & **KINZER**, Elizabeth 23 Jun 1829 surety C.F. KINZER (OB)

**ATKINS**, James & **PIGG**, Anny both of St. Thomas Parish 29 Apr 1777 by banns (OB)

**ATKINS**, James & **POE**, Elizabeth; 6 Apr 1792 surety John SMITH (OB)(OM)

**ATKINS**, James Jr. & **ATKINS**, Fanny; 22 Nov 1803 surety Wisdon ATKINS (OB)

**ATKINS**, John & **BURRASS**, Ann d/o Edmund BURRASS 9 Feb 1778 surety Joseph ATKINS (OB) 11 Feb 1778 (OM)

**ATKINS**, John & **CAMPBELL** Peggy; 20 Dec 1806 Peggy's guardian, William TATUM of Albemarle Co. is surety (OB)

**ATKINS**, John s/o Walter ATKINS & **WEBB**, Susan 27 Oct 1823 surety William T. BURRUSS who is also guardian by Rev. George MORRIS (OB) (OMR)

**ATKINS**, Jonathan & **QUISENBERRY**, Milly d/o George QUISENBERRY 7 Feb 1813 (OM)

**ATKINS**, Joseph & **ATKINS**, Ann 9 Jan 1787 surety John ATKINS Jr. (OB)

**ATKINS**, Joseph & **JAMES**, Milly; 22 Sept 1775 both of St. Thomas Parish (OB)

**ATKINS**, Malachi & **MONTAGUE**, Sally; 7 Jun 1797 surety Roger BELL (OB)

**ATKINS**, Robert H. age 23 s POB POR Orange s/o Henry C. ATKINS and Maria L. LAYTON farmer & **PEARCE**, Phillippa age 21 s POB POR Orange d/o John PEARCE and Amanda TAMPLIN 20 Jul 1880 POM Orange by W.H. CAMPER (OMR)

**ATKINS**, Robert POC age 24 s POB Louisa POR Orange s/o Rosa _____ r.r. hand & **NICHOLAS**, Bettie POC age 22 s POB Louisa POR Orange d/o Frank NICHOLAS and Nancy _____ 28 Oct 1880 POM Gordonsville, Orange by C.T. VAUGHAN (OMR)

**ATKINS**, Silence & **JENNINGS**, Frances d/o John JENNINGS 1 Mar 1786 surety Luke JENNINGS (OB)

**ATKINS**, Waller over 21 & **ATKINS**, Sally over 21; 16 Jan 1803 surety James MORTON (OM)

**ATKINS**, William & **BRIANT**, Wintifred 4 Feb 1777 by banns (OMR)

**ATKINS**, William C. & **BUSICK**, Martha Ann d/o Samuel BUSICK 26 Mar 1835 surety John S. KING who is also guardian (OB)

ATKINS, William G. & NEWMAN, Elizabeth 25 Jan 1849 by Richard
STEPHENS surety Reuben NEWMAN (OMR)
ATKINS, William Henry age 21 S POB POR Orange s/o Charles D.
ATKINS & Mary EVANS farmer & LAYTON, Lucy A. age 25 S POB
POR Orange d/o James NELSON & Maria L. LAYTON DOM 31 Dec
1868 POM Orange by Thos. R. HAWKINS (OMR)
ATKINS, Wisdom & ATKINS, Nancy over 21; 24 Oct 1800 (OM)
ATKINS, Wisdom & ATKINS, Nancy; 24 Sep 1800 surety Edward
ATKINS (OB)
ATKINSON, Thomas & SYLVIE, Sally d/o Sarah SILBY 19 Jan 1802
surety Bernard ATKINSON (OB)
AUSBUM, Robert & CUDDEN, Milly; 27 Feb 1775 both of St. Thomas
Parish (OB)
AUSTIN, David & WILLIAMS, Fanny 27 Dec 1810 by Jacob WATTS
(OM)
AUSTIN, David s/o Nancy AUSTIN of Albemarle & WILLIAMS, Fanny
d/o John WILLIAMS 22 Dec 1810 surety James BEAZLEY (OB)
AUSTIN, John, & BURRUS, Justina; 24 Dec 1807 by George BINGHAM
(OM)
AUSTIN, Richard & SNOW, Mary; 25 Dec 1804 by George BINGHAM
(OM)
AUSTIN, Richard D. & MANSFIELD, Susannah W. 18 Dec 1826 surety
Joseph A. MANSFIELD (OB)
AUSTIN, Samuel G. s/o William AUSTIN and Susan THOMPSON age 29
s farmer POB POR Orange & BOND, Lucy A. d/o Joseph BOND and
Mildred WHITLOCK age 24 s POB Louisa POR Orange; POM Orange
23 Feb 1863 (OMR) 21 Feb 1863 (OML)
AUSTIN, William & THOMPSON, Susan 5 Feb 1833 surety James G.
LINDSAY (OB)
AUSTIN, Willis & MELONE, Jane 18 Aug 1823 surety James MELONE
(OB)
BABER, Robert & SPRADLING, Nancy d/o David SPRADLING 17 Dec
1782 (Orange Consent) 9 Jun 1797 surety William BARTON (OB)
BÄECKMAN, John & HANCOCK, Rebecca d/o William HANCOCK 24
Jun 1809 (OB)
BAILES, Joseph & OLLIVER, Cency d/o Frances OLLIVER 14 Oct
1807 surety David OLLIVER (OB)
BAILES, Joseph & OLLIVER, Cency; 16 Oct 1807 by Jacob WATTS
(OM)
BAILEY, Edward D. age 23 s farmer POB POR Culpeper s/o Samuel
BAILEY and Martha PARKS & RICHARDS, Mary E.W. age 22 s
POB POR Orange d/o Robinson C. RICHARDS and Elizabeth
TINDER POM Orange 25 Dec 1877 (OMR)

9

BAILEY, Lewis & MALLORY, Lucy; 18 Nov 1801 by George
  BINGHAM (OM)
BAILEY, Samuel & PURKS, Martha; POM Orange 3 Feb 1853 (OMR) 1
  Feb 1853 (OML)
BAILEY, William P. & GRIMES, Mary L. 21 years old 28 Oct 1800
  surety Garnett PEYTON (OB) (OM)
BAILY, James & MALLORY, Nancy; 2 Jun 1805 by George BINGHAM
  (OM)
BAKER, Linneaus M. age 21 s POB POR Louisa s/o Joseph M. BAKER
  and Louisa M. MANSFIELD farmer & BURRUSS, Kate H. age 21 s
  POB POR Orange d/o Robert B. BURRUSS and Ann E. GRAVES 27
  Apr 1880 POM Orange by L.A. CUTLER (OMR)
BAKER, Thomas S. s/o William and Lucinda BAKER age 31 s farmer
  POB POR Louisa Co & DAVIS, Maria Jane d/o William J. and
  Elizabeth DAVIS s POB POR Orange; POM Orange 25 May 1858
  (OMR) 21 May 1858 (OML)
BALLARD, David C. & HUCKSTEP, Elizabeth POR Orange John
  HUCKSTEP consent 26 Aug 1811 Isaac GOODALL surety (OB)
BALLARD, Elias W. s/o Edward and Lora A. BALLARD age 20 s farmer
  POB Louisa Co POR Orange & CLARK, Mildred d/o William and
  Lucy CLARK age 30 s POB POR Orange; POM Orange 22 Apr 1856
  (OMR) 14 Apr 1856 (OML)
BALLARD, Larkin & GAINES, Elizabeth d/o Sally GAINES 13 Jan 1786
  surety Curtis BALLARD (OB)
BALLARD, Medley & DEHONEY, Jane d/o Thomas & Hannah
  DEHONEY; 25 Dec 1797 surety Uriah ANDERSON (OB)
BALLARD, Thomas & SMITH, Elizabeth both of St. Thomas Parish 8
  Mar 1778 by banns (OB)
BALLARD, Washing & THORNHILL, Elizabeth; 5 Oct 1802 by George
  BINGHAM (OM)
BALLARD, William & SNOW, Mary; 7 Mar 1795 by George
  BINGHAM (OM)
BALLARD, William S. s/o Edwin BALLARD and Lora Ann HARRIS age
  21 s farmer POB POR Orange & SCHYLER, Mary E. d/o William
  SCHYLER and Mary A. SOVILL age 25 s POB POR Orange; POM
  Orange 16 Oct 1866 (OMR) 8 Oct 1866 (OML)
BALMAINE, Alexander & TAYLOR, Lucy d/o Erasmus TAYLOR 30
  Oct 1786 surety Francis TAYLOR (OB) 31 Oct 1786 at St. Thomas
  Parish (papers of Rev. J. EARNEST)
BANKHEAD, Charles L. s/o Charles S. and Mary Ann BANKHEAD age
  22 s farmer POB Albemarle Co POR Orange & BANKHEAD, Mary
  C. d/o William and Dorothea BANKHEAD age 23 s POB Caroline
  POR Orange; POM Orange 26 Sep 1855 (OMR) 25 Sep 1855 (OML)

**BANKS**, Gerard James s/o Adam BANKS of Madison Co. & **DAVIS**, Ann 17 Jan 1805 by George BINGHAM (OM)

**BANKS**, John POC age 21 s labourer POB POR Orange s/o Sampson BANKS and Harriet BROWN & **STEARNS**, Lizzie age 18 s POB POR Orange d/o James STEARNS POM Mt. Calvary Church, Orange 19 May 1878 by W.J. BARNETT (OMR)

**BARBER**, Thomas & **TAYLOR**, Mary; 22 Mar 1787 surety James TAYLOR (OB)

**BARBOUR**, Ambrose of Bromfield Parish & **THOMAS**, Catherine of St. Thomas Parish 24 Sep 1773 (OB)

**BARBOUR**, James & **JOHNSON**, Lucy; 15 Oct 1795 surety James TAYLOR Jr. (OB) 20 Oct 1795 by George EVE (OM)

**BARBOUR**, Philip C.S. & **POLLOCK**, Peggy d/o William POLLOCK 28 Nov 1808 surety John MOORE (OB) 29 Nov 1808 by Robert JONES (OM)

**BARBOUR**, Philip D. POR Kentucky & **NEWMAN**, Fanny B. d/o James NEWMAN; POM Orange 11 Mar 1852 (OMR) 8 Mar 1852 (OML)

**BARBOUR**, Philip P. & **JOHNSON**, Frances T. 4 Oct 1804 by Hamilton GOSS (Misc Min Ret)

**BARBOUR**, Philip Pendleton & **JOHNSON**, Frances T.; 24 Sep 1804 surety Thomas BARBOUR (OB) 4 Oct 1804 by Hamilton GOSS (OM)

**BARBOUR**, Richard & **MOORE**, Mary; 22 Mar 1796 surety Thomas BARBOUR Jr. (OB)(OM)

**BARBOUR**, Thomas & **THOMAS**, Mary; Jul 1771 (OM)

**BARKER**, James & **MAZE**, Sarah w 12 Jul 1791 surety William RUMSEY by Nathaniel SANDERS (OM)

**BARKER**, Leonard & **ROBINSON**, Keturah d/o Francis ROBINSON 29 Jan 1810 surety Jesse WEBB by Jeremiah CHANDLER (OB) (OM)

**BARKSDALE**, Nathaniel & **DOUGLAS**, Anne; 24 Sep 1772 both of St. Thomas Parish (OB)

**BARNES**, Edward age 25 s POB POR Orange s/o Lewis BARNES laborer & **ROBINSON**, Hannah age 21 s POB POR Orange d/o Charles ROBINSON 7 Jan 1869 POM Orange by H.M. LINNEY (OMR)

**BARNETT**, William & **CARRER**, Elizabeth; 1771 (Orange Memo Book)

**BARNETT**, William J. POC age 38 w POB Africa POR Orange s/o John BARNETT and Sarah BARNETT minister & **DUKE**, Mary A. POC age 24 s POB Greene POR Orange d/o Isaac DUKE and Ellen DUKE 18 Mar 1880 POM Gordonsville, Orange by D. PARKER (OMR)

**BARRETT**, Patrick & **BRIDWELL**, 23 Nov 1819 surety Edward HOLDAY (OB)

**BARTLETT**, Thomas & **URQUHART**, Elizabeth 24 Jan 1831 surety Peter R. JOHNSON (OB) 1 Feb 1831 by William HITER (OM)

11

**BARTLEY**, Nathan T. age 25 s POB Louisa Co. POR Orange s/o Oliver BARTLEY and Elizabeth D. GILLAM miller & **TINSLEY**, Sarah B. age 27 s POB POR Orange d/o Edw. TINSLEY and Lucy A. ROACH 13 Feb 1868 POM Orange by Sanders MASON (OMR)

**BARTON**, John & **MAY**, Milly 27 Jul 1807 surety Joel MAY by Nathaniel SANDERS (OB) (OM)

**BATES**, Abram POC age 27 farm laborer POB POR Orange s/o Gloucester BATES and Martha BARBOUR & **KENNY** Susan POC age 25 s POB Louisa POR Orange d/o Ben KENNY and Barbara _____ POM Orange 15 Jan 1876 (OMR)

**BATES**, Ned POC age 25 s laborer POB POR Orange s/o Gloucester BATES and Martha WASHINGTON & **NEWMAN**, Lucy POC age 20 s POB POR Orange d/o Reuben NEWMAN and Julia BOLLS POM Orange 29 Dec 1876 (OMR)

**BATLEY**, Alford & **WRIGHT**, Mishel of age 26 Feb 1810 surety Thomas A.DEMPSEY (OB)

**BATTAILE**, James R. s/o Richard BATTAILE and Mary WRIGHT age 28 s saddler POB POR Orange & **NEWMAN**, Jane E. d/o Morris D. NEWMAN and Mary A.TATUM age 21 s POB Madison POR Orange; POM Orange 27 Jul 1865 (OMR) 25 Jul 1865 (OML)

**BATTAILE**, Lawrence & **TALIAFERRO**, Ann Hay 9 Jun 1790 surety James TAYLOR (OB)

**BATTLE**, Alfred & **JONES**, Polley 27 Oct 1823 surety Fielding JONES (OB)

**BAUGHAN**, Richard A. age 40 s POB Louisa CO POR Orange s/o John BAUGHAN and Mary SNELSON carpenter & **SHEPHERD**, Elizabeth M.I. age 22 s POB Albemarle Co POR Orange d/o C.R. SHEPHERD and Mildred A. MAHANES 13 Dec 1869 POM Orange by J.W. MCCORAN (OMR)

**BAUKERAND**, Jacob & **DAVIS**, Poly 2 Jan 1823 by George BINGHAM (OM)

**BAXTER**, James & **PAYNE**, Sally; 31 Jul 1812 (OB)

**BAYLOR**, William M. age 25 s POB POR Augusta Co s/o Jacob BAILEY and Rebecca HULL carpenter & **KINZER**, Mildred C. age 23 s POB POR Orange d/o John KINZER and Eunice POINDEXTER 24 Oct 1872 POM Orange by L.A. CUTLER (OMR)

**BEACH**, Bailey & **VAUGHN**, Nancy d/o James VAUGHN who is also surety 12 Jan 1793 (OB)

**BEACH**, Henry & **TRUE**, Delila d/o Martin TRUE 21 Dec 1803 surety Joseph BEACH (OB) 27 Dec 1803 by William CALHOUN (OM)

**BEADLES**, James & **WINSLOW**, Elizabeth surety Edward WINSLOW 15 Nov 1817 (OB)

**BEADLES**, John Jr. & **HAYNES**, Lucinda d/o Jasper HAYNES 17 Dec 1810 surety Robert M. BEADLES (OB)

**BEADLES**, Robert M. & **WINSLOW**, Sarah of age, 5 Feb 1807 surety Fortunatus WINSLOW (OB)

**BEADLES**, William & **MILLER**, Lurenna permission from Thomas MILLER 29 Mar 1824 surety William MILLER (OB)

**BEALE**, Charles & **GORDON**, Mary d/o Nathan GORDON surety Livingston WADDELL 15 Feb 1820 (OB) 18 Feb 1820 by William J. ARMSTRONG (OM)

**BEALE**, Charles W. & **BAKER**, Clementine V. surety R.H. MOSBY 17 Oct 1848 (OB)

**BEALE**, John G. s/o John G.BEALE and Eliza DIGGS age 22 s farmer POB POR Fauquier Co & **GORDON**, Susan V. d/o Reuben L.GORDON and Eliza BEALE age 20 s POB Albemarle Co POR Orange; POM Orange 27 Nov 1867 (OMR) 18 Nov 1867 (OML)

**BEALE**, Richard and **WILLIS**, Elizabeth 1 Jan 1753 (Orange Fee Book)

**BEALE**, William Jr. & **GORDON**, Hannah d/o John & Hannah GORDON sister of James GORDON Jr. 30 Mar 1786 surety John GORDON (OB)

**BEALLE**, Richard H. age 41 s POB Berkley Co. POR Albemarle Co. s/o Richard BEALL and Jane BLAKE miller & **COLLINS**, Elizabeth A. age 35 s POB Louisa Co. POR Orange d/o William O. COLLINS and Nancy COPPAGE 12 Jul 1869 POM Orange by Herndon FRAZER (OMR)

**BEASLEY**, Bennett & **BRYAN**, Mary; 24 Jul 1797 surety Jeremiah BRYAN, Edward BRYAN consents (OB)

**BEASLEY**, John s/o Augustine BEASLEY & **EAVES**, Sally d/o William EAVES who is also surety 8 Jun 1791 (OB) 9 Jun 1791 by Nathaniel SANDERS (OM)

**BEAZLEY**, Charles & **WAIT**, Elizabeth; 1 Oct 1792 surety William PHILIPS (OB) 30 Oct 1792 by George EVE (OM)

**BEAZLEY**, James E. age 29 s farmer POB POR Greene s/o R.S. BEAZLEY and Sarah E. EASLEY & **GRAVES**, Eddie W. age 21 s POB POR Orange d/o James W. GRAVES and Sarah J. GRAVES POM Orange 18 Feb 1879 by L.A. CUTLER (OMR)

**BEAZLEY**, John & **PORTER**, Lucy d/o Abner PORTER 18 Dec 1802 (OB) 23 Dec 1802 by Jacob WATTS (Misc Min Ret)

**BEAZLEY**, Valentine & **POWELL**, Franky d/o Joice POWELL 21 Jun 1803 (OB) 30 Jun 1803 (OM)

**BEAZLEY**, William & **POWELL**, Betsy d/o Benjamin POWELL 25 Dec 1797 (OB) (OM)

**BEAZLEY**, William s/o Charles BEAZLEY & **GRAVES**, Susan aka Susanna d/o Thomas GRAVES POR Orange 25 Nov 1811 Edmund ROW surety (OB) by Jeremiah CHANDLER (OM)

**BECKET**, Richard & **KEA**, Jemima 3 Jan 1815 by George BINGHAM (OM)

**BECKETT**, Richard & **THORNHILL**, Nancy; 26 Dec 1805 by George BINGHAM (OM)

**BECKHAM**, Abner & **THOMAS**, Frances d/o Elizabeth THOMAS 21 Dec 1791 (OB) (OM)

**BECKHAM**, Benjamin & **PORTER**, Mary Ann d/o John PORTER 23 May 1811 Dabney C. MORRIS surety (OB)

**BECKHAM**, Benjamin & **PORTER**, Nancy C. 9 Mar 1824 surety Benjamin F. PORTER 10 Mar 1824 by J. GOSS (OM)

**BECKHAM**, James & **CANADAY**, Sarah 29 Jan 1840 surety Edward CANADAY (OB)

**BECKHAM**, Philip S. age 27 s POB Jefferson Co. POR Orange s/o Fountain BECKHAM and Ann STEPHENSON merchant & **BECKHAM**, Annie age 24 s POB POR Orange d/o James BECKHAM and Sarah KENNEDY 9 Jan 1868 POM Orange by J.W. McCOWN (OMR)

**BECKMAN**, John & **HANCOCK**, Rebecca d/o William HANCOCK 24 Jun 1809 surety William HANCOCK 25 Jun 1809 by Robert JONES (OM)

**BEEDLE**, John & **CASSEN**, Elizabeth; 16 Mar 1777 (OB)

**BEESLEY**, Valentine & **POWELL**, Frankey 30 Jun 1803 by George BINGHAM (Misc Min Ret)

**BELFIELD**, Henry & **KIRTLEY**, Elizabeth 13 Feb 1802 by George BINGHAM (OM)

**BELL**, Brockman & **BROCKMAN**, Rebecca d/o John BROCKMAN 17 Sep 1810 (OB) (OM)

**BELL**, Francis K. s/o William BELL and Fanny BOSTON & **POWELL**, Mary d/o William L. POWELL who is also surety 23 Feb 1831 (OB)

**BELL**, Granville s/o John B. BELL and Mary BROCK age 28 s farmer POB POR Orange & **WRIGHT**, Sally Ann d/o Dabney WRIGHT and Jane M. ESTES age 26 POB Louisa Co POR Orange; POM Orange 7 Mar 1867 (OMR) 4 Mar 1867 (OML)

**BELL**, Henry & **ADKINS**, Susanna probably d/o John and Nancy ADKINS 19 Sep 1796 (OM) (OB)

**BELL**, Henry C. & **BULLOCK**, Sophia 1 Oct 1849 surety John M. BAKER (OB)

**BELL**, Henry C. & **KENDALL**, Elizabeth Ann 5 Dec 1837 surety Robert KINDELL (OB)

**BELL**, Jacob & **TALIAFERRO**, Martha H. d/o Ann TALIAFERRO of Madison Co 4 Jan 1808 (OM)

**BELL**, James R. s/o Henry C. and Betsy Ann BELL age 19 s school teacher POB POR Orange & **PAYNE**, Mary E. d/o Charles and Mary PAYNE age 18 s POB POR Orange; POM Orange 5 Feb 1857 (OMR) 27 Jan 1857 (OML)

**BELL**, John & **BURNLEY**, Judith 3 Jul 1787 surety Reuben BURNLEY (OB)

**BELL**, John & **MINTON**, Fanny d/o John MINTON 4 Dec 1804 (OB)

**BELL**, John B. & **BROCKMAN**, Mary d/o Curtis L. BROCKMAN who is also surety 31 Jan 1837 (OB)

**BELL**, Joseph H. & **REYNOLDS**, Mary T. d/o John T. REYNOLDS who is also surety 7 Nov 1836 by J. GOSS (OB) (OM)

**BELL**, Joshua G. age 26 s farmer POB POR Orange s/o H.C. BELL and Sophia KENDALL & **LEE**, Sarah I. age 21 s POB POR Orange d/o George LEE and Malinda LEE POM Orange 30 Sep 1879 (OMR)

**BELL**, Larkin G. & **COLLINS**, Ann d/o Lewis D. COLLINS who is also surety 4 Feb 1830 (OB)

**BELL**, Nelson H. s/o John H. and Elizabeth BELL age 30 s merchant POB Augusta Co POR Baltimore, MD & **CAVE**, Hannah Jane d/o Richard and Maria CAVE age 26 s POB POR Orange; POM St. Thomas Ch, Orange 10 Oct 1854 (OMR)

**BELL**, Patrick & **QUISENBERRY**, Polly; 13 May 1793 surety Roger BELL (OB) (OM)

**BELL**, Robert A. age 25 s POB POR Orange s/o John B. BELL and Emily A. GILLESPIE school teacher & **WRIGHT**, Ariadne C, age 24 s POB POR Orange d/o Dabney WRIGHT and Jane M. ESTES 15 Apr 1880 by Charles P. SCOTT (OMR)

**BELL**, Robert S. age 25 s farmer POB POR Orange s/o Henry C. BELL and Sophia KENDALL & **MARTIN**, Lucy M. age 19 s POB POR Orange d/o William H. MARTIN and Bettie FITZPATRICK POM Orange 20 Dec 1877 (OMR)

**BELL**, Robert W. & **SHENK**, Anne T. 6 Apr 1810 by James GOSS (OM)

**BELL**, Thomas & **BURNLEY**, Sally; 28 Dec 1795 (OM) (OB)

**BELL**, Thomas & **MILBURN**, Sarah; 19 Nov 1804 (OM)

**BELL**, Thomas D. age 27 s farmer POB POR Orange s/o John B. BELL and Emily A. GILLESPIE & **WRIGHT**, Louisa A. age 21 s POB POR Orange d/o Dabney WRIGHT and _____ ESTES POM Orange 25 Mar 1878 by W.H. CAMPBELL (OMR)

**BELL**, Thomas Jr. & **REYNOLDS**, Lucy (d/o William & Elizabeth REYNOLDS); 30 Mar 1799 (OB) (OM)

BELL, Thomas s/o Ralph and Dorcus BELL age 23 s farmer POB Orange
POR ADAMS Co, Pa POC & **WRIGHT**, Amanda age 21 s POB POR
Orange POC; POM Orange C.H.22 Nov 1865 (OMR) (OML)

BELL, William & **ATKINS**, Rhoda (d/o John & Susannah ATKINS); 21
Dec 1795 (OB) 24 Dec 1795 (OM),

BELL, William & **JOHNSON**, Elizabeth Cave w d/o Benjamin CAVE 23
Feb 1786 (OB)

BELL, William & **SCRIVENER**, Mary W. d/o Samuel SCRIVENER 31
Jan 1825 surety Fountain C. BOSTON (OB)

BELL, William B. Jr. & **NEWMAN**, Frances d/o Andrew NEWMAN 17
Dec 1821 surety Thomas R. HAWKINS (OB)

BELL, William s/o John BELL & **BOSTON**, Fanny d/o Reubin BOSTON
16 Nov 1803 (OB) 17 Nov 1803 (Misc Min Returns)

BELLAMY, James & **LONG**, Jane F.; 14 Feb 1852 (OML)

BELLOMY, James W. age 41 s POB POR Louisa Co s/o Ambrose F.
BELLOMY and Elizabeth FLANNAGAN carpenter & **MAHANES**,
Sarah Jane age 28 s POB Albemarle Co POR Orange d/o William C.
MAHANES and Mary B. HARRIS 24 Mar 1873 POM Orange by
L.A.CUTLER (OMR)

BELZER, Edw. A. age 23 s POB Richmond POR Port Rely, KS [probably
Fort Riley, KS] s/o William F. BELZER and Alice S. ASHBY U.S.
Army & **PAYNE**, Willie S. age 23 s POB Prince William Co POR
Orange d/o William W. PAYNE and Mary S. FARROW 29 Apr 1868
POM Orange by J.W.K. HANDY (OMR)

BENT, Daniel & **SAMPSON**, Elizabeth 15 Jan 1818 surety Daniel
NORMAN (OB)

BERKELEY, Winston POC age 25 s POB Hanover Co POR Louisa Co
s/o Was BERKELEY and Matilda RAGLAND laborer & **MILLS**,
Hannah POC age 22 POB Louisa Co POR Orange 25 Dec 1873 POM
Orange by Frank TIBBS (OMR)

BERRY, Anthony & **LEE**, Jane 20 Dec 1813 surety Nathaniel LEE by
George MORRIS (OB) (OM)

BERRY, Gibbs & **HARRISON**, Harriett Jane d/o Lewis HARRISON who
is also surety 24 Aug 1830 (OB)

BERRY, William P. & **CLARK**, Josephine 8 May 1837 surety Joseph
EDWARDS (OB)

BERRY, William S. & **ROW**, Rachel d/o Thomas ROW who is also
surety 11 Feb 1807 by Nathaniel SANDERS (OB) (OM)

BIBB, Thomas & **BROCKMAN**, Sarah d/o Samuel BROCKMAN Jr. 14
Sep 1785 surety Joseph WOOLFOLK (OB)

BIBB, William & **GROOM**, Mourning 14 Nov 1822 surety Solomon R.
GROOM by George MORRIS (OB) (OM)

BICKERS, Abner & SCOTT, Nancy 23 Feb 1829 surety George LEWIS (OB)

BICKERS, Alexander & JONES, Mary 27 Sep 1830 surety Moses ROBINSON (OB)

BICKERS, Benjamin & MARTIN, Joannah 26 Sep 1815 surety Mallory MARTIN (OB)

BICKERS, George & MALLORY, Nance/Nancy; 22 Nov 1791 (OB) 25 Nov 1791 (OM)

BICKERS, Jairus & BERRY, Eliza 5 May 1836 surety John EDWARDS (OB)

BICKERS, Joel & ATKINS, Rosanna d/o John ATKINS 19 Mar 1805 (OB) 20 Mar 1805 by Robert JONES (Misc Min Ret)

BICKERS, John & LANDRUM, Nancy 5 Nov 1788 surety James TAYLOR (OB)

BICKERS, Joseph & LLOYD, Ellen 4 Oct 1836 surety John HUSTON (OB)

BICKERS, Proctor & OVERTON, Lucy 18 Jan 1823 surety Thomas MARTIN (OB)

BICKERS, Samuel s/o Thomas and Judy BICKERS age 61 w farm laborer POB POR Louisa Co POC & DICKINSON, Nelly age 39 s POB POR Orange POC; POM 27 Dec 1866 (OMR) 24 Dec 1866 (OML)

BICKERS, William & HAWKINS, Elizabeth 14 Jan 1825 surety Benjamin HAWKINS (OB)

BICKERS, William & LEATHERS, Sally; 3 Jun 1794 surety Caleb BICKERS (OB)

BIGGS, William & GOODLOE, Sally Ann 6 Apr 1846 surety Wythe P. CAMPBELL (OB)

BINGHAM, Josias & HUCKSTEP, Matilda d/o Josiah HUCKSTEP 27 Nov 1818 surety Anderson WHITE (OB) 31 Dec 1818 by Jacob WATTS (OM)

BINGHAM, Wyatt s/o Josias BINGHAM & BINGHAM, Rebecca d/o George BINGHAM 12 Jul 1812 surety Samuel ESTES (OB)

BIRCHETT, George K. & SKINKER, Ann D. d/o Samuel T. SKINKER 13 Sep 1834 surety Samuel L. URQUHART (OB)

BIRD, Harrison POC age 22 s POB POR Orange s/o Nelson BIRD and Nellie _____ farm laborer & JONES, Gillie POC age 21 s POB POR Orange d/o San JONES and Dinah _____ 28 Dec 1869 POM Orange by Franklin TIBBS (OMR)

BISCOE, William E. & WRIGHT, Susan R.; 27 Nov 1854 (OML)

BISHOP, Joseph & CLARK, Ann d/o John and Mary CLARK 28 Mar 1791 surety William CLARK (OB) 31 Mar 1791by Nathaniel SANDERS (OM)

**BISHOP**, Joseph & **TERRELL**, Jane; 28 Sep 1793 surety Edmund TERRILL (OB) 29 Mar 1793 by James GARNETT (OM)

**BISHOP**, Joseph Jr. s/o Joseph BISHOP & **TERRILL**, Elizabeth d/o Reuben TERRILL 24 Mar 1825 (OB)

**BISHOP**, Samuel & **VIA**, Sarah 29 Feb 1816 by George BINGHAM (OM)

**BLACK**, Jacob s/o Jacob BLACK Sr. who is also surety & **CAVE**, Nancy d/o William CAVE Jr. 9 Aug 1811 (OB) 22 Aug 1811 by George BINGHAM (OM)

**BLACK**, Joshua & **RAINS**, Alpha 30 Sep 1814 by George BINGHAM (OM)

**BLACK**, William & **SEBREE**, Nancy 5 Sep 1816 by George BINGHAM (OM)

**BLACKERBY/BLACKERLY**, Thaddeus & **MARSHALL**, Jane d/o Merrineau MARSHALL 4 Dec 1795 (OM) (OB)

**BLACKERLY**, Thomas & **HERRING**, Elizabeth d/o Thomas HARRING 23 Dec 1801 surety Thaddeus BLACKERLY (OB) 24 Dec 1801by Jacob WATTS (OM)

**BLACKEY**, Solomon G. POC age 31 s trader POB Albemarle POR Orange s/o Gilbert BLACKEY and Aggy ____ & **WATSON**, Rhoda POC age 28 s POB POR Orange d/o Maria WATSON POM Gordonsville 20 Jan 1876 (OMR)

**BLACKWELL**, James & **BURTON**, Elizabeth d/o William and Sarah BURTON surety Augustine SANFORD 30 Oct 1816 (OB) 3 Nov 1816 (OM)

**BLACKWELL**, Leland & **BURTON**, Nancy d/o William BURTON 1 Sep 1810 surety Robert BURTON (OB) 11 Oct 1810 by Jacob WATTS (OM)

**BLACKWELL**, William POR Fauquier Co s/o Joseph BLACKWELL & **GORDON**, Ann S. permission written by John WALKER 13 Aug 1819 surety William H. DIGGS (OB)

**BLAIR**, James & **SHEPHERD**, Helen; 27 Apr 1791 surety Alexander SHEPHERD (OB)

**BLAKE**, Jacob Jr. s/o Jacob BLAKE Sr. surety & **CAVE**, Nancy d/o William CAVE 9 Aug 1811 (OB)

**BLAKEY**, George Smith & **DAVIS**, Susannah Winston d/o Isaac DAVIS 5 Feb 1821 surety Elijah DAVIS (OB)

**BLAKEY**, James & **BRANHAM**, Nancy d/o Robert BRANHAM who is also surety 22 Oct 1807 (OB) 11 Nov 1807 by George BINGHAM (OM)

**BLAKEY**, James G. & **SORRILLE**, Maria Ann d/o Thomas SORRILLE 6 Nov 1820 surety Robert PRITCHETT (OB)

**BLAKEY**, John & **COWHERD**, Sarah d/o Jonathan COWHERD surety James COWHERD 30 Oct 1780 (OB)

**BLAKEY**, Lewis POC age 21 s labourer POB POR Greene s/o Doctor BLAKEY & **CAMPBELL**, Milly POC age 21 s POB POR Orange d/o Edmund CAMPBELL and Fanny GARNETT POM Orange 26 Dec 1878 by Joseph A. MANSFIELD (OMR)

**BLAKEY**, Reubin & **STROTHER**, Polly; 12 Feb 1807 by William DOUGLASS (OM)

**BLAKEY**, William & **BRANHAM**, Polly d/o Robert BRANHAM 2 Jan 1811 Wm BLAKEY surety (OB) 2 Jan 1811 by James GARNETT (OM)

**BLAKEY**, William & **DAVIS**, Elizabeth w 18 Jan 1798 surety Elijah GRAVES (OB) (OM)

**BLAKEY**, Yelverton C. & **BURTON**, Judith d/o Capt. May BURTON 26 Oct 1803 surety Alexander BRADFORD (OB)

**BLANK**, William P. s/o Robert BLANK and Amanda SMITHSON age 34 s merchant POB Campbell Co POR Gordonsville & **PARROTT**, Sallie A. d/o Samuel H. PARROTT and Mary HARTSOOK age 24 s POB Madison Co POR Orange; POM Orange 21 Dec 1865 (OMR) 18 Dec 1865 (OML)

**BLANTON**, John & **GRADY**, Mary d/o Nathaniel SANDERS 9 Mar 1792 surety William GRADY Jr. (OB) 29 Mar 1792 by Nathaniel SANDERS (OM)

**BLEDSOE**, Bennett age 19 s POB POR Orange s/o George BLEDSOE and Jane TINDER farmer & **APPERSON**, Lucy D. age 21 s POB Culpeper Co POR Orange d/o Thomas APPERSON and Evelina PALMER 12 Nov 1868 POM Orange by Sanders MASON (OMR)

**BLEDSOE**, Franklin s/o John and Margaret BLEDSOE age 20 s farmer POB Culpeper POR Orange & **PROCTOR**, Madaline d/o Thomas and Frances PROCTOR age 22 s POB POR Orange; POM Orange 17 Aug 1856 (OMR) 14 Aug 1856 (OML)

**BLEDSOE**, George & **PITCHER**, Joanna d/o William PITCHER POR Orange 23 Dec 1811 John BLEDSOE surety (OB)

**BLEDSOE**, George & **TINDER**, Jane Ann Frances d/o James R. TINDER 25 Nov 1847 surety Arthur R. TINDER (OB)

**BLEDSOE**, John & **PERRY**, Margaret d/o Peter PERRY who is also surety 1 Mar 1815 (OB) 3 Mar 1815 by Jeremiah CHANDLER (OM)

**BLEDSOE**, John & **PITCHER**, Susanna d/o William PITCHER, Sr. 14 Dec 1809 surety Edmund PITCHER (OB) (OM)

**BLEDSOE**, John A. & **BROWN**, Emily 1 Jan 1840 surety Richard HIGGASON (OB)

**BLEDSOE**, John s/o Aaron BLEDSOE & **DEAR**, Polly d/o Thomas DEAR 5 Jun 1797 surety Thomas WILLIAMSON (OB) (OM)

**BLEDSOE**, John T. & **WOOD**, Lucy Jane d/o James WOOD 28 Mar 1839 (OB)

**BLEDSOE**, John T. s/o Howard BLEDSOE and Julia YAGER age 49 w tailor POB Madison POR Orange & **THOMPSON**, Amanda C. d/o Samuel S.THOMPSON and Lucy A. M. SNELL age 24 s POB Davidson Co, Tennessee POR Orange; POM Orange 11 Mar 1863 (OMR) 9 Mar 1863 (OML)

**BLEDSOE**, Moses & **PERRY**, Ann; 10 Oct 1777 by banns both of St. Thomas Parish (Deed Book 17)

**BLEDSOE**, Moses & **WRIGHT**, Sindy 13 Dec 1831 surety Robert ADAMS (OB)

**BLEDSOE**, Salathiel W. s/o Howard BLEDSOE & **WHITE**, Martha Jane d/o William WHITE who is also surety 23 Dec 1839 (OB)

**BLEDSOE**, William & **MORTON**, Sally d/o Elijah MORTON 21 Jul 1785 surety Aaron BLEDSOE (OB)

**BLEDSOE**, William & **PERRY**, Rachel permission written by Peter PERRY surety Benjamin PERRY 26 Mar 1831 (OB)

**BLEDSOE**, William J. & **SOMMERVILLE**, Jane E. 7 Dec 1857 (OML)

**BLOCK**, Henry age 27 s POB France POR Orange s/o Emanuel BLOCK and Sarah EISANMAN cattle dealer & **GUNDERSHEIMER**, Henrietta age 24 POR Orange d/o Jacob GUNDERSHEIMER and L. KAUFMAN 26 Oct 1870 by Dr. A.L. MAYER (OM)

**BLOWS**, George POR Augusta Co & **FEEN**, Catharina POR St. Thomas Parish 12 Sep 1773 (Deed Book 17)

**BOGGS**, Lewis A. age 21 s farmer POB POR Spotsylvania s/o S.L. BOGGS and Elizabeth RAWLINGS & **WALLACE**, Frances C. age 16 s POB Stafford POR Orange d/o G.B. WALLACE and Elizabeth MCFARLANE POM Worrel Church, Orange 27 Jun 1878 by S.K. WINN of Culpeper (OMR)

**BOHANNON**, Thomas & **MARQUESS**, Lavinia d/o John MARQUESS 26 Mar 1799 surety Isaac PETIT (OB) 31 Mar 1799 by Nathaniel SANDERS (OM)

**BOLING**, John Jr. & **BELL**, Susannah; 19 Apr 1791 permission from Thomas BELL surety William BOLING (OB)

**BOLING**, William & **HAWKINS**, Phebe consent by Phebe Hawkins POINDEXTER 1 Oct 1788 surety James GAINES (OB)

**BOLLS**, Franklin s/o William BOLLS and Elizabeth LEBOW age 24 s farmer POB Cleveland Co, Tennessee POR Union Co, Tennessee & **SEE**, Lucy Ellen d/o John H. SEE and Frances HUGHES age 17 s POB POR Orange; POM Orange 29 Apr 1864 (OMR) 28 Apr 1864 (OML)

**BOND**, Joseph W. & **GROOM**, Virginia Ann 8 May 1858 (OML)

**BOND**, Robert H. age 31 s POB POR Orange s/o Joseph BOND and Mildred WHITLOCK farmer & **COSBY**, Mary E. age 23 s POB POR

Orange d/o William S. COSBY and Lelia WHARTON 18 Jan 1870
POM Orange by Melzi S. CHANCELLOR (OMR)

**BOND**, Thomas W. & **KINGER**, Virginia W. POM Orange 6 Mar 1851
(OMR) 4 Mar 1851 (OML)

**BOND**, William J. age 42 w POB POR Louisa farmer s/o Joseph BOND
and Mildred WHITLOCK & **MEEKS**, Martha A. age 35 w POB
Louisa POR Orange 25 Mar 1880 POM Gordonsville, Orange by P.S.
RHOADES (OMR)

**BOOTH**, Joseph & **GRACE**, Polly d/o George GRACE 5 Mar 1792
surety Mark LAMPTON (OB) (OM)

**BOOTON**, ( aka BOSTON) Reubin & **ANDERSON**, Mary d/o Jacob
ANDERSON who is also surety 18 Dec 1809 (OB) 21 Dec 1809 by
George BINGHAM (OM)

**BOSTON**, Abraham & **CLARKE**, Barsheba surety William CLARKE by
J.C. GORDON 20 Dec 1819 (OB)

**BOSTON**, Alexander & **TERRILL**, Ann d/o John TERRILL who is also
surety 20 Dec 1831 (OB)

**BOSTON**, George & **VAUGHN**, Elizabeth 11 May 1796 surety Joseph
VAUGHN (OB)

**BOSTON**, Henry L. age 21 s POB Orange POR Greene Co s/o William B.
BOSTON and Sarah POWELL farmer & **MCMULLEN**, Eudora B.
age 21 s POB POR Greene Co. d/o James W. MCMULLEN and Mary
JARRELL 24 Mar 1872 POM Orange by H.M. LINNEY (OMR)

**BOSTON**, James N. s/o William B. BOSTON and Sarah POWELL age 22
s farmer POB POR Orange & **BRAGG**, Mary Y. d/o Joseph BRAGG
and Sarah F. BROUGHAN age 17 s POB Albemarle Co POR Orange;
POM Orange 11 Jul 1867 (OMR) 10 Jul 1867 (OML)

**BOSTON**, John & **MOSELEY**, Sarah 13 Jan 1803 POM Orange by
Robert JONES (Misc Min Ret)

**BOSTON**, John & **PETTY**, Frankey d/o George PETTY 19 Mar 1793
surety Joseph WAUGH (OB)

**BOSTON**, John G. age 24 s farmer POB POR Orange s/o John P.
BOSTON and Jane Frances WAUGH & **MARTIN**, Lucy E. age 23 s
POB Caroline POR Orange d/o Henry P. MARTIN and Mary COBB
POM Orange 28 Dec 1876 (OMR)

**BOSTON**, John P. & **WAUGH**, Frances d/o Gourty WAUGH who is also
surety 22 Aug 1842 (OB)

**BOSTON**, Reuben & **HAWKINS**, Sarah 13 Sep 1783 surety George
PETTY (OB)

**BOSTON**, Robert & **WRIGHT**, Lucy; 30 Jan 1778 both of St. Thomas
Parish (Deed Book 17)

**BOSTON**, William s/o Reuben BOSTON & **POWELL**, Sarah d/o
William POWELL Jr. surety William L. POWELL 7 Nov 1831 (OB)

**BOSWELL**, Charles & **THOMPSON**, Lucy; 31 Mar 1795 surety Henry WOOD (OB) (OM)

**BOSWELL**, Garrett & **DOLIN**, Patsy surety John DOLIN 22 Nov 1819 (OB)

**BOSWELL**, Samuel T. & **MIDDLEBROOK**, Martha d/o Nathaniel MIDDLEBROOK who is also surety 22 Apr 1822 (OB)

**BOSWELL**, William s/o Charles BOSWELL & **SLEET**, Mary d/o John SLEET surety Joseph PORTER 21 Mar 1816 (OB)

**BOTHIGHEIMER**, Elias age 23 s POB Germany POR Louisa s/o Emanuel BOTTIGHEIMER and Bettie GUNDERSHEIMER merchant & **GUNDERSHEIMER**, Amelia age 22 s POB Germany POR Orange d/o Jacob GUNDERSHEIMER and Lea KAUFFMAN 16 Nov 1870 by M.J. MICHALBACHER (OM)

**BOTT**, John & **SPOTSWOOD**, Susannah C. 1 Apr 1802 surety Robert SPOTSWOOD (OB)

**BOUGHAN**, Nathaniel J. s/o John BOUGHAN and Polly SNELSON age 44 s carpenter POB POR Louisa Co & **McMULLEN**, Ann B. d/o William B. BOSTON and Sarah POWELL age 28 w POB POR Orange; POM Orange 28 Feb 1867 (OMR) 25 Feb 1867 (OML)

**BOULWARE**. Richard S. & **MOORE**, Mary T. 8 Jan 1833 surety W.M. CHAPMAN (OB)

**BOURN**, Andrew & **BOSWELL**, Sarah surety Brook SIMES 22 Jul 1833 (OB)

**BOURN**, Andrew & **SLEET**, Ann w 5 Oct 1826 surety Weedon SLEET 5 Oct 1826 (OB) 15 Oct 1826 by James GARNETT (OM)

**BOURN**, John & **NEWMAN**, Jane d/o Thomas NEWMAN who is also surety 3 May 1824 (OB)

**BOURNE**, Ambrose & **NEWMAN**, Jane d/o Frances NEWMAN 22 Feb 1796 surety William MORTON (OB) 5 Mar 1796 by Nathaniel SANDERS (OM)

**BOUSE** (or BOASE), Simon s/o James BOUSE and Eliza YARON age 21 s miner POB England POR Orange & **SANDERS**, Virginia d/o Nathaniel and Ann SANDERS age 21 s POB POR Orange; POM Orange 31 Dec 1867 (OMR) 27 Dec 1867 (OML)

**BOUTWRIGHT**, John L. s/o John H. BOUTWRIGHT and Mary E. LORD (or SOREL) age 21 s lieutenant in regular Confederate Army POB POR Columbia, South Carolina & **TALIAFERRO**, Annie P. d/o Edmund T. TALIAFERRO and Octavia H. ROBERTSON age 19 s POB POR Orange; POM Orange C.H. 25 Aug 1863 (OMR) (OML)

**BOWCOCK**, Tandy & **DOUGLASS**, Judith d/o John DOUGLASS 25 Nov 1799 (OB) 26 Nov 1799 by B. BENNETT (OM)

**BOWEN**, Ephraim & **LEATHERS**, Polly d/o John LEATHERS who is also surety 27 Dec 1813 (OB)

**BOWEN**, Francis & **CHRISTOPHER**, Frances 2 Jan 1758 (Orange Fee Book)

**BOWEN**, John & **BRADY**, Sarah surety William G. PAYNE 7 Jul 1830 (OB)

**BOWEN**, John & **SEAL**, Sally 3 Jan 1811 Philip SEAL surety (OB)

**BOWER**, Thomas & **LANDRUM**, Margaret 15 Sep 1789 surety John BICKERS (OB)

**BOWLER**, George W. & **SAUNDERS**, Sarah J. age over 21 POR Orange; 20 Feb 1854 (OML)

**BOWLING**, Charles & **MCKENNEY**, Sarah d/o William MCKENNEY 10 Oct 1791 surety William THOMAS (OB) 13 Oct 1791by Nathaniel SANDERS (OM)

**BOWLING**, John & **BALLARD**, Mary; 22 Aug 1773 both of St. Thomas Parish (Deed Book 17)

**BOWMAN**, N.W. age 31 s POB POR Rockingham s/o Abraham BOWMAN and Rebecca BOWMAN merchant & **JONES**, Laura A. age 22 s POB POR Orange d/o Timothy JONES and Susan B. WINSLOW 23 Nov 1870 POM Orange by L.A. CUTLER (OM)

**BOXLEY**, George & **GRAVES**, Drucilla d/o Isaac GRAVES 16 Jan 1797 surety Jonathan GRAVES (OB)

**BOYER**, Thomas & **THOMPSON**, Martha; 6 Mar 1801 surety James WILLIAMS (OB) 8 Mar 1801 by Hamilton GOSS (OM)

**BOYKIN**, Robert Virginius s/o Robert M. BOYKIN and Sarah V.B. YOUNG age 31 s formerly ch.clk naval store Gosport navy yard & capt. A.C.of C.S.A. POB Isle of Wight Co POR Portsmouth & **CHAPMAN**, Emma d/o John M. CHAPMAN and Susan COLE age 20 s POB POR Orange; POM Orange C.H. 25 Feb 1864 (OMR) (OML)

**BRADEN**, Joseph & **NEALE**, Polly d/o Fielding NEALE, dec'd 18 Mar 1808 consent by James BEAZLEY who is her uncle and guardian surety James ARCHER (OB) 22 Mar 1808 by George BINGHAM (OM)

**BRADFORD**, Alexander over 21 years & **BURTON**, Hannah d/o Capt. May BURTON 16 Nov 1802 surety Benjamin BURTON (OB) 18 ___ 1802 by William CARPENTER Jr, Lutheran (Misc Min Ret)

**BRADFORD**, S. Slaughter age 58 w farmer POB POR Culpeper s/o Samuel K. BRADFORD and Emilie SLAUGHTER & **BATTLE**, Fannie age 30 s POB Mobile, AL POR Orange d/o A.M. BATTLE and Fannie CLITHERALL POM St. Thomas Church, Orange 18 Dec 1879 (OMR)

**BRADLEY**, Demarcus L. & **BROWN**, Susan d/o John BROWN who is also surety 26 Nov 1849 (OB)

**BRADLEY**, George & **RICE**, Lucy; 29 Jul 1775 by banns both of St. Thomas Parish (Deed Book 17)

BRADLEY, James & WELLS, Elizabeth consent by George WELLS 20
Oct 1803 surety John SLEET (OB)
BRADLEY, James & WILLIS, Elizabeth 22 Oct 1803 by Nath.
SANDERS (Misc Min Ret)
BRADLEY, James H. & TERRILL, Lucilla S. 23 Jan 1843 surety
William MALLORY (OB)
BRADLEY, John & HANCOCK, Sally; surety William HANCOCK 16
May 1801 (OB) 18 May 1801 by Robert JONES (OM)
BRADLEY, John & NEWMAN, Jane E. 28 Feb 1844 surety William J.
HERRING (OB) 29 Feb 1844 by J. EARNEST (OMR)
BRADLEY, William & MARSHALL, Polly 15 Jan 1802 surety Thomas
MARSHALL (OB) 18 Jan 1802 by Hamilton GOSS (Misc Min Ret)
BRADLEY, William N. age 22 s POB POR Orange s/o John BRADLEY
and Maria NEWMAN farmer & MCGHEE, Susan A. age 17 s POB
POR Orange d/o William G. MCGHEE and Amanda LANCASTER 13
Mar 1873 POM Orange by W.H. CAMPER (OMR)
BRADLEY, William s/o Richard BRADLEY and Sarah LLOYD age 26 s
farmer POB Bedford Co POR Orange & BATTAILE, Elizabeth B. d/o
Mary BATTAILE age 19 s POB POR Orange; POM Orange 9 May
1865 (OMR) 8 May 1865 (OML)
BRAGG, Benjamin & TWENTYMEN, Polly; 1 Sep 1785 surety William
JAMESON (OB) 4 Sep 1785 by John PRICE (OM)
BRAGG, Joseph M. s/o Joseph BRAGG and Sarah F. BOUGHAN age 22
s farmer POB POR Orange & BOSTON, Clementine V. d/o William B.
BOSTON and Sarah POWELL age 20 s POB POR Orange; POM
Orange 28 Feb 1867 (OMR) 25 Feb 1867 (OML)
BRAGG, Moore & YORK, Jenny; 25 Oct 1801 surety Armistead YORK
(OB) 5 Nov 1801 by Nathaniel SANDERS (OM)
BRAGG, William A. age 32 s POB POR Petersburg s/o William A.
BRAGG and Ann Eliza JONES tobacconist & LEE, Lizzie M. age 25 s
POB Madison Co POR Orange d/o John H. LEE and Fanny WILLIS 11
Dec 1872 POM Orange by J.S. HANSBROUGH (OMR)
BRANCH, Walker POC age 33 w labourer POB Culpeper POR Orange
s/o Nelson BRANCH and Malinda WARD & WILLIAMS, Bettie
POC age 24 s POB Caroline POR Orange d/o Mat WILLIAMS POM
Nazareth Baptist Church, Orange 12 Dec 1878 by Willis ROBINSON
(OMR)
BRANCH, Walker s/o Nelson BRANCH and Malinda WARD age 26 w
blacksmith POB Culpeper Co POR Orange POC & BOWLER, Ellen
d/o Addison and Winney BOWLER age 21 s POB POR Orange POC;
POM Orange 3 Oct 1867 (OMR) 28 Sep 1867 (OML)
BRANHAM, Andrew & MCCAULLY, Nancy surety Mordecai
SHIFLETT 3 Mar 1849 (OB)

**BRANHAM**, John H. & **DADE**, Ann W. d/o Albert G. DADE POM Orange 7 Feb 1851 (OMR) 4 Feb 1851 (OML)

**BRANHAM**, Marmaduke & **HUGHES**, Fanny d/o Francis HUGHES 16 Aug 1791 surety Thomas CHISHAM (OB) 18 Aug 1791 by Nathaniel SANDERS (OM)

**BRANHAM**, Tavner & **SISSON**, Polly d/o Sarah SISSON 5 Sep 1792 surety Morgan FINNELL (OB)

**BRANHAM**, William & **DODSON**, Amanda surety Andrew BRANHAM 23 Jan 1850 (OB)

**BRAXTON**, Carter M. s/o Carter M. BRAXTON and Elizabeth MAYO age 28 s civil engineer POB Norfolk POR Fredericksburg & **HUME**, Fannie P. d/o David HUME and Fannie DADE age 26 s POB POR Orange ; POM Orange 16 Feb 1865 (OMR) (OML)

**BRAXTON**, Cornelius POC age 33 s labourer POB POR Orange s/o _____ and Ony BRAXTON & **PAYNE**, Matilda POC age 26 s POB POR Orange d/o Eliza PAYNE POM Orange Courthouse 23 Jul 1878 by F.L. GIBSON (OMR)

**BRAXTON**, Emmanuel POC age 24 s laborer POB POR Orange s/o Jack BRAXTON and Fanny GIBSON & **TAYLOR**, Dinah POC age 26 s POB POR Orange d/o Jacob TAYLOR and Malinda POWELL POM Orange 6 Oct 1876 (OMR)

**BRAXTON**, Simon POC age 45 w POB POR Orange s/o Nat BRAXTON and Mary _____ laborer & **FRY**, Betsy POC w POB POR Orange d/o Patsy GAINES 27 Mar 1869 POM Orange by John H. ROBINSON (OMR)

**BRAY**, Patrick & **STOCKS**, Mary d/o Thomas STOCKS 24 Aug 1786 surety Francis DADE (OB)

**BREEDING**, Ephraim & **HANEY**, Fanny surety Matthew WRIGHT 2 Mar 1824 (OB)

**BREEDING**, Ephriam & **FRANKLIN**, Molly d/o Edward FRANKLIN 7 Dec 1789 surety Jonathan FRANKLIN (OB)

**BREEDING**, Ezekiel & **HANEY**, Betsy d/o James and Nancy HANEY surety Bazel HANEY 3 Feb 1812 (OB) by George BINGHAM 6 Feb 1812 (OM)

**BREEDING**, James & **GIBBENS**, Rachel 8 Apr 1816 surety Lewis G. POWELL (OB)

**BREEDING**, Richard & **FRANKLYN**, Elizabeth d/o Edward FRANKLYN 31 Jul 1790 surety Jonathan FRANKLYN(OB)

**BREEDLOVE**, Broadus & **DOVELL**, Nancy over 21 years 3 Jan 1809 surety Martin THOMAS (OB) 12 Jan 1809 by Ambrose BROCKMAN of Albemarle Co. (OM)

**BREEDLOVE**, Churchill & **ARCHER**, Amanda M. d/o James ARCHER surety James HIGGERSON 20 Feb 1832 (OB)

BREEDLOVE, Edward & HARVEY, Haney Martin THOMAS surety 21 Jan 1811 (OB)

BREEDLOVE, Madison & BUCKNER, Judy of St. Thomas Parish 11 Feb 1784 surety Francis BUSH (OB)

BREEDLOVE, Martin & HARVEY, Lucinda 9 Jan 1832 surety Layton HARVEY (OB) 12 Jan 1832 by J. GOSS (OM)

BREEDLOVE, Nathaniel & MITCHELL, Elender; 27 Nov 1809 surety William MITCHELL by Ambrose BROCKMAN of Albemarle Co (OB) (OM)

BREEDWELL, Thomas s/o Thomas BREEDWELL & BLACKWELL, Anny w 10 Aug 1796 surety Joshua KENDELL (OB)

BREMER, John F. & DEMSEY, Polly surety Allen DEMSEY 23 May 1814 (OB)

BRENT, George Lee s/o William BRENT Jr. and Winifred B. LEE age 37 s lawyer POB Fairfax Co POR Richmond & JOHNSON, Betsy S. d/o Benjamin V. JOHNSON and Amanda DUKE age 18 s POB POR Orange; POM Montebello, Orange 11 Jan 1865 (OMR) 9 Jan 1865 (OML)

BRENT, Jacob POC age 21 s POB POR Orange s/o Aaron BRENT and Maria LINDSAY r.r. hand & LINDSAY, Susan age 20 s POB POR Orange d/o Absalom LINDSAY and Milly WILSON 26 Dec 1872 POM Orange by Philip JOHNSON (OMR)

BRENT, Joseph POC & QUARLES, Winnie POC 28 Mar 1879 POM Mt. Pleasant, Orange by C.T. JOHNSON (OMR)

BRENT, Joseph POC age 30 s laborer POB POR Orange s/o Aaron BRENT and Maria WILLIS & QUARLES, Winnie POC age 21 s POB POR Orange d/o Martin QUARLES and Ellen REDD POM Orange 23 Feb 1879 (OMR)

BRENT, Kendal C. & BURTON, Polly d/o James BURTON 30 Oct 1808 surety William BURTON Jr. by Jacob WATTS (OB) (OM)

BRIDGES, Matthew & ROW, Mary; 30 Dec 1795 surety Edmund ROW by Nathaniel SANDERS (OB) (OM)

BRIDGES, William & ROW, Ann d/o Edmund ROW 4 Jul 1788 surety Thomas ROW (OB)

BRIDWELL, John & GUARD, Elizabeth surety John GUARD 24 Jan 1835 (OB)

BRIDWELL, O.H. age 28 s POB Culpeper Co POR Orange s/o William H. BRIDWELL and Amanda T. HAWLEY carpenter & THOMPSON, Sallie E. age 21 POB POR Orange d/o Reuben S. THOMPSON and Marina QUISENBERRY 21 May 1872 POM Orange by Herndon FRAZER (OMR)

BRIGHTWELL, Absalom & PINES, Winifred; 24 Feb 1800 surety John MONTAGUE by Nathaniel SANDERS (OB) (OM)

**BRIGHTWELL**, John D. Jr. s/o John D. BRIGHTWELL Sr. and Drucilla PULLIAM age 35 s farmer POB Spotsylvania POR Orange & **COOPER**, Malvina D. d/o Owen COOPER and Jane HUMPHRIES age 32 s POB POR Orange; POM Orange 21 Mar 1867 (OMR) 20 Mar 1867 (OML)

**BRISCOE**, John Henry age 21 s farmer POB Spotsylvania POR Orange s/o William E. BRISCOE and Susan R. CHEWNING & **WRIGHT**, Mollie V. age 19 s POB POR Orange d/o George W. WRIGHT and Martha J. COSBY POM Orange 24 Dec 1878 by William A. HILLE (OMR)

**BRITT**, Charles G. & **KENNEDY**, Teressa d/o John KENNEDY surety Benjamin WALKER 18 Dec 1834 (OB) by Charles P. MOORMAN 18 Mar 1835 (OM)

**BRITTON**, Joseph F. age 21 s miller POB Madison POR Orange s/o William A. BRITTON and Rhoda A. BREEDON & **BUSICK**, Annie R. age 21 s POB Louisa POR Orange d/o James BUSICK and Mary E. MICHEL POM Orange 14 Feb 1878 by C.P. SCOTT (OMR)

**BROCK**, Ansalem & **BUCKNER**, Elizabeth B. 8 Dec 1824 by E.G. SHIP (OM)

**BROCK**, Archibald & **MOYERS**, Sarah d/o Michael MOYERS 15 Mar 1813 surety William KEZEL (OB) by George BINGHAM 18 Mar 1813 (OM)

**BROCK**, Benjamin POC age 23 s POB POR Orange s/o Harvey BROCK and Phoebe ___ laborer & **JACKSON**, Amanda age 26 s POB Louisa Co POR Orange 25 Dec 1870 POM Orange by Frank TIBBS (OM)

**BROCK**, Jack POC age 35 w POB POR Orange s/o Jacob BROCK and Maggy WATSON farmer & **HUME**, Nelly POC age 30 w POB Greene Co POR Orange d/o Eveline BECKHAM 6 Jan 1873 POM Orange by F.L. GIPSON (OMR)

**BROCK**, Robert S. s/o John C. and Elizabeth BROCK age 25 s carpenter POB POR Hanover Co & **DAVIS**, Margaret R. d/o William J. and Elizabeth DAVIS age 21 POB Orange POR Gordonsville, Orange Co; POM Orange 13 Apr 1854 (OMR) 12 Apr 1854 (OML)

**BROCK**, Winfield & **WEBB**, Sarah Mason permission by Jesse B. WEBB surety Richard B. WEBB 12 Mar 1824 (OB)

**BROCKMAN**, Albert T. s/o Samuel BROCKMAN and Frances GRAVES age 24 s farmer POB POR Orange & **BURRUSS**, Alice d/o Robert B. BURRUSS and Ann GRAVES age 18 s POB POR Orange; POM Orange 27 Nov 1866 (OMR) 24 Nov 1866 (OML)

**BROCKMAN**, Andrew & **BROCKMAN**, Amelia d/o William BROCKMAN 22 Apr 1793 surety Samuel BROCKMAN (OB)

**BROCKMAN**, Asa & **QUISENBERRY**, Lucy E. 18 Jan 1819 surety John HENDERSON permission by George ELLIS (OB)

BROCKMAN, Belfield & **DOLEN**, Julia P. niece of H. HOUCK; 2 Jan 1851 (OML)

BROCKMAN, Bledsoe & **LANDRUM**, Elizabeth ( d/o Thomas LANDRUM) ; 2 Jun 1802 (OM)

BROCKMAN, Bledsoe & **LANDRUM**, Elizabeth d/o Thomas LANDRUM who is also surety 2 Jun 1802 (OB)

BROCKMAN, Curtis & **QUISENBERRY**, Nancy POR Orange 28 Oct 1811 William T. BURRUSS surety and guardian of Nancy (OB)

BROCKMAN, Curtis L. & **DANIEL**, Sally w surety Brockman BELL 27 Jul 1840 (OB)

BROCKMAN, Elijah & **TOMLINSON**, Sally 9 Jan 1795 surety William TOMLINSON (OB)

BROCKMAN, James & **BLEDSOE**, Nancy 6 Dec 1790 surety Aaron BLEDSOE (OB)

BROCKMAN, James & **TURNER**, Milly 18 Jul 1806 by Robert JONES (OM)

BROCKMAN, John & **LONG**, Nancy; 2 Dec 1788 by George EVE (OM)

BROCKMAN, John H. age 21 s POB Albemarle Co POR Orange s/o Belfield BROCKMAN and Julia F. DOLIN brick layer & **MAY**, Columbia A. age 21 s POB Madison Co POR Orange d/o Benjamin F. MAY and Mary SUTHAND 29 Jan 1874 POM Orange (OMR)

BROCKMAN, Joseph age 37 s farmer POB POR Orange s/o Asa BROCKMAN and Lucy QUISENBERRY & **WRIGHT**, Eliza J. age 24 s POB Louisa POR Orange d/o Dabney WRIGHT and Jane M. ESTES POM Orange 22 Jan 1878 by Charles QUARLES (OMR)

BROCKMAN, Joshua L. & **GRAVES**, Ann E. 8 Nov 1852 (OML)

BROCKMAN, Lucian T. s/o William L.BROCKMAN and Elizabeth GRAVES age 21 s farmer POB POR Orange & **SAMUEL**, Adaline C. d/o Trenton E.SAMUEL and Bettie COLEMAN age 21 s POB POR Orange; POM Orange 12 Jan 1863 (OMR) (OML)

BROCKMAN, Major & **PATTERSON** , Mary d/o Turner and Susannah PATTERSON 9 Nov 1779 both of St. Thomas Parish surety Sam BROCKMAN (OB)

BROCKMAN, Moses & **BROCKMAN**, Nelly; 25 Apr 1796 surety William DOLLINS (OB)

BROCKMAN, Samuel & **GRAVES**, Frances d/o Claibourn GRAVES who is also surety 22 Nov 1825 (OB) by Jeremiah CHANDLER 23 Nov 1825 (OM)

BROCKMAN, Samuel Jr. & **DURRETT**, Nancy; 24 Oct 1791 surety Joel DURRETT (OB)

BROCKMAN, William & **SMITH**, Mary POR St. Thomas Parish 23 Nov 1784 surety George SMITH (OB)

**BROCKMAN**, William A. s/o William L. and Elizabeth C. BROCKMAN age 30 s farmer POB POR Orange & **MOORE**, Elizabeth T. d/o Robert and Harriet MOORE age 18 s POB POR Orange; POM Orange 6 Dec 1855 (OMR) 5 Dec 1855 (OML)

**BROCKMAN**, William Joel age 20 s farmer POB POR Louisa s/o John BROCKMAN and Martha P. ESTES & **ESTES**, Mary H. age 19 s POB POR Orange d/o William B. ESTES and Rachel A. TATUM POM Orange 14 Nov 1878 by Charles QUARLES (OMR)

**BROCKMAN**, William Jr. & **GRAVES**, Elizabeth C. d/o Claibourn GRAVES who is also surety 21 Feb 1821 (OB) by William G. HITER 22 Feb 1821 (OM)

**BROCKMAN**, William s/o Asa BROCKMAN and Lucy QUISENBERRY age 39 s farmer POB POR Orange & **BICKERS**, Lucy M. d/o William BICKERS and Elizabeth HAWKINS age 25 s POB POR Orange; POM Orange 20 Dec 1866 (OMR) 18 Dec 1866 (OML)

**BRONAUGH**, Charles & **DANIEL**, Mary over 21 23 Jan 1805 surety Caleb LINDSAY (OB)

**BRONAUGH**, Charles B. & **BROCKMAN**, Elizabeth d/o William BROCKMAN 3 Apr 1810 surety Joshua L. BROCKMAN (OB)

**BROOKE**, George & **YANCEY**, Rachel surety Charles YANCEY by James GARNETT 10 Mar 1825 (OB) (OM)

**BROOKING**, Charles R. & **SANDERS**, Susan M. d/o Benjamin SANDERS surety Francis J. SANDERS 16 Dec 1842 (OB)

**BROOKING**, Charles R. age 20 s POB POR Orange s/o Charles R. BROOKING and Susan N. SANDERS farmer & **MORRIS**, Leona age 16 s POB POR Orange d/o John F. MORRIS and Mary A. BLEDSOE 21 Feb 1869 by Sanders MASON (OMR)

**BROOKING**, Robert & **RUSSELL**, Patsey 8 Apr 1788 surety John SCOTT (OB) 11 Apr 1788 by James WADDELL Presbyterian (OM)

**BROOKING**, Robert U. & **WILHOIT**, Mildred d/o Ezekiel WILHOIT surety Jacob WATTERS 8 Apr 1822 (OB)

**BROOKING**, Samuel & **TAYLOR**, Mary; 22 Dec 1785 surety Chapman TAYLOR (OB)

**BROOKING**, William F. & **PETTIS**, Eliza S. POM Orange 22 Jan 1851 (OMR) 20 Jan 1851 (OML)

**BROOKING**, William POR St. Thomas Parish & **THOMPSON**, Anne POR St. Thomas Parish 21 Jan 1778 (Deed Book 17)

**BROOKMAN**, James Jr. & **STEVENS**, Mildred 18 Jun 1833 surety Reuben KENNEDY (OB)

**BROOKS**, Anthony POC age 60 s farm labourer POB POR Orange s/o Daniel BURRUSS and Celia _____ & **GORDON**, Susan POC age 35 w POR Orange 30 Jan 1879 by Robert R. WOODSON (OMR)

29

**BROOKS**, Barwell POC age 58 w POB Culpeper Co POR Orange s/o George BROOKS and Silva _____ laborer & **JOHNSON**, Ellen POC age 25 s POB POR Orange d/o William JOHNSON and Martha JOHNSON 14 May 1870 POM Orange by Philip JOHNSON (OMR)

**BROOKS**, Frederick POC age 23 s farm laborer POB POR Orange s/o Frederick BROOKS and Maria _____ & **THOMAS**, Sarah POC age 22 s POB POR Orange POM Gordonsville, Orange 23 Oct 1878by F. TIBBS (OMR)

**BROOKS**, George & **TAYLOR**, Dorothy; 13 Mar 1789 by George EVE (OM)

**BROOKS**, James & **FISHER**, Mary; 9 Aug 1853 (OML)

**BROUGHTON**, Thomas & **KEMP**, Sarah; 28 Oct 1786 surety James NEWMAN Jr. (OB)

**BROWN**, Allen POC age 23 s labourer POB POR Orange s/o Edgar BROWN and Hannah BARBOUR & **GORDON**, Mildred POC age 19 s POB Albemarle POR Orange d/o Lucy GORDON POM Orange 30 Dec 1879 (OMR)

**BROWN**, Bernis & **BURTON**, Nancy d/o James BURTON surety John M. BURTON 15 May 1815 (OB) by Jacob WATTS 25 May 1815 (OM)

**BROWN**, Bezabel & **PRICE**, Elizabeth d/o George PRICE who is also surety 10 Sep 1817 (OB)

**BROWN**, Bushrod W. & **SMITH**, Ellen H. ward of William T. SMITH 17 Dec 1850 (OB) by Herndon FRAZER 19 Dec 1850 (OM)

**BROWN**, Charles B. & **JACKSON**, Jane E.L. d/o Joseph S. JACKSON surety Miles B. LIPSCOMB 9 Oct 1848 (OB)

**BROWN**, Daniel & **JOHNSON**, (aka Johnston) Mary d/o Elizabeth JOHNSTON POM Orange 19 Mar 1852 (OMR) 18 Mar 1852 (OML)

**BROWN**, Hamet POC age 38 w POB POR Orange s/o Walker BROWN and Mary _____ farmer & **WILLIS**, Virginia POC age 33 s POB POR Orange 14 Dec 1880 POM Orange by Joseph A. MANSFIELD (OMR)

**BROWN**, Harry POC 23 s farm laborer POB Albemarel POR Orange s/o James BROWN and Milly JACKSON & **MADISON**, Tislee POC age 22 s POB Albemarle POR Orange POM Orange 3 Jun 1876 (OMR)

**BROWN**, Henry & **BOSTON**, Polly d/o John BOSTON surety Gowry WAUGH 25 Dec 1820 (OB)

**BROWN**, Henry J. & **BOND**, Ann M. d/o Thomas BOND surety James O. BROWN 16 Oct 1844 (OB)

**BROWN**, Horace & **PARROTT**, Lucy C. d/o Sarah PARROTT surety William T. PARROTT 6 Nov 1833 (OB) by Albert G. BURTON 12 Nov 1833 (OM)

**BROWN**, James & **HARROD**, Nancy; 11 Nov 1788 surety John HARROD (OB)

**BROWN**, James E. age 21 s POB POR Orange s/o John BROWN and Frances HOLBURT miller & **AMOS**, Emily L. age 16 s POB POR Orange d/o George A. AMOS and Jennie DARNALL 7 May 1873 POM Orange by H.E. HATCHER (OMR)

**BROWN**, James O. & **COOPER**, Sarah d/o Owen COOPER surety John M. COLEMAN 18 Dec 1838 (OB)

**BROWN**, James R. & **HANEY**, Mary Ann d/o James HANEY surety Benjamin HIGGERSON 17 Jul 1843 (OB)

**BROWN**, James W. & **DEMPSEY**, Mary C. surety John GREEN 30 Oct 1841 (OB)

**BROWN**, James W. s/o James O. BROWN and Sarah M. COOPER age 23 s farmer POB POR Orange & **BOWLER**, Mary E. d/o Robert BOWLER and Caroline E. BOLLING age 22 s POB POR Orange; POM Orange 29 Mar 1866 (OMR) 26 Mar 1866 (OML)

**BROWN**, John & **WALLER**, Judith surety Spencer J. ATKINS 22 Feb 1820 (OB)

**BROWN**, John G. s/o John BROWN & **HOLBERT**, Martha Frances d/o Elijah HOLBERT surety Carter B. FAULCONER 18 Dec 1834 (OB)

**BROWN**, John POC age 20 s POB Louisa Co. POR Orange s/o Armistead BROWN & Fanny BROOKS laborer & **SCOTT**, Hulda POC age 20 s POB Louisa Co POR Orange d/o Lewis SCOTT & Emily JACKSON DOM 2 Jun 1868 POM Orange by H.M. LINNEY (OMR)

**BROWN**, Joseph F. age 25 s farmer POB POR Orange s/o Henry BROWN and Ann BONO & **CHEWNING**, Mary E. age 26 s POB POR Orange d/o R.W. CHEWNING and Ellen HOPKINS POM Orange 29 Jan 1878 by Melzi S. CHANCELLOR (OMR)

**BROWN**, Lewis POC age 27 s farm laborer POB Louisa POR Orange s/o Adam BROWN and Mary THURSTON & **WADDY**, Mary age 24 s POB POR Orange d/o Harry WADDY POM Orange 6 Sep 1876 by Richard STEPHENS (OMR)

**BROWN**, Matthew B. POC age 24 s barker POB POR Orange s/o Charlotte FIDO & **FISHER**, Jane POC age 23 s POB Culpeper POR Orange d/o Sylvester FISHER POM Orange 3 Nov 1879 by C.T. VAUGHN (OMR)

**BROWN**, Opian POC age 34 s POB POR Orange carpenter & **CLARK**, Catherine [POC] age 25 s POB POR Orange d/o Nicholas CLARK and Elizabeth LONG 8 Jan 1874 POM Orange (OMR)

**BROWN**, Page POC age 27 s POB Louisa Co POR Orange s/o Adam BROWN and Mary THURSTON farmer & **CARTER**, Miranda POC age 21 s POB POR Orange d/o Tom CARTER and Louisa LUCAS 31 Aug 1873 POM Orange by Richard STEPHENS (OMR)

**BROWN**, Preston POC age 24 s POB Albemarle Co POR Orange s/o James BROWN and Milly JACKSON farm laborer & **GREEN**,

31

Winney age 25 w POB POR Orange d/o Andy STEWART and Sarah
Ann _____ DOM 4 Dec 1869 POM Orange by Franklin TIBBS (OMR)

**BROWN**, Sanderson & **BICKERS**, Nancy surety Abner BICKERS 26
Dec 1816 (OB)

**BROWN**, Seth C. age 37 s POB Rappahannock Co. POR Orange s/o John
BROWN and Elizabeth JONES saddler & **BECKHAM**, Jennie E. age
18 POB POR Orange d/o James BECKHAM and Sarah A. KENNEDY
1 Mar 1870 POM Orange by J.W. MCCOWN (OMR)

**BROWN**, Thomas H. age 21 s POB POR Orange s/o Henry J. BROWN
and Ann M. BOND farmer & **ESTES**, Mildred T. age 23 w POB POR
Orange d/o Dabney WRIGHT and Jane M. ESTES 16 Jul 1868 POM
Orange by Charles QUARLES (OMR)

**BROWN**, William & **HANCOCK**, Mary surety Joseph P. COONS 25 Sep
1824 (OB) by George MORRIS 25 Sep 1824 (OM)

**BROWN**, William & **HORD**, Ann d/o Jesse HORD surety Edward
FAULCONER 19 Jun 1822 (OB)

**BROWN**, Wilson POC age 23 s POB Louisa Co. POR Orange s/o Adam
BROWN and Mary THURSTON laborer & **ELLIS**, Malinda POC age
21 s POB Louisa Co POR Orange d/o Joseph ELLIS and Frances
LUCAS 27 Apr 1873 POM Orange by Richard STEPHENS (OMR)

**BROWN**, Wilson POC age 24 s labourer POB POR Orange s/o Edgar
BROWN and Hannah BARBOUR & **JACKSON**, Cornelia POC age
23 s POB POR Orange d/o John JACKSON and Gabriella TAYLOR
POM Orange 17 Dec 1879 (OMR)

**BROWNING**, Cornelius R. s/o Joshua BROWNING and Lilly GODDIN
age 24 s POB Brooks Co, GA POR Colquett Co, GA farmer &
**JONES**, Frances A. d/o John JONES and Susan BICKERS age 26 s
POB POR Orange POM Orange 22 Dec 1863 (OMR) 21 Dec 1863
(OML)

**BROWNING**, John A. s/o Willis and Elizabeth BROWNING age 25 s
farmer POB POR Rappahannock Co. & **WILLIS**, Mary Lewis d/o
George and Martha P. WILLIS age 18 s POB Florida POR Orange
POM Orange 5 Oct 1853 (OMR) 4 Oct 1853 (OML)

**BRUCE**, Loudoun B. & **ESTES**, Milly; 10 Sep 1807 surety William
ESTES by George BINGHAM (OB) (OM)

**BRUCE**, Mordecai & **AHEART**, Christina both of St. Thomas Parish by
banns (Deed Book 17)

**BRUNER**, Peter & **KIBLINGER**, Catey; 3 Aug 1801surety Daniel
KIBLINGER (OB)

**BRUSCH**, John J. age 25 s POB Switzerland POR Staunton s/o John
BRUSCH and Maggy WIGGLE butcher & **JOHNSTON**, Hannah B.

age 17 s POB Newbury POR Orange d/o William W. JOHNSTON 29 Jun 1873 POM Orange by J.W.MCCOWEN (OMR)

**BRYAN,** Daniel & **BARBOUR,** Mary T. d/o Thomas BARBOUR surety Nathaniel T. WELCH by J. GOSS 8 Apr 1818 (OB) (OM)

**BRYAN,** Edward & **HAMBLETON,** Polly; 15 Mar 1793 consent by Edward HAMBLETON surety William STOWERS (OB)

**BRYAN,** James & **FULK,** Elizabeth surety William SMITH 30 Sep 1834 (OB)

**BRYAN,** Jeremiah & **LONG,** Frankey surety Armstead LONG 27 Mar 1813 (OB) by George BINGHAM 28 Mar 1813 (OM)

**BRYANT,** Charles & **SNOW,** Polly 27 Mar 1823 by George BINGHAM (OM)

**BRYANT,** John s/o William BRYANT and Elizabeth GLASSIM age 31 s miner POB England POB Orange & **SMITH,** Ann E. d/o William SMITH and Sarah HAWKINS age 17 s POB Fauquier Co POR Orange; POM Orange 26 Nov 1867 (OMR) 23 Nov 1867 (OML)

**BRYANT,** Norris POC age 22 s labourer POB Albemarle POR Orange s/o Lewis and Rebecca BRYANT & **BANKS,** Nellie POC age 21 s POB Greene POR Orange POM Mt. Pisgah Church, Orange 24 Jul 1878 by Elliott TIBBS (OMR)

**BRYANT,** Thomas POR St. Thomas Parish & **THORNTON,** Frankie POR St. Thomas Parish 23 Dec 1775 by banns (Deed Book 17)

**BUCHANAN,** John M. age 23 s watchman on railroad POB Spotsylvania POR Fredericksburg s/o William S. BUCHANAN and Malvina STEWART & **FAULCONER,** Lucy F. age 26 s POB POR Orange d/o William FAULCONER and Catherine A. CHEWNING POM Orange 13 Dec 1877 (OMR)

**BUCK,** Anthony & **SHEPHERD,** Mary; 15 Dec 1796 surety Andrew SHEPHERD Jr. (OB)

**BUCKHANNON,** John & **SMITH,** Mary surety Henry SMITH POM St. Thomas Parish 27 Jan 1785 (OB)

**BUCKNER,** Baldwin & **BURTON,** Fanny; 12 Nov 1794 surety James COLLINS (OB) by George EVE 16 Nov 1794 (OM)

**BULL,** Marcus Jr. & **DADE,** Sarah T. surety Garland BALLARD 5 Apr 1843 (OB) by J. EARNEST 19 Apr 1843 (OM)

**BULLOCK,** Oswald s/o William R. and Sophia BULLOCK age 23 s student POB POR Orange & **QUISENBERRY,** Ann F. d/o Hezakiah and Emily QUISENBERRY age 21 s POB POR Orange; POM Orange 27 Nov 1855 (OMR) 26 Nov 1855 (OML)

**BULLOCK,** Walter age 22 s farmer POB Louisa POR Spotsylvania s/o Robert N. BULLOCK and Ann E. JONES & **MILLS,** Jennie C. age 22 s POB POR Orange d/o Thomas M. MILLS and Mary S. GRAVES POM Orange 20 Sep 1877 (OMR)

**BULLOCK**, William K. & **KENDALL**, Sophia d/o Robert KENDALL surety James M. KENDALL 23 Jan 1832 (OB)

**BULLS**, Alfred age 40 w farm laborer POB Essex Co POR Albemarle Co POC & **JACKSON**, Ellen age 26 w POB POR Orange POC; POM Orange 17 Nov 1866 (OMR)

**BUMPASS**, Joseph & **TERRILL**, Nancy; 24 May 1823 (OB)

**BUNDY**, William & **ROLLS**, Ophelia Ann surety William ROLLS 21 Dec 1832 (OB)

**BURDON**, Willis age 39 s POB Albemarle Co POR Orange s/o Willis BURDON and Maria _____ farmer & **STILLMIN**, Mary age 21 w POB Madison Co POR Orange d/o Matilda STEDWIN 13 Mar 1869 POM Orange by T.M. CARSON (OMR)

**BURKE**, Isaac & **MILLER**, Jane over 21 years surety Robert MILLER by George BINGHAM 4 Feb 1809 (OB) (OM)

**BURN**, James & **KNIGHT**, Elizabeth permission from William B. KNIGHT surety John LAMB 21 Apr 1818 (OB)

**BURNAM**, Charles s/o Charles BURNAM and Mercie WEIMER age 39 s farmer POB Canada POR Orange & **GABBOT**, Lucinda d/o James GABBOT POB POR Orange; POM Orange 13 Jun 1867 (OMR) 12 Jun 1867 (OML)

**BURNLEY**, Garland & **TAYLOR**, Frances; 8 Nov 1779 both of St. Thomas Parish surety Robert TAYLOR (OB)

**BURNLEY**, James & **PARSONS**, Nancy; 1 Nov 1798 surety Andrew SHEPHERD Jr. (OB)

**BURNLEY**, Jonas POC age 21 s farm labourer POB POR Orange s/o John BURNLEY and Sarah WALKER & **GORDON**, Eliza POC age 21 s POB POR Orange POM Hopewell Church, Orange 2 Jan 1879 by W.H. CAMPER (OMR)

**BURNLEY**, Richard & **JONES**, Eliza Swan both of St. Thomas Parish (Orange Fee Book)

**BURNS**, James & **PEYTON**, Peachey d/o William PEYTON surety James KNIGHT 21 May 1836 (OB)

**BURRUS**, Alfred POC age 23 s POB POR Orange s/o Sam BURRUS and Mary MANSFIELD laborer & **WHITE**, Nelly POC age 24 s POB POR Orange d/o Thomas WHITE and Sarah ELLIS 8 Mar 1873 POM Orange by Thomas R. HAWKINS (OMR)

**BURRUS**, Joseph & **TERRILL**, Nancy; 24 May 1823 surety William S. FRAZER (OB)

**BURRUS**, Roger s/o Thomas BURRUS and Frances TANDY & **MILLS**, Cynthia d/o Nathaniel MILLS and Frances THOMPSON [b. 19 Sep 1772] 8 Jan 1790 surety Roger TANDY (OB)

**BURRUS**, Samuel & **RUCKER**, Catey 24 Oct 1788 by George EVE (OM)

**BURRUSS,** Lancelot & **SLAUGHTER,** Frances M. ward of Lunsford H. LONG who is also surety 26 Nov 1827 (OB)

**BURRUSS,** Minor POC age 22 s POB POR Orange s/o Sam BURRUSS and Mary _____ wagoner & **ELLIS,** Lucy POC age 17 s POB POR Orange d/o James ELLIS and Lucinda DANIEL 21 Aug 1880 POM Orange by Albert THURSTON (OMR)

**BURRUSS,** Robert B. & **GRAVES,** Ann E. d/o Lewis GRAVES who is also surety 22 Nov 1847 (OB) by Herndon FRAZER 30 Nov 1847 (OM)

**BURRUSS,** William T. s/o Joseph BURRUSS and Nancy TERRILL age 34 s farmer POB POR Orange & **SEE,** Almyra A. d/o James SEE and Gracie E. PROCTOR age 20 s POB POR Orange; POM Orange 2 Feb 1865 (OMR) (OML)

**BURTON,** Aylett & **WILLIAMS,** Patsy 1 Nov 1832 surety Southy SIMPSON (OB)

**BURTON,** Bezabel & **JARRELL,** Frances d/o Mildred JARRELL surety Reuben KENNEDY 2 Jul 1833 (OB)

**BURTON,** Fleming POC age 42 s POB Caroline Co POR Orange s/o Jesse BURTON and Betsy _____ laborer & **MORRIS,** Elizabeth POC age 31 s POB POR Orange d/o Ben MORRIS and Betsy PAYNE 14 Aug 1869 POM Orange by Theo M. CARSON (OMR)

**BURTON,** James & **GOODRIDGE,** Betsy 2 Apr 1799 surety James TAYLOR (OB) 3 Apr 1799 by Hamilton GOSS (OM)

**BURTON,** James & **WHITE,** Mary d/o Jeremiah WHITE both of St. Thomas Parish surety Francis TAYLOR 19 Jan 1779 (OB)

**BURTON,** John & **MAY,** Milly; 27 Jul 1807 surety Joel MAY by Nathaniel SANDERS (OB)(OM)

**BURTON,** John M. & **GOODRIDGE,** Mildred surety George C. GOODRIDGE by Jacob WATTS 10 Feb 1812 (OB) (OM)

**BURTON,** May & **HEAD,** Sarah 29 Sep 1776 both of St. Thomas Parish (Deed Book 17)

**BURTON,** William & **GOODRICH,** Ann b.d. 14 Dec 1785 certified by Betsy BURTON 24 Dec 1806 surety William RUCKER (OB) by Jacob WATTS 25 Dec 1806 (OM)

**BUSH,** Caleb & **TAYLOR,** Lucinda surety StClair TAYLOR 24 Oct 1812 (OB) by George BINGHAM 29 Oct 1812 (OM)

**BUSH,** Edmund & **WARKER,** Elizabeth; 5 Sep 1798 by George BINGHAM (OM)

**BUSH,** Francis & **DAVIS,** Lucy both of St. Thomas Parish 27 Jul 1773 (Deed Book 17)

**BUSH,** Thomas & **BREADWELL,** Liddy; 22 Mar 1802 surety Henry WOOD (OB) by Nathaniel SANDERS, Baptist 25 Mar 1802 (Misc Min Returns)

35

BUSICK, Nathan S. & **LLOYD**, Berlinda d/o Eliz. LLOYD surety
William BUSICK 25 Feb 1832 (OB)

BUTLER, Alexander F. & **ANDREWS**, Elizabeth Ann d/o Lewis
ANDREWS; 23 Feb 1852 (OML)

BUTLER, George W. age 20 y 11 mo 15 days s POB Louisa Co POR
Orange s/o William R. BUTLER and Mary K. HAWKINS wheelwright
& **GIBSON**, Mary E. age 19 s POB POR Orange d/o William GIBSON
and Martha J. KRISE 1 Sep 1870 POM Orange by H.M. LINNEY
(OMR)

BUTLER, Matthew & **KRISE**, Mary Ann d/o Elizabeth KRISE surety
Samuel H. PARROTT 14 Oct 1843 (OB)

BUTLER, Robert E. age 24 s POB POR Louisa Co s/o Elijah BUTLER
and Mary GENTRY farmer & **GRADY**, Mary W. age 14 s POB Louisa
Co POR Orange d/o Joseph GRADY and Sallie ESTES 31 Jan 1869
POM Orange Thomas R. HAWKINS (OMR)

BUTLER, Robert L. age 23 s POB Louisa Co POR Orange s/o David F.
BUTLER and Martha J. POINDEXTER farmer & **GIBSON**, Angelina
age 19 s POB POR Orange d/o William GIBSON and Martha J. KRISE
17 Dec 1868 POM Orange by H.M. LINNEY (OMR)

BYERS, David H. s/o David MYERS and Nancy MUMLY(?) age 35 w
merchant POB Albemarle Co POR Orange & **KEITH**, Helen J. d/o
Daniel KEITH age 32 s POB POR Orange; POM Orange 23 May 1867
(OMR) 22 May 1867 (OML)

BYRUM, John & **SOUTHERLAND**, Mildred surety Robert
SOUTHERLAND 9 Aug 1848 (OB)

CAHOE, Patrick s/o Richard & Nancy CAHOE age 25 s laborer POB
County Waterford, Ireland POR Orange & **STITZER**, Elizabeth d/o
William & Elizabeth STITZER age 24 s POB & POR Orange; POM
Orange 9 Oct 1855 (OMR)

CALDWELL, Porter D. age 22 s POB POR King William Co. s/o J.T. &
B.R. CALDWELL merchant & **WILLIAMS**, Mamie C. age 22 POB
POR Orange Co. d/o L.B. & Mary C. WILLIAMS 27 Jan 1869 POM
Orange by T.M. CARSON (OMR)

CAMP, James & **WOOD**, Mary 16 Sep 1803 POM Orange by Robert
JONES (Misc Min Ret)

CAMP, William POR Culpeper Co. & **WILLIS**, Frances 27 Nov 1772
marriage date of 1 Dec but no minister named (Deed Book 17)

CAMPBELL, Alexander & **MALLORY**, Anna surety George LAWSON
7 Nov 1822 (OB)

CAMPBELL, Archibald & **ARNOLD**, Susannah; 1 Nov 1786 surety
William HANCOCK (OB)

**CAMPBELL**, Benjamin POC age 26 s POB POR Orange s/o Absalom CAMPBELL and Lucy JOHNSON laborer & **LINDSAY**, Mary POC age 21 s POB Madison Co POR Orange 5 Feb 1873 POM Orange by Philip JOHNSON (OMR)

**CAMPBELL**, James A. POC age 23 s POB POR Orange s/o Absalom CAMPBELL and Winnie _____ farm hand & **SMITH**, Laura POC age 21 s POB POR Orange d/o Jane JOHNSON 28 Oct 1869 POM Orange by Philip JOHNSON (OMR)

**CAMPBELL**, Joseph D. physician & **ATKINS**, Sarah M. d/o Joseph ATKINS surety Hugh M. DICKINSON 23 Sep 1847 by J. EARNEST (OB) (OM)

**CAMPBELL**, Larkin POC age 22 s POB POR Orange s/o Isaac CAMPBELL and Amy CAMPBELL farm laborer & **GREEN**, Ellen POC age 21 s POB POR Orange d/o William GREEN and Mary GREEN 30 Dec 1869 POM Orange by Philip JOHNSON (OMR)

**CAMPBELL**, Ned POC age 21 s POB Bedford Co POR Orange s/o Edward CAMPBELL and Violet _____ r.r. hand & **HIGGENBOTHAM**, Mildred POC age 17 s POB POR Orange d/o John MILLER and Lucy BROOKS 28 Aug 1873 POM Orange by E.R. PERRY (OMR)

**CAMPBELL**, Robert & **ATKINS**, Ann Maria d/o Spencer J. ATKINS 7 May 1818 surety Robert DUNCAN and James WALLER (OB)

**CAMPBELL**, William J. age 20 s farmer POB POR Orange s/o James S. CAMPBELL and Mary MCCLARY & **HUGHES**, Mildred A. age 17 s POB POR Orange d/o Jefferson HUGHES and Mary A. HERNDON POM Orange 20 Dec 1877 (OMR)

**CAMPBELL**, William J. POC age 30 s clerk in a store POB POR Orange s/o John CAMPBELL and Minerva JOHNSON & **WORMLEY**, Rachel age 22 s POB POR Orange d/o Fayette WORMLEY and Fanny WILLIAMS POM Orange 19 Oct 1879 (OMR)

**CAMPBELL**, Willis POC age 23 s POB POR Orange s/o Isaac CAMPBELL laborer & **JAMES**, Maria POC age 21 s POB Fauquier Co POR Orange d/o Isaac JAMES 12 Dec POM Orange by John H. ROBERTSON (OMR)

**CAMPER**, William H. s/o John CAMPER and Mary J. JONES age 30 s minister POB Botetourt Co. POR Orange & **JERDONE**, Mary C. d/o Francis JERDONE and Eliza M. WATKINS age 22 s POB POR Orange; POM Orange 18 Dec 1866 (OMR) 12 Dec 1866 (OML)

**CANADAY**, James & **TINDER**, Ann d/o Anthony TINDER surety Robinson TINDER 17 Apr 1834 (OB)

**CANADAY**, James D. s/o James CANADAY and Ann TINDER age 26 s farmer POB POR Orange & **MASON**, Ellen A. d/o Charles MASON and Lucy JONES age 24 s POB POR Orange; POM Orange 25 Jan 1866 (OMR) 23 Jan 1866 (OML)

**CANNADAY**, James D. age 29 w POB POR Orange d/o James CANADAY and Ann TINDER farmer & **MASON**, Lucy H. age 30 w POB POR Orange d/o Charles MASON and Lucy JONES 12 Sep 1868 POM Orange by Sanders MASON (OMR)

**CARBERRY**, Patrick s/o William and Margaret CARBERRY w laborer POB Ireland POR Orange & **JOHNSON**, Susan d/o William B. and Martha LEWIS w POB POR Orange; POM Orange 16 Feb 1856 (OMR) 15 Feb 1856 (OML)

**CARD**, Abraham POR St. Thomas Parish & **ARCHER** Ann POR St. Thomas Parish 25 Sep 1773 (Deed Book 17)

**CAREY**, Albert POC age 27 s POB POR Orange s/o Wilson CAREY and Elizabeth BROWN farmer & **WALLACE**, Caroline POC age 35 w POB POR Orange d/o Nancy ___ 26 Mar 1880 POM Blue Run Church, Orange by William ROBINSON (OMR)

**CAREY**, George POC age 24 s POB POR Orange laborer s/o Wilson CAREY and Lizzie DAVIS & **KELLEY**, Alice POC age 21 s POB Albemarle POR Orange d/o James KELLEY 9 Dec 1880 POB Barboursville, Orange by William ROBINSON (OMR)

**CARNEEL**, John s/o James CARNEEL and Betsy WRIGHT age 57 w farmer POB POR Caroline Co & **THACKER**, Ann d/o Benjamin THACKER and Lucy LOWRY age 35 s POB Hanover Co POR Orange; POM Orange 20 Oct 1867 (OMR) 18 Oct 1867 (OML)

**CARPENTER**, Fountain & **CARPENTER**, Martha F. d/o Pleasant CARPENTER surety James CARPENTER by Edward G. SHIP 24 Jun 1833 (OB) (OM)

**CARPENTER**, John F. & **DULANEY**, Sarah G. surety William DULANEY 22 May 1837 (OB)

**CARPENTER**, Philip M. & **EHEART**, Lucy C. d/o Michael L. EHEART 18 Nov 1841 surety Henry A. SNEED (OB)

**CARPENTER**, Reuben POC age 22 s POB Culpeper POR Orange s/o Henry CARPENTER and Susan WISE laborer & **TOWNS**, Mary Ella POC age 25 s POB POR Orange d/o Absalom TOWNS and Betsy POAGUE 22 Jul 1880 POM Orange by Willis ROBINSON (OMR)

**CARPENTER**, William B. & **JOHNSON**, Susan F. d/o Martha A. JOHNSON surety James W. CARPENTER 18 Nov 1839 (OB)

**CARPENTER**, Willis H. s/o Jonas CARPENTER age 25 s farmer POB POR Madison Co & **MURRAY**, Carolina S. d/o Joseph and Lutecia MURRAY age 20 s POB Dublin, Ireland POR Orange; POM Orange 7 Sep 1854 (OMR) (OML)

**CARR,** Albert POC age 30 w POB Albemarle Co POR Orange s/o Dick
CARR and Fanny CARR laborer & **WRIGHT,** Mattie POC age 31 s
POB POR Orange d/o Daniel WRIGHT 11 Sep 1869 POM Orange by
H.M. LINNEY (OMR)

**CARR,** David & **CAVE,** Emily A. ward of Philip C. CAVE who is also
surety 13 Oct 1826 (OB) by J. GOSS 19 Oct 1826 (OM)

**CARROL,** Jacob & **REYNOLDS,** Tabitha permission from Rachel
REYNOLDS 14 Jan 1783 surety Benjamin GRIFFITH (OB)

**CARROLL,** William & **CLARKE,** Elizabeth d/o William CLARKE
surety Abraham BOOTEN 20 Aug 1823 (OB)

**CARRUTHERS,** William H. & **CLARKE,** Ann H. d/o William D.
CLARKE who is also surety by M.A. DUNN 1 Sep 1847 (OB) (OM)

**CARTER,** Adcock POR Spotsylvania & **DANIEL,** Elizabeth POR Orange
Co 12 Sep 1811 John CORTHON security (OB)13 Oct 1811 by Philip
PENDLETON (OMR)

**CARTER,** Benjamin & **DANIEL,** Polly surety Adcock CARTER 30 Sep
1813 (OB) by Philip PENDLETON 13 Oct 1813 (OM)

**CARTER,** Burwell POC age 24 s POB POR Orange s/o Burwell CARTER
and Amy SMITH laborer & **ALLENS,** Sally POC age 22 s POB Louisa
Co POR Orange d/o William ALLENS 7 Nov 1872 POM Orange by
H.E. HATCHER (OMR)

**CARTER,** Cassius s/o William Fitzhugh and Elizabeth Lucy CARTER age
30 s physician POB POR Fairfax & **TALIAFERRO,** Jane A. d/o
Charles and Louisa G.TALIAFERRO age 17 s POB Caroline Co POR
Orange; POM Orange 18 Jun 1856 (OMR) (OML)

**CARTER,** Charles R. & **NEWMAN,** Jane d/o Alexander NEWMAN who
is also surety 28 Nov 1825 (OB) by John HALES 30 Nov 1825 (OM)

**CARTER,** Cyrus POC age 21 s POB POR Orange s/o Thomas CARTER
and Gray TIBBS laborer & **WAUGH,** Mary Jane POC age 21 s POB
POR Orange d/o Reuben WAUGH and Eliza KELLY 28 Nov 1868
POM Orange by John H. ROBERTSON (OMR)

**CARTER,** George POC age 21 s farm labourer POB POR Orange s/o Tom
CARTER and Hennetta COLLINS & **LEWIS,** Sally POC age 21 s
POB POR Orange d/o James LEWIS and Milly LEWIS ages of both
parties sworn to by Mat LEWIS, brother of Sally LEWIS POM Orange
17 Apr 1878 by Sanders MASON (OMR)

**CARTER,** Harry W. age 38 s painter POB Kentucky POR Orange s/o
Harry W. CARTER and Laura W. PUFFER & **MAYHUGH,** Mary
Alice age 22 s POR Orange d/o Coffer MAYHUGH and Ann E.
BRADLEY POM Gordonsville 27 Nov 1877 (OMR)

**CARTER,** Howard P. POC age 21 s labourer POB POR Orange s/o
Edmund CARTER and Betsy GREEN & **WILSON,** Nora POC age 22

s POB Richmond POR Orange d/o John WILSON and Lucy ___ POM
Orange 26 Jun 1878 (OMR)

**CARTER,** James & **NEWCOM,** Jane 14 May 1822 by George
BINGHAM (OM)

**CARTER,** John POC age 27 s railroad hand POB Albemarle POR Orange
s/o William DOUGLASS and Ann GRADY & **CHANDLER,** Lucy
POC age 21 s POB POR Orange d/o Fred. CHANDLER POM Orange
24 Dec 1879 by W.J. BARNETT (OMR)

**CARTER,** John POC age 41 w labourer POB Madison POR Orange s/o
Robert and Celie CARTER & **JACKSON,** Lucy POC age 23 s POB
POR Orange d/o Gabriel and Eliza JACKSON POM Mt. Pleasant
Church, Orange 31 Dec 1879 by C.T. JOHNSON (OMR)

**CARTER,** Joseph & **BELL,** Polly; 23 Apr 1792 surety John CARTER
(OB)

**CARTER,** Lewis POC age 21 s POB POR Orange s/o Edmund CARTER
and Kitty BARBOUR laborer & **SMITH,** Mary A. age 17 s POB POR
Orange d/o Albert SMITH 8 Nov 1873 POM Orange by F.L. GIPSON
(OMR)

**CARTER,** Thomas W. age 32 s POB Fauquier POR Richmond s/o
William CARTER and Martha NELSON nurseryman & **FLETCHER,**
Bettie B. age 23 s POB Fauquier POR Orange d/o Alex D. FLETCHER
and Louisa WEBSTER 7 Jan 1880 (marriage register gives the 1880
date; marriage license says 6 Jan 1879 but it is filed with 1880) POM
Orange by H.E. HATCHER (OMR)

**CARTER,** William C. & **NEWMAN,** Mary Ann surety George
NEWMAN 8 Aug 1833 (OB)

**CARY,** Barney & **LEATHERS,** Alice surety Richard HAYES 21 May
1825 (OB)

**CASEBOLT,** Andrew M. & **SAMPSON,** Louisa permission from John
SAMPSON surety James JOLLETT 25 Sep 1834 (OB)

**CASEY,** William & **TAYLOR,** Agnes permission from Charles TAYLOR
24 Mar 1788 surety Jeremiah SIMS (OB) by George EVE 6 Apr 1788
(OM)

**CASH,** James & **HENSHAW,** Ann surety John BROWN 6 Sep 1825 (OB)

**CASH,** Joseph B. age 54 w POB Orange POR Madison s/o James CASH
and Anna HENSHAW farmer & **SMITH,** Sarah J. age 35 s POB
Fluvanna POR Orange d/o William S. SMITH and Carthagena DAVIS
30 Dec 1880 POM Orange by J.C. PAINTER (OMR)

**CASON,** Benjamin & **GRAVES,** Nancy surety Jonathan GRAVES 28 Sep
1818 (OB)

**CASON,** M.H. age 21 s farmer POB Albemarle POR Orange s/o William
CASON and Mary A. HALL & **MAY,** Sarah F. age 30 s POB Madison

POR Orange d/o B.F. MAY and Mildred SOUTHARDS POM Orange 25 Dec 1878 (OMR)

**CASON**, William & **THOMPSON**, Mary d/o John and Catherine THOMPSON 17 Feb 1795 surety Frederick THOMPSON (OB)

**CATES** (possibly COTES), David S. s/o David H. CATES and Elizabeth MORRIS age 30 s boot & shoemaker POB POR Orange & **HUTCHISON**, Mattie E. d/o William F. HUTCHISON and Martha L. BRAWNER age 21 s POB Fauquier Co POR Orange; POM Orange 6 Dec 1866 (OMR) (OML)

**CATTERTON**, Benjamin W. & **AUSTIN**, Ann 8 Feb 1827 by George BINGHAM (OM)

**CATTERTON**, Benjamin W. & **PRICE**, Elizabeth 31 Dec 1821 surety James SIMMS (OB) 3 Jan 1822 by George BINGHAM (OM)

**CATTERTON**, Francis & **CLARKSON**, Nancy 12 Oct 1815 by George BINGHAM (OM)

**CAVE**, Abner s/o William CAVE Sr. & **SIMS**, Betsey d/o William SIMS 8 Jan 1803 surety Thomas CAVE (OB) 13 Jan 1803 by George BINGHAM (Misc Min Ret)

**CAVE**, Bartlett Jr. & **SNOW**, Jenny 22 Dec 1796 by George BINGHAM (OM)

**CAVE**, Benjamin Jr. & **WHITE**, Elizabeth 21 Jan 1794 surety William WHITE (OB) by George EVE 22 Jan 1794 (OM)

**CAVE**, Nathan POC age 21 s farm labourer POB Madison POR Orange s/o Isaac CAVE and Eliza ____ & **MILLER**, Emma POC age 22 s POB Richmond POR Orange POM Orange C.H. 26 Mar 1878 by Willis ROBINSON (OMR)

**CAVE**, Richard & **PORTER**, Maria; 25 Nov 1805 surety Abner PORTER by Robert JONES (OB) (OM)

**CAVE**, Richard & **SHELTON**, Lucy by Nathaniel SANDERS, Baptist 12 Dec 1806 (OM)

**CAVE**, Robert over 21 years & **BRADLEY**, Lucy over 21 years 19 Aug 1806 surety George BRADLEY(OB)

**CAVE**, Robert C. s/o Robert P.CAVE and Sarah F. LINDSAY age 20 s farmer POB POR Orange & **DANIEL**, Fannie S. d/o William F. DANIEL and Julia TERRILL age 18 s POB POR Orange; POM Sycamore Church, Richmond, VA 15 Jan 1863 Richmond (OMR) 12 Jan 1863 (OML)

**CAVE**, Robert P. s/o Robert CAVE who is also surety & **LINDSAY**, Sarah F. ward of James G. LINDSAY 25 Jul 1836 (OB) by Joseph A. MANSFIELD 2 Aug 1836 (OM)

**CAVE**, Sinclair & **ANDERSON**, Sary 13 Mar 1814 by George BINGHAM (OM)

**CAVE**, Thomas & **SIMS**, Nancy 4 Nov 1797 surety William SIMS (OB)

41

**CAVE**, Thomas B. s/o Richard CAVE and Maria PORTER age 56 s farmer POB Madison Co POR Orange & **DOWNER**, Lucy F. d/o Robert DOWNER and Frances DANIEL age 32 s POB POR Orange; POM Orange 27 Jul 1865 (OMR) 24 Jul 1865 (OML)

**CAVE**, William & **JOLLETT**, Judy permission from Mary JOLLETT 22 Nov 1791 surety James JOLLETT (OB)

**CAVE**, William & **MALLORY**, Mary 28 Dec 1761 both of St. Thomas Parish (Orange Fee Book)

**CAVE**, William & **SNOW**, Sarah over 21 years 16 Jul 1810 surety Bartlett CAVE (OB) 16 Jul by George BINGHAM (OM)

**CAVE**, William s/o John CAVE POR Brumfield Parish, Culpeper Co. & **CHRISTY**, Frances d/o Julius CHRISTY POR St. Thomas Parish 6 Jun 1783 surety Belfield CAVE (OB) 11 Jun 1783 by George EVE (OM)

**CAZA**, William & **SLAUGHTER**, Mary surety Jeremiah HENRY by John GARNETT 12 May 1812 (OB) (OM)

**CHAMBERS**, Abraham & **DAWSON**, Mary d/o John DAWSON 17 Nov 1790 surety William DAWSON (OB) 18 Nov 1790 by Nathaniel SANDERS (OM)

**CHAMBERS**, Thomas & **ROBINSON**, Milly d/o Artimus ROBINSON 15 Jul 1790 surety Francis HUGHES (OB)

**CHAMBERS**, Willis & **HOUSTON**, Mary surety Lewis HOUSTON 10 Oct 1836 (OB)

**CHAMHART**, Henry & **DAWSON**, Fanny surety Baldwin TALIAFERO 4 Feb 1816 by William HAWLEY . The groom's signature is in German (OB)

**CHAMP**, Philip POC age 24 s rail road hand POB Culpeper POR Orange s/o Robert CHAMP and Mary ___ & **DABNEY**, Susan POC age 21 s POB POR Orange d/o John DABNEY and Rhoda _____ POM Orange 20 Dec 1877 (OMR)

**CHAMPE**, Lewis POC age 22 s labourer POB Madison POR Orange s/o Robert and Mary CHAMPE & **CARTER**, Nannie POC age 21 s POB Louisa POR Orange d/o Reuben CARTER and Maria DANIEL POM Gordonsville, Orange 25 Nov 1879 by M. WASS (?) (OMR) There is a letter filed with this marriage license from Nannie CHAMPE in which she states that her parents' names are supposed to read "Reuben Carter and Maria Carter instead of Reuben Carter and Maria Daniel". This may be a misunderstanding on her part regarding the use of a maiden name in this record.

**CHANDLER**, Frederick POC age 23 s POB POR Orange s/o Frederick CHANDLER and Camomile COLEMAN farmer & **PARSON**, Polly POC age 20 s POB POR Orange d/o Mittie PARSON 21 Feb 1869 POM Orange by Philip JOHNSON (OMR)

CHANDLER, James & **MCNEAL,** Frances d/o Martha MCNEAL surety
Samuel THOMPSON Jr. 22 Dec 1789 (OB)

CHANDLER, John & **TERRELL,** Elizabeth permission from William
TERRELL surety William LINDSAY 26 Dec 1791 (OM)

CHANDLER, Joseph & **HOMES,** Nancy 15 Jan 1794 surety George
SCOTT (OB)

CHANDLER, Robert & **ROBINSON,** Sukey 24 Feb 1774 both of St.
Thomas parish by banns (Deed Book 17)

CHANDLER, Uriel POC age 25 s labourer POB POR Orange s/o Nelson
CHANDLER and Lucy BROOKS & **GRAVES,** Phillipa POC age 22 s
POB POR Orange d/o Robert GRAVES and Mary LINDSAY POM
Orange 26 Apr 1877 (OMR)

CHANDLER, William POC age 21 s POB POR Orange s/o Robert
CHANDLER and Eve BURKES laborer & **JAMES,** Willie Ann POC
age 18 s POB POR Orange d/o Elijah JAMES and Sarah Ann BURKS
21 Dec 1873 POM Orange by C. GILLUM (OMR)

CHAPMAN, Albert POC age 23 s POB POR Fauquier Co s/o Albert
CHAPMAN and Lena SMITH laborer & **GORDON,** Amanda POC age
21 POB Madison Co POR Orange d/o Abraham GORDON and Fanny
GORDON 26 Dec 1873 POM Orange by Frank TIBBS (OMR)

CHAPMAN, James Henry s/o Edmund CHAPMAN and Phinella WOOD
age 22 s POB POR Orange POC & **ROBINSON,** Caroline age 18 s
POR Orange POC; POM Orange 28 Dec 1867 (OMR) 25 Dec 1867
(OML)

CHAPMAN, John M. & **COLE,** Susan d/o William COLE surety John
WILLIS 2 Aug 1841 (OB) by James D. MCCABE 3 Aug 1841(OM)

CHAPMAN, Joshua & **YANCY,** Catharine surety Stephen YANCY 26
Nov 1816 (OB)

CHAPMAN, Nathaniel s/o Pearson CHAPMAN and S.M. ALEXANDER
age 25 s POB POR Charles Co, MD & **CHAPMAN,** Mary d/o John M.
CHAPMAN and Susan COLE age 24 s POB POR Orange; POM
Orange 23 Oct 1867 (OMR) 22 Oct 1867 (OML)

CHAPMAN, Richard M. & **VERDIER,** Maria d/o Paul VERDIER who is
also surety 7 Feb 1813 (OB)

CHAPMAN, Thomas & **EARLY,** Elizabeth d/o James EARLY; 23 Nov
1803 (OB) 29 Nov 1804 by George BINGHAM (Misc Min Ret)

CHAPMAN, William Henry & **STANARD,** Mary E.; POM Orange 1 Apr
1852 (OMR) 31 Mar 1852 (OML)

CHEWNING, George & **HILMAN,** Delilah 27 May 1839 surety Joseph
HILMAN (OB)

CHEWNING, George W. age 27 s POB POR Spotsylvania Co s/o George
CHEWNING and Delilah HILMAN carpenter & **YOUNG,** Sarah A.

age 25 s POB POR Orange d/o Charles YOUNG and Ann E.
BROCKMAN 4 Jan 1874 POM Orange(OMR)

**CHEWNING**, George W. s/o Henry and Branchy CHEWNING age 24 s
POR Louisa Co & **DIGGS**, Mary age 18 S; POM Orange 27 Dec 1853
(OMR) 26 Dec 1853 (OML)

**CHEWNING**, Isham B. & **COCKERILL**, Margaret d/o Thompson
COCKERILL 4 Apr 1829 surety Alex WHITELAW (OB)

**CHEWNING**, Joseph S. & **REYNOLDS**, Emily G. d/o Daniel G.
REYNOLDS 1Dec 1849 surety Charles R. CHEWNING by A.H.
BENNETT (OB)(OMR)

**CHOWNING**, Lorimer & **CARTER**, Judith surety George SHARMAN
11 Dec 1788 (OB)

**CHEWNING**, Thomas S. age 25 s farmer POB POR Spotsylvania s/o
Joseph S. CHEWNING and Emily G. REYNOLDS & **BELL**, Nannie
R. age 18 s POB POR Orange d/o Orville BELL and Mary F. ESTES
POM Orange 12 Apr 1877 (OMR)

**CHEWNING**, William J. age 25 s POB POR Spotsylvania s/o Joseph S.
CHEWNING and Emily G. REYNOLDS farmer & **REYNOLDS**,
Laura H. age 20 s POB POR Orange d/o Lewis H. REYNOLDS and
Lucy RHOADES 31 Mar 1880 POM Orange by W.H.CAMPER
(OMR)

**CHILDRES**, John & **JARRELL**, Mildred surety John DOTSON 11 Dec
1834 (OB)

**CHILDRESS**, Giles R. age 24 s POB POR Spotsylvania Co s/o Giles R.
CHILDRESS and Sarah E. PATTON farmer & **GRADY**, Sallie J. age
17 POB Louisa Co POR Orange 23 Jan 1872 POM Orange by Thomas
R. HAWKINS (OMR)

**CHILDRESS**, Giles R. & **PATTON**, Sarah E. d/o Elliott PATTON surety
Samuel POMFRET 7 Nov 1836 (OB)

**CHILDRESS**, Johnson E. age 22 s POB POR Orange s/o George W.
CHILDRESS and Wilhelma SHIFLETT lawyer & **VAUGHAN**,
Harriet E. age 19 s POB Madison Co POR Orange d/o Pascal
VAUGHAN and Henrietta DOWELL 25 Jan 1872 POM Orange by
Sam HARRIS (OMR)

**CHILDRESS**, William A. s/o William CHILDRESS and Elizabeth ELLIS
age 47 s carpenter POB Louisa Co POR Orange & **CHILDRESS**,
Wilhelma C. d/o Archibald SHIFLETT and Barlinda VAUGHN POB
Louisa Co POR Orange POM Orange 28 Dec 1865 (OMR) 18 Dec
1865 (OML)

**CHILDRESS**, William E. age 27 s POB Spotsylvania POR Orange s/o
Giles R. CHILDRESS and Sarah E. PATTON farmer & **TINDER**,
Lydia J. age 22 s POB POR Orange d/o Robinson G. TINDER and Ann

G. MASON 13 Feb 1868 POM Orange by Melzi S. CHANCELLOR (OMR)

**CHILES,** Henry L. & **MORRIS,** Louisa A. d/o George MORRIS surety Tandy G. MORRIS 19 Dec 1836 (OB)

**CHILES,** James & **LAND,** Jenny both of St. Thomas Parish surety John LEATHERS 28 Jan 1779 (OB)

**CHILES,** Walter G. & **HEAD,** Emily A. d/o John HEAD who is also surety 1 Jun 1827 (OB)

**CHILES,** William & **MORRIS,** Ann C. d/o George MORRIS surety Tandy G. MORRIS 26 Oct 1827 (OB)

**CHISAM,** Benjamin & **BECKHAM,** Elizabeth d/o Henry BECKHAM 27 Aug 1796 (OM) (OB)

**CHISHAM,** James & **RAINES,** Catherine surety Francis HUGHES 1 Dec 1789 (OB)

**CLARK,** Ambrose & **THOMAS,** Mary d/o Joseph THOMAS who is also surety 1 Nov 1797 (OB)

**CLARK,** Edmund & **NORMAN,** Lucy Cary w 26 Mar 1838 surety Elhanon ROW (OB)

**CLARK,** Edward M. & **NALLE,** Jane S. 7 Oct 1847 surety Joseph HIDEN by S.J. MOORMAN (OB) (OM)

**CLARK,** Franklin W. age 25 s POB POR Orange s/o James T. CLARK and Mary Ann WILTSHIRE blacksmith & **WAUGH,** Mildred W. age 22 s POB POR Orange Charles S. WAUGH and Mary F. FAULCONER 26 Dec 1872 POM Orange by Edw. M. JORDAN (OMR)

**CLARK,** Henry & **GRASTY,** Nanney 28 Dec 1801 surety G.L. GRASTY (OB) 5 Jan 1802 by Nathaniel SANDERS (OM)

**CLARK,** Henry & **JOHNSON,** Elizabeth w 25 Mar 1805 surety Thomas GRASTY (OB)

**CLARK,** James & **GRAVES,** Elizabeth; 5 Feb 1807 (OM)

**CLARK,** James & **PAYNE,** Sally over 21 years surety Gabriel PAYNE 5 Mar 1804 (OB) 20 Mar 1804 by Nath. SANDERS (Misc Min Ret)

**CLARK,** James A. age 27 s POB POR Orange s/o James T. CLARK and Mary Ann WILTSHIRE farmer & **BRITTON,** Emma F. age 19 s POB Page POR Orange d/o S.F. BRITTON and Virginia FRANKLIN 11 Nov 1880 POM Orange by E.R. PERRY (OMR)

**CLARK,** James F. age 19 s POB POR Orange s/o John J. CLARK and Lucy HUGHES cooper & **HUGHES,** Sarah E. age 22 s POB POR Orange d/o Alexander HUGHES and Jane LEE 11 Sep 1873 POM Orange by E.R. PERRY (OMR)

**CLARK,** John & **POWELL,** Winney d/o John POWELL surety Adam MANSPOILE 5 Nov 1794 (OB)

**CLARK**, John Z. s/o John H. CLARK and Martha E. CONNER age 22 s carpenter POB POR Spotsylvania & **JONES**, Amanda S. d/o Churchill JONES and Emiline LONG age 22 s POB POR Orange; POM Orange 9 Feb 1865 (OMR) 30 Jan 1865 (OML)

**CLARK**, Larkin & **BELL**, Rebecca d/o Thomas and Sally BELL surety Roger BELL 30 Jan 1797 (OB)

**CLARK**, Nathaniel & **HALL**, Nancy 8 Feb 1804 by George BINGHAM (Misc Min Ret)

**CLARK**, Reuben & **PETTY**, Lizey d/o George PETTY 31 Jan 1801 surety Abner PETTY (OB)

**CLARK**, Reubin & **CLARK**, Martha E. d/o Joseph CLARK surety Larkin CLARK 16 Dec 1801 (OB) 17 Dec 1801 by Isham TATUM (OM)

**CLARK**, William & **HARRIS**, Frances 6 Feb 1832 surety Thomas HARRIS (OB)

**CLARK**, William & **TERRILL**, Jane 15 Jan 1818 surety Eliphalet JOHNSON by J.C. GORDON (OB) (OM)

**CLARK**, William O. s/o S.T. and Susan CLARK age 24 s farmer POB POR Orange & **JONES**, Angelina d/o John and Susan JONES age 32 s POB POR Orange; POM Orange 5 Nov 1857 (OMR) 4 Nov 1857 (OML)

**CLARKE**, Henry & **GRASTY**, Nancy 28 Dec 1801 surety G.L. GRASTY (OB) 5 Jan 1802 by Nath. SANDERS (Misc Min Ret)

**CLARKE**, Henry James & **MANSFIELD**, Mary Lewis d/o Robert MANSFIELD who is also surety 25 Dec 1815 (OB)

**CLARKE**, John J. & **HUGHES**, Lucy Ann d/o Elizabeth HUGHES 22 Feb 1847 surety Archibald MIDDLEBROOK (OB) 24 Feb 1847 by Joseph S. JACKSON (OM)

**CLARKE**, John Jr. & **SLEET**, Frances d/o John SLEET who is also surety 21 Jan 1826 (OB)

**CLARKE**, Richard S. & **REYNOLDS**, Mary F. d/o D.G. REYNOLDS 18 Mar 1847 surety R.H. REYNOLDS (OB)

**CLARKE**, Stokely T. & **NEWMAN**, Susan d/o John NEWMAN who is also surety 29 Aug 1833 (OB)

**CLARKE**, Thomas & **JAMESON**, Catharine R. 23 Aug 1813 surety John CLARKE and Philemon SAMUEL (OB) 5 Sep 1813 by J. GOSS (OM)

**CLARKE**, Walker & **VAWTER**, Elizabeth d/o William VAWTER 26 Jan 1802 surety Thomas LANDRUM (OB)

**CLARKE**, William & **COOK**, Betsy s 7 Nov 1792 surety Edward PAGETT (OB)

**CLARKE**, William & **LEE**, Lucy 8 Jan 1821 surety Ambrose LEE (OB)

**CLARKSON**, Anselm & **JONES**, Milly surety Thomas JAMES 29 Jun 1789 (OB)

**CLAXTON**, Benjamin s/o Reuben CLAXTON and Nancy TAYLOR age 23 s farm laborer POB POR Orange POC & **TAYLOR**, Catherine d/o Bennet TAYLOR and Barbara JACKSON age 21 s POB POR Orange POC POM Orange 9 Nov 1867 (OMR) 4 Nov 1867 (OML)

**CLAY**, Henry POC age 30 labourer POB Madison POR Orange s/o Kitty MADISON & **WAUGH**, Lucy Ann POC age 24 s POB POR Orange d/o Henry WAUGH and Winney _____ POM Orange 30 Dec 1879 by Robert WOODSON (OMR)

**CLAYTON**, Philip & **STUBBLEFIELD**, Elizabeth Hackley d/o George STUBBLEFIELD 17 May 1794 surety Daniel F. STROTHER (OB)

**CLAYTON**, Philip s/o Philip CLAYTON & **CONWAY**, Margaret surety Isaac H. WILLIAMS 3 Nov 1827 (OB)

**CLEMMER**, David F.B. s/o George L. CLEMMER & **KINZER**, Mildred Jane d/o Christian F. KINZER who is also surety 23 Feb 1841 (OB) 25 Feb 1841 by J. EARNEST (OM)

**CLOPTON**, Nathaniel A. age 43 s farmer POB POR Fauquier s/o N.V. CLOPTON and Sarah G. SKINKER & **LAPTON**, Mollie D. age 22 s POB Albemarle POR Orange d/o Henry LAPTON and Sarah COCKERELL POM Orange 7 Nov 1878 by J.S. HAMSBROUGH (OMR)

**CLORE**, Silas F. & **NEWMAN**, Lucetta A. d/o Thomas NEWMAN who is also surety 6 Nov 1846 (OB)

**CLORE**, William POC age 19 s POB POR Madison s/o Charles CLORE and Mary TUTT farmer & **STEWARD**, Violet POC age 18 s POB POR Orange d/o Jeanne TAYLOR 6 Jul 1880 POM Orange by Willis ROBINSON (OMR)

**COATS**, Jeremiah & **WEBSTER**, Sally; 15 Feb 1791 surety Francis WEATHERALL (OB)

**COATES**, John & **THOMPSON**, Sarah both of St. Thomas Parish surety Edward THOMPSON 27 Mar 1783 (OB)

**COBBS**, Peter N. & **HENSHAW**, Cortney A. d/o Edmund HENSHAW who is also surety 28 Feb 1825 (OB) by J. GOSS 10 Mar 1825 (OM)

**COCKBURN**, Robert & **BROWN**, Sarah 23 Jan 1776 both of St. Thomas Parish by banns (Deed Book 17)

**COCKE**, Alexander & **EVANS**, Margaret C. d/o John W. EVANS who is also surety 29 Aug 1831 (OB)

**COCKERILL**, James A. & **ROUTT**, Mary F. d/o William P. ROUTT, surety Elbert ROUTT 27 Feb 1834 (OB)

**COCKRANE**, Patrick & **SPENCER**, Winifred 9 Apr 1774 by banns both of St. Thomas Parish (Deed Book 17)

**COCKRELL**, John & **DOWELL**, Lucy d/o Atwell DOWELL who is also surety 18 Feb 1845 (OB)

**COFFMAN**, William S. age 23 s POB POR Page Co. s/o David C. COFFMAN and Emily THORNHILL farmer & **KITE**, Eliza J. age 22 s POB Page Co POR Orange d/o William H. KITE and Rebecca BLOSSER 18 Nov 1869 POM Orange by L.A. CUTLER (OMR)

**COGWELL**, Ralph & **REYNOLDS**, Sarah surety John DAWSON 29 Jan 1785 (OB) 1 Feb 1785 by Nathaniel SANDERS (OM)

**COLE**, Wesley & **WATKINS**, Lucy surety Taliaferro KNIGHTING 13 Jun 1835 (OB) by Peter CRAWFORD 14 Jun 1835 (OM)

**COLE**, William J. age 25 s POB POR Madison Co s/o John W. COLE and Bathsheba ANDERSON farmer & **HERNDON**, Emma J. age 23 s POB POR Orange d/o R.I. HERNDON, and Ellen HUTCHINSON 24 Dec 1872 POM Orange by Thomas F. GRIMSLEY (OMR)

**COLEMAN**, Ambrose & **HILMAN**, Fanny d/o Joseph HILMAN who is surety 24 Apr 1810 (OB)

**COLEMAN**, Burrell s/o Ambrose COLEMAN and Fanny HILLMAN age 43 s blacksmith POB POR Orange & **SMITH**, Sarah L. d/o James SMITH and Sarah A. HAWKINS age 21 s POB Fauquier Co POR Orange; POM Indiantown, Orange 4 Mar 1864 (OMR) 2 Mar 1864 (OML)

**COLEMAN**, David P. age 27 s POB POR Orange s/o John COLEMAN and Mary A. WRIGHT farmer & **WAUGH**, Josie M. age 21 s POB POR Orange d/o Charles S. WAUGH and Mary Frances FAULCONER 28 Dec 1880 POM Orange by William A. HILL (OMR)

**COLEMAN**, Edmand M. age 33 s hotel keeper POB POR Orange s/o Thomas F. COLEMAN and Sarah DILLARD & **WOOLFOLK**, Eva F. age 25 s POB POR Orange d/o John L. WOOLFOLK and Sarah J. MORTON POM Orange 25 Nov 1878 (OML) 30 Dec 1878 by J.W. MCCOWN (OMR)

**COLEMAN**, Francis & **DAVIS**, Betty d/o Joseph and Elizabeth DAVIS surety Francis TAYLOR 7 Jan 1786 (OB)

**COLEMAN**, George W. & **GRASTY**, Mary Ann surety John GRASTY 2 Jan 1841 (OB)

**COLEMAN**, James & **CHEW**, Milly; 18 Dec 1786 surety James TAYLOR (OB)

**COLEMAN**, James of St. Thomas Parish & **TAYLOR**, Sarah of St. Thomas Parish 14 Apr 1780 surety Moses HAYES (OB)

**COLEMAN**, James L. & **DAVIS**, Elizabeth P.F. surety Thomas DAVIS 19 Sep 1839 (OB)

**COLEMAN**, James & **QUISENBERRY**, Sarah d/o Vivion QUISENBERRY surety John QUISENBERRY 13 Dec 1842 (OB)

**COLEMAN**, John & **BRADLEY**, Elizabeth d/o George and Lucy BRADLEY surety Samuel SMITH 19 Dec 1794 (OB) 24 Dec 1794 by George EVE (OM)

COLEMAN, John P. & **COLEMAN**, Frances M. d/o Thomas
COLEMAN surety George W. COLEMAN 12 Nov 1839 (OB)

**COLEMAN**, John POC age 23 s labourer POB Goochland POR Orange
s/o Jim COLEMAN and Rachel MOSELY & **STEWART**, Ellen POC
age 23 s POB POR Orange d/o Sancho STEWART and Lucinda
LUCAS POM Orange 17 Jun 1877 (OMR)

**COLEMAN**, John & **WRIGHT**, Mary A. d/o Benjamin WRIGHT surety
William A. WRIGHT 18 Oct 1844 (OB)

**COLEMAN**, John T. & **ANDREWS**, Emily S. d/o Lewis ANDREWS
suretyJesse B. BLADES 24 Feb 1849 (OB)

**COLEMAN**, Littleton L. s/o Reuben L. COLEMAN and Mary WALKER
age 25 s POB Spotsylvania POR Orange & **SAMUEL**, Carrie V. d/o
Thornton V. SAMUEL and Bettie COLEMAN age 18 s POB POR
Orange; POM Orange 20 Dec 1866 (OMR) 18 Dec 1866 (OML)

**COLEMAN**, Reuben L. s/o Reuben L. COLEMAN and Mary WALLER
age 28 farmer POB Spotsylvania POR Orange & **BROCKMAN**,
Adaline d/o Trenton V. SAMUEL and Bettie COLEMAN age 25 w
POB POR Orange; POM Orange 28 Feb 1867 (OMR) (OML)

**COLEMAN**, Robert & **COLEMAN**, Sarah d/o Elizabeth COLEMAN 24
Nov 1800 surety Thomas COLEMAN (OB)

**COLEMAN**, Robert age 33 s POB POR Caroline Co s/o Addison S.
COLEMAN and Ann Maria REDD on railroad & **HUFFMAN**, Sallie
age 18 POB POR Orange d/o John HUFFMAN and Mary J. ROACH
22 Feb 1873 POM Orange by J.S. HANSBROUGH (OMR)

**COLEMAN**, Samuel age 22 s farmer POB POR Orange s/o John
COLEMAN and Mary Ann WRIGHT & **MASSEY**, Laura J. age 18 s
POB POR Orange d/o A.J. MASSEY and Sally A. SWIFT POM
Orange 18 Dec 1878 by Melzi S. CHANCELLOR (OMR)

**COLEMAN**, Thomas & **HAWKINS**, Susannah w 28 Jun 1781 both of St.
Thomas Parish surety James TAYLOR (OB)

**COLEMAN**, Thomas & **SNOW**, Saluda 23 Oct 1816 by George
BINGHAM (OM)

**COLEMAN**, Thomas age 35 S POB POR Orange s/o Ambrose
COLEMAN and Frances HILLMAN carpenter & **TINSLEY**, Mary F.
age 34 S POB POR Orange d/o Edward TINSLEY and Lucy A.
ROACH 21 Dec 1871 POM Orange by John C. WILLIS (OMR)

**COLEMAN**, Wesley POC age 22 s farm labourer POB POR Orange s/o
Wilson COLEMAN and Martha A. BROWN & **PRESLEY**, Courtenay
POC age 17 s POB POR Orange d/o Thornton PRESLEY and Dicey
____ POM Shady Grove Church, Orange 21 Dec 1878 by C.T.
JOHNSON (OMR)

**COLEMAN**, Wilson & **HOWARD**, Catharine surety Moses BLEDSOE
24 Nov 1834 (OB)

**COLES,** Washington POC age 32 w POB Albemarle Co POR Orange s/o Daniel COLES and Harriet EVANS servant & **TRICE,** Mary F. [POC] age 22 s POB Louisa CO POR Orange d/o Samuel TRICE [and Susan _____] 14 Mar 1872 POM Orange by F.L. GIPSON (OMR) [Orange death file cards]

**COLLIER,** Eli & **SHOTWELL,** Arena d/o Jeremiah SHOTWELL who is also surety 7 Apr 1835 (OB) 17 Apr 1835 by E.G. SHIP (OM)

**COLLIER,** Hudson & **HAM,** Betsy 29 Jan 1811 Joseph HAM surety (OB)

**COLLINS,** Daniel POC age 22 s farm laborer POB POR Orange s/o William COLLINS and Mary GIBSON & **RALLS,** Betty POC age 18 s POB POR Orange d/o John RALLS and Mary WILLIAMS 1 Jan 1876 POM Orange (OMR)

**COLLINS,** Edward & **COLLINS,** Ann; 24 May 1781 both of St. Thomas Parish surety James COLEMAN (OB)

**COLLINS,** Francis T. & **WILLIAMS,** Margaret d/o Jacob WILLIAMS who is also surety 22 Dec 1817 (OB)

**COLLINS,** Francis & **DAHONEY,** Peggy d/o Thomas DEHONEY 27 Apr 1794 by George EVE (OM)

**COLLINS,** George & **MITCHELL,** Elizabeth; 10 Feb 1794 surety William MITCHELL (OB)

**COLLINS,** James & **BURTON,** Lucy d/o Capt. May BURTON Jr. 26 Aug 1793 surety William RUCKER (OB)

**COLLINS,** James S. age 27 s POB Albemarle Co POR Staunton s/o William A. COLLINS and Nancy A. MAHANES & **MAHANES,** Lucy Davis age 21 POB Albemarle Co POR Orange d/o William C. MAHANES and Mary A. HARRIS 22 Nov 1869 POM Orange by R. L. COLEMAN (OMR)

**COLLINS,** James s/o George COLLINS & **HARVIE,** Sarah d/o John HARVIE 13 Jan 1792 surety William MITCHELL (OB)

**COLLINS,** James Jr. & **JOHNSON,** Mildred C. d/o Valentine JOHNSON surety Robert C. JOHNSON 20 May 1824 (OB) 23 May 1824 by J. GOSS (OM)

**COLLINS,** Jerome B. & **BURRUS,** Jane surety Hezekiah QUISENBERRY 7 Dec 1831 (OB)

**COLLINS,** John & **BECKHAM,** Rebecca surety John GREEN 10 Nov 1829 (OB)

**COLLINS,** John & **CAVE,** Frances B. ward of Philip C. CAVE who is also surety 17 Dec 1823 (OB)

**COLLINS,** John & **KIRTLEY,** Elizabeth 4 Jan 1803 by George BINGHAM (Misc Min Ret)

**COLLINS,** John & **YAGER,** Betty; 28 Dec 1803 surety Benjamin COLLINS (OB)

COLLINS, John A. age 24 s POB POR Orange s/o Robert COLLINS and Jane J. ROBINSON r.r. hand & **RICHARDS**, Sallie M. age 23 s POB POR Orange d/o William RICHARDS and Susan LANCASTER 25 Jan 1880 POM Orange by W.H. CAMPER (OMR)

COLLINS, Lewis Dillard & **WILLIAMS**, Elizabeth; 24 Dec 1792 surety Jacob WILLIAMS (OB)

COLLINS, Peter s/o Peter and Elizabeth COLLINS age 31 w miner POB England POR Orange & **WILLIAMS**, Ann C. d/o James and Elizabeth WILLIAMS age 27 s POB England POR Orange; POM Orange 24 Aug 1856 (OMR) 22 Aug 1856 (OML)

COLLINS, Reubin & **RIDDLE**, Fanny d/o James RIDDLE 13 May 1807 surety Valentine RIDDLE (OB) 21 May 1807 by George BINGHAM (OM)

COLLINS, Robert D. age 21 s POB POR Orange s/o Robert COLLINS and Jane ROBINSON farmer & **PAYNE**, Louisa E. age 18 s POB POR Orange d/o Charles G. PAYNE and Mary COOPER 18 Dec 1873 POM Orange by Charles QUARLES (OMR)

COLLINS, Roswell & **JOHNSON**, Verlinday J. surety Eliphalet JOHNSON 15 Nov 1827 (OB)

COLLINS, Tandy & **BEAZLEY**, Ann d/o James BEAZLEY Sr. 7 Feb 1809 surety Sanford BEASLEY (OB) 9 Feb 1809 by Jacob WATTS (OM)

COLLINS, William & **QUISENBERRY**, Sally; 18 Oct 1813 (OM)

COLLINS, William & **BREEDWELL**, Anky surety Thomas MCBRIDE 3 Jan 1826 (OB)

COLLINS, William & **MAHANES**, Nancy surety Pleasant DOWELL 12 Dec 1828 (OB)

COLLINS, William & **SNELL**, Patty both of St. Thomas Parish by banns 16 Sep 1776 (Deed Book 17)

COLLINS, William H. & **BARBOUR**, Frances Cornelia surety Stephen COLLINS 24 Jul 1834 (OB)

COLLINS, William W. & **WILLIAMS**, Frances d/o Jacob WILLIAMS 7 Apr 1818 (OM)

COLSTON, Wallace s/o William COLSTON and Harriet BAYLOR age 25 s laborer on farm POB Albemarle Co POR Orange POC & **BROCK**, Courtney d/o Alex. BROCK and Grace JONES age 23 s POB POR Orange POC; POM Orange 8 Sep 1866 (OMR) 6 Sep 1866 (OML)

COLVIN, William F. s/o John D. and Frances Colvin age 20 s carpenter POB POR Culpeper & **HAWLEY**, Lucy M. d/o Thomas and L.A. Hawley age 22 s POB Culpeper POR Orange; POM Orange 15 Feb 1855 (OMR)

**COLVIN**, John W. age 49 w POB Culpeper Co POR Orange s/o Gabriel COLVIN and Mary ROBERTS farmer & **SIMS**, Lucy Ann age 40 s POB POR Orange d/o Richard SIMS and Polly _____ 21 Dec 1871 POM Orange by J.W. MCCOWN (OMR)

**COLVIN**, John R. & **MARSHALL**, Sarah Frances d/o Coleman MARSHALL who is also surety by Hernden FRAZER 6 Aug 1844 (OB) (OM)

**COLY**, William & **MCCLARY**, Milly 3 Jun 1819 by George BINGHAM (OM)

**COLYER**, Chapman & **MORRIS**, Charlotte d/o William MORRIS surety Bluford MORRIS 20 Jan 1830 (OB)

**COLYER**, Preston & **HAYNA**, Eliza 8 Nov 1804 by George BINGHAM (Misc Min Ret)

**CONALTY**, Patrick & **HILL**, Polly d/o Richard HILL who is also surety 25 Oct 1820 (OB)

**CONDON**, John s/o David and Mary CONDON age 33 s laborer POB Ireland POR Orange & **BROWN**, Sarah F. d/o William and Mary BROWN age 24 s POB POR Orange; POM Orange 24 Dec 1853 (OMR) (OML)

**CONNER**, John & **DANIEL**, Lucy d/o Reubin DANIEL 20 Nov 1776 both of St. Thomas Parish (Deed Book 17)

**CONNER**, John & **LANCASTER**, Mary d/o Mary LANCASTER surety Robert LANCASTER Jr. 7 Feb 1785 of St Thomas Parish (OB)

**CONNER**, John & **TERRILL**, Sarah surety Robert TERRILL Jr. by James GARNETT Sr. 22 Nov 1821 (OB) (OM)

**CONNER**, William ward of Zeph TURNER & **SMITH**, Emily surety Fayette SMITH 6 Jan 1823 (OB) by James GARNETT Sr. 7 Jan 1823 (OM)

**CONWAY**, Catlett Jr.[b.d. 1786 s/o Catlett CONWAY & Susanna FITZHUGH of "Hawfield"] & **TALIAFERRO**, Verlinda; 26 Sep 1810 surety George CONWAY (OB) [W & M Quarterly]

**CONWAY**, Catlett & **TAYLOR**, Harriet d/o Charles TAYLOR who is also surety 4 May 1816 (OB)

**CONWAY**, Charles C. age 28 s POB Greene Co POR Culpeper s/o William H. CONWAY and Marion GLASSEL physician & **JONES**, Bettie S. age 30 s POB Richmond POR Orange d/o Philip B. JONES and Elizabeth SUTTON 16 Nov 1871 POM Orange by J.S. HANSBROUGH (OMR)

**CONWAY**, Edgar POC age 26 s labourer POB POR Orange s/o Edgar CONWAY and Emily _____ & **SHEPHERD**, Lucy age 22 s POB POR Orange d/o Wash. SHEPHERD POM Orange 18 Dec 1877 (OMR)

**CONWAY**, Henry C. age 21 s farmer POB POR Madison s/o B. F. T. CONWAY and Cornelia BUCHANAN & **MANN**, Mattie M. age 19 s

POB POR Orange d/o William H. MANN and Belle KEETH POM
Gordonsville, Orange 23 Jan 1878 by Herbert M. HOPE (OMR)

**CONWAY**, Oregon POC age 22 s POB POR Orange s/o Edmund
CONWAY and Lucy KELLEY (?) laborer & **WASHINGTON**,
Hannah POC age 20 s POB POR Orange d/o Lewis WASHINGTON
and Fanny MCINTOSH 24 Nov 1872 POM Orange by W.H. CAMPER
(OMR)

**CONWAY**, Reuben & **MACON**, Lucy H. d/o Thomas MACON who is
also surety 24 Jul 1811 (OB)

**COOK**, Elijah & **TURNER**, Polly d/o Ann TURNER surety Samuel HILL
16 May 1796 (OB)

**COOK**, Marshall & **SCOTT**, Susan d/o George SCOTT surety Caleb
SCOTT 14 Dec 1831 (OB)

**COOK**, Noah & **ROACH**, Hetty d/o William ROACH who is also surety
11 Feb 1840 (OB)

**COOK**, Thomas & **CHILES**, Mary; 10 Apr 1797 surety Reuben
GARTON (OB)

**COOK**, William & **GARTON**, Susannah d/o Uriah GARTON 13 Jun
1785 surety William PAGE (OB)

**COOK**, William H. age 22 s POB POR Orange s/o Noah COOK and
Hettie R. ROACH mechanic & **BRADFORD**, Mollie M. age 23 s POB
Green Co POR Orange d/o John E. BRADFORD and Virginia FRY 18
Dec 1873 POM Orange by H.E. HATCHER (OMR)

**COOK**, William J. s/o Marshall and Susan COOK age 24 s bricklayer
POB Culpeper POR Orange & **SMITH**, Angelina d/o Caleb and
Elizabeth SMITH age 20 s POB POR Orange; POM Orange 19 Feb
1856 (OMR) 14 Feb 1856 (OML)

**COONS**, John P. & **BRIDENHEART**, Susan surety James VERDIER 12
Mar 1818 (OB)

**COOPER**, Alfred age 25 s POB POR Orange s/o Owen COOPER and
Jane HUMPHRIES farmer & **REYNOLDS**, Mary E. age 21 s POB
POR Orange d/o Robert E. REYNOLDS and Elizabeth F. TERRILL 17
Dec 1868 POM Orange by Herndon FRAZER (OMR)

**COOPER**, Benjamin & **LANCASTER**, Susannah d/o John LANCASTER
18 Dec 1804 surety William ROBINSON (OB)

**COOPER**, Benjamin & **WATKINS**, Sarah P. surety P.S. FRY by Joseph
S. JACKSON 16 Nov 1848 (OB) (OM)

**COOPER**, Elijah A. s/o Elijah COOPER and Julia A. BROWNING age
25 s seaman POB Gloucester Co. POR Hampton & **CLARK**, Martha
E. d/o William CLARK and Frances ESTES age 17 s POB POR
Orange; POM Orange 21 Feb 1865 (OMR) 20 Feb 1865 (OML)

**COOPER**, James & **SMITH**, Mildred d/o James SMITH 18 Dec 1798
surety Elisha ADAMS (OB)

**COOPER**, James POC age 34 s POB Madison POR Orange s/o Elizabeth COOPER farmer & **STROTHER**, Lucinda POC age 36 s POB Greene POR Orange 13 Dec 1880 POM Orange by Joseph A. MANSFIELD (OMR)

**COOPER**, Owen & **WEBB**, Mary Mason POR Orange consent by Jesse B. WEBB 20 Dec 1811 Benjamin LANCASTER surety (OB)

**COOPER**, William & **QUISENBERRY**, Mary d/o Moses QUISENBERRY 24 Nov 1787 surety James QUISENBERRY (OB)

**COOPER**, William J. & **BROCKMAN**, Sarah E. d/o Asa BROCKMAN; 10 Nov 1853 (OML)

**COPPAGE**, Charles & **WAYT**, Lydia 24 Oct 1803 by Jacob WATTS (Misc Min Ret)

**CORNELIUS**, Augustine & **TERRELL**, Sarah d/o Peggy TERRELL 10 Mar 1790 surety Edmund TERRILL (OB)

**COTTOM**, Peter & **GRYMES**, Judith Robinson over 21 years 25 Jan 1808 surety James PULLIAM (OB)

**COUNSELLOR**, Franklin & **MILLER**, Elizabeth M. surety John S. THORNTON 1 Aug 1832 (OB) by J. GOSS 2 Aug 1832 (OM)

**COVINGTON**, Abraham POC age 25 s POB POR Orange s/o Ben COVINGTON and Rhoady LINDSAY laborer & **BROWN**, Julia POC age 25 s POB POR Orange d/o Jim BROWN 8 Jun 1872 POM Orange by Philip JOHNSON (OMR)

**COWGILL**, Daniel & **MARTIN**, Betsy d/o Ann BOWEN 1 Aug 1785 surety John BOWEN (OB)

**COWGILL**, George & **WAIT**, Phoebe; 15 Sep 1792 surety Edward WAIT (OB)

**COWGILL**, Isaac & **GILLOCK**, Sally d/o Elizabeth GILLOCK 3 May 1794 surety Lawrence GILLOCK (OB) 15 May 1794 by James GARNETT (OM)

**COWHERD**, Coleby & **COWHERD**, Mary Jane; POM Orange 4 Nov 1852 (OMR) 2 Nov 1852 (OML)

**COWHERD**, Francis & **SCOTT**, Lucy d/o Johnny SCOTT who is also surety 13 Aug 1787 (OB)

**COWHERD**, Francis K. & **HENSHAW**, Sarah A. d/o John HENSHAW who is also surety 23 Oct 1815 (OB)

**COWHERD**, John S. & **DANIEL**, Lucy W. ward of Coleby COWHERD surety William COWHERD 15 Mar 1826 (OB)

**COWHERD**, Reuben & **WOOLFOLK**, Frances d/o Thomas WOOLFOLK 28 Jun 1794 surety James TAYLOR Sr. (OB)

**COX**, Benjamin F. age 21 s POB Albemarle Co POR Louisa Co. s/o Abner COX and Caroline F. ESTES farmer & **ESTES**, Martha D. age 24 s POB POR Orange d/o William B. ESTES and Sarah BRUCE 28 Nov 1871 POM Orange by Charles QUARLES (OMR)

**COX,** Francis S. & **EVE,** Mary d/o Sarah EVE surety William WHITE 6 Apr 1826 (OB)

**COX,** Joab & **ESTES,** Lucy; 3 Jan 1803 surety William ESTES (OB)

**COX,** John & **BRYSON,** Mary s both of St. Thomas Parish surety John BELL 6 Feb 1782 (OB)

**COX,** Thomas & **OLLIVER,** Milley d/o Tabitha OLLIVER both of St. Thomas Parish 10 Mar 1783 surety Joel STODGHILL (OB)

**COX,** Warner & **COX,** Leah surety Garrett ESTES 31 Dec 1827 (OB)

**COX,** William & **ESTES,** Betsy; 29 Jan 1791 surety John BELL (OB)

**COX,** William D. & **WHITE,** Fanny surety John WHITE 16 Feb 1813 (OB)

**CRAIG,** Elijah & **MAUPIN,** Sarah by George BINGHAM 17 Nov 1819 (OM)

**CRAIG,** James & **SHIP,** Martha surety Benjamin BURTON 29 Sep 1825 (OB)

**CRAIG,** Samuel & **THOMAS,** Frances d/o James THOMAS who is also surety 11 Apr 1821 (OB)

**CRANE,** Jonas & **BURRUSS,** Catharine S.F. ward of Thomas F. BURRUSS; POM Orange 7 Jul 1853 (OMR) 6 Jul 1853 (OML)

**CRANE,** Thomas J. & **BURRUS,** Frances d/o Joseph BURRUS surety Thomas F. BURRUS 8 May 1843 (OB)

**CRASK,** James & **COLLINS,** Jane; 25 Apr 1796 surety Edward COLLINS (OB)

**CRAWFORD,** Charles Y. & **ELLIS,** Frances H. d/o Thomas ELLIS surety Thomas J. ELLIS 24 Oct 1831 (OB)

**CRAWFORD,** Jeremiah & **CRAWFORD,** Janey d/o Archelan CRAWFORD 31 May 1792 by George EVE (OM)

**CRAWFORD,** Martin & **LAMB,** Susanna; 9 Dec 1801 by George BINGHAM (OM)

**CRAWFORD,** Reuben & **ALMOND,** Margaret L. d/o William ALMOND surety Mason B. ALMOND 12 Jan 1833 (OB)

**CRAWFORD,** Zachariah & **RAINS,** Cibba by George BINGHAM 10 May 1818 (OM)

**CREBBS,** John C.s/o John and Hannah CREBBS age 30 w architect/builder POB Winchester POR Louisa Co & **BICKERS,** Bettie A.d/o William and Elizabeth BICKERS age 22 s POB POR Orange; POM Orange 11 Feb 1858 (OMR) 8 Feb 1858 (OML)

**CREEL,** Benjamin F. age 40 s POB Madison POR Albemarle s/o Benjamin CREEL and Mary E. CARPENTER farmer & **MCMULLAN,** Arabella T. age 23 s POB Greene POR Orange d/o James W. MCMULLAN and Mary JARRELL 7 Jun 1880 POM Orange by John R. JOYNER, Episcopalian minister (OMR)

CRENSHAW, Spotswood Dabney & **GRAVES,** Winifred d/o Isaac
GRAVES Sr. surety Coalby GRAVES 18 Jun 1816 (OB)
CRENSHAW, Thomas & **PARROTT,** Nancy d/o William PARROTT
POR Orange 21 Dec 1811 Woodson PARROTT surety (OB)
CRENSHAW, William G. & **GRAVES,** Fanny E.H. d/o Jonathan
GRAVES surety Richard P. GRAVES 24 May 1847 (OB)
**CREW,** Jacob & **DOLLINS,** Martha age 21 2 Feb 1790 surety William
DOLLINS (OB) (OM)
**CRIGLER,** Peter & **PRATT,** Fanny d/o Jonathan PRATT who is also
surety 14 Jul 1819 (OB)
**CROCKETT,** Thomas R. s/o Thomas J. CROCKETT and Margaret
ROBINSON age 30 s bricklayer POB District of Columbia POR
Orange & **SACRA,** Sarah A.d/o Thomas J. SACRA and Lucinda
ROBINSON age 18 s POB Spotsylvania POR Orange; POM Orange 9
Aug 1864 (OMR) 8 Aug 1864 (OML)
**CROCKFORD,** William H. age 31 w POB Jersey City, NJ POR
Warrenton, s/o John CROCKFORD and Ellen WINDHAM agent &
**JONES,** Mattie G. age 29 s POB POR Orange d/o James L. JONES
and Martha PORTER 23 Jun 1874 POM Orange (OMR)
**CROOKS,** Joseph B. & **HENNESEY,** Kitty M. surety William P. ROUTT
4 Jan 1815 (OB) by James GARNETT 5 Jan 1815 (OM)
**CROSS,** Charles H. s/o George CROSS and Rosa A. BETTS age 27 s
farmer POB England POR Orange & **HANSFORD,** Mary G. d/o John
HANSFORD and Sarah KING age 30 s POB POR Orange; POM
Orange 30 Nov 1865 (OMR) 24 Nov 1865 (OML)
**CROSS,** Joshua & **DANIEL,** Nancy surety James B. DANIEL 14 Oct
1818 (OB)
**CROSTHWAIT,** Aaron & **BROCKMAN,** Nelly d/o John BROCKMAN
17 Aug 1792 surety Caleb LINDSAY (OB) (OM)
**CROXTON,** Joseph & **TURNER,** Delphy surety Ezekiel TURNER 8 Nov
1802 (OB)
**CRUMP,** Benjamin & **BARBER/ BARBOUR,** Mary Price; 12 Apr 1757
both of St. Thomas Parish (Orange Fee Book)
**CRUMP,** Benjamin & **PRICE,** Mary Barber 12 Apr 1756 (Orange Fee
Book) The entries for this and the previous were both in the fee book. I
couldn't determine which was correct so I included both entries.
**CRUTCHFIELD,** Albert G. & **MOORE,** Frances T. surety William C.
MOORE Sr. 27 Feb 1843 (OB) by Albert ANDERSON 2 Mar 1843
(OM)
**CRUTCHFIELD,** Thomas & **TAYLOR,** Ann Pendleton; 18 Jan 1799
surety James TAYLOR (OB)
**CULLEN,** George Jr. s/o George and Barbara CULLEN age 23 s jeweler
POB POR Orange C.H. & **HANSBROUGH,** Martha S. d/o Alexander

HAMILTON and Elizabeth HANSBROUGH age 18 s POB Culpeper
C.H. POR Orange C.H.; POM Orange 15 Jun 1858 (OMR) 14 Jun 1858
(OML)

**CUNNINGHAM,** Henry & **BROOKMAN,** Courtney surety James
SHIFLETT 18 Jan 1845 (OB)

**CUNNINGHAM,** James H. age 22 s POB POR Orange Co s/o Henry H.
CUNNINGHAM and Courtney F. BROOKMAN farmer & **PETTETT,**
Martha A. age 21 s POB POR Orange d/o Fountain PETTETT and
Sallie ROACH 11 Feb 1869 POM Orange by James A. MANSFIELD
(OMR)

**CUNNINGHAM,** Peyton POC age 31 s farm laborer POB Danville POR
Orange s/o Bob CUNNINGHAM and Louisa _____ & **GREEN,** Eliza
POC age 22 s POB POR Orange d/o Jim GREEN and Martha____
POM Orange 31 Dec 1875 (OMR)

**CUNNINGHAM,** William F. age 21 s POB POR Orange s/o Henry F.
CUNNINGHAM and Courtenay BROOKMAN farmer & **MILLER,**
Julia S. age 21 s POB Goochland POR Orange d/o J.H. MILLER 20
Dec 1868 POM Orange by Joseph A. MANSFIELD (OMR)

**CURTIS,** Elijah & **DANIEL,** Nancy; 23 Jan 1801 surety John D. LONG
(OB)

**DABNEY,** Alexander & **BELL,** Sally; 25 Aug 1776 (OB)

**DADE,** Albert G. s/o Langhorn DADE and Ann HARRISON age 50 w
farmer POB King George Co POR Orange & **BROOKING,** Mary R.
d/o Jacob WALTERS and _____ BROOKING [Belinda was written
in at a later date] age 34 w POB POR Orange; POM Orange 15 May
1866 (OMR) 9 May 1866 (OML)

**DADE,** Francis & **TALIAFERRO,** Sarah d/o Lawrence TALIAFERRO
13 Mar 1782 surety Hay TALIAFERRO (OB)

**DADE,** Lewis POC age 55 s farmer POB POR Orange s/o Billy TAYLOR
& **WOOLFOLK,** Caroline POC age 35 s POB Louisa POR Orange
POM Orange 18 Sep 1879 (OMR)

**DADE,** Spencer POC age 29 s labourer POB POR Orange s/o Richard
DADE and Fanny BARTON & **WAGNER,** Mary POC age 19 s POB
POR Orange POM Orange 13 Dec 1877 (OMR)

**DADE,** William POR Prince William & **DADE,** Sarah 6 Nov 1792 surety
Townsend DADE (OB)

**DAHONEY,** Rhodes & **CHAPMAN,** Jinney d/o Joseph CHAPMAN 19
Oct 1790 (OB)

**DAILEY,** Alexander & **BRENT,** Sarah A. d/o George P. BRENT who is
also surety 19 Jan 1847 (OB) 21 Jan 1847 by S. WATKINS (OM)

**DAILY,** Charles Riggs age 23 s merchant POB POR Montgomery Co.,
MD s/o Samuel DAILY and Mary J. NANIS & **HERNDON,** Sarah
Virginia age 24 POB POR Orange d/o William T. HERNDON and

Henrietta VAUGHAN POM Orange 9 Jul 1879 by H.E. HATCHER (OMR)

**DALEY**, Alexander s/o John DALEY and Elizabeth DUNN age 53 w leather dealer POB Kings Co, Ireland POR Orange & **RAWLINGS**, Sarah J. d/o Richard RAWLINGS and Lucy S. RAWLINGS age 41 s POB POR Orange; POM Spotsylvania 28 May 1863 SPMR 26 May 1863 (OML)

**DALTON**, John & **EARLES**, Polly; 23 Jun 1800 surety Rodham EARLES (OB)

**DALTON**, John & **EARLES**, Polly; 24 Jun 1800 by Hamilton GOSS (OM)

**DANCE**, Beverley POC age 27 w blacksmith POB Prince Edward POR Culpeper s/o Ed. JACKSON and Amy ____ & **WILLIAMS**, Narcissa age 17 s POB POR Orange d/o Thornton WILLIAMS and Ellen ____ POM Orange 30 Dec 1875 (OMR)

**DANIEL**, Abel M. age 23 s POB POR Orange rail roading s/o John M. DANIEL and Mildred JACKSON & **BROCKMAN**, Maria E. age 21 s d/o Ira S. BROCKMAN and Lucy B. DAVIS 17 Nov 1880 POM Pamunkey Church, Orange by J.W. MCCOWN (OMR)

**DANIEL**, Albert POC age 38 w engineer POB North Carolina POR Orange s/o Phil DANIEL and Annika ____ & **PORTER**, Angelina POC age 35 w POB Louisa POR Orange POM Gordonsville 13 Feb 1876 (OMR)

**DANIEL**, Beverly & **HIATT**, Jane; 28 Feb 1786 surety Benjamin HIATT (OB)

**DANIEL**, Beverly R. & **ANDREWS**, Mary d/o Lewis ANDREWS 20 Dec 1847 surety John L. ANDREWS (OB) 23 Dec 1847 by Herndon FRAZER (OM)

**DANIEL**, Cornelius O. & **PLUNKETT**, Peggy w 6 Apr 1793 surety John O. BRIAN (OB)

**DANIEL**, James & **DAVIS**, Lucy; 5 Apr 1772 (Orange Fee Book)

**DANIEL**, James & **FINNELL**, Alse; 8 Apr 1797 surety James DANIEL (OB)

**DANIEL**, John & **MARSHALL**, Lucy Mary 25 Jul 1776 (Deed Book 17)

**DANIEL**, John M. & **JACKSON**, Mildred A. d/o Joseph S. JACKSON surety Charles B. BROWN 4 Oct 1848 (OB)

**DANIEL**, John POC age 21 s r.r. hand POB POR Orange s/o John DANIEL and Winney ____ & **TIMBERLAKE**, Rachel POC age 22 s POB Louisa POR Orange d/o Cornelia ____ POM Orange 24 May 1879 by F. TIBBS (OMR)

**DANIEL**, John POC age 62 w labourer POB Stafford POR Orange s/o Lucy GRIFFIN & **LEE**, Martha age 27 s POB Madison POR Orange d/o Henry and Milly LEE POM Orange 17 Dec 1879 (OMR)

**DANIEL**, John T. age 36 w POB POR Orange farmer & **PIERCE,** Amanda M. age 22 s POB Spotsylvania POR Orange d/o John PIERCE and Frances TAMPLIN 1 Apr 1869 POM Orange by I.W.K. HANDY (OMR)

**DANIEL**, Joseph S. age 22 y 9 mo farmer POB POR Orange s/o John M. DANIEL and Mildred A. JACKSON & **LIPSCOMB,** Mary Ella age 21 s POB POR Orange d/o M.B. LIPSCOMB and Octavia M. WILROY POM Orange 31 Oct 1877 (OMR)

**DANIEL**, Reuben & **MCCLAMROCK,** Elizabeth 23 Sep 1835 surety David MCCLAMROCK (OB)

**DANIEL**, Reuben & **MERRY,** Elizabeth 16 Sep 1760 (Orange Fee Book)

**DANIEL**, Reuben & **MERRY,** Elizabeth; Nov 1760 both of St. Thomas Parish (Orange Fee Book)

**DANIEL**, Reuben R. & **REYNOLDS,** Elizabeth 21 Dec 1804 surety Thomas DANIEL (OB)

**DANIEL**, Robert & **HUMPHRIES,** Frances Head 23 Nov 1772 (Deed Book 17)

**DANIEL**, Samuel A. & **ROBINSON,** Sarah J. d/o Thomas ROBINSON 14 Apr 1847 surety Richard G. ROBINSON (OB)

**DANIEL**, William & **GAINES,** Mary; 3 Feb 1785 surety Henry CHILDS (OB)

**DANIEL**, William M. & **ESTES,** Maria Ellen 28 Nov 1836 surety James W. ESTES (OB) 1 Dec 1836 by William HITER (OM)

**DANIEL**, William Travers & **TERRILL,** Mary Julia d/o Uriel TERRILL 9 Apr 1842 surety William J. STEVENS (OB)

**DARBY**, Adam & **SHEPHERD,** Catherine d/o Andrew SHEPHERD 15 Nov 1796 surety Daniel GRINNAN Jr. (OB)

**DARGAN**, Edwin C. age 25 s minister of the gospel POB Darlington Co., SC POR Roanoke s/o J.O.B. DARGON and Jane F. SYDE & **GRAVES,** Lucy A. age 25 s POB POR Orange d/o William C. GRAVES and Martha A. HIDEN POM Orange 11 Jun 1878 by J. Ad. FRENCH (OMR)

**DARLINGTON**, John T. s/o Henry DARLINGTON and Charlotte BLEDSO age 21 s newspaper publisher POB Edgefield District, S.C. POR Elbert Co, GA & **ADAMS,** Arianna H. d/o Thomas J. ADAMS and Martha OWNES age 15 s POB POR Orange; POM Verdiersville, Orange 19 Mar 1863 (OMR) 17 Mar 1863 (OML)

**DARNELL**, Abraham & **DARNELL,** Elizabeth permission by Abraham DARNELL Sr. for both 19 Dec 1797 surety George MCDANIEL (OB) 20 Dec 1797 by Hamilton GOSS (OM)

**DARNELL**, Ancell & **MORRISS,** Virginia d/o Reuben MORRISS who is also surety 29 Dec 1829 (OB) 30 Dec 1829 by J. GOSS (OM)

**DARNELL**, Nelson & **MALLORY**, Cintha d/o Henry MALLORY who is also surety 23 Jan 1809 (OB) 24 Jan 1809 by Robert JONES (OM)

**DARNELL**, Rice & **AHART**, Polly 25 Dec 1804 by Hamilton GOSS (Misc Min Ret)

**DARNELL**, Thomas & **EHART**, Elizabeth d/o Captain GAINES surety James ALEXANDER 13 Aug 1794 (OB) 21 Aug 1794 by George MARTIN (OM)

**DARNELL**, Zachariah & **WILLIAMS**, Ann 28 Dec 1838 surety John FEARNEYHOUGH (OB)

**DAUNEY**, Alexander POR St. Thomas Parish & **BELL**, Sally POR St. Thomas Parish 25 Aug 1776 (Deed Book 17)

**DAVENPORT**, John H. & **BRENT**, Eliza F. 18 Dec 1848 surety P.S. FRY (OB) 20 Dec 1848 by Daniel B. EWING (OM)

**DAVENPORT**, John Tanner s/o Peter and Martha DAVENPORT age 24 s painter POB POR Richmond & **BELL**, Mary Margaret d/o Francis and Mary BELL age 19 s POB POR Orange; POM Orange 27 May 1856 (OMR) 26 May 1856 (OML)

**DAVENPORT**, Lewis s/o William DAVENPORT and Phebe DAY age 28 s carpenter POB New York City POR Orange & **LOURY**, Sarah C. d/o Jefferson WRIGHT and Sarah WRIGHT age 21 s POB POR Orange; POM Orange 26 Dec 1865 (OMR) (OML)

**DAVIS**, Absolem & **DAVIS**, Jerusha; 25 Dec 1796 by George BINGHAM (OM)

**DAVIS**, Alexander POC age 25 s POB Madison Co POR Orange s/o Robert D. TWYMAN and Harriet DAVIS farm laborer & **ALLEN**, Lizzie POC age 18 s POB POR Orange d/o John ALLEN and Amanda SAMUEL 25 Dec 1873 POM Orange by F.L. GIPSON (OMR)

**DAVIS**, Andrew J. & **FERNEYHOUGH**, Susan E. d/o Elizabeth FERNEYHOUGH; POM Orange 2 Feb 1852 (OMR) 22 Dec 1851 (OML)

**DAVIS**, Asa & **SNOW**, Mary d/o Bird SNOW 25 May 1818 surety William COLLINS (OB)

**DAVIS**, Bartlett & **LOWRY**, Sally; 31 Jan 1799 by George BINGHAM (OM)

**DAVIS**, Benjamin & **JONES**, Jane 25 Jan 1806 by William DOUGLASS, Methodist (OM)

**DAVIS**, Edward A. s/o Abraham DAVIS and Sarah SMITH age 42 s carpenter POB Colinton District, S.C. POR Orangeburg District, S.C. & **BROWN**, Mary D. d/o Robinson BROWN and Ann BISHOP age 28 s POB Culpeper Co POR Orange; POM Walnut Farm, Orange married by chaplain of 27th VA infantry, Stonewall Brigade 18 Mar 1864 (OMR) 17 Mar 1864 (OML)

**DAVIS**, Edward s/o Parke B. DAVIS and Maria KING age 35 s farmer POB POR King William Co. & **BROCKMAN**, Fannie d/o William L. BROCKMAN and Elizabeth C. GRAVES age 27 s POB POR Orange; POM Orange 1 Mar 1866 (OMR) 28 Feb 1866 (OML)

**DAVIS**, Elijah & **JONES**, Elizabeth 24 Dec 1806 by George BINGHAM (OM)

**DAVIS**, Evan & **HILMAN**, Polly surety Joseph HILMAN 31 Jan 1817 (OB) 3 Feb 1817 by J.C. GORDON (OM)

**DAVIS**, Frank POC age 23 s farm laborer POB POR Orange s/o Edward DAVIS and Rachel OATS & **ROLLS**, Eliza POC age 19 s POB POR Orange d/o John ROLLS and Mary CHRISTIAN POM Orange 29 Aug 1877 (OMR)

**DAVIS**, Frederick D. & **EDDINS**, Mildred surety Thomas EDDINS 7 Dec 1822 (OB)

**DAVIS**, George W. s/o Thomas and Susan DAVIS age 24 s carpenter POB Orange POR Green Co & **CASON**, Sallie M. d/o Benjamin and Elizabeth CASON age 23 s POB POR Orange; POM Orange 15 Apr 1858 (OMR) 14 Apr 1858 (OML)

**DAVIS**, Henry POC age 22 s labourer POB Spotsylvania POR Orange s/o Pleasant and Betsy DAVIS & **GRASTY**, Peachy POC age 21 s POB POR Orange POM Orange 17 Nov 1878 by John C. WILLIS (OMR)

**DAVIS**, Horace POC age 21 s farm labourer POB Greene POR Orange s/o Willis DAVIS and Kitty BEAZLEY & **SNEED**, Alice POC age 18 s POB Fluvanna POR Orange d/o William SNEED and Willie Ann BANKS POM Nazareth Baptist Church, Orange 21 May 1879 by William ROBINSON (OMR)

**DAVIS**, James & **JOHNSON**, Mary surety John BELL 1 Mar 1780 (OB)

**DAVIS**, James & **MODISET**, Ann d/o Mary MODISET 17 Aug 1785 surety Patrick COCHRAN (OB)

**DAVIS**, James M. & **SALE**, Catharine E. d/o John W. SALE surety George PANNILL Jr. 23 Jun 1845 (OB)

**DAVIS**, James s/o Robert DAVIS and Harriet SANDERS age 25 s shoemaker POB Madison Co POR Orange POC & **SNEED**, Milly d/o Winston SNEED and Lucy CARTER age 22 s POB POR Orange POC; POM Orange 11 Oct 1866 (OMR) 10 Oct 1866 (OML)

**DAVIS**, Jenkinias & **LOWRIE**, Babby; 21 Dec 1794 by George BINGHAM (OM)

**DAVIS**, John & **DEAR**, Sally surety David GOODALL 16 May 1816 (OB) 18 May 1816 by George BINGHAM (OM)

**DAVIS**, John & **EASTIN**, Mary; 27 Jul 1789 (OM)

**DAVIS**, John & **PANNILL** Elizabeth d/o William PANEL 10 Jan 1789 (OB)

**DAVIS**, John POR St. Thomas Parish & **JONES**, Mary POR St. Thomas Parish 25 Feb 1772 (Orange Fee Book)

**DAVIS**, Joseph POC age 23 s POB POR Orange s/o Joe DAVIS laborer & **HILL**, Laura POC age 21 s POB POR Orange d/o Robert HILL and Tamer TYLER 23 Sep 1868 POM Orange by Philip JOHNSON (OMR)

**DAVIS**, Leman & **TINDER**, Catharine d/o Anthony TINDER 26 Aug 1834 surety Robinson TINDER (OB) 28 Aug 1834 by Joseph A. MANSFIELD (OM)

**DAVIS**, Leonard & **BURROWS**, Suzanna; 1 Jan 1776 (OB)

**DAVIS**, Lewis & **HAM**, Dashia (prenuptial agreement with Theodocius HAM) 13 May 1814 surety William B. KNIGHT (OB)

**DAVIS**, Mitchell & **HARVEY**, Elizabeth 15 Apr 1816 surety Robert G. DOUGLAS (OB) 18 Apr 1816 by George BINGHAM (OM)

**DAVIS**, Mitchell & **MALLORY**, Elizabeth surety John MALLORY 24 Dec 1821 (OB) 30 Dec 1821 by George BINGHAM (OM)

**DAVIS**, Ransom & **ADAMS**, Polly surety Leman DAVIS 19 Apr 1850 (OB) 21 Apr 1850 by Joseph S. JACKSON (OM)

**DAVIS**, Reuben & **GRADY**, Lucy d/o William GRADY Sr. and Lucy GRADY surety Alexander GRADY 1 Apr 1816 (OB)

**DAVIS**, Richard T. age 39 w POB Albemarle Co POR Loudon Co. s/o John A.G. DAVIS and Mary Jane TERRELL Episcopal Minister & **FROST**, Louisa T. age 32 s POB Prince William Co POR Orange d/o _____ FROST and Elizabeth CARTER 7 Oct 1869 POM Orange by T.M. CARSON (OMR)

**DAVIS**, Thomas POR Spotsylvania & **HIATT**, Susannah; 1 May 1783 (OB)

**DAVIS**, Thomas & **BOWCOCK**, Susan d/o Tandy BOWCOCK surety P.S. FRY 19 Jul 1825 (OB) 2 Aug 1825 by George MORRIS (OM)

**DAVIS**, Thomas & **COLEMAN**, Eliza J. surety James L. COLEMAN by K. ADAMS 20 May 1840 (OB) (OM)

**DAVIS**, Thomas & **EARLY**, Elizabeth d/o Theodosia EARLY 24 Apr 1783 (OB)

**DAVIS**, Thomas & **PANNILL**, Elizabeth d/o William PANNILL Sr. surety William PANNILL Jr. 10 Jan 1789 (OB)

**DAVIS**, Thomas J. & **JACKSON**, Mary E.; 26 Jan 1857 (OML)

**DAVIS**, Thornton s/o Benjamin and Nelly DAVIS age 25 s laborer on farm POB POR Orange POC & **MAGRUDER**, Judy d/o Peter and Phoebe MAGRUDER age 21 s POB POR Orange POC: POM Orange 19 Oct 1867 (OMR) 16 Oct 1867 (OML)

**DAVIS**, Washington POC age 22 s laborer POB Spotsylvania POR Orange s/o William P. DAVIS & **WILLIS**, Ellen POC age 21 s POB POR

Orange d/o James WILLIS and Louisa WILLIS POM Orange 25 Oct
1876 (OMR)

**DAVIS,** William & **BOSTON,** Sally d/o Reuben BOSTON who is also
surety 27 Nov 1809 (OB)

**DAVIS,** William & **EASTON,** Nancy; 5 Feb 1789 (OB)

**DAVIS,** William & **GOODRIDGE,** Harriett ward of William DAVIS
surety James BECK 23 Feb 1818 (OB)

**DAVIS,** William & **ROGERS,** Auley d/o John ROGERS who is also
surety 24 Feb 1818 (OB)

**DAVIS,** William J. & **RENNOLDS,** Sarah Ann d/o John T. RENNOLDS
who is also surety 4 Jan 1849 (OB)

**DAVISON,** Percey G. age 24 s farmer POB POR Lexington s/o D. G.
DAVISON and Annie WHITE & **PALMER,** Maggie C. age 23 s POB
Lexington POR Orange d/o M.J. WALLACE POM Orange 11 Sep
1877 (OMR)

**DAWSON,** Isaac POC age 25 s labourer on C. & O. Railroad POB Greene
POR Orange s/o Lewis DAWSON and Caroline MICHENS &
**TAYLOR,** Maria age 22 s POB POR Orange d/o Albert TAYLOR and
Emily POWELL POM Orange 4 Sep 1879 by F. TIBBS (OMR)

**DAWSON,** James (over 21 years) & **HUGHES,** Nancy d/o Francis
HUGHES (over 21 years) 22 Dec 1803 by Nath. SANDERS (Misc Min
Ret)

**DAWSON,** James POC age 60 w farm laborer POB POR Orange &
**GORDON,** Susan POC age 20 s POB POR Orange d/o Ceasar
GORDON and Tena WHITE POM Orange 20 Aug 1877 (OMR)

**DAWSON,** John & **CHISM,** Ann; 19 Oct 1775 both of St. Thomas Parish
by banns (Deed Book 17)

**DAWSON,** John & **POLLARD,** Nancy 3 Aug 1795 surety Benjamin
HAWKINS (OB) 25 Aug 1795 by Nathaniel SANDERS (OM)

**DAWSON,** Musgrave clerk & **WAUGH,** Mary 31 May 1757 (Orange Fee
Book)

**DAY,** Henry C. age 30 s POB Macon Co, GA POR Brunswick, GA s/o
Charles DAY and Mary Jane CRACKER lawyer & **LAMAR,** Jane A.
age 30 w POB Caroline Co. POR Orange d/o Charles C.
TALIAFERRO and Louisa G. ARMISTEAD 19 Sep 1870 POM
Orange by John S. HANSBOROUGH (OMR)

**DAY,** James F. & **NEWMAN,** Mary Frances d/o Thomas NEWMAN
surety George O. NEWMAN 24 Jul 1832 (OB)

**DEANE,** Charles & **BOSTON,** Elizabeth d/o John BOSTON who is surety
by James GARNETT 15 May 1816 (OB) (OM)

**DEANE,** George s/o William DEANE & **KINDLE,** Mary 11 Feb 1811
Jeremiah BRYAN surety (OB)

**DEANE**, George W. & **SLEET**, Louisa surety William C. SLEET 27 Aug 1840 (OB) by K. ADAMS 8 Sep 1840 (OM)

**DEANE**, John & **LAMB**, Polly d/o James LAMB who is also surety 24 Jul 1821 (OB)

**DEANE**, John & **MAYS**, Elizabeth surety Zachary JONES by Nathaniel SANDERS 18 Aug 1790 (OB) (OM)

**DEANE**, Reuben s/o William DEANE & **LONG**, Mary d/o James LONG who is also the minister surety Everit SULLIVAN 29 Dec 1828 (OB) (OM)

**DEANE**, William & **BOSTON**, Sarah; 2 Jun 1789 surety Joseph BOSTON (OB)

**DEANE**, William (Jr.) & **DEANE**, Mary surety Jeremiah BRIANT 30 May 1816 (OB) 9 Jun 1816 no minister listed (OM)

**DEAR**, John & **SMITH**, Catharine both of St. Thomas Parish by banns 1 Nov 1774 (Deed Book 17)

**DEAR**, Thomas & **FENNELL**, Lucy; 27 Jan 1778 by banns both of St. Thomas Parish (Deed Book 17)

**DEERING**, Thomas & **RUMSEY**, Mary of lawful age, permission by Mary TREASEY surety James DEERING 19 Jun 1783 (OB)

**DELANY**, John & **WATTS**, Susannah POR St. Thomas Parish 5 Mar 1773 (Deed Book 17)

**DEMAINE**, Charles W. s/o William DEMAINE and Elizabeth MANKIN age 21 s fireman on O.& A. Railroad POB Alexandria City POR Orange & **MUSE**, Annie E. d/o Edward and Mary MUSE age 21 s POB New York City, NY POR Orange; POM Gordonsville 15 Mar 1864 (OMR) 11 Mar 1864 (OML)

**DEMPSEY**, James & **BATLEY**, Catharine 30 Dec 1834 surety John DEMPSEY (OB)

**DEMPSEY**, James A. & **SMITH**, Elizabeth; 20 Dec 1852 (OML)

**DEMPSEY**, Joseph D. age 23 s POB Orange POR Spotsylvania farmer s/o Pleasant DEMPSEY and Nancy WRIGHT & **JACKSON**, Laura A. age 23 s POB POR Orange d/o Ryland JOHNSON and Ann HANEY 25 Nov 1880 POM Orange by Melzi S. CHANCELLOR (OMR)

**DEMPSEY**, Lewis & **MCCLARNEY**, Polly 17 Mar 1823 surety Ike RICHARDS (OB)

**DEMPSEY**, Pleasant & **HANEY**, Lucinda d/o James HANEY who is also surety 20 Aug 1834 (OB)

**DEMPSEY**, Pleasant R. & **WRIGHT**, Nancy d/o Eliz. WRIGHT 5 Feb 1848 surety James A. DEMPSEY (OB)

**DEMPSEY**, Robert D. & **WATSON**, Mary E. d/o Benjamin WATSON 22 May 1850 surety William MORRIS (OB) 1 Jun 1850 by B.L. HUME (OMR)

**DEMPSEY,** Thomas J. age 25 s farmer POB POR Orange s/o James A. DEMPSEY and Elizabeth W. SMITH & **QUANE,** Mary J. age 16 s POB POR Orange d/o Daniel QUAN and Bridget O'NEAL POM Orange 6 Oct 1878 by Sanders MASON (OMR)

**DEMPSEY,** Wellford age 22 s farmer POB POR Orange s/o Robert DEMPSEY and Elizabeth WATSON & **MORRIS,** Mary J. age 22 s POB POR Orange d/o Thomas MORRIS and Hannah WATSON POM Orange 18 Dec 1878 by John C. WILLIS (OMR)

**DEMPSEY,** William A. & **MORRIS,** Margaret F.; POM Orange 6 Jan 1852 (OMR) 2 Jan 1852 (OML)

**DEMPSEY,** William A. age 52 w miller POB POR Orange s/o Lewis DEMPSEY and Mary MCCLARY & **MORRIS,** Ann E. age 28 s POB POR Orange d/o James MORRIS and Elizabeth WILTSHIRE POM Orange 16 Mar 1879 by Sanders MASON (OMR)

**DENNISON,** James & **LUCAS,** Nancy w 8 Mar 1822 surety Jacob RUMBOUGH (OB)

**DEREY,** Lavey & **WYE,** Ann; 7 Sep 1785 surety James HEAD (OB)

**DICKENSON,** Allen & **JOHNSON,** Salley Ann 20 Dec 1831 by J. GOSS (OMR)

**DICKENSON,** Allen & **JOHNSON,** Sally Ann d/o Valentine JOHNSON 17 Dec 1831 surety Belfield JOHNSON (OB)

**DICKENSON,** Bennett & **CARPENTER,** Mildred d/o Pleasant CARPENTER 23 Dec 1822 surety Douglass DICKENSON (OB)

**DICKERSON,** Thomas & **WOOD,** Nancy 22 Oct 1810 surety Reubin TWYMAN by Jacob WATTS (OB)(OMR)

**DICKIE,** William L. & **GRASTY,** Elizabeth L. 3 Apr 1849 (OB)

**DICKINSON,** James s/o William DICKINSON and Matilda MATTHEWS age 48 w farmer POB Essex Co. POR Richmond Co. & **TAYLOR,** Ann M. d/o Richard S. TAYLOR and Eleanor GWATHWAY age 43 s POB King William Co. POR Orange; POM Orange 31 Oct 1867 (OMR) 30 Oct 1867 (OML)

**DICKINSON,** Ralph & **QUISENBERRY,** Ann ward of Mary QUISENBERRY surety Charles DICKINSON 24 Mar 1815 26 Mar 1815 by John A. BILLINGSLEY (OB) (OMR)

**DICKINSON,** Robert & **PARISH,** Ruth d/o Joseph PARISH 10 Feb 1787 (OB)

**DIGGES,** Brice POC age 23 s farm labourer POB Louisa POR Orange s/o Boswell DIGGES and Clara HARRISON & **HALL,** Matilda POC age 22 s POB POR Orange d/o Henry HALL and Judy WILLIAMS POM Shady Grove Church, Orange 10 Mar 1878 by B.T. JOHNSON (OMR)

**DIGGES,** Cole C. & **CASH,** Matilda A. d/o James CASH surety William BROWN 12 Oct 1825 (OB) by James GARNETT 13 Oct 1825 (OM)

**DIGGS**, Cole C. & **GARTON**, Jemima A. d/o Mary GARTON surety Philip HUNT 17 Sep 1831 (OB)

**DILLY**, Richard & **DEVENNEY**, Mary M. d/o C. DEVENNEY 22 Mar 1819 (OB)

**DIXON**, John & **RUMSEY**, Lucy permission from William RUMSEY surety Benjamin HUME 27 Sep 1813 (OB) by Jeremiah CHANDLER 30 Sep 1813 (OM)

**DIXON**, Samuel & **BROWN**, Charlotte both of St. Thomas Parish 3 Oct 1773 (Deed Book 17)

**DOANE**, John & **MAYS**, Elizabeth; 18 Aug 1790 (OB)

**DOD**, John / William [the bond is made out to William DOD but is signed by John DOD] & **LEE**, Susanna; 31 Dec 1792 surety Zachariah WOOD (OB)

**DODD**, James & **COOK**, Nancy 9 Jun 1803 by Nath. SANDERS (Misc Min Ret)

**DODD**, John age 21 s POB POR Louisa farmer s/o Joseph H. DODD and Frances Jane HUNDLEY & **SPROUSE**, Angelina age 20 s POR Orange d/o Alexander SPROUSE and Louisa GILSON 14 Jan 1877 POM Orange (OMR)

**DODD**, John over 21 years & **JOHNSON**, Sally over 21 years surety William DODD 13 Feb 1804 (OB)

**DOHONEY**, Rhodes & **CHAPMAN**, Jenny permission from Joseph CHAPMAN surety Francis COLLINS 19 Oct 1790 (OB)

**DOHONY**, James & **VAWTER**, Winifred 23 Feb 1775 both of St. Thomas Parish (Deed Book 17)

**DOLAND**, Thomas & **STOCKDELL**, Elizabeth 25 Nov 1850 (OB)

**DOLLINS**, Reuben & **HENSLEY**, Elizabeth d/o William HENSLEY 30 Dec 1789 surety Lewis HENSLEY (OB)

**DONALD**, William & **QUINN**, Lucinda d/o Garland QUINN who is also surety 23 Oct 1831 by J. GOSS (OB) (OM)

**DONATHAN**, John & **ELUCK**, Polly 14 Mar 1803 by Nathl. SANDERS (Misc Min Ret)

**DONOVER**, John & **GAER**, Sally d/o Nathaniel GAER 27 Jan 1790 surety William GAER (OB)

**DOOLEY**, Harden B. s/o Thomas DOOLEY and Susan DOOLEY age 19 s farmer POB POR Bedford Co. & **BOWLER**, Harriet A. d/o Robert BOWLER and Caroline V. BOWLING age 21 s POB POR Orange; POM Orange 16 Feb 1864 (OMR) 12 Feb 1864 (OML)

**DOOLING**, Thomas & **FINNELL**, Elizabeth; 15 Mar 1791 surety John QUINN (OB)

**DOUGLAS**, Charles & **PAYNE**, Mary; 25 Apr 1796 surety John PAYNE (OB)

**DOUGLASS,** Carter POC age 21 s farm labourer POB Fauquier POR
Orange s/o Delphia DOUGLASS & **CAMPBELL,** Celas POC age 25 s
POB POR Orange d/o John CAMPBELL and Minerva JOHNSON
POM Orange 3 Jan 1878 by W.J. BARNETT (OMR)

**DOUGLASS,** James M. & **CLASBY** (?), Courtney 7 Aug 1845 surety
Zachariah DARNELL (OB)

**DOUGLASS,** James P. & **BOWLER,** Elizabeth G. d/o Davis BOWLER
19 Dec 1832 surety David BOWLER (OB)

**DOUGLASS,** John & **BURTON,** Margaret 30 May 1831 surety John M.
BLAKEY (OB)

**DOUGLASS,** Lewis Porterfield s/o John B. DOUGLASS & **BARNETT,**
Ann E. 31 Dec 1838 surety Edwin T. DOUGLASS (OB)

**DOUGLASS,** Rice J. & **REYNOLDS,** Lucy Ann 22 May 1850 surety
Joseph D. REYNOLDS (OB) 28 May 1850 by Joseph A. MANSFIELD
(OMR)

**DOWELL,** Berryman & **HILL,** Margaret 24 Dec 1838 surety John HILL
(OB)

**DOWELL,** John & **GARITSON,** Elizabeth 14 Jan 1819 by George
BINGHAM (OM)

**DOWELL,** Madison & **HUCKSTEP,** Elizabeth M. d/o Josiah
HUCKSTEP 29 Oct 1831 surety William G. HUCKSTEP (OB)

**DOWELL,** Maj. M. & **DOWELL,** Mary M.; 26 Oct 1857 (OML)

**DOWELL,** Nathan & **VAUGHN,** Lucy d/o Joseph VAUGHN 29 Apr
1819 surety Richard DOWELL of Albemarle Co. by J.C. GORDON
(OB) (OM)

**DOWLING,** John & **LUCAS,** Frances d/o Ann LUCAS 4 Apr 1816 surety
Benjamin HERNDON (OB)

**DOWNER,** Reuben C. s/o Robert G. DOWNER and Frances A. DANIEL
age 24 s bricklayer /plasterer POB POR Orange & **DANIEL,** Mary C.
d/o James B. DANIEL and Margaret BESME (?) age 16 s POB POR
Orange POM Orange 7 Jan 1864 (OMR) 1 Jan 1864 (OML)

**DOWNER,** Robert G. & **DANIEL,** Frances A. d/o James B. DANIEL 6
Dec 1830 surety John HENDERSON (OB)

**DOWNER,** William W. & **REYNOLDS,** Lucy Mary ward of Robert E.
REYNOLDS POM Orange 15 Dec 1852 (OMR) 13 Dec 1852 (OML)

**DOWNIN,** Virgil age 30 s POB Washington Co., MD POR Orange s/o
S.S. DOWNIN and Nancy FLETCHER saddler & **DOWNEY,** Mary J.
age 18 s POB POR Orange d/o John DOWNEY and Mildred MASON
7 Oct 1873 POM Orange by J.W. MCCOWEN (OMR)

**DRAPER,** Chiswell G. & **SMITH,** Eliza d/o John SMITH 13 Sep 1827
surety Thomas P. RIPPETO (OB)

**DRAPER,** Richard & **BOSTON,** Martha d/o Reuben BOSTON who is
also surety 12 Nov 1816 (OB)

**DREWRY**, Giles B. age 34 s POB Bedford Co POR Orange s/o Isaac N. DREWRY and Sallie DONDIE lawyer & **WRIGHT**, Amanda M. age 18 s POB POR Orange d/o Dabney WRIGHT and Jane M. ESTES 23 Dec 1873 POM Orange by Charles QUARLES (OMR)

**DUKE**, William & **GIBBS**, Lini 28 Feb 1803 surety John H. GIBBS (OB)

**DULANEY**, George age 25 s POB Rockingham Co s/o Arnold DULANEY and Polly BURKE saddler & **BRADLEY**, Almeda W. age 15 s POB Louisa Co. d/o D.S. BRADLEY and Susan BROWN 20 Aug 1868 POM Orange by T.R. DUNN (OMR)

**DULANEY**, William & **CAMPBELL**, Catharine H. 3 Oct 1838 surety William COLLINS (OB)

**DUNAVANT**, George & **HANY**, Peggy 27 Oct 1814 by George BINGHAM (OM)

**DUNAWAY**, George & **HAINEY**, Peggy d/o James HAINEY who is also surety Oct 1814 by George BINGHAM (OM)

**DUNAWAY**, John & **SUTHERLAND**, Polly; 9 Jan 1816 surety Alexander SUTHERLAND (OB) 12 Jan 1816 by Jeremiah CHANDLER (OM)

**DUNAWAY**, Richard & **MASSEY**, Sarah Frances 29 Sep 1841 surety Richard L. RICHARDS (OB)

**DUNAWAY**, Thomas & **WRIGHT**, Mary; 3 Jul 1826 (OB)

**DUNCAN**, Joseph & **STEVENS**, Nancy; 22 May 1772 both of St. Thomas Parish (Orange Fee Book)

**DUNN**, Benjamin F. s/o John DUNN and Mildred WATTS age 47 s physician POB POR Louisa Co. & **GRAVES**, Hattie F. d/o Abner GRAVES and Pamela EDWARDS age 27 s POB Chesterfield Co. POR Orange; POM Orange 19 Dec 1867 (OMR) 7 Dec 1867 (OML)

**DUNN**, Fountain D. & **VIA**, Nancy Craig 23 Dec 1819 by George BINGHAM (OM)

**DUNN**, Garland & **MILLER**, Raweana d/o Sarah MILLER 25 Feb 1813 surety John MILLER Jr. (OB)

**DUNN**, John & **MAUPIN**, Susanna 4 Feb 1813 by George BINGHAM (OM)

**DUNN**, Martin A. & **WALKER**, Mary d/o Benjamin WALKER 6 Feb 1839 surety William MALLORY (OB)

**DUNN**, William & **BLEDSOE**, Mary; 24 Jan 1775 (OB)

**DUNN**, William G. & **WALKER**, Elizabeth V. d/o Benjamin WALKER surety Martin A. DUNN 23 Oct 1844 (OB)

**DUNOVAN**, William & **KNIGHT**, Fanny 10 Mar 1825 permission by William KNIGHT surety Matthew KNIGHT (OB)

**DURRETT**, Achilles & **QUISENBERRY**, Lydia over 21 surety Moses QUISENBERRY 25 Sep 1805 (OB)

**DURRETT,** Davis & **DAVIS,** Elizabeth 8 Feb 1817 surety Isaac DAVIS Jr. (OB) 11 Feb 1817 by Jacob WATTS (OM)

**DURRETT,** John D. & **DAVIS,** Frances 20 Nov 1797 surety James WATTS (OB)

**DURRETT,** Killian & **THOMPSON,** Elizabeth POR Orange 6 may 1802 by Robert JONES (Misc Min Ret)

**DURRETT,** William POC age 22 s POB POR Green s/o Dawson DURRETT and Ann ___ & **BANKS,** Susan POC age 21 s POB Green POR Orange d/o Ezekiel BANKS and Sophia FRY POM Orange 31 May 1877 (OMR)

**DUVALL,** Clabourn & **FAULCONER,** Polly d/o David FAULCONER who is also surety 24 Feb 1812 (OB) 3 Mar 1812 by Jeremiah CHANDLER (OM)

**DUVALL,** John P. age 19 s POB POR Orange rail road laborer s/o John P. DUVALL and Bettie WOOLFRY & **BROWN,** Roberta E. age 25 s d/o James O. BROWN and Sarah M. COOPER 11 Feb 1880 POM Orange by C.R. SCOTT (OMR)

**EAGAN,** James & **PRITCHETT,** Lucinda 27 Feb 1826 surety Robert PRITCHETT (OB)

**EARLY,** James & **CARR,** Sarah 9 Jul 1812 by George BINGHAM (OM)

**EARLY,** Job & **THOMPSON,** Elizabeth 9 Dec 1813 by George BINGHAM (OM)

**EARLY,** Joel & **SMITH,** Lucy; 23 Jun 1772 both of St. Thomas Parish (Orange Fee Book)

**EARLY,** John & **TIMBERLAKE,** Margaret 6 Mar 1823 by George BINGHAM (OM)

**EARLY,** William & **GRAVES,** Sarah 12 Nov 1812 by George BINGHAM (OM)

**EARNEST,** Joseph minister & **TAYLOR,** Betsy Hord; POM Orange 30 Dec 1851 (OMR) (OML)

**EASTHAM,** Edward & **THORNTON,** Ann; 5 Jun 1798 surety William RUCKER Jr. permission by George THORNTON (OB)

**EASTIN,** John & **GRIFFITH,** Sarah s 28 Apr 1785 surety David GRIFFITH (OB)

**EASTIN,** Philip & **HENDERSON,** Elizabeth d/o Alexander HENDERSON 23 Mar 1782 surety William TOMLINSON (OB)

**EASTING,** Stephen POR St. Thomas Parish & **JOHNSON,** Susannah POR St. Thomas Parish 2 Apr 1773 (Deed Book 17)

**EASTIS,** John & **COX,** Sarah age 21 26 Dec 1799 surety Joan COX (OB)

**EATON,** William & **DUNNIVEN,** Elizabeth 18 Jun 1812 by George BINGHAM (OM)

**EAVES,** William & **HIGHLANDER,** Nancy d/o George HIGHLANDER 9 Jan 1797 surety George WEBSTER (OB)

69

**EDDINS, Alfred & WINSLOW,** Mary Miller d/o Valentine WINSLOW 13 Dec 1828 surety Valentine M. HOUSEWORTH (OB)

**EDDINS, Allen & PARROTT,** Judith 8 Jan 1833 surety Thomas J. EDDINS (OB)

**EDDINS, Elijah & OSBORN,** Nancy d/o Robert OSBORN surety George COLLINS 12 Feb 1798 (OB) 15 Feb 1797 by Hamilton GOSS (OM)

**EDDINS, Fountain & ANDERSON,** Emily d/o Joel ANDERSON 26 May 1835 surety Jeremiah GARNETT (OB)

**EDDINS, Hiram S. & MOYERS,** Sarah P. d/o William H. MOYERS surety Michael P. MOYERS 10 Dec 1833 by E.G. SHIP (OM) (OB)

**EDDINS, Joseph Jr. & DAVIS,** Nancy d/o Mary DAVIS 31 Dec 1808 surety Joseph DAVIS (OB) 3 Jan 1809 by Jacob WATTS (OM)

**EDDINS, Smith & BURTON,** Maria d/o May/Mary BURTON surety Benjamin BURTON 24 Jul 1820 (OB)

**EDDINS, Tandy & SIMS,** Amelia d/o John and Eliz SIMS 10 Nov 1823 surety William H. SIMS (OB)

**EDDINS, Theophilus & HERNDON,** Lucy D. 15 Dec 1828 surety B.P. HERNDON (OB)

**EDDINS, Thomas & COLLINS,** Frances d/o William COLLINS 25 Dec 1798 surety John HERNDON (OB) 26 Dec 1798 by Hamilton GOSS (OM)

**EDDINS, William & MANSFIELD,** Sarah H. 23 Dec 1816 surety William H. MANSFIELD (OB)

**EDDINS, William A.** s/o A.J. EDDINS and Amanda J. MILLER age 23 s clerk in store POB Rockingham POR Albemarle **& GLENN,** Susan C. d/o William GLENN and Samantha TAYLOR age 18 s POB Page POR Orange; POM Orange 31 May 1866 (OMR) (OML)

**EDINGTON, Edmund & GORDON,** Priscilla; 24 Sep 1798 surety Samuel GORDON (OB)

**EDWARDS, Brice Jr. & RHOADES,** Mary Ann 23 Dec 1848 surety William WOOD by G.W. ABELL (OB) (OM)

**EDWARDS, Daniel** age 21 s POB POR Orange s/o William EDWARDS and Jonath _____ laborer **& SPOTSWOOD,** Winnie age 21 s POB POR Orange d/o Pleasant SPOTSWOOD and Winnie _____ 27 Mar 1869 POM Orange by John H. ROBINSON (OMR)

**EDWARDS, Elisha** s/o William EDWARDS **& EATON,** Elizabeth 28 Aug 1798 surety William EATON (OB)

**EDWARDS, Horace B. & WOOD,** Mary J. 23 Mar 1844 surety E.T. DOUGLASS (OB)

**EDWARDS, Jefferson** s/o William EDWARDS who is also surety **& LONG,** Courtnay 23 Apr 1832 (OB)

**EDWARDS, John & BICKERS,** Selina Anna d/o George BICKERS who is also surety 15 Mar 1815 (OB)

**EDWARDS**, Samuel age 42 w POB POR Albemarle Co s/o Thomas EDWARDS and Agnes BROCKMAN farmer & **SHOTWELL**, Sallie J. age 24 s POB POR Orange d/o Caswell SHOTWELL and Columbia WOOD 15 Feb 1872 POM Orange by W. S. BRIGGS (OMR)

**EDWARDS**, William & **OLIVER**, Lydia d/o Francis OLIVER who is also surety 17 Jan 1817 (OB) 19 Jan 1817 by J. GOSS (OM)

**EGER**, Leonard & **ATKINS**, Sarah d/o Dickinson ATKINS 9 May 1849 surety Richard S. BOULWARE (OB) 22 May 1849 by Burruss DULIN (OM)

**EGGLESTON**, Robert I. s/o Richard S. EGGLESTON and Jane SAUNDERS age 24 s farmer POB New Kent POR Charles City Co. & **EDDINS**, Emma J. d/o A. EDDINS and Julia STANARD age 16 s POB Powhatan POR Orange; POM Orange 2 Nov 1865 (OMR) (OML)

**EHART**, Michael & **EHART**, Sarah 26 Jan 1814 surety Adam EHART (OB) 28 Jan 1814 by Hamilton GOSS (OM)

**EHEART**, Michael L. & **CAVE**, Lavinia B. d/o Robert CAVE who is also surety 24 Mar 1823 (OB)

**EHEART**, Robert W. age 50 w farmer POB POR Orange s/o M.L. EHEART and Lavinia CAVE & **BLEDSOE**, Amanda C. age 42 w POB POR Orange d/o Samuel THOMPSON and Mildred SNELL POM Orange 22 Dec 1879 (OMR)

**ELAM**, Thomas J. s/o Odiga ELAM and Mary J.DAVENPORT age 22 s farmer POB Trout Co, GA POR Steward Co, GA & **LANCASTER**, Sarah Jane d/o James M. JACOBS & Lucy FINNEY age 18 w POB POR Orange; POM Orange 9 Jul 1863 (OMR) 6 Jul 1863 (OML)

**ELIASON**, William P. & **PANNILL**, Susan G. 24 Feb 1840 surety George PANNILL (OB)

**ELIOTT**, George & **MARTIN**, Judith 31 Jan 1816 (OB)

**ELLIOT**, William & **HALL**, Mary Knight 20 Dec 1821 by George BINGHAM (OM)

**ELLIOTE**, Allen & **GAINES**, Percilia 18 Jun 1803 by Nath SANDERS (Misc Min Ret)

**ELLIOTT**, Albin & **GAINES**, Urcilla 11 Jun 1803 surety William ROBERSON (OB)

**ELLIOTT**, James & **HIGDON**, Elizabeth d/o John HIGDON 13 Dec 1828 surety William G. HUCKSTEP (OB)

**ELLIS**, Alexander s/o Nelson ELLIS and Sady HILL age 25 s laborer POB POR Orange POC & **GILES**, Eliza d/o Edmund and Maria GILES age 28 s POB POR Orange POC; POM Orange 17 Dec 1866 (OMR) (OML)

**ELLIS**, Frank POC age 27 s POB POR Orange laborer & **MAY**, Polly age 19 s POB POR Orange d/o Squire MAY and Clio MADISON sister of

Thomas A. MAY (who testifies to her age) 1 Feb 1874 POM Orange (OMR)

**ELLIS**, George POC age 21 s POB Louisa Co POR Orange s/o Joseph ELLIS and Frances LUCAS laborer & **MCINTOSH**, Harriet age 21 s POB POR Orange d/o William MCINTOSH and Randall YOUNG 4 Jan 1874 POM Orange (OMR)

**ELLIS**, George POC age 26 s laborer POB POR Orange s/o James ELLIS and Lina CORBINS & **LINDSEY**, Matilda POC age 16 s POB POR Orange d/o Absalom LINDSAY and Nancy PRESLEY POM Orange 22 Oct 1876 (OMR)

**ELLIS**, Harrison POC age 22 s POB POR Orange farm laborer s/o Walker ELLIS and Mary _____ & **TAYLOR**, Lucy POC age 16 POB POR Orange d/o Barbour TAYLOR and Mary _____ POM Orange 3 Mar 1877 (OMR)

**ELLIS**, Harrison s/o Edmund ELLIS and Nancy DADE age 20 s laborer POB Orange C.H. POR Orange POC & **HUGHES**, Alice d/o Ellen WAUGH age 22 s POB POR Orange POC; POM Orange C.H. 29 Sep 1866 (OMR) (OML)

**ELLIS**, Horace age 23 s farm laborer POB POR Orange POC & **PRESLEY**, Emily age 25 s POB POR Orange POC; POM Orange 26 Dec 1867 (OMR) (OML)

**ELLIS**, Horace POC age 23 s labourer POB POR Orange s/o Horace and Laura ELLIS & **WALKER**, Mary POC age 18 s POB POR Orange d/o George and Nancy WALKER POM Orange 18 Dec 1879 (OMR)

**ELLIS**, Jack POC age 45 s farm labourer POB POR Orange s/o Lewis WILLIAMS and Myra _____ & **KINNY**, Ella POC age 40 w POB Albemarle POR Orange d/o Rachel KENNY POM Orange 23 Aug 1879 by F. TIBBS (OMR)

**ELLIS**, James H. & **WOOLFOLK**, Mary C. d/o Thomas WOOLFOLK 25 Mar 1816 surety John THOMPSON (OB)

**ELLIS**, Joseph POC age 21 s labourer POB Louisa POR Orange s/o Samuel ELLIS and _____ HICKS & **ELLIS**, Susan POC age 21 s POB POR Orange d/o Punch ELLIS and Polly _____ POM Orange 7 Sep 1879 by L.W. CAVE (OMR)

**ELLIS**, Lewis B. s/o Hezekiah ELLIS and Malinda CARRIES age 25 s farmer POB POR Prince William Co & **BROWN**, Philippa J. d/o John G. BROWN and Patsy F. HOLBERT age 18 s POB POR Orange; POM Orange 7 Dec 1865 (OMR) 6 Dec 1865 (OML)

**ELLIS**, Lewis POC age 21 s labourer POB Louisa POR Orange s/o Joe ELLIS and Frances HUNTER & **PRYOR**, Alice POC age 20 s POB POR Orange d/o William PRYOR and Mary A. SHAPE (?) POM Orange 26 Dec 1878 by W.S. CAMPBELL (OMR)

ELLIS, Mike POC age 24 s POB POR Orange s/o Walker ELLIS and
Mary _____ farm laborer & **LINDSAY**, Abby POC age 25 s POB POR
Orange d/o Squire LINDSAY and Melvina WOOD 28 Dec 1871 POM
Orange by Philip JOHNSON (OMR)

ELLIS, Richard P. & **FERGUSON**, Margaret 22 Nov 1830 surety James
H. ELLIS (OB)

ELLIS, Robert POC age 22 s POB POR Orange farm laborer s/o James
ELLIS and Lucinda LEWIS & **GRAVES**, Sallie POC age 17 s POB
POR Orange d/o Joseph GRAVES 28 Dec 1880 POM Thornhill,
Orange by A.W. GRAVES, baptist (OMR)

ELLIS, Samuel POC age 21 s labourer POB Louisa POR Orange s/o
Samuel ELLIS and Charlotte CLARK & **WASHINGTON**, Polly POC
age 19 s POB POR Orange d/o Milton WASHINGTON and Emily
ELLIS POM Orange 20 Dec 1879 (OMR)

ELLIS, Thomas J. brother of John ELLIS who is surety & **FERGUSON**,
Cynthia Ann d/o Vivion FERGUSON 1 Jan 1829 (OB)

ELLIS, William N. age 23 s POB POR Orange s/o Edmund ELLIS and
Nancy JOHNSON laborer & **THORNTON**, Mary Ella age 19 POB
POR Orange d/o William THORNTON and Caroline JACKSON 10
Aug 1870 POM Orange by J.S. HANSBOROUGH (OMR)

EMBREE, Richard & **PAYNE**, Judith; 17 Jan 1785 surety George
PAYNE of St. Thomas Parish (OB)

EMBREY, John A. s/o Joseph EMBREY and Catherine PEYTON age 23
s farmer POB Rappahannock POR Culpeper & **PRIEST**, Eliza A. d/o
Fellows PRIEST and Lucy HICKERSON age 23 s POB Culpeper Co
POR Orange; POM Orange 5 Dec 1865 (OMR) 27 Nov 1865 (OML)

EMMANUEL, Preston B. age 22 s farmer POB POR South Carolina s/o
W.P. EMMANUEL and R.F. MING & **SANFORD**, Lizzie H. age 21 s
POB POR Orange d/o Law. SANDFORD and Lucy WALKER POM
Orange 10 Dec 1879 (OMR)

EMMERSON, James & **TINDER**, Jemimah permission from Alepain(?)
and Jesse TINDER surety Ephraim TINDER 12 Feb 1818 (OB)

EMMONS, James s/o James S. and Ann EMMONS age 21 s farmer POB
POR Fauquier & **COLLINS**, Rebecca E. d/o Francis and Margaret
COLLINS age 27 s POB Madison POR Orange; POM Orange 23 Dec
1856 (OMR) 16 Dec 1856 (OML)

ENGLAND, George W. & **HANEY**, Mary 17 Dec 1836 surety John C.
THORNTON (OB)

ENGLAND, John & **JOHNSON**, Elisabeth 21 Dec 1832 surety Benjamin
P. JOHNSON (OB)

ENGLAND, William S. & **SUTHERLAND**, Mary 1 Mar 1837 surety
William JOHNSON (OB)

ESQUE, William [possibly William ESSEX] & **BICKERS**, Mary F.;
POM Orange 23 Dec 1851 (OMR)

**ESTES**, Abraham & **COX**, Sally W. 6 Aug 1810 surety William COX
(OB) 26 Aug 1810 by George BINGHAM (OM)

**ESTES**, Andrew F. s/o Robert ESTES and Sally E. COSBY age 22 s
farmer POB Louisa POR Orange & **HAYES**, Lucy C. d/o Thomas
HAYES and Bettie BROCKMAN age 19 s POB POR Orange; POM
Orange 24 Jan 1867 (OMR) 22 Jan 1867 (OML)

**ESTES**, Elisha & **BINGHAM**, Maria d/o George BINGHAM 5 Aug 1815
surety John BINGHAM (OB)

**ESTES**, Garrett & **COX**, Sarah 16 Dec 1826 surety Warner COX (OB)

**ESTES**, Isaac L. age 26 s POB POR Orange s/o William B. ESTES and
Sarah BRUCE farmer & **GILBERT**, Dorothea C. age 18 s POB
Albemarle Co POR Orange d/o William GILBERT and Ellen PAYNE
6 Feb 1872 POM Orange by A.M. POINDEXTER (OMR)

**ESTES**, James R. s/o Thomas ESTES who is also surety & **BELL**,
Elizabeth M. d/o Brockman BELL 19 Nov 1838 (OB)

**ESTES**, John & **DANIEL**, Maria d/o Reubin DANIEL who is also surety
16 Apr 1821 (OB) 10 May 1821 by George BINGHAM (OM)

**ESTES**, John H. age 37 s farmer POB Louisa POR Orange s/o Thomas
ESTES and Nancy PORTER & **GRAVES**, Julia A. age 26 s POB POR
Orange d/o Isaac W. GRAVES and Eliza BROCKMAN POM Orange
14 Dec 1876 (OMR)

**ESTES**, Littleton & **HARVEY**, Frances whose guardian is Littleton
ESTES 23 Feb 1818 surety Thomas SORRILLE (OB)

**ESTES**, Samuel & **HOLLADAY**, Winifred; 21 Jul 1776 both of St.
Thomas Parish (Deed Book 17)

**ESTES**, Samuel & **OGG**, Jane 17 Aug 1818 surety James OGG (OB)

**ESTES**, Thomas B. s/o Thomas ESTES age 48 s farmer POB POR Orange
& **ESTES**, Mary E. d/o John ESTES age 38 s POB POR Orange; POM
Orange 10 Dec 1866 (OMR)

**ESTES**, William & **BRUCE**, Sarah 26 Sep 1842 surety Robert U.
BROOKING (OB) 29 Sep 1842 by Benjamin CREEL (OM)

**ESTES**, William & **HARVEY**, Polly 23 Oct 1804 surety Anthony
HARVEY (OB)

**ESTES**, William T. age 34 w farmer POB Louisa POR Orange s/o Robert
ESTES and Sally COSBY & **BELL**, Ida F. age 17 s POB POR Orange
d/o Orville BELL and Mary T. ESTES POM Orange 8 Jan 1878 by
W.H. CAMPER (OMR)

**ESTES**, William T. s/o Robert ESTES and Sally COSBY age 24 s farmer
POB Louisa POR Orange & **WRIGHT**, Mary V. d/o Dabney
WRIGHT and Jane M. ESTES age 23 s POB POR Orange; POM
Orange 18 Apr 1867 (OMR) 9 Apr 1867 (OML)

ETHERTON, Thomas E. age 25 s POB POR Albemarle Co s/o Anderson
ETHERTON and Millicent HALL farmer & **MADISON**, Mary F. age
25 s POB POR Orange d/o Jack MADISON and Lucy ROUTT 11 Dec
1873 POM Orange by H.E. HATCHER (OMR)

EUBANK, Elias D. s/o George W. EUBANK and Mary C. HILL age 23 s
farmer POB POR Nelson & **BECKHAM**, Mary O. d/o James
BECKHAM and Sarah CANADAY age 16 s POB POR Orange; POM
Gordonsville, Orange 5 Nov 1863 (OMR) 4 Nov 1863 (OML)

EVANS, John & **KING**, Nancy d/o Julian KING who is also surety 2 Mar
1809 (OB) 24 Mar 1809 by Robert JONES (OM)

EVE, Joseph & **SMITH**, Polly d/o Raif and Patty SMITH 19 Aug 1799
surety John SMITH (OB)

EVES, Thomas & **JENKINS**, Fanny d/o William JENKINS 18 Mar 1805
surety James ATKINS (OB)

FABER, Lewis J. age 19 years 6 months s merchant POB Albemarle POR
Orange s/o John G. FABER and A.M. WINGFIELD & **JORDAN**,
Mary Lucy age 18 s POB POR Orange d/o John M. JORDAN and
Susan A. GENTRY POM Gordonsville 12 Apr 1876 (OMR)

FACKLER, Henry & **TERRILL**, Frances 25 Jan 1812 surety Reubin
TERRILL (OB) 26 Jan 1812 by Jeremiah CHANDLER (OM)

FAIRFAX, Edward s/o Minor FAIRFAX and Malinda TANSEL age 21 s
engineer POB Prince William Co POR Gordonsville & **DICKINSON**,
Flora J. d/o Robert W. DICKINSON and Julia CRAIG age 17 s POB
Augusta Co POR Gordonsville; POM Gordonsville, Orange 19 Jan
1864 (OMR) 18 Jan 1864 (OML)

FALLIN, John A. s/o H.H. FALLIN and Eleanor S. WALTERS age 28 s
farmer/cost engineer POB Halifax Co. POR Danville & **ROGERS**,
Elizabeth F. d/o Joseph ROGERS and Malinda NEWMAN age 23 s
POB POR Orange; POM Orange 30 Oct 1865 (OMR) 28 Oct 1865
(OML)

FALLIS, Thomas & **JAMES**, Polly; 29 May 1797 surety James
COLEMAN (OB)

FANDREE, Joseph & **KINSER**, Susan 10 Dec 1831 surety Richard
HOLBERT (OB)

FANT, John T. & **JAMES**, Fanny d/o Joseph and Lucy JAMES who is
also surety 1 Feb 1806 (OB) 18 Feb 1806 by Nathaniel SANDERS
(OM)

FARGUSON, John & **LUCAS**, Frances 12 May 1788 surety William
LUCAS who also consents (OB)

FARGUSON, Vivion s/o William FERGUSON and Margaret VIVION &
**MILLS**, Mary A. d/o Nathaniel MILLS b. 16 Nov 1780 surety Jackson
MILLS 15 Nov 1803 (OB)

**FARISH,** John D. & **ROACH,** Mary K. 4 Dec 1848 surety Thomas J.
ROACH who is also guardian (OB)

**FARISH,** William H. POR Caroline County & **ROACH,** Nancy Jane 23
Sep 1850 surety Thomas J. ROACH (OB) 2 Oct 1850 by A.H.
BENNETT (OM)

**FARISH,** William P.T. age 37 w POB POR Caroline s/o George B.
FARISH and Clementine DILLARD farmer & **COLEMAN,** Mollie E.
age 33 s POB POR Orange d/o Thomas F. COLEMAN and Susan
DILLARD 11 Mar 1874 POM Orange (OMR)

**FARRAR,** David S. s/o Garland and Mary L. FARRAR age 32 s teacher
POB Goochland Co. POR Fluvanna & **ATKINS,** Martha J. d/o Joseph
and Mary ATKINS age 27 s POB POR Orange; POM Orange 18 Oct
1857 (OMR) 27 Oct 1857 (OML)

**FAULCONER,** Alfred M. & **BOWCOCK,** Madeline 19 Apr 1828 surety
Edmund N. KENNEDY (OB)

**FAULCONER,** Ambrose & **TINDER,** Lucy d/o Anthony TINDER 2 Mar
1831 surety Robinson TINDER (OB)

**FAULCONER,** Benjamin & **MASSEY,** Mary Ann d/o James O.
MASSEY 17 Feb 1845 surety Edmund PEACHER (OB) 20 Feb 1845
by John MASSEY (OM)

**FAULCONER,** Carter B. & **FAULCONER,** Nancy 27 Dec 1813 by
Ambrose BROCKMAN of Albemarle County (OM)

**FAULCONER,** Carter B. Jr. & **HERRING,** Elizabeth M. 27 Nov 1849 by
Joseph S. JACKSON (OM)

**FAULCONER,** David & **GRADY,** Sarah d/o William GRADY 30 Mar
1794 surety John PARTLOW (OB)

**FAULCONER,** E.N. s/o Alfred FAULCONER and Madaline BOCOCK
age 25 s carpenter POB POR Orange & **HANSFORD,** Sallie J. d/o
William TERRILL and Fanny BOSTON age 25 w POB POR Orange;
POM Orange 30 Aug 1866 (OMR) 27 Aug 1866 (OML)

**FAULCONER,** Edward S. & **HORD,** Melindy d/o Jesse HORD 25 Mar
1818 surety Carter B. FAULCONER (OB)

**FAULCONER,** Elias & **NEWMAN,** Polley 27 Nov 1802 POM Orange by
Robert JONES (Misc Min Ret)

**FAULCONER,** Elias over 21 & **NEWMAN,** Polly over 21 surety Robert
B. LONG 27 Nov 1802 (OB)

**FAULCONER,** Frederick W. s/o Alfred M. FAULCONER and Madaline
BOCOCK age 23 s farmer POB POR Orange & **APPERSON,** Evelina
d/o Thomas APPERSON and Eveline SALMER age 22 s POB
Culpeper Co POR Orange; POM Orange 31 Oct 1867 (OMR)

**FAULCONER,** George & **COLEMAN,** Nancy d/o James COLEMAN 8
Jun 1793 (OM)

**FAULCONER**, George & **JACOBS**, Sarah 25 Jul 1849 surety James B.
JACOBS (OB)

**FAULCONER**, George s/o William and Elizabeth FAULCONER age 37
w day laborer POB POR Orange & **WATSON**, Sarah J. d/o Benjamin
and Fannie WATSON age 20 s POB POR Orange; POM Orange 15
Mar 1858 (OMR) (OML)

**FAULCONER**, Hugh & **FAULCONER**, Elizabeth d/o Ann
FAULCONER 20 Mar 1816 surety William FISHER (OB) 22 Mar
1816 by John C. GORDON (OM)

**FAULCONER**, James & **SISSON**, Milly 23 Jun 1794 permission by
Sayrey [Sarah] SISSON surety Morgan FINNELL (OB)

**FAULCONER**, James F. s/o James F. FAULCONER and Priscilla
TINDER age 29 w farmer POB Culpeper POR Orange &
**CANNADAY**, Bettie D. d/o James CANNADAY and Ann TINDER
age 21 s POB POR Orange; POM Orange 14 Dec 1865 (OMR) 13 Dec
1865 (OML)

**FAULCONER**, James W. age 26 s POB POR Orange s/o Benjamin
FAULCONER and Mary MASSIE merchant & **REYNOLDS**, Lillie E.
age 18 s POB POR Orange d/o Joseph D. REYNOLDS and Elizabeth
HENDERSON 15 Jan 1874 POM Orange (OMR)

**FAULCONER**, John & **LAY**, Elizabeth 16 Jan 1835 by Joseph A.
MANSFIELD (OM)

**FAULCONER**, John & **MORRISON**, Margaret; 16 Jan 1775 (OB)

**FAULCONER**, John & **QUISENBERRY**, Mary Ann d/o George
QUISENBERRY 26 Nov 1832 surety Albert QUISENBERRY (OB)

**FAULCONER**, John A. age 20 s POB POR Orange s/o L.T.D.
FAULCONER and Mary F. NEWMAN carpenter & **MUNDY**, Betty
A. age 19 s POB POR Orange d/o Albert MUNDY and Mary A.
JOHNS 22 Dec 1869 POM Orange by H.M. LINNEY (OMR)

**FAULCONER**, John C. s/o Alfred N. FAULCONER and Madaline
BOCOCK age 32 s carpenter POB POR Orange & **PETITT**, Columbia
F. d/o Fountain P. PETTIT and Martha A. ROACH age 20 s POB POR
Orange; POM Orange 19 Dec 1867 (OMR) 18 Dec 1867 (OML)

**FAULCONER**, John H. age 23 s POB POR Orange s/o John
FAULCONER and Elizabeth LAY carpenter & **FAULCONER**, Mary
R. age 21 s POB POR Orange d/o Alfred M. FAULCONER and
M.F.D. BOCOCK 1 Dec 1870 POM Orange by H.M. LINNEY (OM)

**FAULCONER**, Kemp & **PERRY**, Elizabeth d/o Peter PERRY 31 Mar
1819 surety Nicholas FAULCONER (OB) 1 Apr 1819 by J.C.
GORDON (OM)

**FAULCONER**, Lawrence T.D. & **NEWMAN**, Mary F. d/o John
NEWMAN who is also surety 13 Dec 1848 (OB) 14 Dec 1848 by
Richard STEPHENS (OM)

FAULCONER, Newman & **NEWMAN,** Maria 17 Mar 1814 surety
Thomas NEWMAN by J. GOSS (OB) (OM)

FAULCONER, Nicholas & **FAULCONER,** Frances 18 Dec 1804 surety
Reubin FAULCONER (OB)

FAULCONER, Oswald N. age 22 s POB POR Orange s/o Carter B.
FAULCONER and Elizabeth HERRING r.r. employee &
**WHITLOCK,** Mary E. age 16 s POB Louisa Co POR Orange d/o
William W. WHITLOCK and Sarah E. CHEWNING 4 Dec 1873 POM
Orange by Samuel HARRIS (OMR)

FAULCONER, Reuben & **FAULCONER,** Jenny d/o Thomas
FAULCONER; 1 Nov 1796 (OM)

FAULCONER, Richard & **SANDERS,** Nancy d/o Nathaniel SANDERS 9
Apr 1792 surety William FISHER (OB)

FAULCONER, Richard & **WRIGHT,** Julian d/o John WRIGHT who is
surety 28 Nov 1826 (OB)

FAULCONER, Robert B. age 45 s POB POR Orange s/o Carter B.
FAULCONER and Nancy FAULCONER carpenter & **KENNEDY,**
Nannie age 34 s POB POR Orange d/o Hiram P. KENNEDY and Mary
FAULCONER 12 Apr 1869 POM Orange by James A. MANSFIELD
(OMR)

FAULCONER, Robert B. s/o Carter B. and Nannie FAULCONER age 45
s carpenter POB POR Orange & **KENNEDY,** Fannie d/o Hiram P.
KENNEDY and Mary FAULCONER age 34 s POB POR Orange; 14
Apr 1867 (OML)

FAULCONER, Samuel & **BURGES,** 14 May 1798 surety Edmund
BURGES (OB)

FAULCONER, Spencer & **WRIGHT,** Margaret d/o John WRIGHT
surety Thomas R. WRIGHT 30 Sep 1834 (OB)

FAULCONER, Thomas & **JONES,** Elizabeth d/o James JONES 16 Oct
1811 Dudley HARPER surety (OB)

FAULCONER, Thomas & **JONES,** Elizabeth d/o James JONES surety
Dudley HARPER 16 Oct 1811 by Jeremiah CHANDLER (OB) (OM)

FAULCONER, William & **CHISHOLM** Betsy; 23 Jan 1797 surety
William DAWSON (OB)

FAULCONER, William & **JACOBS,** Elizabeth d/o Benjamin JACOBS 2
Jun 1818 by J.C. GORDON (OM)

FAWKNER, John C. & **FAULCONER,** Ann Jr. d/o Ann FAULCONER
surety Joseph STEVENS 19 Jul 1828 (OB)

FEARNEY, Lough Lewis & **JOHNS,** Sarah d/o Mason JOHNS; POM
Orange May 1851 (OMR) 6 May 1851 (OML)

FEARNEY, Thomas & **LUCAS,** Agy; 19 Feb 1776 by banns both of St.
Thomas Parish (Deed Book 17)

**FEARNEY,** William & **MORTON,** Sarah 19 Nov 1775 by banns both of St. Thomas Parish (Deed Book 17)

**FEARNEYHOUGH,** John & **DARNELL,** Jincy surety James D. DARNELL guardians Michael L. EHEART and Elizabeth FEARNEYHOUGH 21 Dec 1838 (OB)

**FEARNEYHOUGH,** John & **JENNINGS,** Eliza 6 Jan 1848 surety William F. BROOKING (OB)

**FEARNEYHOUGH,** John & **JONES,** Elizabeth 22 Sep 1819 surety Holland OZBORNE (OB)

**FELTNER,** George W. s/o John D. FELTNER and Jane E.TALLEY age 23 s blacksmith POB POR Jefferson Co. & **WOOD,** Louisianna d/o Thomas WOOD and Sarah F.BERRY age 23 s POB POR Orange; POM Orange C.H.17 Sep 1863 (OMR) (OML)

**FENNEL,** Charles & **SAUNDERS,** Nancy; 9 Nov 1775 by banns both of St. Thomas Parish (Deed Book 17)

**FENNELL,** William Jr. & **BOURN,** Jenny both of St. Thomas Parish 5 Feb 1778 (Deed Book 17)

**FERGUSON,** Thomas S. age 27 s POB Clark Co. POR Fauquier Co. s/o John D. FERGUSON and Emily GREEN merchant & **PAGE,** Mary E. age 25 s POB Fauquier Co POR Orange Co. d/o C.T. PAGE and Lucy MCPARROW (?) 23 Jul 1869 POM Orange by H.E. HATCHER (OMR)

**FERRELL,** George & **WOLF,** Polly d/o Leonard WOOLF; 13 May 1795 surety Joseph CANTERBERRY (OB)

**FETE,** William W. age 21 s telegraph business POB Lancaster, PA POR Orange s/o Jacob FETE and Elizabeth SLOVAM & **RILES,** Missouri age 18 s POB Fairfax POR Orange d/o Alex RILES and Julia A. SOUTHERLAND POM Orange 30 Apr 1876 By James DOUGHERTY (OMR)

**FIELD,** Ambrose POC age 24 s POB Madison Co POR Orange s/o Harry FIELD laborer & **BARNES,** Sarah POC age 25 w POB Albemarle Co POR Orange 3 Sep 1873 POM Orange by F.L. GIPSON (OMR)

**FIELD,** Richard H. POR Culpeper & **BARBOUR,** Philippi 10 Dec 1840 surety Presley N. SMITH by John COLE (OB) (OM)

**FIELDS,** Thomas POC age 27 w laborer POB POR Orange s/o Hamson FIELDS and Celie NORRIS & **BLAKE,** Edmonia POC age 18 s POB POR Orange d/o Benjamin BLAKE POM Orange 31 Mar 1877 (OMR)

**FIELDS,** William POC age 20 s POB POR Orange s/o Harrison FIELDS & Ceylon MORRIS laborer & **CARTER,** Ellen POC age 17 s POB Fauquier Co. POR Orange d/o Aaron CARTER & Mary GRAYSON 25 Jun 1868 POM Orange by Franklin TIBBS (OMR)

**FILLINGER,** Henry & **FERRELL,** Betsy; 1 Jan 1799 by Hamilton GOSS (OM)

**FINKS, J.F. & DULANEY, Mary E.** d/o William DULANEY surety William J. DULANEY 10 Oct 1829 (OB)

**FINKS, Stephen** POC age 23 s labourer POB POR Albemarle s/o Edmund FINKS and Lucinda FINKS & **CAVE, Irena** POC age 18 s POB Albemarle POR Orange d/o Horace and Amanda CAVE POM Orange 27 Dec 1877 (OMR)

**FINNEL, Reuben & BOWEN** Elizabeth d/o Henry BOWEN 12 Dec 1784 by Nathaniel SANDERS (OM)

**FINNELL, Benjamin & ROBINSON,** Elizabeth d/o Artemis and Phoebe ROBINSON; 28 Dec 1799 surety Moses ROBINSON (OB)

**FINNELL, Benjamin & SLEET,** Sarah Carter w both of St. Thomas Parish 25 Aug 1775 (Deed Book 17)

**FINNELL, George & DAWSON,** Sally 27 Jan 1794 surety Lawrence GILLOCK (OB)

**FINNELL, James & CHAMBERS,** Rebecca; 18 Aug 1791 by Nathaniel SANDERS (OM)

**FINNELL, James** s/o Simon FINNELL & **CHAMBERS,** Rebecca; 13 Jun 1793 surety Marmaduke BRANHAM (OB)

**FINNELL, John & CHAMBERS,** Elizabeth; 11 Jan 1797 (OB)

**FINNELL, John & SURRY,** Caty; 2 Feb 1797 (OM)

**FINNELL, Reubin & BOURNE,** Elizabeth d/o Henry BOURNE; 13 Dec 1784 (OM)

**FISHER, Addison & APPERSON,** Frances surety Richard APPERSON 26 Oct 1832 (OB)

**FISHER, Daniel A.** s/o Daniel FISHER and Malinda REAGAN age 22 s farmer POB Rockingham Co POR Orange & **COLE,** Josephine C. d/o Philip COLE and Edith BRYAN age 21 s POB Rockingham Co POR Orange; POM Orange 19 Jun 1866 (OMR) 16 Jun 1866 (OML)

**FISHER, James & MASON,** Fanny surety Peter MASON Jr. by Nathaniel SANDERS 26 Dec 1805 (OB) (OM)

**FISHER, William & COX,** Sally surety George COX 25 Dec 1825 (OB)

**FISHER, William & FAULCONER,** Margaret; 25 Sep 1815 surety Isaac JOHNSON (OB) 5 Oct 1815 by Jeremiah CHANDLER (OM)

**FITZGERAL, Easom & SELF,** Mary 28 Jan 1802 by George BINGHAM (OM)

**FITZGERRELL, Stephen** s/o James FITZGERRELL & **BRUCE,** Catherine; 14 Nov 1787 surety William FITZGERRELL (OB)

**FITZHUGH, Battaile & TALIAFERRO,** Elizabeth surety Lewis TALIAFERRO 12 Mar 1804 (OB)

**FITZHUGH, Henry Jr. & CONWAY,** Elizabeth; (May 2 or Apr 17) 1792 guardian John B. FITZHUGH surety Charles TAYLOR (OB)

**FITZHUGH, William & TALIAFERRO,** Ann d/o Lawrence TALIAFERRO; 24 Feb 1783 surety Francis DADE (OB)

**FLEAK,** Andrew & **RHOADS,** Frankey d/o Epaphroditus RHOADS; 22 Oct 1795 by George EVE (OM)

**FLECK,** Henry & **SMATTS,** Betsy surety Peter SEKLE 6 May 1797 (OB)

**FLEEK,** Andrew & **LOWER,** Rachel; 8 Nov 1793 surety John COLEMAN (OB)

**FLETCHER,** Madison & **WILTSHIRE,** Sarah d/o Benjamin WILTSHIRE who is also surety 9 Dec 1844 (OB)

**FLETCHER,** Washington & **PAYNE,** Elizabeth surety Willis OVERTON by Nathaniel SANDERS 5 Jan 1807 (OB) (OM)

**FLETCHER,** William & **SULLIVAN,** Delilah d/o William SULLIVAN surety Gusty PATES by Nathaniel SANDERS 17 Dec 1807 (OB) (OM)

**FLICK,** Henry & **BRYAN,** Pauline d/o Jeremiah BRYAN surety James BRYAN 7 Aug 1837 (OB)

**FLICK,** John & **KIBLINGER,** Barbary 4 Jun 1796 surety Jacob KIBLINGER (OB) 9 Jun 1796 by George EVE (OM)

**FLICK,** William & **LOWER,** Catherine d/o Michael LOWER Sr.; 5 Sep 1798 surety Charles PERCY (OB)

**FLOWERS,** George & **HERNER,** Sarah surety Peter MARSH 20 Oct 1829 (OB)

**FLOYD,** Samuel & **HERRING,** Jane d/o Thomas HERRING; 16 Apr 1799 surety William BRADLEY (OB)

**FLURY,** Christian age 39 s POB Switzerland POR Gordonsville, VA s/o John FLURY and Margaret REIDI vinter & **BRUSH,** Anna age 25 s POB Switzerland POR Gordonsville d/o John BRUSH and Margaret WIGGLE 5 Jul 1873 POM Orange by J.C. DINWIDDIE (OMR)

**FORD,** Absolem & **RANSDELL,** Molly 11 Jan 1792 surety Sanford RANSDELL (OB) 17 Jan 1792 by Nathaniel SANDERS (OM)

**FORD,** Benjamin & **ATKINS,** Rhody d/o Annie ATKINS; 29 Dec 1813 (OM)

**FORD,** Harlin & **GRADY,** Margaret permission given by William and Margaret GRADY surety Walker GRADY 26 Jan 1821 (OB)

**FORD,** William & **MOORE,** Ann; 14 Dec 1785 by J. PRICE (OM)

**FORD,** William & **STUBBLING** Susanna 16 Nov 1805 surety James LANTON (OB)

**FORTSON,** Benjamin & **HEAD,** Sally d/o James HEAD; 6 Dec 1790 surety Shelton WHITE (OB)

**FORTUNE,** Armistead & **MCINTOSH,** Sarah Ann 11 Oct 1841 surety William THORNTON (OB)

**FOSTER,** Andrew & **SHIFLETT,** Sarah; 5 Oct 1852 (OML)

**FOSTER,** Anthony POR St. Thomas Parish & **PRICE,** Elizabeth POR St. Thomas Parish; 4 Apr 1776 by banns (Deed Book 17)

**FOSTER**, Haskew & **SNELL**, Caty 28 Jul 1793 surety John WILLIAMS (OB) 21 Aug 1794 by George MARTIN (OM)

**FOSTER**, James A. age 21 s farmer POB POR Orange s/w Andrew FOSTER and Sarah F. SHIFFLETT & **NORFORD**, Mary F. age 22 s POB Louisa POR Orange d/o James M. NORFORD and Julia F. GILBERT POM Orange 11 Nov 1877 (OMR)

**FOSTER**, John & **DEERING**, Susannah d/o Robert Deering; 15 Oct 1793 by George EVE (OM)

**FOSTER**, Thomas & **JONES**, Frances; 25 Feb 1777 both of St. Thomas Parish by banns (Deed Book 17)

**FOSTER**, Thomas POR St. Thomas Parish & **SAWYER** Mary POR ST. Thomas Parish 8 Oct 1774 by banns (Deed Book 17)

**FOSTER**, William & **HAWKINS**, Tabitha; 19 Apr 1793 surety Richard HORD (OB)

**FOUTAINE**, George POC age 28 s brick layer POB Hanover POR Orange s/o Richard FOUNTAINE and _____ & **SIMS**, Jane POC age 25 s POR Orange OM Gordonsville 16 Feb 1876 by C. T. JOHNSON (OMR)

**FOUSHEE**, John A. & **HERRING**, Lucy M. d/o Benjamin HERRING 5 Feb 1849 surety William Daniel HERRING (OB)

**FOUSHEE**, Robert & **HENELY**, Mary Ann d/o Pleasant HENELY who is also surety 28 Sep 1835 (OB)

**FOUSHEE**, Thomas A. & **MASON**, Susan M.F. 22 Jul 1844 surety Thomas GRAVES (OB)

**FOUSHEE**, Thornton & **GRAVES**, Nancy d/o Richard Graves; 23 Jul 1791 surety John GRAVES (OB) 28 Jul 1791 Nathaniel SANDERS (OM)

**FOX**, Stephen & **HERNDON**, Elizabeth; 7 Mar 1796 (OM)

**FRANCIS**, Richard & **PHILLIPS**, Emily d/o Thomas PHILLIPS 19 Dec 1849 surety John R. GRYMES (OB) 20 Dec 1849 by J.M. HENRY (OMR)

**FRANCIS**, French s/o Joe and Lizzy FRANCIS age 46 s blacksmith POB Culpeper Co. POR Orange POC & **TAYLOR**, Rebecca d/o Ben TAYLOR and Barbara JACKSON age 24 s POB POR Orange POC; POM Orange 21 Sep 1867 (OMR) (OML)

**FRANKLYN**, John & **PEARSON**, Mary; 11 Mar 1785 (OB)

**FRANKLYN**, Jonathan & **BREEDING**, Susannah d/o Job BREEDING 31 Jul 1790 surety Richard BREEDING (OB)

**FRAZER**, Herndon & **RAWLINGS**, Mary Lucetta d/o Richard RAWLINGS who is also surety 23 May 1848 (OB)

**FRAZER**, John s/o William S. FRAZER and Ann BURRUSS age 29 s farmer POB POR Orange & **MORTON**, Susan M. d/o George W. MORTON and Susan TERRILL, age 25 s POB POR Orange; POM Orange 18 Dec 1866 (OMR) 12 Dec 1866 (OML)

**FRAZER,** Leland & **MALLORY,** Ann Smith d/o Henry MALLORY who is also surety 23 Apr 1827 (OB) 17 May 1827 by George BINGHAM (OMR)

**FRAZER,** William S. & **BURRUS,** Ann d/o William T. BURRUS who is also surety 28 Jun 1819 (OB)

**FRAZIER,** Shadrack & **MORRIS,** Polly d/o William MORRIS surety James MORRIS 4 Jun 1807 (OB) 9 Jun 1807 by George BINGHAM (OM)

**FREDERICK,** Philip & **BAUGHER,** Betsy 24 Nov 1808 by George BINGHAM (OM)

**FREEMAN,** Frederick & **BADGER,** Philadelphia 14 May 1838 surety James TUELL (OB)

**FREEMAN,** Henry POC age 29 s POB Louisa Co POR Orange laborer & **TURNER,** Charlotte POC age 20 w POB POR Orange d/o Lewis LINDSAY and Ellen GREEN 30 Jan 1873 POM Orange by Philip JOHNSON (OMR)

**FREEMAN,** Thomas POC & **CLARK,** Louisa POC; 2 Jun 1853 (OML)

**FRENCH,** Benjamin F. age 30 s POB Amherst POR Orange carpenter s/o John S. FRENCH and Dorothea G. ALCOCK & **WOOD,** Virginia F. age 25 s POB Amherst POR Orange d/o Thomas WOOD and Sarah F. BERRY 27 Oct 1880 POM Liberty Mills, Orange by P.S. RHODES (OMR)

**FRENCH,** J. Adolphus age 31 POB Powhatan POR Orange s/o John W. FRENCH and Judith F. BLANTON minister & **MADISON,** Fannie T. age 26 s POB POR Orange d/o James A. MADISON and Lucy M. HIDEN 25 May 1880 POM Orange by J.W. MCCOWN (OMR)

**FRY,** Meade POC age 24 s POB Albemarle POR Orange farm laborer s/o Clara FRY & **LEWIS,** Nancy POC age 19 s POB POR Orange d/o Cato LEWIS and Amy GRYMES 27 Nov 1880 POM Orange by Dabney PARKER (OMR)

**FRY,** Oscar age 25 S POB Madison Co POR Gordonsville s/o Wesley FRY and Lucinda FRY depot porter & **GIBSON,** Margaret age 17 S POB POR Orange d/o Albert GIBSON and Levina GIBSON 3 Mar 1870 POM Orange by J.W. MCCOWN (OMR)

**FRY,** Philip S. & **ANDERSON,** Pamelia M. 31 Jul 1833 surety W.M. CHAPMAN (OB)

**FRY,** Robert POC age 23 s POB POR Orange laborer s/o Henry FRY & **JACKSON,** Maria POC age 22 s POB POR Orange d/o Moses JACKSON and Milly TURNER 28 Aug 1880 POM Orange by W.J. BARNETT (OMR)

**FRY,** William POC age 22 s labourer POB POR Orange s/o Alex FRY and Amanda MEEKS & **SHEPHERD,** Mollie POC age 17 s POB POR

Orange d/o Wash SHEPHERD and Susan BRAY POM Orange 30 Dec
1878 by Willis ROBINSON (OMR)

**FRYE,** John & **BAUGHER,** Catharine 2 Jun 1808 by George BINGHAM
(OM)

**FRY,** Thornton F. POC age 18 s labourer POB POR Orange s/o Henry
FRY and Peggy MANSFIELD & **HOWARD,** Georgianna POC age 22
s POB POR Orange d/o Daniel HOWARD and Ann GRAVES POM
Orange 29 Nov 1879 (OMR)

**FURNACE,** John POR St. Thomas Parish & **DUNCOME,** Elizabeth POR
St. Thomas Parish 24 Jan 1773 (Deed Book 17)

**FURNIS,** Jacob & **PAGE,** Mary d/o John PAGE both POR St. Thomas
Parish 5 Dec 1782 surety William GLASS (OB)

**GABBOTT,** James M. & **HERNDON,** Leah F. 17 Dec 1849 surety
William G. HERNDON (OB)

**GAINES,** Andrew J. & **LEE,** Frances 5 May 1845 surety Reuben
KENNEDY (OB)

**GAINES,** Augustine & **WHITE,** Polly 30 Sep 1804 by Hamilton GOSS
(Misc Min Ret)

**GAINES,** Francis & **LEWIS,** Betsy 21 Jul 1776 both of St. Thomas Parish
by banns (Deed Book 17)

**GAINES,** George POC age 22 s POB POR Orange s/o Guilford GAINES
and Daphne _____ laborer & **JOHNSON,** Lydia POC age 18 s POB
POR Orange d/o Charles JOHNSON and Lucy _____ DOM 23 Jan
1869 POM Orange by Philip JOHNSON (OMR)

**GAINES,** John & **GAINES,** Jenny d/o Edward GAINES 13 Mar 1793
surety Richard COLLINS (OB)

**GAINES,** John & **SANDERS,** Joanna d/o Nathaniel SANDERS surety
George MASON 5 Mar 1800 by Nathaniel SANDERS (OB) (OM)

**GAINES,** Reuben & **JONES,** Sarah surety Benjamin SANDERS 17 Oct
1826 (OB)

**GAINES,** Richard & **ADAMS,** Sarah d/o Thomas ADAMS POR Orange
17 Sep 1811 William ROBINSON surety (OB)

**GAINES,** Richard & **EASTIN,** Elizabeth d/o Elizabeth EASTIN surety
Philip EASTIN both of St. Thomas Parish 6 Feb 1782 (OB)

**GAINES,** Richard & **SANDERS,** Malinda 22 Jun 1818 surety John
SANDERS (OB) 24 Jun 1818 by J.C. GORDON (OM)

**GAINES.** Thomas & **ROW,** Milley d/o Thomas ROW surety William
ROW 26 Dec 1800 (OB)

**GALASBY,** John & **GOODRIDGE,** Betsy surety Richard GOODRIDGE
14 Sep 1795 (OB)

**GALISPIE,** John N. s/o Jonathan and Matilda GILLISPIE, age 22 s
wheelwright POB Albemarle POR Orange & **WRIGHT,** Lavinia A. d/o

Dabney and Matilda WRIGHT age 25 s POB POR Orange; POM Orange 15 Jan 1857 (OMR) 13 Jan 1857 (OML)

**GALLARY**, George POC age 35 w farm laborer POB POR Orange s/o Sam GALLARY and Judy WHITE & **WILSON**, Millie POC age 28 w POB POR Orange d/o Nannie _____ POM Orange 20 Aug 1876 (OMR)

**GAMBLE**, Matthew & **BELL**, Nancy surety David HOLMES 1 Jan 1796 (OB)

**GAMBOE**, Samuel & **CHISHAM**, Catherine d/o John CHISHAM surety John DAWSON 23 Dec 1796 (OB)

**GAMBREL**, Walter & **LEE**, Betsy surety William LEE 27 May 1801 (OB)

**GAMBUL**, Walter & **HUTCHERSON**, Martha 6 Oct 1821 surety Washington HUTCHERSON (OB)

**GARDE**, William & **YATES**, Mary w 3 Nov 1795 surety Edward BRACKEN (OB)

**GARDENER**, Alexander Z. age 26 s POB POR Orange s/o Daniel GARDENER and Minerva RICHARDS farmer & **YOUNG**, Edmonia C. age 18 s POB POR Orange d/o Charles YOUNG and Ann BROCKMAN 13 Feb 1873 POM Orange by Herndon FRAZER (OMR)

**GARDENER**, James M. age 23 s POB POR Orange s/o David GARDNER and Minerva RICHARDS farmer & **MALLORY**, Mary E. age 19 POB POR Orange d/o William P. MALLORY and Margaret BICKERS 25 Feb 1868 POM Orange by H.E. HATCHER (OMR)

**GARDNER**, Daniel & **HARRIS**, Matilda POR Orange 23 Dec 1811 Joseph HARRIS "the above bound J. ATKINS is guardian also to the said Gardner" Joseph ATKINS surety (OB)

**GARDNER**, Dowell L. & **RICHARDS**, Minerva 23 Oct 1843 surety Ezekial RICHARDS (OB)

**GARDNER**, Nathan & **GARTON**, Truesy surety Churchill H. GARTON 26 Jan 1825 (OB)

**GARDNER**, Zachariah & **MARTIN**, Lucinda 12 Dec 1816 (OM)

**GARNER**, William A. age 23 s telegraph operator POB Richmond city POR Fauquier s/o E.W. GARNER and M.A. GARRETT & **RUNKLE**, Susan M. age 19 s POB Greene POR Orange d/o George W. RUNKLE and _____ GENTRY POM Albemarle 9 Oct 1877 (OMR)

**GARNET**, Thomas & **HAWKINS**, Rachel 13 Oct 1760 (Orange Fee Book)

**GARNETT**, Andrew & **BELL**, Sally B.; 19 Nov 1808 surety William BELL (OB)

**GARNETT**, James & **CHILES**, Frances d/o James CHILES who is also surety 7 Oct 1807 (OB) 23 Dec 1807 by Robert JONES (OM)

**GARNETT,** Joel s/o James and Elizabeth GARNETT age 33 s farmer
POB POR Culpeper & **SCOTT,** Ann E. d/o John and Ann SCOTT age
31 s POB POR Orange; POM Orange 16 Oct 1855 (OMR)

**GARNETT,** John O. s/o James J. GARNETT & **WILLIS,** Mary Elizabeth
d/o Larkin WILLIS 21 Jul 1846 surety Owen T. WILLIS (OB)

**GARNETT,** Larkin & **BELL,** Elizabeth d/o Joseph and Elizabeth BELL
surety Roger BELL 22 Dec 1802 (OB)

**GARNETT,** Milton s/o James and Elizabeth GARNETT age 33 s farmer
POB Culpeper Co POR Orange & **COBBS,** Mary Ann d/o Peter N. and
Courtney COBBS age 22 s POB Albemarle Co POR Orange; POM
Orange 3 Nov 1857 (OMR) 2 Nov 1857 (OML)

**GARNETT,** Thomas & **BROCKMAN,** Suckey/Susanna both of St.
Thomas Parish surety Adam LINDSAY 15 Nov 1780 (OB)

**GARNETT,** Thomas & **GORDON,** Lucy H. d/o John Churchill
GORDON surety J.C. GORDON 1 Dec 1832 (OB)

**GARR,** Willis POC age 45 s farm labourer POB Albemarle POR Orange
s/o Joe EHEART & **GWATHMEY,** Lucinda POC age 25 s POB POR
Orange d/o Alfred and Sally GWATHMEY POM Orange 27 Jan 1878
(OMR)

**GARREL,** James & **TAYLOR,** Sarah; 14 Mar 1797 (OM)

**GARRELL,** Demey & **STANTON,** Sally d/o Christy STANTON surety
James TAYLOR 27 Dec 1788 (OB) 15 Jan 1789 by George EVE (OM)

**GARRELL,** Elisha & **BRADLEY,** Nancy surety Samuel SMITH 19 Dec
1797 (OB) 21 Dec 1797 by Hamilton GOSS (OM)

**GARRETT,** Benjamin F. age 19 s farmer POB Culpeper POR Orange s/o
Jackson GARRETT and Lucy M. LLOYD & **BUTLER,** Malinda C.
age 21 s POB Louisa POR Orange d/o John J. BUTLER and Ann C.
BASICK 14 Feb 1877 POM Orange (OMR)

**GARTH,** D.C. & **HEAD,** Amanda d/o John HEAD who is also surety 15
Sep 1824 (OB)

**GARTON,** Charles & **KENNEDAY,** Louisa d/o Reuben KENNEDAY
who is also surety 25 Apr 1835 (OB)

**GARTON,** John & **DOLING,** Elizabeth surety Estes W. AMOS 28 Jun
1841 (OB)

**GARTON,** Spencer & **HANCOCK,** Polly d/o William HANCOCK 15
Feb 1797 surety James TAYLOR (OB)

**GARTON,** Zachary & **JONES,** Evelina surety Rice DARNELL 18 Mar
1829 (OB)

**GATES,** Charles & **LOYD,** Betsey; 12 Mar 1810 (OB)

**GATEWOOD,** Henry & **QUISENBERRY,** Amy d/o Moses
QUISENBERRY; 10 Aug 1805 (OM)

**GAY,** William E. & **DOLING,** Nancy surety Edward HOACK by E.G.
SHIP (OB) (OM)

**GAYDEN,** John & **COLLINS,** Catey both of St. Thomas Parish 9 Mar 1773 (Deed Book 17)

**GEAR,** William & **ROGERS,** Polly d/o John ROGERS who is also surety 15 Aug 1798 (OB)

**GEAR,** Joshua & **WATSON,** Jane d/o Isaac WATSON 27 Oct 1800 (OM)

**GEAR,** William & **HAM,** Sally granddaughter of Sam HAM; 21 Aug 1792 surety James HANEY(OB)

**GEE,** Joseph C. & **NEWMAN,** Sarah A.B. surety Thomas NEWMAN 13 Aug 1829 (OB)

**GEE,** Samuel M. & **HUME,** Hannah M. d/o William W. HUME surety William C. HUME 6 Aug 1839 (OB)

**GEER,** John & **MCDANIEL,** Betsy surety Reynolds CHAPMAN 11 Apr 1823 (OB) 13 Apr 1823 by George BINGHAM (OM)

**GEER,** Jonathan & **THRACKWELL,** Sarah 28 Jan 1802 by George BINGHAM (OM)

**GEER,** Nathaniel & **LAMB,** Sarah d/o John LAMB who is also surety 19 Mar 1836 (OB)

**GEER,** Ransom & **LAMB,** Polly 23 Feb 1802 by George BINGHAM (OM)

**GENTRY,** Aaron & **OGG,** Peggy 13 Jan 1803 by George BINGHAM (Misc Min Ret)

**GENTRY,** Charles H. age 34 w wagonmaker POB Louisa POR Orange s/o Robert H. GENTRY and Louisa J. HAMILTON & **LEE,** Elizabeth age 24 s POB POR Orange d/o Alexander LEE and Virinda BLEDSOE POM Orange 24 Nov 1878 by H.E. HATCHER (OMR)

**GENTRY,** James & **GIBSON,** Nelly 6 Aug 1816 by George BINGHAM (OM)

**GENTRY,** James & **LANGFORD,** Peachy 3 Oct 1823 by George BINGHAM (OM)

**GENTRY,** John R. & **MANSFIELD,** Mary Jane d/o Thomas M. MANSFIELD 17 Feb 1851 (OML)

**GEORGE,** Isaac & **SPENCER,** Catharine 1771-1774 (Orange County Memo Book)

**GEORGE,** John & **LONG,** Elizabeth 22 Dec 1803 by Nath. SANDERS (Misc Min Ret)

**GEORGE,** William & **HAWKINS,** Lucy 13 Feb 1793 surety Edward GEORGE (OB)

**GIBBS,** Alex. L. s/o John and Pinkston A.GIBBS age 27 s merchant POB Richmond Co. POR Fredericksburg & **MALLORY,** Eveline T. d/o Philip and Sarah C.MALLORY age 28 s POB POR Orange; POM Orange 28 Jan 1858 (OMR) 28 Dec 1857 (OML)

**GIBBS,** James & **JOHNSON,** Ann w 8 Jul 1771 (Orange County Memo Book)

**GIBBS,** Julius & **DAVIS,** Aggie d/o Joseph DAVIS surety James DAVIS both of St. Thomas Parish 27 Dec 1779 (OB)

**GIBBS,** William & **WAYT,** Mary Ann d/o William WAYT surety Christopher CRIGLER 19 Dec 1815 (OB)

**GIBBS,** William C. & **WAYT,** Kissy surety William CRIGLER 23 Dec 1818 (OB)

**GIBBS,** Zachariah & **WAYT,** Lucy d/o James WAYT surety William WAYT 14 Feb 1805 (OB)

**GIBSON,** B.F. age 24 s POB POR Orange s/o William GIBSON and Martha J. KRISE farmer & **HUGHES,** Sarah E. age 18 POB POR Orange d/o Robert HUGHES and Margaret A. JONES 13 Dec 1870 POM Orange by Thomas R. HAWKINS (OM)

**GIBSON,** E. Dorsey s/o Thomas G. GIBSON and Puryfee(?) GRAY age 34 s physician POB Orange POR Culpeper Co & **TOWLES,** Bettie C. d/o Thomas W. GRAY and Sallie LUCAS age 28 w POB POR Orange; POM Orange C.H. 10 Oct 1865 (OMR) (OML)

**GIBSON,** John & **COLLINS,** Eliza 31 Jan 1822 by George BINGHAM (OM)

**GIBSON,** John & **HARVEY,** Elizabeth; 7 Aug 1798 (OM)

**GIBSON,** Joseph H. POC age 22 s POB POR Orange laborer & **WEST,** Tabitha age 19 s POB POR Orange d/o Nelson WEST 31 Dec 1873 POM Orange by Charles P. SCOTT (OMR)

**GIBSON,** Joseph M. age 29 s farmer POB POR Orange s/o William GIBSON and Martha J. KRISE & **JONES,** Fannie W. age 20 s POB POR Orange d/o William A. JONES and Delilah SEE POM Orange 18 Mar 1877 (OMR)

**GIBSON,** Joshua & **STONE,** Elizabeth 20 Dec 1821 by George BINGHAM (OM)

**GIBSON,** Nathan & **GIBSON,** Mary Jane d/o Burwell GIBSON; 3 Oct 1854 (OML)

**GIBSON,** Peter & **ESTES,** Fanny surety William ESTES 23 Dec 1809 (OB)

**GIBSON,** Peter E. age 19 s POB POR Albemarle Co. s/o Jesse GIBSON and Lizzie SANDERS farmer & **THOMAS,** Susan V. age 17 s POB POR Orange d/o Fountain THOMAS and Lucinda WOOD 21 Sep 1873 POM Orange by Levi GARBER (OMR)

**GIBSON,** Robert age 25 s POB POR Louisa lawyer s/o William GIBSON and Mary FLEMING & **WHITE,** Lizzie age 21 s POB Rockingham POR Orange d/o Isaac WHITE and Jane GORDON 16 Dec 1880 POM Gordonsville Orange by P.S. RHODES (OMR)

**GIBSON,** Thomas & **GENTRY,** Fanny 29 Nov 1827 by George BINGHAM (OM)

**GIBSON**, William & **CARTY**, Betsey 14 Mar 1803 by Nathaniel SANDERS (Misc Min Returns)

**GIBSON**, William & **MORRIS**, Elizabeth d/o William MORRIS Jr. 14 Nov 1817 (OB) by George BINGHAM 14 Nov 1818 (OM)

**GIBSON**, William E. & **GIBSON**, Susan H. 10 Oct 1838 surety Edwin E. GIBSON (OB) 11 Oct 1838 by John W. WOODVILLE (OM)

**GIBSON**, William s/o Nathan GIBSON & **JRISE**, Martha Jane d/o Eliz. JRISE surety Matthew BUTLER 10 Sep 1845 (OB)

**GIFFORD**, Edward W. age 24 s farmer POB Bucks Co., PA POR Cecil Co., MD s/o Samuel GIFFORD and Sarah McDOWELL & **ENGLAND**, Georgie age 24 s POB Cecil Co., MD POR Orange d/o R.H. ENGLAND and Sarah A. NEWTON POM Orange 4 Nov 1879 (OMR)

**GILBERT**, Aquila & **NEWMAN**, Fanny surety Thomas NEWMAN 17 May 1809 by Robert JONES 17 May 1809 (OB) (OM)

**GILBERT**, Charles E. age 20 s POB POR Greene Co s/o Thomas A. GILBERT and Ann E. WETSEL farmer & **CLARK**, Cornelia M. age 18 POB POR Orange d/o William S. CLARK and Susan GARTH 19 Dec 1872 POM Orange by J.W. MCCOWN (OMR)

**GILBERT**, Joseph & **FEARNEYHOUGH**, Agness surety John FEARNEYHOUGH 29 Dec 1817 (OB) by J. GOSS 30 Dec 1817 (OM)

**GILBERT**, Thomas & **FEARNEAUGH**, Ann d/o Thomas FEARNEAUGH both of St. Thomas Parish 11 May 1778 surety James TAYLOR (OB)

**GILBERT**, Thomas s/o Weston GILBERT & **EHEART**, Harriet d/o Michael L. EHEART who is also surety 26 Mar 1849 (OB)

**GILLABERT**, Don Pedro y. & **GARTON**, Frances S. surety Cole C. DIGGS 15 Sep 1838 (OB)

**GILLABERT**, Peter age 59 w POB Spain POR Orange s/o William C. GILLABERT and Elizabeth CORDONA laborer & **STAPLES**, Elizabeth age 24 s POB POR Orange Co d/o William E. STAPLES and Mary J. GARTON 28 Feb 1869 POM Orange by Thomas R. HAWKINS (OMR)

**GILLASPY**, John & **WHITE**, Ann d/o John WHITE Sr. 7 Jul 1796 surety Benjamin CAVE Jr. her brother in law (OB)

**GILLETT**, Samuel & **PANNILL**, Sally 3 Jun 1790 by John LELAND (OM)

**GILLIAM**, William & **PARROTT**, Martha A. d/o George PARROTT; 9 Jun 1851 (OML)

**GILLISPIE**, William G. & **DOUGLAS**, Sarah A. d/o William DOUGLAS; 28 Apr 1851 (OML)

**GILLOCK**, John & **WOLFENGERGER**, Hannah both of St. Thomas Parish 7 Jan 1778 (Deed Book 17)

**GILLOCK,** Lawrence & **TWENTYMEN,** Betsy surety John ORANT 26
May 1788 (OB)

**GILLOCK,** Thomas & **MORGAN,** Elizabeth surety Joseph THOMAS
POM St. Thomas Parish 8 Jan 1784 (OB)

**GILLUM,** Thaddeus O. age 24 s POB Albemarle Co POR Orange s/o
Frederick W. GILLUM and Martha J. JONES merchant & **MUNDY,**
Sarah Elizabeth age 18 s POB POR Orange d/o Burruss MUNDY and
Harriet LANCASTER 15 Jan 1874 POM Orange (OMR)

**GILMER,** John & **MINOR,** Sarah surety Dabney MINOR 27 Jun 1808
(OB) by Robert JONES 28 Jun 1808 (OM)

**GILMER,** John T. & **TALIAFERRO,** Julia Ann d/o George G.
TALIAFERRO who is also surety 12 Sep 1838 (OB)

**GILSON,** Edward POC age 23 s POB POR Orange s/o David GILSON
and Mary ___ farmer & **JOHNSON,** Phillis POC age 25 s POB POR
Orange d/o Isaac JOHNSON and Mary ____ 8 Jun 1874 POM Orange
(OMR)

**GLADWELL,** John W. age 35 w farmer POB Hardy, WV POR Albemarle
s/o J.W. GLADWELL and Eliza BEAM & **SEAY,** Annie S. age 36 w
POB POR Albemarle d/o ____POLLOCK POM Gordonsville 1 Feb
1876 (OMR)

**GLASSELL,** Andrew & **TAYLOR,** Elizabeth; 21 Oct 1777 (OM)

**GOFF,** James M. s/o James GOFF and Martha JONES age 33 w house
carpenter /ship joiner POB Richland District, S.C. POR Clarke Co,
Alabama & **SKINNER,** Eliza A. d/o William SKINNER and Jane
WEBB age 25 s POB Madison Co POR Orange; POM Orange 10 Aug
1864 (OMR) 6 Aug 1864 (OML)

**GOFFNEY,** Ebenezer s/o William GOFFNEY and Leanna THORNTON
age 26 s POB POR Orange POC & **JACKSON,** Anna d/o Monroe and
Eliza JACKSON age 19 s POB POR Orange POC; POM Orange 28
Dec 1867 (OMR) 26 Dec 1867 (OML)

**GOFORTH,** Thomas & **FOSTER,** Milly; 9 Sep 1788 (OM)

**GOLDBACK,** Abraham age 30 s POB Germany POR Richmond s/o Judah
GOLDBACK and Theresa ROSEMBAUM manufacturer & **BEAR,**
Henrietta age 22 s POB New York City POR Orange d/o Bernard
BEAR and Helena WOLF 29 Apr 1874 POM [Gordonsville by S. M.
BETTERMANN ?] (OMR)

**GOLDEN,** Richard & **WALTON,** Ann; 3 May 1798 (OM)

**GOLDING,** Reuben & **PRICE,** Polly d/o George PRICE surety John
PRICE 28 Jul 1804 (OB)

**GOLDMAN,** James R. age 24 s POB Fredericksburg POR Orange s/o
Lunsford GOLDMAN and Nancy ALLEN farmer & **HUGHES,**
Virginia age 26 w POB POR Orange d/o Larkin HERNDON and Jane
HERNDON DOM 21 Oct 1869 POM Orange by E.R.PERRY (OMR)

GON, John Jr. & **GRACE,** Gracey d/o George GRACE 9 Dec 1793 (OM)
**GOOCH,** William T. & **MORTON,** Mary E. d/o Eliz. MORTON surety
L.B. GRASTY 22 Jan 1849 (OB)
**GOOD,** Jacob & **LONG,** Evelina surety Lewis GOOD 4 Mar 1829 (OB)
**GOOD,** James s/o Lewis GOOD & **HARRIS,** Catherine surety Littleton
HARRIS 24 Oct 1836 (OB)
**GOOD,** Simeon & **EDDINS,** Sarah surety Theophilus EDDINS 5 Nov
1827 (OB)
**GOODALL,** David & **CLARK,** Tabitha 21 Feb 1809 by George
BINGHAM (OM)
**GOODALL,** David & **DAVIS,** Elizabeth d/o Joseph DAVIS surety John
DAVIS 8 Apr 1793 (OB) by George EVE 10 Apr 1793 (OM)
**GOODALL,** Fontaine & **SEAL,** Peggy d/o Philip SEAL surety John
RIDDLE 3 Nov 1817 (OB) 6 Nov 1818 by George BINGHAM (OM)
**GOODALL,** Isaac & **HUCKSTEP,** Milly surety John HUCKSTEP 18 Jan
1808 (OB) by Jacob WATTS 20 Jan 1808 (OM)
**GOODALL,** James & **HARVEY,** Sally both of St. Thomas Parish surety
John BELL 23 Jan 1782 (OB)
**GOODALL,** James & **RIDDLE,** Lucy surety Charles GOODALL 27 Feb
1815 (OB) by George BINGHAM 23 Mar 1815 (OM)
**GOODALL,** John & **DAVIS,** Sally by George BINGHAM 20 Dec 1804
(OM)
**GOODALL,** Jonathan & **RUSSELL,** Patsy surety Caleb SMOOT 19 Dec
1798 (OB) by George BINGHAM 23 Dec 1798 (OM)
**GOODALL,** Parks & **COX,** Franky surety Thomas COS 9 Feb 1788 (OB)
by George EVE 14 Feb 1788 (OM)
**GOODALL,** William & **DAVIS,** Lucy d/o Jonathan DAVIS surety John
DAVIS 15 Mar 1785 (OB)
**GOODALL,** William W. & **GOODALL,** Virenda L.E. d/o Isaac
GOODALL surety Henry B. WINSLOW 10 Feb 1834 (OB) by Willis
HUCKSTEP 27 Feb 1834 (OM)
**GOODLOE,** Judson C. age 28 s POB Albemarle Co POR Nelson Co. s/o
John H. GOODLOE and Ann WINN farmer & **DOWNER,** Maria E.
age 19 POB POR Orange d/o Robert G. DOWNER and Frances A.
DANIEL 8 Dec 1870 POM Orange by Charles QUARLES (OM)
**GOODLOE,** Spotswood H. age 34 w POB Albemarle Co POR Nelson Co
s/o John H. GOODLOE and Ann WINN hotel keeper & **EDDINS,**
Charlotte J. age 20 s POB Powhatan Co POR Orange d/o Alfred
EDDINS and Julia STANARD 5 Dec 1872 POM Orange by Charles
QUARLES (OMR)
**GOODRICH,** John & **DEER,** Betty 14 Mar 1775 both of St. Thomas
Parish (OB)

**GOODRIDGE,** George C. & **BURTON,** Fanny surety John LUCAS 25 Mar 1809 (OB) by Jacob WHITE 26 Mar 1809 (OM)

**GOODWIN,** Charles E. s/o John and Mary Ann GOODWIN age 25 s gangsman on railroad POB Prince William Co. POR Orange & **MASON,** Sarah Margaret d/o Sanders and Catherine MASON age 20 s POB Rockingham Co. POR Orange; POM Orange 20 Dec 1855 (OMR) 19 Dec 1855 (OML)

**GOODWIN,** James A. s/o John and Mary Ann GOODWIN age 23 s farmer POB Prince William Co. POR Orange & **MASON,** Emily Frances d/o Sanders and Catherine MASON age 18 s POB Rockingham POR Orange; POM Orange 4 Sep 1856 (OMR) (OML)

**GOODWIN,** John F. s/o John and Mary A.GOODWIN age 25 s POB Prince William Co. POR Orange & **DUVALL,** Sarah E. d/o William L. and Comfort DUVALL age 19 s POB Ann Arundle Co, MD POR Orange; POM Orange 18 Jun 1857 (OMR) (OML)

**GOODWIN,** John M. & **STEVENS,** Eliza T. d/o William STEVENS surety Robert TERRILL Jr. 17 Nov 1824 (OB)

**GOODWIN,** John T. s/o Dr. William and Frances GOODWIN age 27 farmer POR Louisa Co & **TERRILL,** Betsy Veranda d/o Dr. William TERRILL age 18; POM Orange 22 Dec 1853 (OMR) 12 Dec 1853 (OML)

**GOODWIN,** John T. s/o Dr. William and Frances GOODWIN age 27 farmer POR Louisa Co & **TERRILL,** Betty O. d/o Dr. U. TERRILL age 18 POR Orange; POM Orange 22 Dec 1853 (OMR)

**GOODWIN,** Robert J. s/o John GOODWIN and Mary A. ARNOLD age 28 s engineer on O.& A. railroad POB Prince William Co POR Orange & **DAVIS,** Bettie W. d/o William J. DAVIS age 22 s POB POR Orange; POM Orange 5 Sep 1867 (OMR) 3 Sep 1867 (OML)

**GOOLSBY,** William E. age 21 s brakeman on C. & O. railroad POB Nelson POR Albemarle s/o G.R. GOOLSBY and M.J. WOMELDORF & **DAVIS,** Sarah E. age 19 s POB POR Orange d/o James DAVIS and Sarah A. OGG POM Orange 19 Dec 1876 (OMR)

**GORDALL,** Andrew POC age 23 s farm laborer POB POR Orange s/o Andrew GORDALL and Rhoda ____ & **GRYMES,** Clara POC age 20 s POB POR Orange d/o Jim GRYMES and Frances ____ POM Orange 7 Apr 1877 (OMR)

**GORDEN,** Charles POC age 22 s farm labourer POB Madison POR Orange s/o Henry GORDEN and Biddy ROW & **FRY,** Elizabeth POC age 17 s POB Madison POR Orange d/o Alexander FRY and Amanda MEEKS POM Orange 19 Jan 1878 (OMR)

**GORDON,** Edmund POC age 22 s POB POR Orange saw miller s/o James GORDON and Tabitha JACKSON & **JACKSON,** Sarah POC age 21 s

92

POB POR Orange d/o Jeff WHARTON and Amanda JACKSON 25
Dec 1880 POM Orange by Joseph A. MANSFIELD (OMR)

GORDON, John A.B. s/o John A. GORDON and Jane HERNDON age 23
s farmer POB POR Spotsylvania & **GORDON**, Fanny F. d/o Edward
GORDON and Fanny HERNDON age 23 s POB Culpeper Co POR
Orange; POM Orange 12 Nov 1867 (OMR) 4 Nov 1867 (OML)

GORDON, John C. & **TERRILL,** Mary Ann surety William MALLORY
25 May 1839 (OB)

GORDON, John H. & **GRASTY,** Eliza ward of John TERRILL who is
surety 29 Sep 1823 (OB)

GORDON, Joseph H. s/o John A. and Jane GORDON age 23 s farmer
POB POR Spotsylvania & **WILLIS**, Hannah E. d/o James and
Elizabeth WILLIS age 24 s POB POR Orange; POM Orange 3 Mar
1857 (OMR) 2 Mar 1857 (OML)

GORDON, Nathaniel & **GORDON,** Mary; 18 Oct 1785 (OB)

GORDON, Thomas C. s/o John A. GORDON and Jane S. HERNDON age
26 s farmer POB POR Spotsylvania & **BALLARD**, Lucy J. d/o Charles
B. BALLARD and Sarah CHANCELLOR age 23 s POB Spotsylvania
POR Orange; POM Orange 9 Nov 1865 (OMR) 27 Oct 1865 (OML)

GORDON, William A. age 25 s physician POB Spotsylvania POR Orange
s/o John A. GORDON and Jane L. HERNDON & **WILLIS**, Irene G.
age 21 s POB POR Orange d/o James WILLIS and Louisa WILLIS
POM Orange 9 Nov 1876 (OMR)

GORDON, William POC age 59 w laborer POB Louisa POR Orange s/o
William GORDON and Fanny BAGLEY & **GREEN,** Lucy age 24 s
POB POR Orange POM Orange 2 Nov 1876 (OMR)

GORE, John Jr. & **GRACE,** Gracey d/o George GRACE surety Joseph
BOOTH 9 Dec 1793 (OB) by James GARNETT 11 Dec 1793 (OM)

GOSNEY, Reubin & **MCKINNEY,** Elizabeth surety William
MCKINNEY 19 Apr 1809 (OB)

GOSS, Ebenezer & **NALLE,** Ann C.W. surety David HUME 12 Sep 1846
(OB) by J. EARNEST 15 Sep 1846 (OM)

GOSS, Hamilton & **MAJOR,** Martha (w/o ?); 24 Dec 1798 (OM)

GOSS, Jesse H. s/o J.H. and Mary GOSS age 27 s lawyer POB Georgia
POR LaGrange, Georgia & **NEWMAN**, Julia d/o J.B. and S.B.
NEWMAN age 25 s POB POR Orange; POM Orange 2 Sep 1857
(OMR) 1 Sep 1857 (OML)

GOSS, John W. & **MACON,** Sarah F.; POM Orange 15 Sep 1853 (OMR)
13 Sep 1853 (OML)

GRACE, George & **MCNEAL,** Ann; 9 Jan 1774 both of St. Thomas
Parish by banns (Deed Book 17)

GRADY, Andrew & **DUNAWAY,** Susannah d/o Thomas DUNAWAY
surety William DUNAWAY 9 May 1826 (OB)

**GRADY,** Benjamin & **ADAMS,** Catherine; 1 Jan 1800 (OM)
**GRADY,** John & **PROCTOR,** Sarah d/o John PROCTOR surety George
PROCTOR Jr. 8 Dec 1807 (OB) 18 Dec 1807 by Nathaniel SANDERS
(OM)
**GRADY,** Richmond & **MONTAGUE,** Hannah; 24 Oct 1801 (OB)
**GRADY,** Samuel & **MONTAGUE,** Caty surety John HENDERSON who
also certifies her age 27 Aug 1801 (OB) 29 Aug 1801 by Duke W.
HULLUM (OM)
**GRADY,** William & **DUNAWAY,** Martha d/o Thomas DUNAWAY
surety William DUNAWAY 21 Dec 1827 (OB)
**GRAHAM,** David & **COWHERD,** Eliza permission given by Coleby
COWHERD surety Reuben NEWMAN 29 Sep 1834 (OB)
**GRAMMER,** Rolley POC age 21 s POB Sussex Co. POR Orange s/o Jim
and Rose GRAMMER laborer & **SPOTSWOOD,** Edmonia POC age
19 s POB POR Orange 3 Oct 1868 POM Orange by John H.
ROBERTSON (OMR)
**GRANT,** Jesse & **FAULCONER,** Sally d/o John FAULCONER surety
Reubin FAULCONER 21 Sep 1804 (OB)
**GRANT,** John R. age 24 s merchant POB POR Fauquier s/o John N.
GRANT and Lucy A. LATHAM & **ESKEW,** Annie C. age 22 s POB
Louisa POR Orange d/o William J. ESKEW and Mary F. BICKERS
POM Orange 30 Mar 1876 (OMR)
**GRANT,** Samuel & **CRAIG,** Lidia; 22 Jul 1784 (OB)
**GRASTY,** George & **PAYNE,** Elizabeth d/o John PAYNE surety John G.
WRIGHT 22 Dec 1809 (OB)
**GRASTY,** Goodrich Lightfoot & **MORTON,** Elizabeth w 26 Mar 1804
surety Thomas COLEMAN (OB)
**GRASTY,** Isaac B. age 28 s photographer POB Chickasaw Co.,
Mississippi POR Nelson s/o George G. GRASTY and Mary S.
BRINKER & **THOMPSON,** Laura H. age 27 s POB POR Orange d/o
William L. THOMPSON and Susan GRASTY POM Orange 13 Jul
1876 (OMR)
**GRASTY,** John & **COOKE,** Tabitha Virginia d/o George M. COOKE
surety William C. MOORE by Herndon FRAZER 5 Dec 1842 (OB)
(OM)
**GRASTY,** John Thomas age 21 s POB POR Orange s/o John GRASTY
and Virginia CORK farmer & **SALE,** Mollie E. age 22 s POB POR
Orange d/o Robert C. SALE and Mary M. DAVIS 3 Nov 1868 POM
Orange by R.C. CAVE (OMR)
**GRAVATT,** Ellis W. s/o John C. and Anada GRAVATT age 24 s coach
trimmer POB Caroline Co POR Fredericksburg & **TERRILL,** Mary T.
d/o Oliver and Susan E. TERRILL age 19 s POB POR Orange; POM
Orange 23 Dec 1856 (OMR) 8 Dec 1856 (OML)

**GRAVES,** Absolem & **WHITE,** Felicia d/o John WHITE 19 Dec 1789 surety William WHITE (OB)

**GRAVES,** Benjamin & **COLLINS,** Elizabeth d/o William COLLINS surety George COLLINS 13 Sep 1796 (OB)

**GRAVES,** Benton V. s/o Colby GRAVES and Jane FERGUSON age 33 s farmer POB POR Spotsylvania & **STUBBLEFIELD**, Susan d/o Thomas STUBBLEFIELD and Mary HILMAN age 29 s POB POR Orange; POM Orange 19 Dec 1865 (OMR) 14 Dec 1865 (OML)

**GRAVES,** Charles T. & **CAMPBELL,** Susan 29 Sep 1836 surety Samuel H. STOUT (OB)

**GRAVES,** Charles T. & **WEBB,** Ann R. d/o Augustine WEBB 15 Sep 1821 surety John V. WEBB (OB)

**GRAVES,** Isaac & **MANSFIELD,** Nancy H. 14 Sep 1826 by J. GOSS (OM)

**GRAVES,** Isaac & **MANSFIELD,** Nancy H. 30 Aug 1826 surety Joseph A. MANSFIELD (OB)

**GRAVES,** Isaac & **PLUNKETT,** Elizabeth 28 May 1821 surety James WHITE (OB)

**GRAVES,** Isaac F. & **STEVENS,** Margaret A. d/o William STEVENS who is also surety 25 Nov 1835 (OB)

**GRAVES,** Isaac L. & **GRAVES,** Amanda M. 12 Dec 1845 surety Richard P. GRAVES permission by Jacob GRAVES (OB)

**GRAVES,** Isaac L. & **GRAVES,** Amanda M. 18 Dec 1845 by Herndon FRAZER (OMR)

**GRAVES,** Isaac W. & **BROCKMAN,** Elisa C. d/o Curtis BROCKMAN who is also surety 14 Nov 1831 (OB)

**GRAVES,** Jacob & **WHITE,** Fanny surety John WHITE who also certifies her age 22 Sep 1800 (OB) 8 Oct 1800 by Jacob WATTS (OM)

**GRAVES,** James W. & **GRAVES,** Sarah Jane d/o Charles T. GRAVES permission by Jacob GRAVES 9 Jan 1847 surety C.E.L. GRAVES (OB)

**GRAVES,** Joel & **GRAVES,** Sarah s surety Isaac GRAVES 20 Dec 1794 (OB)

**GRAVES,** Joseph POC age 51w POB POR Orange blacksmith & **HENDERSON,** Betsy POC age 48 w POB POR Orange 5 Jan 1868 POM Orange by R.C. CAVE (OMR)

**GRAVES,** Lewis & **WHITE,** Fanny d/o Richard WHITE 18 Feb 1819 surety Joseph BOXLEY (OB)

**GRAVES,** Paschal & **GRAVES,** Elizabeth W. d/o Jacob GRAVES who is also surety by Jeremiah CHANDLER 25 Aug 1830 (OB) (OM)

**GRAVES,** Paschal & **GRAVES,** Elizabeth W. d/o Jacob GRAVES who is also surety 25 Aug 1830 by Jeremiah CHANDLER (OB) (OMR)

**GRAVES,** Richard & **OAKES,** Sarah A.T. d/o John OAKS 2 Dec 1828 surety Thomas A. OAKS (OB)

**GRAVES,** Richard P. & **GRAVES,** Lucy F. 7 May 1847 by E.G. SHIP (OMR)

**GRAVES,** Richard P. & **GRAVES,** Lucy F. d/o Charles T. GRAVES who is also surety 22 Mar 1847 (OB)

**GRAVES,** Roda & **MARQUESS,** Marian d/o John MARQUESS surety Moses ROBINSON 24 Nov 1800 (OB)

**GRAVES,** Rufus E. age 21 s farmer POB POR Orange s/o Isaac W. GRAVES and Eliza E. BROCKMAN & **ESTES,** Fannie L. age 24 s POB Louisa POR Orange James R. ESTES and Martha R. WRIGHT POM Orange 27 Aug 1876 (OMR)

**GRAVES,** Thomas & **GRADY,** Ann d/o William GRADY surety Lincfield GRADY 18 Jun 1788 (OB)

**GRAVES,** Thomas & **STUBBLEFIELD,** Bettie Ellen 16 Dec 1848 surety Charles W. HUME (OB)

**GRAVES,** Thomas E. s/o Lewis GRAVES and Fanny WHITE age 22 s farmer POB POR Orange & **BROCKMAN,** Lou d/o Samuel BROCKMAN and Frances A. GRAVES age 29 s POB POR Orange; POM Orange 26 Dec 1867 (OMR) 23 Dec 1867 (OML)

**GRAVES,** Thomas Jr. & **BURROUGHS** Mourning d/o Frances BURRUS [Mourning is the daughter of Thomas BURRUSS and Frances TANDY; Thomas Jr. is the son of Thomas GRAVES and Sarah DELANEY as per Catherine Knorr] surety Christopher DICKIN 5 Feb 1791 (OB)

**GRAVES,** Waller & **RUCKER,** Polly d/o Mary RUCKER surety William RUCKER 12 Jun 1805 (OB)

**GRAVES,** William & **HILMAN,** Betsy surety Uriel HILMAN 12 Jun 1805 (OB)

**GRAVES,** William & **THOMPSON,** Eliza d/o Sarah THOMPSON 28 Jan 1833 surety Jacob GRAVES (OB)

**GRAVES,** William & **WHITE,** Peggy 9 Feb 1804 by Hamilton GOSS (Misc Min Ret)

**GRAVES,** William C. & **HIDEN,** Martha A. d/o Joseph HIDEN 18 Jul 1850 surety William SCOTT by Daniel B. EWING (OB) (OMR)

**GRAY,** Gabriel & **BARBOUR,** Sarah d/o Thomas BARBOUR 18 Jun 1813 surety Jeremiah PANNILL (OB)

**GRAY,** Gabriel & **DABNEY,** Emmely A. 9 Oct 1824 surety Samuel H. STOUT (OB)

**GREEN** Willis POC age 40 w farm labourer POB Madison POR Orange s/o Sam GREEN and Hannah GREEN & **WILLIAMS,** Rosa POC age 25 s POB Louisa POR Orange d/o William COOK and Sarah HARRIS POM Nazareth Baptist Church, Orange 19 Nov 1878 by Willis ROBINSON (OMR)

**GREEN**, Bolling POC age 37 w POB POR Orange s/o Jim GREEN and Ann GREEN laborer & **ROBINSON**, Violet POC age 23 w POB POR Orange d/o Daniel HOWARD and Courtena LINDSAY DOM 12 Sep 1869 POM Orange by Thomas R. HAWKINS (OMR)

**GREEN,** John & **STEPHENSON,** Susan w 24 Mar 1829 Robert CAMPBELL surety (OB)

**GREEN**, Littleton POC age 21 s POB Bedford Co POR Orange s/o Adam GREEN and Fanny _____ laborer & **WRIGHT**, Delia POC age 23 s POB Nelson Co. POR Orange 31 Dec 1868 POM Orange by Frank NICHOLAS (OMR)

**GREEN**, Nicholas & **PRICE,** Elizabeth 6 Jan 1757 both of St. Thomas Parish (Orange County Fee Book)

**GREEN,** Otho POC age 22 s farm labourer POB Louisa POR Orange s/o Bolling GREEN and Senora RICHARDSON & **DAVIS,** Ida age 21 s POB Richmond POR Orange POM Shady Grove Church, Orange Jul 1879 by C.T. JOHNSON (OMR)

**GREEN,** Pleas POC age 22 s farm laborer POB Spotsylvania POR Orange s/o Robert JORDAN and Aggy GREEN & **TAYLOR,** Adeline POC age 15 s POB POR Orange d/o Spencer TAYLOR and Sally _____ POM Orange 2 Apr 1877 (OMR)

**GREEN,** Richard POC age 24 s POB POR Orange s/o Elijah GREEN and Lucy _____ laborer & **GOODALL,** Martha age 20 s POB Madison Co POR Orange d/o John BROODUS 18 Aug 1870 POM Orange by Frank TIBBS (OMR)

**GREEN,** Robert s/o Harrison and Caroline GREEN age 21 s farm laborer POB POR Orange POC & **JACKSON,** Caroline age 24 s POB POR Orange POC; POM Orange 29 Dec 1866 (OMR) 27 Dec 1866 (OML)

**GREEN,** Spotswood POC age 22 s POB POR Orange s/o Overson GREEN and Caroline LONG laborer & **QUARLES,** Lucy POC age 16 POB POR Orange d/o Bartlett QUARLES and Patsy PORTER 27 Mar POM Culpeper Co by Philip JOHNSON (OMR)

**GREEN,** Stephen & **RECTOR,** Martha; 21 Oct 1854 (OML)

**GREEN,** Stephen G. age 40 w POB Westmoreland Co. POR Orange s/o George GREEN and Sallie BRIMMER farmer & **HERNDON,** Sarah F. age 23 s POB POR Orange d/o Edward F. HERNDON and Susan LANCASTER 2 Dec 1869 POM Orange by Melzi S. CHANCELLOR (OMR)

**GREEN,** Stephen G. s/o George GREEN and Sally BRIMMER age 35 w POB Westmoreland Co POR Culpeper & **PIERCE,** Delphia A. d/o John PIERCE and Frances TAMPLIN age 30 s POB Spotsylvania POR Orange; POM Orange 20 Dec 1866 (OMR) 19 Dec 1866 (OML)

**GREEN,** William N. age 26 s POB Fauquier Co. POR Shenandoah Co. s/o A.G. GREEN and Rachel A. ROGERS merchant & **GRAVES,** Kate F.

age 26 s POB POR Orange d/o Lewis GRAVES and Fanny WHITE 20
Feb 1868 POM Orange by Herndon FRAZER (OMR)

**GREENING,** Nehemiah & **KEYSER,** Elizabeth surety Robert THOMAS
9 Nov 1831 (OB)

**GREGORY,** Isaac & **SAMPSON,** Lucy d/o John SAMPSON who is also
surety 27 Jun 1814 by George BINGHAM (OB) (OM)

**GREGORY,** Obediah & **LANCASTER,** Nancy d/o Benjamin
LANCASTER who is also surety 7 Nov 1812 by Jeremiah
CHANDLER 8 Nov 1812 (OM)

**GREVIERS,** Henry POC age 25 s POB POR Albemarle Co s/o Fountain
GREVIERS and Jane BINS laborer & **GOODALL,** Rebecca POC age
19 s POB POR Orange d/o Andrew GOODALL and Rhoady
JOHNSON 12 Aug 1872 POM Orange by Frank TIBBS (OMR)

**GRIFFE,** John s/o Harris GRIFFE and Sethe WOOD age 19 s farmer POB
POR Dekalb Co, GA & **PIERCE,** Eliza H. d/o John W. PIERCE age
19 s POB POR Orange; POM Orange 4 Sep 1863 (OMR) 2 Sep 1863
(OML)

**GRIFFEY,** Abell & **SUTTON,** Catherine surety William SUTTON 23
Sep 1793 (OB)

**GRIFFEY,** Joseph & **WISDOM,** Fanny s surety Edmund BURRUS 15
Oct 1789 (OB)

**GRIFFIN,** James H. s/o James GRIFFIN and Ann OGLESBY age 46 s
blacksmith POB Buford District, S.C. POR Irvine Co, GA & **SMITH,**
Mary A. d/o John and Patience SMITH age 47 w POB Culpeper Co
POR Orange; POM Orange 23 Jun 1864 (OMR) 20 Jun 1864 (OML)

**GRIFFIN,** Richard I. age 22 s farmer POB Fluvanna POR Orange s/o
Joseph W. GRIFFIN and Sarah S. GRUBBS & **BYRUM,** Annie E. age
21 s POB POR Orange d/o John BYRUM and Mildred
SOUTHERLAND POM Orange 29 Mar 1877 (OMR)

**GRIFFIN,** William E. age 24 s rail road hand POB Goochland POR
Orange s/o Joseph W. GRIFFIN and Sarah F. GRUBBS POM Orange
24 Jun 1877 (OMR)

**GRIGSBY,** Elisha & **PORTER,** Elizabeth d/o Abner PORTER surety
John PORTER 24 May 1796 (OB) 27 May by George EVE (OM)

**GRIGSBY,** Reuben & **PORTER,** Burlinda A. surety William PORTER
24 Feb 1817 (OB) by J. GOSS 26 Feb 1817 (OM)

**GRIMSLEY,** John & **SMITH,** Sarah d/o Gasper SMITH surety William
SMITH 13 Oct 1826 (OB)

**GRIMSLEY,** Richard s/o George and Pollie GRIMSLEY age 21 s
overseer POB Rappahannock POR Culpeper & **SMITH,** Ellen d/o
Harrison and Susan SMITH age 25 s POB Culpeper POR Orange;
POM Orange 3 Dec 1854 (OMR)

**GRINNAN,** William S. & **SHEPHERD,** Mary Miller d/o George SHEPHERD surety Paul VERDIER 4 Feb 1817 (OB)

**GROOM,** John & **DELANEY,** Dise 22 Jan 1797 surety Jacob WILLIAMS (OB)

**GROOM,** John Z. age 30 w saw miller POB Louisa POR Orange s/o James GROOM and Virginia STUBBS & **RHOADES,** Mary age 22 s POB POR Orange d/o Thomas N. RHOADES and Susan A. HILMAN POM Orange 2 Nov 1879 (OMR)

**GROOM,** Solomon & **CHILES,** Elisabeth surety Achilles ATKINS 20 Dec 1831 (OB)

**GROOM,** Solomon & **HARRIS,** Elizabeth surety Overton HARRIS 10 Sep 1823 (OB) by George MORRIS (OM)

**GRYMES,** Benjamin A. & **BEALE,** Harriet H. POM Orange 5 Jan 1853 (OMR) 3 Jan 1853 (OML)

**GRYMES,** Jacob POC age 21 s POB POR Orange s/o Abraham GRYMES and Nettie TAYLOR laborer & **FRY,** Amanda POC age 21 s POB POR Orange d/o Philip FRY and Polly MILLS 26 Dec 1868 POM Orange by Jos. A. MANSFIELD (OMR)

**GRYMES,** Jacob POC age 23 w POB Orange POR Albemarle Co. s/o Abram GRYMES and Milly TAYLOR farming & **KINNEY,** Lucy POC age 20 s POB POR Orange d/o Shelton KINNEY and Fanny TOWLES 21 Dec 1873 POM Orange by Frank TIBBS (OMR)

**GRYMES,** Peyton & **CATLETT,** Catharine R. surety N.P. CATLETT by J. EARNEST 29 Apr 1845 (OB) (OM)

**GRYMES,** Peyton & **DADE,** Harriett w surety Blackwell CHILTON 4 Oct 1819 (OB)

**GRYMES,** Thomas M. & **WORMELEY,** Rebecca Tayloe surety Peter GRYMES 9 Dec 1822 (OB)

**GRYMES,** William S. age 44 s POB POR Orange s/o Peter GRYMES and Harriet SHEPHERD physician & **BERNARD,** Mary Ann age 25 s POB Petersburg, POR Orange d/o D.M. BERNARD and Sarah FIELD 1 Jun 1870 POM Orange by J.S. HANSBOROUGH (OMR)

**GULLEY,** John & **LAND,** Mary d/o John LAND surety Enoch GULLEY [the consent gives her name as Elizabeth] 22 Mar 1781 (OB)

**GUNNELLS,** James POC age 21 s laborer POB Fluvanna POR Orange s/o Patrick GUNNELLS and Mary JOHNSON & **WALKER,** Charlotte POC age 19 s POB POR Orange d/o Champ WALKER and Judy GORDON POM Orange 21 Apr 1879 (OMR)

**GWATHMEY,** Stork POC age 22 s labourer POB POR Orange s/o Philip GWATHMEY and Silvia RUFFLES & **TURNER,** Texana POC age 18 s POB POR Orange d/o John TURNER and Louisa WEBB POM Orange 22 Nov 1877 (OMR)

**GWATHMEY,** William POC age 21 s labourer POB POR Orange s/o Philip GWATHMEY and Silva RUFFIN **& SMITH,** Annie POC age 20 s POB POR Orange d/o Isaac SMITH and Milly JACKSON POM Orange 8 Oct 1879 (OMR)

**GWATHMEY,** Wortham POC age 20 s POB POR Orange laborer s/o Philip GWATHMEY and Sylvia RAFFLE **& WHITE,** Virginia POC age 18 s POB POR Orange 29 Aug 1880 POM Orange by W.J. BARNETT (OMR)

**GWYNN,** Henry B. age 27 s POB Baltimore, MD POR Orange teacher s/o Charles R. GWYNNN and Mary SANGETON **& SCOTT,** Mary A. age 19 s POB Baltimore, MD POR Orange d/o William C. SCOTT and Pamilia A. GRAVES 25 Aug 1880 POM Orange by Herbert M. HOKE, M.E. Church S. (OMR)

**HACKETT,** Reuben POC age 25 s POB Madison Co POR Orange s/o Reuben HACKETT and Lucy _____ blacksmith **& STEWART,** Mary POC age 23 s POB Madison Co POR Orange d/o Washington STEWART 1 Nov 1872 POM Orange by F.L. GIPSON (OMR)

**HAINES,** Jacob **& NICHOLS,** Sarah surety Absalom HAND 12 Aug 1835 (OB)

**HAINEY,** May **& RUNKLE,** Mary Macklin d/o Jacob RUNKLE who is also surety 2 Nov 1811 (OB)

**HALE,** Daniel W. s/o Jacob HALE and Elizabeth ERMON age 28 s blacksmith POB Rockingham Co POR Orange **& DAVIS,** Mary E. d/o William J. DAVIS age 29 s POB POR Orange; POM Gordonsville, Orange 20 Dec 1866 (OMR) 17 Dec 1866 (OML)

**HALE,** Ermon C. age 22 s machinist POB POR Orange s/o Jacob HALE and Elizabeth ERMON **& COLVIN,** Emma S. age 18 s POB POR Orange d/o William G. COLEMAN and Lucy A. COLVIN POM Gordonsville, Orange 9 Dec 1879 (OMR)

**HALES,** John **& BLACKWELL,** Mary E. surety William HUGHES Jr. 10 Apr 1822 (OB)

**HALEY,** William S. **& STEPHENS,** Maria Priscilla d/o Joseph STEPHENS who is also surety 11 Jun 1850 (OB)

**HALL,** Ambrose **& MARR,** Elizabeth 27 Dec 1807 by George BINGHAM (OM)

**HALL,** Andrew POC age 21 s POB POR Orange s/o Ben HALL and Lucy HILL laborer **& JOHNSON,** Fanny POC age 21 s POB POR Orange d/o Joseph JOHNSON and Lettie TYREE 2 Dec 1868 POM Orange by Philip JOHNSON (OMR)

**HALL,** Bazel **& MAIDEN,** Doria 2 Dec 1802 by George BINGHAM (Misc Min Ret)

**HALL,** Dudley **& LANCASTER,** Susannah surety Benjamin LANCASTER who also gives his permission 18 Feb 1819 (OB)

**HALL,** Ferrill ward of James H. ELLIS & **GRUBBS,** Mary Ann d/o Thomas GRUBBS surety Albert S. GRUBBS 12 Jan 1832 (OB)

**HALL,** Joseph s/o Hasten and Lucy HALL age 26 s farmer POB Albemarle Co POR Green Co & **RINER,** Mary E. d/o Jacob and Matilda RINER age 18 s POB POR Orange POM Orange 25 Feb 1858 (OMR) 22 Feb 1858 (OML)

**HALL,** Peter A. & **BURTON,** Lucinda d/o William BURTON surety Robert BURTON 1 May 1819 (OB) 4 May 1819 by Jacob WATTS (OM)

**HALL,** Richard & **PEARL,** Sally 2 May 1829 surety Ephraim ROSSER (OB) 10 May 1829 by Jeremiah CHANDLER (OM)

**HALL,** Richard P. & **GRUBBS,** Martha S. d/o Thomas GRUBBS surety Alfred S. GRUBBS 16 May 1838 (OB)

**HALL,** Thomas & **PICKET,** Elizabeth 25 Feb 1819 by George BINGHAM (OM)

**HALL,** Timothy A. age 25 s minister of the gospel POB POR Orange s/o James HALL and Hardenia BUNNELL & **ALLISON,** Mary F. age 27 s POB POR Orange d/o Robert ALLISON and Maria FARMER POM Orange 27 May 1879 by Melzi S. CHANCELLOR (OMR)

**HALL,** William & **DAVIS** Susannah 2 Jan 1800 (OM)

**HALL,** William J. & **SHEPHERD,** Elizabeth Bell d/o Andrew SHEPHERD surety William SHEPHERD 18 Jun 1801 (OB)

**HAM,** Bennett & **HAM,** Lurinna surety Samuel HAM 27 Mar 1821 (OB) by George BINGHAM 12 Apr 1821 (OM)

**HAM,** Joseph & **HEAREN,** Sarah d/o Francis and Sarah HEAREN; 12 Dec 1783 surety William GLASS (OB)

**HAM,** Joseph & **SMOOT,** Nancy surety Caleb SMOOT 5 Mar 1804 (OB)

**HAM,** Samuel & **WISDOM,** Clary both of St. Thomas Parish 18 Jan 1773 (Deed Book 17)

**HAM,** Vernon & **SAMPSON,** Virginia Ann d/o William SAMPSON who is also surety 3 Dec 1831 (OB)

**HAMBLETON,** Edward & **RIPPITO,** Elizabeth consent by John RIPPITO surety William RIPPITO 9 Aug 1793 (OB)

**HAMBLETON,** Elige & **BAYLE,** Polly [d/o John BALY] 30 Dec 1802 by Nathl. SANDERS (Misc Min Ret)

**HAMBLETON,** Elige & **BAYLE,** Polly d/o John BAYLE (she is under age) surety Alford BATTLE 28 Dec 1802 (OB) 30 Dec 1802 by Nathaniel SANDERS (OM)

**HAMBLETON,** LeRoy & **BLUNT,** Suckey d/o Michael BLUNT surety John FINNELL by James GARNETT 12 Jan 1800 (OB) (OM)

**HAMBLETON,** Theophilus & **POWELL,** Nutty surety John HAMBLETON 23 Mar 1796 (OB) 25 Mar 1796 by Nathaniel SANDERS (OM)

**HAMBLETON,** Thomas & **COLEMAN,** Margaret d/o John COLEMAN who is also surety 23 Jun 1803 (OB)

**HAMILTON,** John & **RICHARD,** Frances d/o William RICHARD surety James JONES 23 Dec 1788 (OB) by John LELAND 24 Dec 1788 (OM)

**HAMILTON,** John & **RIPPETOE,** Sarah W. surety Edward HAMBLETON who is also her guardian 25 Aug 1801 (OB) 27 Aug 1801 by Hamilton GOSS (OM)

**HAMILTON,** William & **OLIVE,** Jensy d/o Elizabeth OLIVE surety Francis JONES 24 Dec 1799 (OB)

**HAMS,** John & **OFFALL,** Elizabeth d/o John OFFALL surety James BEAZLEY 25 Jan 1830 (OB)

**HANCOCK,** James & **HANCOCK,** Elender d/o William HANCOCK who is also surety 10 Oct 1805 (OB) by Robert JONES 11 Oct 1805 (OM)

**HANCOCK,** Munroe B. & **OVERTON,** Sidney surety William MALLORY 11 Nov 1818 (OB)

**HANCOCK,** William B. & **BRIDEHART,** Mary surety Paul VERDIER 23 Sep 1816 (OB) by Robert JONES 24 Sep 1816 (OM)

**HANCOCK,** William POR Trinity Parish & **BROCK,** Jemima POR St. Thomas Parish by banns 4 May 1775 (Deed Book 17)

**HANDY,** Frederick A.G. age 30 s POB Worcester Co., MD POR Richmond s/o Isaac W.K. HANDY and Mary I.R. PURNELL lawyer & **COWHERD,** S. Lelia age 21 s POB POR Orange d/o Edwin F. COWHERD and Susan L. FREEMAN 7 Nov 1872 POM Orange by I.W.K. HANDY (OMR)

**HANEY** James & **PETROS,** Nancy d/o Mathew PETROS surety John GOODALL 1 May 1784 (OB)

**HANEY,** Bazle & **DEANE,** Elizabeth d/o William DEANE surety William DEANE Jr. 14 Jan 1817 (OB) 23 ___ 1818 by George BINGHAM (OM)

**HANEY,** John I. & **JACOBS,** Elizabeth surety Tandy B. MCCLARY 29 Feb 1836 (OB)

**HANEY,** William J. s/o John J. HANEY and Huldah JACOBS age 27 s POB Orange POR Albemarle Co & **HARLOW,** Lucy Mary d/o Julius B. HARLOW and Winney P. CROOKS age 24 s POB POR Orange POM Orange 15 Jan 1867 (OMR) (OML)

**HANKINS,** D.R. s/o Matthew C. HANKINS and M.P. GRISSIM age 34 s POB Wilson Co, Tennessee POR Lebanon, Tennessee & **CLARK,** Novella V. d/o William D. CLARK and Jane M. ELIASON age 22 s POB POR Orange; POM Orange 6 Jun 1866 (OMR) (OML)

**HANLEY,** Benjamin & **EDWARDS,** Frances 15 Sep 1803 POM Orange by Robert JONES (Misc Min Ret)

**HANSBROUGH**, Georgie G. age 19 s POB POR Orange d/o John S. HANSBROUGH and Mary E. BALLARD POM Orange 12 Oct 1876 (OMR)

**HANSBROUGH**, John S. s/o Alexander HAMILTON and Elizabeth HANSBROUGH age 25 s teacher POB Culpeper POR Fredericksburg & **BALLARD**, Mary E. d/o Garland and Georgianna BALLARD age 22 s POB POR Orange; POM Orange 5 Aug 1856 (OMR) (OML)

**HANSBROUGH**, Peter A. & **MILLER**, Frances d/o James MILLER surety William B. TAYLOR by J. GOSS 6 Oct 1831 (OB) (OM)

**HANSFORD**, John & **KING**, Sarah surety John W. EVANS 7 Dec 1812 (OB)

**HANY**, John & **WATSON**, Elizabeth 17 Dec 1822 by George BINGHAM (OM)

**HARDIMAN**, James E. & **KINZOR**, Elizabeth surety K. Steurman KINZOR 21 Oct 1820 (OB)

**HARDY**, Charles W. s/o William J.HARDY and Ann TRUEBLOOD age 29 s merchant POB POR Norfolk & **TALIAFERRO**, Victoria d/o Edmund P.TALIAFERRO and Octavia H. ROBERTSON age 26 s POB Culpeper Co POR Orange; POM Orange C.H.24 Oct 1865 (OMR) (OML)

**HARLEY**, Batt & **MURPHY**, Joanna 17 Oct 1853 (OML)

**HARLOW**, James G. age 23 s POB Louisa Co. POR Orange s/o Richard F. HARLOW and Rebecca WHITE farmer & **TINDER**, Susan Ann age 16 POB POR Orange d/o James R. TINDER and Emily SANDERS 14 Jan 1869 POM Orange by H.E.HATCHER (OMR)

**HARLOW**, John W. age 23 s POB Louisa Co POR Orange s/o Richard HARLOW and Rebecca WHITE farmer & **MORRIS**, Zalemma H. age 16 s POB POR Orange d/o Burruss MORRIS and Julia M. BICKERS 13 Jan 1874 POM Orange (OMR)

**HARLOW**, Joseph C. s/o Julius B. HARLOW and Winney B. CROOKS age 21 s miller POB POR Orange & **ESTES**, Eliza M. d/o William B. ESTES and Sarah BRUCE age 22 s POB Madison Co POR Orange; POM Orange 13 Feb 1866 (OMR) 10 Feb 1866 (OML)

**HARLOW**, Julius B. & **CROOKS**, Winnifred P. surety Joseph B. CROOKS 15 Apr 1840 (OB)

**HARLOW**, Lucian M. s/o Richard and Rebecca HARLOW age 26 s farmer POB Louisa Co POR Orange & **BICKERS**, Serena d/o Proctor and Lucy BICKERS age 29 s POB POR Orange; POM Orange 3 Feb 1858 (OMR) 2 Feb 1858 (OML)

**HARRELL**, Theodore s/o Richard HARRELL and Sarah ADAMS age 26 s carpenter POB Loudon Co POR Fauquier & **GRAVES**, Nannie B.

d/o Isaac W. GRAVES and Eliza BROCKMAN age 18 s POB POR
Orange; POM Orange 6 Dec 1865 (OMR) 14 Nov 1865 (OML)

**HARRIS,** Calvin D. & **BOWLER,** Mary Frances d/o David BOWLER
surety Valentine M. HOUSEWORTH 14 Dec 1833 (OB)

**HARRIS,** Charles M. age 21 s POB POR Spotsylvania s/o R.M.C.
HARRIS and Mary F. KISHPAUGH farmer & **FAULCONER,**
Margaret V. age 21 s POB POR Orange d/o Benjamin FAULCONER
& Mary A. MASSEY 5 Apr 1868 POM Orange by Melzi S.
CHANCELLOR (OMR)

**HARRIS,** Frank POC age 25 s laborer POB Prince Edward POR Orange
s/o Gilbert HARRIS and Amanda COX & **STROTHER,** Lucy age 20 s
POB POR Orange d/o Willis STROTHER and Mary GILFORD POM
Orange 2 Apr 1877 (OMR)

**HARRIS,** James & **ESTES,** Fanny d/o William ESTES Jr. who is also
surety 24 Dec 1827 (OB)

**HARRIS,** James & **ESTES,** Sally surety William ESTES 23 Dec 1805
(OB) 25 Dec 1805 by George BINGHAM (OM)

**HARRIS,** John & **PRICE,** Milly w 3 Nov 1800 surety Thomas BELL
(OB)

**HARRIS,** John & **ROWZIE,** Frances; 17 Nov 1774 (OML)

**HARRIS,** John C. & **TIMBERLAKE,** Mary A.E. surety William M.
CHAPMAN 13 Nov 1834 (OB)

**HARRIS,** Lewis & **SMITH,** Martha; 17 Nov 1816 surety William ELLIS
(OB)

**HARRIS,** Littleton & **ESTES,** Sarah surety Triplett H. ESTES 26 Dec
1836 (OB)

**HARRIS,** Moses T. & **BOWCOCK,** Elvira M. surety A.M.
BARKSDALE Jr. 27 May 1822 (OB)

**HARRIS,** Peter & **ESTES,** Mary Stanfield surety Willaim ESTES 27 Feb
1797 (OB)

**HARRIS,** Philip POC age 24 s POB Albemarle Co POR Orange s/o Philip
HARRIS and Mary _____ tanner & **SMITH,** Frances age 22 s POB
POR Orange d/o George SMITH and Mary FITZHUGH 28 Dec 1869
POM Orange by Philip JOHNSON (OMR)

**HARRIS,** Richard H. s/o Calvin D. HARRIS and Mary F. BOWLER age
25 s carpenter POB POR Orange & **DAVIS,** Lucy M. d/o William I.
DAVIS and Bettie BOLLES age 24 s POB POR Orange; POM
Gordonsville, Orange 22 Jan 1863 (OMR) (OML)

**HARRIS,** Samuel J. age 30 s POB Albemarle Co POR Orange s/o Samuel
J. HARRIS and Catherine W. GARRISON carpenter & **MADISON,**
Lucy M. age 22 s POB POR Orange d/o John R. MADISON and Lucy
S. ROUTT 25 Nov 1869 POM Orange by L.A. CUTLER (OMR)

**HARRIS,** William & **GIBSON,** Peggy ward of Peter GIBSON who is also surety 24 Jan 1820 (OB)

**HARRIS,** William D. & **FAULCONER,** Rachel V. 11 Jun 1856 (OML)

**HARRIS,** William M. POC age 40 w POB Richmond POR Orange s/o Samuel M. HARRIS and Catharine JONES barber & **JOHNSON,** Sarah J. POC age 18 s POB POR Orange d/o George JOHNSON and Fanny _____ 22 Jan 1874 POM Orange (OMR)

**HARRISON,** Jabez & **TAYLOR,** Elizabeth d/o William TAYLOR Sr. surety William TAYLOR Jr. 8 Feb 1820 (OB)

**HARRISON,** John R. b.d. 11 Aug 1817 s/o John C. HARRISON & **WALTERS,** Sarah ward of Robert W. BROOKING who is also surety 2 Oct 1839 (OB)

**HARRISON,** Lewis & **HARRISON,** Nancy by William DOUGLAS Methodist 3 May 1806 (OM)

**HARRISON,** Thomas B. age 24 s POB Richmond POR Orange printer s/o Thomas BOTTS HARRISON and Sarah S. FREEMAN & **GRYMES,** Alice Beale age 22 s POB POR Orange d/o Benjamin A. GRYMES and Harriet H. BEALE 15 Dec 1880 POM Orange C.H. by L.B. JOHNSON (OMR)

**HARRISON,** William & **SIMS,** Polly; 14 Oct 1816 surety William SIMMS (OB)

**HARRISON,** Zachariah E. & **CHEWNING,** Mary C. surety Elisha CHEWNING 20 Mar 1844 (OB)

**HARROD,** Benjamin & **BLAIR,** Betsy 20 Apr 1796 (OM)

**HARROD,** Richard & **ARNOLD,** Joanna d/o Willis ARNOLD who is also surety 3 Aug 1803 by William CALHOUN (OB) (OM)

**HART,** John & **TAYLOR,** Jane F. surety James SHEPHERD 6 Aug 1826 (OB) by Edward C. MCGUIRE 15 Aug 1826 (OM)

**HARTSOOK,** James W. & **QUINN,** Mary surety Rice DARNELL 4 Oct 1837 (OB)

**HARVEY,** Anthony & **BINGHAM,** Polly d/o George BINGHAM surety Richard GOLDING 22 Feb 1808 (OB)

**HARVEY,** Benjamin & **HARVEY,** Susanna; 23 Feb 1775 both of St. Thomas Parish by banns (Deed Book 17)

**HARVEY,** John & **ESTES,** Lucy both of St. Thomas Parish by banns 19 Apr 1778 (Deed Book 17)

**HARVEY,** John & **FELIX,** Elizabeth d/o William FELIX surety William BRADLEY by Hamilton GOSS 22 Jan 1800 (OB) (OM)

**HARVEY,** Layton & **DOVELL,** Elizabeth surety Jeremiah PIERCE 6 Aug 1822 (OB)

**HARVEY,** Thomas & **GOODALL,** Eleanor d/o James GOODALL Sr. surety Park GOODALL 22 Feb 1814 (OB) 24 Feb 1814 by George BINGHAM (OM)

**HARVEY,** Thomas & **HOBBS,** Sarah both of St. Thomas Parish by banns 19 Apr 1778 (Deed Book 17)

**HARVEY,** William & **WOOD,** Alley d/o Hopeful WOOD surety Charles COPPEDGE 12 Jul 1800 (OB)

**HARVY,** Jonathan & **ROSS,** Margaret by George BINGHAM 16 Mar 1802 (OM)

**HARWOOD,** Moses & **SUTTON,** Elizabeth; 7 Mar 1791 surety William SUTTON (OB)

**HASEY,** Michael & **LEATHERS,** Elizabeth surety James T. LEATHERS 9 Feb 1823 (OB)

**HATCHER,** Hilary E. s/o Uriel HATCHER and Susan WITT age 33 s minister POB Bedford POR Orange & **JONES,** Gillie Frances d/o James L. JONES and Martha A. PORTER age 26 s POB POR Orange; POM Beaumont, Orange 2 Oct 1866 (OMR) 27 Sep 1866 (OML)

**HAUSE,** Conrad & **THOMPSON,** Susannah 2 Apr 1796 (OM)

**HAWKINS,** Alexander & **SCOTT,** Anna surety George SCOTT 15 Oct 1807 (OB) 17 Oct 1807 by Nathaniel SANDERS (OM)

**HAWKINS,** Benjamin & **BICKERS,** Polley 17 Mar 1802 by Frederick KABLER (Misc Min Ret)

**HAWKINS,** Benjamin & **BICKERS,** Polly surety Nicholas BICKERS by Frederick KABLER 16 Mar 1802 (OB) (OMR)

**HAWKINS,** Benjamin & **SCOTT,** Sally; 7 Mar 1799 by Nathaniel SANDERS (OM)

**HAWKINS,** Benjamin F. age 22 s POB POR Orange s/o Benjamin J. HAWKINS and Betsy HAWKINS farmer & **RICHARDSON,** Ann Eliz. age 18 s POB POR Orange d/o John A. RICHARDSON and Margaret HAWKINS 27 Feb 1872 POM Orange by Sanders MASON (OMR)

**HAWKINS,** Benjamin J. & **HAWKINS,** Elizabeth J. surety William GRAVES 7 Aug 1843 (OB)

**HAWKINS,** Elijah & **SCOTT,** Elizabeth surety George SCOTT by Nathaniel SANDERS Baptist 8 Jan 1807 (OB) (OM)

**HAWKINS,** Henry S. & **FINNELL,** Elizabeth surety Benjamin S. PERRY 8 Jan 1848 (OB)

**HAWKINS,** James & **COLEMAN,** Betsy d/o James COLEMAN surety Joseph BLEDSOE 3 Sep 1799 (OB)

**HAWKINS,** James & **RECTOR,** Elizabeth surety Ikey RICHARDS 11 Nov 1799 (OB)

**HAWKINS,** Jehu & **GAINES,** Mary w both of St. Thomas Parish surety John HAWKINS and Areulues HAWKINS 28 Oct 1780 (OB)

**HAWKINS,** John B. & **FORD,** Ann; 2 Oct 1812 surety William FORD (OB) 4 Oct 1812 by Jeremiah CHANDLER (OM)

**HAWKINS,** John T. age 47 s lumber merchant POB POR Spotsylvania s/o James H. HAWKINS and Frances R. PENDLETON & **TANNER,** Mollie T. age 29 s POB POR Orange d/o James and Eunice TANNER POM Orange 27 Feb 1879 by John MCGILL (OMR)

**HAWKINS,** Moses & **QUISENBERRY,** Joice 23 Apr 1803 surety Moses QUISENBERRY (OB)

**HAWKINS,** Moses & **STROTHER,** Susanna both of St. Thomas Parish 3 Mar 1770 (Orange Fee Book)

**HAWKINS,** Nicholas & **MASON,** Frances H. surety Thomas MASON 19 Dec 1825 (OB)

**HAWKINS,** Reuben & **RICHARDSON,** Susan d/o Josiah and Sarah RICHARDSON surety John A. RICHARDSON 1 Sep 1849 (OB) 2 Sep 1849 by J. EARNEST (OM)

**HAWKINS,** Roddy & **JONES,** Elizabeth d/o Francis JONES surety Charles PAYNE 26 Feb 1817 (OB) 28 Feb 1817 by J.C. GORDON (OM)

**HAWKINS,** Roddy s/o Reuben HAWKINS & **CHAMBERLAIN,** Alice 31 Mar 1803 by Nathaniel Sanders (Misc Min Ret)(OB)

**HAWKINS,** Roddy s/o Reuben HAWKINS & **CHAMBERLANE,** Alice surety Richard GAINES 26 Mar 1803 (OB) 31 Mar 1803 by Nathaniel SANDERS, Baptist (OM)

**HAWKINS,** Thomas & **BLEDSOE,** Ann d/o John BLEDSOE surety George BLEDSOE 13 Mar 1848 (OB)

**HAWKINS,** Thomas & **PERRY,** Mary d/o Peter PERRY surety Thomas STUBBLEFIELD 23 Dec 1816 (OB) 24 Dec 1816 by John C. GORDON (OM)

**HAWKINS,** William & **DAVIS,** Harriot d/o Evers DAVIS surety William GRAVES 4 Jan 1837 (OB)

**HAWLEY,** Benjamin & **EDWARDS,** Frances surety Joseph EDWARDS 14 Sep 1803 (OB) by Robert JONES 15 Sep 1803 (OM)

**HAWLEY,** George W. s/o Abram and Mary A. HAWLEY age 44 w POB Albemarle Co POR Orange & **CROOKS,** Elvira S. d/o Joseph BOND and Catherine CROOKS age 40 s POB POR Orange POM Orange 28 May 1857 (OMR) 25 May 1857 (OML)

**HAWS,** John & **MITCHELL,** Sarah surety William HUFFMAN 16 Feb 1828 (OB)

**HAYES,** Moses & **PETTY,** Sarah; 28 Oct 1780 (OM)

**HAYES,** Thomas & **BROCKMAN,** Elizabeth d/o Asa BROCKMAN, who is also surety 30 Mar 1846 (OB) 2 Apr 1846 by Herndon FRAZER (OM)

**HAYES,** Thomas & **WINSLOW,** Martha surety Blueford S. WILLIAMS 19 Oct 1844 (OB)

**HAZLEHURST,** William s/o Robert HAZELHURST and Frances S. NUSLOW age 29 s banker and broker POB Glynn Co, GA POR Macon, GA & **CROCKFORD,** Rosa E. d/o John CROCKFORD and Ellen WENDHAM age 24 s POB Alexandria, VA POR Orange; POM Woodley, Orange 14 Dec 1865 (OMR) 13 Dec 1865 (OML)

**HEAD,** Benjamin Jr. & **GAAR,** Margaret d/o Lewis GAAR; 21 Aug 1784 surety William HEAD (OB)

**HEAD, G.** Edgar age 23 s POB POR Albemarle Co s/o Valentine HEAD and Lucy KINSOLVING farmer & **MUNDY,** Jennie A. age 20 s POB POR Orange d/o James D. MUNDY and Julia PRATT 22 Dec 1870 POM Orange by John W. TUCKER (OM)

**HEAD,** George Marshall & **RUCKER,** Milly d/o John and Mary RUCKER surety Joel RUCKER 11 Nov 1789 (OB)

**HEAD,** Henry & **SANFORD,** Elizabeth d/o Ann SANFORD surety Durrett SANFORD 5 Nov 1794 (OB)

**HEAD,** James POR St. Thomas Parish & **KIRTLEY,** Elizabeth Jannet POR Brumfield Parish [in what is now Madison County] by banns 5 Dec 1775 (Deed Book 17)

**HEAD,** John & **SANFORD,** Nancy d/o Ann SANFORD surety Richard SANFORD 26 Nov 1787 (OB)

**HEAD,** Tavenah & **PLUNKETT,** Jenney d/o Jesse PLUNKETT surety John PLUNKETT 20 Dec 1798 (OB)

**HEAD,** Valentine & **HUCKSTEP,** Elina d/o John HUCKSTEP surety Willis HUCKSTEP 21 Mar 1815 (OB) by Jacob WATTS 23 Mar 1815 (OM)

**HEAD,** Wilton s/o Marshall HEAD & **HUCKSTEP,** Fanny d/o John HUCKSTEP surety Valentine HEAD 17 Feb 1823 (OB) by George BINGHAM 18 Feb 1823 (OM)

**HEASTINE/ HESTIN,** Monroe N. & **COLLINS,** Eliza 20 Jun 1835 surety John B. HARTSOOK (OB)

**HEASTON/HESTIN,** Lewis & **COLLINS,** Drucilla d/o Mordecai COLLINS surety Nimrod R. COLLINS 14 Feb 1826 (OB)

**HELM,** William & **TALIAFERRO,** Matilda d/o Francis TALIAFERRO surety Hay TALIAFERRO 31 May 1784 (OB)

**HENDERSON,** Ambrose & **ACREE,** Lucy d/o William ACREE who is also surety 16 Apr 1810 by Ambrose BROCKMAN of Albemarle Co. (OM)

**HENDERSON,** Ceasar POC age 27 w labourer POB POR Orange s/o Jacob HENDERSON and Dinah WEBB & **BROADUS,** Addie POC age 27 s POB Louisa POR Orange d/o Andrew BROADUS and Agness _____ POM Orange 14 Sep 1879 (OMR)

**HENDERSON,** Daniel POC age 21 s labourer POB POR Orange s/o Minor HENDERSON & **HENDERSON,** Louisa age 21 s POB POR

Orange d/o Dick HENDERSON and Lucy HALL POM Orange 27 Nov
1878 by Elder Robert R. WOODSON (OMR)

**HENDERSON,** Henry POC age 22 s farm labourer POB POR Orange s/o
Dick HENDERSON and Lucy HALL & **MARSHALL,** Nancy POC
age 21 s POB POR Orange d/o Edmund MARSHALL and Jane
SPENCER POM Hopewell Baptist Church, Orange 20 Nov 1879 by
C.T. VAUGHN (OMR)

**HENDERSON,** John & **DANIEL,** Frankey surety Caleb LINDSAY 2 Jan
1797 (OB)

**HENDERSON,** John & **QUISENBERRY,** Salley POR Orange 28 Oct
1811 William T. BURRUSS surety and guardian of Salley (OB)

**HENDERSON,** John H. Jr. s/o John HENDERSON & **GRAVES,** Frances
Ann d/o Jacob GRAVES 5 Nov 1832 (OB)

**HENDERSON,** John POC age 21 s POB POR Orange s/o Lewis
HENDERSON laborer & **GREEN,** Betty Ann POC age 17 POB POR
Orange d/o Anderson GREEN and Susan HENDERSON 29 Dec 1868
POM Orange by Thos. R. HAWKINS (OMR)

**HENDERSON,** John POC age 29 w POB POR Orange s/o Lewis
HENDERSON and Martha GRAHAM laborer & **WHITE,** Julia POC
age 19 s POB POR Orange d/o Thomas WHITE and Sarah ELLIS
dated 25 Dec 1880 however the notation stated that the woman refused
to marry him (OMR)

**HENDERSON,** Jos. POC age 21 s POB POR Orange s/o Minor
HENDERSON and Chaney _____ farm laborer & **SMITH** Frances
POC age 17 s POB POR Orange d/o Maria SMITH DOM 30 Dec 1869
POM Orange by Philip JOHNSON (OMR)

**HENDERSON,** Joseph M. s/o John and Sarah HENDERSON age 21-22 s
farmer POB POR Orange & **ELLIS,** Sarah E. d/o Robert S. and Emily
A. ELLIS age 17-18 s POB POR Orange; POM Orange 9 May 1854
(OMR) 2 May 1854 (OML)

**HENDERSON,** Minor POC age 22 s POB Louisa Co POR Orange s/o
Minor HENDERSON and Jeanne CLARK farm laborer & **DADE,**
Mary age 22 s POB POR Orange d/o Albert DADE and Eliza _____ 30
Dec 1872 POM Orange by Philip JOHNSON (OMR)

**HENDERSON,** Nelson POC age 21 s POB Louisa Co POR Orange s/o
Minor HENDERSON and Chaney CLARK laborer & **COVINGTON,**
Rebecca POC age 21 s POB POR Orange d/o Ben COVINGTON and
Rhoda WATKINS 31 May 1873 POM Orange by E.R. PERRY (OMR)

**HENDERSON,** William POC age 20 s farmer POB POR Orange s/o
Lewis HENDERSON and Martha GRAVES & **THURSTON,** Nellie
POC age 20 s POB POR Orange d/o William THURSTON and Nancy
WASHINGTON POM Orange 6 Jan 1877 (OMR)

109

**HENDERSON**, William POC age 21 s labourer POB POR Orange s/o Jacob HENDERSON and Dinah POLK & **JOHNSON**, Belle POC age 22 s POB POR Orange d/o Lewis JOHNSON and Martha JACKSON POM Orange 2 Jun 1879 by Sanders MASON (OMR)

**HENDERSON**, William s/o John and Sally HENDERSON age 42 w farmer POB POR Orange & **YOUNG**, Sarah E. d/o Curtis and Nancy BROCKMAN age 36 w POB POR Orange; POM Orange 24 Oct 1854 (OMR) 23 Oct 1854 (OML)

**HENISON**, Abram POC age 24 s POB POR Orange s/o Neptune HENISON and Sallie _____ laborer & **DAWSON**, Fanny POC age 24 s POB POR Orange d/o Laughter DAWSON and Anna _____ 11 Jul 1869 POM Orange by John. H. ROBERTSON (OMR)

**HENLEY**, Osborn & **WINSLOW**, Martha of Orange 25 Nov 1804 by Robert JONES (Misc Min Ret)

**HENNESSY**, Peter POR Albemarle & **ROUTT**, Winney w surety James TAYLOR 25 Nov 1793 (OB)

**HENRY**, Belfield & **KIRTLEY**, Elizabeth 1 Feb 1803 by George BINGHAM (Misc Min Ret)

**HENRY**, Belfield & **KIRTLEY**, Elizabeth by George BINGHAM 13 Feb 1802 (OM)

**HENRY**, Benjamin & **ROBERTS**, Nancy d/o Hugh ROBERTS surety Thomas ROBERTS by George EVE 17 May 1792 (OB) (OM)

**HENRY**, Benson & **WALKER**, Peachy Ann surety John S. WALKER 31 Jan 1837 (OB) 7 Feb 1837 by Benjamin CREEL (OM)

**HENRY**, William & **WARREN**, Elizabeth w; 22 Apr 1793 surety Thomas ROBERTS (OB) by George EVE 25 Apr 1793 (OM)

**HENRY**, Zachary & **KIRTLEY**, Lucy by George BINGHAM 17 Nov 1801 (OM)

**HENSHAW**, Edmund & **NEWMAN**, Mary d/o James NEWMAN surety James NEWMAN Jr. 22 Sep 1785 (OB)

**HENSHAW**, George T. & **DAVIS**, Martha H. (Martha arrived at 21 years old on 28 Sep 1837) surety Albert EARLY 18 Nov 1837 (OB)

**HENSHAW**, John & **COWHERD**, Sarah d/o Francis COWHERD surety John SCOTT 5 Dec 1818 (OB) by J. GOSS 8 Dec 1818 (OM)

**HENSHAW**, John & **NEWMAN**, Elizabeth d/o James and Elizabeth NEWMAN surety Thomas NEWMAN 20 Aug 1792 (OB)

**HENSHAW**, John & **NEWMAN**, Patty d/o James NEWMAN surety William NEWMAN both of St. Thomas Parish 4 Dec 1780 (OB)

**HENSHAW**, John S. s/o Philip T. and Sarah A. HENSHAW age 27 w farmer POB POR Oldham Co, Kentucky & **COLE**, Ann E. d/o William and Mary F. COLE age 23 s POB POR Orange; POM Orange 28 Nov 1854 (OMR) 27 Nov 1854 (OML)

**HENSHAW,** Philip T. & **SCOTT,** Sarah Ann d/o Sarah SCOTT surety Garrett SCOTT 19 Jul 1824 (OB) 20 Jul 1824 (OM)

**HENSHAW**, Thomas P.G. s/o Edward and Jane HENSHAW (now Mrs. ROYSTER) age 26 s farmer POB POR Richmond & **PORTER**, Virginia O.S. d/o William and Mary Ann PORTER age 32 s POB POR Orange; POM Orange 5 Apr 1855 (OMR)

**HENSLEY,** Cypress & **THOMPSON,** Caty surety John THOMPSON 18 Sep 1809 (OB) by Jacob WATTS 24 Sep 1809 (OM)

**HENSLEY**, James & **MAIDEN**, Elizabeth 23 Dec 1802 by George BINGHAM (Misc Min Ret)

**HENSLEY,** Jeder & **THOMPSON,** Winney d/o George THOMPSON surety Armistead BROWN 16 Jan 1808 (OB) by Jacob WATTS 21 Jan 1808 (OM)

**HENSLEY,** John & **OLIVER,** Elizabeth d/o Francis OLIVER who is also surety by Ambrose BROCKMAN of Albemarle 8 Dec 1810 (OB) (OM)

**HENSLEY,** Lewis & **FOSTER,** Mary surety Eastham SNELL 28 Oct 1785 (OB)

**HERMAN,** Frederick & **JAMASON,** Mary w surety Philemon DAVIS by Robert JONES 4 Jan 1810 (OB) (OM)

**HERNDON,** Andrew J. & **DUNAWAY,** Jane d/o Mildred DUNAWAY surety Edmund DUNAWAY 21 Sep 1841 (OB)

**HERNDON,** Benjamin & **BLEDSOE,** Hannah surety Moses BLEDSOE 17 Dec 1822 (OB)

**HERNDON**, Benjamin & **EHART,** Catherine; 20 Nov 1787 by George EVE (OM)

**HERNDON,** Benjamin & **LUCAS,** Nancy 28 Dec 1813 by George EVE (OM)

**HERNDON,** Benjamin & **STEPHENS,** Mary d/o Benjamin STEPHENS surety Thomas HERNDON by Robert JONES 9 Oct 1805 (OB) (OM)

**HERNDON**, Benjamin Jr. of age POR Orange & **ANDERSON**, Sally age over 21 POR Orange; POM Orange 26 Jan 1854 (OMR) 25 Jan 1854 (OML)

**HERNDON**, Davis C. s/o Benjamin HERNDON and Hannah BLEDSOE age 26 s farmer POB POR Orange & **APPERSON**, Lucy P. d/o Joseph APPERSON and Lucinda PERRY age 25 s POB POR Orange; POM Orange 1 Jan 1867 (OMR) 31 Dec 1866 (OML)

**HERNDON**, E. Frazer age 23 s POB POR Orange s/o Edward F. HERNDON and Susan LANCASTER farmer & **SLEET,** Lucy J. age 22 s POB POR Orange d/o John P. SLEET and Elizabeth DAVIS 2 Dec 1869 POM Orange by Melzi S. CHANCELLOR (OMR)

**HERNDON,** Edward & **BRADLEY,** Mary B. surety Pollard BRADLEY 19 Oct 1822 (OB)

**HERNDON,** Edward & **LANCASTER,** Susan d/o Edmund LANCASTER who is also surety 17 Dec 1828 (OB)

**HERNDON,** Edward F. s/o James and Esther HERNDON age 25 s farmer POB POR Madison Co & **WAYLAND,** Julia A. d/o William and Frances W. WAYLAND age 19 s POB POR Orange; POM Orange 27 Jul 1858 (OMR) 24 Jul 1858 (OML)

**HERNDON,** Ezekiel & **JONES,** Sarah d/o Elliott JONES who is also surety 29 Jan 1821 (OB)

**HERNDON,** Fielding & **MONTAGUE,** Mildred surety David MONTAGUE 11 Sep 1822 (OB)

**HERNDON,** George & **TEALE,** Sarah d/o Henry TEALE who is also surety 26 Mar 1806 (OB) by Nathanial SANDERS 1 Apr 1806 (OM)

**HERNDON,** Harrison s/o John and Mahala HERNDON age 24 s mechanic POR Orange POR North Carolina & **MASON,** Aby d/o Charles and Lucy B. MASON age 18 s POB POR Orange; POM Orange 5 Nov 1854 (OMR)

**HERNDON,** Henry & **WOOD,** Sidney 16 Dec 1802 by Hamilton GOSS (Misc Min Ret)

**HERNDON,** Henry Jr. & **LLOYD,** Elizabeth d/o Robert LLOYD who is also surety 24 Sep 1827 (OB)

**HERNDON,** Henry POC age 22 s farm labourer POB Madison POR Orange s/o George HERNDON and Fanny ___ & **JOHNSON,** Wilhelmina age 21 s POB POR Orange d/o Celia JOHNSON POM Mt. Calvary Baptist Church, Orange 19 Sep 1878 by W.J. BARNETT (OMR)

**HERNDON,** J. H. age 21 s farmer POB POR Greene s/o W.P. HERNDON and Sarah E. PARROTT & **YOWELL,** Sarah J. age 22 s POB Greene POR Orange d/o A. G. YOWELL and Lucy J. QUINN POM Orange 30 Jan 1879 by P.S. RHODES(OMR)

**HERNDON,** James & **FERNEYHOUGH,** Esther d/o Thomas FERNEYHOUGH who is also surety 22 Dec 1823 (OB) by Leroy CANADAY 30 Dec 1823 (OM)

**HERNDON,** James & **QUISENBERRY,** Elizabeth d/o George QUISENBERRY who is also surety 24 Jul 1815 (OB) by John A. BILLINGSLEY 30 Jul 1815 (OM)

**HERNDON,** James C. & **FAULCONER,** Emily J.; POM Orange 3 Aug 1853 (OMR) 2 Aug 1853 (OML)

**HERNDON,** James s/o James and Elizabeth HERNDON age 24 s mechanic POB POR Orange & **PEACHER,** Mary F. d/o Alexander and Nicy PEACHER age 19 s POB POR Orange; POM Orange 15 Oct 1854 (OMR)

**HERNDON,** Joel & **HUME,** Lucy w surety Richard JOHNSON 24 Apr 1843 (OB)

112

**HERNDON,** John & **ADAMS,** Nancy d/o William ADAMS who is also surety 15 Dec 1809 (OB)

**HERNDON,** John & **LANDRUM,** Mahala d/o Lewis LANDRUM who is also surety 15 Dec 1821 (OB)

**HERNDON,** John & **PENCE,** Mary d/o John PENCE surety Benjamin HERNDON 7 Sep 1815 (OB)

**HERNDON,** John & **WRIGHT,** Elizabeth d/o John WRIGHT surety William WRIGHT 19 Apr 1781 (OB) 25 Apr 1781 by Nathaniel SANDERS (OM)

**HERNDON,** John B. s/o John HERNDON Jr. and Mahala LANDRUM age 20 s millwright POB POR Orange & **WEBB,** Sarah A.E. d/o Richard C. WEBB and Mary S. LANCASTER age 22 s POB POR Orange; POM Orange 21 Dec 1865 (OMR) 27 Nov 1865 (OML)

**HERNDON,** John D. POC age 48 w POB POR Orange s/o John HERNDON and Allie SACEY (or LACEY) carriage driver & **COOPER,** Anne E. POC age 60 w POB POR Orange d/o Martha WEST 9 Apr 1874 POM [Gordonsville Baptist Church by George NALLEY] (OMR)

**HERNDON,** John W. & **MIDDLEBROOK,** Lucy C.; 9 Jan 1851 (OML)

**HERNDON,** Joseph & **HERNDON,** Mary d/o James HERNDON (dec'd of Orange Co.) surety Benjamin QUISENBERRY 28 Sep 1846 (OB)

**HERNDON,** Larkin & **WRIGHT,** Jane surety George HERNDON 9 Mar 1826 (OB)

**HERNDON,** Robert N. s/o Richard T. HERNDON and Ellen W. HUTCHISON age 26 s farmer POB POR Orange & **BLEDSOE,** Georgianna F. d/o John BLEDSOE and Jane WOOD age 23 s POB Madison Co POR Orange; POM Orange 13 Dec 1866 (OMR) 19 Dec 1866 (OML)

**HERNDON,** Tandy & **SCOTT,** Mary 1771 (Orange Fee Book)

**HERNDON,** Thomas & **BELL,** Elizabeth; 3 Aug 1852 (OML)

**HERNDON,** William & **PERRY,** Sukey; 5 May 1786 surety Moses BLEDSOE (OB)

**HERNDON,** William & **YOUNG,** Lucy J. d/o Daniel YOUNG surety Benjamin QUISENBERRY 15 Dec 1845 (OB)

**HERNDON,** Wyatt POC age 21 s farm labourer POB POR Orange s/o Emanual HERNDON and Milly CHAPMAN & **HUNTER,** Milly POC age 24 w POB POR Orange POM Mt. Zion Church, Orange 1 Jun 1879 by Richard STEPHENS (OMR)

**HERNSON,** Richard A. age 22 s POB POR Orange s/o Edward HERNSON and Susan LANCASTER farmer & **TINDER,** Amanda L. age 27 s POB POR Orange d/o Thomas TINDER and Nancy MASON 28 Nov 1872 POM Orange by Melzi S. CHANCELLOR (OMR)

**HERRING**, Franklin T. age 32 s carpenter POB POR Orange s/o George HERRING and Sarah S. HOLBERT & **GIBSON**, Amarilous age 19 years 8 months POB POR Orange d/o William GIBSON and Martha J. KRISE POM Orange 16 Mar 1876 (OMR)

**HERRING**, James & **COFER**, Judah d/o James COFER surety Peter RUCKER 2 Apr 1784 (OB)

**HESTAND**, John & **NOWELL**, Tanlipy; 4 Nov 1799 (OM)

**HEUSTEN**, John & **BROWN**, Ann surety Philip S. FRY 22 Sep 1847 (OB)

**HIATT**, Jonathan & **CONNER**, Mary d/o Rachel CONNER surety Lewis CONNER 27 May 1784 both of St. Thomas Parish (OB)

**HICKS**, Charles M. age 21 s POB Spotsylvania Co POR Orange s/o Charles M. HICKS and Lucy J. SORRELL farmer & **SCHUYLER**, Cassandra D. age 18 POB POR Orange d/o William SCHUYLER and Mary Ann SORRELL DOM 13 Oct 1868 POM Orange by Thomas R. HAWKINS (OMR)

**HICKS**, John R. s/o Robert HICKS and Bettie WHITLOCK age 25 s POB POR Spotsylvania farmer & **BOND**, Martha C. d/o Joseph BOND and Mildred WHITLOCK age 21 s POB Louisa Co POR Orange; POM Orange 15 Mar 1866 (OMR) 5 Mar 1866 (OML)

**HICKS**, Peter W. s/o Robert HICKS and Marina WHITLOCK age 22 s farmer POB Spotsylvania POR Orange & **BOND**, Lucy M. d/o Thomas W. BOND and Virginia KINZER age 14 s POB POR Orange; POM Orange 7 Feb 1867 (OMR) 6 Feb 1867 (OML)

**HIEATT**, John & **ARNOLD**, Sarah; 30 Dec 1783 surety Nicholas ARNOLD POM St. Thomas Parish (OB)

**HIEATT**, Lewis & **ALLEN**, Barbary s surety Thomas DAVIS 24 Dec 1783 POM St. Thomas Parish (OB)

**HIGHLANDER**, Thomas age 26 s POB POR Orange s/o Madison HIGHLANDER and Sarah PETTIS farmer & **FAULCONER**, Lucy F. age 27 w POB POR Orange d/o John TINDER 29 Mar 1870 POM Orange by Sanders MASON (OMR)

**HILL**, Benjamin F. s/o Samuel and Sucky HILL age 27 s farm laborer POB Culpeper Co POR Orange POC & **MURPHY**, Lucinda d/o John and Polly MURPHY age 21 s POB POR Orange POC; POM Orange C.H. 27 Dec 1866 (OMR) (OML)

**HILL**, Horace s/o Edward SHEPHERD and Martha BANKS age 19 s laborer on farm POB POR Orange POC & **OWENS**, Mary J. d/o Lewis and Matilda OWENS age 18 s POB POR Orange POC; POM Orange 24 Dec 1866 (OMR) (OML)

**HILL**, Richard POC age 30 s POB Halifax Co POR Orange s/o Bill PRINDLE and Mary HILL wagoner & **CARTER**, Dinah POC age 25 POB POR Orange 2 Aug 1873 POM Orange by F.L. GIPSON (OMR)

**HILL**, Samuel & **TATE**, Nancy surety Uriah TATE 24 Dec 1788 (OB)

**HILMAN**, Uriel & **GRAVES**, Sally; 11 Jul 1797 surety Thomas GRAVES (OB)

**HITE**, Carter s/o Major HITE and Harriet COONS age 25 s farm laborer POB POR Orange POC & **RUCKER**, Columbia d/o Legrand RUCKER and Harriet E. WASHINGTON age 18 s POB POR Orange POC; POM Orange 26 Dec 1867 (OMR) 23 Dec 1867 (OML)

**HITE**, Isaac Jr. & **MADISON**, Nelly d/o Col. James MADISON and Eleanor CONWAY both of St. Thomas Parish surety Ambrose MADISON [her brother] 31 Dec 1782 (OM)

**HITT**, John M. age 28 s farmer POB Wood Co., WV POR Orange s/o Martin HITT and Ann M. HAWKINS & **HAWKINS**, Columbia age 28 s POB POR Orange d/o Ben J. HAWKINS and Elizabeth J. HAWKINS POM Orange 13 Jul 1876 (OMR)

**HITZ**, Bartholomew age 24 s POB Switzerland POR Gordonsville, VA s/o Bartholomew HITZ and Ursula MULTNER cooper & **BARTSH**, Ann age 26 s POB Switzerland POR Gordonsville, VA d/o John BARTSH and Lucie WEBER 21 Apr 1873 POM Gordonsville by Louis LOCHNER (OMR)

**HOBDAY**, John & **DAVIS**, Mary; 16 Aug 1790 by Nathaniel SANDERS (OM)

**HODGSON**, William B. s/o Joseph HODGSON & **PANNILL**, Louisa D. d/o George PANNILL Jr.; 28 Apr 1851 (OML)

**HOILE**, James s/o Charles HOILE and Sally KILSH age 24 s farmer POB North Carolina POR Orange & **GILLABERT**, Mary A. d/o Peter GILLABERT and Frances GARDNER age 17 s POB POR Orange; POM Orange 2 Aug 1866 (OMR) 30 Jul 1866 (OML)

**HOLLADAY**, Benjamin L. age 23 s farmer POB POR Spotsylvania s/o Henry A. HOLLADAY and Mary F. JENKINS & **JENNINGS**, Mary Ida age 20 s POB POR Orange d/o William A. JENNINGS and Mary A. WHARTON POM Orange 6 Nov 1878 by J. A. FRENCH (OMR)

**HOLLADAY**, Henry T. s/o Lewis S. HOLLADAY and Jane THOMPSON age 36 w miller POB Spotsylvania POR Orange & **PORTER**, Fannie W. d/o John A. PORTER and Mary CRUMP age 26 s POB POR Orange; POM Orange 3 May 1865 (OMR) 28 Apr 1865 (OML)

**HOLLADAY**, Lewis L. s/o Waller HOLLADAY and Huldah LEWIS age 61 w physician POB Spotsylvania POR Orange & **GARNETT**, Mary E. d/o Larkin WILLIS and Mary GORDON age 38 w POB POR Orange; POM Locust Dale, Madison Co 24 Jun 1864 Madison (OMR) 23 Jun 1864 (OML)

**HOLLADAY**, Robert POC age 23 s POB Spotsylvania Co POR Orange
s/o Moses HOLLADAY and Patsy SMITH laborer at sawmill &
**WILLIS**, Eliza age 21 s POB Albemarle Co POR Orange 4 Dec 1869
POM Orange by Franklin TIBBS (OMR)

**HOLLADAY**, Samuel J. s/o William HOLLADAY and Martha WRIGHT
age 23 s farmer POB POR Butler Co, Alabama & **CLARK**, Mary H.
d/o William CLARK and Frances ESTES age 18 s POB POR Orange;
POM Orange 1 Jun 1865 (OMR) 30 May 1865 (OML)

**HOLLAND**, George & **COLEMAN**, Mary; 21 Mar 1757 both of St.
Thomas Parish (Orange Co. Fee Book)

**HOLLIDAY**, Henry POC age 21 s POB POR Louisa blacksmith s/o
Joseph HOLLIDAY and Martha LEWIS & **DANIEL**, Louisa POC age
18 s POB POR Orange d/o Travis DANIEL and Ellen LEWIS 4 Dec
1880 POM Shady Grove Church, Orange by C.J. JOHNSON (OMR)

**HOLLIDAY**, Waller L. & **TALIAFERRO**, Elizabeth; 22 May 1852
(OML)

**HOLMES**, Albert POC age 22 s POB POR Orange s/o Albert HOLMES
and Ann SPENCER wagoner & **HENDERSON**, Ann POC age 21 s
POB POR Orange d/o Jacob HENDERSON and Diana ____ 15 Mar
1874 POM Orange (OMR)

**HOLMES**, Albert POC age 27 w labourer POB POR Orange s/o Albert
HOLMES and Ann SPENCER & **FRY**, Barbara A. POC age 22 s POB
POR Orange POM Orange 25 Dec 1877 (OMR)

**HOLMES**, Russell s/o Jacob HOLMES and Nancy TAYLOR age 22 s
farm laborer POB Hanover Co POR Orange POC & **THORNTON**,
Rebecca d/o Moses THORNTON age 16 s POB Albemarle Co POR
Orange POC; POM Gordonsville, Orange 29 Dec 1866 (OMR) 27 Dec
1866 (OML)

**HOLMES**, Samuel POC age 35 s farm labourer POB POR Orange s/o
Paul HOLMES and Vina HOWARD & **SMITH**, Nancy POC age 22 s
POB Albemarle POR Orange d/o Archie SMITH and Patsy ___ POM
Orange 27 Jan 1878 (OMR)

**HOLT**, William W. s/o Joel HOLT and Sarah PARKERSON age 23 s
wheelwright POB Pulaski Co, GA POR Dooly Co, GA & **BOSTON**,
Mary E. d/o John P.BOSTON and Frances WAUGH age 17 s POB
POR Orange; POM Orange 15 Mar 1864 (OMR) (OML)

**HOMES**, Abraham s/o Paul HOMES and Vina POWELL age 26 s laborer
POB POR Orange POC & **BROCK**, Alice age 25 s POB POR Orange
POC; POM Gordonsville 20 Oct 1866 (OMR) 19 Oct 1866 (OML)

**HOMES**, James & **HILMAN**, Sally d/o Joseph HILMAN 22 Dec 1795
surety William GRAVES (OB)

**HOOMES**, George POC age 23 s POB POR Orange s/o Albert HOOMES
and Ann SPENCER wagoner & **THURSTON**, Maria POC age 21 s

POB Spotsylvania POR Orange d/o Anthony THURSTON and Betsy SMITH 21 Jun 1873 POM Orange by M.C. WILLIS (OMR)

**HOPKINS**, Marshall s/o Lawson HOPKINS and Lucinda CHEWNING age 22 s farmer POB Spotsylvania POR Orange & **HUGHES**, Jane J. d/o James FORD and Ellen HUGHES age 21 s POB POR Orange; POM Orange 18 Oct 1866 (OMR) 16 Oct 1866 (OML)

**HOPKINS**, Samuel C. s/o Lawson HOPKINS and Lucinda HOPKINS age 23 s farmer POB Spotsylvania POR Orange & **BOSTON**, Susan F. d/o John BOSTON and Jane F. WAUGH age 18 s POB POR Orange; POM Orange 7 Apr 1863 (OMR) 6 Apr 1863 (OML)

**HOPKINS**, William POC age 22 s POB POR Orange s/o George HOPKINS and Betsy HILL laborer & **GRYMES**, Alberta POC age 21 s POB POR Orange d/o Spotswood GRYMES and Mary _____ 14 May 1869 POM Orange by John ROBERTSON (OMR)

**HOPKINS**, Zebulen s/o John HOPKINS and Lucinda OVERTON age 23 s POB Spotsylvania POR Orange & **DOOLEY**, Harriet A. d/o Robert BOWLER age 25 w POB POR Orange; POM Orange 26 Dec 1865 (OMR) 25 Dec 1865 (OML)

**HOPLEY**, Dennis S. s/o Dennis S. HOPLEY and Mary E. SPRAGLE age 22 s patent maker POB POR Vickburg, Mississippi & **CLARK**, Minerva A. d/o James T. CLARK and Mary A. WILTSHIRE age 22 s POB POR Orange; POM Unionville, Orange 15 Sep 1863 (OMR) 14 Sep 1863 (OML)

**HORD**, Miles POC age 23 s farm labourer POB POR Orange s/o James HORD and Elizabeth JONES & **WALKER**, Sarah Frances POC age 22 s POB POR Orange d/o George WALKER and Nancy _____ POM Nazareth Baptist Church, Orange 20 Dec 1878 by Willis ROBINSON (OMR)

**HORSLEY**, James & **CHILES**, Jane d/o James CHILES who is also surety 4 Aug 1809 (OB)

**HOSSLEY**, Dennis S. s/o Dennis HOSSLEY and Mary E. SPANGLER age 26 wheelwright w POB Warren Co., Mississippi POR Orange & **AUSTIN**, Sallie B. d/o William C. AUSTIN and Susan THOMPSON age 22 s POB POR Orange; POM Orange 24 Sep 1867 (OMR) (OML)

**HOUSEWORTH**, Joseph H. s/o V.M. and S.W. HOUSEWORTH age 23 s gentleman POB POR Orange & **BRENT**, Harriet M. d/o George P. and Harriet BRENT age 25 s POB POR Orange; POM Orange 12 Mar 1857 (OMR) 9 Mar 1857 (OML)

**HOUSEWORTH**, Valentine A. age 41 s POB POR Orange s/o Valentine M. HOUSEWORTH and Susan WINSLOW farmer & **WINSLOW**, Mary M. age 28 s POB POR Orange d/o George WINSLOW and Martha COCKRELLE 11 Mar 1874 POM Orange (OMR)

HOWARD, Alexander POC age 22 s POB POR Orange s/o Jack
HOWARD and Elizabeth HOWARD laborer & TIBBS, Mary age 21 s
POB POR Orange d/o George TIBBS and Frances TIBBS 28 Aug 1869
POM Orange by Philip JOHNSON (OMR)
HOWARD, Alexander POC age 35 w farm labourer POB POR Orange s/o
Jack HOWARD and Elizabeth ____ & TIBBS, Jane POC age 21 s
POB POR Orange d/o George TIBBS and Frances ____ POM Orange
26 Jun 1879 (OMR)
HOWARD, Charles P. & TAYLOR, Jane; 11 Mar 1793 surety Charles
WARDELL (OB)
HOWARD, Richard & SULLIVAN, Margaret 28 Dec 1790 surety
William FAULCONER (OB)
HOWARD, William J. POC age 22 s barber POB Spotsylvania POR
Washington City s/o William J. HOWARD and Sarah S. HERNDON &
BROWN, Alverta S. POC age 21 s POB POR Orange d/o Albert
BROWN and Winny SIMPSON POM Orange 19 Oct 1876 (OMR)
HUBBARD, Carter & DURRETT, Betsy; 16 Jan 1793 surety Joel
DURRETT (OB)
HUDGINS, George W. age 39 s farmer s/o Churchill HUDGINS and
Louisa HALEY POB POR Orange & WIATT, Mary Ann age 43 w
POB POR Orange d/o Richard RICHARDS and Nancy OVERTON
POM Orange 27 Oct 1878 by William A. HILL (OMR)
HUDSON, John & DEDMAN, Mary 2 Apr 1793 surety Francis TAYLOR
(OB)
HUDSON, William & CHILES, Nancy; 14 Sep 1816 permission by James
CHILES surety Benjamin VAWTER (OB)
HUGHES, Alexander & LEE, Jane 27 Dec 1847 surety Lemuel WRIGHT
by M.A. DUNN (OB) (OMR)
HUGHES, Alexander & MITCHELL, Elizabeth 22 Dec 1803 by Nath.
SANDERS (Misc Min Ret)
HUGHES, Alexander & MITCHELL, Elizabeth d/o West MITCHELL 3
Dec 1803 surety Marmaduke BRANHAM (OB)
HUGHES, Armistead & CHISHAM, Salley d/o John CHISHAM 23 Apr
1800 surety William DAWSON (OB)
HUGHES, Armistead & FLEET, Sarah Ann 8 Dec 1836 surety Charles
DEAN (OB)
HUGHES, Armistead & HICKS, Sarah Frances surety John HICKS 24
Sep 1846 (OB)
HUGHES, Armisted & CHISHAM, Sally; 27 Apr 1800 surety William
DANSON (OB)
HUGHES, Armstead age 60 w farmer POB POR Orange s/o Alex.
HUGHES and Elizabeth MITCHELL & GIBSON, Mary age 39 w

POB Louisa POR Orange d/o _____ GIBSON POM Orange 5 Jun
1879 by E.R. PERRY (OMR)

**HUGHES**, David P. age 26 s carpenter POB POR Orange s/o Armistead
HUGHES and Sarah F. HICKS & **HUGHES**, Elizabeth age 20 s POB
POR Orange d/o Jefferson HUGHES and Mary A. HERNDON POM
Orange 21 Dec 1876 (OMR)

**HUGHES**, Edward B. age 34 w POB POR Orange s/o Nancy HUGHES
carpenter & **MASON**, Susan S. age 32 s POB POR Orange d/o Sanders
MASON 7 Oct 1873 POM Orange by J.W. MCCOWEN (OMR)

**HUGHES**, George H. s/o Pancy WOOD age 24 s carpenter POB POR
Orange & **HERNDON**, Virginia d/o L. and Jane HERNDON age 22 s
POB POR Orange; POM Orange 11 Feb 1858 (OMR) 10 Feb 1858
(OML)

**HUGHES**, George W. & **HARVEY**, Polly 10 Jan 1812 (there is an error
in the original bond that gives the year as 1813) surety James SNOW
(OB)

**HUGHES**, Humphrey L. and **MARSHALL**, Lucy Ann d/o Coleman
MARSHALL who is also surety 3 Dec 1838 (OB)

**HUGHES**, Jefferson & **HERNDON**, Mary A.; POM Orange 17 Mar 1853
(OMR) (OML)

**HUGHES**, Robert & **JONES**, Margaret 26 Oct 1840 surety John
GRASTY (OB) 5 Jan 1841 by R.L. COLEMAN (OMR)

**HUGHES**, Thomas & **DAVIS**, Mary; 8 Jun 1775 (OML)

**HUGHES**, William Jr. & **BLACKWELL**, Ann G. 10 Apr 1822 surety
John HALES (OB)

**HUGHES**, William W. 21 s POB Orange POR Louisa carpenter s/o
Armistead HUGHES and Fanny HICKS & **GIBSON**, Virginia age 19 s
POB POR Orange 29 Apr 1880 POM Orange by E.R. PERRY (OMR)

**HULL**, Peter POC age 30 s coachman POB POR Orange s/o Spencer
HULL and Maria _____ & **BROWN**, Alice POC age 23 s POB Fluvanna
POR Orange d/o Ben BROWN and Anna WEST POM Zion Hill
Church, Orange 26 Dec 1879 by Robert HUGHES (OMR)

**HUMBLE**, William & **OVERTON**, Mary d/o Willis OVERTON 9 Jun
1808 surety Eliphalet JOHNSON (OB)

**HUME**, Benjamin & **TALIAFERRO**, Elizabeth w of Col. William
TALIAFERRO 25 Aug 1801 surety William W. HUME by Frederick
KORBLAR (OB) (OMR)

**HUME**, Charles F. s/o Francis and Lucy HUME age 25 s carpenter POB
POR Orange & **HAYNES**, Sarah N. d/o John and Jane L. BOURNE
age 30 w POB POR Orange; POM Orange 13 Nov 1856 (OMR) 11
Nov 1856 (OML)

**HUME**, Charles W. & **KENNEDY**, Louisa W.S. POM Orange 12 Apr
1853 (OMR) (OML)

**HUME,** David & **DADE,** Frances E. d/o Harriett S. Grymes DADE 21 Feb 1833 surety P.S. FRY (OB) 3 May 1833 by E.G. SHIP (OMR)

**HUME,** Francis & **JONES,** Lucy 23 Jun 1820 surety John RICHARDS (OB)

**HUME,** Francis age 37 w POB Rockingham Co. POR Orange Co s/o John HUME and Nancy JONES carpenter & **DEMPSEY,** Virginia A. age 31 s POB POR Orange d/o Lewis DEMPSEY and Polly MCCLARY 20 May 1869 POM Orange by John C. WILLIS (OMR)

**HUME,** Francis s/o John HUME and Nancy JONES age 34 w miller POB Rockingham POR Orange & **CHEWNING,** Amanda P. d/o P. Wesley CHEWNING age 26 s POB POR Orange; POM Orange 31 Dec 1865 (OMR) 29 Dec 1865 (OML)

**HUME,** Frank & **BATTAILE,** Martha Ann d/o Mary BATTLE; POM Orange 1 Sep 1852 (OMR) 30 Aug 1852 (OML)

**HUME,** Henry S. & **MASON,** Sally 18 Apr 1845 surety Adon C. MORRIS (OB)

**HUME,** James A. & **JOHNSON,** Marietta d/o Richard JOHNSON 11 Dec 1849 surety John SCOTT (OB)

**HUME,** John & **JONES,** Nancy 24 Mar 1823 surety Fielding JONES (OB)

**HUME,** John H. age 22 s farmer POB Rockingham POR Orange s/o Benjamin HUME and Eliza HUME & **KNIGHTON,** Maggie L. age 21 s POB POR Orange d/o William KNIGHTON POM Orange 30 Aug 1877 (OMR)

**HUME,** John M. & **GOODALL,** Harriet J. d/o Isaac GOODALL who is also surety 7 Dec 1826 (OB)

**HUME,** Newton & **STANARD,** Elizabeth Janeiro d/o William H. STANARD 8 Apr 1831 surety Jennings MAUPIN (OB)

**HUME,** Paul POC age 29 s POB POR Orange s/o Enoch HUME and Rebecca _____ farm laborer & **PORTER,** Nellie POC age 25 s POB Greenbrier POR Orange d/o George BECKHAM and Evelina BECKHAM 29 Dec 1869 POM Orange by Philip JOHNSON (OMR)

**HUMES,** Francis & **PAIN,** Elizabeth d/o Reubin PAIN 30 Jan 1801 surety William FOSTER (OB)

**HUMES,** James & **DODD,** Margaret d/o James DODD 30 Dec 1812 surety Henry DODD (OB) 31 Dec 1812 by Jeremiah CHANDLER (OM)

**HUMPHREYS,** John B. & **CHILD,** Susan Jane d/o Isabella CHILDS 17 Dec 1838 surety Thomas J. HUMPHREYS (OB)

**HUMPHRIES,** William & **WEBB,** Susannah 26 Nov 1774 both of St. Thomas Parish by banns (Deed Book 17)

**HUNDLEY,** John & **LOYD,** Nancy 12 Jul 1794 surety Nehemiah HUNDLEY (OB)

HUNDLEY, Joshua & GRESSOM, Betsey 9 Feb 1798 surety James
HUNDLEY (OB)

HUNDLEY, Nehemiah & CAVE, Elizabeth permission from Benjamin
CAVE 4 Aug 1790 surety Coalby SMITH (OB)

HUNLEY, James & CHILES, Susannah 23 Jan 1797 surety Benjamin
CAVE (OM)

HUNLEY, Wyatt & LLOYD, Sarah 22 Oct 1839 (OB)

HUNT, James & DARNELL, Susanna 26 Aug 1802 by Hamilton GOSS
(Misc Min Ret)

HUNTER, Pleasant & HARRIS, Jane d/o Lindsay HARRIS who is surety
25 Nov 1799 (OB)

HUNTER, Stephen POC age 21 s POB Louisa Co. POR Orange s/o Isaac
HUNTER and Ellen _____ laborer & PAYNE, Anna POC age 18
POB POR Orange d/o William PAYNE and Georgianna WILLIAMS
16 Apr 1870 POM Orange by Philip JOHNSON (OMR)

HURLOCK, J.H. age 28 s farmer POB Berks Co., PA POR Orange s/o
William J. HURLOCK and Mary Ann HAWK & MORRIS, Laura V.
age 21 s POB POR Orange d/o Thomas MORRIS and Hannah
WATSON POM Orange 19 Dec 1878 by John C. WILLIS (OMR)

HUSBANDS, W.A.C. s/o James HUSBANDS and Rebecca LEWIS age 22
s physician POB Charlston, SC POR Dallas Co, Alabama &
MALLORY, Columbia d/o Ichabod MALLORY and Mary
KENNEDY age 16 s POB POR Orange; POM Orange C.H. 7 Jan 1864
(OMR) 6 Jan 1864 (OML)

HUTCHEN, William & ROBINSON, Siler d/o John ROBINSON 23 Mar
1795 surety William ROBINSON (OB)

HUTCHERSON, Washington & LANCASTER, Elizabeth 12 Dec 1816
surety Thomas LANCASTER (OB)

HUTCHESON, Charles POC age 26 s cabinet maker POB Amherst POR
Orange s/o Adeline HUTCHESON & BURRUSS, Fannie POC age 21
s POB Greene POR Orange d/o Thomas BURRUSS and Elizabeth ___
POM Gordonsville 13 Jul 1876 (OMR)

HUTCHISON, Robert L. age 31 s POB Fauquier POR Orange s/o
William HUTCHISON and Martha L. BRONOUGH farmer &
ATKINS, Helen G. age 20 s POB POR Orange d/o William G.
ATKINS and Elizabeth NEWMAN 29 Nov 1871 POM Orange by
James L. FISHER (OMR)

HYER, Henry s/o Henry and Catherine HYER age 23 s gunsmith POB
Richmond POR Petersburg & LIPSCOMB, Martha F. d/o Fitzhugh
and Martha LIPSCOMB age 17 s POB POR Orange C.H.; POM
Orange 5 Aug 1856 (OMR) 4 Aug 1856 (OML)

HYTE, Jacob & BEALE, Frances 15 Dec 1760 both of St. Thomas Parish
(Orange Fee Book)

**INSKEEP,** John A. age 54 w farmer POB POR Culpeper s/o Joel
INSKEEP and Mary E. BENTLEY & **BOSWELL,** Sarah E. age 35 s
POB Madison POR Orange d/o William J. BOSWELL and Martha M.
TALIAFERRO (?) POM Orange 21 May 1878 by H.M. HOPE (OMR)

**ISAAC,** George & **SPENCER,** Caroline married between May 14-17 and
between the years 1771-1774) (OM)

**JACKSON,** Allen POC age 23 s POB POR Orange s/o Andrew
JACKSON and Sally WHITE laborer & **TARRY,** Lila POC age 19 s
POB Madison Co POR Orange d/o Fountain TARRY and Mary
JACKSON 6 Jan 1872 POM Orange by Frank TIBBS (OMR)

**JACKSON,** Andrew POC age 21 s labourer POB Madison POR Orange &
**GALLERY,** Fanny age 19 s POB POR Orange d/o George GALLERY
and Sallie BARKS POM Orange 25 Dec 1877 (OMR)

**JACKSON,** Andrew POC age 26 s POB Fauquier Co POR Albemarle Co.
s/o Thomas JACKSON and Ailsy WAINGER brick moulder &
**DOUGLASS,** Sallie POC age 25 s POB Albemarle Co POR Orange 15
Nov 1871 POM Orange by H.E. HATCHER (OMR)

**JACKSON,** Charles s/o Andrew JACKSON age 23 s farm laborer POB
POR Orange POC & **PORTER,** Alice d/o Allen LONG age 17 s POB
POR Orange POC; POM Orange 9 Nov 1867 (OMR) 4 Nov 1867
(OML)

**JACKSON,** Daniel POC age 21 s POB Louisa Co POR Orange s/o David
JACKSON and Judy TAYLOR farm laborer & **BELL,** Harriet POC
age 20 s POB POR Orange d/o Jeffrey BELL and Nancy DADE 5 Apr
1874 POM Orange (OMR)

**JACKSON,** Edward POC age 28 s POB Louisa CO POR Orange s/o
Lewis JACKSON and Peggy _____ laborer & **PATTERSON,** Nancy
POC age 21 s POB Nelson Co POR Orange 30 Dec 1868 POM Orange
by H. BLAIR (OMR)

**JACKSON,** Frank POC age 63 s farmer POB POR Orange s/o Randal
JACKSON and Patsy or Betsy _____ & **FREEMAN,** Emily POC age
45 w POB Louisa POR Orange POM Orange 12 Dec 1878 by Willis
ROBINSON (OMR)

**JACKSON,** George POC age 22 s labourer POB Greene POR Orange s/o
Mary JACKSON & **BROWN,** Bettie POC age 21 s POB Augusta POR
Orange d/o Jake BROWN and Jinny CARTER POM Orange 29 Dec
1879 by F. TIBBS (OMR)

**JACKSON,** George POC age 44 s POB POR Orange s/o Thomas
JACKSON and Mary MANSER laborer & **JACKSON,** Ellen POC age
44 s POB Louisa Co POR Orange d/o Lucy JACKSON 22 Apr 1873
POM Gordonsville by J.W. MCCOWEN (OMR)

**JACKSON,** Henry POC age 21 s laborer POB POR Orange s/o Thomas
JACKSON and Matilda POINDEXTER & **SMITH,** Tabby age 16 s

POB POR Orange d/o Albert SMITH POM Shady Grove Orange 30
Sep 1876 by C.T. JOHNSON (OMR)

**JACKSON,** Henry POC age 22 s labourer POB Hanover POR Orange s/o
John MINOR and Louisa COLE & **MINOR,** Hannah POC age 21 s
POB Hanover POR Orange d/o Watson MINOR and Jane ___ POM
Orange 19 Dec 1877 (OMR)

**JACKSON,** Henry POC age 22 s labourer POB Louisa POR Orange s/o
Patrick JACKSON and Milly MILLS & **ELLIS,** Mary POC age 20 s
POB POR Orange d/o William ELLIS and Lucinda MANSFIELD
POM Shady Grove Church, Orange 27 Dec 1879 by C. T. JOHNSON
(OMR)

**JACKSON**, Henry POC age 22 s POB POR Orange s/o Gabriel
JACKSON and Rachel GREEN farmer & **KINNEY**, Massey POC age
21 s POB Augusta POR Orange d/o Marshall KINNEY and Eliza
_____ 7 Aug 1873 POM Orange by F.L. GIPSON (OMR)

**JACKSON**, Horace POC age 21 s POB POR Orange s/o Andrew
JACKSON and Sally GOLDING laborer & **TAYLOR**, Virginia POC
age 18 s POB Green POR Orange 27 Sep 1873 POM Orange by Frank
TIBBS (OMR)

**JACKSON**, Jacob POC age 22 s laborer POB Louisa POR Orange s/o
Patrick JACKSON and Milly ANDERSON & **WILLIS**, Milly POC age
17 s POB Louisa POR Orange d/o Thornton WILLIS and Maria BIBB
POM Orange 26 Dec 1876 (OMR)

**JACKSON,** James POC age 21 s labourer POB POR Orange s/o Robert
JACKSON and Ester GRAVES & **HENDERSON,** Hannah POC age
21 s POB POR Orange d/o Doc HENDERSON and Lucy MAY POM
Mt. Pleasant Church, Orange 22 Jun 1878 by C.T. JOHNSON (OMR)

**JACKSON**, James POC age 21 s POB POR Orange s/o Lewis JACKSON
and Mary _____ farm laborer & **GAINES**, Clara POC age 20 s POB
Madison Co POR Orange d/o Albert GAINES and Charlotte _____ 27
Jan 1870 POM Orange by Philip JOHNSON (OMR)

**JACKSON,** John & **HERNDON,** Mary (Polly) d/o Edward HERNDON
and Mary Ann GAINES by George BINGHAM 19 Jan 1809 (OM)

**JACKSON**, John age 28 s in U.S. government service, Gordonsville POB
POR Orange POC & **WALKER**, Mary age 30 w POB Albemarle Co
POR Orange POC; POM Orange 25 Dec 1867 (OMR) (OML)

**JACKSON**, John H. age 27 s POB Orange POR Madison s/o James
JACKSON and Pamelia HARRISON farmer & **BROOKING**, Jane M.
age 19 s POB POR Orange d/o Robert W. BROOKING and C.A.
WILLHOIT 3 Mar 1868 POM Orange by W.S. BRIGGS (OMR)

**JACKSON,** John M. & **DANIEL,** Nancy R. surety Landon LINDSAY 17
Dec 1823 (OB)

**JACKSON**, John POC age 25 w rail road hand s/o Mat. POINDEXTER and Lizzie ___ & **LEACH**, Anna POC age 21 s POB POR Orange POM Orange 17 Apr 1876 (OMR)

**JACKSON**, Joseph POC age 23 s farm labourer POB POR Orange s/o Andrew JACKSON and Sally WHITE & **JOHNSON**, Irma POC age 18 s POB POR Orange d/o Reuben JOHNSON and Rachel WHITE POM Orange 6 May 1877 (OMR)

**JACKSON**, Lewis POC age 26 w POB POR Orange s/o Andrew JACKSON and Sarah ____ butler & **OWENS**, Fanny POC age 28 s POB POR Orange d/o Lewis OWENS and Matilda _____ 31 Jul 1869 POM Orange by Frank TIBBS (OMR)

**JACKSON**, Lewis POC age 26 w POB POR Orange s/o Andrew JACKSON and Sarah WILLIAMS laborer & **PATRICK**, Caroline POC age 23 s POB POR Orange d/o Henry PATRICK and Tabby PATRICK 14 Jan 1872 POM Orange by Frank TIBBS (OMR)

**JACKSON**, Major POC age 21 s farm laborer POB POR Orange s/o Monroe JACKSON and Judy GREEN & **JACKSON**, Barbara POC age 22 s POB POR Orange d/o Monroe JACKSON and Courtnay THORN POM Orange 20 Aug 1877 (OMR)

**JACKSON**, Marshall M. age 28 s bricklayer POB POR Louisa Co POC & **WILLIAMS**, Hardenia age 18 s POB POR Orange POC; POM Orange 20 Dec 1866 (OMR) 17 Dec 1866 (OML)

**JACKSON**, Moses POC age 22 s labourer POB Culpeper POR Orange s/o Frank JACKSON and Rebecca HILL & **GOODALL**, Laura POC age 21 s POB POR Orange d/o George GOODALL and Jane GRYMES POM Orange 30 Jan 1879 by Joseph A. MANSFIELD (OMR)

**JACKSON**, Oscar s/o John JACKSON and Gabriella TAYLOR age 19 s laborer on farm POB POR Orange POC & **MILLS**, Alice d/o Edgar and Lucilla MILLS age 18 s POB Louisa Co POR Orange POC; POM Orange 18 May 1867 (OMR) (OML)

**JACKSON**, Polk POC age 27 s POB POR Orange s/o Thomas JACKSON and Mary MENSER farm laborer & **ARMISTEAD**, Ellen POC age 16 s POB POR Orange d/o Hilliard ARMISTEAD and Kitty MCDANIEL 26 Dec 1873 POM orange by F.L. GIPSON (OMR)

**JACKSON**, Tandy & **MILLS**, Sarah d/o Nathaniel MILLS Sr. surety Reubin LINDSAY 27 Mar 1809 (OB)

**JACKSON**, Thomas POC age 20 s POB POR Orange s/o Henry JACKSON and Martha PORTER laborer & **JACKSON**, Mary POC age 19 s POB POR Orange d/o Monroe JACKSON and C. THOMS 26 Jul 1868 POM Orange by Robert C. CAVE (OMR)

**JACKSON**, Thomas POC age 21 s farm laborer POB Greene POR Orange s/o Ham JACKSON and Sarah TERRILL & **HUGHES**, Mary age 20 s

POB POR Orange d/o Caleb HUGHES and Sally BURRUSS POM
Orange 6 Sep 1876 (OMR)

JACKSON, William & **MILLER,** Ann; 20 Dec 1824 surety Thomas
MITCHELL (OB) by Jeremiah CHANDLER 24 Dec 1824 (OM)

JACKSON, William E. & **GENTRY,** Susan Jane surety George A.
GENTRY 18 Dec 1830 (OB)

JACKSON, William s/o John JACKSON and Malinda WILLIS age 22 s
laborer POB POR Orange POC & **LEE,** Alice d/o Jeny LEE and Maria
STATELY age 15 s POB POR Orange POC; POM Orange C.H.1 Dec
1866 (OMR) (OML)

JACKSON, Wilson POC age 22 s labourer POB POR Orange s/o Wilson
JACKSON and Harriet BROWN & **ELLIS,** Bettie POC age 21 s POB
POR Orange d/o Sam ELLIS and Charlotte LINDSAY POM Mt.
Calvery Church, Orange 9 Jun 1878 by W.H. CAMPER (OMR)

JACOB, William & **MARTIN,** Polly d/o Henry MARTIN 21 Aug 1802
surety Benjamin JACOBS (OB) 24 Aug 1802 by Nathaniel SANDERS
(OM)

JACOBS, Benjamin & **FAULCONER,** Ann d/o John FAULCONER
surety William FAULCONER 10 Jan 1818 (OB) by J.C. GORDON 13
Jan 1818 (OM)

JACOBS, Benjamin & **MARTIN,** Sarah d/o Henry MARTIN surety
Matthew BRIDGES 30 Dec 1799 (OB) 2 Jan 1800 by Nathaniel
SANDERS (OM)

JACOBS, Daniel & **DEMPSEY,** Almira d/o Thomas A. DEMPSEY
surety John J. HANEY 21 Dec 1846 (OB)

JACOBS, George s/o Benjamin JACOBS & **SMITH,** Catharine d/o
George SMITH surety Hugh M. FAULCONER 10 Feb 1824 (OB)

JACOBS, James & **HOWARD,** Matilda d/o Washington HOWARD who
is also surety 17 Apr 1834 (OB)

JACOBS, James M. & **FINNELL,** Lucy surety John MORRIS 25 Dec
1837 (OB)

JACOBS, Joel b.d. 31 Mar 1795 s/o Thomas JACOBS of Madison Co.,
KY & **TAYLOR,** Mary d/o James TAYLOR surety Thomas COLLINS
12 Feb 1818 (OB)

JACOBS, Nathan & **STRAGHAN,** Nancy (born 14 May 1783) surety
Albin ELLIOTT by Nathaniel SANDERS 19 Dec 1806 (OB) (OM)

JACOBS, Richard F. s/o James M. JACOBS and Lucy MORRIS age 20 s
miller POB POR Orange & **FAULCONER,** Susan J. d/o William
FAULCONER and Elizabeth JACOBS age 25 s POB POR Orange;
POM Orange 24 Dec 1867 (OMR) 23 Dec 1867 (OML)

JACOBS, Solomon & **FAULCONER,** Margaret ward of George
FAULCONER; 3 Oct 1854 (permission certificate, Orange)

**JACOBS**, William & **MARTIN**, Polly 24 Aug 1803 by Nath. SANDERS (Misc Min Ret)

**JACOBS**, William & **WRIGHT**, Sarah permission from Thomas WRIGHT who is also surety 15 Dec 1836 (OB)

**JACOBS**, William P. & **HANEY**, Emily d/o Jacob HANEY who is also surety 29 Nov 1842 (OB)

**JACOBS**, William s/o George and Catherine JACOBS age 26 s farmer POB POR Orange & **RICHARDSON**, Sarah F. d/o Josiah and Sarah RICHARDSON age 28 s POB POR Orange; POM Orange 6 Jul 1856 (OMR) 5 Jul 1856 (OML)

**JACOBS**, Absalom E. s/o Nathaniel & Nancy H. JACOBS age 20 s blacksmith POB POR Orange & **FAULCONER**, Margaret Elizabeth d/o William and Elizabeth FAULCONER age 20 s POB POR Orange; POM Orange 5 Oct 1854 (OMR)

**JAMAR**, Richard & **ADAMS**, Betsy POR Orange 16 Dec 1811 Thomas ADAMS surety (OB)

**JAMES**, Daniel & **DAVIS**, Lucy 5 Apr 1773 (Orange Fee Book)

**JAMES**, Daniel POR St. Mark's Parish & **DAVIS**, Lucy POB Culpeper (now of St. Thomas Parish) 6 Apr 1773 (Deed Book 17)

**JAMES**, Richard & **ADAMS**, Betsey surety Thomas ADAMS by Jeremiah CHANDLER 16 Dec 1811 (OB)

**JAMES**, Spencer & **DAVIS**, Frances surety Philomen DAVIS 21 Aug 1780 both of St. Thomas Parish (OB)

**JAMESON**, Joseph & **ROGERS**, Maria N. d/o Joseph ROGERS surety John R. NEWMAN 3 Jan 1843 (OB)

**JAMESON**, Thomas R. & **SAMUEL**, Polly s surety Henry SAMUEL 12 Dec 1792 (OB)

**JAMESON**, William & **MAUPIN**, Rebecca by George BINGHAM 22 Sep 1814 (OM)

**JARRALD**, Jeremiah & **SIMS**, Lucretia surety James JARRALD 30 Sep 1816 (OB) 2 Oct 1816 by George BINGHAM (OM)

**JARRELL**, Adam & **MILLER**, Adiliza surety Jesse MILLER 14 Dec 1843 (OB)

**JARRELL**, Anderson & **RAINES**, Polly surety John DOLSON 23 Dec 1834 (OB)

**JARRELL**, Elisha & **BRADLEY**, Nancy permission from George BRADLEY surety Samuel SMITH 19 Dec 1797 (OB) by Hamilton GOSS 21 Dec 1797 (OM)

**JARRELL**, James & **SIMS**, Frances surety Zachariah TAYLOR 23 May 1793 (OB) 13 Jun 1793 by George EVE (OM)

**JARRELL**, James & **TAYLOR**, Sarah by George BINGHAM 14 Mar 1797 (OM)

**JARRELL,** James & **YOWELL,** Mary D. surety James P. SIMS 4 Nov 1837 (OB)

**JARRELL,** Jefferson & **SIMS,** Nancy surety James SIMS 4 Nov 1837 (OB)

**JARRELL,** Joseph & **SIMS,** Olivia d/o John and Eliz. R. SIMS surety William H. SIMS 12 Dec 1829 (OB)

**JARRELL,** Reuben & **STOWERS,** Nancy surety Rice DARNELL 25 Dec 1826 (OB)

**JARRELL,** William (Jr) & **CAMPBELL,** Jane A. surety Joseph ATKINS 20 Apr 1842 (OB) by J. EARNEST 21 Apr 1842 (OM)

**JARRELL,** Zachariah & **SIMS,** Fanny d/o William and Nancy SIMS surety Sanders WALKER 24 Nov 1797 (OB)

**JENKINS,** David & **DARNELL,** Elizabeth surety Rice DARNELL 19 Apr 1821 (OB)

**JENKINS,** John & **TERRY,** Sarah surety Reubin OAKES 26 Nov 1810 (OB)

**JENKINS,** Quire & **HAWKINS,** Lucy surety Alfred BATTAILE 1 Aug 1812 (OB)

**JENKINS,** Thomas & **TAYLOR,** Elizabeth G. surety Charles TAYLOR 14 Jan 1800 (OB)

**JENKINS,** William S. & **PETTIS,** Sally d/o John PETTESS surety Edmund B. PETTYS 19 Dec 1808 (OB)

**JENKINS,** William T. & **ELLIS,** Mary Ann d/o Hezekiah ELLIS surety Garland B. TAYLOR 8 Oct 1828 (OB)

**JENNINGS,** James J. age 26 s farmer POB Culpeper POR Orange s/o R.S. JENNINGS and Susan SMITH & **WRENN,** Ella J. age 20 s POB Culpeper POR Orange d/o Philip M. WRENN and Elizabeth BRAMMER POM Orange 30 Oct 1877 (OMR)

**JENNINGS,** John & **WILLIS,** Mary E. surety Augustine WILLIS 9 Dec 1817 (OB)

**JENNINGS,** William C. & **SHEARMAN,** Alice permission by George SHEARMAN surety John H. SHEARMAN 23 Dec 1825 (OB)

**JERDONE,** John age 37 s farmer POB New Kent Co. POR Orange s/o Francis JERDONE and Eliza M. WATKINS & **ROBINSON,** Lillie E. age 23 s POB POR Orange d/o John H. ROBINSON and Tabitha E. CLARK POM Orange 15 Nov 1876 by Charles QUARLES (OMR)

**JOHNS,** James F. s/o Mason JOHNS ( who is also surety) & **MUNDAY,** Mildred d/o Burroughs MUNDAY ( who is also surety) 24 Nov 1845 (OB)

**JOHNS,** William C. age 20 s POB Orange POR Albemarle Co s/o Jamese F. JOHNS and Mildred J. MUNDAY farmer & **MITCHELL,** Nancy Ann age 18 s POB Greene Co POR Orange d/o I.N. MITCHELL and

Nancy POINDEXTER 6 Sep 1868 POM Orange by R.L. COLEMAN (OMR)

**JOHNSON**, Abner age 23 s POB POR Orange s/o _____ JOHNSON and Sallie MINGER laborer & **GREEN**, Pelina age 18 s POB POR Orange d/o Anderson GREEN and Susan HENDERSON 10 Apr 1870 POM Orange by Thomas R. HAWKINS (OMR)

**JOHNSON**, Abram POC age 48 w POB Greene Co POR Orange s/o Jesse ___ & Peggy ___ farm laborer & **BROOKS**, Sarah POC age 56 w POB Spotsylvania POR Orange 26 Dec 1873 POM Orange by F.L. GIPSON (OMR)

**JOHNSON,** Allen POC age 24 s farm labourer POB POR Orange s/o Ira JOHNSON and Malvina JOHNSON & **WORMLEY,** Sallie POC age 22 s POB POR Orange d/o Reuben WORMLEY and Resin SHELLY POM Orange 22 Jul 1877 (OMR)

**JOHNSON,** Charles POC age 21 s farm labourer POB POR Orange s/o Mildred Ann JOHNSON & **MCINTOSH,** Ann POC age 17 s POB POR Orange d/o William MCINTOSH and Martha YOUNG POM Orange 13 Nov 1879 by Philip JOHNSON (OMR)

**JOHNSON,** Colin & **ELLIS,** Mary Ann surety Thomas J. ELLIS 20 Dec 1824 (OB)

**JOHNSON,** Edward R. & **HANEY,** Ann T. d/o James HANEY surety John L. WEBB 24 Dec 1838 (OB)

**JOHNSON,** Frank age 21 s POB POR Orange laborer & **DADE,** Alice age 18 POB POR Orange d/o Jack DADE and Amy DADE 26 Apr 1868 POM Orange by R.D. HERNDON (OMR)

**JOHNSON,** Frank age 28 s POB Orange POR Madison Co. s/o Reuben HACKETT and Lucy JOHNSON ditcher & **GREEN,** Mary age 16 s POB Madison Co. POR Orange d/o Willis GREEN and Martha A. TWYMAN 3 Apr 1870 POM Orange by H.E. HATCHER (OMR)

**JOHNSON,** Frank s/o Aaron JOHNSON and Lilly HOMES age 28 w farm laborer POB POR Orange POC & **MASON,** Cally age 21 s POB Madison Co POR Orange POC POM Gordonsville, Orange 27 Dec 1866 (OMR) 24 Dec 1866 (OML)

**JOHNSON,** Frank[lin] POC age 26 w POB POR Orange s/o Charlotte TOWNS laborer on farm & **KELTSER,** Eliza [POC] age 29 w POB Spotsylvania Co POR Orange d/o John MORRIS and Rachel _____ 14 Jul 1872 POM Orange by E.R. PERRY (OMR)

**JOHNSON,** Frederick POC age 22 s POB Louisa Co POR Orange s/o William JOHNSON and Mildred WATSON laborer on farm & **GWATHMEY,** Robinette POC age 18 s POB POR Orange d/o William GWATHMEY and Seamia THORNTON 23 Jun 1872 POM Orange by F.L. GIPSON (OMR)

**JOHNSON**, George POB POR Orange s/o Solomon JOHNSON and Sarah JOHNSON waiter & **STANARD**, Mary E. age 24 POB Greene Co. POR Orange d/o Adam STANARD and Cassie STANARD 27 Oct 1870 by J.W. MCCOWN (OM)

**JOHNSON,** Horace POC age 22 s POB Culpeper POR Orange labourer s/o Baylor JOHNSON and Charlotte WHITE & **WASHINGTON,** Mary Ann age 20 s POB Spotsylvania POR Orange d/o James WASHINGTON and Edith WALLER POM Orange 20 Oct 1877 (OMR)

**JOHNSON**, Isaac Jr. & **TERRILL,** Elizabeth surety Archibald TERRILL 5 Jun 1795 (OM)

**JOHNSON**, Isaac L. s/o George T. JOHNSON and Zalinda L. JOHNSON age 47 w house painter POB POR Lynchburg & **GRAVATT**, Mary T. d/o Oliver TERRILL and Susan PROCTOR age 30 w POB POR Orange; POM Orange 19 Jun 1867 (OMR) 18 Jun 1867 (OML)

**JOHNSON**, James POC age 31 s farmer s/o Lewis JOHNSON and Mary GREEN & **JOHNSON**, Harriet POC age 21 s POB POR Orange d/o Stephen JOHNSON and Ann E. _____ 1 Jan 1876 POM Orange (OMR)

**JOHNSON,** James & **QUISENBERRY,** Nancy d/o Mary QUISENBERRY surety Spencer ATKINS 21 May 1807 (OB) by Robert JONES 22 May 1807 (OM)

**JOHNSON**, James B. s/o Belfield and Eliza JOHNSON age 24 s merchant POB Barboursville POR Culpeper C.H. & **MARSHALL**, Sarah Cordelia d/o James MARSHALL age 18 s POB Orange C.H. POR Barboursville; POM Orange 9 Jun 1858 (OMR) 4 Jun 1858 (OML)

**JOHNSON**, James S. s/o Richard JOHNSON and Priscilla JONES age 35 s farmer POB POR Orange & **CHEWNING**, Anna S. d/o Pereguine W. CHEWNING and Ellen A. HOPKINS age 21 s POB Spotsylvania POR Orange; POM Orange 24 Oct 1867 (OMR) 21 Oct 1867 (OML)

**JOHNSON**, James s/o Carter JOHNSON and Charlotte A. CHARITY age 32 w laborer on farm POB POR Orange POC & **GRAVES**, Lucinda d/o Dick and Dinah RICHARDS age 31 w POB POR Orange POC; POM Orange 18 Aug 1867 (OMR) 14 Aug 1867 (OML)

**JOHNSON**, John B. & **RICHARDS,** Nancy surety John W. RICHARDS 16 Nov 1825 (OB)

**JOHNSON,** John P. A. & **ESTES,** Sarah R. d/o Thomas ESTES surety William ESTES 19 Dec 1846 (OB)

**JOHNSON,** John POC age 21 s farm laborer POB POR Orange s/o Albert STROTHER and Matilda TAYLOR & **HERNDON,** Linnia POC age 21 s POB Albemarle POR Orange d/o John D. HERNDON POM Gordonsville 18 Apr 1877 (OMR)

**JOHNSON**, John T. s/o Richard and P.U. JOHNSON age 25 s POB POR Orange & **JOHNSON**, Mary d/o John B. JOHNSON age 22 s POB POR Orange; POM Orange 26 Dec 1854 (OMR)

**JOHNSON**, Jones POC age 21 s farm laborer POB POR Orange s/o Isaac JOHNSON and Ann TESC & **BELL**, Hannah POC age 18 s POB POR Orange d/o Jeff BELL and Nancy ___ POM Mt. Pleasant, Orange 18 Mar 1876 (OMR)

**JOHNSON**, Joseph & **HANEY**, Buly E. d/o James HANEY surety Edward R. JOHNSON 21 Dec 1840 (OB)

**JOHNSON**, Joseph age 21 s POB POR Orange s/o Amos JOHNSON and Aggie ___ farm laborer & **CHELTON**, Dolly Ann age 21 POB POR Orange d/o Robert CHILTON and Sally ___ 18 Nov 1871 POM Orange by Daniel BROWN (OMR)

**JOHNSON**, Joseph Bain & **SHROPSHIRE**, Elizabeth both of St. Thomas Parish 31 Jan 1773 (Deed Book 17)

**JOHNSON**, Joseph POC age 21 s labourer POB POR Orange s/o Davy JOHNSON and Ginnie WILLIAMS & **HENDERSON**, Eliza POC age 21 s POB POR Orange d/o Samuel and Betsy HENDERSON POM Hopewell Baptist Church, Orange 8 Sep 1878 by Willis ROBINSON (OMR)

**JOHNSON**, Joseph W. & **BLEDSOE**, Lucy H. JONES surety William S. BLEDSOE 23 Dec 1850 (OB)

**JOHNSON**, Lewis POC age 40 w POB POR Orange laborer & **JOHNSON**, Frimendzas age 38 s POB POR Orange d/o Lewis JOHNSON and Betty RAWLS 28 May 1868 POM Orange by John H. ROBERTSON (OMR)

**JOHNSON**, Peter POC age 27 s labourer POB Louisa POR Orange s/o Edmund JOHNSON and Clara ___ & **GRAVES**, Susan POC age 22 s POB POR Orange d/o Peter GRAVES POM Hopewell Church, Orange 8 Aug 1878 by W.H. CAMPER (OMR)

**JOHNSON**, Peter R. & **ALCOCK**, Patsy surety Robert H. ROSE 9 Jan 1818 (OB) by William G. HITER 11 Jan 1818 (OM)

**JOHNSON**, Peter T. physician & **CLARK**, Nancy; POM Orange 24 Mar 1853 (OMR) 22 Mar 1853 (OML)

**JOHNSON**, Peyton POC age 24 s labourer POB POR Orange s/o Ellen POWELL & **SPENCER**, Fanny POC age 24 s POB POR Orange William and Laura SPENCER POM Orange 29 Oct 1879 (OMR)

**JOHNSON**, Philip POC age 23 s labourer POB POR Orange s/o Joe JOHNSON & **PRESLEY**, Susan POC age 21 s POB POR Orange d/o George and Emily PRESLEY POM Shady Grove Church, Orange 28 Dec 1878 by C.T. JOHNSON (OMR)

**JOHNSON**, Philip s/o William JOHNSON and Milly GREEN age 21 s ditcher POB POR Orange POC & **MADISON**, Ellen age 22 s POB

POR Orange POC; POM Orange 26 Dec 1867 (OMR) 24 Dec 1867 (OML)

**JOHNSON**, Randall age 24 farm laborer POB POR Orange POC & **McINTOSH**, Alvia d/o Gus MCINTOSH and Lucinda HENDERSON age 17 s POB POR Orange POC; POM Orange 29 Dec 1867 (OMR) 23 Dec 1867 (OML)

**JOHNSON**, Richard & **ALCOCKE**, Lucy surety Joseph ALCOCKE 1 Feb 1809 (OB)

**JOHNSON**, Richard & **JONES**, Priscilla d/o James JONES surety Eliphalet JOHNSON 20 Jan 1829 (OB)

**JOHNSON**, Richard POC age 24 s labourer POB Nelson POR Orange s/o Isaac and Lucinda JOHNSON & **MARSHALL**, Henrietta POC age 23 s POB Louisa POR Orange d/o Frank MARSHALL and Milly CARTER POM Orange 24 Apr 1878 by Willis ROBINSON (OMR)

**JOHNSON**, Robert POC age 21 s POB Spotsylvania POR Orange laborer s/o Reuben JOHNSON and Lucy CRUMP & **BURKES**, Ella age 21 s POB POR Orange d/o James BURKES and Mary _____ 3 Jan 1880 POM Orange by D.T. CONOWAY (OMR)

**JOHNSON**, Samuel POC age 24 s POB POR Orange s/o Richard JOHNSON and Viney GREEN cook & **DAY**, Alice POC age 21 s POB POR Orange d/o Adam DADE and Maria TALIAFERRO 22 May 1880 POM Orange (OMR)

**JOHNSON**, Stephen POC age 24 s POB POR Orange laborer s/o Joseph JOHNSON and Jeanetta WILLIS & **DADE**, Mary POC 22 s POB POR Orange d/o Benjamin DADE and Sally BURDINE 15 Sep 1880 POM Nazareth Baptist Church, Orange by William ROBINSON (OMR)

**JOHNSON**, Thomas & **FINNELL**, Jane 24 Dec 1840 surety John F. MORRIS (OB)

**JOHNSON**, Thomas & **RICHARDS**, Diannah d/o William RICHARDS surety Philomen RICHARDS 31 Jan 1797 (OM)

**JOHNSON**, Thomas H. & **MASON**, Julie surety William S. FRASER 28 Sep 1840 (OB)

**JOHNSON**, Thomas POC age 36 s farm laborer POB Hanover POR Orange s/o Major JOHNSON and Charlotte COLEMAN & **GOLDING**, Mary POC age 37 w POB Greene POR Orange d/o Kitty _____ POM Orange 3 Jun 1876 by Willis ROBINSON (OMR)

**JOHNSON**, Thomas s/o Jacob JOHNSON and Nancy JARRELL age 66 w farmer POB POR Spotsylvania & **MARTIN**, Julia d/o William MARTIN and Malinda FAULCONER age 23 s POB POR Orange; POM Orange 4 Apr 1865 (OMR) 3 Apr 1865 (OML)

**JOHNSON**, Valentine & **BENNETT**, Nancy; 31 Jan 1791 surety Howard BENNETT (OB) by George EVE 7 Feb 1791 (OM)

**JOHNSON,** Valentine (Captain) & **CAVE,** Elizabeth d/o Belfield CAVE surety Richard CAVE 30 Aug 1803 (OB)

**JOHNSON,** William & **BARNETT,** Ann 10 Feb 1770 both of St. Thomas Parish (Orange Fee Book)

**JOHNSON,** William & **FITZHUGH,** Ann surety Henry FITZHUGH 22 Sep 1802 (OB)

**JOHNSON,** William G. & **DAVENPORT,** Evelina B. surety Peter T. JOHNSON 23 Oct 1849 (OB) by J. EARNEST 24 Oct 1849 (OM)

**JOHNSON,** William H. s/o Thomas JOHNSON who is also surety & **WEBB,** Susan d/o Benjamin H. WEBB 12 Feb 1845 (OB)

**JOHNSON,** William Henry POC age 35 w blacksmith POB Washington Co., NC POR Orange s/o William Henry JOHNSON & **MORETON,** Matilda POC age 30 w POB POR Orange POM Orange 19 Aug 1877 (OMR)

**JOHNSON,** William M. s/o J.P. JOHNSON and Martha FLOYD age 22 s farmer POB Coveta Co, GA POR Whitfield Co, GA & **SOUTHERLAND,** Mary E. d/o Alex SOUTHERLAND and Dinah HOWARD age 21 s POB POR Orange; POM Orange 15 Jan 1863 (OMR) 12 Jan 1863 (OML)

**JOHNSON,** William POC age 24 s POB POR Orange s/o Clara JOHNSON farm laborer & **REDD,** Adelaide POC age 22 s POB POR Orange d/o Henry REDD and Fanny WORMLEY 26 Jun 1880 POM Orange (OMR)

**JOHNSON,** William POC age 27 s rail road hand POB POR Orange s/o Jeffrey JOHNSON and Gillie Ann DAVIS & **WALKER,** Sophia POC age 23 s POB POR Orange d/o James WALKER and Emily GRINNAN POM Orange 25 Dec 1878 (OMR)

**JOHNSON,** William s/o Ben CARTER and Gracie WILLIAMS age 25 s laborer POB POR Orange POC & **TIBBS,** Frances d/o Charles BOWLER and Mary HOOMES age 40 w POB POR Orange POC; POM Orange C.H. 22 Aug 1866 (OMR) (OML)

**JOHNSON,** William s/o Garrick JOHNSON and Mary A. RICHARDSON age 25 s working at sawmill POB Savannah, GA POR Orange POC & **ROBINSON,** Ann d/o Beverley ROBINSON and Harriet TIBBS age 19 s POB POR Orange POC POM Orange 26 Dec 1867 (OMR) 23 Dec 1867 (OML)

**JOHNSON,** William W. & **ANDERSON,** Harriet Ann d/o Joel ANDERSON surety Fountain EDDINS 20 Jul 1835 (OB) by David FISHER 4 Aug 1835 (OM)

**JOHNSON,** Wyatt age 46 s POB Orange POR Spotsylvania Co. s/o Eliphalett JOHNSON and Sarah BRIGHTWELL farmer & **COOPER,** Eliza J. age 32 s POB POR Orange d/o Owen COOPER and Jane M.

HUMPHRIES 10 Dec 1871 POM Orange by Herndon FRAZER (OMR)

**JOHNSTON,** James & **SMITH,** Elizabeth d/o Absalem SMITH who is also surety 18 May 1801 (OB)

**JOLLETT,** Simson permission from James JOLLETT & **GLASS,** Nancy surety Daniel BENT 8 Jul 1822 (OB)

**JONES**, Benjamin & **FOSTER,** Elizabeth; 12 May 1774 by banns both of St. Thomas Parish (Deed Book 17)

**JONES,** Benjamin F. & **CROOKS,** Mary F. d/o Joseph B. CROOKS who is also surety 12 May 1847 (OB)

**JONES,** Benjamin H. & **WHITELAW,** Elizabeth surety Alexander WHITELAW 27 Mar 1815 (OB) 25 Apr 1815 (OM)

**JONES,** Benjamin POC 23 s POB POR Orange farm laborer s/o Lane JONES and Ellen GRYMES & **CLARK,** Harriet POC age 22 s POB POR Orange 30 Dec 1880 POM Orange by Dabney PARKER (OMR)

**JONES,** Benjamin POC age 26 w POB POR Orange s/o Harrison JONES and Susan MCDANIEL laborer & **ARMISTEAD,** Lucy POC age 21 s POB POR Orange d/o Louis ARMISTEAD and Fanny WACKER 30 Aug 1872 POM Orange by J. S. HANSBROUGH (OMR)

**JONES,** Benjamin R. & **BOSTON,** Sarah d/o John BOSTON 16 Aug 1825 (OB)

**JONES,** Burkett & **WRIGHT,** Polly d/o Nancy WRIGHT surety William WRIGHT 17 Mar 1818 (OB)

**JONES**, Charles POC age 21 s POB Madison Co POR Orange s/o Jackson JONES and Rachel GRAVES farm laborer & **CARPENTER**, Ellen POC age 19 POB POR Orange d/o Jo. CARPENTER and Morice THOMPSON 2 May 1874 POM Orange [by Frank TIBBS] (OMR)

**JONES,** Churchill age 24 s farmer POB POR Orange s/o Churchill JONES and Kisie PATSY & **ADAMS,** Bertie H. age 24 s POB POR Orange d/o Thomas J. ADAMS and Martha J. CLARK POM Orange 27 Dec 1877 (OMR)

**JONES,** Douglass G. age 24 s farmer POB POR Orange s/o Nathaniel S. JONES and Mildred A. TINDER & **TINDER,** Nannie J. age 24 s POB POR Orange d/o Thomas R. TINDER and E.J. TINDER POM Orange 29 Nov 1877 (OMR)

**JONES,** Edmund & **SHELAR,** Caty surety John SHELAR Jr. 23 Jun 1823 (OB) by George BINGHAM 3 Jul 1823 (OM)

**JONES,** Fielding POR Spotsylvania & **JOHNSON,** Mary d/o Isaac JOHNSON surety Eliphalet JOHNSON by J.C. GORDON 10 Feb 1817 (OB) (OM)

**JONES**, George S. s/o Benjamin P. and Sarah F. JONES age 23 s farmer POB Madison Co. POR Orange & **TALLEY**, Mary J. d/o Meriwether and Delilah TALLEY age 19 s POB POR Orange; POM Orange 12 Jun 1855 (OMR)

JONES, Gillard age 21 s blacksmith POB Albemarle POR Madison s/o Sam JONES and Margaret NELSON & **WASHINGTON,** Lucy Ann age 17 s POB Madison POR Orange d/o Aaron WASHINGTON 10 Feb 1877 POM Orange (OMR)

JONES, Henry W. age 47 w POB Fluvanna Co POR Orange s/o Cavy JONES and Ann OMOHUNDRO farmer & **BROCKMAN,** Lucy B. age 35 w POB King William Co. POR Orange d/o Parker B. DAVIS and Maria F. KING 23 Aug 1870 POM Orange by Charles QUARLES (OMR)

JONES, Hudson POC age 23 s labourer POB POR Orange s/o Virginia BUCK & **TERRILL,** Cornelia POC age 17 s POB POR Orange Horace TERRILL and Margaret HALL POM Orange 29 Oct 1879 (OMR)

JONES, James & **ROBINSON,** Caty d/o John ROBINSON surety John JONES 7 Sep 1785 (OB)

JONES, James age 25 s POB POR Orange s/o Benj. R. JONES and Sarah F. BOSTON farmer & **GRAVES,** Susan B. age 21 s POB POR Orange d/o William GRAVES 2 Jan 1870 POM Orange by John C. WILLIS (OMR)

JONES, James B. age 26 s farmer POB Louisa POR Albemarle s/o Charles E. JONES and Martha A. SMITH & **SUPTON,** Kate E. age 22 s POB Albemarle POR Orange d/o Daniel N. SUPTON and Sarah E. COCKRILL POM Orange 22 Mar 1876 (OMR)

JONES, James L. s/o John R. JONES & **PORTER,** Martha A. d/o William PORTER surety James W. GOSS 17 Jan 1834 (OB)

JONES, James POC age 22 s POB POR Madison Co. s/o Reuben JONES and Emily ARRINGTON farmer & **ALLEN,** Peachy POC age 22 POB POR Orange d/o John T. ALLEN and Amanda SAMUEL 26 Dec 1872 POM Orange by J.S. HANSBROUGH (OMR)

JONES, James W. & **WEBB,** Martha S. d/o William B. WEBB who is also surety 22 Oct 1844 (OB)

JONES, John & **ABELL,** Margaret w [ possibly Margaret TINDER, widow of John ABEL] surety James JONES 7 Sep 1785 (OB)

JONES, John & **BICKERS,** Susan d/o Joseph BICKERS who is also surety 23 Dec 1811 (OB)

JONES, John & **MASON,** Elizabeth d/o George MASON who is also surety 21 Dec 1818 (OB) J.C. GORDON 26 Dec 1818 (OM)

JONES, John (under 21 years) permission from Thomas JONES of Spotsylvania Co. & **FAULCONER,** Milley d/o Richard FAULCONER of Orange who is also surety 18 Jan 1813 (OB)

**JONES**, John W. s/o Micajah and Susan JONES age 21 s blacksmith POB Madison Co POR Orange & **HEATWELL**, Eliza d/o David and Eliza HEATWELL age 18 s POB Rockingham Co POR Orange; POM Orange 15 Jan 1857 (OMR) 14 Jan 1857 (OML)

**JONES**, Micajah & **WRIGHT**, Susan surety Fielding JONES 24 Nov 1817 (OB) by J.C. GORDON 27 Nov 1817 (OM)

**JONES**, Mosias & **SLAYTOR**, Frances by George BINGHAM 25 Sep 1818 (OM)

**JONES**, Nathaniel S. & **TINDER**, Mildred S. d/o Thomas TINDER who is also surety 19 Dec 1846 (OB)

**JONES**, Reuben & **STOWERS**, Patty s surety Jeremiah BRYANT permission by Mary STOWERS 3 Aug 1789 (OB)

**JONES**, Richard & **LEONARD**, Grace both of St. Thomas Parish 10 Mar 1760 (Orange Fee Book)

**JONES**, Robert minister & **HERNDON**, Mary w surety Hamilton GOSS by Hamilton GOSS 3 Jun 1800 (OB) (OM)

**JONES**, Samuel W. & **LANDRUM**, Sarah S. d/o Daniel LANDRUM who is also surety 30 Jan 1846 (OB)

**JONES**, Silas B. age 24 s hoop pole gatherer POB POR Orange s/o Nathaniel JONES and Mildred TINDER & **TINDER**, Mary E. age 17 s POB POR Orange d/o Thomas R. TINDER and Elizabeth TINDER POM Orange 28 Sep 1876 (OMR)

**JONES**, Stephan POC age 22 s POB Green Co.,VA POR Orange s/o Ambrose JONES and Harriet STANARD farm laborer & **COOPER**, Alberta POC age 21 s POB POR Orange d/o Ezekial COOPER and Betsy COOPER DOM 18 Sep 1869 POM Orange by T.M. CARSON (OMR)

**JONES**, Thad M. age 22 s POB Hanover Co. POR Spotsylvania Co. s/o Eli JONES and Mary E. CHEWNING farmer & **CHEWNING**, Maretta J. age 19 s POB POR Orange d/o William B. CHEWNING and Susan OVERTON DOM 2 Dec 1869 POM Orange by Melzi S. CHANCELLOR (OMR)

**JONES**, Thomas & **OVERTON**, Peggy d/o Willis OVERTON who is also surety 20 Nov 1811 (OB)

**JONES**, Timothy & **WINSLOW**, Susan B. surety Robert M. HIGGINS 11 May 1846 (OB)

**JONES**, Walter & **FREEMAN**, Sally by George BINGHAM 25 Mar 1802 (OM)

**JONES**, Walter free POC & **BROOKS**, Catharine free POC d/o Sarah BROOKS surety Lawrence T.D. FAULCONER 18 Dec 1848 (OB) by J. EARNEST 19 Dec 1848 (OM)

**JONES**, William & **ADAMS**, Catharine surety William CLARK 23 Mar 1830 (OB)

**JONES,** William A. & **LEE** Delilah 11 Jul 1846 surety Lemuel WRIGHT (OB) by Joseph S. JACKSON 15 Jul 1846 (OM)

**JONES,** William Jr. POC age 30 s farmer POB POR Orange s/o Robert JONES and Judy JONES & **BANKS,** Emma POC age 26 s POB POR Orange d/o John BANKS and Winny ___ POM Orange 15 Mar 1877 (OMR)

**JONES,** William L. & **ARNETT,** Jane Ellen d/o William ARNETT who is also surety 25 Nov 1816 (OB)

**JONES,** William R. s/o Michael R. JONES & **WEBB,** Elizabeth d/o Richard B. WEBB who is also surety 1 Oct 1830 (OB)

**JONES,** William W. & **FARISH,** Elizabeth surety Thomas GRAY 29 Oct 1822 (OB)

**JONES,** William W. & **TOWLES,** Frances surety Smith STUBBLEFIELD 8 Dec 1840 (OB)

**JONES,** Zachariah & **DEAN,** Rebecca surety John JONES 15 Nov 1787 (OB)

**JORDON,** John M. & **GENTRY,** Susan A. d/o Sarah GENTRY; POM Orange 30 Jun 1853 (OMR) 27 Jun 1853 (OML)

**JOSEPH,** Jonathan & **DEERING,** Sarah surety Thomas DEERING permission by Robert DEERING Sr. 11 Mar 1786 (OB)

**KEAGAN,** James age 50 w POB Ireland, Almor Co [sic] POR Orange s/o Patrick KEAGAN merchant & **SULLIVAN,** Ann age 35 w POB Ireland [?] Co. POR Orange d/o Patrick CONWAY 25 Sep 1872 POM Orange by John DOHERTY (OMR)

**KEATON,** Horace M. & **JENNINGS,** Lucy surety William A. JENNINGS 16 Dec 1828 (OB)

**KEATON,** Nelson & **DAVIS,** Edna by George BINGHAM 7 Jan 1802 (OM)

**KEENIN,** Robert s/o James and Jane W. KEENIN age 24 s laborer POB Ireland POR Orange & **TAMPLIN,** Sarah d/o Peter MAGOVERIN and Sarah TAMPLIN age 28 s POB POR Orange; POM Orange 26 Sep 1853 (OMR) (OML)

**KEETON,** John J. age 27 s POB POR Orange s/o James KEETON and Lucy JENNINGS mechanic & **HERNDON,** Susan A. age 20 s POB POR Orange d/o Richard T. HERNDON and Ella HUTCHINSON 29 Mar 1869 POM Orange by James A. MANSFIELD (OMR)

**KEETON,** John Sr. & **CHANCELLOR,** Elizabeth w surety John KEETON Jr.15 Jan 1812 (OB) by Jeremiah CHANDLER 2 Feb 1812 (OM)

**KEGS,** Charles M. s/o Thomas KEGS and Lucy WRIGHT age 24 s engineer on O.& A. railroad POB Prince William Co POR Alexandria & **KING,** Music D. age 20 s POB POR Orange POM Orange 26 Sep 1867 (OMR) 21 Sep 1867 (OML)

**KEISTER,** Ely & **THOMAS,** Nancy surety Broadus THOMAS 7 Mar 1832 (OB)

**KEITH**, Nelson POC age 29 w POB POR Fauquier Co s/o Austin CHECK and Dinah KEITH farm laborer & **DADE**, Emma J. POC age 16 s POB POR Orange d/o Benjamin DADE and Lucy _____ 25 Dec 1872 POM Orange by F.L. GIPSON (OMR)

**KEITH,** Peyton & **PETTY**, Sally d/o George PETTY surety Thomas PROCTER, by James GARNETT 18 May 1803 (OB) (OM)

**KELLY**, Joseph age 27 s POB POR Orange s/o John KELLY and Maria KELLY farm laborer & **ROBINSON**, Maria age 19 s POB POR Orange d/o Scylla ROBINSON DOM 18 Oct 1869 POM Orange by I.W.K. HANDY (OMR)

**KELLY**, Spencer & **RUMSEY**, Lianna surety John SLEET 19 Feb 1805 (OB)

**KENDALL**, Robert G. & **BROCKMAN**, Virginia A.; 12 Jan 1852 (OML)

**KENNEDY**, Fountain & **PEYTON**, Eliza P.; POM Orange 24 Jan 1852 (OMR) (OML)

**KENNEDY**, Hiram P. & **FAULCONER**, Mary surety Carter B. FAULCONER 25 Oct 1830 (OB) by J. GOSS 31 Oct 1830 (OM)

**KENNEDY**, Isaac & **BARTLEY**, Virginia A. d/o Oliver BARTLEY; 23 Apr 1852 (OML)

**KENNEDY**, Littleton s/o Reuben KENNEDY & **HILL**, Martha d/o Richard HILL who is also surety 11 Apr 1820 (OB)

**KENNEDY,** Livingston & **ADAMS**, Martha Ann w surety Thomas J. MARTIN 23 Dec 1847 (OB)

**KENNEDY,** Reuben & **GARTON**, Mary surety W.M. CHAPMAN 24 Jun 1834 (OB)

**KENNEY**, Mickleberry POC 46 s POB Louisa POR Orange laborer s/o Winston KENNEY and Betsey KANE & **QUARLES,** Henrietta POC age 26 s POB POR Orange 13 Mar 1880 POM Orange by Frank TIBBS (OMR)

**KENNEY**, William H. s/o William H. BROCKENBROUGH and America A. KENNEY age 27 s carpenter POB POR Albemarle Co POC & **MADISON**, Nelly d/o James and Louisa MADISON age 18 s POB POR Orange POC; POM Orange 12 Mar 1866 (OMR) (OML)

**KENNIDAY,** Newman & **LEE,** Sidney surety Joseph LEE 17 Jan 1825 (OB)

**KENNON,** Ira & **MCCLANNOCK,** Mary J. d/o John McCLANNOCK surety John ESTES 16 May 1827 (OB)

**KENNON,** Jos. D. age 29 s engineer POB Louisa POR Baltimore Co., MD s/o Richard KENNON and Ann HORDE & **MOORE,** Ella H. age 25 s

POB POR Orange d/o William C. MOORE Jr. and Marian HORDE
POM Orange 2 Jan 1878 by J.W. MCCOWN (OMR)

**KENNON,** Philip & **HORD,** Sarah d/o Jesse HORD surety Peter HORD
22 Dec 1823 (OB)

**KENNON,** Richard & **HORD,** Ann E. d/o Daniel HORD Sr. surety John
HOUSTON 7 Dec 1847 (OB)

**KERSEY,** William & **TAYLOR,** Agnes permission from Charles
TAYLOR surety Jeremiah SIMS 24 Mar 1788 (OB) by George EVE 6
Apr 1788 (OM)

**KEY,** Walter & **DANIEL,** Martha permission from Martha DANIEL
surety John WHITE 14 Dec 1812 (OB)

**KEYTT,** Peyton & **PETTY,** Sally POR Orange 18 May 1803 by James
GARNETT (Misc Min Ret)

**KINCHELOE,** Remand S. age 24 s POB Fairfax Co POR Orange s/o Paul
KINCHELOE and Manifred CALVERT clerk in store & **DADE,** Mary
O. age 25 s POB King George Co POR Orange d/o Sarcossan T.
DADE and Mildred J. POPE 7 Jan 1869 POM Orange by Theo M.
CARSON (OMR)

**KINCHELOE,** Robert E. age 28 s POB Fairfax Co POR Culpeper Co s/o
Daniel KINCHELOE and Winnie _____ merchant & **FLETCHER,**
Alice L. age 20 POB Fauquier Co POR Orange d/o A.D. FLETCHER
and Louisa MCALLISTER 3 May 1870 POM Orange by H.E.
HATCHER (OMR)

**KINDALL,** Robert & **GARNETT** Ursula; 15 Dec 1796 surety Adam
LINDSAY (OB)

**KINDELL,** Thomas G. & **MEREDITH,** Elizabeth surety Roger
SLAUGHTER 24 Feb 1823 (OB)

**KING,** Azariah & **ABEL,** Mary; 1780 surety Caleb ABEL (OB)

**KING,** Gabriel & **BIGGERS,** Huldah d/o Macon BIGGERS surety
William BIGGERS by James GARNETT 6 Dec 1799 (OB) (OM)

**KING,** Holcombe R. s/o William KING & **PEACHER,** Mary Ann D. d/o
William PEACHER who is also surety 22 Dec 18232 (OB)

**KING,** John & **ROW,** Cynthia d/o Edmund ROW surety Abner ROW 3
Jul 1804 (OB) 5 Jul 1804 by Nath. SANDERS (Misc Min Ret)

**KING,** John F. & **BROCKMAN,** Mary Ann d/o William L. BROCKMAN
who is also surety 21 Dec 1846 (OB)

**KING,** John s/o Julian KING & **YATES,** Frances surety James YATES 27
Apr 1807 (OB) by Robert JONES 27 Apr 1807 (OM)

**KING,** Miles Edward & **LIPSCOMB,** Willie Ann surety Fleming
LIPSCOMB 6 Dec 1848 (OB) 7 Dec 1848 by Daniel B. EWING (OM)

**KING,** Reuben & **JOLLETT,** Elizabeth permission from James JOLLET
surety Simeon JOLLETT 20 May 1822 (OB)

**KING,** Robert & **GORDON,** Priscilla C. surety Charles BEALE 18 Jan 1834 (OB)

**KING,** Sadrut & **WAYT,** Mary d/o James WAYT surety Richard WHITE 15 Dec 1785 (OB)

**KING,** Virginius B. age 23 s POB POR Orange s/o John F. KING and Mary BROCKMAN farmer & **DANIEL,** Virginia age 28 s POB POR Orange d/o William F. DANIEL and Julia TERRELL 23 Sep 1873 POM Orange by Herndon FRAZER (OMR)

**KINNEY,** William & **BEALE,** Fanny over 21 surety Cornelius DEVENNEY by Robert JONES 20 Dec 1806 (OB) (OM)

**KINNY,** Dudley POC age 27 s labourer POB POR Orange s/o Shelton and Charity KENNY & **DAVIS,** Rebecca POC age 26 s POB POR Orange d/o Pleasant DAVIS and Betsy TIBBS POM Orange 13 Dec 1879 (OMR)

**KINZER,** Christian T. & **SUTTON,** Mildred POR Orange 9 Oct 1811 Willis ARNOLD surety (OB)

**KINZER,** Christian T. & **SUTTON,** Mildred surety Willis ARNOLD by Robert JONES 9 Oct 1811 (OB) (OM)

**KINZER,** George C. age 22 s POB POR Orange s/o Philip S. KINZER and Susan E. LONG r.r. hand & **BROWN,** Mollie G. age 23 s POB POR Orange d/o James O. BROWN and Sarah M. COOPER 12 Nov 1868 POM Orange by Charles QUARLES (OMR)

**KINZER,** John & **BROOKING,** Jane surety Charles R. BROOKING 17 Dec 1827 (OB)

**KINZER,** John H. s/o Christian F. KINZER and Mildred SUTTON age 43 w farmer POB POR Orange & **WAYLAND,** Susan C. d/o Clement WAYLAND age 37 s POB Madison Co POR Orange; POM Orange 7 Aug 1866 (OMR) 6 Aug 1866 (OML)

**KINZER,** Philip F. & **LONG,** Susan E. d/o Joshua LONG who is also surety 3 Jun 1845 (OB) by Joseph A. MANSFIELD 5 Jun 1845 (OM)

**KINZER,** Steurman & **WRIGHT,** Susan surety William WRIGHT 3 Nov 1834 (OB)

**KIRTLEY,** Jonathan & **ANDERSON,** Theodoshia by George BINGHAM 13 Oct 1801 (OM)

**KIRTLEY,** Joseph & **SIMS,** Elizabeth d/o Jeremiah SIMS surety Pemperton SIMS 20 Nov 1810 (OB) by George BINGHAM 6 Dec 1810 (OM)

**KIRTLEY,** Sinclear/ St. Clair & **PANNILL** Ann d/o William PANNILL surety Morton PANNILL 16 Nov 1800 (OB)

**KIRTLEY,** Willis & **THORNTON,** Mary Presley permission by George THORNTON surety Peter THORNTON 31 Dec 1802 (OB) 2 Jan 1803 by Jacob WATTS (Misc Min Ret)

**KITE,** Henry & **HOUSTON,** Sarah Ann d/o John HOUSTON surety Lewis HOUSTON 26 Nov 1835 (OB)

**KITE,** Siram age 28 s POB Page Co POR Madison Co s/o George KITE and Susan HANSDEN farmer & **KITE,** Emma age 25 s POB Page Co POR Orange d/o William H. KITE and Rebecca BLOSSER 16 Aug 1870 POM Orange by J.W. MCCOWN (OMR)

**KLEE/CLEE,** John & **PRICE,** Catherine widow 16 Apr 1811 Thomas LOVILL surety (OB)

**KNIGHT,** Lewis & **COLEMAN,** Matildah 15 Jun 1828 surety John PAYNE Jr. (OB)

**KNIGHT,** Matthew & **HANEY,** Nancy d/o James HANEY 15 Dec 1823 surety Ezekial BREEDING (OB)

**KNIGHT,** William & **HANEY,** Luraney d/o James HANEY Sr. 13 Oct 1828 surety Ezekial BREEDING (OB)

**KNIGHT,** William & **OAKES,** Delphia; 23 Feb 1797 surety Thomas OAKES (OB)

**KNIGHT,** William & **ROGERS,** Elizabeth 29 Jan 1799 by George BINGHAM (OM)

**KNIGHT,** William Butcher & **CAVE,** Frances surety William CAVE 23 Aug 1791 (OB) 25 Aug 1791 by George EVE (OM)

**KNIGHTEN,** Benjamin F. age 27 s farmer POB POR Orange s/o R. T. KNIGHTEN and Elizabeth CHEWNING & **SCHUYLER,** Helen W. age 20 s POB POR Orange d/o William SCHUYLER and Mary Ann SORRELL POM Orange 24 Dec 1879 by W. F. CAMPER (OMR)

**KNIGHTEN,** Robert A. s/o Taliaferro and E. Watkins KNIGHTEN age 21 s mechanic POB POR Orange & **HERRING,** Georgianna d/o George and Sarah Holbert HERRING age 28 s POB POR Orange; POM Orange 22 Oct 1857 (OMR) 5 Oct 1857 (OML)

**KNIGHTEN,** Roderick H. age 29 s wagonmaker POB POR Orange s/o Roderick T. KNIGHTON and Elizabeth WATKINS & **TALLEY,** Lucy V. age 19 s POB Spotsylvania POR Orange d/o Richard TALLEY and Mary J. ROBINSON POM Orange 23 Dec 1877 (OMR)

**KNIGHTEN,** William & **BROWN,** Mary 4 May 1825 surety Benjamin VAWTER (OB) 6 May 1825 by George MORRIS (OM)

**KNIGHTEN,** William J. s/o Mordecai KNIGHTEN & **OAKS,** Elizabeth A. 16 Aug 1843 surety Samuel ATKINS (OB)

**KNIGHTEN,** William s/o Mordecai and Frances KNIGHTEN age 30 w shoemaker POB POR Orange & **SANFORD,** Nancy d/o Jefferson and Sarah WRIGHT age 25 w POB POR Orange; POM Orange 23 Jan 1855 (OMR)

**KNOX,** John physician & **MACON,** Lucy d/o James MACON 29 Jun 1846 surety James L. JONES (OB) 2 Jul 1846 by J. EARNEST (OM)

**KRISE,** Jacob & **WILLIAMS,** Mildred d/o Jacob WILLIAMS surety
Major WILLIAMS 4 Jun 1827 (OB)

**KUBE,** Cornelius W. age 24 s carpenter POB POR Orange s/o George
MASTIN and Mary KUBE & **JONES,** Mary A. age 24 s POB POR
Orange d/o William A. JONES and Delilah SEE POM Orange 15 Mar
1877 (OMR)

**KUBE,** John B. age 24 S POB POR Orange s/o John KUBE and
Fredericka STUNZ farmer & **APPERSON,** Malvina age 21 S POB
Culpeper Co POR Orange d/o Thomas APPERSON and Evelina
PALMER 22 Dec 1870 POM Orange by Richard STEPHENS (OM)

**KUBE,**(aka KUBA) William s/o Henry & Katherine KUBE age 25 s
farmer POB Germany POR Orange & **DOWNEY,** Mildred C. d/o
Sanders and Catherine MASON age 27 w POB POR Orange; POM
Orange 19 Nov 1857 (OMR) 18 Nov 1857 (OML)

**LACY,** Allan R. & **ANCELL,** Elizabeth surety Robert ANCELL 21 Oct
1816 (OB)

**LAHONEY,** Daniel & **FURNEY,** Fanny surety William GARDE 16 Nov
1794 (OB) by George EVE 11 Dec 1794 (OM)

**LAMB,** Benjamin & **LAMB,** Peggy d/o John LAMB who is also surety 19
Jan 1797 (OB)

**LAMB,** Ezekiel & **WOOD,** Rebecka E.; POM Orange 24 Dec 1863
(OMR)

**LAMB,** William & **HERRING,** Elizabeth 26 Aug 1804 by George
BINGHAM (Misc Min Ret)

**LANCASTER,** Alexander & **WEBB,** Milly surety Benjamin
LANCASTER 23 Oct 1826 (OB)

**LANCASTER,** George E. age 29 w farmer POB POR Orange s/o William
C. LANCASTER and Polly OAKS & **SUTHERLING,** Eliza M. age 22
s POB POR Orange d/o William SUTHERLING and Sarah HARRIS
POM Orange 3 Jul 1877 (OMR)

**LANCASTER,** Henry & **WRIGHT,** Mary surety George FINNELL 26
Jul 1794 (OB)

**LANCASTER,** James & **LANCASTER,** Nancy surety Richard
RICHARDS 16 Jul 1816 (OB)

**LANCASTER,** Joseph M. age 20 s POB POR Orange s/o William C.
LANCASTER and Mary F. OAKS farmer & **TINDER,** Eugene E. age
23 s POB POR Orange d/o Thomas TINDER and Nancy MASON 7
Jan 1868 POM Orange by Melzi CHANCELLOR (OMR)

**LANCASTER,** Marshall T. age 26 s farmer POB POR Orange s/o Owen
C. LANCASTER and Jane HERNDON & **REYNOLDS,** Octavia C.
age 29 s POB Louisa POR Orange POM Orange 5 Jun 1877 (OMR)

**LANCASTER,** Owen C. s/o Edmund LANCASTER and Sarah COOPER
age 42 w farmer POB POR Orange & **HERNDON,** Mary d/o James

HERNDON and Elizabeth QUISENBERRY age 44 w POB POR
Orange; POM Orange 3 Oct 1865 (OMR) 25 Sep 1865 (OML)

**LANCASTER**, Reuben & **CONNER,** Betsy surety John CONNER 2 Jun
1792 (OB)

**LANCASTER**, Richard O. age 25 s POB POR Orange s/o Owen C.
LANCASTER and Jane HERNDON farmer & **HERNDON**, Ella S. age
25 s POB POR Orange d/o Joseph HERNDON and Mary HERNDON
1 Jun 1873 POM Orange by Richard STEPHENS (OMR)

**LANCASTER**, Robinson S. s/o William C. LANCASTER and Mary C.
OAKES age 29 s farmer POB POR Orange & **FAULCONER,**
Catherine J. d/o James F. FAULCONER and Priscilla TINDER age 33
s POB Culpeper Co POR Orange; POM Orange 24 Dec 1866 (OMR)
19 Dec 1866 (OML)

**LANCASTER**, William s/o Jonathan and Sarah LANCASTER age 25 s
farmer POB POR Orange & **TINDER**, Adaline Tutt d/o Thomas and
Nancy TINDER age 19 s POB Orange POR Locust Hill; POM Orange
29 May 1856 (OMR) 28 May 1856 (OML)

**LANDRUM**, John & **COLLINS,** Mary d/o Edward COLLINS surety
Thomas LANDRUM 7 Feb 1794 (OB)

**LANDRUM**, Willis POC age 21 s POB Albemarle Co POR Orange
William LANDRUM and Ann VERDUR laborer & **GRAY**, Courtenay
POC age 19 s POB Albemarle POR Orange d/o John GRAY and
Harriet BAYLOR 6 Jun 1868 POM Orange by Frank NICHOLS
(OMR)

**LANE**, John & **CREW,** Tabitha by George BINGHAM 23 Dec 1798
(OM)

**LANE**, Robert G. & **WHITELAW**, Polley 17 Mar 1803 by Wm
DOUGLASS (Meth.Epis.Ch) (Misc Min Ret)

**LANSLEY**, John & **PITCHER**, Catherine POR Orange 23 Dec 1811 John
BLEDSOE surety (OB)

**LANTON**, Thomas & **WALKER,** Mary by Aaron BLEDSOE 28 Aug
1783 (OM)

**LARMAND**, John & **WRIGHT**, Ann C.; POM Orange 27 Apr 1852
(OMR) 26 Apr 1852 (OML)

**LARMAND**, John s/o Frances and Lucy LARMAND age 38 w tinsmith
POB Richmond, VA POR Orange C.H. & **BRADLEY**, Maria F. d/o
William and Lucy NEWMAN age 32 w POB POR Orange; POM
Orange 12 Apr 1855 (OMR)

**LAWSON**, John D. s/o Daniel and Jane LAWSON age 36 s commercial
POB Orange Co, New York POR New York City & **BALLARD**, Helen
Peyton d/o Garland and Georgiana BALLARD age 25 s POB POR
Orange; POM Orange 10 Jan 1855 (OMR)

**LAYTON,** John L. age 34 s farmer POB Rockingham POR Orange s/o Lewis LAYTON and Mary LOHR & **LLOYD,** Comora F. age 34 s POB Madison POR Orange d/o Robert LLOYD and Lucetta HILL POM Orange 6 Apr 1879 by W.H. CAMPBELL (OMR)

**LEA,** Gideon & **COFFERY,** Amey/Anny 14 Jul 1777 both of St. Thomas Parish by banns (Deed Book 17)

**LEAK,** Robert & **LEAK,** Susannah; 21 Dec 1784 surety Lewis WILLIS (OB)

**LEAKE,** Lewis W. & **MITCHELL,** Jane d/o Mary MITCHELL 9 Oct 1837 surety William T. MITCHELL (OB)

**LEAKE,** Shelton F. & **GREY,** Rebecca 11 Jun 1843 surety James B. NEWMAN (OB) 13 Jul 1843 by J. EARNEST (OM)

**LEATHERER,** John & **WHITE,** Sarah 4 Mar 1777 both of St. Thomas Parish (Deed Book 17)

**LEATHERS,** Alexander & **MITCHELL,** Lucy d/o Henry MITCHELL who is also surety 26 Nov 1821 (OB)

**LEATHERS,** Franklin P. age 27 s POB POR Orange carpenter s/o Levi H. LEATHERS and Elizabeth C. YANCEY & **ATKINS,** Hennitta age 22 s POB POR Orange d/o Charles D. ATKINS and Mary EVANS 14 Sep 1880 by W.H. HAMPER (OMR)

**LEATHERS,** James & **MALLORY,** Dolly surety Uriel MALLORY 30 Dec 1816 (OB)

**LEATHERS,** James F. & **JENKINS,** Lucy surety Edmund D. LONGAR by George MORRIS 23 Sep 1822 (OB) (OM)

**LEATHERS,** Jonathan & **PAYNE,** Betsy d/o Thomas PAYNE Elijah MALLORY surety 23 Sep 1807 (OB)

**LEATHERS,** William & **FINNELL,** Nancy surety Roger BELL 18 Apr 1792 (OB)

**LEATHERS.** Levy & **YANCY,** Elizabeth; 17 Feb 1851 (OML)

**LEAVELL,** Lewis & **BELL,** Frances d/o John BELL surety John W. POWELL by Hamilton GOSS 28 Jan 1805 (OB) (OM)

**LECKIE,** William L. & **REDDIS,** Ann V. surety Thomas MILLER 12 Apr 1817 (OB)

**LEE,** Abner & **LEE,** Sally surety Samuel LEE by Nathaniel SANDERS 6 Jan 1808 (OB)

**LEE,** Alexander & **BLEDSOE,** Verrinda ward of Alex WRIGHT surety Abner LEE 16 Nov 1840 (OB)

**LEE,** Byrd H. age 22 s farmer POB POR Orange s/o James LEE and Elizabeth PROCTOR & **BROOKS,** Virginia age 21 s POB Goochland POR Orange POM Orange 24 Oct 1876 (OMR)

**LEE,** David P. age 22 s POB POR Orange s/o Alexander LEE and Virnada BLEDSOE farm laborer & **STITZER,** Lucy A. age 28 s POB POR

Orange d/o Addison STITZERE and Mary A. CLARK 31 Dec 1872
POM Orange by H.E. HATCHER (OMR)

**LEE**, George & **BOAR,** Melinda d/o Mary BOAR surety Edward N.
CANADAY 9 Sep 1839 (OB)

**LEE**, George & **FOSTER,** Caty d/o William FOSTER who is also surety
10 Nov 1800 (OB)

**LEE**, Henry & **LAMB**, Fannie by George BINGHAM 10 Aug 1814 (OM)

**LEE**, James & **PROCTOR,** Elisabeth d/o Lucy Ann PROCTOR surety
Addison STITZER 30 Dec 1840 (OB)

**LEE**, James & **SANFORD,** Harriett surety William LEE 5 Mar 1816 (OB)

**LEE**, John & **BELL,** Elizabeth d/o Thomas BELL surety Ambrose
MADISON both of St. Thomas Parish 18 Dec 1781 (OB)

**LEE**, John H. & **WILLIS,** Frances surety Ambrose MADISON who is
also her guardian 18 Nov 1839 (OB)

**LEE**, John H. & **WILLIS,** Mary Lee d/o Nelly C. WILLIS who is also
surety 2 Mar 1826 (OB)

**LEE**, John Henry & **HUGHES,** Frances surety Robert HUGHES 25 Feb
1841 (OB)

**LEE**, Joseph & **LEE,** Polly surety Zachariah WOOD 31 Dec 1811 (OB)

**LEE**, Kendall & **GORDON,** Sarah surety James GORDON Jr. 17 Jun
1785 (OB)

**LEE**, Lafayette & **MASSEY**, Eliza; 24 Feb 1851 (OML)

**LEE**, Lewis H. age 27 s farmer POB Madison POR Orange s/o John H.
LEE and Fanny M. WILLIS & **HANSBROUGH,** Georgie G. age 19 s
POB POR Orange d/o John S. HANSBROUGH and Mary E.
BALLARD POM Orange 12 Oct 1876 (OMR)

**LEE**, Luther age 21 s POB POR Orange farmer s/o James LEE and Martha
WOOD & **WOOD,** Eliza J. age 16 s POB POR Orange d/o John F.
WOOD and Lucy A. BERRY 22 Jul 1880 by W.H. HAMPER (OMR)

**LEE**, Moses & **TERRILL,** Elizabeth surety Henry CLARKE 17 Jun 1820
(OB)

**LEE**, Richard & **DODD,** Anna surety Mordecai MASTIN 24 Feb 1789 by
John LELAND (OB) (OM)

**LEE**, Sylvester S. age 37 s POB Rockingham POR Orange farmer s/o
James LEE and Lucy J. SPINDLE & **LUCK,** Virginia C. age 27 s POB
Spotsylvania POR Orange d/o Richard A. LUCK and Mary M. BARR
19 Feb 1880 POM Orange by E.R. PERRY (OMR)

**LEE**, Timothy & **JONES,** Susan surety Churchill JONES 4 Nov 1844
(OB) 13 Nov 1844 by Joseph S. JACKSON (OM)

**LEE**, William & **HUGHES,** George Ann surety Lemuel WRIGHT by
Joseph S. JACKSON 1 Jan 1846 (OB) (OM)

**LEE**, William & **SIMECO,** Polly age 21 surety John SIMECO 23 Dec
1799 (OB)

**LEE,** William & **TERRILL,** Sally surety John TERRILL 16 May 1812 (OB) 19 May 1812 by Jeremiah CHANDLER (OM)

**LEE,** William age 23 s POB POR Orange cooper s/o John H. LEE and Fanny HUGHES & **HUGHES,** Victoria P. age 17 s Lewis A. HUGHES and Jane LEE 22 Jul 1880 POM Orange by W.H. HAMPER (OMR)

**LEE,** William H. age 42 s farmer POB POR Orange s/o William LEE and Sarah TERRILL & **TERRILL,** Georgia E. age 30 s POB POR Orange d/o William H. TERRILL and M. Ann BOSTON POM Orange 14 Dec 1876 (OMR)

**LEE,** Zachary & **MANSPOIL,** Sara d/o Adam and Mary MANSPOILE surety Abner WATSON 25 May 1790 (OB)

**LEMOINE,** John E. & **SPOTSWOOD,** Mary B. d/o John SPOTSWOOD surety Robert G.W. SPOTSWOOD 30 Jun 1825 (OB)

**LEWIS,** Ed POC age 22 s POB POR Orange s/o Putner LEWIS and Eliza GRYMES saw mill hand & **MORTON,** Mary POC age 22 s POB Greene Co POR Orange d/o Susan _____ 13 Apr 1873 POM Orange by Thomas WALKER (OMR)

**LEWIS,** George POC age 27 s POB POR Orange s/o Kemp LEWIS and Susan GRYMES carpenter & **MARSHALL,** Nancy POC age 26 s POB POR Orange 15 Nov 1871 POM Orange by Philip JOHNSON (OMR)

**LEWIS,** James & **WATKINS,** Nancy d/o Isham WATKINS surety James LANDRUM 20 Aug 1794 (OB)

**LEWIS,** James POC age 21 s farm labourer POB POR Orange s/o Adam LEWIS and Aggy TIBBS & **TERRILL,** Georgianna POC age 21 s POB POR Orange d/o Robert TERRILL and Martha GOODALL POM Orange 16 Mar 1878 by John MANSFIELD (OMR)

**LEWIS,** Johnson POC age 23 s farm labourer POB POR Orange s/o Buller LEWIS and Eliza GRYMES & **DUKE,** Amanda POC age 22 s POB POR Orange d/o Lee DUKE and Lucy JOHNSON POM Mt. Vella, Orange 13 Dec 1878 by Willis ROBINSON (OMR)

**LEWIS,** Madison POC age 21 s POB POR Orange s/o Jim LEWIS and Milly LEWIS farm laborer & **HENDERSON,** Fanny POC age 21 s POB Louisa Co. POR Orange d/o Jake HENDERSON and Dinah HENDERSON 21 May 1872 POM Orange by John C. WILLIS (OMR)

**LEWIS,** Philip P. & **HERNDON,** Pamelia; 25 Jun 1858 (OML)

**LEWIS,** Thomas M. & **WYMAN,** Emeline ward of Walter KEY who is also surety 25 Sep 1820 (OB)

**LEWIS,** Thomas POC age 45 s carpenter POB Culpeper POR Orange s/o Thornton LEWIS and Lucy _____ & **BARBOUR,** Betsy POC age 23 s POB Culpeper POR Orange d/o Walker BARBOUR and Jane _____ POM Orange 31 Aug 1879 by William B. LEE (OMR)

**LEWIS,** Warner POC age 30 w labourer POB Albemarle POR Orange &
**BRANHAM,** Dora POC age 21 s POB POR Orange d/o Bashnor (?)
and Matilda BRANHAM POM Orange 29 Sep 1877 (OMR)
**LEWIS,** William & **HARTSOOK,** Ann M. surety William A.
LANDRUM 26 Nov 1844 (OB) 29 Nov 1844 by James D. ROBERTS
(OM)
**LEWIS,** William L. s/o John Wesley LEWIS and Ann H. DUVALL age
30 s express agent POB Prince George Co, MD POR Orange &
**COLVIN,** Elizabeth F. d/o Howard COLVIN and Elizabeth
HENSHAW age 18 s POB Culpeper Co POR Orange; POM
Gordonsville, Orange 12 Apr 1866 (OMR) (OML)
**LEWIS,** Willis & **WILTSHIRE,** Catharine d/o Benjamin WILTSHIRE
who is also surety 28 Sep 1839 (OB)
**LIMMANDS,** Elijah & **SANDAGE,** Lucy; 13 Oct 1796 (OM)
**LINDSAY,** Caleb & **STEVENS,** Sally d/o John STEVENS who is also
surety 3 Mar 1785 (OB)
**LINDSAY, Daniel Jr.** POC age 23 s POB POR Orange farm laborer s/o
Daniel LINDSAY and Courtenay STEARN & **JACKSON,** Jane POC
age 25 w POB POR Orange d/o Robert JACKSON and Esther
GRAVES 27 Nov 1880 POM Mt. Pleasant Church, Orange by C.J.
JOHNSON (OMR)
**LINDSAY,** Henry s/o Minor LINDSAY and Ann WASHINGTON age 24
s POB POR Orange POC & **MINOR,** Sarah d/o Thornton and Louisa
POINDEXTER age 22 w POB Spotsylvania POR Orange POC; POM
Orange 28 Aug 1867 (OMR) 27 Aug 1867 (OML)
**LINDSAY,** James POC age 22 s labourer POB POR Orange s/o Daniel
LINDSAY and Courtney STEARNS & **MORTON,** Annie Bell age 20
s POB POR Orange d/o Bell MORTON and Ann WILLIS POM
Orange 14 Dec 1879 (OMR)
**LINDSAY,** John & **DANIEL,** Henrietta surety William REYNOLDS 24
Oct 1825 (OB) by Jeremiah CHANDLER 25 Oct 1825 (OM)
**LINDSAY,** Lancelot & **NEWMAN,** Jane d/o John NEWMAN Sr. surety
John S. LINDSAY 3 Apr 1832 (OB)
**LINDSAY,** Landon & **MILLS,** Cely d/o Nathaniel MILLS POR Orange
26 Aug 1811 Reuben LINDSAY surety (OB)
**LINDSAY, Minor Jr.** POC age 27 s labourer POB POR Orange s/o Minor
LINDSAY and Ann WILLIS & **CARTER,** Lucinda POC age 17 s POB
POR Orange d/o Burwell CARTER and Amy SMITH POM Mt.
Pleasant, Orange 22 Jun 1878 by C.T. JOHNSON (OMR)
**LINDSAY,** Moses & **DONALDSON,** Mary 9 Jan 1754 (Orange Fee
Book)
**LINDSAY,** Robert & **DANIEL,** Minerva guardian William REYNOLDS
who is also surety 25 Oct 1824 (OB)

**LINDSAY,** William & **SHEPHERD,** Nancy surety William BROCKMAN 3 Oct 1781 (OB)

**LINDSAY,** William POC age 21 s POB POR Orange s/o Billy LINDSAY and Franky _____ farmer & **FRY,** June POC age 17 s POB POR Orange d/o Henry FRY and Margaret Ann E. TAYLOR 13 Dec 1873 POM Orange by Calmon GILLUM (OMR)

**LINDSEY,** Moses and **DONSTON,** Mary 9 Jan 1754 (Orange Fee Book)

**LINNEY,** Henry B. age 30 s tobacconist POB POR Orange s/o Henry M. LINNEY and Lucy G. BEALE & **EVANS,** Virginia Taylor age 28 s POB Prince William POR Orange d/o James A. EVANS and Anna M. NORVILL POM Gordonsville 2 Jan 1878 by P.F. AUGUST (OMR)

**LINNEY,** Henry M. & **BEALE,** Lucy G. d/o Charles BEALE 4 Nov 1844 surety Charles BEALE (OB)

**LINNEY,** William & **BELL,** Ann both of St. Thomas Parish 4 Sep 1773 (Deed Book 17)

**LINNEY,** William & **BURRUS,** Anne w POR St. Thomas Parish 20 Nov 1780 (OM)

**LINTON,** Moses & **REED,** Nancy surety Joel DURRETT 17 Dec 1800 (OB)

**LIPSCOMB,** Fleming & **ATKINS,** Elizabeth d/o Joseph ATKINS who is also surety 5 Nov 1835 (OB)

**LIPSCOMB,** William J. s/o Arthur B. LIPSCOMB and Mary A. STROTHER age 29 w painter POB Campbell Co POR Orange & **FAULCONER,** Dolly M. d/o Alfred FAULCONER and Madalina BOCOCK age 32 s POB POR Orange; POM Orange 28 Dec 1865 (OMR) 27 Dec 1865 (OML)

**LLOYD,** Belfield s/o Robert LLOYD who is also surety & **KINZER,** Rachel d/o C.F. KINZER 27 Nov 1830 (OB)

**LLOYD,** Calvin age 26 s farmer POB Madison POR Orange s/o Robert LLOYD and Lucetta HILL & **BROCKMAN,** Martha age 21 s POB Madison POR Orange POM Orange 8 Dec 1878 by Joseph S. MANSFIELD (OMR)

**LLOYD,** George H. s/o James and Eliza LLOYD age 20 s farmer POB POR Madison Co & **MARTIN,** Christianna Mary d/o Jacob RILEY and Mary HICKS age 20 w POB Spotsylvania POR Orange; POM Orange 17 Oct 1867 (OMR) (OML)

**LLOYD,** John & **MONTAGUE,** Nancy surety Andrew MONTAGUE 12 Nov 1793 (OB)

**LLOYD,** Reuben & **BADGER,** Lucy 27 Jun 1829 surety John SULIVAN (OB)

**LLOYD,** Robert A. age 22 s farmer POB Madison POR Orange s/o Robert H. LLOYD and Parthenia HILL & **BROOKMAN,** Martha age 22 s

POB POR Orange d/o Pleasant BROOKMAN POM Orange 31 Dec 1878 by Joseph A. MANSFIELD (OMR)

**LLOYD,** Thompson & **MOUBRY,** Sarah 15 Oct 1809 by George BINGHAM (OMR)

**LLOYD,** William s/o Henry LLOYD who is also surety & **LLOYD,** Fanny d/o George LLOYD who is also surety 19 Dec 1827 (OB)

**LOBAN,** James & **ROBINSON,** Frances 7 Nov 1829 surety Philip ROBINSON (OB) 19 Nov 1829 by J. GOSS (OMR)

**LOCKETT,** Robert s/o Sam and Peggy LOCKETT age 23 s farm laborer POB POR Orange POC & **MURPHY,** Kittie d/o Benja. MURPHY age 25 s POB POR Orange POC; POM Orange 26 Dec 1867 (OMR) 21 Dec 1867 (OML)

**LOGAN,** Joseph P. physician & **PANNILL,** Ann Eliza d/o Jeremiah PANNILL who is also surety 13 Feb 1843 (OB) 16 Feb 1843 by John COLE (OMR)

**LOGGINS,** Joseph age 24 s POB Spotsylvania Co POR Orange s/o Pash LOGGINS and Huldy HENDERSON laborer & **HALL,** Lucy M. age 16 s POB POR Orange d/o ____HALL and Maria HALL 18 Apr 1870 POM Orange by Herndon FRAZER (OMR)

**LOGGINS,** Robert age 21 s POB Spotsylvania Co POR Orange s/o P. LOGGINS and Huldy HENDERSON farm laborer & **HALL,** Ann age 21 POB POR Orange d/o Maria HALL 31 Dec 1869 POM Orange by Herndon FRAZER (OMR)

**LOHR,** James H. age 21 farmer POB POR Madison s/o Michael LOHR and Rachel BAZZEL & **SWANN,** Annie W. age 24 POB Madison POR Orange d/o Charles W. SWANN and Agnes A. PENDLETON POM Orange 13 Apr 1876 (OMR)

**LONG,** Abraham POC age 22 s POB POR Orange s/o Spencer LONG and Jane PROCTOR laborer & **MCINTOSH,** Mollie POC age 16 s POB POR Orange d/o Joe MCINTOSH and Patsey WILLIS 16 Jan 1869 POM Orange by Philip JOHNSON (OMR)

**LONG,** Abram POC age 27 s farm labourer POB POR Orange s/o Spencer LONG and Jane PROELER & **JOHNSON,** Emma POC age 25 s POB Culpeper POR Orange d/o Baylor JOHNSON 20 Nov 1879 POM Hopewell Church, Orange by C.T. VAUGHN (OMR)

**LONG,** Armistead & **KINDELL,** Betsy ward of James MCMULLAN surety William DEAN by George BINGHAM 4 Apr 1816 (OB) (OM)

**LONG,** Henry & **MANSPOIL,** Lucy surety John LONG 7 Nov 1785 (OB)

**LONG,** Henry POC age 23 s farm labourer POB POR Orange s/o Austin LONG and Evelina ____ & **GIBSON,** Ida POC age 23 s POB Culpeper POR Orange d/o Ben GIBSON POM Orange 31 Aug 1879 by William B. LEE (OMR)

**LONG**, James & **REYNOLDS**, Elizabeth by Nathaniel SANDERS 10 Feb 1785 (OM)

**LONG**, Joshua & **DAWSON**, Frances d/o John DAWSON surety Caleb WEBB by Robert JONES 16 Jan 1821 (OB) (OM)

**LONG**, Richard & **STEVENSON**, Nancy surety Joseph STEVENSON 29 Dec 1796 (OB)

**LONG**, Spotswood & **HARRIS**, Sabina surety Thomas HARRIS by George MORRIS 29 Jun 1824 (OB) (OM)

**LONG**, Weir & **SMITH**, Ann; 20 Nov 1775 both of St. Thomas Parish by banns (Deed Book 17)

**LONG**, William & **BICKERS**, Elizabeth over 21 years surety Joseph BICKERS 3 May 1804 (OB)

**LONG**, William & **FARISH**, Mary Stevens d/o Thomas FARISH surety James FARISH 3 Jun 1812 (OB)

**LONGAN**, Edmund & **EDWARDS**, Sally over 21 years surety Joseph EDWARDS 25 Oct 1809 (OB)

**LORRILL**, Thomas & **CLEE**, Elizabeth d/o John CLEE surety William DUKE 7 Jul 1800 (OB) by George BINGHAM 10 Jul 1800 (OM)

**LOVELL**, James & **HARVEY**, Elizabeth over 21 years surety William HARVEY 13 Apr 1802 (OB) 15 Apr 1802 by Hamilton GOSS (Misc Min Ret)

**LOVING**, Thomas & **VAWTER**, Mary surety Benjamin VAWTER 1 Nov 1813 (OB)

**LOWER**, Michael & **GIBBENS**, Ann d/o Thomas GIBBENS surety Michael MOYERS 27 Apr 1812 (OB) by George BINGHAM 2 May 1812 (OM)

**LOWER**, Peter & **HAM**, Judith by George BINGHAM 2 Jan 1806 (OM)

**LOWINS**, Francis & **DAVIS**, Sarah both of St. Thomas Parish 24 Jun 1773 (OM)

**LOWRY**, Abner & **LOWRY**, Nancy 13 Jun 1803 by George BINGHAM (Misc Min Ret)

**LOWRY**, Thomas & **DEDMAN**, Nancy permission given by John DEDMAN surety Philip DEDMAN 20 Nov 1805 (OB) by Nathaniel SANDERS 21 Nov 1805 (OM)

**LOYD**, George over 21 years & **BELL**, Betsy over 21 years surety William PULLIAM 18 Dec 1805 (OB)

**LOYD**, Thomas & **GRESHAM**, Sally w both of St. Thomas Parish surety John LOYD 27 Apr 1780 (OB)

**LOYD**, Willis & **AYHEART**, Felicia by George BINGHAM 25 Dec 1809 (OM)

**LUCAS**, James & **HENDERSON**, Nancy 24 Oct 1788 (OM)

**LUCAS**, Edmund s/o Jim LUCAS and Amy NACY age 25 s laborer POB POR Orange POC & **WEAVER**, Jane d/o Edmund WEAVER age 28 w POB POR Orange POC; POM Orange 27 May 1866 (OMR) 21 May 1866 (OML)

**LUCAS,** Elijah & **BROCKMAN,** Nancy d/o William BROCKMAN who is also surety 24 Aug 1801 (OB)

**LUCAS,** Ezekiel & **AHART,** Catharine over 21 years surety John FARGUSON 24 Mar 1801 (OB) by Hamilton GOSS (29 Mar 1801 (OM)

**LUCAS,** John H. age 34 s farmer POB Albemarle POR Orange s/o William W. LUCAS and Diana MARSHALL & **MILLER,** Cornelia R. age 23 s POB Madison POR Orange d/o Alonzo MILLER and Mary Jane MOORE POM Orange 27 Nov 1877 (OMR)

**LUCAS,** Thomas & **SNELL,** Sally Garnett surety Eastman SNELL 25 Jan 1789 (OB) by John LELAND 9 Mar 1789 (OM)

**LUCAS,** Titus POC age 21 s POB POR Orange s/o William LUCAS and Matilda LUCAS laborer & **BROWN,** Patsey POC age 21 s POB Louisa Co POR Orange d/o Adam BROWN 22 Jul 1872 POM Orange by Richard STEPHENS (OMR)

**LUCAS,** Zachariah & **WOOD,** Nancy 31 Jan 1799 by Hamilton GOSS (OM)

**LUCK,** George A. & **KENDALL,** Mary Louisa surety Joshua KENDALL 22 Nov 1819 (OB) by Jeremiah CHANDLER 24 Nov 1819 (OM)

**LUCK,** William A. age 45 w farmer POB Spotsylvania POR Orange s/o Richard A. LUCK and Lucy J. SPINDLE & **WAUGH,** Ella S. age 22 s POB POR Orange d/o Robert G. WAUGH POM Orange 20 Nov 1879 by E.R. PERRY (OMR)

**LUMSDEN,** James F. s/o Richard M. LUMSDEN and Martha HILMAN age 25 s farmer POB Spotsylvania POR Orange & **JACOBS,** Annie E. d/o George JACOBS and Catharine SMITH age 24 s POB POR Orange; POM Orange 20 Dec 1866 (OMR) 18 Dec 1866 (OML)

**LYNCH,** George W. s/o Jeremiah LYNCH and Cresy SIMMONS age 25 s engineer on O.& A. railroad POB York Co, Pa POR Alexandria, VA & **GOODWIN,** Lucy A. d/o John GOODWIN and Mary ARNOLD age 23 s POB Prince William Co POR Orange; POM Gordonsville, Orange 10 May 1866 (OMR) 9 May 1866 (OML)

**LYNN,** Lucian age 26 s farmer POB POR Fairfax Co. s/o James E. LYNN and Jane POMEROY & **DAVIS,** Mary L. age 23 s POB POR Orange d/o William I. DAVIS and Sarah A. OGG POM Gordonsville 22 Nov 1876 by John C. DINWIDDIE (OMR)

**MACKONEY,** James & **SLEET,** Patsey d/o James SLEET 31 Dec 1801 by Nath. SANDERS (Misc Min Ret) (OB)

**MACON,** James H. & **NEWMAN,** Lucetta T. d/o W.E. NEWMAN surety Robert L. MADISON 9 Oct 1815 (OB)

**MACON**, Thomas & **MADISON**, Sarah [b.d. 17 Aug 1764 d/o Col. James MADISON and Eleanor CONWAY] surety James MADISON (brother of Sarah) 30 Jan 1790 (OM)

**MADEN**, Jacob & **DAVIS**, Julia d/o John DAVIS surety James MAIDEN 25 Aug 1817 (OB) 4 Sep 1817 by George BINGHAM (OM)

**MADISON**, Ambrose & **WILLIS**, Jane d/o William C. WILLIS who is also surety 11 Sep 1819 (OB)

**MADISON**, Catlett & **ROUTT**, Winney surety William TINSLEY and Stuart SANFORD by Robert JONES 17 Mar 1807 (OB) (OM)

**MADISON**, Francis & **BELL**, Susanna POR Orange d/o William BELL 9 Oct 1772 both of St. Thomas Parish (Orange Fee Book)

**MADISON**, Frank POC age 60 w POB POR Orange s/o Anthony MADISON and Sarah MADISON laborer & **YARHER**, Mary POC age 40 w POB POR Orange 6 Jun 1868 POM Orange by Philip JOHNSON (OMR)

**MADISON**, Garland POC age 24 s POB POR Orange laborer s/o Mat MADISON and Louisa ___ & **CAMPBELL**, Priscilla POC age 21 s POB POR Orange d/o Philip CAMPBELL and Betsy ___ POM Orange CH 4 Apr 1877 (OMR)

**MADISON**, James A. physician & **HEIDEN**, Lucy M. d/o Joseph HEIDEN; POM Orange 2 Jan 1851 OMR 1 Jan 1851 OML

**MADISON**, James POC age 21 s POB Orange POR Albemarle s/o Walker MADISON and Eliza HOLMES laborer & **CAMPBELL**, Emma T. age 19 s POB POR Orange d/o Wesley CAMPBELL and Malissa JOHNSON 18 Dec 1880 POM Calvary Baptist Church, Orange by William ROBINSON (OMR)

**MADISON**, Robert L. physician POR Petersburg & **LEE**, Lititia R.; POM Orange 3 May 1853 (OMR) 2 May 1853 (OML)

**MADISON**, Walker POC age 22 s labourer POB POR Orange s/o Henry MADISON and Julia QUARLES & **JOHNSON**, Ophelia POC age 16 s POB POR Orange POM Mt. Calvary Baptist Church, Orange 21 Mar 1878 by W. J. BARNETT (OMR)

**MADISON**, William POC age 21 s farmer POB POR Orange s/o Timothy MADISON and Jane MINOR & **WASHINGTON**, Betsy POC age 18 s POB POR Orange d/o Lewis WASHINGTON and Fanny MACINTOSH POM Orange 16 Mar 1878 by W. J. BARNETT (OMR)

**MAGGARD**, Henry & **LAMB**, Betsy s surety George ARGEBRIGHT 30 Dec 1791 (OB) by George BINGHAM 1 Jan 1792 (OM)

**MAHANES**, Samuel over 21 years & **BROCKMAN**, Elizabeth d/o William BROCKMAN who is also surety 20 Nov 1802 (OB) 25 Nov 1802 by Hamilton GOSS (Misc Min Ret)

**MAHONEY**, Daniel & **FINNEY**, Fanny surety William GARDE 24 Nov 1794 (OB) by George EVE 11 Dec 1794 (OM)

**MALLORY,** Alfred M. & **WILLIAMS,** Nancy surety John MALLORY Jr. 27 Dec 1833 (OB)

**MALLORY,** Elijah & **PAYNE,** Judith over 21 years surety John PAYNE 4 Apr 1804 (OB)

**MALLORY,** Henry & **JONES,** Ann 18 Jan 1795 by George BINGHAM (OM)

**MALLORY,** Henry & **LONG,** Lucy w both of St. Thomas Parish surety John DEAR 24 Dec 1781 (OB)

**MALLORY,** Ichabod & **KENEDY,** Jane surety Carter B. FAULCONER 21 Jul 1834 (OB)

**MALLORY,** Ichabod & **MARTIN,** Lucinda surety Mallory MARTIN by George BINGHAM 22 Jan 1816 (OB) (OM)

**MALLORY,** James & **BROCKMAN,** Polly permission from John BROCKMAN Sr. who is also surety 21 Dec 1801 (OB)

**MALLORY**, John & **MORTON**, Frances surety William MORTON 27 Feb 1804 (OB) 28 Feb 1804 by Nath. SANDERS (Misc Min Ret)

**MALLORY,** John & **SAWYER,** Sarah both of St. Thomas Parish 17 Feb 1778 (Deed Book 17)

**MALLORY,** Nathan & **THOMPSON,** Elizabeth by George BINGHAM 23 Oct 1821 (OM)

**MALLORY,** Philip & **MORTON,** Sally ward of William MORTON who is also surety 19 Aug 1812 (OB)

**MALLORY,** Reuben & **CARTEE/CARTER(?),** Dorothy surety John BLEDSOE 9 Jun 1789 (OB)

**MALLORY,** Robert & **MALLY,** Nancy 17 Oct 1798 by George BINGHAM (OM)

**MALLORY,** Roger & **PAYNE,** Mary d/o Thomas PAYNE surety Moses LEATHERS 16 May 1797 (OB)

**MALLORY,** William & **GIBSON,** Mary permission from John GIBSON surety Uriel MALLORY 8 Dec 1797 (OB)

**MALLORY,** William & **HOLBERT,** Mary d/o Elijah HOLBERT who is also surety 19 Apr 1828 (OB)

**MALLORY,** William P. & **EDWARDS,** Lucy Ann surety Davis ATKINS 26 Jul 1842 (OB)

**MALONE,** George A. s/o James MALONE and Ellen CUNNINGHAM age 22 s machinist POB Saline Co, Mo POR St.Louis, Mo & **SMITH,** Frances S. d/o Ambrose A. SMITH and Catharine JACOBS age 24 s POB POR Orange POM Orange 29 Sep 1864 (OMR) 27 Sep 1864 (OML)

**MANDIN,** Lewis age 23 s POB POR Richmond s/o Doran A. MANDIN and Ann HOWARD engineer & **HARRIS,** Sarah E. age 22 s POB

Hanover Co POR Orange d/o W.V. HARRIS 3 Apr 1872 POM Orange by J.W. MCCOWN (OMR)

**MANN**, James J. age 25 s farmer POB Hanover POR Orange s/o Jonathan T. MANN and Sarah J. SPENCER & **HATCH**, Mabel Estelle age 21 s POB POR Orange d/o Henry HATCH and Mary C. GARDNER POM Orange C.H. 12 Jan 1876 by H. E. HATCHER (OMR)

**MANNEN**, John & **HILL**, Elizabeth d/o Harriett S. GRYMES surety P.S. FRY 7 Jan 1833 (OB)

**MANNONI**, Anthony age 24 s POB Island of Corsica POR Richmond s/o Louis A. MANNONI and Mary Catherine PAULENTINI merchant & **FAULCONER**, Alma E. age 21 s POB POR Orange d/o E.J. FAULCONER and Louisa ALLEN 29 Jun 1880 POM Methodist Church, Gordonsville, Orange by Herbert M. HOKE (OMR)

**MANOR**, James & **KEESAER**, Mary Ann surety Isaac KEESAER 10 Dec 1832 (OB)

**MANSFIELD**, James W. s/o Robert MANSFIELD & **CLARK**, Mildred d/o John CLARK surety Henry J. CLARK by J. GOSS 18 Nov 1813 (OB) (OM)

**MANSFIELD**, Joseph A. & **LINDSAY**, Susan Ann surety James G. LINDSAY 24 Mar 1835 by P. CRAWFORD (OB) (OM)

**MANSFIELD**, Joseph A. & **MANSFIELD**, Nancy d/o Robert MANSFIELD surety Robert CAVE 25 Aug 1828 (OB)

**MANSFIELD**, Reuben s/o John MANSFIELD and Lydia WHITE age 34 w carpenter POB POR Orange POC & **BANKS**, Lucy d/o Garrett JOHNSON and Nelly BERKELEY age 30 w POB POR Orange POC: POM Orange 17 Aug 1867 OMR 9 Aug 1867 OML

**MANSFIELD**, William H. & **EDDINS**, Selina permission from Thomas EDDINS surety William EDDINS 30 Dec 1817 (OB)

**MANSPOILE**, Johny & **WOOD**, Sally d/o Catey WOOD surety Zachariah LEE 17 Feb 1796 (OB) by Nathaniel SANDERS 19 Feb 1796 (OM)

**MARKES**, Joseph & **MIDDLEBROOK**, Mary Ann d/o Archibald MIDDLEBROOK who is also surety by Joseph S. JACKSON 9 Dec 1843 (OB) (OM)

**MARKSPILE**, Michael & **LONG**, Ann both of St. Thomas Parish 9 Dec 1772 (Deed Book 17)

**MARR**, Alexander & **RUCKER**, Sarah 5 Jan 1760 (Orange Fee Book)

**MARR**, Henry & **RUCKER**, Frances d/o William RUCKER who is also surety 4 Sep 1820 (OB)

**MARR**, Joel & **MILLER**, Betsy over 21 years surety Robert MALLORY 232 Apr 1810 (OB) by Jacob WATTS 10 May 1810 (OM)

**MARR,** Thomas & **HARVEY,** Sally over 21 years surety Thomas
HARVEY 24 Dec 1810 (OB) 3 Jan 1811 by George BINGHAM (OM)

**MARSH,** Alexander & **LEE,** Ann Eliza d/o Sarah LEE surety Lafayette
LEE 19 Nov 1846 (OB)

**MARSH,** Peter & **JOLLETT,** Lucy Walker d/o James JOLLETTE who is
also surety by William DOUGLAS, Methodist 24 Mar 1806 (OB)
(OM)

**MARSH,** Thomas & **JOLLETT,** Malindey permission from James
JOLLETT surety Simeon JOLLETT 12 Mar 1822 (OB)

**MARSHALL,** Archalus Lewis s/o James and Elizabeth MARSHALL age
22 s merchant POB Orange POR Barboursville & **FITZHUGH,** Estell
d/o Madison and Mary F. FITZHUGH age 18 s POB Green Co POR
Barboursville POM Orange 22 May 1855 OMR

**MARSHALL,** Coleman & **BICKERS,** Joanna permission from Nicholas
BICKERS surety Benjamin C. BICKERS 3 Aug 1815 (OB)

**MARSHALL,** George & **BOSWELL,** Ann surety William LOYD 30 Sep
1787 (OB)

**MARSHALL,** Henry & **WALTON,** Elizabeth by George BINGHAM 25
Jan 1810 (OM)

**MARSHALL,** Henry & **WOOD,** Elenor 27 Dec 1804 by George
BINGHAM (Misc Min Ret)

**MARSHALL,** Loudon & **LANGFORD,** Jincy by George BINGHAM 18
Feb 1827 (OM)

**MARSHALL,** Smith POC age 30 s POB POR Orange s/o Mingo
MARSHALL and Nancy HOLMES laborer & **JOHNSON,** Milly POC
age 20 s POB Madison Co POR Orange d/o Richard JOHNSON and
Lucy JOHNSON 5 Sep 1869 POM Orange by Frank TIBBS (OMR)

**MARSHALL,** Thomas & **ANCELL,** Nancy surety Robert ANCEL 26
Dec 1804 (OB) 27 Dec 1804 by George BINGHAM (Misc Min Ret)

**MARSHALL,** Thomas A. s/o James and Elizabeth MARSHALL age 22 s
POB Orange POR Barboursville & **FITZHUGH,** Louisa C. d/o James
M. and Mary F. FITZHUGH age 17 s POB Green Co POR
Barboursville; POM Orange 24 Dec 1857 OMR 23 Dec 1857 OML

**MARSHALL,** Valentine H. & **LOYD,** Frances d/o Robert LOYD who is
also surety 22 Dec 1830 (OB)

**MARSHALL,** Willis & **WHITELAW,** Sarah surety Alexander
WHITELAW 29 May 1820 (OB)

**MARTIN,** Benjamin & **KNIGHT,** Mary d/o Ephriam KNIGHT [in his
permission, Ephraim calls his daughter Eliza Ann] surety Bejamin
JACOBS 6 Jan 1796 (OB)

**MARTIN,** Brice & **LUCAS,** Rachel 8 Jul 1793 surety Isaac DAVIS (OB)
7 Aug 1793 by George EVE (OM)

**MARTIN**, George & **BURKET**, Elizabeth R. 29 Apr 1828 surety David C. WATTS (OB)

**MARTIN**, George & **JONES**, Elizabeth d/o Thomas JONES surety John YOUNG 14 Jun 1783 (OB)

**MARTIN**, George permission from Henry MARTIN & **SISSON**, Fanny permission from Sary SISSON 30 Jul 1804 surety Abner SISSON (OB) 2 Aug 1804 by Nath. SANDERS (Misc Min Ret)

**MARTIN**, James age 45 w POB POR Orange s/o William MARTIN and Malinda FAULCONER farmer & **LEE**, Fanny G. age 22 s POB POR Orange d/o George LEE and Malinda BALLS 17 Oct 1872 POM Orange by E.R. PERRY (OMR)

**MARTIN**, James s/o William and Malinda MARTIN age 25 s cooper POB POR Orange & **MARTIN**, Mary Ann d/o Thomas and Sarah MARTIN age 25 s POB POR Orange POM Orange 17 Oct 1854 OMR

**MARTIN**, John age 21 y 5 mo telephone operator POB POR Albemarle s/o William MARTIN and Eliza A. PURCEL (?) & **FAULCONER**, Susie age 17y 7 mo POB POR Orange d/o E.J. FAULCONER and Maria L. ALLEN POM Gordonsville 29 May 1877 (OMR)

**MARTIN**, Lewis A. age 27[b. 6 Feb 1850] s shoemaker POB POR Spotsylvania s/o James MARTIN and Mary J. MASTIN & **SULLIVAN**, Laura Jane age 19 [b. 17 Jun 1858] s POB POR Orange d/o George SULLIVAN and Lucy Ann FISHER POM Orange 9 Dec 1877 (OMR)

**MARTIN**, Mallory s/o Thomas and Sarah MARTIN age 22 s carpenter POB POR Orange & **BROWN**, Lucy Ann d/o John and Martha BROWN age 21 s POB POR Orange; POM Orange 18 Oct 1857 (OMR) 17 Oct 1857 (OML)

**MARTIN**, Mallory s/o Thomas MARTIN and Sarah COLLINS age 31 w carpenter POB POR Orange & **MARTIN** Lucilla d/o William MARTIN and Malinda FAULCONER age 21 s POB POR Orange; POM Orange 28 Dec 1865 (OMR) 25 Dec 1865 (OML)

**MARTIN**, Millard F. age 22 s cooper POB POR Orange s/o James MARTIN and Mary Ann MARTIN & **TALLEY**, Lucy M. age 21 s POB POR Orange d/o William E. TALLEY and Mary F. BOND POM Orange 15 Oct 1876 by E. R. PERRY OMR

**MARTIN**, Thomas & **COLLINS**, Sarah G. 26 May 1828 surety William CLARK (OB)

**MARTIN**, Thomas age 75 w farmer POB POR Orange s/o William H. MARTIN and Mary MALLORY & **RILEY**, Dorothea V. age 21 s POB POR Orange d/o Jacob RILEY and _____ HICKS POM Orange 1 Oct 1879 (OMR)

**MARTIN**, William & **ATKINS**, Patsy; 3 Dec 1808 (OM)

**MARTIN,** William & **FAULCONER,** Melinda d/o Elias FAULCONER who is surety 19 Dec 1821 (OB) 20 Dec 1821 by George MORRIS (OM)

**MARTIN,** William & **FERNEYHOUGH,** Nancy 24 Dec 1812 surety John FERNEYHOUGH (OB) 27 Dec 1812 by J. GOSS (OM)

**MARTIN,** William & **SNELL,** Margaret 27 Dec 1810 surety John SNELL by J. GOSS (OB) (OM)

**MARTIN,** William H. & **MALLORY,** Phebe 29 Jun 1829 surety Davis ATKINS (OB)

**MARTIN,** William H. s/o James MARTIN and Sidney WILLOUGHBY age 48 [b. 1818] w farmer POB Spotsylvania POR Orange & **POWELL,** Elizabeth H. d/o William POWELL age 28 s POB Spotsylvania POR Orange; POM Orange 15 Dec 1864 (OMR) 5 Dec 1864 (OML)

**MARTIN,** William H. s/o Thomas and Sarah MARTIN age 24 s carpenter POB POR Orange & **BROWN,** Sarah F. d/o John G. and Martha F. BROWN age 17 s POB Madison POR Orange; POM Orange 23 Oct 1855 OMR

**MARTIN,** William J. age 22 s carpenter POR Orange & **KENNEDY,** Lucy M. d/o Hiram P. and Mary KENNEDY age 27 s POB POR Orange; POM Orange 3 Dec 1857 OMR 1 Dec 1857 OML

**MARTIN,** William James & **WOOD,** Catharine 23 Dec 1839 surety Albert G. PALMER (OB)

**MARYE,** Robert B. & **MADISON,** Mary F. 16 Jun 1843 surety Robert T. WILLIS (OB) 22 Jun 1843 by J. EARNEST (OM)

**MASON,** Baylor & **CLARKE,** Catey d/o John CLARKE surety Zachariah WOOD 10 May 1813 (OB)

**MASON,** C.R. Jr. age 35 s POB Hanover POR Orange s/o C.R. MASON Sr. and Drusilla BOXLEY farmer & **WOOLFOLK,** Mary M. age 19 s POB POR Orange d/o James T. WOOLFOLK and Sarah M. F. MOORE 9 Nov 1880 POM Orange by L.A. CUTLER (OMR)

**MASON,** Charles & **JONES,** Lucy surety George MASON 22 Dec 1820 (OB)

**MASON,** Charles G. age 22 farmer POB Culpeper POR Orange s/o James S. MASON and Sarah C. MASON & **WILTSHIRE,** Mary E. age 22 s POB POR Orange d/o Alfred WILTSHIRE and Sarah A. FAULCONER POM Orange 5 Mar 1876 by Melzi S. CHANCELLOR (OMR)

**MASON,** Charles T. & **JONES,** Milly d/o James JONES surety Richard R. JONES 11 Aug 1832 (OB)

**MASON,** Edwin & **SAUNDERS,** Mary d/o B. SAUNDERS surety Benjamin T. SAUNDERS 22 Feb 1847 (OB) by Herndon FRAZER 25 Feb 1847 (OM)

**MASON,** Enoch & **PAYNE,** Frances surety Charles H. AMOS 17 Dec 1831 (OB)

**MASON,** George & **ROACH,** Mary d/o Christian F. ROACH 5 Jun 1829 (OB)

**MASON,** George permission from brother Charles MASON & **SANDERS,** Millisent d/o Nathaniel SANDERS surety Jonathan PEACHER 10 Aug 1797 (OB)

**MASON,** Isam B. & **SEBREE,** Lucy s permission from Martin JOHNSON surety William WATTS 25 Dec 1797 (OB) by Hamilton GOSS 27 Dec 1797 (OM)

**MASON,** James & **JONES,** Ann surety Jefferson ALMOND 6 Sep 1842 (OB)

**MASON,** James & **OAKS,** Nancy surety Charles MASON 24 Aug 1795 (OB) by Nathaniel SANDERS 26 Aug 1795 (OM)

**MASON,** John & **FAULCONER,** Elizabeth d/o Thomas FAULCONER surety Samuel MASON 16 Aug 1796 (OB)

**MASON,** John & **SEBREE,** Lucy 27 Dec 1795 by Hamilton GOSS (OM)

**MASON,** John A. age 35 s soldier POB Spotsylvania POR Washington DC s/o James W. MASON and Ann R. JONES & **MASON,** Elizabeth E. age 28 s POB Culpeper POR Orange d/o James L. MASON and Eleanor B. FIELD POM Maple Spring Orange 13 Aug 1879 by Sanders MASON (OMR)

**MASON,** John E. s/o Sanders MASON and Catherine JONES age 19 s farmer POB POR Orange & **BROWN,** Martha C. d/o John BROWN and Martha F. HOLBERT age 22 s POB POR Orange; POM Orange 20 Dec 1866 (OMR) (OML)

**MASON,** Joseph & **TANDY,** Ann d/o Henry TANDY Sr.[ and Ann MILLS] surety Will TANDY, brother 26 Jun 1809 (OB)

**MASON,** Major & **OVERTON,** Elizabeth surety Willis OVERTON 15 Oct 1827 (OB)

**MASON,** Peter s/o George MASON & **RICHARDS,** Lucy d/o Ike RICHARDS surety Fielding JONES 26 Dec 1827 (OB)

**MASON,** Richard R. s/o Charles and Lucy MASON age 21 s farmer POB POR Orange & **CANADY,** Ann C. d/o James and Ann CANADAY age 18 s POB POR Orange; POM Orange 5 Apr 1855 (OMR)

**MASON,** Robert & **HUTCHERSON,** Sarah d/o Washington HUTCHERSON surety Richard TINDER 19 Dec 1837 (OB)

**MASON,** Samuel & **GRAVES,** Lyddia over 21years surety Thomas GRAVES 29 Oct 1804 (OB)

**MASON,** Samuel age 68 w farmer POB POR Orange s/o James MASON and Nancy OAKS & **BOULLING,** Susan age 34 s POB Spotsylvania POR Orange POM Orange 9 Apr 1876 (OMR)

**MASON,** Samuel Jr. ward of Samuel MASON & **PERRY,** Sally
permission from Peter PERRY surety George MASON 26 Nov 1827
(OB)

**MASON,** Sanders permission from George MASON & **JONES,** Caty d/o
James JONES surety Fielding JONES 10 Dec 1821 (OB)

**MASON,** Thomas s/o Bailey MASON who is also surety & **CLARKE,**
Nancy 1 Oct 1814 (OB) 20 Oct 1814 by John GARNETT (OM)

**MASON,** William G. & **SANDERS,** Lucy Ann; POM Orange 14 Dec
1852 (OMR) (OML)

**MASTIN,** Thomas J. age 55 w POB POR Spotsylvania Co. s/o John
MASTIN and Mary JONES farmer & **DAVIS,** Lucinda M. age 47 w
POB Tennessee POR Orange d/o Abner LILE and Martha CATE 17
Oct 1869 POM Orange Richard STEPHENS (OMR)

**MASTIN,** William F. age 23 s POB POR Spotsylvania Co s/o Thomas
MASTIN and Elizabeth HICKS farmer & **DUNAWAY,** Margaret age
28 s POB POR Orange d/o Edmund DUNAWAY and Sarah KNIGHT
22 Aug 1872 POM Orange by Melzi CHANCELLOR (OMR)

**MATTHEWS,** Clayton & **CHILES,** Susan d/o James CHILES surety
Walter G. CHILES 23 May 1825 (OB)

**MATTHEWS,** Drury C. & **ROBINSON,** Martha E. 26 May 1856 (OML)

**MAUPIN,** David & **DAVIS,** Jerusha by George BINGHAM 5 Feb 1812
(OM)

**MAUPIN,** Gabriel & **BURTON,** Virginia d/o William BURTON surety
Robert BURTON 22 Apr 1826 (OB) by J. GOSS 11 May 1826 (OM)

**MAUPIN,** Gabriel & **HUCKSTEP,** Lucy E. d/o Josiah HUCKSTEP
surety William HUCKSTEP 18 Sep 1826 (OB)

**MAUPIN,** Jennings & **MILLER,** Sally; 25 Dec 1797 surety Thomas
MILLER (OB)

**MAUPIN,** Jennings & **SORRILLE,** Sarah Ophelia d/o Thomas
SORRILLE surety William R. ROBINSON 12 Nov 1829 (OB)

**MAUPIN,** Tyre & **BEADLES,** Jane d/o John BEADLES 14 Jun 1824
surety William MILLER (OB)

**MAURY,** Leonard H. & **CAMPBELL,** Virginia M. d/o William
CAMPBELL surety Robert WILSON 24 Jan 1803 (OB)

**MAXWELL,** John & **HENRY,** Agatha surety Benson HENRY by George
EVE 6 Feb 1792 (OB) (OM)

**MAXWELL,** Samuel M. age 30 s farmer POB Wilkes Barre, PA POR
Orange s/o James L. MAXWELL and Elizabeth MEREDITH &
**TALIAFERRO,** Mary V. age 25 s POB POR Orange d/o John F.
TALIAFERRO and Rebecca MALLORY POM Taylor tsp. [sic]Orange
24 Oct 1878 by R.L. MAXWELL (OMR)

**MAXWELL**, Thomas & **HENRY,** Dulley d/o William HENRY surety James MAXWELL 27 Mar 1792 (OB) by George EVE 3 Apr 1792 (OM)

**MAY**, Alexander POC age 21 s POB POR Orange s/o Squire MAY and Clio MADISON farm laborer & **JOHNSON,** Lucy POC age 18 s POB POR Orange d/o Thomas JOHNSON and Polly MCINTOSH 8 Jan 1874 POM Orange (OMR)

**MAY**, Beverley POC age 23 s POB POR Orange s/o Esquire MAY and Clia MADISON laborer & **JACKSON,** Jane POC age 23 POB POR Orange d/o Robert JACKSON and Esther DANIEL 25 Dec 1873 POM Orange by C. GILLUM (OMR)

**MAY**, Jeremiah POC age 21 s labourer POB POR Orange s/o Squire MAY and Cleo MADISON & **MADISON,** Emily POC age 19 s POB POR Orange POM Mt. Pleasant, Orange 24 Dec 1878 by C.T. JOHNSON (OMR)

**MAY**, Squire POC age 41 w POB POR Orange s/o Aaron MAY and Hannah _____ farmer & **TERRILL,** Rosanna POC age 27 s POB POR Orange d/o Amy _____ 8 Jun 1873 POM Orange by R.B. SULLIVAN (OMR)

**MAYO**, Robert A. s/o William MAYO & **TALIAFERRO,** Sarah D. d/o Hay TALIAFERRO Sr. surety Lawrence T. DADE 6 Oct 1819 (OB)

**MAYO**, William P. s/o Allen L. MAYO & **ROUTT,** Dorenda A. 13 Oct 1851 (OML)

**MCALISTER**, John & **TURNER,** Cary/Clary d/o Ann TURNER; 13 Nov 1798 surety James TURNER (OB)

**MCALISTER,** Thomas C. age 28 s farmer POB Madison POR Orange s/o Arthur MCALISTER and Sarah E. JONES & **JONES,** Sarah E. age 27 s POB POR Orange d/o B.F. JONES and Mary E. CROOKS POM Orange 21 Nov 1878 by Thomas W. LENOX, Baptist minister (OMR)

**MCCLAMROCK,** John & **ESTES,** Jenny d/o Elisha ESTES surety Caleb SMOOT 15 Aug 1802 (OB) by George BINGHAM 18 Aug 1802 (OM)

**MCCLARNE,** John age 23 s POB Pennsylvania POR Orange s/o Thomas MCCLARNE and Clementine DOLBY farmer & **CAMPBELL,** Ursulia age 21 POB POR Orange d/o James S. CAMPBELL and Mary MCCLARY 27 Jan 1870 POM Orange by E.R. PERRY (OMR)

**MCCLARNEY,** Robert & **LONG,** Elizabeth surety Samuel FLINN 28 Oct 1822 (OB)

**MCCLARNEY,** Roger & **MORRIS,** Sarah 17 Dec 1795 surety Arculus HAWKINS (OB)

**MCCLARY,** Charles L. s/o Tandy B. MCCLARY and Mary F. JACOBS age 24 s blacksmith POB Orange POR Madison Co & **BLEDSOE,** Lucy d/o John BLEDSOE and Peggy PERRY age 22 s POB POR Orange; POM Orange 26 Jul 1866 (OMR) 25 Jul 1866 (OML)

**MCCLARY**, David & **PICKER,** Catey by George BINGHAM 5 Nov 1801 (OB)

**McCLARY**, James F. s/o William and Mary MCCLARY age 22 s boot & shoemaker POB POR Orange & **BICKERS**, Susan A. d/o Proctor and Lucy BICKERS age 24 s POB POR Orange; POM Orange 16 Nov 1854 (OMR)

**MCCLARY**, William F. & **DEMPSEY,** Phebe d/o Daniel DEMPSEY surety Tandy B. MCCLARY 28 Aug 1822 (OB)

**MCCOMRICK** (aka MCCOMRACK), William & **NEWMAN,** Wilhelmina; POM Orange 8 Jun 1852 (OMR) (OML)

**MCCONE**, Daniel G. age 23 s farmer POB Lancaster Co., PA POR Orange s/o Samuel MCCONE and Sarah KHEEN & **TINDER,** Cornelia A. age 27 s POB POR Orange d/o Arthur TINDER and Margaret H. BLEDSOE POM Orange 28 Dec 1876 (OMR)

**MCCORD**, Samuel A. age 26 s POB Lancaster Co. PA POR Orange s/o Samuel MCCORD and Sarah KEEN cooper & **TINDER,** Lucy R. age 21 s POB POR Orange d/o Arthur TINDER and Margaret H. BLEDSOE 31 Dec 1872 POM Orange by Sanders MASON (OMR)

**MCCOY**, George & **NICKINGS,** Elizabeth d/o Nathaniel NICKINGS; age 24 years surety George MARSHALL 10 Mar 1788 (OB) 11 Mar 1789 by George EVE (OM)

**MCCOYLE**, Michael over 21 years & **MCKINNEY,** Mary d/o William MCKINNEY who is also surety 18 Dec 1809 (OB)

**MCCRACKEN**, Patrick s/o Thomas and Ellen MCCRACKEN age 28 s farmer POB Ireland POR Spotsylvania & **DICKEY,** Elizabeth B. d/o James and Joanna DICKEY age 41 s POB Nelson Co POR Orange POM Orange 2 Mar 1857 (OMR) 28 Feb 1857 (OML)

**MCCRACKER**, Michael & **ALMOND,** Martha Jane M. 16 Dec 1856 (OML)

**MCDANIEL**, Derenzey & **BROOKS,** Susanna d/o John BROOKS surety Joshua KENDLE 25 Sep 1793 (OB)

**MCDANIEL**, Jeremiah & **BROOKS,** Rachel over 21 years d/o Jane BROOKS surety Derenzy MCDANIEL 4 Dec 1799 (OB)

**MCDANIEL**, John L. & **WEBSTER,** Elizabeth Mildred d/o Shadrack WEBSTER who is also surety 25 May 1829 (OB)

**MCDANIEL,** Samuel POC age 34 s farm labourer POB POR Orange s/o Samuel MCDANIEL and Phoebe BARRETT & **BROADUS,** Betsy POC age 23 s POB POR Orange POM Orange 16 Jul 1879 (OMR)

**MCDANIEL**, Stacy & **LAMB,** Sally; 11 Apr 1799 by George BINGHAM (OM)

**MCDANIEL,** Thomas & **LAMB,** Polly d/o Richard LAMB who is also surety 23 Apr 1827 (OB) by George BINGHAM 31 Apr 1827 (OM)

**MCDANIEL,** William POC age 29 s blacksmith POB POR Orange s/o Benjamin MCDANIEL and Patsy PIERCE & **SANDERS,** Sally POC age 29 w POB POR Orange d/o Horace ELLIS POM Tatton, Orange 5 Dec 1878 by John S. HANSBROUGH (OMR)

**MCDONALD** (or MCDANIEL), Patrick & **MILLER,** Elizabeth d/o Judith MILLER surety John MILLER 25 Jul 1792 (OB)

**MCDONALD,** John s/o Thomas and Mary MCDONALD age 28 s conductor POB Fauquier Co POR Shenandoah Co & **CULLEN,** Marietta d/o George and Barbara Ann CULLEN age 24 s POB Shenandoah Co POR Orange; POM Orange 18 Nov 1857 (OMR) 17 Nov 1857 (OML)

**MCFARLANG,** William s/o John MCFARLANG & **ALSOP,** Fanny surety Daniel COKELY 6 Jan 1808 (OB)

**MCFARLING,** John & **DEDMAN,** Frances age 23 years on 23 Feb 1811 surety George HERNDON 14 Dec 1810 (OB)

**MCGEE,** William G. & **LANCASTER,** Amanda M. surety Burruss MUNDAY 11 Dec 1848 (OB)

**MCGEHEE,** William G. age 23 s POB Louisa POR Orange s/o A.J. MCGEHEE and Mary Jane HAMILTON farmer & **WIGGLESWORTH,** Mary Jane age 23 s POB POR Orange d/o Claiborne WIGGLESWORTH and Eliza REYNOLDS 25 Apr 1880 POM Orange by Melzi S. CHANCELLOR (OMR)

**MCGHEE,** John S. POR Louisa Co. & **HARRIS,** Lucy d/o Frances HARRIS POR Orange 25 Nov 1811 Hezekiah ATKINS surety (OB) 11 Dec 1811 by George MORRIS (OMR)

**MCINTIRE,** Solomon H. & **CLARKE,** Eunice H. surety John H. RIADON 17 Aug 1826 (OB)

**MCINTOSH,** Jacob s/o Albert MCINTOSH and Frances ELLIS age 21 s laborer/farmer POB POR Orange POC & **WASHINGTON,** Martha age 19 s POB POR Orange POC POM Orange 12 Aug 1866 (OMR) 11 Aug 1866 (OML)

**MCINTOSH,** Joe POC age 24 s POB POR Orange s/o William MCINTOSH and Martha YOUNG laborer & **CARPENTER,** Mary POC age 21 s POB POR Orange 8 Jan 1880 POM Orange (OMR)

**MCINTOSH,** William POC age 21 s POB POR Orange s/o Joseph MCINTOSH and Patsy WILLIS laborer & **GAINES,** Cora POC age 19 s POB Madison Co POR Orange d/o Gilford GAINES 10 Feb 1872 POM Orange by Philip JOHNSON (OMR)

**MCKIM,** Charles G. age 29 s farmer POB Richmond city POR Orange s/o William A. MCKIM and Caroline MASON & **HUGHES,** Jessie age 19 s POB POR Orange d/o Jefferson HUGHES and Mary A. HERNDON POM Orange 20 Dec 1877 (OMR)

**MCKINLEY**, Hugh & **FINNELL**, Anna Rita surety William FINNELL 26 Dec 1796 (OB)

**MCKINNEY**, Travis & **POLLARD**, Betsy surety Edmund POLLARD 7 Jan 1801 (OB)

**MCMULLAN**, William s/o James MCMULLAN & **CAVE**, Ann d/o Abner CAVE who is also surety 27 Mar 1825 (OB)

**MCMULLAN**, Henry & **TAYLOR**, Lurenna surety William S. WALKER 8 Dec 1831 (OB)

**MCMULLAN**, James  John MCMULLAN states James is of age & **KENDALL**, Edy d/o Henry and Ruth KENDALL surety James HARVEY 14 Mar 1796 (OB)

**MCMULLAN**, Jeremiah s/o James MCMULLAN & **SHELTON**, Frances D. d/o Thomas SHELTON surety William SHELTON 14 Dec 1835 (OB)

**MCMULLAN**, Patrick permission by John MCMULLAN and Theodora Beasley MCMULLEN & **WALKER**, Sarah surety Thomas WALKER 2 Jan 1792 (OB) 5 Jan 1792 by George EVE (OM)

**MCMULLAN**, Thomas Walker s/o James and Frances MCMULLAN age 22 farmer POB Green Co & **BELL**, Eliza Ann d/o Francis (dec) and Mary BELL age 21 POB Orange; POM Orange 8 Feb 1854 (OMR) 4 Feb 1854 (OML)

**MCMULLIN**, James Jr. & **WALKER**, Frances surety William WALKER 31 Jan 1825 (OB)

**MCMULLIN**, John POR Greene Co. s/o James MCMULLIN & **WALKER**, Peachy POR Madison Co. d/o John WALKER Jr. who was a farmer 26 Jan 1818 (OB)

**MCMURRAN**, Edwin M. age 30 s POB Frederick Co. POR Culpeper Co s/o Samuel MCMURRAN and Ann S. SNODGRASS druggist & **THOMSON**, Mary Eliza age 25 s POB POR Orange Co. d/o Alfred THOMSON and Sarah E. SNEED 6 Jan 1869 POM Orange by R.L. MCMURRAN (OMR)

**MEADE**, James N. s/o Madison MEADE and Sarah E. ROBINSON age 30 s carpenter POB Louisa Co POR Orange & **LANCASTER**, Eliza A. d/o John LANCASTER and Malissa BRIGHTWELL age 25 s POB POR Orange POM Orange 19 Dec 1865 (OMR) 15 Dec 1865 (OML)

**MEADE**, Richard N. s/o Madison MEADE and Sarah A. ROBINSON age 27 s farmer POB Louisa Co POR Orange & **LANCASTER**, Amanda C. d/o John LANCASTER and Malicia BRIGHTWELL age 24 s POB POR Orange; POM Orange 3 Oct 1867 (OMR) 2 Oct 1867 (OML)

**MEADOWS**, Jacob & **ROACH**, Nancy by George BINGHAM 8 Dec 1815 (OM)

**MEDLEY**, Ambrose POR Brumfield Parish [now in Madison County] & **BURTON**, Frankie POR St. Thomas Parish surety Capt. May BURTON 12 Dec 1775 (OB)

**MEDLEY**, Jacob & **HEAD**, Fanny 15 Jul 1804 by Hamilton GOSS (Misc Min Ret)

**MELBURN**, William & **TAYLOR**, Sarah surety Charles TAYLOR 1 Oct 1801 (OB)

**MELONE**, Eli & **DUKE**, Eveline d/o William DUKE surety Barnett SMITH 27 Dec 1826 (OB)

**MELONE**, John & **GOLDING**, Nancy d/o Richard GOLDING surety Edmund ESTES 6 Mar 1820 (OB)

**MELONE**, William & **WAYLAND**, Mary permission from Henry WAYLAND surety Matthew MARQUESS by George BINGHAM 14 Jan 1809 (OB) (OM)

**MELTON**, Samuel N. age 21 s POB POR Louisa Co s/o J.H. MELTON and Louisa A. BURRUSS farmer & **OGG**, Laura age 21 s POB Louisa Co POR Orange d/o Thomas OGG and Jenette MELTON 12 Dec 1872 POM Orange by James O. MOSS (OMR)

**MENEFEE**, Spencer & **BOSTON**, Ritta surety Joseph BOSTON 20 Nov 1786 (OB)

**MEREDITH**, Jaquelin M. s/o Reuben and Mary MEREDITH age 22 s farmer POB Hanover Co POR Stafford & **BANKHEAD**, Ellen d/o William and Dorothea BANKHEAD age 19 s POB Caroline Co POR Orange; POM Orange 5 Jan 1858 (OMR) (OML)

**MERIWETHER**, Charles H. physician & **ANDERSON**, Ann Eliza d/o William ANDERSON surety Dabney MINOR 25 Sep 1815 (OB)

**MERIWITHER**, Garrett M. & **MINOR**, Mary Ann d/o Dabney MINOR surety William M. ANDERSON 24 Sep 1819 (OB)

**MERRIWETHER**, Charles & **MINOR**, Ann surety and guardian is Dabney MINOR 11 Sep 1800 (OB)

**MERRYMAN**, William over 21 years & **STEVENS**, Elizabeth over 21 years surety Merryman STEVENS 10 Oct 1804 (OB)

**MICHIE**, James H. age 23 s conductor C. & O. railroad POB Louisa POR Orange s/o James M. MICHIE and Mildred POWERS & **LYNN**, Laura E. age 19 s POB POR Orange d/o A.J. LYNN and Nannie GOODWIN POM Gordonsville, Orange 10 Oct 1878 by J. Ad. FRENCH (OMR)

**MICHIE**, James s/o Lewis MICHIE and Rachel THOMSON age 25 s r.r. laborer POB Louisa Co POR Orange POC & **WALKER**, Jane d/o Joe Walker POB POR Orange POC; POM Orange 23 Sep 1867 (OMR) (OML)

**MICHIE**, John & **EARLY**, Frances d/o Theodoshe EARLEY surety James EARLEY 23 Jul 1787 (OB)

**MIDDLEBROOK,** Archibald & **BOSWELL,** Lucy surety Charles BOSWELL 27 Nov 1820 (OB)

**MILLER,** Aylett & **SPILMAN,** Mary d/o Robert B. SPILMAN surety Alex H. SPILMAN 22 Mar 1827 (OB)

**MILLER,** Christian & **BEAZLEY,** Elizabeth 7 Jun 1808 by George BINGHAM (OM)

**MILLER,** Daniel & **SORRILLE,** Elizabeth d/o Thomas SORRILLE surety William SIMS 4 Mar 1823 (OB)

**MILLER,** George Henry age 23 s POB Goochland Co POR Orange s/o Andrew J. MILLER and Sarah Ann ANDERSON farmer & **SMITH,** Arianner age 21 s POB Albemarle Co POR Orange d/o John SMITH and Lucy _____ 4 Jan 1872 POM Orange by J.W. MCCOWN (OMR)

**MILLER,** Henry & **PIGLEN,** Margaret both of St. Thomas Parish 11 Feb 1778 by banns (Deed Book 17)

**MILLER,** Henry s/o John and Mary MILLER age 29 s gardener POB Germany POR Orange & **SKINNER,** Leanna d/o John SKINNER & _____ WEBB age 30 s POB POR Orange; POM Orange 5 Jun 1867 (OMR) 1 Jun 1867 (OML)

**MILLER,** James K. & **JENNINGS,** Ann Chapman d/o Berryman JENNINGS and Ann CHAPMAN surety William C. JENNINGS 18 Jun 1831 (OB)

**MILLER,** James & **LLOYD,** Sarah d/o Robert LLOYD who is also surety 23 Jan 1821 (OB) by Leeroy CANADAY 25 Jan 1821 (OM)

**MILLER,** Jesse & **STEVENS,** Ann d/o Joseph STEVENS surety William STEVENS 19 Jan 1796 (OB) 11 Feb 1796 by Nathaniel SANDERS (OM)

**MILLER,** John E. age 24 s farmer POB Goochland POR Orange s/o John MILLER and Mildred WARE & **WOOD,** Isabella M. age 19 s POB Madison POR Orange d/o William WOOD and Catharine A. MITCHELL POM Orange 14 Dec 1876 (OMR)

**MILLER,** John Jr. & **MILLER,** Anna d/o John MILLER surety Thomas SORRILLE 2 Jun 1823 (OB)

**MILLER,** John A. & **RUCKER,** Sarah A. surety Jonathan TWYMAN 10 Feb 1838 (OB) by E.G. SHIP 16 Feb 1838 (OM)

**MILLER,** John & **LLOYD,** Mary surety Henry LLOYD 8 Mar 1823 (OB)

**MILLER,** Robert & **JENNINGS,** Ann surety George WETHERALL 6 Jan1816 (OB)

**MILLER,** Thomas & **PLUNKETT,** Sarah d/o Jesse PLUNKETT surety William CLARK 22 Dec 1794 (OB) by George EVE 13 Jan 1795 (OM)

**MILLS,** Mitchell POC age 27 w (he has no profession due to blindness) POB Louisa POR Orange s/o James MILLS and Eliza A. ROBINSON & **HENDERSON,** Lucy M. POC age 19 s POB POR Orange d/o

Alfred HENDERSON and Lucy _____ POM Orange 25 Sep 1879 (OMR)

**MILLS**, Thomas M. POB Louisa Co & **GRAVES**, Mary S.(?); 21 Aug 1852 (OML)

**MILLS,** William POC age 22 s farm laborer POB Upsher Co. WV POR Madison s/o George MILLS and Susan FRY & **BANKS,** Celia POC age 22 s POB Greene POR Orange d/o Ezekiel BANKS and Sophia BANKS POM Orange 22 Sep 1877 (OMR)

**MILTON**, James C. & **TAYLOR**, Mary 14 Jul 1802 POM Orange by Robert JONES (Misc Min Ret)

**MINICH**, Daniel & **WOOLFREY**, Peggy M. d/o Richard WOOLFREY surety James W. WOOLFREY 12 Jan 1847 (OB)

**MINION**, John M. & **SCOTT**, Elizabeth ward of George JACOBS; 20 Dec 1852 (OML)

**MINNICK**, John C. age 19 s POB POR Orange s/o Daniel MINNICK and Margaret WOOLFREY farmer & **MCLEAREN**, Charlotte age 20 s POB Lancaster, PA POR Orange d/o Thomas MCLEAREN and Clementina DOBBINS 12 Oct 1873 POM Orange by Sanders MASON (OMR)

**MINOR**, Aaron POC age 24 s POB Louisa Co POR Orange s/o Daniel MINOR and Julia A. WASHINGTON laborer & **TAYLOR**, Mollie POC age 17 s POB POR Orange d/o Jacob TAYLOR and Melinda POWELL 2 Apr 1873 POM Orange by F.L. GIPSON (OMR)

**MINOR**, Addison POC age 22 s POB Spotsylvania POR Orange s/o Thomas MINOR and Lizzie LEWIS laborer & **CARPENTER**, Mary POC age 21 s POB Culpeper POR Orange d/o Henry CARPENTER and Susan WISE 2 Sep 1880 POM Orange by William CAMPBELL (OMR)

**MINOR**, Henry POC age 21 s POB Spotsylvania POR Orange s/o George MINOR and Sarah POINDEXTER laborer & **EVANS**, Septener age 17 s POB Richmond POR Orange d/o George EVANS and Courtney BAYLOR 4 Apr 1880 POM Shady Grove Church, Orange by Willis ROBINSON (OMR)

**MINOR**, Lucius POC age 26 s rail road hand POB Louisa POR Orange s/o Lansy MARSHALL and Betty MARSHALL & **ROBINSON,** Mary POC age 23 w POB POR Orange d/o Rosa GALLERY POM Orange 25 Sep 1877 (OMR)

**MINOR**, Sandy age 22 s POB POR Orange s/o John MINOR and Clara _____ laborer & **DAVIS**, Kesiah age 19 POB Spotsylvania POR Orange d/o Pleasant DAVIS and Bettie DAVIS 24 Apr 1870 POM Orange by John C. WILLIS (OMR)

**MITCHEL**, William & **GRINNELS,** Rebecca; d/o Sarah GRINNELS surety George MARSHALL 21 Dec 1790 (OB)

**MITCHELL,** Benjamin & **PRITCHETT,** Elizabeth surety Jennings MAUPIN 21 Oct 1827 (OB)

**MITCHELL,** Benjamin & **SORRILLE,** Nancy d/o Thomas SORRILLE, surety Walter HOUSEWORTH 26 Mar 1832 (OB)

**MITCHELL,** Henry & **LUCAS,** Molly d/o William LUCAS Jr. who is also surety [Molly is called Mary in her father's permission] 18 Mar 1794 (OB)

**MITCHELL,** Henry & **TURNER,** Peggy surety Edward FAULCONER 19 Mar 1825 (OB) by Abraham TINSLEY 20 Mar 1825 (OM)

**MITCHELL,** Isaac N. s/o John MITCHELL and Ella WOOD age 37 w saddler POB Green Co POR Orange & **JOHNS,** Ann Maria d/o Mason JOHNS and Ann WALKER age 28 s POB Albemarle Co POR Orange; POM Orange 6 Sep 1866 (OMR) 27 Aug 1866 (OML)

**MITCHELL,** Isaac N. s/o John MITCHELL and Ellen WARD age 35 w saddler POB Green Co POR Orange & **SHOTWELL,** Sarah J. d/o Tazwell SHOTWELL and Columbia WOOD age 21 s POB POR Orange 20 Dec 1865 (OML)

**MITCHELL,** John s/o William MITCHELL & **WOOD,** Nelly surety Thomas DICKERSON 22 Sep 1813 (OB) by Jacob WATTS 30 Sep 1813 (OM)

**MITCHELL,** Robert POC age 26 w POB Albemarle Co POR Orange s/o Newton MITCHELL and Ellen CARTER & **BROOKS,** Ellen POC age 20 s POB Albemarle Co POR Orange d/o Frederick BROOKS & Maria ___ 29 Dec 1868 POM Orange by Frank NICHOLAS (OMR)

**MITCHELL,** Robert & **PARROTT,** Nancy Y. permission from John BEAZLEY surety Jonathan TWENTYMEN 21 Jan 1823 (OB) by George BINGHAM 23 Jan 1823 (OM)

**MITCHELL,** Thomas & **RUMSEY,** Nancy d/o Thomas RUMSEY surety Marmaduke BRANHAM 4 Feb 1805 (OB)

**MITCHELL,** William F. s/o John MITCHELL and Nelly WOOD age 39 s silversmith POB Green Co. POR Orange & **DAVIS,** M.S. d/o James DAVIS and Sarah J. AWL age 21 s POB POR Orange; POM Orange 3 Oct 1867 (OMR) (OML)

**MITCHELL,** William & **PARROTT,** Elizabeth permission from Larkin RUCKER surety Alfred TWYMAN 5 Apr 1825 (OB)

**MODENA,** Benjamin J. s/o Thomas H. MODENA and Mary A. HOPKINS age 26 s lawyer POB Fluvanna Co. POR Orange & **GAY,** Bettie F. d/o William GAY and Nancy DORAND age 22 s POB POR Orange POM Orange 29 Mar 1863 (OMR) 28 Mar 1863 (OML)

**MONCURE,** Henry W. age 18 s POB POR Stafford s/o Henry MONCURE and Julia WARWICK farmer & **HENDERSON,** Sadie L.

age 20 s POB POR Orange d/o Joseph M. HENDERSON and Hannah I. TERRILL 27 Jul 1880 POM Orange by L.A. CUTLER (OMR)

**MONCURE,** William age 27 s engineer POB Culpeper POR Orange s/o Charles P. MONCURE and Ann L. DANIEL & **CHAPMAN,** Belle age 22 s POB POR Orange d/o John M. CHAPMAN and Susan COLE 12 Dec 1878 by John S. HANSBROUGH (OMR)

**MONCURE,** William E. s/o John and Easter MONCURE age 28 s farmer POB POR Stafford & **BANKHEAD,** Georgianna Cary d/o William and Dorothea B. BANKHEAD age 22 s POB Caroline Co POR Orange; POM Orange 18 Oct 1853 (OMR) 17 Oct 1853 (OML)

**MONROE,** James s/o Man MONROE age 26 s servant POB POR Martin Co., N.C. POC & **ELKINS,** Mary Eliza d/o Frank ELKINS age 25 w POB POR Orange POC POM Orange 22 Feb 1866 (OMR) (OML)

**MONTAGUE,** David & **HERNDON,** Nancy surety Fielding HERNDON 27 Dec 1819 (OB)

**MONTAGUE,** William & **PERRY,** Sukey surety William DODD 1 Sep 1812 (OB) 3 Sep 1812 by Jeremiah CHANDLER (OM)

**MOOBRAY,** James & **BROCKMAN,** Mary Ann; 13 Jul 1852 (OML)

**MOOBRAY,** Zachariah & **CLATTERBUCK,** Mary d/o William CLATTERBUCK who is also surety 7 Feb 1820 (OB)

**MOODY,** John & **STOWERS,** Betsy d/o Mark STOWERS who is also surety 31 Mar 1808 (OB)

**MOORE,** Alexander & **FORD,** Lucy d/o William FORD surety Gowry WAUGH 13 May 1807 (OB) by Nathaniel SANDERS, Baptist 15 May 1807 (OM)

**MOORE,** Benjamin POC age 24 s labourer on C. & O. railroad s/o Nelson and Susan MOORE & **DANIEL,** Laura POC age 19 s POB POR Orange d/o Eveline DANIEL POM Orange 18 Apr 1878 (OMR)

**MOORE,** Bernard & **PRICE** Catey both of St. Thomas Parish 3 Oct 1770 (Orange Fee Book)

**MOORE,** Bernard POR Orange & **PRICE,** Catharine d/o Agalon PRICE 3 Oct 1770 (OML)

**MOORE,** C.W. age 34 s POB Culpeper Co POR Orange s/o Reuben MOORE and Ellen PETTY farmer & **BELL,** Virginia A. age 26 POB Louisa Co POR Orange d/o John B. BELL and Emily GILLESPIE 17 Feb 1870 POM Orange by H.E. HATCHER (OMR)

**MOORE,** Edmund C. s/o Robert L. & Mary MOORE age not certain w farmer POB POR Orange & **MOORE,** Fannie B. d/o W.C. and Matilda MOORE age 23 s POB & POR Orange; POM Orange 14 Aug 1855 (OMR) 10 Aug 1855 (OML)

**MOORE,** Francis Jr. & **HAWKINS,** Lucy 9 Nov 1761 (Orange Fee Book)

**MOORE,** Francis & **WARD,** Lucy 29 Apr 1788 by George EVE (OM)

**MOORE,** Greenville POC age 24 s POB POR Orange laborer & **GREEN,** Susan POC age 18 s POB POR Orange d/o Frank GREEN and Henrietta RIDLEY 16 May 1880 POM Orange (OMR)

**MOORE,** James & **JAMES,** Nancy 20 Jan 1803 by Nathl. SANDERS (Misc Min Ret)

**MOORE,** James S. & **SLAUGHTER,** Jane surety Jonathan GRAVES by Albert ANDERSON 26 May 1834 (OB) (OM)

**MOORE,** James S. age 27 s farmer POB Kentucky POR Orange s/o John MOORE and Anna CRITCHFIELD & **SALE,** Virginia M. age 22 s POB POR Orange d/o Robert C. SALE and Mary DAVIS POM Orange 16 Mar 1876 by R. Lin CAVE (OMR)

**MOORE,** John & **SMITH,** Elizabeth; 23 Jan 1797 surety William LOYD (OB)

**MOORE,** John T. age 31 s POB New Kent POR Hanover s/o R.P. MOORE and Eliza W. RATLIFF & **YOUNG,** Mary C. age 35 w POB POR Orange d/o R. H. WILLIS and Mary NALLE 20 Feb 1877 POM Orange (OMR)

**MOORE,** Nathaniel & **ADAMS,** Sally d/o John ADAMS surety Richard RICHARDS 1 Jun 1800 (OB)

**MOORE,** Richard B. age 57 w POB POR Orange s/o John MOORE and Fanny BARBOUR farmer & **CRUMP,** Susan age 49 s POB Fredericksburg POR Orange d/o John CRUMP and Susan HART 21 Nov 1871 POM Orange by C.Y. STEPTOE (OMR)

**MOORE,** Richard B. & **MALLORY,** Hannah C. permission from Philip MALLORY surety James B. MOORE 3 Sep 1841 (OB)

**MOORE,** Robert L. age 27 s POB Orange POR Bath Co. s/o William C. MOORE and Marian P. HORD merchant & **PARROTT,** Emma L. age 18 s POB Louisa Co POR Orange s/o Samuel H. PARROTT and Mary HARTSOOK 18 Mar 1869 POM Orange by Charles QUARLES (OMR)

**MOORE,** Robert T. & **BURRUSS,** Hariett d/o William T. BURRUSS surety Benjamin HAWKINS 7 Jan 1826 (OB)

**MOORE,** Robert & **SPENCER,** Elizabeth Gaines d/o Joseph SPENCER surety Reubin GAINES 28 Jun 1793 (OB)

**MOORE,** Thomas R. & **CROW,** Elizabeth ward of Obediah OVERTON surety John PAYNE 16 Aug 1804 (OB)

**MOORE,** William & **DAY,** Susanna 20 Jun 1803 POM Orange by Robert JONES (Misc MIn Ret)

**MOORE,** William & **GRYMES,** Betty Johnson surety Ludwell GRYMES 10 Apr 1781 (OB)

**MOORE,** William & **SMITH,** Rebecca Hite 5 Apr 1804 by Nath. SANDERS (Misc Min Ret)

**MOORE,** William A. & **WRIGHT,** Mary d/o William WRIGHT who is also surety 2 Sep 1816 (OB) 5 Sep 1816 by John C. GORDON (OM)

**MOORE,** William C. & **HORD,** Marion d/o Daniel HORD Sr. surety Robert T. MOORE 25 Dec 1834 (OB)

**MOORE,** William C. & **TAYLOR,** Matilda R. surety Robert T. MOORE 11 Dec 1826 (OB)

**MOORE,** Yelly & **BROWN,** Elizabeth d/o John BROWN surety Cornelius MOORE 29 Dec 1802 (OB) 30 Dec 1802 POM Orange by Robert JONES (Misc Min Ret)

**MORACE,** Linza & **MORACE,** Virinda 4 Jan 1838 by banns by James LONG (OM)

**MORRIS,** Aden C. & **FINNELL,** Nancy 13 Apr 1824 surety William B. WEBB (OB)

**MORRIS,** Ashton B. age 22 s farmer POB POR Orange s/o John F. MORRIS and Mary A. BLEDSOE & **RHOADES,** Lillian M. age 19 s POB POR Orange d/o John RHOADES and Ann E. HATCH POM Orange 2 Jan 1879 (OMR)

**MORRIS,** Benjamin s/o Dick and Roseanna MORRIS age 22 s laborer on farm POB Louisa Co POR Orange POC & **HENDERSON,** Louisa d/o Lewis HENDERSON age 18 s POB POR Orange POC 27 Oct 1867 (OML)

**MORRIS,** Blackly s/o Reuben MORRIS & **TATTUM,** Elizabeth 17 Dec 1833 surety Richard HILL (OB)

**MORRIS,** Charles R. POR Spotsylvania & **MASON,** Elizabeth B. d/o Samuel MASON 5 Dec 1825 John MITCHELL surety (OB)

**MORRIS,** Dabney & **PETTY,** Polly 29 Feb 1816 surety Patrick PETTY (OB)

**MORRIS,** David & **GRUNTER,** Jemima; 18 Feb 1776 (OM)

**MORRIS,** David & **SHIFLETT,** Patsy d/o William SHIFLETT who is also surety 26 Apr 1813 (OB)

**MORRIS,** Elijah & **GEER,** Elizabeth 9 Feb 1802 by George BINGHAM (OB)

**MORRIS,** George & **GRAVES,** Susannah d/o Richard GRAVES 7 Apr 1795 (OM)

**MORRIS,** George & **HOUSTON,** Mary 5 Mar 1847 surety P.S. FRY (OB)

**MORRIS,** George & **SIMMONDS,** Mary d/o Bazzel SIMMONDS who is also surety 23 Dec 1811 (OB) 24 Dec 1811 by J. GOSS (OMR)

**MORRIS,** George & **SOUTHERLAND,** Sarah Jane 22 Nov 1847 surety Richard C. WEBB (OB)

**MORRIS,** George W. POC age 24 s POB POR Orange s/o William MORRIS and Dorcas _____ laborer & **KINNEY,** Louisa POC age 27

w POB POR Orange d/o Marshall KINNEY and Eliza _____ 28 Mar
1869 POM Orange by Theo M. CARSON (OMR)

**MORRIS**, James B. s/o Lewis MORRIS age 29 s bricklayer POB POR
Orange & **BICKERS**, Julia M. d/o Proctor and Lucy BICKERS age 22
s POB POR Orange POM Orange 16 Nov 1854 (OMR)

**MORRIS**, James H. age 29 s POB POR Orange s/o George MORRIS and
Sarah J. SUTHERLIN lumber man & **RHOADES**, Ella R. age 18 s
POB POR Orange d/o John R. RHOADES Jr. and Anna E. HATCH 14
Apr 1880 POM Orange by John C. WILLIS (OMR)

**MORRIS**, James L. & **BATTLEE**, Lavenia 23 May 1836 surety Fielding
JONES (OB)

**MORRIS**, James s/o Reubin MORRIS & **SHIFLETT**, Sarah d/o
Mordecai SHIFLETT who is also surety 19 Jan 1844 (OB)

**MORRIS**, John & **BROWN**, Linny; 21 Sep 1775 both of St. Thomas
Parish by banns (Deed Book 17)

**MORRIS**, John & **SHIFLETT**, Fanny d/o William SHIFLETT 13 Apr
1824 surety May HANEY (OB)

**MORRIS**, John F. & **BLEDSOE**, Mary Ann; 2 Jul 1852 (OML)

**MORRIS**, John Jr. & **DOLLINS**, Sucky d/o William DOLLINS who is
also surety 14 Oct 1809 by J. GOSS (OB)

**MORRIS**, John Thomas s/o James L. MORRIS & **WATSON**, Frances; 12
May 1853 (OML)

**MORRIS**, Josiah & **SHIFLETT**, Sukey 28 Jan 1802 by George
BINGHAM (OMR)

**MORRIS**, Peter POC age 21 s farm laborer POB POR Orange s/o Louisa
JACKSON & **BROOKS**, Ellen POC age 22 s POB POR Orange d/o
Anthony BROOKS and Violet ____ POM Orange 3 Feb 1876 (OMR)

**MORRIS**, Reuben & **ACREE**, Sally d/o William ACREE who is also
surety 22 Dec 1806 (OB) 24 Dec 1806 by Robert JONES (OMR)

**MORRIS**, Reuben J. s/o Benedict & Elizabeth MORRIS age 29 s
gentleman POB Albemarle Co. POR Gordonsville, Orange Co &
**DAVIS**, Sally Ann d/o William J. and Elizabeth W. DAVIS age 19
POB Orange POR Gordonsville; POM Orange 13 Apr 1854 (OMR) 12
Apr 1854 (OML)

**MORRIS**, Reuben Jr. & **JONES**, Pamela d/o Susan JONES 17 Sep 1838
surety John FERNEYHOUGH (OB)

**MORRIS**, Reubin & **COLEMAN**, Molly d/o James COLEMAN surety
Jilson MORRIS 10 Jun 1793 (OB)

**MORRIS**, Thomas & **ACREE**, Elizabeth 22 Jan 1803 (Misc Min Ret)

**MORRIS**, Thomas & **AERY**, Betsy 20 Jan 1803 surety William AERY
(OB)

**MORRIS**, Thomas & **WRIGHT**, Sally 3 Dec 1807 surety Elisha
WRIGHT (OB) 14 Dec 1807 by Robert JONES (OMR)

170

**MORRIS**, William & **ROACH,** Molly 19 Feb 1813 by George BINGHAM (OMR)

**MORRIS**, William A. & **MASON**, Sarah Jane d/o Charles MASON; POM Orange 8 Apr 1852 (OMR) 29 Mar 1852 (OML)

**MORRIS**, William A. age 23 s farmer POB POR Orange s/o James MORRIS and Elizabeth WILTSHIRE & **DAVIS,** Susan A.T. age 20 s POB POR Orange d/o John DAVIS and Susan M. SISLEE POM Orange 20 Apr 1879 by John C. WILLIS (OMR)

**MORRIS**, William Anderson & **QUISENBERRY,** Winneyfret d/o Aaron QUISENBERRY surety Roger SLAUGHTER 6 Feb 1802 (OB)

**MORRISON**, George & **SISSON**, Sally surety James COLEMAN 13 Apr 1791 (OB) by Nathaniel SANDERS 14 Apr 1791 (OM)

**MORRISON**, Thomas & **DAWSON**, Nancy d/o John DAWSON surety William DAWSON 31 Jul 1797 (OB)

**MORRISS**, William L. s/o Aden C. MORRISS and Milly LEE age 29 s carpenter POB POR Orange & **GAINES**, Annie E. d/o Andrew GAINES and Frances LEE age 20 s POB POR Orange; POM Orange 9 May 1867 (OMR) (OML)

**MORSE**, Francis & **WARD**, Lucy; 12 May 1789 (OM)

**MORTON**, Bell POC age 36 s POB Essex POR Orange s/o Fannie MORTON dining room servant & **BOWLER**, Silah POC age 37 s POB POR Orange d/o Addison BOWLER 26 Dec 1880 POM Rapidan, Culpeper Co. by William B. LEE (OMR)

**MORTON**, Elijah & **WEBB**, Mary G.; 22 Jun 1812 surety Goodrich L. GRASTY (OB) 25 Jun 1812 by Jeremiah CHANDLER (OM)

**MORTON**, George & **TANDY**, Amanda d/o Henry TANDY who is also surety 11 May 1827 (OB)

**MORTON**, George & **WILLIAMS**, Elizabeth S. ward of George PANNILL who is also surety 20 Jun 1823 (OB)

**MORTON**, George Jr. & **COLEMAN**, Elizabeth d/o Eliz. COLEMAN surety Thomas COLEMAN 25 Sep 1797 (OB)

**MORTON**, George W. & **TAYLOR**, Evelina M. ward of Robert TAYLOR Jr. who is also surety 28 May 1824 (OB)

**MORTON**, George W. & **TERRILL**, Susan E. surety Oliver TERRILL 18 Dec 1834 (OB)

**MORTON**, George W. age 27 s POB POR Orange s/o George W. MORTON and Susan TERRILL farmer & **FRAZIER**, Laura age 19 s POB POR Orange d/o W.F.B. FRAZER and Lucinda D. MILLS 5 Sep 1872 POM Orange by Charles QUARLES (OMR)

**MORTON**, H.W. age 26 s POB Scotland POR Orange s/o Garvin MORTON and Jennett DYX farmer & **THAYER**, Emma age 20 s POR Orange d/o John C. THAYER 12 May 1870 POM Orange by John N. JONES (OMR)

**MORTON**, John [s/o John MORTON and Elizabeth HAWKINS] & **TANDY,** Mary [d/o Henry TANDY and Ann MILLS] surety Henry TANDY 24 Apr 1789 (OB)

**MORTON,** Robert & **CURTIS,** Margaret over 21 years surety James MORTON 26 Oct 1803 (OB)

**MORTON**, Thomas D. age 32 s POB Orange POR Culpeper s/o Dr. George MORTON and Betsy WILLIAMS farmer & **PANNILL**, Sallie W. age 26 s POB POR Orange d/o James B. PANNILL and Fannie WILLIAMS 2 Jul 1873 POM Orange by W.F. ROBINS (OMR)

**MORTON,** William & **TAYLOR,** Milly both of St. Thomas Parish 5 Jan 1775 (Deed Book 17)

**MOSBY**, Lawrence s/o Winston and Fanny MOSBY age 22 s POB POR Orange laborer POC & **YERBER**, Rose d/o George and Penny YERBER age 18 s POB POR Orange POC; POM Orange 18 Aug 1866 (OMR) (OML)

**MOSBY**, Robert s/o Winston & Fanny MOSBY age 26 s laborer on farm POB POR Orange POC & **MALLORY**, Cornelia d/o Reuben & Lucy HACKETT age 28 w POB Madison Co POR Orange POC; POM Orange 21 Apr 1867 (OMR) 20 Apr 1867 (OML)

**MOTHERSHEAD**, John & **BURRUS,** Sukey; 8 Dec 1789 (OM)

**MOTHERSHED**, Nathaniel & **BIRT,** Ruthy d/o Moses BIRT surety John COOK 11 Aug 1781 (OB)

**MOTHERSHED**, Nathaniel & **MINOR,** Mary 18 Nov 1761 (Orange Fee Book)

**MOYER,** William H. & **BEADLES,** Lurinna surety Thomas MILLER Jr. 25 Nov 1816 (OB) by George BINGHAM 28 Nov 1816 (OM)

**MOYERS,** Michael P. & **MELONE,** Susan surety John H. MELONE 7 Mar 1836 (OB)

**MOZINGO,** James & **CLEMMONS,** Mildred d/o Henry CLEMMONS surety John HERNDON by Robert JONES 23 Jun 1806 (OB) (OM)

**MUDDYMAN**, Edmund s/o Thomas MUDDYMAN age 38 w mason POB England POR Orange & **MASON,** Catherine d/o Abner CLARK age 35 s POB POR Orange; POM Orange 19 Aug 1866 (OMR) 13 Aug 1866 (OML)

**MUGLER,** Philip s/o Philip and Catherine MUGLER age 21 s painter POB Strausburg, France POR Richmond, Va & **FAUDREE**, Lucy M. d/o Joseph and Susan FAUDREE age 20 s POB POR Orange; POM Orange 29 Apr 1856 (OMR) 24 Apr 1856 (OML)

**MUNDAY,** Albert & **JONES,** May F. 28 Aug 1848 surety Mason JONES (OB)

**MUNDAY,** Burruss & **CROSTHWAIT,** Elizabeth d/o John CROSTHWAIT 13 Feb 1815 surety Joseph CROSTHWAIT (OB) 14 Feb 1815 by J. GOSS (OMR)

**MUNDAY,** Burruss & **LANCASTER,** Harriet A. d/o Thomas LANCASTER 24 Jan 1848 surety James W. GOSS and Thomas LANCASTER (OB)

**MUNDAY,** Burruss age 51 w farmer POB Albemarle POR Orange s/o Burruss MUNDAY and Elizabeth CROSSWHITE & **GOODWIN,** Mary C. age 21 s POB POR Orange d/o Charles E. GOODWIN and Sarah MASON POM Orange 23 Jan 1878 by H.E. HATCHER (OMR)

**MUNDAY,** Burruss s/o Burruss and Elizabeth MUNDAY age 31 w farmer POB Albemarle Co POR Orange & **LANCASTER,** Ann E. d/o Thomas and Mary LANCASTER age 23 s POB POR Orange; POM Orange 21 Jan 1858 (OMR) 15 Jan 1858 (OML)

**MUNDAY,** Samuel & **CROSSWHITE,** Milly d/o John CROSSWHITE 31 Aug 1816 surety Stephen ESTREGE (OB) 5 Sep 1816 (OM)

**MUNDAY,** Wilson & **OLIVER,** Nancy d/o Francis OLIVER who is also surety 26 Aug 1816 (OB)

**MURPHY,** Ben POC age 25 s carpenter POB POR Orange s/o Phil MURPHY and Polly COVINGTON & **NALLE,** Jane POC age 22 s POB POR Orange d/o John NALLE and Livinia LUCAS POM Orange 7 Feb 1878 by E.R. PERRY (OMR)

**MURPHY,** James POC age 25 s POB Nelson Co POR Orange s/o Randall MURPHY and Charlotte MAYS laborer & **SHARPE,** Esther POC age 19 s POB POR Orange d/o Dany SHARPE and Martha MINOR 26 Dec 1868 POM Orange by Charles QUARLES (OMR)

**MURPHY,** William L. s/o John MURPHY and Ellen EDMONDSON age 50 s farmer POB Fredericksburg POR Orange & **GARDNER,** Minerva d/o Ezekiah RICHARDS and Betsy LANCASTER age 41 w POB POR Orange; POM Orange 26 Nov 1864 (OMR) 24 Nov 1864 (OML)

**MURPHY,** Zachariah & **ATKINS,** Lucy d/o James ATKINS Jr. surety Nathaniel MIDDLEBROOK 23 Mar 1801 (OB)

**MURRAY,** Robert POC age 21 s POB Madison Co POR Culpeper s/o Nehemiah MURRAY and Caroline _____ laborer & **HALL,** Susan POC age 17 s POB POR Orange d/o Henry HALL and Judy _____ 4 Apr 1874 POM Orange (OMR)

**MURRAY,** Washington POC age 35 w farm labourer POB POR Orange s/o York MURRAY and Rebecca BELL & **JACKSON,** Louisa POC age 27 s POB POR Orange d/o Moses JACKSON and Minnie MURRAY POM Mt. Pleasant Church, Orange 22 Sep 1878 by C.T. JOHNSON (OMR)

**MUSGROVE,** Alexander & **MORRIS,** Polly d/o George MORRIS surety Dabney MORRIS 28 Jan 1813 (OB) by J. GOSS 12 Feb 1813 (OM)

**MUSICK,** John & **BERRY,** Mary both of St. Thomas Parish by banns 22 Jul 1776 (Deed Book 17)

**MUZINGO,** Joseph & **CLEMENS,** Polly surety Henry CLEMENS 31 Mar 1800 (OB)

**MYERS,** Levi E. age 21 s POB Page POR Culpeper s/o John S. MYERS and Catharine GRIFFIE blacksmith & **HEFLIN,** Ella V. age 19 s POB POR Orange d/o George W. HEFLIN and Lucy E. DEMPSEY 14 Oct 1880 POM Orange by John C. WILLIS (OMR)

**NALLE,** Gustavus B.W. age 27 s POB POR Culpeper Co s/o P.P. NALLE and Elizabeth WALLACE merchant & **PORTER,** Nannie H. age 26 s POB POR Orange d/o John A. PORTER and Mary CRUMP 10 Dec 1872 POM Orange by C.Y. STEPTOE (OMR)

**NALLE,** Martin & **BARBOUR,** Nelly 15 Sep 1809 surety J.W. BARBOUR (OB)

**NALLE,** Martin & **MALLORY,** Elizabeth w 2 Dec 1831 surety Jeremiah PANNILL (OB)

**NASH,** Thomas W. & **CLARKE,** Virginia d/o William CLARKE who is also surety 15 Jan 1824 (OB)

**NAYLOR,** Thomas & **WALTON,** Jane 4 Jan 1814 by George BINGHAM (OM)

**NEAL,** Charles & **MILLER,** Ann permission from Robert MILLER surety Francis COLLINS 23 Aug 1785 (OB)

**NEAL,** Fielding & **BEAZLEY,** Catherine (d/o James BEAZLEY surety Charles NEAL 22 Oct 1787 (OB) by George EVE 12 Nov 1787 (OM)

**NEAL,** Miscajah & **BEAZLEY,** Milly d/o James BEAZLEY surety Mace PICKETT 3 Aug 1782 (OB)

**NELSON,** James & **ADAMS,** Ann; 11 Jul 1823 surety Richard RICHARDS (OB)

**NELSON,** Smith POC age 38 s labourer POB Frederick POR Orange s/o Peter NELSON & **HILL,** Ellen POC age 25 s POB Madison POR Orange POM Nazareth Baptist Church, Orange 16 Jan 1878 by Willis ROBINSON (OMR)

**NELSON,** Thomas & **QUISENBERRY,** Elizabeth 25 Jan 1813 surety James NELSON (OB) 28 Jan 1813 by Jeremiah CHANDLER (OM)

**NELSON,** William s/o James NELSON & **SMITH,** Sarah d/o James SMITH surety Elisha ADAMS 13 Jun 1803 (OB)

**NEWMAN,** Alexander & **SLEET,** Lucy d/o James SLEET Sr. who is also surety 14 Mar 1803 (OB) 17 Mar 1803 by Nathl. SANDERS (Misc Min Ret)

**NEWMAN,** Andrew & **GARNER,** Jinnette surety James FLEET or SLEET Jr. 21 Jul 1801 (OB)

**NEWMAN,** Andrew & **WRIGHT,** Eleanor d/o William WRIGHT who is also surety 14 Jul 1813 by J. GOSS (OB) (OM)

**NEWMAN,** Charles & **CHILES,** Catharine d/o James CHILES who is also surety 20 Dec 1820 (OB) 21 Dec 1820 by James GARNETT Jr. (OM)

**NEWMAN,** Conway age 31 s POB POR Orange s/o James B. NEWMAN and Sallie B. FITZHUGH merchant & **TAYLOR,** Eleanor age 23 s POB King William Co POR Orange d/o Robert TAYLOR and Barbara TILDEN 13 Jan 1869 POM Orange by I.W.K.HANDY (OMR)

**NEWMAN,** George & **WILTSHIRE,** Sarah Jane; POM Orange 1 Jan 1853 (OMR) 27 Dec 1852 (OML)

**NEWMAN,** George Jr. & **TUTMAN,** Elizabeth ward of John TUTMAN who is also surety 2 Jun 1818 (OB)

**NEWMAN,** George S. & **LINDSAY,** Eveline A. ward of James G. LINDSAY who is also surety 30 Jul 1840 (OB)

**NEWMAN,** George & **NEWMAN,** Ann C. surety Thomas NEWMAN 28 Mar 1837 (OB)

**NEWMAN,** George & **WAUGH,** Elizabeth surety John BOSTON 10 Jan 1825 (OB)

**NEWMAN,** George s/o John NEWMAN and Mildred QUISENBERRY age 40 w farmer POB POR Orange & **JONES,** Malvina d/o James JONES and Elizabeth OVERTON age 36 s POB POR Orange; POM Orange 14 Mar 1867 (OMR) 25 Feb 1867 (OML)

**NEWMAN,** Harden POC age 21 s POB POR Orange s/o Hardin NEWMAN and Lucinda BARKER laborer & **WINSTON,** Georgia A. POC age 17 s POR Orange d/o Betsy NEWMAN 19 Apr 1869 POM Orange by H.M. LINNEY (OMR)

**NEWMAN,** Henry & **NEWMAN,** Sarah d/o Andrew NEWMAN surety George LEWIS 11 Apr 1825 (OB)

**NEWMAN,** James F. s/o George and Bettie NEWMAN age 33y 4mo 28days s farmer POB Madison Co POR Orange & **WINSLOW,** Martha E. d/o Thompson and Eleanor COCKERILLE age 35y 5mo 9days w POB POR Orange; POM Orange 11 May 1856 (OMR) 10 May 1856 (OML)

**NEWMAN,** James & **SCOTT,** Mary d/o Sarah SCOTT surety John F. DANIEL 24 Sep 1828 (OB)

**NEWMAN,** John & **QUISENBERRY,** Sidnah d/o George QUISENBERY Sr. 3 Jul 1803 surety Moses HAWKINS (OB)

**NEWMAN,** John R. s/o William S. and Lucy NEWMAN age 35 s farmer POB POR Orange & **RODGERS,** Margaret R. d/o Joseph and Malinda RODGERS age 24 s POB POR Orange; POM Orange 13 Dec 1857 (OMR) 12 Dec 1857 (OML)

**NEWMAN,** John Sr. & **WAUGH,** Milly surety Stokely CLARKE 2 Oct 1833 (OB)

**NEWMAN,** John & **ATKINS,** Mildred surety Alexander NEWMAN and Moses PEREGORY 18 May 1819 (OB)

**NEWMAN,** Reuben & **CLARKE,** Mary Jane d/o Henry T. CLARKE surety James CLARKE 12 May 1831 (OB)

**NEWMAN,** Reuben & **HACKNEY,** Nancy surety P.S. FRY 8 Jul 1844 (OB)

**NEWMAN,** Robert G. & **NEWMAN,** Mary 15 Aug 1835 surety John NEWMAN Sr. (OB)

**NEWMAN,** Thomas & **BARBOUR,** Lucy 7 Mar 1798 surety John HENSHAW (OB)

**NEWMAN,** Thomas & **HACKNEY,** Jane S. 29 Apr 1837 surety Joseph STEPHENS (OB)

**NEWMAN,** Thomas & **MORRIS,** Patsy Oliver d/o George MORRIS surety William MORTON 22 Oct 1798 (OB)

**NEWMAN,** William Jr. & **FAULCONER,** Lucy 24 Aug 1809 surety Nicholas FAULCONER by Robert JONES (OB) (OM)

**NICHOLAS,** James s/o Ned NICHOLAS and Rose WORMLEY age 28 w farm laborer POB Culpeper CO POR Orange POC & **MYERS,** Milly d/o Jeny and Emily MYERS age 22 s POB POR Orange POC; POM Orange 28 Dec 1866 (OMR) 27 Dec 1866 (OML)

**NICHOLS,** Edwin & **SIMS,** Eveline d/o William SIMS who is also surety 29 May 1832 (OB)

**NICHOLS,** John & **PRITCHETT,** Sarah 30 Apr 1822 surety Robert PRITCHETT (OB)

**NIPPER,** Jacob & **FLECK,** Elizabeth surety Andrew FLECK 5 Mar 1796 (OB) by George EVE 15 Mar 1796 (OM)

**NIXON,** Harrison POC age 21 s POB Buckingham Co. POR Orange laborer & **JOHNSON,** Sarah POC age 19 s POB POR Orange d/o Joseph JOHNSON and Betty TYREE 16 Aug 1868 POM Orange by Philip JOHNSON (OMR)

**NOLAN,** Thomas & **AMES,** Alice J. POM Orange 17 Oct 1852 (OMR) (OML)

**NOLAND,** Cuthbert P. age 29 s farmer POB POR Loudoun s/o R.P. NOLAND and Susan WILSON & **HAXALL,** Rosalie age 27 s POB Richmond POR Orange d/o R. Barton HAXALL and Octavia ROBINSON POM Orange 22 Oct 1879 (OMR)

**NOOMES,** Joseph & **DAVIS,** Rachel; 23 Aug 1776 both of St. Thomas Parish (Deed Book 17)

**NORFORD,** James M. age 49 w POB Albemarle Co POR Green Co. s/o Isaac OXFORD and Elizabeth NORFORD cabinet maker & **BROCKMAN,** Julia F. age 38 w POB POR Orange d/o John DOLIN and Frances DOLIN 3 Oct 1869 POM Orange by John N. FOX (OMR)

**NORFORD,** James T. age 19 s POB Green Co. POR Orange s/o James M. NORFORD and Frances GILBERT farmer & **BROCKMAN**, Elizabeth F.M. age 16 s POB Albemarle Co POR Orange d/o Belfield BROCKMAN and Julia F. DOLIN 20 Jan 1870 POM Orange by E.P. HAWKINS (OMR)

**NORFORD**, Thomas G. age 25 s POB Greene Co. POR Orange s/o Matthew NORFORD and Frances GILBERT farmer & **DULANY**, Sarah N. age 25 POB Rockingham Co POR Orange 24 Mar 1872 POM Orange by Jos. S. MANSFIELD (OMR)

**NORMAN**, Cuthbert & **JOLLETT,** Sophia surety James JOLLETT 1 Aug 1791 (OB) 2 Aug 1791 by George EVE (OM)

**NORMAN,** Daniel & **WARKIN,** Betsy surety Peter MARSH 26 Nov 1818 (OB)

**NORRIS,** Caleb & **HARRIS,** Ally 18 Jun 1812 by George BINGHAM (OM)

**NORRIS,** Henry H. & **JOHNSON,** Lucie A. M. d/o Belfield C. JOHNSON surety Philip S. FRY by E.G. SHIP 13 May 1850 (OB) (OM)

**NORRIS,** William & **WALTON,** Margaret B. 4 Feb 1819 by George BINGHAM (OM)

**NUN,** Willis POC age 40 w labourer POB Madison POR Orange s/o Sam NUN and Hannah GREEN & **WILLIAMS,** Ana age 25 POB POR Orange d/o William COOK and Sarah HARRIS POM Orange 17 Nov 1878 (OMR)

**O'SULLIVAN**, John s/o Jeremiah and Mary O'SULLIVAN age 24 s tinsmith POB Richmond POR Orange & **SARMAND**, Josephine d/o Francis and Lucy SARMAND age 21 s POB Richmond POR Orange; POM St.Thomas Ch., Orange 2 Jul 1855 (OMR)

**OAKES**, Mainyard & **LANCASTER,** Polly d/o John and Susannah LANCASTER surety James MASON 22 Sep 1806 by Nathaniel SANDERS (OM)

**OAKS,** John & **BELL,** Mary Ann surety Henry C. BELL 26 Nov 1839 (OB)

**OAKS,** John & **GRAVES,** Joanna over 21 years d/o Thomas GRAVES who is also surety 7 Apr 1807 (OB) by Nathaniel SANDERS 14 Apr 1807 (OM)

**OAKS,** Major & **OAKS,** Weltha surety Reuben OAKS 25 Jan 1814 (OB)

**OGG,** John Jr. & **GOODALL,** Sally surety John GOODALL 21 Dec 1792 (OB)

**OGG,** William & **LAMB,** Franky d/o John LAMB who is also surety 7 Jun 1793 (OB)

**OLIVE**, James & **MINOR,** Susannah both of St. Thomas Parish surety Nathaniel MOTHERSHED 24 Aug 1781 (OB)

**OLIVER,** Caleb & **WHITE,** Nancy d/o Thomas WHITE surety Richard WHITE 10 Sep 1792 (OB) 15 Sep 1792 by George EVE (OM)

**OLIVER,** Ealey & **RHOADES,** Martha d/o Clifton RHOADES surety Valentine RIDDLE 31 Sep [sic] 1836 (OB)

**OLIVER,** James & **SIMS,** Lucretia d/o Margarite SIMS surety Joseph KIRTLEY 22 Nov 1824 (OB)

**OLIVER,** Killis & **RIDDLE,** Winney d/o James RIDDLE surety Richard WHITE 23 Jan 1797 (OB) 26 Jan 1797 by George BINGHAM (OM)

**ORANT,** John & **LINTOR,** Peggy; 11 Dec 1783 surety Benoni HANSFORD (OB)

**OSBORNE,** Fielding & **MASSEY,** Mary d/o Edmund MASSEY who is also surety 5 Apr 1803 (OB)

**OTT,** Michael & **PENCE,** Catharine surety William CAMPBELL 27 Aug 1798 (OB)

**OVERPACK,** George & **CARNS,** Martha; George WALTERS is guardian of Martha and surety 27 Jun 1803 (OB)

**OVERTON,** Beverly & **CONNER,** Elizabeth surety Willis OVERTON 2 Oct 1788 (OB)

**OVERTON,** Beverly & **RICHARDS,** Patty d/o William RICHARDS surety James JONES 15 Sep 1789 (OB) by John LELAND 14 Oct 1789 (OM)

**OVERTON,** John & **CARLETON,** Martha surety Willis OVERTON 2 Feb 1797 (OB)

**OVERTON,** Joshua & **PALMER,** Frances surety Willis OVERTON 15 Jan 1797 (OB)

**OVERTON,** Willis & **BRADLY,** Nancy surety Reuben BOSTON 1 Sep 1788 (OB)

**OWEN,** Chichester & **CLARKE,** Frances d/o Robert CLARKE surety Charles S. STERN 10 Nov 1817 (OB)

**OWENS,** John & **HAMBLETON,** Sarah w surety William RICHARDS 31 Dec 1790 (OB)

**OWENS,** Lee A. d/o William OWENS and Jane CHANDLER age 23 w farmer POB Mecklenburg Co. POR s POB POR Orange; POM Orange 9 Apr 1865 (OMR) 8 Apr 1865 (OML)

**OWENS,** Lewis POC age 21 s labourer POB POR Orange s/o Daniel OWENS and Eliza MANSFIELD & **WHITE,** Grace POC age 23 s POB POR Orange Harry WHITE and Dicey BANKS POM Shady Grove Church, Orange 4 Aug 1878 by C.T. JOHNSON (OMR)

**OWENS,** Lewis s/o Lewis and Matilda OWENS age 31s laborer POB POR Orange POC & **BRAXTON,** Hannah d/o Polly GILMOR age 21 s POB POR Orange POC; POM Orange 13 Oct 1865 (OMR) 28 Aug 1865 (OML)

**OWENS,** Sturd & **HARRIS,** Caty; 31 Mar 1795 by George BINGHAM (OM)

**OZBORN,** Braxton & **TALIAFERRO,** Ann surety John TALIAFERRO 9 Jan 1813 (OB) by Isham TATUM 13 Jan 1813 (OM)

**OZBORNE,** Holland s/o Robert OZBORNE who is also surety & **FEARNEYHOUGH,** Sally 22 Nov 1812 (OB) by J. GOSS 3 Dec 1813 (OM)

**OZBORNE,** Churchwell C. & **OZBORNE,** Mildred d/o Holland OZBORNE surety Benjamin L. MITCHELL 12 Mar 1831 (OB) by J. GOSS 22 Mar 1831 (OM)

**OZBORNE,** Holland Jr. & **MITCHELL,** Isabella M. surety John T. RENNOLDS 8 Apr 1835 (OB)

**PADGETT,** John & **BECKHAM,** Nancy surety Benjamin CHISHOLM 21 Aug 1799 (OB)

**PAGE,** Elijah & **SISK,** Nelly d/o Martin SISK surety Jacob ANDERSON 25 Dec 1800 (OB)

**PAGE,** James & **LONG,** Burlinda d/o William LONG who is also surety 15 Sep 1819 (OB)

**PAGE,** James permission from Elizabeth PAGE & **SHIFLETT,** Winny d/o Elizabeth SHIFLETT surety Lewis STOWERS 3 Dec 1789 (OB)

**PAGE,** John & **MIDDLEBROOK,** Elizabeth; 7 Oct 1777 both of St. Thomas Parish (Deed Book 17)

**PAGE,** John Jr. s/o John & Elizabeth PAGE Sr. & **COLLINS,** Mary d/o Mary COLLINS; 22 Dec 1783 (OB)

**PAGE,** John POC age 21 s POB POR Orange s/o Gilbert PAGE and Anice PAGE laborer & **QUARLES,** Ona P. POC age 22 s POB POR Orange d/o Bartlett QUARLES and Patsy ROSS 28 Dec 1868 POM Orange by E.R. PERRY (OMR)

**PAGE,** Mann A. & **WILLIS,** Mary Champe d/o William C. WILLIS who is also surety 14 Nov 1827 (OB)

**PAGE,** Sinclair & **LONG,** Elizabeth d/o William LONG surety is William L. LONG 15 Jan 1818 (OB)

**PAGE,** Tandy & **SMITH,** Judith d/o Benjamin SMITH who is also surety 29 Dec 1815 (OB)

**PAGE,** William & **ALEXANDER,** Elizabeth permission from James and Elizabeth ALEXANDER surety James MCMULLEN 27 Mar 1793 (OB)

**PAGGETT,** James & **BEECON,** Phillis permission from Elizabeth BEECON, guardian of Phillis surety Benjamin CHISHOLM 30 Jan 1800 (OM)

**PAGGETT,** William & **CLARKE,** Ann 17 Aug 1804 by Nath. SANDERS (Misc Min Ret)(permission)

**PAGGETT,** William s/o Ann PAGGETT & **CLARK,** Ann d/o Patrack CLARK surety Ikey RICHARDS 15 Aug 1804 (OB) by Nathaniel SANDERS 17 Aug 1804 (OM)

**PALMER,** Albert G. & **BOSWELL,** Lucy Ann d/o William BOSWELL who is also surety 12 Jul 1833 (OB)

**PALMER,** Benjamin & **LEFOE,** Judah d/o Danel LEFOE 24 Sep 1811 Willis OVERTON surety (OB)

**PALMER,** William & **HORD,** Ellen surety William A. MARTIN 29 Sep 1835 (OB)

**PANNILL,** David & **HENSHAW,** Lucy Walker d/o John HENSHAW surety Benjamin WALKER 14 Mar 1835 (OB)

**PANNILL,** Philip POR Culpeper Co & **PORTER,** Martha d/o John A. Porter; 12 Jul 1851 (OML)

**PARKER,** Richard POR St. Thomas Parish & **CAVE,** Hannah d/o William CAVE POR St. Thomas Parish surety Roland THOMAS Jr. 17 Apr 1780 (OB)

**PARKER,** Winslow & **THOMAS,** Mary; 4 Aug 1774 both of St. Thomas Parish (Deed Book 17)

**PARKS,** Richard H. & **BURTON,** Clarasa surety Edward CASON 28 Nov 1814 (OB)

**PARROTT,** Bezaleel B. & **STEPHENS,** Julia Ann d/o Joseph STEPEHNS who is also surety 26 Feb 1846 (OB)

**PARROTT,** George & **CATTERTON,** Elizabeth by George BINGHAM 16 Dec 1813 (OM)

**PARROTT,** George & **HARTSOOK,** Elizabeth by J. GOSS 21 Dec 1824 (OM)

**PARROTT,** John & **SIMMONDS,** Fanny d/o John SIMMONDS, surety Robert MILLER by George BINGHAM 25 Dec 1811 (OB) (OM)

**PARROTT,** Samuel H. & **HARTSOOK,** Mary surety John B. HARTSOOK 26 Nov 1832 (OB)

**PARROTT,** Thomas Y. & **HOUSEWORTH,** Martha Jane d/o Valentine M. HOUSEWORTH surety Joseph WILLIAMS 25 Nov 1839 (OB)

**PARROTT,** William & **EHEART,** Mary Lavenia d/o Mildred L. EHEART surety P..M. CARPENTER 9 May 1843 (OB)

**PARROTT,** William & **WAYLAND,** Judith d/o Joshua WAYLAND surety Henry WAYLAND by Jacob WATTS 15 Jan 1810 (OB) (OM)

**PARROTT,** William H. & **WILCOX,** Mary permission from William WILCOX surety George W. SHEARMAN 18 Jan 1834 (OB)

**PARROTT,** Woodson & **WILLIAMS,** Elizabeth d/o John WILLIAMS surety Joseph WILLIAMS 16 Nov 1819 (OB)

**PARSONS,** David & **CLARK,** Elizabeth surety John CLARK 4 Dec 1800 (OB)

**PARTLOW**, Benjamin H. s/o John L. PARTLOW and Martha LILLARD age 30 s merchant POB Rappahannock Co. POR Orange & **JONES**, Edmonia H. d/o James L. JONES and Martha A. PORTER age 24 s POB POR Orange; POM Beaumont, Orange 3 Oct 1866 OMR 28 Sep 1866 OML

**PASCOE**, William age 32 s POB England POR Orange s/o William PASCOE and Marjorie _____ miner & **RICHARDSON**, Emma J. age 22 s POB England POR Orange d/o Charles S. RICHARDSON and Sophia BOXALL 29 Mar 1869 POM Orange by Theo. M. CARSON (OMR)

**PATRICK**, Henry POC age 21 s farm labourer POB POR Orange s/o Monmouth PATRICK and Tabby TIBBS & **GUNNERS**, Bettie POC age 18 s POB Louisa POR Orange d/o Patrick GUNNER and Leana ALLENS POM Orange 20 Feb 1879 by Willis ROBINSON (OMR)

**PATTERSON**, John C. & **COBBS**, Lucetta N. d/o Peter N. COBBS who is also surety 8 Aug 1849 (OB)

**PATTERSON**, John POR Berkely Co. & **CUDDING**, Peggy POR St. Thomas Parish 3 Mar 1776 by banns (Deed Book 17)

**PATTON**, Hugh M. age 29 s POB Richmond POR Alexandria s/o John M. PATTON and Peggy F. WILLIAMS clerk & **BULL**, Fanny D. age 23 s POB Washington POR Orange d/o Marcus BULL and Sarah T. DADE 19 Oct 1870 POM Orange by John S. HANSBRAUGH (OM)

**PAUL**, John & **LEATHERS**, Eliza Ann d/o Jonathan LEATHERS surety Edmund D. LONGAN by George MORRIS 18 Aug 1824 (OB) (OM)

**PAUL**, Jacob & **NEALE**, Catey w surety John HAUSE 28 Jul 1793 (OB) by George EVE 15 Aug 1793 (OM)

**PAUL**, Robert & **EDWARDS**, Rachel surety Charles FINNELL 27 Dec 1790 (OB) 28 Dec 1790 by Nathaniel SANDERS (OM)

**PAWNING**, Edwin age 35 s POB England POR Orange s/o John M. PAWNING and Elizabeth BROWN machinist & **JOHNSON**, Adeline age 20 s POB POR Orange d/o Ryland JOHNSON and Ann HANEY 19 May 1868 POM Orange by Melzi S. CHANCELLOR (OMR)

**PAYNE**, Benjamin C. s/o Charles G.PAYNE and Mary COOPER age 22 s farmer POB POR Orange & **COLLINS**, Elizabeth A. d/o Robert COLLINS and Jane ROBINSON age 19 s POB POR Orange; POM Orange 21 Dec 1865 OMR 15 Dec 1865 OML

**PAYNE**, Charles & **JONES**, Lucy d/o Frances JONES surety William PAYNE 8 Nov 1814 (OB)

**PAYNE**, Charles s/o Robert PAYNE who is also surety & **COOPER**, Mary surety James COOPER 19 Dec 1829 (OB)

**PAYNE**, Henry POC age 28 w POB Fairfax POR Orange s/o George PAYNE sawyer & **JOHNSON**, Virginia POC age 21 s POB POR

Orange d/o Stephen JOHNSON and Nelly FRY 30 Oct 1880 POM
Orange by W.H. CAMPER (OMR)

**PAYNE**, James T. & **WALLER**, Elizabeth; 31 Jan 1853 (OML)

**PAYNE**, James W. s/o Charles G. PAYNE & **LANCASTER**, Sarah Ann
d/o James G. LANCASTER; 20 Sep 1852 OML

**PAYNE**, Jesse age 30 s POB POR Spotsylvania s/o James PAYNE and
Mary WHEELER farm laborer & **SOVRELL**, Laura E. age 17 s POB
POR Orange d/o Jos. SORVELL and Nannie DUNAWAY 8 Jul 1874
POM Orange [by Sanders MASON] (OMR)

**PAYNE**, John & **BLEDSOE**, Elizabeth w surety Ambrose RICHARDS 27
Aug 1801 (OB)

**PAYNE, John** & **CHISSOM**, Mildred surety Samuel GAMBOE 1 Jan
1802 (OB)

**PAYNE, John** & **LINDSAY**, Sucky surety Adam LINDSAY 6 Aug 1793
(OB)

**PAYNE, John** & **MALLORY**, Elizabeth surety Elijah MALLORY 8 Jan
1805 (OB) by Robert JONES 10 Jan 1805 (OM)

**PAYNE**, John T. s/o Charles PAYNE and Lucy JONES age 30 s lumber
business POB POR Orange & **ROACH**, Ann d/o Robert ROACH and
Milly JONES age 24 s POB POR Orange; POM Orange 17 Jun 1866
OMR 15 Jun 1866 OML

**PAYNE**, Milton & **BURTON**, Sarah d/o May BURTON surety John
PAYNE 4 Nov 1811 (OB) by Jacob WATTS 7 Nov 1811 (OM)

**PAYNE**, Philip POC age 27 s POB POR Orange s/o Thornton PAYNE
and Ellen PAYNE laborer & **WILLIAMS**, Fanny POC age 22 s POB
POR Orange d/o Thomas WILLIAMS 21 Mar 1872 POM Orange by
E.R. PERRY (OMR)

**PAYNE**, Philip POC age 29 w labourer POB POR Orange s/o Thornton
PAYNE and Ellen JOHNSON & **SMITH**, Caroline POC age 20 s POB
POR Orange d/o Margaret SMITH POM Orange 13 Dec 1879 (OMR)

**PAYNE**, Robert & **COLLINS**, Ann surety Lewis D. COLLINS 24 Jun
1809 (OB)

**PAYNE**, Thomas & **JONES**, Sidney ward of Fielding JONES who is also
surety 25 Jul 1825 by George MORRIS (OB) (OM)

**PAYNE**, Thomas POC age 24 s POB Orange Co POR Culpeper Co s/o
Gilbert PAGE and Ann BROCK farmer & **BANKS**, Fanny POC age 21
s POB Culpeper Co POR Orange d/o Henry BANKS and Mary
ROBINSON 11 Feb 1869 POM Orange by J.W. MCCOWN (OMR)

**PAYNE**, William G. & **WELLS**, Mary M. surety Richard H. ROBINSON
11 Apr 1832 (OB)

**PAYNE**, William s/o Richard PAYNE & **FOSTER**, Nancy surety Joseph
CANTERBERRY 25 Mar 1795 (OB)

**PEACHER,** Edmund & **HILMAN,** Lucy d/o Joseph HLMAN surety
Uriah HILMAN 17 Oct 1801 (OB) by Nathaniel SANDERS 20 Oct
1801(Misc Min Ret)

**PEACHER,** James & **BRENT,** Judith A. ward of Thomas PROCTER
surety Alexander GRADY 21 Jun 1826 (OB)

**PEACHER,** Joseph W. & **BROCK,** Elizabeth  Robert BROCK is her
guardian and surety 23 Nov 1829 (OB)

**PEACHER,** Peter M. & **PEACHER,** Sarah W. surety William PEACHER
25 Nov 1827 (OB)

**PEACHER,** Reuben & **JOHNSON,** Sarah d/o Nancy JOHNSON surety
James JONES 27 Dec 1791 (OB) 29 Dec 1791 by Nathaniel
SANDERS (OM)

**PEARL,** Ned age 22 s POB Madison Co POR Orange s/o Lewis PEARL
and Ninna JOHNSON laborer & **MADISON,** Jane age 22 s POB POR
Orange d/o Thomas PAYNE and Martha HOWARD 16 Apr 1870 POM
Orange by Thomas R. HAWKINS (OMR)[death of a son in 1883
indicated that this couple is of color] [] information taken from Orange
courthouse card file on deaths

**PEARSON,** Joel s/o William H. PEARSON and Sarah PORTER age 23 s
student POB South Caroline POR Fairfield District, S.C. & **MANN,**
Georgia Anna d/o William H. MANN and Arabella R. KEITH age 20 s
POB Albemarle Co POR Orange; POM Gordonsville, Orange 20 Aug
1866 OMR 17 Aug 1866 OML

**PEARSON,** John & **GOODRICH,** Betsy age 21surety Killis OLIVER 10
Sep 1789 (OB)

**PECK,** Jacob POR Staunton & **COURSEY,** Polly POR St. Thomas Parish
24 Feb 1778 (Deed Book 17)

**PENCE,** John & **LUCAS,** Elizabeth surety Zachariah LUCAS 13 Apr
1795 (OB)

**PENDLETON,** Benjamin & **QUISENBERRY,** Elizabeth d/o William
QUISENBERRY surety James TAYLOR 2 Jun 1796 (OB)

**PENDLETON,** John & **TAYLOR,** Elizabeth surety James TAYLOR 8
Nov 1785 (OB)

**PENDLETON,** John & **THOMPSON,** Fanny surety Jackson TANDY 22
Dec 1806 (OB)

**PENDLETON,** John S. & **WILLIAMS,** Lucy Ann surety P.S. FRY 24
Nov 1824 (OB)

**PENDLETON,** Rice & **QUISENBERRY,** Elizabeth d/o John
QUISENBERRY surety George QUISENBERRY 3 Nov 1788 (OB)

**PENDLETON,** Robert & **BURRUS,** Elizabeth surety Edmund BURRUS
31 Jan 1797 (OB)

**PENNY,** John H. & **SEARS,** Mary G. surety John W. SEARS 11 Sep
1835 (OB)

**PERCEY,** Charles & **LOWER,** Elizabeth d/o Michael LOWER surety Jacob LOWER 2 Jan 1798 (OB)

**PEREGOY,** John W. age 23 s blacksmith POB Rockingham POR Harrisonburg s/o Eli M. PEREGOY and Louisa E. FLOWERS & **WOOD,** Sarah Emma age 18 s POB POR Orange C.T. WOOD and Jane E. SMITH POM Orange 27 Jun 1878 by E.R. PERRY (OMR)

**PEREGOY,** Moses & **NEWMAN,** Sarah surety Thomas NEWMAN 28 Nov 1814 (OB)

**PERRY,** Abraham & **WHARTON,** Polly d/o George WHARTON surety Moses BLEDSOE 18 Jul 1797 (OB)

**PERRY,** Benjamin & **HAWKINS,** Buly Ann d/o Elijah HAWKINS who is also surety 18 Jul 1831 (OB)

**PERRY,** Edmund A. s/o Benjamin R. PERRY and Martha WHITE age 35 s farmer POB Perquinemons Co, NC POR Orange & **TERRILL,** Ellen d/o Edmund TERRILL and Susan SMITH age 30 s POB POR Orange; POM Orange 23 Dec 1865 OMR 22 Dec 1865 OML

**PERRY,** Elijah R.[Elijah Richard b. 19 May 1840] s/o George PERRY and Mary BROWN [fourth wife of George L. PERRY] age 23 s minister POB POR Orange & **BOSTON,** Sophia S. d/o John [P.] BOSTON and [Jane] Frances WAUGH [b. 23 Oct 1845] age 18 s POB POR Orange; POM Orange 31 Dec 1863 OMR OML [] information taken from William & Mary Quarterly

**PERRY,** Elijah s/o James PERRY & **WEBB,** Ann d/o Richard Crittendon WEBB surety James MASON 9 Jan 1797 (OB)

**PERRY,** George & **BROWN,** Mary P. surety George MORRIS 22 May 1837 (OB)

**PERRY,** George & **WRIGHT,** Sarah surety Micajah JONES 26 Dec 1827 (OB)

**PERRY,** James Lewis & **PERRY,** Jane d/o Peter PERRY who is also surety 12 Sep 1814 (OB) by Jeremiah CHANDLER 13 Sep 1814 (OM)

**PERRY,** James & **TANDY,** Nancy surety Roger TANDY, brother [Nancy b. 6 Oct 1768 d/o Henry TANDY and Ann MILLS] 28 Feb 1791 (OB) [] taken from William & Mary Quarterly and compiler's notes

**PERRY,** Levi L. age 26 s POB POR Orange s/o George PERRY and Mary BROWN merchant & **MUNDY,** Julia Ann age 17 s POB POR Orange d/o Burrus MUNDY and Harriet LANCASTER 7 Jan 1869 POM Orange by H.W. HATCHER (OMR)

**PERRY,** Lewis & **BURROWS,** Mary both of St. Thomas Parish 22 Feb 1773 (Deed Book 17)

**PERRY,** Moses & **BROCKMAN,** Susa surety Samuel BROCKMAN 23 Mar 1786 (OB)

**PERRY,** Peter & **FAULCONER,** Lucy surety David FAULCONER 27 Oct 1790 (OB) by Nathaniel SANDERS 4 Nov 1790 (OM)

**PERRY**, William & **WOOD**, Mary surety Lewis L. POATE 18 Dec 1824 (OB) by Jeremiah CHANDLER 24 Dec 1824 (OM)

**PERRY**, William F. s/o William F. PERRY and Augusta C. FERRIS age 22 s clerk ordinance department POB New York City POR Richmond & **TERRILL**, Virginia d/o Dr. Uriel TERRILL and Jane LOVELL age 26 s POB POR Orange; POM Orange 2 Apr 1863 OMR OML

**PERRY**, William W. & **RIPPETO**, Ann G. 15 Jun 1822 by Leeroy CANADAY (OM)

**PETITT**, Ira W. s/o Fountain P. PETITT and Martha A. ROACH age 23 s bricklayer POB Albemarle Co. POR Orange & **SMITH**, Serrepta A. d/o John and Lucy SMITH age 22 s POB Albemarle Co. POR Orange; POM Orange 19 Dec 1867 OMR 16 Dec 1867 OML

**PETTITT**, Corbin Lee s/o Samuel PETTITT and Louisa NELSON age 21 s farmer POB POR Fairfax Co. & **LAYTON**, Agnes H. d/o Samuel LAYTON and Maria NELSON age 18 s POB POR Orange; POM Orange 18 Aug 1863 OMR OML

**PETTY**, George & **MCNEAL**, Elizabeth both of St. Thomas Parish 2 Sep 1773 (Deed Book 17)

**PETTY**, Zachary & **KENDEL**, Polly d/o John KENDEL surety James SLEET Jr. 26 Mar 1804 (OB)

**PEYTON**, F. Bradley age 29 s depot agent POB POR Orange s/o William S. PEYTON and Willie Ann NEUMAN & **BEALE**, Marian H. age 22 s POB POR Orange d/o Charles W. BEALE and Clementina V. BAKER POM Gordonsville 14 Nov 1877 (OMR)

**PEYTON**, James & **HUFFMAN**, Anna d/o Elijah HUFFMAN who is also surety 12 Feb 1816 (OB) 21 Feb 1816 by George BINGHAM (OM)

**PEYTON**, John S. & **DOWELL**, Harriet Elizabeth d/o Atwell DOWELL who is also surety 22 Apr 1843 (OB) by Herndon FRAZER 26 Apr 1843 (OM)

**PEYTON**, William S. & **NEWMAN**, Willi Anna surety Carter B. FAULCONER 19 Dec 1837 (OB)

**PHILIPS**, Conyers & **FERNEYHOUGH/FEARNEY**, Elizabeth d/o Thomas FERNEYHOUGH surety John FERNEYHOUGH by Jacob WATTS 14 Jul 1806 (OB) (OM)

**PHILIPS**, David & **DAVIS**, Mary; 2 Mar 1778 both of St. Thomas Parish (Deed Book 17)

**PHILIPS**, Hughey & **LECKIE**, Nancy surety Lucy ANDERSON 23 Oct 1829 (OB)

**PHILIPS**, John W. permission from Catharine PHILIPS & **HERNDON**, Martha Ann d/o Fielding and Mildred HERNDON surety Robert RICHARDS 17 Jan 1848 (OB)

**PHILIPS**, Reuben G. s/o Zachariah PHILLIPS and Susanna COLEMAN age 29 s POB Calhoun Co, Alabama POR Pontatock Co, Mississippi &

**HUGHES**, Virginia d/o Armistead HUGHES and Sarah A. SLEET age 25 s POB POR Orange; POM Orange 26 Nov 1863 OMR 24 Nov 1863 OML

**PHILIPS**, Richard & **SOUTHERLAND**, Catharine surety Armistead CLARKE 4 Mar 1826 (OB)

**PHILIPS**, Thomas permission from H. Thomas PHILIPS & **DAVIS**, Milly d/o Jonathan and Milly DAVIS surety David PHILIPS 16 Nov 1791 (OB)

**PHIPS**, Thomas & **MONTAGUE**, Polly surety John MONTAGUE 18 Oct 1799 (OB)

**PIATT**, William & **WHITE**, Nancy 3 Jul 1821 by J. GOSS (OM)

**PICKETT**, Charles & **DOWELL**, Jane by George BINGHAM 8 Mar 1821 (OM)

**PIERCE**, Henry M. s/o John PIERCE and Frances W. TAMPLIN age 22 s railroading POB Spotsylvania POR Orange & **ADAMS**, Eliza Jane d/o Robert ADAMS and Mildred MASON age 22 s POB POR Orange; POM Orange 23 Jan 1866 OMR 22 Jan 1866 OML

**PIERCE**, John W. & **TAMPLIN**, Amanda d/o Edward TAMPLIN who is also surety 11 May 1846 (OB) by J. EARNEST 14 May 1846 (OM)

**PIERCE**, Oscar J. s/o John and Frances PIERCE age 23 s carpenter POB Spotsylvania POR Orange & **ANDERSON**, Charlotte N. d/o Joseph and Mary ANDERSON age 24 s POB "Forkequire County of Va" [sic] POR Orange; POM Orange 5 Apr 1855 OMR 23 Mar 1855 OML

**PIPER**, William & **WHITE**, Elizabeth over 21 surety Willis WHITE 26 Dec 1803 (OB) by Jacob WATTS 29 Dec 1803 (Misc Min Ret)

**PITCHER**, John O. age 21 s farmer POB Pennsylvania POR Orange s/o John PITCHER and Martha PITCHER & **GRADY**, Mary E. age 21 s POB Louisa POR Orange d/o Kate GRADY POM Orange 26 Apr 1879 by Melzi S. CHANCELLOR (OMR)

**PITCHER**, Alexander POC age 38 w POB Madison Co POR Orange s/o Ned PITCHER and Alice TWYMAN blacksmith & **BANKS**, Amanda age 16 s POB POR Orange d/o Sampson BANKS and Caroline GREEN 2 Jun 1874 POM Orange (OMR)

**PITCHER**, Jonathan & **MASON**, Betsy surety Charles MASON 3 Nov 1788 (OB)

**PITCHER**, Robert POC age 31 s POB POR Orange s/o Endeig PITCHER and Jane ELLIS laborer & **DAVIS**, Martha E. POC age 15 s POB POR Orange d/o Albert DAVIS and Sally _____ 10 Oct 1869 POM Orange by Thomas R. HAWKINS (OMR)

**PITCHER**, William & **COLEMAN**, Fanny d/o James COLEMAN who is also surety 19 Nov 1803 (OB)

**PITTMAN**, John & **RUCKER**, Jane surety Albert G. RUCKER 17 Mar 1835 (OB)

**POINDEXTER**, George POC age 21 s POB POR Orange s/o Lewis POINDEXTER and Emily POLAND laborer & **TURNER**, Grace POC age 24 s POB POR Orange d/o Robert TURNER and Mary POR 28 Dec 1871 POM Orange by Philip JOHNSON (OMR)

**POINDEXTER**, James R. & **HANKINS [or HAWKINS]**, Martha D. d/o Thomas R. HANKINS [or HAWKINS] who is also surety 3 Oct 1846 (OB)

**POINDEXTER**, Joseph & **MITCHELL**, Clearissy Jane d/o John MITCHELL surety Griffin MITCHELL 10 Jun 1833 (OB)

**POLLARD**, Charles s/o Charles POLLARD age 27 s laborer in express office POB Culpeper Co POR Orange POC & **TERRILL**, Helen d/o Thornton TERRILL age 16 s POB POR Orange POC; POM Orange 29 Dec 1867 OMR 28 Dec 1867 OMR

**POLLARD**, Edmund & **HERNDON**, Sally surety Benjamin WRIGHT 26 Dec 1794 (OB)

**PORTER**, Albert s/o Moses PORTER age 35 w farm laborer POB POR Orange POC & **COLEMAN**, Sylvia d/o James COLEMAN age 24 s POB POR Orange POC; POM Orange 29 Dec 1867 OMR 27 Dec 1867 OML

**PORTER**, Benjamin & **NEWMAN**, Patsy over 21 years surety William NEWMAN 11 Jan 1803 by Robert JONES (OB) (OM)

**PORTER**, Camp & **ALCOTT**, Fanny permission from John ALCOTT surety John BOURNE 4 Dec 1797 (OB)

**PORTER**, Charles Jr. & **PROCTOR**, Betsy d/o George PROCTOR surety Benjamin HANSFORD 11 Nov 1782 (OB) (OM)

**PORTER**, John & **CARTER**, Catherine surety Pierce SANFORD 24 Dec 1793 (OB)

**PORTER**, John A. & **CRUMP**, Mary d/o John CRUMP surety Horace STRINGFELLOW 2 Nov 1821 (OB)

**PORTER**, John Henry s/o Ruford PORTER and Eliza PENYMAN age 23 s brick mason POB Forsythe Co, NC POR Orange & **BARDEN**, Alverta Ellsworth d/o Lewis H. BARDEN and Lucy P. FAULCONER age 21 s POB POR Orange; POM Orange 24 Oct 1867 OMR 21 Oct 1867 OML

**PORTER**, John POC age 22 s POB POR Orange s/o William PORTER and Susan PORTER laborer & **WASHINGTON**, Emily POC age 18 POB POR Orange d/o John WASHINGTON and Lucy ROBINSON 27 Dec 1873 POM Orange by F.L. GIPSON (OMR)

**PORTER**, Joseph POC age 29 s POB POR Orange s/o Patsy QUARLES farm laborer & **HALL**, Catharine POC age 21 s POB POR Orange d/o Henry HALL and Julia _____ 6 Mar 1870 POM Orange by Philip JOHNSON (OMR)

**PORTER,** Lewis M. age 28 s farmer POB Powhatan POR Staunton s/o John E. PORTER and Sophia DORSCH & **DANIEL,** Mildred A. age 22 s POB POR Orange d/o John M. DANIEL and Ann JACKSON POM Orange 29 Oct 1878 by L.A. CUTLER (OMR)

**PORTER,** William & **HENSHAW,** Mary Newman d/o Edmund HENSHAW 4 Dec 1815 (OB)

**PORTER,** William & **MCCAULEY,** Polly surety Charles URQUET 22 Aug 1796 (OB)

**POULTER,** John & **RANSDELL.** Patty surety Sanford RANSDELL 24 Jan 1786 (OB) by John PRICE 25 Jan 1786 (OM)

**POWELL** Simon & **LAMB,** Clarissa d/o James LAMB surety James LAMB Jr. 28 Aug 1832 (OB)

**POWELL,** Ambrose s/o Thomas POWELL & **BRITT,** Sally d/o Mary BRITT surety James BUSH 8 Sep 1783 (OB)

**POWELL,** Benjamin & **PICKETT,** Esther d/o Mace PICKETT surety Thomas WALKER 20 Dec 1792 (OB) 24 Dec 1792 by George EVE (OM)

**POWELL,** Benjamin & **SHOTWELL,** Martha d/o Jeremiah SHOTWELL who is also surety 12 Aug 1831 (OB)

**POWELL,** E.T. s/o John and Mary POWELL age 23 s merchant POB King William Co POR Ayletts, King William Co. & **CAVE,** Mary A. d/o Robert P. and S.F. CAVE age 18 POB Green Co POR Orange; POM Orange 15 Jan 1857 OMR OML

**POWELL,** Fealden & **BALLARD,** Susannah surety Elijah POWELL 6 Mar 1801 (OB) 8 Mar 1801 by Hamilton GOSS (OM)

**POWELL,** George & **RICHARDS,** Sarah d/o Ezekial RICHARDS surety Jonathan JOHNSON 13 Oct 1849 (OB)

**POWELL,** Jack POC age 22 s POB Madison POR Orange s/o Nelson POWELL and Julianna HENDERSON laborer & **TYLER,** Violet POC age 22 s POB POR Orange d/o Fanny TYLER 24 Jan 1880 POM Orange by Joseph A. MANSFIELD (OMR)

**POWELL,** James & **SHEELOR,** Nancy surety James SHELAR Jr. 23 Sep 1816 (OB) by George BINGHAM 25 Sep 1816 (OM)

**POWELL,** James & **STEVENS,** Julia T. d/o William STEVENS surety John M. GOODWIN 16 Nov 1827 (OB)

**POWELL,** John West POR Madison Co. & **BELL,** Eliza F.P. d/o John BELL surety St. Clair KIRTLEY 1 Feb 1803 (OB)

**POWELL,** Lazarus age 23 s farmer POB Spotsylvania POR Orange s/o James E. POWELL and Sarah F. LANCASTER & **TINDER,** Elizabeth R. age 24 s POB POR Orange d/o George T. TINDER and Susan HERNDON POM Orange 4 Dec 1879 (OMR)

**POWELL**, Lewis G. Jr. & **SMITH**, Jane her guardian is Lewis G. POWELL who also acts as surety 23 Dec 1822 (OB) 26 Dec 1822 by George BINGHAM (OM)

**POWELL**, Lewis Gordon & **POWELL**, Sally d/o Benjamin POWELL surety Thomas WALKER 1 Jan 1793 (OB)

**POWELL**, Ptolemy & **LAVIT** Sidney w surety Robert DANIEL 23 Dec 1793 (OB)

**POWELL**, Reuben & **BALLARD**, Elizabeth d/o Moreman and Martha BALLARD surety Ezekial CRAWFORD 20 Dec 1800 (OB) by Hamilton GOSS 21 Dec 1800 (OM)

**POWELL**, Robert & **BOWLER**, Sarah d/o Robert BOWLER who is also surety 16 Jun 1840 (OB)

**POWELL**, Robert & **SHIFFLET**, Nancy d/o Absalom SHIFFLET surety John DOLLINS 21 Mar 1829 (OB)

**POWELL**, Robert s/o Fielding and Susannah POWELL & **WALKER**, Sabra d/o Thomas and Mishenier WALKER 25 Dec 1825 surety Willis POWELL (OB)

**POWELL**, Simeon & **SAMPSON**, Frances d/o William SAMPSON surety George R. POWELL 17 Mar 1829 (OB)

**POWELL**, William & **BOWLER**, Elizabeth M. d/o Robert BOWLER who is also surety 27 Jul 1842 (OB)

**POWELL**, William Lewis & **MCMULLAN**, Lucy d/o John MCMILLAN who is also surety 19 Sep 1796 (OB) 22 Sep 1796 by George BINGHAM (OM)

**POWELL**, William s/o Sarah POWELL & **RIDDLE**, Frances surety Lewis G. POWELL and John RIDDLE 26 Dec 1825 (OB)

**POWELL**, Willis & **BEASLEU**, Malinda 10 Jan 1827 by George BINGHAM (OM)

**POWELL**, Yancey & **BEADLES**, Elizabeth d/o John BEADLES who is also surety 23 Oct 1833 (OB)

**PRATT**, J.H. age 22 s sawyer POB POR Orange s/o William PRATT and Frances DOUGLASS & **VAUGHAN**, Elmellia age 20 s POB Greene POR Orange d/o Cornelius VAUGHAN and Louisa R. DUFF POM Orange 2 Apr 1878 by W.H. CAMPER (OMR)

**PRATT**, William & **WHITE**, Nancy surety William WHITE 11 Jun 1821 (OB)

**PRESTIGE**, Wilson M. s/o Campbell PRESTIGE and Polly FRANKS age 22 s farmer POB Yalabasha Co., Mississippi POB Lafayette Co, Mississippi & **HERNDON**, Ann V. d/o Benjamin HERNDON and Hannah BLEDSOE age 25 s POB POR Orange; POM Orange 1 Sep 1863 OMR 31 Aug 1863 OML

**PRICE**, George W. & **WILHOIT**, Louisa H.; 25 Jan 1858 (OML)

**PRICE,** John & **SIMS,** Elizabeth surety Richard L. SIMS who is also her
  guardian 24 Feb 1812 (OB) by George BINGHAM 26 Feb 1812 (OM)
**PRICE,** Joshua POC age 52 w POB POR Louisa Co s/o Jeremiah PRICE
  and Uriah _____ r.r. hand & **BERKLEY,** Jane POC age 50 w POB
  Louisa Co POR Orange 25 Jan 1872 POM Orange by H.M. LINNEY
  (OMR)
**PRICE,** Robert POC age 23 s POB Culpeper Co POR Rappahannock Co
  s/o Jeffrey PRICE and Juda SPOTSWOOD laborer & **WILLIAMS,**
  Louisa POC age 21 s POB POR Orange d/o Henry WILLIAMS and
  Sarah ROBINSON 20 Apr 1870 POM Orange by Philip JOHNSON
  (OMR)
**PRICE,** Thomas & **DOHONEY,** Elizabeth 2 Apr 1804 by George
  BINGHAM (Misc Min Ret)
**PRICE,** Thomas & **DOHONEY,** Elizabeth d/o Hanner DOHONEY 29
  Mar 1805 (OB) by George BINGHAM 2 Apr 1805 (OM)
**PRIEST,** Albert T. age 22 s POB POR Orange Co s/o Augustine G.
  PRIEST and Cordelia CLARK farmer & **WAUGH,** Mary E. age 21 s
  POB POR Orange d/o Charles S. WAUGH and Mary E. FAULCONER
  DOM 18 Feb 1869 POM Orange John CLARK (OMR)
**PRIEST,** Augustine & **CLARKE,** Cordelia G. surety Stokely T. CLARKE
  22 Sep 1845 (OB)
**PRIEST,** Henry C. age 23 s farmer POB POR Orange s/o Augustine G.
  PRIEST and Cordelia CLARK & **TALLEY,** Ida I. age 22 s POB
  Louisa POR Orange d/o Peyton TALLEY and Frances A. BOSTON
  POM Orange 13 Nov 1877 by William A. HILL (OMR)
**PRITCHETT,** Benjamin & **HERNDON,** Polly surety William H.
  STANARD 7 Apr 1798 (OB)
**PRITCHETT,** P.B. & **DOWNER,** Ann E. ward of John D. HAWKINS
  surety William C. DOWNER 29 Aug 1850 (OB) by John A.
  BILLINGSLEY 6 Sep 1850 (OM)
**PROCTER,** Oscar & **TERRILL,** Mary Ann surety George F. TERRILL
  27 Jan 1845 (OB)
**PROCTER,** Thomas & **SHADRACH,** Lucy surety P.S. FRY 20 Oct 1825
  (OB)
**PROCTOR,** George Jr. & **GRADY,** Fanny d/o William GRADY Sr.
  surety John GRADY 29 Jun 1807 (OB) by Nathaniel SANDERS 1 Jul
  1807 (OM)
**PROCTOR,** George s/o Abraham PROCTOR and Mary A. CARTER age
  26 s carpenter POB POR Orange POC & **THOMPSON,** Frances age
  16 s POB POR Orange POC; POM Orange 12 Oct 1867 OMR 11 Oct
  1867 OML
**PROCTOR,** Hezikiah & **YOUNG,** Nancy d/o John YOUNG surety John
  TURNLEY 30 Mar 1783 (OB)

**PROCTOR**, Olander s/o Thomas and Mary PROCTOR age 21 farmer POB POR Orange & **BLEDSOE**, Mildred H. d/o John and Margaret BLEDSOE age 17 POB POR Orange; POM Orange 29 Dec 1857 OMR 26 Dec 1857 OML

**PROCTOR**, Uriah & **SINGLETON**, Martha POR Fredericksburg both of St. Thomas Parish 22 Aug 1776 by banns (Deed Book 17)

**PROCTOR**, William & **HIATT**, Elizabeth both of St. Thomas Parish 8 May 1777 by banns (Deed Book 17)

**PROCTOR**, William Jr. & **YOUNG**, Ann H. d/o Daniel YOUNG who is also surety 14 Dec 1842 (OB)

**PRYOR**, Pleasant POC age 27 w laborer POB POR Orange s/o William PRYOR and Mary A. GREEN & **GORDON**, Fanny POC age 17 s POB POR Orange d/o Jere GORDON and Polly ELLIS POM Orange 31 Mar 1877 (OMR)

**PULLIAM**, Absalom & **KING**, Rhoda surety John E. PULLIAM and Thomas ROW (her uncle) 22 Jun 1824 (OB)

**PULLIAM**, David & **WRIGHT**, Lucy Ann d/o John WRIGHT surety Robert WRIGHT 6 Oct 1838 (OB) by Joseph A. MANSFIELD 10 Oct 1838 (OM)

**PURTON**, May & **HEAD**, Sara; 29 Sep 1776 (OM)

**QUANN**, John D. age 22 s farmer s/o Daniel QUANN and Alice O'NEAL POB POR Orange & **SMITH**, Ida I. age 16 s POB POR Orange d/o John C. SMITH and Semea A. POE POM Orange 13 Feb 1876 by Sanders MASON (OMR)

**QUARLES**, Duncan M. s/o John T. and Mary QUARLES age 22 teacher POB Louisa Co POR Orange & **SPOTSWOOD**, Martha P. d/o William L.M. and Catharine H. SPOTSWOOD age 21 POB Spotsylvania POR Orange; POM Orange 21 Jul 1857 OMR 14 Jul 1857 OML

**QUARLES**, Fleet POC age 25 s labourer POB Spotsylvania POR Orange s/o Martin QUARLES and Ellen RAY & **GALLERY**, Urslie age 22 s POB POR Orange d/o George GALLERY and Sally BANK/BARK POM Mt. Pleasant, Orange 25 May 1879 by C.T. JOHNSON (OMR)

**QUARLES**, Hawkins POC age 22 s POB POR Orange s/o Ralph QUARLES and Jane TAYLOR blacksmith & **STAUNTON**, Nellie POC age 21 s POB POR Orange d/o Moses STAUNTON and Patsy ____ 19 Feb 1874 POM Orange (OMR)

**QUARLES**, William & **VIVION**, Frances d/o John VIVION surety Nathaniel MILLS both of St. Thomas Parish 3 Sep 1779 (OB)

**QUICK**, George & **RAINS**, Mildred d/o Reubin RAINS surety Richard LAMB 21 Mar 1809 (OB) by George BINGHAM 22 Mar 1809 (OM)

191

**QUINN,** Garland & **SMITH,** Dealen permission from Hannah HENSLEY surety Cypress HENSLEY 2 Dec 1809 (OB) by Jacob WATTS 24 Dec 1809 (OM)

**QUINN,** Richard & **WOOD,** Ann; 27 Mar 1783 surety William GLASS (OB) 2 Apr 1783 by J. PRICE (OM)

**QUISENBERRY,** Aaron & **REYNOLDS,** Henrietta d/o William REYNOLDS surety George QUISENBERRY by Robert JONES 17 Oct 1805 (OB (OM)

**QUISENBERRY,** Albert & **REYNOLDS,** Sarah d/o William REYNOLDS surety Philip S. REYNOLDS by Jeremiah CHANDLER 18 Apr 1831 (OB) (OM)

**QUISENBERRY,** Benjamin & **GROOM,** Sally B. d/o Major GROOM surety John HENDERSON 11 Jan 1816 (OB) by Jeremiah CHANDLER 14 Jan 1816 (OM)

**QUISENBERRY,** Benjamin s/o Vivion QUISENBERRY & **HERNDON,** Elizabeth d/o Eliz. HERNDON surety William HERNDON 18 Dec 1843 (OB)

**QUISENBERRY,** Bevin aka Vivion s/o George QUISENBERRY surety & **WRIGHT,** Salley d/o Benjamin WRIGHT surety POR Orange 28 Oct 1811 (OB)

**QUISENBERRY,** Daniel & **RHOADES,** Mary d/o George RHOADES surety Jonathan ATKINS 10 Dec 1812 (OB) by J. GOSS 27 Dec 1812 (OM)

**QUISENBERRY,** George & **DANIEL,** Jane both of St. Thomas Parish surety Vivion DANIEL 22 May 1783 (OB)

**QUISENBERRY,** George & **REYNOLDS,** Margaret d/o William REYNOLDS surety John YOUNG 22 Jun 1802 (OB)

**QUISENBERRY,** Hezekiah & **BURRUSS,** Frances Emily d/o William T. BURRUSS by George MORRIS surety Joseph BURRUSS 10 Dec 1824 (OB) (OM)

**QUISENBERRY,** James & **BURROWS,** Jane both of St. Thomas Parish [Jane b.d. 5 Jul 1759 d/o Thomas BURRUSS and Frances TANDY] 2 Dec 1776 (Deed Book 17) [] information taken from compiler's notes.

**QUISENBERRY,** James & **RHOADS,** Elizabeth surety Catlett RHOADS 26 Feb 1844 (OB)

**QUISENBERRY,** James & **SANDERS,** Sarah Frances; 19 Nov 1851 (OML)

**QUISENBERRY,** John & **ROW,** Mary E. d/o Elhanon ROW; POM Orange 23 Sep 1852 OMR 21 Sep 1852 OML

**QUISENBERRY,** Moses ward of Henry QUISENBERRY POR Louisa Co. & **DURRETT,** Milly d/o Joel; DURRETT who is also surety 14 Aug 1805 (OB)

**QUISENBERRY**, Vivian s/o George QUISENBERRY who is also surety & **WRIGHT,** Sally d/o Benjamin WRIGHT who is also surety 28 Oct 1811 (OB)

**QUISENBERRY**, Vivion s/o George QUISENBERRY and Jenny DANIEL age 73 w farmer POB POR Orange & **HERNDON**, Elizabeth d/o Ambrose COLEMAN and Frances HILMAN age 52 w POB POR Orange; POM 29 Nov 1866 OMR 21 Nov 1866 OML

**QUISENBERRY**, Vivion s/o Vivion and Sarah QUISENBERRY age 25 POB POR Orange & **ROBINSON**, Ann E. d/o Thomas and Elizabeth T. ROBINSON age 19 POB POR Orange; POM Orange 10 Dec 1857 OMR 23 Nov 1857 OML

**QUISENBERRY**, William & **TERRILL,** Catharine ward of William QUISENBERRY surety James YOUNG 22 Oct 1832 (OB)

**RABESKY**, Henry s/o Philip and Anna RABESKY age 25 s blacksmith POB Germany POR Orange & **KUBE**, Mary M. d/o Henry KUBE and Cathrin RUBY age 31 s POB Germany POR Orange; POM Orange 7 Sep 1865 (OMR) 4 Sep 1865 (OML)

**RAGLAND**, Philip W. POC age 22 s POB Louisa Co. POR Orange s/o Winston RAGLAND and Judy ELLIS laborer & **WILLIS**, Susan POC age 20 POB POR Orange 26 Dec 1871 POM Orange by Philip JOHNSON (OMR)

**RAGLAND**, Pleasant POC age 22 s POB Albemarle Co POR Orange laborer & **CAVE**, Mary Lou age 21 POB POR Orange d/o Walker CAVE 23 Jan 1872 POM Orange by Jos. A. MANSFIELD (OMR)

**RAINER**, Anderson & **JARRALL,** Patsy d/o John JARRALL who is also surety 19 Jul 1838 (OB)

**RAINES**, Merry & **FLOYD,** Annie surety Samuel FLOYD 19 Mar 1799 (OB) 21 Mar 1799 by Hamilton GOSS (OM)

**RAINS**, Fielding & **WILLIAMS,** Elizabeth surety Matthew LAMB by George BINGHAM 10 Nov 1819 (OB) (OM)

**RAINS**, Richard & **EASTRIDGE,** Theodosia; 22 May 1783 by George EVE, Baptist (OM)

**RAINS**, William POR Rockingham Co. & **EDDINS**, Frances of age d/o Mildred EDDINS POR Orange 23 Oct 1811 William DULANEY surety (OB)

**RALLS,** John POC age 50 w farmer POB POR Orange s/o Minor and Eliza RALLS & **GORDON,** Eveline POC age 38 s POB POR Orange POM Orange 23 Jul 1877 (OMR)

**RALLS**, Robinson & **CLARKE,** Mary Ann d/o Thomas CLARKE surety 26 Nov 1811 (OB) by James GARNETT 28 Nov 1811 (OM)

**RAMSDELL**, Lyman age 48 w POB Hampshire Co., Mass POR Orange s/o Oliver RAMSDELL and Terezah PORTER miner & **BURTON,** Arminta V. age 19 s POB Culpeper Co POR Orange d/o A.S.

BURTON and Frances E. STARKEY 18 Oct 1869 POM Orange by
Melzi S. CHANCELLOR (OMR)
RANDAL, Richard & HUFFMAN, Ruby surety Milton HUFFMAN 27
May 1833 (OB)
RANDOLPH, John POC age 23 s farm laborer POB POR Orange s/o
James RANDOLPH and Nelly ___ & LAWSON, Lucy POC age 21 s
POB POR Orange d/o Daniel LAWSON POM Orange 5 Aug 1876 by
John S. HANSBROUGH (OMR)
RANDOLPH, William & BACK, Lucy surety Rachel BACK 15 Nov
1825 (OB)
RANSON, James & PARROTT, Melvina d/o John PARROTT surety
Dabney LOCKER 21 Dec 1836 (OB)
RAWLS, Ed POC s/o Sam RAWLS and Lucy TERRILL & JACKSON,
Mollie POC age 18 s POB POR Orange d/o Ned JACKSON and Fanny
PAGE 4 Jan 1877 POM Orange (OMR)
RAWLINGS, Edward T. s/o Lewis and Hannah G. RAWLINGS age 30
general agent POB Spotsylvania POR Richmond & PORTER, Susan
d/o John A. and Mary PORTER POB POR Orange; POM Orange 21
Feb 1856 (OMR) 12 Feb 1856 (OML)
RAWLINGS, John L. & SIMMONS, Elizabeth d/o Basel SIMMONS
who is also surety 10 Oct 1825 (OB) by J. GOSS 11 Oct 1825 (OM)
RAWLINS, William age 37 w POB Sheffield, England POR Brooklyn,
NY s/o Benj. RAWLINS and Lydia KNOWLES merchant &
STANARD, Mildred C. age 27 s POB POR Orange d/o Beverley
STANARD and Ellen B. TALIAFERRO 12 Feb 1868 POM Orange by
T.M. CARSON (OMR)
READ, Albert POC age 40 w labourer POB POR Orange s/o Reuben
READ and Mary BURRUS & MCDANIEL, Sarah POC age 23 s POB
POR Orange d/o Benjamin MCDANIEL and Polly ___ POM Orange
18 Oct 1877 (OMR)
READ, Carvel H. & FAULCONER, Mildred d/o William FAULCONER
surety Nicholas FAULCONER 16 Oct 1824 (OB)
READ, John & HERNDON, Margaret surety William S. WALKER 5 Jan
1833 (OB) by E.G. SHIP 3 May 1833 (OM)
READ, William & CRAYTON, Lucinda permission from Sarah
CRATON surety Ezekial RICHARDS 15 May 1826 (OB)
READ, William & RUMSEY, Dysa over 21 years surety Henry TEEL 22
Oct 1802 (OB)
READER, Isaac & MACKELANY, Susannah d/o Susaner
MACKELANY stepdaughter of John WOOLFREY surety William
HUTCHINSON 26 Dec 1796 (OB)

**RED**, Henry POC age 24 s POB POR Orange s/o Henry RED and Annie GALLERY laborer & **CAMPBELL**, Isabella POC age 18 s POB POR Orange d/o George CAMPBELL and Mary JOHNSON 1 Sep 1870 POM Orange by Philip JOHNSON (OMR)

**REED**, Benjamin s/o Dyannah Teal READ & **PAYNE**, Sarah surety Daniel YOUNG 11 May 1826 (OB)

**REESE**, John & **PORTER**, Sarah Frances d/o John PORTER who is also surety 1 Jun 1826 (OB) by James GARNETT 8 Jun 1826 (OM)

**REEVES**, Stafford s/o Timothy and Betsy REEVES age 26 s editor POB Hull, Yorkshire, England POR Woodville, Orange Co. & **SEIDELL**, Elizabeth A. d/o Charles WARD and Mary SEIDELL age 18 s POB Bucks Co, Pa POR Vancluse, Orange Co.; POM Orange 20 Mar 1856 (OMR) 19 Mar 1856 (OML)

**REID**, J. Dorsey lieutenant POR Washington city & **CHAPMAN**, Maria Louisa d/o Richard M. CHAPMAN; POM Orange 1 Aug 1851 (OMR) 31 Jul 1851 (OML)

**REID**, James A. & **NEWMAN**, Ellen E. d/o Reubin NEWMAN who is also surety by J. EARNEST 7 Oct 1845 (OB) (OM)

**REINS**, William & **EDDONS**, Frances 25 Oct 1811 by George BINGHAM (OM)

**RENNOLDS**, William & **JONES**, Hannah 27 Jul 1811 Thomas CLARK sec (OB)

**REVELEY**, Thomas age 30 s farmer POB Lagrange, MO POR Orange s/o Thomas C. REVELEY and Robinette TAYLOR & **BALL**, Annie H. age 33 s POB POR Orange d/o Marcus BALL and Sarah DADE POM Orange 27 Mar 1877 (OMR)

**REVELEY**, Thomas C. & **TAYLOR**, Robinette F. surety Thomas T. TOWLES 7 May 1844 (OB) by J. EARNEST 8 May 1844 (OM)

**REYNOLDS**, Aaron & **CHAMBERS**, Caty surety James ADAMS 13 Aug 1784 (OB)

**REYNOLDS**, Benjamin F. & **WRIGHT**, Virginia T. d/o Benjamin WRIGHT; POM Orange 4 Jul 1853 (OMR) 27 Jun 1853 (OML)

**REYNOLDS**, James S. & **DOUGLASS**, Mary E. d/o William DOUGLASS who is also surety 25 Aug 1834 (OB)

**REYNOLDS**, John & **DARNELL**, Anna both of St. Thomas Parish 23 Jan 1774 by banns (Deed Book 17)

**REYNOLDS**, John & **JACOBS**, Susan d/o Nathan JACOBS surety Daniel G. REYNOLDS 8 Feb 1826 (OB)

**REYNOLDS**, John & **ROBINSON**, Mary d/o Elijah ROBINSON surety George SISSON 5 Jan 1830 (OB)

**REYNOLDS**, John W. s/o John D. REYNOLDS and Elizabeth HENDERSON age 31 s farmer POB POR Orange & **DOWNER**, Mildred A. d/o Robert E. DOWNER and Frances A. DANIEL age 18 s

POB POR Orange; POM Orange 31 May 1866 (OMR) 30 May 1866
(OML)

**REYNOLDS**, Joseph [s/o Joseph REYNOLDS and Elizabeth HERNDON]
& **WRIGHT**, Susanna both of St. Thomas Parish 10 Feb 1774 by
banns (Deed Book 17)

**REYNOLDS**, Joseph D. (his brother is William REYNOLDS) &
**HENDERSON**, Elizabeth M. d/o John HENDERSON who is also
surety 5 Nov 1832 (OB)

**REYNOLDS**, Lewis H. & **RHOADES**, Lucy; POM Orange 21 Dec 1851
(OMR) 19 Dec 1851 (OML)

**REYNOLDS**, Philip S. & **REYNOLDS**, Elizabeth d/o William
REYNOLDS surety Albert QUISENBERRY by Jeremiah CHANDLER
18 Apr 1831 (OB) (OM)

**REYNOLDS**, Richard & **FINNEL**, Lucy d/o Simon FINNEL surety
William DAWSON 24 Dec 1800 (OB)

**REYNOLDS**, Richard & **ROACH**, Ann w both of St. Thomas Parish 24
Aug 1778 surety Thomas Parish (Deed Book 17)

**REYNOLDS**, Richard & **ROW**, Elizabeth K. d/o Elhanon ROW POC
Hansford T. SANDERS surety 18 Oct 1847 (OB)

**REYNOLDS**, Robert E. & **TERRILL**, Elizabeth Frances d/o Nancy
TERRILL surety Joseph D. REYNOLDS 10 Oct 1842 (OB) by
Herndon FRAZER 11 Oct 1842 (OM)

**REYNOLDS**, Washington [s/o Joseph REYNOLDS and Susanna
WRIGHT] & **SWAN**, Catharine [d/o Samuel Hatch SWANN] surety
William W. REYNOLDS 1 Mar 1805 (OB) [] taken from notes of
Catherine Knorr

**REYNOLDS**, William [s/o Joseph REYNOLDS and Elizabeth
HERNDON] & **NIXON**, Nancy both of St. Thomas Parish 22 May
1777 by banns (Deed Book 17) [] taken from the notes of Catherine
Knorr

**REYNOLDS**, William [s/o Joseph REYNOLDS and Susanna WRIGHT]
& **QUISENBERRY**, Jane d/o George QUISENBERRY who is also
surety 27 Nov 1809 (OB) [] taken from the notes of Catherine Knorr

**REYNOLDS**, William s/o William REYNOLDS [and Nancy NIXON] &
**QUISENBERRY**, Joice d/o Sally QUISENBERRY surety Robert
YOUNG 27 Nov 1809 (OB) [] taken from the notes of Catherine Knorr

**REYNOLDS**, William & **RUMSEY**, Peggy d/o Thomas RUMSEY surety
Reuben SCOTT 27 Jul 1797 (OB)

**REYNOLDS**, William & **WEBB**, Delilah surety Oliver TERRILL 17 Feb
18445 (OB) by Joseph S. JACKSON 18 Feb 1845 (OM)

**REYNOLDS**, William A. age 17 s farmer POB Louisiana POR Orange s/o
John N.M. REYNOLDS and Lucy F. RHOADES & **MORRIS**, Lillie

K. age 17 s POB POR Orange d/o George MORRIS and Sarah J. SUTHERLAND POM Orange 5 Oct 1879 (OMR)

**REYNOLDS**, William G. & **ROACH**, Susan M.; POM Orange 25 Nov 1852 (OMR) 22 Nov 1852 (OML)

**REYNOLDS**, William H. s/o William S. REYNOLDS and Ann QUISENBERRY age 25 s farmer POB Spotsylvania POR Orange & **REYNOLDS**, Ann Wise d/o James D. REYNOLDS and Elizabeth HENDERSON age 16 s POB POR Orange; POM Orange 14 Mar 1867 (OMR) 11 Mar 1867 (OML)

**REYNOLDS**, William J. age 27 s farmer POB Fluvanna POR Orange s/o Tobias REYNOLDS and Dolly PARISH & **BROOKS**, Louanna age 21 s POB Goochland POR Orange 13 Oct 1878 by T.A. M. HOPE (OMR)

**REYNOLDS**, William S. & **QUISENBERRY,** Nancy d/o Vivion QUISENBERRY who is also surety 28 Oct 1833 (OB)

**REYNOLDS**, William W. & **YOUNG,** Margaret surety James YOUNG by James G. LINDSAY 28 Dec 1840 (OB) (OM)

**RHINE**, John & **DAVIS**, Edy by George BINGHAM 17 Apr 1827 (OM)

**RHOADES**, Achilles age 45 [b. 6 Jul 1835] s POB POR Orange s/o Catlett RHOADES and Nancy RHOADES[ Nancy b. 8 Jan 1801] farmer & **KUBE**, Bettie [aka Catharine Elizabeth b. 17 May 1836] age 35 s POB POR Orange d/o John KUBE and Fredericka KUBE 19 Oct 1880 POM Orange by Richard STEPHENS (OMR) [] taken from compiler's notes

**RHOADES**, Clifton & **HAM**, Milly d/o Samuel HAM who is also surety 9 Aug 1814 (OB) by Jacob WATTS 6 Oct 1814 (OM)

**RHOADES**, John & **FAULCONER**, Margaret d/o John FAULCONER surety Hugh M. FAULCONER 23 Aug 1819 (OB) by J.C. GORDON 26 Aug 1819 (OM)

**RHOADES**, John & **RHOADES**, Susan d/o George RHOADES surety Thomas RHOADES 12 Dec 1834 (OB)

**RHOADES**, John & **HATCH**, Ann Eliza d/o Henry HATCH; POM Orange 21 Dec 1851 (OMR) 19 Dec 1851 (OML)

**RHOADES**, Nicholas POC age 22 s POB POR Orange s/o Nicholas RHOADES and Sarah HOOMES sawmill hand & **STEWART**, Mary age 21 s POB POR Orange d/o Betsey BANKS 14 Dec 1872 POM Orange by Frank TIBBS (OMR)

**RHOADES**, Richard B. s/o William RHOADES and Elizabeth COUTHRON age 30 s farmer POB POR Orange & **KUBE**, Mary G. d/o John KUBE age 25 s POB POR Orange; POM Orange 29 Mar 1866 (OMR) 22 Mar 1866 (OML)

**RHOADES**, Thomas age 26 s POB Augusta Co POR Orange s/o Sim WILLIAMS and Charity RHOADES laborer & **HOOMES**, Courtney

age 25 s POB POR Orange d/o Nelson HOOMES and Sarah _____ 17
Sep 1870 POM Orange by H.M. LINNEY (OMR)

**RHOADES,** Thomas & **HILMAN,** Susan d/o Joseph HILMAN who is
also surety 26 Oct 1840 (OB)

**RHOADES,** William H. age 26 s blacksmith POB POR Orange s/o John
RHOADES Jr. and Ann E. HATCH & **SANDERS,** Cora J. age 19 s
POB POR Orange d/o John R. SANDERS and Mary J. PAYNE POM
Orange 18 Feb 1879 (OMR)

**RHODES,** Catlett & **RHODES,** Nancy d/o George RHODES surety
Thomas RHODES 13 Jun 1831 (OB)

**RHODES,** Clifton & **WALKER,** Elizabeth surety John FLEET 2 Nov
1829 (OB)

**RHODES,** George & **HAWKINS,** Ann d/o Benjamin HAWKINS surety
Catlett RHODES 10 May 1826 (OB)

**RHODES,** George & **WRIGHT,** Nancy d/o B. BENNETT surety William
WRIGHT 28 Mar 1791 (OB) by Nathaniel SANDERS 1 Apr 1791
(OM)

**RHODES,** John & **PEARSON,** Tabitha d/o Robert PEARSON surety
Joseph BURTON 10 May 1793 (OB)

**RHODES,** Richard & **WRIGHT,** Lucy surety George Bledsoe WRIGHT
9 Feb 1793 (OB)

**RHODES,** Richard & **WRIGHT,** Mary surety Fielding JONES 9 Mar
1829 (OB)

**RHODES,** Robert POR Albemarle Co. & **DELANEY,** Lisza s surety
Andrew SHEPHERD 27 May 1782 (OB)

**RICE or RIFE,** Henry & **BINGHAM,** Milly d/o George BINGHAM
surety John BINGHAM 27 May 1816 (OB)

**RICHARDS,** Ezekial & **HERNDON,** Ann surety John HENDON Jr. 5
Nov 1849 (OB)

**RICHARDS,** Ferdinand s/o Richard RICHARDS Jr. & **QUISENBERRY,**
Jannie d/o Vivion QUISENBERRY; POM Orange 9 Mar 1852 (OMR)
8 Mar 1852 (OML)

**RICHARDS,** Fountain & **MILLS,** Sophia by George BINGHAM 10 Apr
1823 (OM)

**RICHARDS,** George W. & **TINDER,** Sarah E.; POM Orange 30 Dec
1852 (OMR) 29 Dec 1852 (OML)

**RICHARDS,** Hezekiah & **LANCASTER,** Elizabeth permission from John
LANCASTER surety Benjamin COOPER 27 Dec 1813 (OB)

**RICHARDS,** Ike & **ROBINSON,** Elizabeth d/o John ROBINSON surety
William ROBINSON 18 Dec 1797 (OB)

**RICHARDS,** James & **KEYSER,** Sarah surety Jacob KEYSEAR 26 Mar
1832 (OB)

**RICHARDS,** James P. age 33 s merchant POB POR Orange s/o William RICHARDS and Susan RICHARDS & **WRIGHT,** Columbia age 17 s POB POR Orange d/o John WRIGHT and Louisa MASSEY POM Good Hope Church, Orange 2 Nov 1879 (OMR)

**RICHARDS,** John & **WATTS,** Milly both of St. Thomas Parish 3 Apr 1776 by banns (Deed Book 17)

**RICHARDS,** John S. s/o Fountain RICHARDS and Sophia MILLS age 39 s physician POB POR Albemarle Co & **WINSLOW,** Bettie E. d/o George WINSLOW and Martha COCKRELL age 26 s POB POR Orange; POM Orange 22 Dec 1864 (OMR) 21 Dec 1864 (OML)

**RICHARDS,** John W. age 21 s POB Spotsylvania POR Orange s/o Robert RICHARDS and Catherine OVERTON farmer & **SANDERS,** Theodosia C. age 17 s POB POR Orange d/o James SANDERS and Elizabeth MASON Orange by Sanders MASON (OMR)

**RICHARDS,** Morgan age 25 s POB Fairfax Co. POR Orange s/o John RICHARDS and Jane WILT merchant & **HUBAND,** Fanny L. age 17 s POB King William Co. POR Orange d/o E.H. HUBAND and Sarah F. ARMSTRONG 25 Jan 1872 POM Orange by James L. FISHER (OMR)

**RICHARDS,** Philemon & **WOODS,** Susannah both of St. Thomas Parish 3 Feb 1778 by banns (Deed Book 17)

**RICHARDS,** Richard & **ADAMS,** Mary surety Ezekial RICHARDS 26 Jan 1818 (OB) by J.C. GORDON 11 Feb 1818 (OM)

**RICHARDS,** Richard s/o John RICHARDS and Elizabeth TINDER age 33 s carpenter POB Culpeper Co POR Orange & **FAIRFAX,** Flora d/o Robert DICKINSON and Julia CRAIG age 21 w POB Augusta Co POR Orange; POM Gordonsville, Orange 13 Sep 1866 (OMR) (OML)

**RICHARDS,** Robinson C. & **TINDER,** Elizabeth L. d/o James R. TINDER Sr. POM Orange 24 Dec 1851 OMR 22 Dec 1851 OML

**RICHARDS,** Weedon & **MASON,** Mary d/o Ann MASON surety Sanders MASON 23 Dec 1830 (OB)

**RICHARDS,** William W. & **LANCASTER,** Susan; POM Orange 2 Feb 1852 (OMR) 19 Jan 1852 (OML)

**RICHARDSON,** Charles POC age 21 s POB POR Orange s/o Harry RICHARDSON and Nelly JOHNSON r.r. hand & **WATSON,** Anna POC age 21 s POB Louisa Co POR Orange d/o John WATSON and Sophy WINSTON 30 Dec 1871 by Thomas R. HAWKINS (OMR)

**RICHARDSON,** E.E. age 20 s farmer POB Madison POR Orange s/o John A. RICHARDSON and Margaret M. HAWKINS & **HAWK,** Mary R. age 22 s POB Pennsylvania POR Orange d/o William HURLOCK and Mary HAWK POM Orange 9 Jan 1879 (OMR)

**RICHARDSON,** George POC age 48 w labourer POB Louisa POR Orange s/o Charles RICHARDSON and Casey DOWIN & **BATES,**

Julia POC age 32 w POB POR Orange d/o Lewis HARVEY and
Phoebe BROCK POM Orange 25 Oct 1879 (OMR)

**RICHARDSON**, Henry age 22 s POB England POR Orange s/o Charles S.
RICHARDSON and Sophia BOXALL miner & **JOHNSON**, Rosa
Ellen age 18 s POB Orange POR Orange d/o Edwin R. JOHNSON and
Ann HANEY 6 Oct 1870 POM Orange by M.S. CHANCELLOR (OM)

**RICHARDSON**, John A. & **HAWKINS**, Margaret N. d/o Alex
HAWKINS surety John J. HANEY 19 Dec 1846 (OB)

**RICHARDSON**, Josiah & **ABELL**, Sarah d/o Caleb ABELL surety John
LANSLEY 5 Feb 1816 (OB) by John C. GORDON 6 Feb 1816 (OM)

**RICHARDSON**, Quarles POC age 29 w farm labourer POB POR Orange
s/o Harry RICHARDSON and Nelly JOHNSON & **BROCKMAN**,
Eliza POC age 28 s POB Louisa POR Orange d/o Harry BROCKMAN
POM Orange 26 May 1877 (OMR)

**RICHARDSON**, Robert A. & **BLEDSOE**, Elizabeth; POM Orange 29
Dec 1853 (OMR) 27 Dec 1853 (OML)

**RICHARDSON**, Robert M. age 21 s farmer POB POR Orange s/o John A.
RICHARDSON and Margaret HAWKINS & **HIGHLANDER**, Ann H.
age 17 s POB POR Orange d/o Madison HIGHLANDER and Sarah
HIGHLANDER POM Orange 20 Feb 1876 by H.E. HATCHER
(OMR)

**RICHARDSON**, William Henry age 24 s POB Caroline Co POR
Albemarle Co. s/o William RICHARDSON and Martha
SOUTHWORTH shoe and boot maker & **ESTES**, Lucinda C. age 25 s
POB Louisa Co POR Orange Co d/o Thomas ESTES and Nancy
PORTER 6 Jan 1869 POM Orange by Herndon FRAZER (OMR)

**RICKETTS**, William H. s/o H. RICKETTS and Elizabeth FOGG age 25 s
saddler POB Rappahannock Co. POR Orange & **CULLEN**, Emma d/o
George CULLEN age 24 s POB POR Orange; POM Orange C.H.15
Sep 1863 (OMR) 14 Sep 1863 (OML)

**RIDDELL**, James & **RHODES**, Theodosia surety Charles NEALE by
George EVE 27 Nov 1788 (OB) (OM)

**RIDDELL**, William & **RIDDELL**, Joyce permission from her uncle,
Lewis RIDDLE surety John GOODALL both of St. Thomas Parish 25
Dec 1783 (OB)

**RIDDLE**, Charles & **SIMS**, Lucretia surety Jeremiah JARRELL 3 Jan
1818 (OB)

**RIDDLE**, Fielding & **WAITS**, Milly surety William Lewis POWELL 13
Feb 1795 (OB) by George EVE17 Feb 1795 (OM)

**RIDDLE**, Hazelworth & **RIDDLE**, Sarah d/o John RIDDLE surety
William RIDDLE 31 Mar 1835 (OB) by E.G. SHIP 1 May 1835 (OM)

**RIDDLE**, John & **SEAL**, Elizabeth surety John M. BALLARD 24 Sep
1804 (OB)

**RIDDLE,** Tavner & **GOODALL,** Mary d/o David GOODALL surety Charles GOODALL 27 Dec 1813 (OB) by George MORRIS 30 Dec 1813 (OM)

**RIDDLE,** Tavner & **POWELL,** Sally d/o Lewis G. POWELL who is also surety 22 Apr 1822 (OB) by George BINGHAM 25 Apr 1822 (OM)

**RIDDLE,** Thompson & **POWELL,** Mary ward of Thompson RIDDLE surety Valentine RIDDLE 22 Nov 1824 (OB)

**RIDDLE,** Valentine & **GOODALL,** Betsy d/o James GOODALL Sr. surety James GOODALL Jr. and Tavener RIDDLE 11 Nov 1809 (OB) by George BINGHAM (OM)

**RIDLEY,** Emanuel POC age 21 s blacksmith POB POR Orange s/o Uriel RIDLEY and Mary HOMES & **MADISON,** Clara POC age 19 s POB POR Orange d/o Henry MADISON and Julia THOMPSON POM Mt. Pleasant Church, Orange 28 Dec 1878 by C.T. JOHNSON (OMR)

**RIEVES,** William s/o Moses RIEVES and Betty HOGINS age 25 w shoemaker POB Madison Co POR Orange POC & **JOHNSON,** Charlotte d/o John JOHNSON and Lucy HARRISON age 21 s POB POR Orange POC; POM Orange 26 Dec 1867 (OMR) 25 Dec 1867 (OML)

**RIGHT,** Edward & **POWELL,** Frankey d/o John POWELL surety Richard PLAYLE 24 Jan 1787 (OB)

**RIGHT,** James & **RAWSON,** Sarah surety Luke JENNINGS 28 Feb 1785 (OB) by Nathaniel SANDERS 3 Mar 1785 (OM)

**RILEY,** Jacob Frederick age 62 w POB Wertemburg, Germany POR Orange s/o John RILEY and Mary MITCHELL farmer & **HITT,** Mary Ellen age 38 s POB Fauquier POR Orange d/o Martin HITT and M. Mary HAWKINS 16 Sep 1880 POM Orange by W.H. CAMPER (OMR)

**RINER,** Jacob E. s/o Aaron RINER and Mary PLANKENBAKER age 31 s carpenter POB Green Co POR Louisa Co & **ROBINSON,** Martha J. d/o James ROBINSON and Nancy RYAN age 22 s POB Louisa Co POR Orange; POM Orange 21 Sep 1865 (OMR) 18 Sep 1865 (OML)

**RINER,** Jacob s/o Daniel RINER and Elizabeth FLESHMAN age 70 w farmer POB Madison Co POR Orange & **ESTES,** Nancy F. d/o Edward GILBERT and Susan SANDRIDGE age 44 w POB Albemarle Co POR Orange; POM Orange 28 Apr 1867 (OMR) 25 Apr 1867 (OML)

**RINER,** John & **OVERTON,** Fanny d/o Obediah OVERTON who is also surety 12 Dec 1817 (OB)

**RIORDAN,** Lafayette W. age 48 w POB Petersburg, VA POR Orange s/o George F. RIORDAN and Irene DICKERSON gentleman at large & **STAPLES,** Sarah F. age 22 s POB POR Orange d/o William E. STAPLES and Mary GARTON 1 May 1873 POM Orange by Thomas R. HAWKINS (OMR)

**RIPLEY,** William & **EVE,** Elizabeth d/o Sarah EVE surety Francis S. COX 20 Mar 1832 (OB) by J. GOSS 22 Mar 1832 (OM)

**RIPPETO,** Peter & **TAYLOR,** Martha d/o William TAYLOR surety Ellis HAMBLETON 25 May 1801 (OB)

**RIPPETO,** Thomas P. & **MCCALLISTER,** Louisa Henry HOUCK is guardian and security 26 Jan 1824 (OB) by J. GOSS 5 Feb 1824 (OM)

**RIPPITO,** William & **STROW,** Betsy d/o Zanny ARANZY (his consent is written in German) surety William LUCAS Jr. 12 Apr 1797 (OB)

**RIVES,** Moses POC age 50 w POB POR Orange s/o Louis RIVES and Rachel _____ carpenter & **WHITE,** Jane POC age 25 s POB POR Orange d/o Abraham WHITE and Mary _____ 21 Feb 1869 POM Orange by James A. MANSFIELD (OMR)

**RIVES,** Willis POC age 37 s farmer POB POR Orange s/o Phil RIVES and Maria _____ & **FRY,** Mary Ann POC age 24 s POB Albemarle POR Orange d/o Clara FRY POM Orange 31 Dec 1879 by Joseph A. MANSFIELD (OMR)

**RIXEY,** John & **SUTHERLAND,** Betsy surety Joseph SUTHERLAND 25 Jul 1792 (OB)

**ROACH,** Emanuel B. s/o Michael ROACH and Angelina RICKER age 25 s farmer POB Rockingham Co. POR Orange & **FAULCONER,** Mary d/o John FAULCONER and Elizabeth LEE age 24 s POB POR Orange; POM Orange 27 Jun 1867 (OMR) 26 Jun 1867 (OML)

**ROACH,** Henry D. & **PAYNE,** Eliza Ann surety Robert ROACH 24 Nov 1845 (OB)

**ROACH,** James s/o Robert ROACH and Mildred JONES age 29 w sheriff of Orange Co POB POR Orange & **HENDERSON,** Henrietta J. d/o William HENDERSON and Elizabeth J. HANELSON age 19 s POB Randolph Co, Mo POR Orange; POM Ellerslie, Orange 13 Aug 1863 (OMR) 27 Jul 1863 (OML)

**ROACH,** James s/o Robert ROACH and Mildred JONES age 32 w sheriff of Orange POB POR Orange & **WILLIS,** Jane G. d/o James WILLIS and Elizabeth GORDON age 26 s POB POR Orange; POM Orange 19 Feb 1867 (OMR) 15 Feb 1867 (OML)

**ROACH,** James & **LINDSAY,** Betsy surety Caleb LINDSAY 22 Dec 1788 (OB)

**ROACH,** Robert & **JONES,** Milly surety John ROACH 2 May 1828 (OB)

**ROACH,** William & **LEATHERS,** Sarah surety Alexander LEATHERS 24 Dec 1821 (OB)

**ROACH,** William & **ROW,** Tincey d/o Thomas ROW surety Elhanon ROW 6 Feb 1821 (OB)

**ROADS,** Samuel P. age 25 s farmer POB POR Albemarle s/o Horace ROADS and Jane SHIEER & **CLARK,** Gillie M. age 18 s POB POR

Orange d/o William CLARK and Frances ESTES POM Orange 23 Dec 1879 (OMR)

**ROBBINS**, Thomas & **FOSTER,** Mary 24 Dec 1775 both of St. Thomas Parish by banns (Deed Book 17)

**ROBBINS**, Wilber Fiske s/o John S. ROBINS and Drucilla D. CONNER age 32 s minister POB Accomac Co POR Culpeper & **HUME**, Bettie Thompson d/o Benjamin HUME and Mary LOWER age 33 s POB POR Orange; POM Orange 5 Mar 1867 (OMR) 26 Feb 1867 (OML)

**ROBERSON**, William S. & **MALLORY,** Elizabeth surety Robert PAYNE 6 Jul 1815 (OB)

**ROBERTS**, Andrew S. s/o J.P.ROBERTS and Mary l. SEAL age 23 s tanner POB Madison Co POR Orange & **WATKINS**, Mollie B. d/o R.S.WATKINS and Elizabeth M. DANIEL age 21 s POB POR Orange; POM Orange 1 Nov 1866 (OMR) (OML)

**ROBERTS**, Curtis & **CHEWNING,** Sally d/o Robert CHEWNING surety Amos ROBERTS 14 Mar 1814 (OB)

**ROBERTS**, George & **TIPPETT,** Luvina d/o Samuel TIPPETT surety James POWELL 6 Dec 1792 (OB) by George EVE 27 Dec 1792 (OM)

**ROBERTS**, Hugh & **SILK,** Elizabeth by Hamilton GOSS 2 Jan 1799 (OM)

**ROBERTS**, James & **WHITEHEAD,** Catherine surety Thomas SORRILLE by George BINGHAM 23 Dec 1822 (OB) (OM)

**ROBERTS**, John & **KNIGHT,** Agnes d/o Mathew KNIGHT surety Samuel HAM 8 Jan 1796 (OB)

**ROBERTS**, John & **WHITE,** Nancy surety John WHITE by George EVE 30 Jan 1794 (OM)

**ROBERTS**, John & **LAMB,** Lucy d/o Matthew LAMB surety Henry SNOW 5 Jan 1833 (OB)

**ROBERTS**, Robert W. s/o J.P. ROBERTS and Mary L.SEAL age 19 s farmer POB Culpeper Co POR Orange & **ESTES**, Mildred A. d/o James and Elizabeth ESTES age 19 s POB POR Orange; POM Orange 25 Dec 1866 (OMR) 24 Dec 1866 (OML)

**ROBERTS**, Thomas & **HENRY,** Frances d/o William HENRY 27 Dec 1790 (Orange County Permission)

**ROBERTS**, William H. age 22 s farmer POB POR Orange s/o Waller ROBERTS and Fanny OLIVER & **YOWELL,** Bettie E. age 19 s POB Greene POR Orange d/o Albert Z. YOWELL and Jane QUINN 15 Feb 1877 POM Orange (OMR)

**ROBERTS**, William & **ROBINSON,** Martha P. d/o Elijah ROBINSON surety Richard James ROBINSON 10 Sep 1834 (OB)

**ROBERTSON**, John & **PORTER,** Frances surety Joseph THOMAS Jr. 5 Mar 1787 (OB)

**ROBERTSON**, Joseph H. age 35 s bridge builder POB POR Albemarle s/o C.C. ROBERTSON and Sarah GOODMAN & **THOMASSON**, Eudora E. age 29 s POB Louisa POR Orange d/o Garland THOMASSON and Jane Q. TISDALE 9 Jan 1876 POM Orange by J. W. MCCOWN (OMR)

**ROBERTSON**, Richard & **COLLINS**, Elizabeth surety Edward COLLINS 23 Sep 1799 (OB)

**ROBERTSON**, Robert Randolph age 32 s POB Caroline Co POR Austin, TX s/o Mackenzie B. ROBERTSON and Mary HOLT merchant & **TAYLOR**, Bettie T. age 22 POB POR Orange d/o Robert TAYLOR and Barbara TILGHMAN 18 Dec 1873 POM Orange by John S. HANSBROUGH (OMR)

**ROBERTSON**, Willis & **DOLIN**, Elizabeth surety John DOLIN 14 Dec 1821 (OB)

**ROBINSON**, Achilles D. & **BELL**, Sally B. d/o Roger BELL who is also surety 1819 (OB)

**ROBINSON**, Francis & **TERRELL**, Mary d/o William TERRELL surety John MORTON 28 Feb 1788 (OB)

**ROBINSON**, Garland & **ARCHER**, Emily d/o James ARCHER who is also surety by E.G. SHIP 14 Feb 1834 (OB) (OM)

**ROBINSON**, Hugh & **JOHNSON**, Susan surety by Joseph ATKINS who is also her guardian 27 Dec 1822 (OB)

**ROBINSON**, James & **EMBRY**, Judy 16 Jan 1761 (Orange Fee Book)

**ROBINSON**, James E. POC age 22 s farm labourer POB POR Orange s/o George ROBINSON and Mary Jane BALTIMORE & **BREWER**, Violet L. POC age 21 s POB POR Orange d/o Ellis BREWER and Harriet NEWMAN POM Orange 7 Jul 1877 (OMR)

**ROBINSON**, James POC age 19 s labourer POB POR Orange s/o Edmund ROBINSON and Georgianna TAYLOR & **JOHNSON**, Mary POC age 23 s POB POR Orange d/o Philip JOHNSON and Milly GREEN POM Orange 12 Dec 1877 (OMR)

**ROBINSON**, James R. & **PAYNE**, Susan Ann d/o Charles G. PAYNE; 24 Nov 1851 (OML)

**ROBINSON**, John & **SMITH**, Lucy 24 Nov 1757 (Orange Fee Book)

**ROBINSON**, John & **MELONE**, Susan permission from John and Rebeckah MELONE who is also surety 20 Aug 1817 (OB)

**ROBINSON**, John J. & **PEYTON**, Georgianna; POM Orange 12 Oct 1852 (OMR) 11 Oct 1852 (OML)

**ROBINSON**, Joseph & **SNELL**, Philadelphia surety Robert SNELL 28 Dec 1801 (OB)

**ROBINSON**, Lewis D. & **COLLINS**, Sarah d/o Lewis D. COLLINS who is also surety 24 Nov 1845 (OB)

ROBINSON, Michael & **WILLIAMS**, Polly surety William ARNETT 20 Dec 1799 (OB)

ROBINSON, Moses & **JONES**, Fanny d/o Richard JONES surety John CAMPBELL 24 Feb 1806 (OB) 27 Feb 1806 by James GARNETT (OM)

ROBINSON, Richard H. & **HARRISON**, Mary H. d/o Burr HARRISON who is also surety 7 Jun 1832 (OB)

ROBINSON, Richard J. & **OWEN**, Ellen Elizabeth d/o Frances I. OWEN surety Benjamin W. ROBINSON 23 Oct 1839 (OB)

ROBINSON, Thomas & **HOLMES**, Mary Susan Samuel H. STOUT is her guardian and security 11 May 1835 (OB)

ROBINSON, Thomas & **LANCASTER**, Sarah surety Edmund LANCASTER 29 Dec 1817 (OB) by J.C. GORDON 31 Dec 1817 (OM)

ROBINSON, Thomas & **ROACH**, Nancy eldest d/o James ROACH surety John ROACH 11 Feb 1813 (OB) by Jeremiah CHANDLER 14 Feb 1813 (OM)

ROBINSON, Thomas & **ROBINSON**, Lucy both of St. Thomas Parish 25 Apr 1777 (Deed Book 17)

ROBINSON, Thomas & **SAUNDERS**, Elizabeth T. d/o John SAUNDERS surety Hansford T. SAUNDERS 26 Nov 1827 (OB)

ROBINSON, Thomas A. & **SHEPHERD**, Maria L. d/o James SHEPHERD 21 Feb 1831 (OB)

ROBINSON, William & **COLLINS**, Margaret d/o Richard COLLINS surety James HERNDON 26 Nov 1794 (OB)

ROBINSON, William & **ADAMS**, Frankey permission from James ADAMS who is also surety 24 Mar 1788 (OB)

ROBINSON, William & **EMBRY**, Joanna 23 Jan 1754 (Orange Fee Book)

ROBINSON, William & **SMITH**, Agnes 27 Jan 1758 (Orange Fee Book)

ROBUKS, Hugh & **SISK**, Elizabeth; 26 Dec 1798 (OM)

ROGERS, Benjamin & **LANE**, Mary by George BINGHAM 13 Sep 1808 (OB)

ROGERS, Charles P. POR Albemarle & **COLE**, Catharine A.; POM Orange 24 May 1853 (OMR) 23 May 1853 (OML)

ROGERS, Chesley & **JARRELL**, Tabitha d/o John and Ann JARRELL w surety Jefferson JARRELL 15 Oct 1830 (OB)

ROGERS, Isaac N. & **WHITE**, Mary A.; 20 Dec 1854 (OML)

ROGERS, James & **JACKSON**, Elizabeth d/o Drury JACKSON surety 15 Apr 1811 (OB)

ROGERS, James & **WOOD**, Margaret by George BINGHAM 1 Jun 1819 (OM)

**ROGERS,** Jermenius & **FARGUSON,** Elizabeth by George BINGHAM 24 Dec 1809 (OM)

**ROGERS,** John & **DARNELL,** Lucy d/o Mary Ann DARNELL; 28 Feb 1803 surety James HUNT (OB) 1 Mar 1803 (Misc Min Ret)

**ROGERS,** John & **KNIGHT,** Elizabeth; 27 Dec 1798 by George BINGHAM (OM)

**ROGERS,** John POR Fredericksville Parish [Louisa County] & **ESTIS,** Barbara POR St. Thomas Parish 31 Oct 1773 (Deed Book 17) [] taken from compiler's notes

**ROGERS,** John & **CHISSOM,** Mildred d/o John CHISSOM 30 Dec 1801 (Orange County permission) [see entry for John PAYNE]

**ROGERS,** Jonathan & **TWYMAN,** Frances by George BINGHAM 13 Nov 1814 (OM)

**ROGERS,** Joseph & **NEWMAN,** Malinda by Robert JONES 28 Jun 1808 (OM)

**ROGERS,** Kelles & **HAM,** Mary d/o Samuel and Eliza HAMM surety Joseph HAM 12 Jan 1807 (OB) by George BINGHAM 15 Jan 1807 (OM)

**ROGERS,** Reuben age 45 S POB POR Orange s/o Jos. ROGERS and Malinda NEWMAN wheelwright & **TERRILL,** Finella H. age 43 POB POR Orange d/o Uriel TERRILL and Jane LOVELL 23 Nov 1870 by R.C. CAVE (OM)

**ROGERS,** Robert H. s/o Joseph ROGERS and Malinda NEWMAN age 32 s POB POR Orange & **TERRILL,** Emma Lovell d/o Oliver TERRIL and Susan PROCTOR age 21 s POB POR Orange; POM Orange 21 May 1867 (OMR) 20 May 1867 (OML)

**ROGERS,** Samuel & **DAVIS,** Sally by George BINGHAM 10 Dec 1796 (OM)

**ROGERS,** Thomas & **CHANCELLOR,** Penelope ward of Thomas ROGERS surety John CHANCELLOR by Jeremiah CHANCELLOR 22 Oct 1810 (OB) (OM)

**ROGERS,** William s/o John ROGERS & **COLYER,** Polly d/o Martin COLYER surety Sinclair WILLIAMS 4 Apr 1821 (OB) by George BINGHAM 6 Apr 1821 (OM)

**ROHR,** John F. age 55 w wheelwright POB Rockingham POR Orange s/o John ROHR and Catharine MILLER & **WEBB,** Susan J. age 40 w POB Louisa POR Orange POM Orange C.H. 23 Nov 1876 (OMR)

**ROHR,** Robert M. age 24 s POB Greene Co., POR Orange s/o John F. ROHR and Isabella KEARNEY blacksmith & **POINDEXTER,** Martha A. age 23 s POB Greene Co POR Orange d/o Joseph POINDEXTER and Clarissa MITCHELL 26 Dec 1871 POM Orange by J.W. MCCOWN (OMR)

**ROLL,** Roberson & **CLARK,** Mary Ann 28 Nov 1811 by James GARNETT (OM)

**ROLLINS,** Richard & **HERNDON,** Lucy John HERNDON is her guardian and her surety 17 Apr 1807 (OB) by Robert JONES 26 Apr 1807 (OM)

**ROLLS,** John POC age 29 s labourer POB POR Orange s/o Frank ROLLS and Maria HOLMES & **VAUGHN,** Ada age 19 s POB Augusta POR Orange d/o William VAUGHN and Venia COLES POM Orange 26 Dec 1877 (OMR)

**ROOT,** Herbert A. age 25 s farmer POB Munson, Massachusetts POR Orange s/o George ROOT and Delphia BACON & **DOWNER,** Phoebe G. age 36 s POB POR Orange d/o Robert G. DOWNER and Frances A. DANIEL POM Orange 14 Mar 1878 by Charles QUARLES (OMR)

**ROSE,** Allen POC age 29 s railroad hand POB POR Orange s/o Henry ROSE and Lucy GRIFFIN & **EAST,** Charlotte POC age 18 s POB Nelson POR Orange d/o Robert EAST and Margaret _____ POM Orange 25 Sep 1879 (OMR)

**ROSE,** James POC age 22 s rail road hand POB POR Orange s/o Henry ROSE and Lucy ___ & **WHITE,** Josephine POC age 19 s POB POR Orange d/o Ben WHITE and Julia _____ POM Orange 17 Aug 1876 by W. J. BARNETT (OMR)

**ROSE,** Robert H. & **MADISON,** Frances F. [b. 4 Oct 1774 youngest d/o James MADISON and Eleanor CONWAY] surety Reynolds CHAPMAN 26 Jan 1801 (OB)

**ROSE,** Robert N. & **OFFIELD,** Sarah surety John HAUS 10 Nov 1834 (OB)

**ROSSON,** Archelaus & **WARREN,** Haney Ritter d/o Elizabeth WARREN surety William MOORE 23 Jan 1797 (OB)

**ROTHROCK,** George & **POLLOCK,** Elizabeth d/o William POLLOCK surety William COOPER 30 Oct 1793 (OB)

**ROTHWELL,** Benjamin C. permission from John ROTHWELL & **BROCKMAN,** Harriet C. d/o Sims BROCKMAN surety F.D. BROCKMAN 2 Apr 1835 (OB)

**ROTHWELL,** John s/o Captain John ROTHWELL & **WHITE,** Ann surety Dabney O. SHACKELFORD 29 Nov 1841 (OB)

**ROUTT,** Ancel P. & **SWAN,** Ellen A. d/o Alexander SWAN Jr. who is also surety 9 Jan 1847 (OB)

**ROW,** Elhanon s/o Thomas ROW [POC see entry for Richard REYNOLDS] & **SANDERS,** Mary D. d/o John SANDERS who is also surety 10 Nov 1818 (OB) by J.C. GORDON 12 Nov 1818 (OM)

**ROW,** Thomas & **SHADRACH,** S. surety Robert SANDERS 3 Feb 1829 (OB)

**ROWE**, James W. s/o Keeling ROWE and Fannie BATES age 28 s farmer POB POR Caroline Co & **SANFORD**, Jennie B. d/o Lawrence SANFORD and Lucy WALKER age 21 s POB POR Orange; POM Orange 12 Dec 1867 OMR 26 Nov 1867 OML

**ROWE**, John S. age about 22 deputy sheriff of Orange Co POR Orange & **WALKER**, Eliza d/o Benjamin WALKER age about 22; POM Orange 20 Dec 1853 (OMR) 17 Dec 1853 (OML)

**ROWLAND**, William H. s/o Isaac ROWLAND and Winney BECKSLEY age 26 s farmer POB Soundes Co.,Ga POR Clynch(?)Co, Ga & **KNIGHT**, Ann E. d/o Lewis KNIGHT age 25 s POB Madison Co POR Orange; POM Orange 23 Mar 1864 (OMR) 22 Mar 1864 (OML)

**RUCKER**, Albert & **PARROTT**, Sarah; Robert MITCHELL is her guardian and surety 19 Apr 1831 (OB)

**RUCKER**, Allen & **PRITCHETT**, Harriett surety William WHITE 7 Nov 1836 (OB)

**RUCKER**, Belfield s/o Joel RUCKER & **WHITE**, Nancy d/o Richard and Nancy WHITE surety William RUCKER 23 May 1809 (OB) by Ambrose BROCKMAN of Albemarle Co. 28 May 1809 (OM)

**RUCKER**, Elliot & **SMITH**, Nancy surety Samuel SMITH 6 May 1789 (OB)

**RUCKER**, Ellzy & **BURTON**, Mary P. d/o Joseph BURTON surety James WHITE 16 Jan 1809 (OB) 19 Jan 1809 by Jacob WATTS (OM)

**RUCKER**, Ephriam & **RANDALL**, Elizabeth both of St. Thomas Parish 25 Jun 1775 by banns (Deed Book 17)

**RUCKER**, Joel & **OLIVER**, Nancy d/o Tabitha OLIVER surety Joseph BURTON 15 Dec 1786 (OB) by George EVE 20 Dec 1786 (OM)

**RUCKER**, John & **TINSLEY**, Betty permission from John TINSLEY surety James RUCKER both of St. Thomas Parish 27 Apr 1780 (OB)

**RUCKER**, Minor & **HEAD**, Harriett surety John HEAD 25 Nov 1822 (OB)

**RUCKER**, Peter & **CRAWFORD**, Jemima both of St. Thomas Parish 3 Jan 1773 (Deed Book 17)

**RUCKER**, Thornton & **SNYDOR**, Patsy ward of Henry HILL surety Zachariah TAYLOR 31 Aug 1819 (OB)

**RUCKER**, William & **THORNTON**, Catey Taliaferro d/o George THORNTON surety George M. HEAD 22 Dec 1794 (OB) by George EVE 25 Dec 1794 (OM)

**RUCKER**, Wisdom & **BURRUS**, Rosanna d/o Mary BURRUS surety Vincent VASS 29 Sep 1787 (OB)

**RUMBAUGH**, Jacob & **SOUTHERLAND**, Nancy surety William P. SOUTHERLAND 25 Nov 1823 (OB)

**RUMSEY**, Elijah & **HUGHES**, Sally d/o Francis HUGHES surety Marmaduke BRANHAM 30 Jul 1805 (OB)

**RUMSEY,** James & **DEERING,** Mary permission from Robert DEERING 7 Apr 1790 surety William LEATHERS (OB)

**RUMSEY,** Thomas & **COPE,** Patty both of St. Thomas Parish by banns 15 Mar 1777 (Deed Book 17)

**RUMSEY,** Walker & **CAMIKE,** Polly b. 15 May 1786 surety Spencer KELLY 28 Jul 1807 (OB)

**RUMSEY,** William & **BARRETT,** Peggy surety William LEATHERS 12 May 1790 (OB) by John LELAND 20 May 1790 (OM)

**RUNKEL,** George & **POWELL,** Frances d/o William L. POWELL who is surety 5 Feb 1828 (OB)

**RUNKLE,** Emanuel & **GOODALL,** Mary d/o John GOODALL surety St. Clair RUNKLE 26 Mar 1829 (OB)

**RUNKLE,** George M. age 41 w POB Greene Co POR Orange s/o George RUNKLE and Frances POWELL agricultural machinist & **MASSEY,** Lydia F. age 35 w POB Louisa POR Orange d/o _____ OGG and Jenetta MELTON 16 Dec 1873 POM Orange by J.O. MOSS (OMR)

**RUNKLE,** William H. & **POWELL,** Elizabeth d/o William Lewis POWELL who is also surety 1 Feb 1827 (OB)

**RUNNOLDS,** William & **JONES,** Hannah 4 Aug 1811 by James GARNETT (OMR)

**RUSSELL,** Nehemiah & **COLLINS,** Sally both of St. Thomas Parish 11 Aug 1775 by banns (Deed Book 17)

**RUSSELL,** William & **MERRY,** Mary surety Thomas HERNDON 21 Mar 1789 (OB)

**RUSSELL,** William POC age 25 w POB Hanover POR Orange s/o John WILLIAMS and Fanny ANDERSON farm laborer & **ROBINSON,** Lucinda POC age 30 s POB Louisa POR Orange d/o Henry THOMPSON 4 Sep 1880 POB Gordonsville, Orange by Dabney PARKER (OMR)

**RUSSELL,** William POC age 33 s farm labourer POB Hanover POR Orange s/o Jacob STUBBS and Nancy ANDERSON & **BATES,** Amy POC age 22 s POB POR Orange d/o Gloster BATES and Martha w 26 May 1877 (OMR)23 Feb 1872 POM Orange (OML)

**SACRA,** Charles R. age 24 s POB Spotsylvania POR Orange s/o Charles R. SACRA farmer & **RICHARDS,** Amanda J. age 24 s POB POR Orange 9 Jan 1873 POM Orange by E.R. PERRY (OMR)

**SACRE,** Beverley s/o Thomas J. SACRE & Lucinda ROBINSON age 21 s farmer POB Spotsylvania POR Orange & **CHEWNING,** Emma R. d/o C.W. CHEWNING and Ellen HOPKINS age 21 s POB Spotsylvania POR Orange; POM Orange 20 Oct 1867 (OMR) 17 Oct 1867 (OML)

**SALE,** John W. & **COLEMAN,** Catharine surety Wilson COLEMAN 13 Jun 1814 (OB)

**SALE,** Robert C. & **DAVIS,** Mary M. her brother Thomas DAVIS is her guardian surety James M. DAVIS 18 Jan 1842 (OB)

**SALE,** William B. age 27 s farmer s/o Robert C. SALE and Mary M. DAVIS & **SPOTSWOOD,** Mary S. age 22 s POB POR Orange d/o Phil A. SPOTSWOOD and Columbia YERBY POM Orange 1 Feb 1876 by W. E. PAYNE (OMR)

**SAMAR,** John H. s/o John SAMAR and Mary L. HILL age 35 s planter POB Bibb Co,GA POR Macon, GA & **CARTER,** Jane A. d/o Charles C.TALIAFERRO and Louisa G. ARMISTEAD age 25 w POB Caroline Co POR Orange; POM Orange 11 Jan 1864 (OMR) 6 Jan 1864 (OML)

**SAMPSON,** Elijah & **ROGERS,** Amy d/o John ROGERS surety Alexander ROGERS 6 Jun 1804 (OB)

**SAMPSON,** George & **JOLLETT,** Drada surety Fielding JOLLETT 17 Dec 1818 (OB) by George BINGHAM 6 Jan 1819 (OM)

**SAMPSON,** James & **JAMES,** Anney by George BINGHAM 27 Jun 1800 (OM)

**SAMPSON,** John & **JOLLETT,** Clarissa permission from James JOLLETT surety Peter MARSH 26 Feb 1813 (OB) by George BINGHAM 2 Mar 1813 (OM)

**SAMPSON,** Thomas & **POWELL,** Winny surety Thomas WALKER 23 Jul 1791 (OB) by George EVE 28 Jul 1791 (OM)

**SAMPSON,** William Jr. & **SAMPSON,** Sally d/o William SAMPSON Sr. surety Cornelius BEAZLEY 25 Sep 1810 (OB)

**SAMPSON,** William & **JOLLETT,** Sally by George BINGHAM 8 Jan 1809 (OM)

**SAMS,** John & **BLEDSOE,** Mary d/o Aaron BLEDSOE surety George TERRILL 22 Sep 1785 (OB)

**SAMUEL,** Meshach & **TAYLOR,** Lucretia d/o Zachariah TAYLOR surety Pascal TAYLOR 24 Nov 1825 (OB)

**SAMUEL,** Trenton E. & **COLEMAN,** Elizabeth F. d/o Eliz. L. TERRILL surety Andrew C. SAMUEL 25 May 1840 (OB) by William Y. HETER (OM)

**SANDERS,** Benjamin T. age 44 w POB POR Orange s/o Benj. SANDERS and Nancy JONES farmer & **DEMPSEY,** Isabella age 20 s POB POR Orange d/o John L. DEMPSEY and Susan NASH 30 Aug 1868 POM Orange by Sanders MASON (OMR)

**SANDERS,** Benjamin s/o Nathaniel SANDERS & **JONES,** Nancy d/o Francis JONES surety John GAINES 18 Dec 1804 (OB)

**SANDERS,** Dudley T. & **PERRY,** Nancy surety Benjamin PERRY 27 Oct 1828 (OB)

**SANDERS,** Dudley T. s/o Benjamin SANDERS and Nancy JONES age 59 w miller POB POR Orange & **BROOKING,** Mary Ann d/o Charles R.

BROOKING & Amanda CLARK age 25 s POB POR Orange; POM Orange 14 Feb 1865 (OMR) 30 Jan 1865 (OML)

SANDERS, James & **MASON**, Elizabeth J.; POM Orange 23 Oct 1851 (OMR) (OML)

SANDERS, Nathaniel & **SANDERS**, Ann surety Hansford T. SANDERS 9 Jan 1834 (OB)

SANDERS, William Preston age 23 s POB POR Orange s/o Francis J. SANDERS and Lucy I. BROCKMAN farmer & **COSBY**, Letitia W. age 22 s POB POR Orange d/o William S. COSBY and Livinia WHARTON 2 Dec 1869 POM Orange by Melzi S. CHANCELLOR (OMR)

SANDRIDGE, Austin & **HALL**, Ann 11 Jan 1816 by George BINGHAM (OM)

SANER, Charles H. age 34 s POB POR Louisa Co. s/o Josiah SANER and Rebecca PORTER r.r. hand & **PARISH**, Amanda A. age 26 s POB Louisa Co POR Orange 27 Feb 1868 POM Orange by Charles QUARLES (OMR)

SANFORD, Augustus C. & **WRIGHT**, Ann d/o Jefferson WRIGHT who is also surety 31 Aug 1844 (OB)

SANFORD, Hamlet & **BIGGERS**, Phebe d/o Macon BIGGERS surety Thornton TUCKER 17 Jan 1810 (OB)

SANFORD, Hamlet & **CLARK**, Nancy d/o William CLARK who is also surety 14 Sep 1815 (OB) by George MORRIS 17 Sep 1815 (OM)

SANFORD, Henry A. POC 22 s farmer POB POR Westmorland s/o William H. SANFORD and Mary SANDS & **WYATT**, Edmonia age 21 s James M. WYATT and Mary A. RICHARDS POM Orange 5 Oct 1876 by H. E. HATCHER (OMR)

SANFORD, John & **RANSDELL**, Betsy d/o John RANSDELL Sr. surety Ambrose CLARK 30 Jun 1788 (OB)

SANFORD, Lawrence & **FORD**, Catharine d/o William FORD surety James FORD 27 Jan 1817 (OB) by J.C. GORDON 30 Jan 1817 (OM)

SANFORD, Lawrence & **WALKER**, Lucy H. d/o Benjamin WALKER surety William H. WALKER 16 May 1844 (OB)

SANFORD, Muse & **SCOTT**, Betsey [d/o George SCOOT of Orange] surety John LUCAS 3 Jan 1804 (OB) 4 Jan 1804 by Jacob WATTS (Misc Min Ret) [] taken from notes of Catherine Knorr

SANFORD, Reuben & **WEBB**, Frances d/o William Crittendon WEBB and Vivian WEBB surety John SNELL 2 Mar 1789 (OB) 5 Mar 1789 by George EVE (OM)

SANFORD, Reuben & **WALLACE**, Nancy d/o James WALLACE Sr. surety Thomas ARNOLD 24 Dec 1800 (OB)

**SANFORD,** Robert & **GRYMES,** Hannah permission from Ludwell GRYMES surety James TAYLOR 28 Apr 1792 (OB)

**SANFORD,** Stewart & **ARNOLD,** Anna d/o Benjamin and Sally ARNOLD surety Willis ARNOLD 27 Oct 1803 (OB)

**SANFORD,** Walker age 28 s POB POR Orange s/o Lawrence SANFORD and Lucy H. WALKER farmer & **JOHNSON,** Lelia age 23 s POB POR Orange d/o Joseph H. JOHNSON and Elmira E. ANDREWS 29 Jan 1880 POM Orange by W.E. CAVE (OMR)

**SAUNDERS,** Francis J. & **BROCKMAN,** Lucy d/o Curtis L. BROCKMAN who is also surety 10 Nov 1845 (OB)

**SAUNDERS,** Hansford T. & **RHOADES,** Mary V. d/o Richard RHOADES surety John RHOADES 17 Dec 1827 (OB)

**SAUNDERS,** James W. & **BLAIR,** Barbara G. d/o Helen BLAIR surety W.F. GOOCH 23 Jan 1823 (OB)

**SAWYER,** William & **WRIGHT,** Elizabeth both of St. Thomas Parish 21 Feb 1775 by banns (Deed Book 17)

**SCALES,** Peter POR Cabell Co. & **MINOR,** Ann M. d/o Lucy MINOR surety P.S. FRY 21 Jun 1827 (OB)

**SCHLOSSER,** George W. age 30 s physician POB Franklin Co., MD [sic] POR Orange s/o Peter G. SCHLOSSER and Catherine MCCOLLUM & **MCCOLLUM,** Mary Bell age 26 s POB Baltimore, MD POR Orange Ephraim MCCOLLUM and Rebecca HILDERBRAND POM Orange 11 Oct 1876 by F. G. SCOTT (OMR)

**SCHOOLER,** Joseph H. & **QUISENBERRY,** Dolly surety Henry QUISENBERRY 8 Mar 1810 (OB) by Jeremiah CHANDLER 13 Mar 1810 (OM)

**SCOTT,** Andrew (aka Daniel) s/o John SCOTT and Charlotte WILLIAMS age 23 s farm laborer POB POR Orange POC & **JOHNSON,** Ellen d/o Isaac JOHNSON and Mary SMITH age 21 s POB POR Orange POC; POM Orange 26 Dec 1867 (OMR) 23 Dec 1867 (OML)

**SCOTT,** Caleb & **SMITH,** Sarah Ann Elizabeth surety Marshall COOK 30 Sep 1836 (OB)

**SCOTT,** Charles & **COWHERD,** Harriet d/o Francis COWHERD surety John S. COWHERD 21 Oct 1823 (OB)

**SCOTT,** Charles & **LANDRAM,** Mary L. d/o Daniel LANDRAM surety William A. LANDRAM 3 Jul 1837 (OB)

**SCOTT,** Edmund W. age 25 s farmer POB POR Orange s/o Garrett SCOTT and Sarah Ellen NALLE & **GRAVES,** Eudora C. age 27 s POB POR Orange d/o James W. GRAVES and Sarah GRAVES POM Orange 24 Oct 1877 (OMR)

**SCOTT,** George & **LEE,** Ann s 22 Sep 1825 (OB)

**SCOTT,** George & **ABELL,** Nancy surety George SMITH 15 Oct 1807 (OB)

**SCOTT,** George & **WOOD,** Nancy surety William SCOTT 29 Dec 1787 (OB)

**SCOTT,** George s/o Reubin and Peggy SCOTT age 70 w farmer POB POR Orange & **BLEDSOE,** Rosa d/o Godfrey and Mary YAGES (?) age 70 w POB Madison Co POR Orange; POM Orange 14 Dec 1854 (OMR)

**SCOTT,** James M. age 32 s POB POR Orange s/o Garrett SCOTT and Sara E. NOLLE farmer & **GRAVES,** Catharine Single POB POR Orange d/o Charles T. GRAVES and Susan CAMPBELL 10 Feb 1870 POM Orange by I.W.K. HANDY (OMR)

**SCOTT,** John & **COWHERD,** Ann d/o Coleby COWHERD surety William COWHERD 10 Apr 1822 (OB)

**SCOTT,** John & **HILMAN,** Joannah d/o Uriel HILMAN surety Richard S. ABELL 7 Jun 1824 (OB)

**SCOTT,** John S. & **THOMPSON,** Sarah E. surety William AUSTIN 7 Dec 1838 (OB)

**SCOTT,** John Wickliffe s/o John and Ann SCOTT age 28 s farmer POB POR Orange & **HACKLEY,** Sarah F. d/o Robert and Mary Ann HACKLEY age 25 s POB Florida POR Orange; POM Orange 29 Jan 1856 (OMR) 28 Jan 1856 (OML)

**SCOTT,** Larkin & **FAULCONER,** Elizabeth surety William FAULCONER 30 Jul 1817 (OB) by J.C. GORDON 2 Aug 1817 (OM)

**SCOTT,** Minor POC age 26 w farm laborer POB Louisa POR Orange s/o David SCOTT and Rose HART & **TOWNS,** Malinda POC age 19 s POB POR Orange d/o Absalom TOWNS and Bettie POGUE POM Orange 5 Mar 1876 by R. WOODSON (OMR)

**SCOTT,** Reuben & **COPE,** Margaret s both of St. Thomas Parish surety Lewis COOK 7 Feb 1781 (OB)

**SCOTT,** Thomas POC age 24 w POB Richmond City POR Orange laborer s/o Thomas SCOTT and Martha MOODY & **GAINES,** Rosa POC age 21 w POB POR Orange d/o James SMITH POM Orange 20 Feb 1877 (OMR)

**SCOTT,** Thomas & **HENSHAW,** Virginia O. d/o Edmund HENSHAW surety George NEWMAN Jr. 25 Nov 1817 (OB) 26 Nov 1817 by J. GOSS (OM)

**SCOTT,** William & **SHADRACK,** Nelly surety John SHADRICK by Nathaniel SANDERS 10 Feb 1791 (OM) (OB)

**SCOTT,** William C. & **GRAVES,** Pamela A. d/o Charles T. GRAVES surety William C. GRAVES 9 Jan 1850 (OB) by Joseph H. FOX 10 Jan 1850 (OM)

**SCOTT,** William C. Jr. age 24 s farmer POB POR Orange s/o William C. SCOTT and Pamela A. GRAVES & **COWHERD,** Susan E. age 19 s

POB POR Orange E.F. COWHERD and Susan FREEMAN POM
Orange 23 May 1876 by F.G. SCOTT (OMR)

**SCOTT**, William W. age 24 s POB POR Orange s/o Garnett SCOTT and
Sarah Ellen NALLE lawyer & **WILLIS**, Claudia M. age 23 s POB
POR Orange d/o John WILLIS and Lucy T. MADISON 29 Sep 1869
POM Orange by T.M. CARSON (OMR)

**SEAL**, Thomas permission from Philip SEAL & **POWELL**, Elizabeth d/o
Lewis G. POWELL surety James POWELL 10 Aug 1818 (OB)

**SEAL**, Thomas & **TAYLOR**, Nancy surety St. Clair TAYLOR 13 Jan
1827 (OB) by George BINGHAM 16 Jan 1827 (OM)

**SEBREE**, John s/o Richard SEBREE & **JOHNSON**, Sally surety William
TOMLINSON 17 Mar 1791 (OB)

**SEBREE**, William & **KAVENNER**, Hannah; 31 May 1774 both of St.
Thomas Parish by banns (Deed Book 17)

**SEBREE**, William & **STROTHER**, Mary; 27 Jun 1775 both of St.
Thomas Parish by banns (Deed Book 17)

**SEE**, Dallas POC age 27 s POB POR Orange s/o Jacob SEE and Hannah
ARMISTEAD farmer & **BANKS**, Sarah POC age 19 s POB POR
Orange d/o Hannah BANKS 21 Mar 1874 POM Orange (OMR)

**SEE**, John H. s/o Willis SEE and Mary RICHARDS age 58 w farmer POB
Fauquier Co POR Orange & **JONES**, Mary B. d/o A.S. JONES and
Mary J. OVERTON age 21 s POB Petersburg, VA POR Orange; POM
Orange 19 Nov 1863 (OMR) 18 Nov 1863 (OML)

**SEEDS**, George W. age 27 s farmer POB Salem, NJ POR Cumberland, NJ
s/o Benjamin SEEDS and Eunice LANGLEY & **DOUGLASS**, Delia E.
age 21 s POB POR Orange d/o F.E. DOUGLASS and Selma HEAD
POM Orange 23 May 1878 (OMR)

**SEEF** (or LEEF), William F. s/o Henry LEEF or Seef and Julia
GAMBRILL age 26 s engineer on O.& A. railroad POB Baltimore, MD
POR Gordonsville & **GOODWIN**, Margaret C. d/o John GOODWIN
and Mary S. ARMCOL(?) age 18 s POB Prince William Co. POR
Gordonsville; POM Gordonsville 26 Nov 1863 (OMR) 24 Nov 1863
(OML)

**SEEVERS**, Christopher & **PIERCE**, Sarah surety Adam MANSPOILE,
15 Jul 1796 (OB) by Nathaniel SANDERS 18 Jul 1796 (OM)

**SELDEN**, Samuel M. age 23 s POB Lynchburg, VA POR Buckingham
Co. s/o Samuel M. SELDEN and Caroline E. HARE gentleman &
**BLAND**, Emma Randolph age 17 POB Prince Edward Co. POR
Orange d/o John R. BLAND and Emily SAUDON 24 Jun 1873 POM
Orange by J.C. DINWIDDIE (OMR)

**SELF**, Matthew & **BEAZLEY**, Katy surety John SHIFLETT 23 Apr 1827
(OB)

**SELF,** Samuel & **SHIFLETT,** Frances d/o Elizabeth SHIFLETT surety Mace PICKETT 21 Dec 1787 (OB) 26 Dec 1787 by George EVE (OM)

**SEPIN,** Joseph Q. age 26 s farmer POB Mississippi POR Orange s/o George W. SEPON and Mildred C. ROW & **TINSLEY,** Milly S.V. age 16 s POB POR Orange d/o Edward TINSLEY and Molly SANDERS (Molly Sanders is crossed out and the name Lucy A. ROACH is noted as the correct mother of the bride) POM Orange 25 Oct 1877 (OMR)

**SEWERS,** Christopher & **PIERCE,** Sarah; 18 Jul 1796 by Nathaniel SANDERS (OM)

**SHACKELFORD,** Uriel & **HILMAN,** Diadema her guardian is Uriel HILMAN who also acts as surety 23 Feb 1818 (OB) by J.C. GORDON 25 Feb 1818 (OM)

**SHACKELFORD,** Zachariah & **CLEAVE,** Sarah ward of Philip C. CAVE who also is surety 13 Apr 1822 (OB)

**SHACKLEFORD,** Edmund & **HOLLIDAY,** Sally surety James EARLY 23 Jul 1794 (OB)

**SHADRACH,** John & **SANDERS,** Elizabeth surety James TINDER 7 Jan 1789 by John LELAND (OM)(OB)

**SHADRACK,** Thomas & **SANDERS,** Sarah d/o Nathaniel SANDERS surety John WHARTON 21 Jul 1795 (OB)

**SHARMARARD,** Elisha & **POWELL,** Elisa; 11 Jul 1783by George EVE, Baptist (OM)

**SHARP,** David POC age 22 s rail road hand POB POR Orange s/o David SHARP and Martha HOLMS & **GRIFFIN,** Phillipa A. age 20 s POB POR Orange d/o Edmund GRIFFIN POM Gordonsville 28 Nov 1877 (OMR)

**SHAW,** Thomas J. age 43 s engineer POB Prince William Co. POR Orange & **STANARD,** Fanny P. d/o Robert Beverley STANARD and Ellen B. STANARD age 18 s POB POR Orange; POM Orange 29 Nov 1853 (OMR) 28 Nov 1853 (OML)

**SHEARMAN,** John H. & **RUCKER,** Margaret S. permission from William RUCKER surety is Thornton RUCKER 27 Feb 1822 (OB) by George BINGHAM 7 Mar 1822 (OM)

**SHELLER,** John & **COX,** Ann surety Thomas COX 25 May 1788 (OB)

**SHELTON,** Thomas & **BEADLES,** Clary d/o John BEADLES surety is Robert M. BEADLES 2 Feb 1808 (OB)

**SHEPHERD,** Alexander & **BURNLEY,** Mary d/o Zachary BURNLEY surety James BURNLEY 7 May 1793 (OB)

**SHEPHERD,** George & **PORTER,** Ann surety Camp PORTER 18 Nov 1793 (OB)

**SHEPHERD,** James POC age 23 s farm labourer POB POR Orange s/o Abram SHEPHERD and Nancy WILLIAMS & **ROSS,** Judy POC age

215

26 s POB Madison POR Orange d/o Lewis ROSS and Anna WARE
POM Rackoon Ford, [sic] Orange 20 Dec 1878 by Willis ROBINSON
(OMR)

**SHEPHERD**, James V. & **JACKSON**, Jane D. surety Andrew T.
SHEPHERD who is also guardian 6 Mar 1847 (OB) by E.G. SHIP 7
May 1847 (OM)

**SHEPHERD**, James & **TAYLOR**, Lucinda surety P.S. FRY 14 Oct 1824
(OB)

**SHEPHERD**, James ward of William SHEPHERD who is also surety &
**VERDIER**, Susan 8 Nov 1810 (OB)

**SHEPHERD**, John M. & **BENSON**, Judith d/o G. BENSON; 28 May
1808 (OB)

**SHEPHERD**, Robert W. & **CONWAY**, Susan Fitzhugh d/o Francis
CONWAY surety Henry CONWAY 14 Jan 1822 (OB)

**SHER**, Robert & **ADDISON**, Jean; 31 Jul 1796 by Nathaniel SANDERS
(OM)

**SHERICK**, Philip B. & **GARTON**, Martha ward of Jacob RUMBOUGH
who is also surety 7 Oct 1819 (OB)

**SHERMAN**, Jesse & **BREEDING**, Sarah surety Berryman BREEDING
by George BINGHAM 23 Sep 1805 (OB)(OM)

**SHIFFLET**, Bennett & **SHIFFLET**, Polly 2 Jan 1816 by George
BINGHAM (OM)

**SHIFFLET**, Edmund & **WIAN**, Milly 2 Jan 1823 by George BINGHAM
(OM)

**SHIFFLET**, Edward & **HENING**, Joice d/o William HENING 28 Feb
1811 James R. HENING surety (OB)

**SHIFFLET**, Felix & **SHIFFLET**, Phebe by George BINGHAM 27 Jan
1822 (OM)

**SHIFFLET**, James & **HERRIN**, Milly 5 Jul 1815 by George BINGHAM
(OM)

**SHIFFLET**, John & **DAVIS**, Susanna; 27 Oct 1796 by George
BINGHAM (OM)

**SHIFFLET**, John & **SHIFFLET**, Rhoda; 29 Dec 1798 no surety listed
(OB)

**SHIFFLET**, John & **SHIFFLET**, Vina 24 Dec 1816 by George
BINGHAM (OM)

**SHIFFLET**, Overton & **HERRING**, Sally d/o William R. HERRING 19
Jan 1809 (OB)

**SHIFFLET**, Slaton & **DAVIS**, Justian 6 Apr 1827 by George BINGHAM
(OM)

**SHIFFLETT**, Archibald & **MORRIS**, Mary surety Rice DARNELL 4 Jan
1836 (OB)

**SHIFFLETT,** Archibald & **VAUGHN,** Birlinda d/o Joseph VAUGHN surety Pleasant DOWELL 8 Feb 1819 (OB) by J. GOSS 11 Feb 1819 (OM)

**SHIFFLETT,** James & **RAINER,** Frances surety Thomas BROOKMAN 31 Mar 1836 (OB)

**SHIFFLETT,** John & **MARTIN,** Frances by George BINGHAM 2 Dec 1813 (OM)

**SHIFFLETT,** John & **RAINES,** Polly 10 Sep 1812 by George BINGHAM (OM)

**SHIFFLETT,** John & **SHIFFLETT,** Polly surety Mordecai SHIFFLETT 7 Aug 1824 (OB)

**SHIFFLETT,** Merry & **SNOW,** Icy 13 May 1813 by George BINGHAM (OM)

**SHIFFLETT,** Pickett & **POWELL,** Lucretia; 25 Jun 1795 by George EVE (OM)

**SHIFFLETT,** Pleasant & **POWEL,** Mary 11 Jan 1827 by George BINGHAM (OM)

**SHIFFLETT,** Powell & **MCMULLAN,** Catharine d/o John and Theodocie MCMULLAN 1 Aug 1797 (Orange Co. permission)

**SHIFFLETT,** Richard & **MORRIS,** Nancy d/o William MORRIS Jr. surety Simpson MORRIS 14 Nov 1817 (OB) by George BINGHAM 14 Nov 1818 (OM) [this is the date that Rev. BINGHAM put on the marriage return. He may have been in error with the year]

**SHIFFLETT,** Slaten & **MORRIS,** Susanna d/o Ikey MORRIS 21 Dec 1818 (OB)

**SHIFFLETT,** Trice & **SNOW,** Raney d/o John SNOW surety John MALLORY by George BINGHAM 26 Feb 1823 (OB) (OM)

**SHIFLET,** John & **HICKS,** Ann 15 Sep 1798 by George BINGHAM (OM)

**SHIFLETT,** Bluford P. s/o Archer and Malinda SHIFLETT age 24 s tailor POB Louisa Co POR Orange & **FAUDREE,** Jane C. d/o Joseph and Susan Ann FODEREE age 21 s POB POR Orange; POM Orange 4 Oct 1853 (OMR) (OML)

**SHIFLETT,** Stephen & **HICKS,** Rachel; 18 Jan 1795 by George BINGHAM (OM)

**SHIFLETT,** Waller C. (aka SHEFLET) age 22 s carpenter POB Rockingham Co. POR Orange & **DUVALL,** Albzerah (aka Altizerah DUVALL) d/o William L. and Comfort DUVALL age 15 s POB Annarundel Co., MD POR Orange; 14 Jul 1858 (OML)

**SHIP,** James T. & **PRICE,** Mary Jane d/o George W. PRICE surety George N. THRIFT 14 Jun 1837 (OB)

**SHIP**, Robert M. & **BURTON**, Martha d/o May BURTON surety
  Benjamin BURTON 26 Feb 1816 (OB)

**SHIPP**, John M. s/o Edward G. SHIPP and Harriet MAUZEY age 31 s
  farmer POB Green Co POR Madison Co & **MANSFIELD**, Susan M.
  d/o Joseph A. MANSFIELD and Susan M. LINDSAY age 32 s POB
  POR Orange; POM Orange 10 Oct 1865 (OMR) 3 Oct 1865 (OML)

**SHIRLEY**, Beverley POC age 22 s POB Spotsylvania POR Orange s/o
  Barnaby SHIRLEY and Nicey DILLARD laborer & **HAWKINS**,
  Louisa POC age 29 s POB POR Orange d/o Henry HAWKINS and
  Milly MANSFIELD 1 Jan 1880 POM Orange by A.W. GRAVES
  (OMR)

**SHIRLEY**, Dabney POC age 24 s POB Spotsylvania POR Orange s/o
  Barnaby SHIRLEY and Nicey DILLARD laborer & **HAWKINS**, Julia
  POC age 32 s POB POR Orange d/o Henry HAWKINS and Milly
  MANSFIELD 1 Jan 1880 POM Orange by A.W. GRAVES (OMR)

**SHIRLEY**, Scott POC age 21 s POB Spotsylvania POR Orange s/o
  Barnaby SHIRLEY and Nicey _____ laborer & **RAWLINGS**, Liddy
  POC age 17 s POB POR Orange d/o Henry RAWLINGS and Milly
  DADE 27 Dec 1872 POM Orange by Herndon FRAZER (OMR)

**SHISLER**, James M. age 29 s farmer POB Louisiana POR Orange s/o
  Thomas SHISLER and M.C. BECK & **PAYNE**, Burdie V. age 20 s
  POB North Carolina POR Orange d/o William H. PAYNE and E.C.
  GAOR (?) 19 Nov 1879 POM Orange (OMR)

**SHISLER**, Lewis & **CLARK**, Sally d/o Joseph CLARK who is also surety
  27 Mar 1809 (OB)

**SHISLER**, William F. & **WOOD**, Mary Elizabeth surety Edmund WOOD
  20 Feb 1837 (OB)

**SHOLES**, Solomon & **WALKER**, Nancy surety Milton BEASLEY 9 Sep
  1835 (OB)

**SHROPSHIRE**, Edward & **PORTER**, Jane d/o John PORTER who is
  also surety 28 Nov 1825 (OB) 4 Dec 1825 by John HALES (OM)

**SHROPSHIRE**, John & **PORTER**, Mary 4 Dec 1757 both of St. Thomas
  Parish (Orange Fee Book)

**SHROPSHIRE**, John & **PORTER**, Mary 21 Dec 1757 (Orange Fee
  Book)

**SHROPSHIRE**, John P. & **REESE**, Catharine 26 Oct 1846 ward of John
  PORTER who is also surety; Edward SHROPSHIRE surety (OB)

**SILVEY**, Stephen & **DEAN**, Frankey; 14 Oct 1785 (OB)

**SILVEY**, Stephen & **DEAR**, Frankey 14 Oct 1785 (OM)

**SILVEY**, William & **ADKISSON**, Mary d/o John ADKISSON surety
  Barnett ADKISSON 13 Oct 1801 (OB) by Hamilton GOSS 15 Oct
  1801 (OM)

**SIM,** Reuben & **GRAVES,** Frances 11 Nov 1812 by George BINGHAM (OM)

**SIMCO,** Brooks & **BOSWELL,** Polly d/o Charles BOSWELL who is also surety 22 Nov 1813 (OB)

**SIMMANDS,** Elijah & **SANDAGE,** Lucy by George BINGHAM 13 Oct 1796 (OM)

**SIMMANDS,** Ephriam & **HANES,** Sarah by George BINGHAM 25 Feb 1797 (OM)

**SIMMONDS,** John & **TATHAM,** Jane surety John CAMPBELL 12 Feb 1825 (OB)

**SIMMONS,** George & **DARNELL,** Mary surety Rice DARNELL 22 Dec 1817 (OB)

**SIMMS,** James & **EARLY,** Lucy T. d/o James EARLY Sr. who is also surety 21 Dec 1818 (OB) by George BINGHAM 21 Jan 1819 (OM)

**SIMPSON,** Aaron & **MULLICAN,** Mary surety John RICHARDS by Jeremiah CHANDLER 14 Mar 1810 (OB)

**SIMPSON,** Daniel & **JONES,** Elizabeth surety James JONES 3 May 1800 (OB)

**SIMPSON,** George & **GOODRIDGE,** Mary surety William DAVIS 9 Jan 1818 (OB)

**SIMPSON,** Horace POC age 40 w labourer POB POR Orange s/o Dennis SIMPSON and Hannah MALLORY & **JOHNSON,** Mary POC age 26 s POB POR Orange POM Orange 20 Feb 1879 (OMR)

**SIMPSON,** Hugh M. s/o Hugh M. SIMPSON and Lucy A. SCHOOLER age 18 s farmer POB POR Orange & **HERNDON,** Eliza J. d/o Edward HERNDON and Susan LANCASTER age 25 s POB POR Orange; POM Orange 25 Jan 1866 (OMR) 18 Jan 1866 (OML)

**SIMPSON,** William & **THOMPSON,** Ann d/o George THOMPSON surety John JOHNSON 8 Dec 1798 (OB)

**SIMS,** Benjamin & **WALKER,** Elizabeth surety William S. WALKER 8 Jan 1827 (OB)

**SIMS,** Brooks & **BOSWELL,** Polly d/o Charles BOSWELL; 22 Nov 1813 (OM)

**SIMS,** Fortunatus age 39 w farmer POB POR Greene s/o John SIMS and Nancy WALKER & **WHITE,** Susan F. age 45 s POB Madison POR Orange d/o _____ WHITE POM Orange 22 Jan 1878 (OMR)

**SIMS,** Hiram A. s/o William T. SIMS & Mary F. PRITCHETT age 24 s physician POB POR Green Co. & **YAGER,** Pamelia W. d/o William YAGER & E.C. WHITLAW age 22 s POB POR Orange; POM Rockingham Co 14 Feb 1867 Rockingham Co. 11 Feb 1867 (OML)

**SIMS,** Isaac & **CATTERTON,** Nancy 5 Jan 1809 by George BINGHAM (OM)

**SIMS**, James P. & **BEAZLEY**, Ann d/o John T. BEAZLEY w POR Madison Co. surety James TAYLOR 23 Sep 1822 (OB)

**SIMS**, James R. & **GOODALL**, Julia Ann d/o Isaac GOODALL surety Benjamin W. BEADLES 7 Aug 1830 (OB)

**SIMS**, James & **MILLER**, Jane surety William MILLER 31 Oct 1829 (OB)

**SIMS**, Jeremiah W. s/o William SIMS who is also surety & **WINSLOW**, Patsy ward of Henry B. WINSLOW who is also surety by E.G. SHIP 28 Aug 1837 (OB) (OM)

**SIMS**, Jeremiah & **TAYLOR**, Margaret 15 Jan 1789 by George EVE (OM)

**SIMS**, John s/o William SIMS & **BEAZLEY**, Betty w 10 Nov 1801 (OB) by George BINGHAM 12 Nov 1801 (OM)

**SIMS**, John & **WALKER**, Nancy surety William H. SIMS 20 Dec 1824 (OB)

**SIMS**, Nathaniel & **JOHNSON**, Susannah; 18 Aug 1796 by George BINGHAM (OM)

**SIMS**, Reuben & **GRAVES**, Frances; 11 Nov 1812 (OM)

**SIMS**, Richard & **WOOD**, Mary surety Henry HERNDON 2 Feb 1819 (OB) by J. GOSS 4 Feb 1819 (OM)

**SIMS**, William Jr. & **SORRILLE**, Virginia d/o Thomas SORRILLE who is also surety by E.G. SHIP 14 Oct 1823 (OB) (OM)

**SIMS**, William Jr. s/o William SIMS Sr. & **WATTS**, Nancy step-d/o John Douglass WATTS surety John PENDLETON 22 Dec 1787 (OB)

**SIMS**, William M. & **PORTER**, Catharine d/o John PORTER who is also surety 28 Jan 1828 (OB)

**SIMS**, William & **JONES**, Susan surety John DOUGLASS 28 Oct 1832 (OB)

**SIMS**, William & **MORGAN**, Eliza by George BINGHAM 15 May 1818 (OM)

**SIMS**, William & **WALKER**, Fannie d/o Elizabeth WALKER surety Elijah PAGE 13 Feb 1796 (OB) by George EVE 24 Feb 1796 (OM)

**SIMSON**, John & **DAWSON**, Polly Stevenson granddaughter of Thomas WELTCH surety John DAWSON 15 Feb 1790 (OB) 18 Feb 1790 by John LELAND (OM)

**SISSON**, ____ & **BRAHAM**, Millie; between 1771 & 1774 (Orange Memo Book)

**SISSON**, C. & **BRANHAM**, Milly; 20 Jul 1771 (OB)

**SISSON**, Abner & **CHAMBERS**, Rachel d/o Thomas CHAMBERS surety George MARTIN 23 Dec 1811 (OB)

**SISSON**, Benjamin & **ROACH**, Susan d/o John ROACH surety Charles W. HUME 9 Oct 1846 (OB)

**SISSON**, Elhanon B. s/o William SISSON and Sarah J. ROW age 21 s farmer POB POR Culpeper Co. & **ELIASON**, Nannie H. d/o William C. ELIASON and Susan V. PANNILL age 22 s POB POR Orange; POM Orange 31 Jan 1867 (OMR) 29 Jan 1867 (OML)

**SISSON**, George W. & **ROW**, Mildred C. d/o Elhanon ROW [POC see entry for Richard REYNOLDS] surety Robert GRAVES 5 Jan 1846 (OB) [] taken from compiler's notes.

**SISSON**, William & **ROW**, Sarah Jane [POC see entry for Richard REYNOLDS] d/o Elhanon ROW surety J.L. ROBINSON 18 Dec 1843 (OB) [] taken from compiler's notes.

**SIZER**, Charles Y. age 20 s POB POR Orange s/o Reuben J. SIZER and Ann YANCY laborer & **SCHOOLER**, Maria age 22 s POB POR Orange d/o William W. SCHOOLER and Mary Ann SORRELL 17 May 1869 POM Orange by Thomas R. HAWKINS (OMR)

**SIZER**, James & **OAKS**, Sarah ward of Benjamin COOPER who is also her surety 27 Nov 1837 (OB) by Jesse POWERS of the Methodist Episcopal Church 27 Nov 1837 (OM)

**SIZER**, James & **YANCEY**, Nancy d/o Charles YANCEY who is also surety 28 Jul 1840 (OB)

**SIZER**, John G. & **BALLARD**, Virginia C. d/o Edwin BALLARD who is also surety 15 Dec 1848 (OB)

**SKINKER**, William free POC & **NICKENS**, Sarah free POC 19 Oct 1820 (OM)

**SKINNER**, Robert age 29 w POB Madison Co. POR Orange s/o William SKINNER and Mary FITZPATRICK farmer & **LONG**, Lydia age 29 s POB Rockingham Co. POR Orange d/o Samuel LONG and Mary HEATWELL 24 Dec 1871 POM Orange by Isaac LONG (OMR)

**SKINNER**, William H. s/o Elijah H. and Mary SKINNER age 24 s mechanic POB Oneida Co., N.Y. POR Orange & **BROOKING**, Jennie E. d/o Charles and Amanda BROOKING age 19 s POB POR Orange; POM Orange 12 May 1857 (OMR) 8 May 1857 (OML)

**SLATER**, Thomas M. & **LAMB**, Martha surety John DEANE 12 Aug 1822 (OB) by George BINGHAM 15 Aug 1822 (OM)

**SLAUGHTER**, Alfred E. age 30 s POB Orange POR Gordonsville s/o Thomas F. SLAUGHTER and Jane M. CHAPMAN physician & **TAYLOR**, Eugenie age 27 s POB Hanover Co. POR Orange d/o Robert TAYLOR and Barbara THILMAN 10 Nov 1869 POM Orange by Philip SLAUGHTER (OMR)

**SLAUGHTER**, Martin & **MOORE**, Lucy Mary R.T. surety Gabriel B. MOORE who is also the minister 3 May 1837 and 4 May 1837 (OB) (OM)

**SLAUGHTER**, Mercer age 26 POB Orange POR Alexandria s/o Thomas
T. SLAUGHTER and Jane M. CHAPMAN & **BULL**, Mary S. age 23 s
POB POR Orange d/o Marcus BULL and Sarah T. DADE 24 Feb 1870
POM Orange by John S. HANSBROUGH (OMR)

**SLAUGHTER**, Nicholas H.C. age 22 farmer POB Danville POR
Pittsylvania s/o Charles B. SLAUGHTER and Julia E. CLEMENT &
**HUNTER**, Pauline A. s POB Appomattox POR Gordonsville d/o
Robert HUNTER and Pauline A. SLAUGHTER POM Gordonsville 10
May 1876 by J. S. HUNTER, Methodist minister (OMR)

**SLAUGHTER**, Thomas T. & **CHAPMAN**, Jane M. surety P.S. FRY 24
Jul 1828 (OB)

**SLEET**, George & **LEE**, Ann d/o Ambrose LEE surety William
GAMBAL 22 Sep 1825 (OB) 25 Sep 1828 by Jeremiah CHANDLER
(OM)

**SLEET**, George A. & **SAMUEL**, Lucy Catharine James WILLIS is
guardian and surety 26 Sep 1842 (OB)

**SLEET**, James Jr. & **PETTY**, Rebecca d/o George PETTY surety Andrew
NEWMAN 27 Oct 1804 (OB)

**SLEET**, John P. & **DAVIS**, Elizabeth M. d/o Lucy DAVIS surety Thomas
PROCTOR 22 Jul 1846 (OB)

**SLEET**, John & **WRIGHT**, Frances d/o William WRIGHT; 22 Jan 1800
(OM)

**SLEET**, Philip J. s/o Philip and Ann SLEET age 32 carpenter POB near
Augusta, Georgia POR Orange & **SAMUEL**, Arkansas C.V. d/o
Philemon and Maria SAMUEL age 33 POB POR Orange; POM
Orange 24 Oct 1854 (OMR) 23 Oct 1854 (OML)

**SLEET**, Philip & **PETTY**, Ann 30 Sep 1816 by John C. GORDON (OM)

**SLEET**, Reuben & **MALLORY**, Frances d/o Henry MALLORY surety
William LONG 22 Dec 1802 (OB) 23 Dec 1802 by Nathl. SANDERS
(Misc Min Ret)

**SLEET**, Weedon & **PETTY**, Patsy d/o George PETTY surety John
PETTY 21 Nov1799 by Nathaniel SANDERS (OB) (OM)

**SLEET**, Weedon Jr. & **THORNTON**, Sydney surety James THORNTON
27 Dec 1830 (OB)

**SMILEY**, William & **NORWELL**, Ester 1 Jun 1776 by banns both of St.
Thomas Parish (Deed Book 17)

**SMITH**, Absolem & **CHANDLER**, Jestin d/o Joseph CHANDLER surety
Edmund CHANDLER 25 Oct 1781 (OB)

**SMITH**, Absalom & **MCNEIL**, Martha surety William TERRILL Jr. 16
Jun 1804 (OB)

**SMITH**, Ambrose s/o George SMITH & **JACOBS**, Catharine d/o
Nathaniel JACOBS surety George JACOBS 12 May 1826 (OB)

**SMITH,** Bradford & **JACOBS,** Nancy d/o Robert JACOBS surety George MARTIN 24 Mar 1812 (OB)

**SMITH,** Caleb A. & **JACOBS,** Elizabeth surety George JACOBS 23 May 1831 (OB)

**SMITH,** Caleb & **BLEDSOE,** Nancy surety George JENKINS 18 Jan 1826 (OB)

**SMITH,** Charles & **MORTON,** Jane d/o Elijah MORTON; 19 Jun 1783 both of St. Thomas Parish surety Joseph MORTON (OB)

**SMITH,** Charles E. age 24 s farmer POB POR Culpeper s/o Peter C. SMITH and Sarah A. NEWTON & **SMITH,** Georgie E. age 22 s POB Culpeper POR Orange d/o Elzy SMITH and Mary A. NASH POM Orange Courthouse 25 Sep 1878 by A.C. BARRON rector of Culpeper Baptist Church (OMR)

**SMITH,** Colby & **KENDALL,** Sally single surety Robert KENDALL 9 Jan 1797 (OB)

**SMITH,** Daniel M. age 24 s POB Orange POR Jacksonport, ARK s/o William T. SMITH and Julia A. BROCKMAN physician & **CAVE,** I. DeLacey age 24 s POB POR Orange d/o William P. CAVE and Isabella DELACY 7 Jan 1873 POM Monte Bello, Orange by J.S. HANSBROUGH (OMR)

**SMITH,** Daniel M. & **STUBBLEFIELD,** Frances d/o George STUBBLEFIELD surety William MORTON Jr. 18 May 1818 (OB) by James GARNETT 20 may 1818 (OM)

**SMITH,** Downing s/o Eliz. SMITH & **GIBSON,** Sarah P. ward of John GIBSON Sr. surety Thomas SMITH 5 Nov 1828 (OB)

**SMITH,** Edmund POC age 21 s POB POR Orange s/o Edmund SMITH and Jane _____ farm laborer & **PRYOR,** Louisa POC age 21 s POB POR Orange d/o William PRYOR and Mary Ann _____ 27 Sep 1880 POM Orange by Albert THURSTON (OMR)

**SMITH,** Edward & **WARREN,** Rose surety Thomas BELL 26 Aug 1786 (OB)

**SMITH,** Edward & **BESS,** Sally surety John ALLBRIGHT 29 Oct 1812 (OB)

**SMITH,** Ernest C. age 23 s telegraph operator POB Spotsylvania POR Louisa s/o D.T. SMITH and Amanda JOHNSON & **HAWKINS,** Alice E. age 19 s POB Hamson Co., KY [sic] POR Orange d/o Elisha HAWKINS and _____ HUGHSON POM Gordonsville 27 Oct 1876 by J. W. MCCOWN (OMR)

**SMITH,** Francis M. age 22 s POB POR Orange s/o James W. SMITH and Mary A. SMITH farmer & **JACOBS,** Elizabeth age 24 w POB POR Orange d/o James M. JACOBS and Lucy MORRIS 23 Jan 1868 POM Orange by Sanders MASON (OMR)

SMITH, George & **ABELL,** Elizabeth; 19 Dec 1798 surety Caleb ABELL (OB)

SMITH, George & **SUGGET,** Elizabeth 26 Feb 1761 (Orange Fee Book)

SMITH, George & **SUGGETT,** Elizabeth; 26 Feb 1760 both of St. Thomas Parish (Orange Fee Book)

SMITH, George & **TERRILL,** Ellen d/o Uriel TERRILL surety William S. TERRILL 16 Dec 1844 (OB) 17 Dec 1844 (OM)

SMITH, James & **CLEVELAND,** Patty 9 Nov 1775 both of St. Thomas Parish by Banns (Deed Book 17)

SMITH, James O. & **GRAY,** Elisa Ann surety Thomas R. HAWKINS 28 Dec 1840 (OB)

SMITH, James Jr. s/o James SMITH Sr. & **BELL,** Mahaloa d/o Henry BELL surety POR Orange 17 Dec 1811 (OB)

SMITH, James O. & **QUINN,** Clarissa surety Charles C. JENNINGS 8 Dec 1847 (OB)

SMITH, James W. age 23 s POB Fauquier Co POR Orange s/o William SMITH and Sarah HAWKINS shoemaker & **BOASE,** Eliza Ann age 19 s POB England POR Orange d/o James BOASE and Eliza EUREN 27 Oct 1870 by John C. WILLIS (OM)

SMITH, James & **SMITH,** Caty surety William LINDSAY 16 Dec 1807 (OB)

SMITH, John & **SMITH,** Jane; 14 Sep 1775 both of St. Thomas Parish (Deed Book 17)

SMITH, John & **SMITH,** Sukey d/o Raife and Sukey SMITH; 20 Apr 1796 surety Absalom TYLER (OB)

SMITH, John & **SUTTON,** Nancy 22 Oct 1798 surety William SUTTON (OB)

SMITH, John & **WARREN,** Elizabeth; 24 Mar 1785 surety Thomas BELL (OB)

SMITH, John & **SYLVEY,** Lucy d/o William SYLVEY surety Joseph GILBERT 11 Jan 1826 (OB) by J. GOSS 12 Jan 1826 (OM)

SMITH, John R. age 22 s merchant POB POR Augusta s/o William F. SMITH and Letitia RANDOLPH & **CARTER,** Frank S. [sic] age 21 s POB Richmond city d/o Daniel H. CARTER POM Orange 25 Apr 1877 (OMR)

SMITH, John R. s/o Thomas and Lucy Ann SMITH (POR Augusta Co) age 22 s coachmaker POR Augusta Co. & **EVANS,** Frances d/o John and Nancy EVANS s POB POR Orange; POM St. Thomas Church, Orange 3 Jul 1853 (OMR) 1 Jul 1853 (OML)

SMITH, John W. age 23 s farmer POB Augusta POR Orange s/o John R. SMITH and Frances A. EVANS & **BRADLEY,** Susan E. age 18 s POB POR Orange d/o Lafayette BRADLEY and Susan A. BROWN POM Orange 12 Feb 1878 by C.P. SCOTT (OMR)

**SMITH**, John W. POC age 48 w POB Rockingham POR Staunton s/o
Wilson SMITH and Lavinie EDWARDS baker & **HARDING**, Mildred
POC age 32 w POB Nelson POR Orange d/o Charlotte MURPHY 5 Jul
1880 POM Gordonsville, Orange by Frank TIBBS (OMR)

**SMITH**, Lewis POC age 22 s farm laborer POB POR Orange s/o Jere
SMITH and Mary ___ & **BLACKEY**, Louisa POC age 22 s POB POR
Orange POM Orange 16 Mar 1876 by Frank TIBBS (OMR)

**SMITH**, Marcellus W. age 22 s POB POR Orange s/o James W. SMITH
and Mary A. SMITH farmer & **REYNOLDS**, Lucy F. age 20 d POB
POR Orange d/o William RHODES 19 Dec 1869 POM Orange by
Sanders MASON (OMR)

**SMITH**, Marion M. age 28 s telegraph repairman POB Albemarle POR
Orange s/o David H. SMITH and Mary A. PARROTT & **RILEY**,
Mary A. age 20 s POB POR Orange d/o Alexander RILEY and Julia
SOUTHERLAND POM Orange 6 Nov 1879 (OMR)

**SMITH**, Noah & **SMITH**, Mary E.M.B. ward of Noah SMITH surety
James BEADLES 25 Mar 1837 (OB) by Benjamin CREEL 12 Apr
1837 (OM)

**SMITH**, Oswald & **QUISENBERRY**, Joice d/o William
QUISENBERRY; 22 Dec 1800 surety Caleb LINDSAY (OB)

**SMITH**, Owen & **JAMESON**, Dolly A. Andrew SAMUEL is her
guardian and her surety 31 Jul 1815 (OB)

**SMITH**, Philip s/o Mathias SMITH & **BICKERS**, Matilda d/o Joseph
BICKERS who is also surety 23 Jul 1804 (OB)

**SMITH**, Presley & **WINSLOW**, Frances d/o Fortunatus WINSLOW
surety Moses WINSLOW 14 Jun 1817 (OB)

**SMITH**, Reuben POC age 26 s POB Louisa Co POR Culpeper Co s/o
Samuel SMITH laborer on farm & **DEALE**, Ann POC age 35 w POB
POR Orange 30 May 1872 POM Orange by Philip JOHNSON (OMR)

**SMITH**, Richard A. s/o William M. SMITH and Eliza BLEDSOE age 25 s
farmer POB Culpeper Co POR Orange & **COOK**, Angelina d/o Caleb
A. SMITH and Betsy JACOBS age 29 w POB POR Orange; POM
Orange 16 Nov 1865 (OMR) (OML)

**SMITH**, Robert POR Spotsylvania Co. & **CONNER**, Ann POR St.
Thomas Parish 15 Jul 1777 by banns (Deed Book 17)

**SMITH**, Robert A. s/o Harris and Susan SMITH age 26 s  no particular
occupation POB Culpeper POR Orange & **ALLISON**, Lucy E. d/o
Robert and Mariah ALLISON age 18 s POB Culpeper POR Orange;
POM Orange 8 Jun 1854 (OMR)

**SMITH**, Robert J. POC age 29 s laborer POB Richmond city POR Orange
s/o Daniel SMITH & **SHEPHERD**, Emma J. age 23 s POB POR
Orange d/o Abraham SHEPHERD and Nancy WILLIAMS POM
Orange 12 Sep 1877 (OMR)

SMITH, Robert POR Spotsylvania & **CONNERS,** Ann POR St. Thomas
Parish 15 Jul 1777 by banns (Deed Book 17)

SMITH, Samuel & **DOUGLASS,** Dorcas; 24 Jun 1774 both of St. Thomas
Parish (Deed Book 17)

SMITH, St. Clair & **POWELL,** Rhoda surety Lewis G. POWELL 26 Mar
1827 (OB) 29 Mar 1827 by George BINGHAM (OM)

SMITH, Stephen & **STEVENS,** Blessing both of St. Thomas Parish 4 Jul
1773 (Deed Book 17)

SMITH, Tartan & **MALLORY,** Lucy d/o Henry MALLORY surety
Francis ABRAHAM 23 Dec 1811 (OB)

SMITH, Timoleon age 38 w POB POR Louisa Co. s/o Origen SMITH and
Mary C. WILKERSON farmer & **GOODWIN,** Betty V. age 31 POB
POR Orange d/o McD TERRILL and Jane LOVELL 5 Mar 1868 POM
Orange by R.C. CAVE (OMR)

SMITH, Thomas & **CAVE,** Polly d/o Abner CAVE who is also surety 25
Oct 1824 (OB)

SMITH, William & **PORTER,** Mary C.; 16 Oct 1799 by James
GARNETT (OM)

SMITH, William B. s/o William M.SMITH and Eliza BLEDSOE age 22 s
farmer POB Madison Co POR Orange & **SUTHERLAND,** Catherine
d/o Alex SUTHERLAND and Dinah HOWARD age 24 s POB POR
Orange; POM Orange 24 Dec 1866 (OMR) 17 Dec 1866 (OML)

SMITH, William Henry age 25 w POB Clarendon Co., NJ POR Orange
s/o Robert and Christiana SMITH farmer & **MCCLEAREN,**
Clementine age 35 w POB Berks Co., PA POR Orange Co 10 Jan 1869
POM Orange by E.R. PERRY (OMR)

SMITH, William J. s/o Robert and Pamelia SMITH age 35 s clerk in store
POB Louisa Co POR Nelson Co. & **PARROTT,** Lucy Jane d/o Samuel
H. and Mary C. PARROTT age24 s POB Louisa Co POR Orange;
POM Orange 29 Oct 1867 (OMR) 23 Sep 1867 (OML)

SMITH, William POC age 19 POB POR Orange s/o Reuben SMITH and
Jennie ROSS brick mason & **POINDEXTER,** Lucy Ann age 21 POB
POR Orange d/o Green POINDEXTER and Melvina HALL 30 Oct
1870 by Herndon FRAZER (OM)

SMITH, William POC age 22 s POB POR Orange s/o George SMITH and
Mary FITZHUGH laborer & **MYERS,** Mary Ann POC age 20 s POB
POR Orange d/o John MYERS 13 Apr 1872 POM Orange by Philip
JOHNSON (OMR)

SMITH, William POR Rockingham Co. & **SMITH,** Lucinda d/o Joseph
SMITH; 2 Jun 1783 surety Rice SMITH (OB)

SMITH, William T. Jr. age 22 s POB POR Orange s/o William T. SMITH
and Julia BROOKMAN & **RILEY,** Sarah A. age 18 s POB Amherst

POR Orange d/o Alexander RILEY and Julia SUTHERLAND 27 Oct
1880 POM Gordonsville, Orange by Patrick DONOHOE (OMR)

**SMITH**, William T. & **BROCKMAN**, Julia surety James YOUNG who is
also her guardian 4 Jan 1847 (OB)

**SMITH**, William & **BRIANT**, Martha d/o Jeremiah BRIANT surety
Armistead LONG 7 Apr 1830 (OB)

**SMITH**, William & **MORRIS**, Nancy 19 Dec 1805 by George
BINGHAM (OM)

**SMITH**, William M. & **BLEDSOE**, Eliza surety Richard S. ABELL 6 Dec
1831 (OB)

**SMITH**, Zachary POC age 21 s POB POR Orange s/o Isaac SMITH and
Milly WILLIAMS laborer & **RUCKER**, Margaret POC age 18 s POB
POR Orange d/o Legrand RUCKER and Harriet LINDSAY 27 Mar
1872 POM Orange by Philip JOHNSON (OMR)

**SMITHERS**, Howard S. age 36 w POB Essex Co POR Orange s/o John S.
SMITHERS and Polly ALLEN telegraph operator & **MANN**, Helen G.
age 19 POB POR Orange d/o William H. MANN and A.R. KEITH 22
Feb 1872 POM Orange by Charles QUARLES (OMR)

**SMOOT**, Caleb & **MCCLAMROCK**, Martha 10 Sep 1795 by George
EVE (OM)

**SMOOT**, James T. age 24 s POB Lynchburg POR New York City s/o
W.H. SMOOT and Mary F. SUTPHIN exporter & **MCCOWN**, Ruth
age 21 s POB Danville POR Orange d/o J.W. MCCOWN and Eliza K.
JOHNSON 28 Dec 1880 POM Baptist Church, Gordonsville, Orange
by J.W. MCCOWN (OMR)

**SMOOT**, Jenifer [sic] & **MELONE**, Rebecca d/o John MELONE surety
Michael LOWER by William DOUGLAS 5 Oct 1805 (OB) (OM)

**SMOOT**, John POR Madison Co. & **THORNTON**, Lucy Buckner d/o
George THORNTON surety Charles THORNTON 9 Jun 1806 (OB)

**SMOOT**, John s/o John SMOOT who is also surety & **DAY**, Jemima d/o
John DAY Sr. 18 Dec 1834 surety John S. PETTY (OB)

**SMOUTS**, John & **FLEEK**, Polly; 7 Oct 1799 surety John FLEEK (OB)
by Jacob WATTS 8 Oct 1799 (OM)

**SNEED**, William T. s/o L.W. SNEED and Elizabeth H. WOOLFOLK age
21 s merchant POB Louisa Co POR Orange & **GOODWIN**, Mary E.
d/o Robert GOODWIN and Susan H. WOOLFOLK age 26 s POB
Louisa Co POR Orange; POM Gordonsville, Orange 6 Nov 1866
(OMR) 1 Nov 1866 (OML)

**SNELL**, Joseph & **MANSFIELD**, Elizabeth Clark d/o Robert
MANSFIELD and Mourning CLARK b. 12 Oct 1788 24 Nov 1806 by
William DOUGLASS Methodist (OM)

**SNELL**, Joseph & **MILLER**, Elizabeth d/o Robert MILLER surety
Reuben SANFORD 22 Aug 1791 (OB)

**SNELL**, Joseph & **WHITE**, Anney surety John CAMPBELL 13 Jan 1821 (OB)

**SNODGRASS**, Paul V. POR Berkely Co. & **RIALL**, Mary surety Edward RIALL 20 Jan 1838 (OB)

**SNORR**, Wiatt & **ROGERS**, Eliza d/o Achilles ROGERS surety Richard WILLIAMS 15 Sep 1827 (OB)

**SNOW**, Augustine & **MALLORY**, Agnes Eggleston d/o Henry MALLORY who is also surety 21 Feb 1816 (OB) by George BINGHAM 27 Feb 1816 (OM)

**SNOW**, Bird & **MAYHUGH**, Polly d/o Polly WATSON; surety Isaac WATSON 9 Jan 1797 (OB) 12 Jan 1797 by George BINGHAM (OM)

**SNOW**, Early & **MALLORY**, Mary Payne surety John MALLORY 26 Feb 1823 (OB) 5 Mar 1823 by George BINGHAM (OM)

**SNOW**, Holand & **MALLORY**, Judith T. surety Thomas MALLORY 28 Aug 1815 (OB) by George BINGHAM 31 Aug 1815 (OM)

**SNOW**, James & **HARVEY**, Jenny 9 Jan 1806 by George BINGHAM (OM)

**SNOW**, John POR Standardsville & **LOWER**, Elizabeth d/o Peter LOWER; 4 Mar 1800 by William CARPENTER Jr. (OM)

**SNYDER**, William & **JENKINS**, Sarah ward of Henry HILL surety William S. JENKINS 6 Dec 1820 (OB) 7 Dec 1820 by James GARNETT Jr. (OM)

**SOMERVILLE**, James s/o James SOMERVILLE and Helen WALLACE age 43 w lawyer POB Madison Co POR Carroll Co, Mississippi & **BARBOUR**, Cornelia C. d/o Quintus BARBOUR and Mary E. SOMERVILLE age 29 s POB Madison Co POR Orange; POM Orange 5 Jun 1867 (OMR) 3 Jun 1867 (OML)

**SOMMERS**, Edgar F. age 21 s POB Madison POR Orange s/o George A. SOMMERS and Rebecca C. HENKLE farmer & **HENSHAW**, Mary V. age 20 s POB POR Orange d/o T.P.G. HENSHAW and Virginia O.S. PORTER 23 Sep 1880 POM Orange by L.A. FOX Evangelical Lutheran minister (OMR)

**SOMMERVILLE**, Harrison & **SLEET**, Nancy surety John SLEET 27 Nov 1822 (OB)

**SORRILLE**, John N. & **STANARD**, Sarah Ann Ophelia d/o William H. STANARD surety Thomas SORRILLE 7 Jan 1823 (OB)

**SORRILLE**, Joseph C. s/o John SORRILLE age 30 s carpenter POB POR Spotsylvania & **DUNAWAY**, Ann d/o Admond DUNAWAY age 18 s POB POR Orange; POM Orange 22 Nov 1857 (OMR) 18 Nov 1857 (OML)

**SOUDER**, Charles M. age 21 s POB POR Gloucester Co., NJ s/o Elias SOWDER and Rebecca EVANS farmer & **WILSON**, Lillie H. age 16 s

POB Forda, NY POR Orange d/o William WILSON and Eliz. S. SALE 6 Nov 1873 POM Orange by J.S. HANSBOROUGH (OMR)

**SOUTHARD**, Elias & **DAVIS**, Elizabeth d/o Walker DAVIS who is also surety 29 Dec 1829 (OB)

**SOUTHERLAND**, James L. & **HIGGERSON**, Mary E. d/o Benjamin HIGGERSON POM Orange 15 Jan 1854 (OMR)

**SOUTHERLAND**, John & **JOHNSON**, Mary surety John B. JOHNSON 17 Dec 1823 (OB)

**SOUTHERLAND**, William & **HUME**, Sarah surety Richard PHILIPS 12 Dec 1836 (OB)

**SOUTHERLIN**, William s/o Alexander and Diana SOUTHERLIN age 25 s laborer POB Louisa Co POR Orange & **JONES**, Sarah E. d/o Fielding and Mary JONES age 18 s POB POR Orange; POM Orange 21 Jun 1856 (OMR) 20 Jun 1856 (OML)

**SPALDING**, Robertson & **JONES**, Fanny surety Elijah JONES 10 Jun 1788 (OB)

**SPENCER**, Edward & **WOOLFOLK**, Eleanor d/o Christo. BROCKMAN (mother) surety Joseph WOOLFOLK 7 Nov 1787 (OB)

**SPENCER**, Francis & **GEORGE**, Wintifred permission from Prettyman MERRY 4 Nov 1790 (OB)

**SPENCER**, George POC age 24 s POB POR Orange s/o James SPENCER and Martha Ann SPENCER laborer & **GREEN**, Polly POC age 17 s POB POR Orange d/o Irison GREEN 27 Sep 1873 by E.R. PERRY (OMR)

**SPENCER**, James & **DAVIS**, Frances surety Philemon DAVIS 21 Aug 1780 (OB)

**SPENCER**, Seth & **THORNTON**, Ann surety Abner BECKHAM 18 Jan 1791 (OB)

**SPICER**, Benjamin & **SNELL**, Caty A. d/o Robert SNELL 26 Oct 1799 surety James COOPER (OB) 9 Jan 1800 by Hamilton GOSS (OM)

**SPICER**, David & **SIMS**, Nancy surety William WILLIAMS 17 Sep 1829 (OB)

**SPICER**, George S. age 24 s farmer POB Louisa POR Orange s/o John S. SPICER and Elizabeth PATTERSON & **WHITTON**, L.R. (?) age 22 s POB Louisa POR Orange d/o Joseph WHITTON and Huldah WHITLOCK POM Orange 21 Feb 1878 by L.W. CAVE (OMR)

**SPICER**, Rawser & **WOOD**, Nancy s stepdaughter of John HENSLEY and daughter of Hanner HENSLEY 27 Aug 1792 surety John WILLIAMS (OB)

**SPINDLE**, John E. age 32 s POB Stafford POR Fauquier s/o Jefferson SPINDLE and Maria PACKETT farmer & **BOSWELL**, Lucy C. age 25 s POB POR Orange William J. BOSWELL and Martha M.

TALIAFERRO 25 Feb 1880 POM Methodist Church, Orange by
Herbert M. HOKE (OMR)

**SPOTSWOOD**, Albert POC age 22 s POB POR Orange s/o Jack
SPOTSWOOD and Fanny NELSON r.r. hand & **WILLIAMS**,
Georgianna POC age 18 s POB POR Orange d/o Ned WILLIAMS and
Mary COLEMAN 28 Dec 1872 POM Orange by Philip JOHNSON
(OMR)

**SPOTSWOOD**, Alexander D. age 33 s POB POR Orange s/o John R.
SPOTSWOOD and Lelia ALLISON farmer & **GORDON**, Lucy H. age
33 s POB Spotsylvania POR Orange d/o John A. GORDON and Jane
HERNDON 15 Dec 1870 POM Orange by Jos. A. BILLINGSLEY
(OM)

**SPOTSWOOD**, Lewis POC age 28 s farm labourer POB Madison POR
Orange s/o John SPOTSWOOD and Mary CLARK & **BOWLER**,
Maria POC age 25 s POB POR Orange d/o Anderson BOWLER and
Winney DUNCAN POM Orange 9 Feb 1878 by Robert R. WOODSON
(OMR)

**SPRADLIN**, John & **FOSTER**, Elizabeth age 18 d/o Lucy FOSTER; 10
May 1798 surety John WORMLEY (OB)

**SPRIGGS**, Ebenezer & **SANFORD**, Mima surety Stewart SANFORD 31
Dec 1804 (OB) by James GARNETT 3 Jan 1805 (OM)

**SPROUSE**, William H. age 20 s POB Albemarle Co POR Amherst Co. s/o
William SPROUSE and Julia A. DUDLEY railroading & **CORKER**,
Bettie A. age 21 s POB Louisa Co POR Orange 11 Mar 1873 POM
Orange by J.W. MCCOWEN (OMR)

**SPROWER**, Charles POC age 22 farm laborer POB Louisa POR Orange
s/o Charles SPROWER and Sally ___ & **JACKSON**, Lottie age 21 s
POB Louisa POR Orange d/o Davy JACKSON POM Orange 20 Feb
1876 (OMR)

**STAGE**, David R. & **MOONEY**, Maryan; 29 May 1777 both of St.
Thomas Parish by banns (Deed Book 17)

**STANARD**, Beverly age 30 s POB POR Orange s/o Charles STANARD
and Aggie PAYNE laborer & **WHITE**, Alice age 20 s POB POR
Orange d/o William WHITE and Susan JOHNSON 19 Nov 1871 POM
Orange by C. GILLUM (OMR)

**STANARD**, Robert B. & **TALIAFERRO**, Ellen B. her surety and
guardian is Edmund P. TAYLOR 19 Jun 1828 (OB)

**STANTON**, Beverly & **STANTON**, Jemimah d/o Betty STANTON; 20
Mar 1786 surety Joseph ROGERS (OB)

**STANTON**, Spencer & **POWELL**, Sally surety Honorias POWELL 18
May 1791 (OB) by George EVE 20 May 1791 (OM)

**STAPLES**, William & **GARTON**, Mary Jane ward of Tandy G. MORRIS
surety William GARTON 4 Nov 1838 (OB)

**STAPP**, Achilles & **VAWTER**, Margaret d/o Mary VAWTER 27 Nov 1782 both of St. Thomas Parish surety Richard WHITE (OB)

**STAPP**, Thomas & **BARBAGE**, Betsy; 4 Jan 1779 both of St. Thomas Parish surety Joel STODGEHILL (OB)

**STARKS**, Lewis POC age 28 s POB POR Orange s/o Lewis STARKS and Lucy COVINGTON farmer & **GREEN**, Margaret age 25 s POB POR Orange d/o Jere GREEN and Mary ___ 31 Dec 1873 POM Orange by E.R. PERRY (OMR)

**STEARNS**, Harvey POC age 24 s labourer POB POR Orange s/o Harvey and Jennie STEARNS & **YANCEY**, Ida POC age 19 s POB Louisa POR Orange d/o Edmund YANCEY and Malinda LEWIS POM Orange 22 Feb 1879 by W.J. BARNETT (OMR)

**STEELE**, Charles G. age 21 s farmer POB Augusta POR Orange s/o Michael STEELE and Mary F. CHANDLER & **DARNELL**, Annie age 18 s POB POR Orange d/o William DARNELL and Harriet DARNELL POM Orange 23 Nov 1879 (OMR)

**STEELE**, Samuel & **MCQUIDDY**, Mary w 24 Nov 1786 surety John ROBINSON (OB)

**STEELY**, Walter S. age 26 s merchant POB Washington DC POR Richmond s/o George S. STEELY and Mary J. MITCHELL & **BAILES**, Lillie H. age 18 s POB Albemarle POR Orange d/o John T. BAILES and Amanda BABER POM Gordonsville 18 Jun 1878 by John R. JOYNER, Presbyterian minister(OMR)

**STEPHENS**, Benjamin & **NELSON**, Agnes d/o James NELSON 28 May 1799 surety Edmund STEPHENS (OB)

**STEPHENS**, Edmund & **ROBINSON**, Agnes d/o Agnes ROBINSON; 31 Dec 1796 surety James NELSON (OB)

**STEPHENS**, George Jr. & **BALL**, Eliza Ann d/o Jesse BALL surety Hugh STEPHENS 24 Dec 1821 (OB) by Edward CANNON 13 Jan 1822 (OM)

**STEPHENS**, George & **EARLY**, Theodosia W. surety James SIMMS 25 Apr 1825 (OB)

**STEPHENS**, James & **GAINES**, Disey; 12 Jan 1795 surety Thomas GAINES (OB)

**STEPHENS**, Newton & **WHITE**, Susanna d/o James WHITE surety Willis WHITE Jr. 13 Mar 1821 (OB) 15 Mar 1821 by George BINGHAM (OM)

**STEPHENS**, William & **NELSON**, Elizabeth d/o James NELSON surety William NELSON 26 Dec 1803 (OB)

**STEPHENSON**, Charles & **HANCOCK**, Susan; 30 May 1809 surety Willis ARNHOLD 31 May 1809 by Robert JONES (OM)

**STEVENS**, Edward & **PETTY**, Betsy d/o John PETTY who is also surety 23 Jun 1817 (OB)

STEVENS, John & STEVENS, Ann S. d/o John STEVENS Jr. who is also surety 22 Nov 1806 (OB)

STEVENS, Joseph L. s/o Joseph L. STEPHENS and Elizabeth S. FLOOD age 29 s planter POB Charleston, SC POR John's Island, SC & FREEMAN, Mary E. d/o A.R. FREEMAN and Mary A. KEMPER age 18 s POB Culpeper Co POR Orange; POM Gordonsville 18 Oct 1864 (OMR) (OML)

STEVENS, Merryman & GRIGRY, Ann d/o John GRIGRY surety William MERRYMAN 10 Oct 1804 (OB) 20 Oct 1804 by Frederick KABLER Lutheran (OM)

STEVENS, Waller & ADAMS, Lucy d/o Thomas ADAMS who is also surety 29 Jun 1801 (OB)

STEVENS, Wesley s/o Indian STEVENS and Virginia BLAND age 35 s laborer on farm POB POR Orange POC & LEWIS, Mary Ann age 31 s POB POR Orange POC; POM Orange 25 Aug 1866 (OMR) (OML)

STEVENS, William & MILLS, Margaret d/o Nathanial MILLS surety James DANIEL 9 Feb 1801 (OB)

STEVENS, William J. & LINDSAY, Julia V. 27 Sep 1847 surety Robert P. CAVE (OB)

STEVENSON, John & PAYNE, Milly; 23 Dec 1793 (OM)

STEVENSON, William H. & YOUNG, Mary d/o John and Mary YOUNG surety John P. COONS and Christian F. KINZER 1 Mar 1832 (OB)

STEWARD, John & REYNOLDS, Catharine d/o William REYNOLDS Sr. 15 Jan 1810 surety George QUISENBERRY (OB)

STEWART, Charles POC age 35 s labourer POB POR Orange s/o Daniel STEWART and Aggy TAYLOR & HENSHAW, Malinda POC age 26 s POB Culpeper POR Orange d/o William and Malinda HENSHAW POM Orange 27 Dec 1877 (OMR)

STEWART, Thornton POC age 21 s labourer POB Spotsylvania POR Orange s/o Nelson STEWART & JACKSON, Mary POC age 25 s POB POR Orange d/o Moses and Vinie JACKSON POM Orange 26 Dec 1877 (OMR)

STITZER, David & WALLER, Sarah Ann d/o James WALLER surety James E. YANCEY 28 Dec 1842 (OB)

STOCKDELL, George H. s/o Thomas STOCKDELL and Brittania BENNETT & WINSLOW, Sarah B. d/o Moses WINSLOW and Ann LONG 20 Jul 1848 surety James F. HERNDON by Benjamin CREEL (OB)(OM)

STOCKDELL, John Jr. & DUVALL, Sally; 2 Nov 1786 surety John STOCKDELL (OB)

STOCKDELL, Robert & GAY, Sally d/o Everett GAY 25 Jan 1839 surety Alfred M. FAULCONER (OB)

**STOCKDELL,** William & **ROSZELL,** Delphea 23 Jan 1793 surety George CHAPMAN (OB)

**STOCKDON,** Henry W. age 30 s POB POR Orange s/o George H. STOCKDON and Sarah WINSLOW carpenter & **HIGGINS,** Lannie J. age 22 s POB POR Orange d/o Robert M. HIGGINS and Ann E. WINSLOW 9 Jun 1880 POM Orange by Herbert HOKE (OMR)

**STOKES,** Moses & **STROTHER,** Susan; 3 Mar 1770 (OB)

**STOKES,** William & **SILVEY,** Lucy s ; 15 Feb 1797 by Hamilton GOSS (OM)

**STONE,** Henry & **GOLDING,** Nancy d/o William GOLDING; 10 Nov 1786 surety Jackie GOLDING (OB)

**STONE,** Henry & **MITCHELL,** Polly d/o William MITCHELL 6 Jan 1823 surety Elijah MITCHELL (OB)

**STONE,** John & **BURTON,** Elizabeth d/o James **BURTON**; 9 Apr 1799 surety James TAYLOR 11 Apr 1799 by Jacob WATTS (OB) (OM)

**STONE,** John & **PARROTT**, Judith 8 Dec 1803 by Jacob WATTS (Misc Min Ret)

**STONE,** John & **PARROTT,** Judith d/o William PARROTT surety William PARROTT Jr. 6 Dec 1803 by Jacob WATTS 8 Dec 1803 (OM)

**STOVIN,** Charles J. s/o Charles STOVIN and Mary LEWIS age 54 w farmer POB Loudon Co POR Orange & **NEWMAN,** Bettie B. d/o Reuben NEWMAN & _____ WELCH age 23 s POB POR Orange; POM Orange 5 Dec 1865 (OMR) 2 Dec 1865 (OML)

**STOWERS,** John & **HERNDON,** Sally 19 Dec 1802 by Jacob WATTS (Misc Min Ret)

**STRAHAN,** Charles s/o Ebenezer STRAHAN and Sarah B. HOLMES age 23 s merchant POB Baltimore, MD POR Fredericksburg & **MORTON,** Jennie C. d/o George W. MORTON and Susan TERRELL age 23 s POB POR Orange; POM Orange 25 Jun 1863 (OMR) 24 Jun 1863 (OML)

**STRATTON,** Richard H. age 25 s POB Staunton POR Orange s/o R.H. STRATTON and A.E. BROWN druggist & **ATKINS,** Betty age 19 s POB POR Orange d/o Samuel G. ATKINS and S.C. PARROTT 3 Nov 1869 POM Orange by J.W. MCCORAN (OMR)

**STRAUGHAN,** John & **SANDERS,** Mary d/o Nathaniel SANDERS; 21 Jul 1783 surety James SANDERS (OB)

**STRONG,** Luther G. age 23 s POB Louisa Co POR Orange s/o William M. STRONG and Lucy Scott WILLIAMS farmer & **HALL,** Alice M. age 22 s POB Louisa Co POR Orange d/o William L. HALL and Agnes CLEVELY 9 Dec 1869 POM Orange by T.M. CARSON (OMR)

**STRONG,** Robert C. s/o Jesse STRONG and Sarah SMITH age 23 s farmer POB Claiborne Co, Mississippi & **HUGHES,** Rebecca A. d/o

Armistead HUGHES and Sarah A. SLEET age 22 s POB POR Orange;
POM Orange 29 Dec 1865 (OMR) 23 Dec 1865 (OML)

**STROTHER,** George F. & **WILLIAMS,** Sarah Green d/o James
WILLIAMS 30 Jul 1807 surety John FARISH (OB) 1 Jul 1807 by
William MASON Sr. (OM)

**STROTHER,** Graves POC age 24 s POB POR Orange laborer &
**THOMPSON,** Eliza POC age 22 s POB POR Orange 2 May 1868
POM Orange by Phil JOHNSON (OMR)

**STROTHER,** John POC age 23 s bark mill hand POB POR Orange s/o
Captain STROTHER and Mary ____ & **YAGER,** Courtenay POC age
21 s POB POR Orange POM Little Zion Baptist Church, Orange 27
Oct 1878 by W.J. BARNETT (OMR)

**STROTHER,** John s/o Charles STROTHER and Diana MCDANIEL age
24 S farm laborer POB POR Orange POC & **WALKER,** Tamar d/o
Horace WALKER and Cornelia MORRIS age 16 s POB POR Orange
POC; POM Orange 27 Dec 1867 (OMR) 26 Dec 1867 (OML)

**STROTHER,** William & **KAVANAUGH,** Ann w 11 Jun 1775 both of St.
Thomas Parish surety William CAVE (Deed Book 17)

**STROW,** John & **WALTERS,** Catharine d/o George WALTERS 24 Feb
1801 by Hamilton GOSS (OM)

**STUART,** Alexander & **REID,** Ann w 3 Aug 1796 surety Robert
STUART (OB)

**STUART,** George POC age33 w POB Green Co POR Orange s/o Adam
STUART laborer & **ROBINSON,** Betsy POC age 30 s POB POR
Orange d/o Peter WRIGHT and Agnes FAMEWOOD 29 Feb 1868
POM Orange by Philip JOHNSON (OMR)

**STUART,** William R. & **BRADFORD,** Lucy Ann d/o Alexander
BRADFORD 16 Sep 1834 surety Joseph B. BRADFORD (OB) 17 Sep
1834 by Edward SHIP (OM)

**STUBBLEFIELD,** George & **HAWKINS,** Ann 20 May 1791 surety
Joseph BISHOP (OB)

**STUBBLEFIELD,** George & **MORRISON,** Sarah 15 Aug 1775 consent
of Richard and Catharine REYNOLDS stepfather and mother of Sarah
surety Joseph SPENCER (OB)

**STUBBLEFIELD,** James & **BECKHAM,** Polley 22 Dec 1803 by Nath.
SANDERS (Misc Min Ret)

**STUBBLEFIELD,** James & **BECKHAM,** Polly 20 Dec 1803 surety
Jeremiah BECKHAM (OB) 22 Dec 1803 by Nathaniel SANDERS
Baptist (OM)

**STUBBS,** Jesse H. Jr. age 28 s POB POR Spotsylvania Co s/o Jesse H.
STUBBS and Sarah PREWETT farmer & **SANDERS,** Ann J. age 19 s
POB POR Orange d/o Francis J. SANDERS and Lucy BROCKMAN
24 Oct 1869 POM Orange by Herndon FRAZER (OMR)

234

**STYERS**, Leonard & **WOLFE**, Elizabeth d/o L. WOLFE; 27 Mar 1800 by Hamilton GOSS (OM)

**SUDDUTH**, George A. s/o Thomas J. SUDDUTH and Maria SPILMAN age 26 s clerk POB POR Culpeper Co & **NEWMAN**, Mary E. d/o Morris D. NEWMAN and Mary A. TATUM age 21 s POB Madison Co POR Orange; POM Orange married by acting chaplain 13th Reg,. Va Infantry Pegrams's Brigade Early's Division Army of Northern Va 5 Feb 1864 (OMR) (OML)

**SULLIVAN**, Dawson & **PAYNE**, Lucy; 13 Jan 1817 (OB)

**SULLIVAN**, Everet & **DEAN**, Nancy 30 Dec 1823 by George BINGHAM (OM)

**SULLIVAN**, Richard B. & **ROBINSON**. Sarah A.; 7 Apr 1857 (OML)

**SUTHERLAND**, Kennith [sic] & **WEBSTER**, Ruth surety Daniel WEBSTER 6 Feb 1789 (OB)

**SUTHERLAND**, Richard W. age 25 s farmer POB POR Orange s/o William SUTHERLAND and Sarah HUME & **WILTSHIRE**, Louisa Virginia age 21 s POB POR Orange d/o Weedon WILTSHIRE and Malinda FAULCONER POM Orange 21 Dec 1876 (OMR)

**SUTTON**, William & **BROWN**, Alice 6 Apr 1775 both of St. Thomas Parish by banns (Deed Book 17)

**SWAIN**, William E. age 50 w POB Prince George Co., MD POR Fauquier s/o James H. SWAIN and Mary HOYLE farmer & **WHARTON**, Ella E. age 23 s POB Culpeper POR Orange d/o Samuel WHARTON and Lucy SIMES 23 Dec 1880 POM Orange by W. H. CAMPER (OMR)

**SWAN**, Robert S. age 29 s POB Madison POR Orange s/o Robert G. SWAN and Catharine M. SIMS gentleman & **NEWMAN**, Corinne T. age 22 s POB POR Orange d/o James F. NEWMAN and Martha COCKRELL 14 Oct 1880 POM Orange by J.M. FRENCH (OMR)

**SWANN**, George W. s/o Frank SWAN and Elizabeth DUKE age 21 s farm laborer POB Petersburg, VA POR Orange POC & **ROBINSON**, Mary age 26 w POB POR Orange POC; POM Orange 7 Dec 1867 (OMR) 30 Nov 1867 (OML)

**SWARTSWELDER**, William & **SEBREE**, Nancy 27 Aug 1816 surety Charles GOODALL (OB) [this may be the same marriage as William BLACK with the German name reported in the English version J.V.]

**SWARTZ**, George s/o Frederick SWARTZ and Elizabeth WILLAST age 25 s farmer POB Germany POR Richmond & **GARNETT**, Lucy M. d/o James and Eliza LLOYD age 25 w POB Madison Co POR Orange; POM Orange 12 Jan 1864 (OMR) (OML)

**SWATS**, Jacob F. & **SMITH**, Sarah E.; POM Orange 24 Jul 1851 (OMR) 21 Jul 1851 (OML)

**SWENEY**, Daniel & **GRIFFETH**, Mary d/o David GRIFFIN surety Edmund GRIFFITH 16 Dec 1791 (OB) 19 Dec 1791 by George EVE (OM)

**SWIFT**, Harlan J. age 25 s POB POR Allegheny Co., NY s/o Calvin SWIFT and Sevilla AULT lawyer & **HIGGINS**, Martha A. age 24 s POB Alleghany Co., NY POR Orange d/o Michael D. HIGGINS and Patty LATHAM 26 May 1869 POM Orange by H.E. HATCHER (OMR)

**SWIFT**, William T. s/o Granville and Jane SWIFT age 21 s farmer POB POR Spotsylvania & **MASSEY**, Lucinda d/o James O. and Elizabeth MASSEY age 27 s POB POR Orange; POM Orange 25 Sep 1856 (OMR) 22 Sep 1856 (OML)

**SWINDELL**, Joel S. s/o Joseph SWINDELL who is also surety POR Madison Co. & **ANDERSON**, Mary Jackson d/o Joel ANDERSON 18 Aug 1821 (OB)

**SWISER**, David & **BAUKER**, Christine 5 Nov 1822 by George BINGHAM (OM)

**SWITZER**, Lawrence & **WHITE**, Nancy 16 Aug 1827 by George BINGHAM (OM)

**SYLVA**, George & **POE**, Lucy; 17 Feb 1796 surety Dennis SHA___(OB)

**TALIAFERRO**, George G. & **JENKINS**, Sarah J. d/o William T. JENKINS who is also surety 12 Feb 1833 (OB)

**TALIAFERRO**, Hay & **THRUSTON**, Lucy Mary w/o William Plummer THRUSTON surety Francis DADE 5 Apr 1791 (OB)

**TALIAFERRO**, Hay & **CONWAY**, Susannah d/o Catlett CONWAY 14 Mar 1797 surety William DADE (OB)

**TALIAFERRO**, Horace D. & **GRYMES**, Lucy N. surety David HUME by J. EARNEST 1 Oct 1844 (OB) (OM)

**TALIAFERRO**, John S. & **BARBOUR**, Maria surety Richard H. TALIAFERRO 8 Jun 1822 (OB)

**TALIAFERRO**, John T. & **CASON**, Mary B. d/o Edward CASON surety Richard CAVE 9 Feb 1829 (OB)

**TALIAFERRO**, John & **MANSFIELD**, Mildred M. surety Joseph A. MANSFIELD 26 May 1828 (OB)

**TAIT**, Moses POC age 21 s farm labourer POB POR Orange s/o Nelson TAIT and Matilda CARR & **STEWART**, Melvina POC age 15 s POB Greene POR Orange d/o George STEWART and Harriet SMITH POM Orange 15 Jul 1877 (OMR)

**TALIAFERO**, Scott POC age 23 s farm labourer POB POR Orange s/o Jackson TALIAFERO and Rachel ANDERSON & **WASHINGTON**, Sally POC age 19 s POB POR Orange d/o Lewis WASHINGTON and Julia HENDERSON POM Shady Grove Church, Orange 3 Feb 1878 by C.T. JOHNSON (OMR)

**TALIAFERRO**, Dick POC age 23 s POB POR Orange s/o Isaac TALIAFERRO & Lucinda _____ farm laborer & **CARTER**, Rena POC age 24 s POB Louisa Co POR Orange d/o Jackson _____ 8 Jan 1870 POM Louisa Co. by William JASPER (OMR)

**TALIAFERRO**, Horace G. age 23 s POB Richmond POR Orange s/o Horace D. TALIAFERRO and Lucy Nelson GRYMES druggist & **BROWN**, Carrie C. age 22 s POB Berkley Co., WV POR Orange d/o James S. BROWN and Margaret E. BURKHART 27 Oct 1869 POM Orange by T.M. CARSON (OMR)

**TALIAFERRO**, John & **STOCKDELL,** Amy/Ann; 12 May 1771 (Orange Fee Book)

**TALIAFERRO**, John Henry POC age 24 s POB Orange POR Culpeper s/o Caroline TALIAFERRO miller & **WILLIS**, Laura POC age 21 s POB POR Orange d/o Kitty WILLIS 30 Sep 1880 POM Orange by John C. WILLIS (OMR)

**TALIAFERRO,** Lawrence & **CHEWNING,** Eliza d/o Robert CHEWNING who is also surety 24 May 1819 (OB)

**TALIAFERRO,** Lawrence H. & **TURNER,** Eliza F. surety Jaq. P. TALIAFERRO 9 May 1843 (OB) by J. EARNEST 15May 1843 (OM)

**TALIAFERRO**, Lewis POC age 37 w POB POR Orange s/o Lewis TALIAFERRO and Maria SMITH laborer & **PAGE**, Eliza POC age 24 s POB POR Orange d/o Gilbert PAGE and Ann WIGGLESWORTH 10 Oct 1880 POM Orange by E.R. PERRY (OMR)

**TALIAFERRO**, Nicholas & **TALIAFERRO,** Ann 3 Oct 1781 surety Francis TALIAFERRO permission from Ann TALIAFERRO (OB)

**TALIAFERRO**, Thomas Garland age 26 s express agent POB Hanover POR Orange s/o J.P. TALIAFERRO and Harriet TINSLEY & **BROWN**, Maggie B. age 20 s POB Berkley Co. VA POR Orange d/o James S. BROWN and Margaret E. BARKHART POM St. Thomas Church, Orange 16 Feb 1876 (OMR)

**TALIAFERRO**, William POC age 22 s farm laborer POB Madison POR Orange s/o Jackson TALIAFERRO and Mary STEWART & **JOHNSON**, Bettie POC age 19 s POB POR Orange d/o Jo. JOHNSON and Nancy HENDERSON POM Orange 7 Oct 1876 by Robert R. WOODSON (OMR)

**TALIAFERRO,** William Q. & **CHAPMAN,** Susan Ann d/o Richard M. CHAPMAN who is also surety 16 Jul 1839 (OB)

**TALIAFERRO**, Willis POC age 21 s POB POR Orange s/o William TALIAFERRO and Sallie GIBSON laborer & **GORDON**, Fanny POC age 23 s POB POR Orange d/o Jack & Eve GORDON 4 Dec 1868 POM Orange by John H. ROBERTSON (OMR)

**TALLEY**, James S. age 22 s POB Louisa Co POR Orange s/o William N. TALLEY and Mary F. BOND farmer & **WEBB**, Mary L. age 21 s POB POR Orange d/o Wyatt B. WEBB and _____ JOHNSON 22 Jan 1874 POM Orange (OMR)

**TALLEY**, Merriweather & **TERRILL**, Delia surety Alex A. BOSTON 22 Dec 1834 (OB)

**TALLEY**, Nathan M. age 23 s farmer POB POR Louisa s/o Anderson TALLEY and Maria NUCKOLLS & **TERRELL**, Mandee P. age 22 s POB POR Orange d/o William H. TERRELL and Martha A. BOSTON POM Orange 23 Nov 1876 by H. E. HATCHER (OMR)

**TALLEY**, Peyton G. s/o Nathan and Prudence W. TALLEY age 23 s farmer POB POR Louisa Co & **BOSTON**, Fannie A. d/o Alexander A. and Ann BOSTON age 22 s POB POR Orange; POM Orange 17 May 1854 (OMR) 1 May 1854 (OML)

**TANDY**, Henry Jr. & **ADAMS**, Betsy; 28 Nov 1796 (OM)

**TANDY**, Roger & **ADAMS**, Mary; 7 Dec 1795 surety Thomas ADAMS (OB)

**TANSIMON**, Lewis POC age 24 s POB POR Orange s/o Thomas TANSIMON and Millie MADISON gold miner & **THURSTON**, Sally POC age 23 s POB Spotsylvania POR Orange d/o Anthony THURSTON and Betsy WHITE 28 Mar 1874 POM Orange (OMR)

**TAPP**, Vincent & **DEMPSEY**, Katharine d/o Daniel DEMPSEY surety Pleasant DEMPSEY 28 Dec 1833 (OB)

**TATE**, John W. age 23 s farmer POB Louisa POR Orange s/o A.L. TATE and Catharine GRUBBS & **BUTLER**, Bettie J. age 19 s POB Louisa POR Orange d/o John J. BUTLER and Anna BUSICK POM Orange 22 Nov 1876 by Charles QUARLES (OMR)

**TATUM**, Alexander G. & **NEWMAN**, Martha d/o Thomas NEWMAN who is also surety 22 Feb 1836 (OB)

**TATUM**, Joseph H. s/o Isham and Mary TATUM age 25 s teacher POB Madison Co POR Orange & **WOOD**, Sarah Jane d/o Richard and Tabitha WOOD age 25 s POB POR Orange; POM Orange 23 Apr 1857 (OMR) 22 Apr 1857 (OML)

**TATUM**, Thomas & **EVANS**, Nancy; 26 Dec 1794 surety John BUCHANAN (OB)

**TAYLOE**, George E. s/o George P. TAYLOE and Mary LANGHOME age 25 s planter & Lt.Col. C.S.A. POB Roanoke Co. POR Marengo Co, Alabama & **WILLIS**, Delia S. d/o George WILLIS and Sallie J. SMITH age 20 s POB Pensacola, Florida POR Orange; POM Wood Park, Orange 9 Feb 1864 (OMR) (OML)

**TAYLOR**, Absolem & **SMITH**, Frances d/o Jeremiah and Elizabeth SMITH; 25 May 1796 (OM)

**TAYLOR**, Alexander POC age 27 s POB Albemarle Co POR Orange s/o Edmund CARTER and Ellen TAYLOR laborer & **RAYLAND**, Mary POC w POB Louisa Co. POR Orange d/o Thomas MORRIS and Sallie MORRIS 16 Apr 1870 POM Orange by Frank TIBBS (OMR)

**TAYLOR**, Alexander s/o Alexander TAYLOR and Nelly JOHNSON age 21 s laborer on farm POB POR Orange POC & **JACKSON**, Betsy d/o Jeny and Barbara JACKSON age 16 s POB POR Orange POC; POM Orange 21 Apr 1867 (OMR) 20 Apr 1867 (OML)

**TAYLOR,** Andrew J. POC age 27 s farm labourer POB POR Orange s/o Spencer TAYLOR and Sally _____ & **MORRIS,** Mary POC age 20 s POB POR Orange d/o Allen LONG and Fanny MORRIS POM Orange 14 May 1879 (OMR)

**TAYLOR**, Andrew POC age 22 s POB POR Orange s/o Albert TAYLOR and Emily _____ dray man & **HARRIS**, Annie POC age 19 s POB POR Orange d/o William HARRIS and Catharine _____ 6 Oct 1880 POM Orange (OMR)

**TAYLOR**, Benjamin W. s/o Thomas N. TAYLOR and Mary N. BROZWELL age 27 s farmer POB Montgomery Co, Alabama POR Tallaporsa Co, Alabama & **BELL**, Minerva C. d/o Henry C. BELL and Elizabeth A. KENDALL age 22 s POB POR Orange; POM Orange 21 Nov 1865 (OMR) 18 Nov 1865 (OML)

**TAYLOR,** Charles POC age 21 farm labourer POB POR Orange s/o Joseph TAYLOR and Eliza _____ & **OLVIN,** Lena age 18 s POB Louisa POR Orange POM Gordonsville 24 Oct 1877 (OMR)

**TAYLOR,** Charles POC age 25 S POB Hanover Co POR Orange s/o Edward TAYLOR and Eloise ALEXANDER farmer & **STROTHER**, Fanny POC age 25 S POB POR Orange d/o Mary _____ 17 Feb 1869 POM Orange by Philip JOHNSON (OMR)

**TAYLOR,** Charles POC age 33 w farm labourer POB Hanover POR Orange s/o Edward TAYLOR and Eloise ALEXANDER & **HORD,** Rebecca POC age 24 s POB POR Orange d/o James HORD and Elizabeth JONES POM Orange 19 Jul 1877 (OMR)

**TAYLOR,** Charles W. age 22 s hoop maker POB Louisa POR Orange s/o George W. TAYLOR and Mary E. GIBSON & **KEENON,** Margaret S. age 16 s POB POR Orange d/o Robert KEENON and Sarah TAMPLIN POM Orange 26 Oct 1879 (OMR)

**TAYLOR**, Conway POC age 45 w POB POR Orange s/o Washington STEWART and Libby _____ farm laborer & **TALIAFERRO,** Fanny POC age 43 w POB POR Orange d/o Ralph HALL and Betsy MORRIS 19 May 1872 POM Orange by F.L. GIPSON (OMR)

**TAYLOR**, Daniel POC age 24 s labourer POB POR Orange s/o Joseph TAYLOR and Eliza ROBINSON & **HUGHES,** Victoria POC age 18 s

239

POB Fluvanna POR Orange d/o James HUGHES and Sally JACKSON
POM Orange 23 Apr 1877 (OMR)

**TAYLOR**, Edmund & **THORNTON,** Nancy 16 Jul 1800 surety Willis
OVERTON (OB)

**TAYLOR**, Edmund POC age 25 s POB POR Orange s/o Frank TAYLOR
and Dinah _____ blacksmith & **CLAXTON**, Harriet POC age 24 s
POB POR Orange d/o Nancy _____ 31 Dec 1872 POM Orange by F.L.
GIPSON (OMR)

**TAYLOR**, Eli & **WARREN,** Rhody d/o Eliz WARREN surety Abraham
JARRELL 24 Oct 1825 (OB)

**TAYLOR**, Elijah & **WALKER,** Dilla; 26 Feb 1795 by George EVE (OM)

**TAYLOR**, Francis & **THOMPSON,** Elizabeth permission from William
THOMPSON and Joel THOMPSON William THOMPSON is surety 9
Feb 1788 (OB)

**TAYLOR**, Garland B. & **MARSHALL**, Angela F. d/o James
MARSHALL surety Richard H. ROBINSON 11 May 1831 (OB)

**TAYLOR**, George & **STANTON,** Ann d/o Charity STANTON surety
Francis TAYLOR by George EVE 1 Aug 1787 (OB) (OM)

**TAYLOR**, James & **ANDERSON,** Nanna w; 27 May 1799 surety Thomas
ROBERTS (OB)

**TAYLOR**, James & **STAUNTON,** Deliah; 20 Dec 1775 by banns both of
St. Thomas Parish (Deed Book 17)

**TAYLOR**, James H. age 22 s POB Madison POR Orange s/o George B.
TAYLOR and Catharine W. WEBSTER farmer & **KEETON**, Laura V.
age 20 s POB POR Orange d/o James P. KEETON and Betti GRUBBS
25 Feb 1880 POM Orange by J.W. MCCOWN (OMR)

**TAYLOR**, James Jr. & **MOORE,** Frances; 21 Dec 1795 surety Gabriel
BARBOUR (OB)

**TAYLOR**, James & **GRAVES,** Frances d/o Maria L. GRAVES surety
Layton G. GRAVES 1 Aug 1835 (OB) by David FISHER 14 Aug 1835
(OM)

**TAYLOR**, James & **HUNT,** Sary surety George BROOK 26 Dec 1789
(OB)

**TAYLOR**, James & **NORMAN,** July Ann permission from Cuthburt
NORMAN surety James JOLLETT 31 Jul 1834 (OB)

**TAYLOR**, James & **WOOD,** Sally surety Richard WOOD 10 Jul 1801
(OB) by Hamilton GOSS 12 Jul 1801 (OM)

**TAYLOR**, John & **JARRELL,** Mary d/o James JARRELL; 21 Dec 1782
surety John JARRELL (OB)

**TAYLOR**, John & **KAVENAUGH,** Elizabeth; 25 Sep 1782 surety John
PRICE (OB)

**TAYLOR**, John & **PEARSON,** Elizabeth 8 Oct 1795 by George EVE
(OM)

**TAYLOR**, Jonathan & **MCDANIEL**, Lizzy Ann 6 Dec 1804 by Hamilton GOSS (Misc Min Ret)

**TAYLOR**, Joseph POC age 23 s POB POR Orange s/o Wilson TAYLOR and Peachy WILSON r.r. hand & **FREEMAN**, Frances age 21 s POB Buckingham Co. POR Orange d/o George FREEMAN and Betty \_\_\_\_\_ 27 Oct 1869 POM Orange by Franklin TIBBS (OMR)

**TAYLOR**, Larkin & **HUME**, Elizabeth; 2 Jun 1808 by George BINGHAM (OM)

**TAYLOR**, Levi G. POC age 24 s POB Louisa CO POR Orange s/o Austin GORDON and Lucinda _____ laborer & **MOSBY**, Dolly A. POC age 20 s POB Louisa CO POR Orange d/o William MOSBY and Delia \_\_\_\_\_ 27 Jun 1869 POM Orange by Thomas R. HAWKINS (OMR)

**TAYLOR**, Patrick D. age 20 s POB Petersburg, POR Spotsylvania Co s/o George G. TAYLOR and Mary HATCHER farmer & **ESTES**, Lizzie K. age 17 POB Spotsylvania Co POR Orange d/o James W. ESTES and Mary E. PULLIAM 3 Dec 1873 POM Orange by Herndon FRAZER (OMR)

**TAYLOR**, Reuben Capt. & **MOORE**, Rebecca 11 Feb 1783 surety James TAYLOR Jr.(OB)

**TAYLOR**, Richard POC age 28 s railroad hand POB Essex POR Orange s/o Nelson TAYLOR and Betsy \_\_\_\_ & **GARDEN**, Lydia POC age 21 s POB Caroline POR Orange d/o Milly \_\_\_\_\_ POM Orange 19 Jun 1879 by F. TIBBS (OMR)

**TAYLOR**, Robert & **KING**, Fanny by Robert JONES 27 Oct 1809 (OM)

**TAYLOR**, Robert & **TAYLOR**, Mary Conway d/o Charles TAYLOR surety John F. CONWAY 31 Jul 1806 (OB)

**TAYLOR**, Stanton & **STANTON**, Elizabeth by George BINGHAM; 23 Jan 1800 (OM)

**TAYLOR**, Washington POC age 22 s POB POR Orange s/o Albert TAYLOR and Emily POWELL laborer & **WILLIS**, Martha POC age 18 s POB POR Orange d/o John WILLIS and Rhody TIBBS 7 Jan 1880 POM Gordonsville, Orange (OMR)

**TAYLOR**, William & **GIBSON**, Susannah d/o Merriman GIBSON 26 Nov 1795 by Nathaniel SANDERS (OM)

**TAYLOR**, William POC age 27 s POB POR Orange s/o Joseph TAYLOR and Eliza WEST laborer & **BROWN**, Margaret POC age 21 s POB Albemarle Co POR orange d/o James BROWN and Milly \_\_\_\_\_ 23 Dec 1873 POM Orange by Frank TIBBS (OMR)

**TAYLOR**, William & **BURNLEY**, Sarah G. surety John TAYLOR 28 Aug 1805 (OB)

**TAYLOR**, William & **WALKER**, Elizabeth surety Zachariah TAYLOR 30 Jan 1789 (OB)

**TAYLOR,** Wilson POC age 21 s POB Albemarle POR Greene laborer s/o Nelson TAYLOR and Sarah JOHNSON & **JACKSON,** Clara POC age 21 s POB Culpeper POR Orange d/o Frank JACKSON and Rebecca HILL POM Orange 11 Mar 1877 (OMR)

**TAYLOR,** Zachariah & **CHEW,** Alice d/o Thomas CHEW between 1771 & 1774 (Orange Fee Book)

**TAYLOR,** Zachary & **GERRELL,** Susanna surety Joel COFER 19 Dec 1792 (OB)

**TEASDALE,** Martin C. age 56 w merchant POB New Jersey POR St. Louis, MO s/o Thomas TEASEDALE and Hannah COSC & **BROCKMAN,** Bettie age 38 s POB POR Orange d/o Samuel BROCKMAN and Frances A. GRAVES POM Greenway, Orange 31 Oct 1878 by J.W. MCCOWN (OMR)

**TEEL,** Henry & **REED,** Dicey surety George HERNDON 26 Apr 1813 (OB) by J. GOSS 5 May 1813 (OM)

**TEEL,** John & **WAUGH,** Nancy d/o Elizabeth WAUGH surety Alexander WAUGH 22 Dec 1817 (OB) by J. GOSS 26 Dec 1817 (OM)

**TEMPLE,** John & **CANTERBERRY,** Mary Ann 29 Jan 1775 by banns both of St. Thomas Parish (Deed Book 17)

**TERRELL,** Edmund & **WILLIS,** Peggy 24 Nov 1760 (Orange Fee Book)

**TERRELL,** Henry C. & **SMITH,** Delpha 19 Nov 1809 surety Samuel TEEL (OB)

**TERRELL,** John & **MILLER,** Caty; 10 Sep 1794 (OM)

**TERRELL,** Oliver & **MALLORY,** Susanna s 5 Jan 1789 surety William MALLORY (OB)

**TERRELL,** William Jr. & **MORTON,** Jane 28 Jan 1793 surety John MORTON (OB)

**TERRILL,** Buckner & **WEBB,** Jane S. 10 Jun 1828 surety P.S. FRY (OB)

**TERRILL,** Edmund & **MORTON,** Ann T.; 19 Jan 1813 surety Elijah MORTON (OB) 21 Jan 1813 by Jeremiah CHANDLER (OM)

**TERRILL,** Edmund & **WILLIS,** Peggy; 24 Nov 1760 both of St. Thomas Parish (Orange Fee Book)

**TERRILL,** Edmund s/o Oliver TERRILL & **SMITH,** Susannah 13 Sep 1810 surety Uriel MALLORY (OB)

**TERRILL,** George F. & **MORTON,** Ann P. d/o John MORTON who is also surety 17 Dec 1844 (OB) by Henrdon FRAZER 19 Dec 1844 (OM)

**TERRILL,** James & **MIDDLEBROOK,** Susan; 1 Oct 1812 (OB)

**TERRILL,** James POC age 22 s labourer POB POR Orange s/o Robin TERRILL and Betsy GORDON & **EDWARDS,** Alice POC age 21 s POB POR Orange POM Orange 20 Feb 1878 by J.W. WALKER (OMR)

242

**TERRILL**, Jesse s/o Nelson Terrill & Patsy PAYNE age 22 s laborer POB Albemarle Co POR Orange POC & **WHITE**, Lucy Ann d/o Benjamin WHITE & Amy WILLIAMS age 18 s POB POR Orange POC; POM Orange 22 Oct 1867 (OMR) (OML)

**TERRILL**, John & **GRASTY**, Susan A. d/o G.S. GRASTY 18 Nov 1820 surety George MORTON (OB)

**TERRILL**, John & **GIBSON**, Elizabeth surety William MALLORY 8 Jun 1835 (OB)

**TERRILL**, John E. & **YOUNG**, Ann d/o John and Mary YOUNG surety James YOUNG 16 Dec 1835 (OB)

**TERRILL**, John G. age 30 s POB POR Orange s/o John TERRILL and Elizabeth GIBSON farmer & **WOOLFOLKS** Sarah M.F. age 31 w POB POR Orange d/o William C. MOORE Sr. and Matilda TAYLOR 15 Jan 1868 POM Orange by R.C. CAVE

**TERRILL**, John s/o Edmund and Susan TERRILL age 35 s mechanic POB POR Orange & **STUBBLEFIELD**, Sarah d/o Thomas and Mary STUBBLEFIELD age 23 s POB POR Orange; POM Orange 6 Nov 1855 (OMR)

**TERRILL**, Oliver T. age 33 s POB POR Orange s/o John TERRILL and Elizabeth E. GIBSON farmer & **FRAZER**, Lucy M. age 27 s POB POR Orange d/o William S. FRAZER and Ann BURRUSS 6 Dec 1870 POM Orange by Charles QUARLES (OM)

**TERRILL**, Peter POC age 27 farm laborer POB POR Orange s/o Robin TERRILL and Betsy JOHNSON & **COLEMAN**, Laura age 22 s POB Louisa POR Orange d/o Winston COLEMAN and Sarah _____ POM Orange 15 Jan 1876 (OMR)

**TERRILL**, Reuben & **GAINES**, Catey 3 Mar 1803 by Nathl. SANDERS (Misc Min Ret)

**TERRILL**, Reubin & **GAINES**, Catey d/o Robert GAINES 28 Feb 1803 surety Benjamin TINDER (OB) 3 Mar 1803 by Nathaniel SANDERS (OM)

**TERRILL**, Reubin & **MORTON**, Susanna 5 Sep 1805 surety William MORTON (OB) 11 Sep 1805 by Nathaniel SANDERS Baptist (OM)

**TERRILL**, Robert Jr. & **COLEMAN**, Elizabeth S. widow 2 Jan 1827 surety Pliney PATTEN (OB)

**TERRILL**, Robert s/o John TERRILL and Ann QUARLES or TOWLES & **MALLORY**, Ann d/o Uriel MALLORY and Hannah CAVE; 22 Feb 1797 surety Uriel MALLORY (OB)

**TERRILL**, Robin POC age 52 w labourer POB POR Orange s/o Peter COONS and Mary COLEMAN & **JONES**, Rachel POC age 44 w POB Madison POR Orange d/o Gibbon GRAY POM Orange 10 Nov 1877 (OMR)

**TERRILL,** Thomas P. age 28 s POB POR Orange s/o Oliver TERRILL and Susan PROCTOR farmer & **DANIEL,** Mary E. age 19 POB POR Orange d/o John M. DANIEL and Mildred JACKSON 30 Nov 1869 POM Orange by W. H. CAMPER (OMR)

**TERRILL,** William & **DANIEL,** Ann s 23 Nov 1780 both of St. Thomas Parish surety James TAYLOR (OB)

**TERRILL,** William H. & **BOSTON,** Ann 15 Nov 1836 ward of John P. BOSTON who is also surety (OB)

**TERRILL,** Zachariah & **WALKER,** Mary 14 May 1771 (Orange Fee Book)

**TERRILL,** Zachariah & **WALKER,** Millie; between 1771 & 1774 (OB)

**TERRY,** Emmanuel & **OAKS,** Nancy 26 Nov 1810 by George MORRIS (OM)

**TERRY,** John & **OAKS,** Lucy; 24 Dec 1795 surety James MASON (OB)

**TERRY,** Overton & **GARNETT,** Sarah; 29 Mar 1808 surety James MORTON (OB)

**THACKER,** Joseph B. age 24 s POB Hanover Co. POR Orange s/o Bej. THACKER and Lucy LOVING farmer & **SCHUYLER,** Eliza E. age 23 s POB POR Orange d/o William SCHUYLER and Mary SOVIELL 9 Jan 1868 POM Orange by Thos. R. HAWKINS (OMR)

**THACKER,** Jospeh T. age 21 s POB Louisa Co POR Orange s/o John THACKER and Elizabeth TATE r.r. hand & **FAULCONER,** Laura B. age 14 s POB Culpeper Co POR Orange d/o Hugh M.B. FAULCONER and Laura N. PILCHER 19 Dec 1871 POM Orange by Thomas R. HAWKINS (OMR)

**THOMAS,** Barbour & **TAYLOR,** Mary; 22 Mar 1787 (OM)

**THOMAS,** Fountain s/o Fountain & Ann THOMAS age 20 s farmer POB POR Orange & **WOOD,** Lucinda d/o James & Rebecca WOOD age 35 s POB Albemarle Co POR Orange; POM Orange 28 Apr 1856 (OMR) (OML)

**THOMAS,** Henry & **WOOD,** Mary 5 Sep 1817 surety Edward THOMAS (OB)

**THOMAS,** James H. age 21 s POB POR Orange d/o David W. THOMAS and Fanny WOOD farmer & **LEAKE,** Alwilda age 16 POB Albemarle Co POR Orange d/o Austin LEAKE and Amanda MAHANES 16 Jan 1873 POM Orange by J.M. MCCOWEN (OMR)

**THOMAS,** Joseph Capt. & **BEAZLEY,** Betsy d/o Augustine BEAZLEY 25 Feb 1802 surety Mark HORNSEY (OB)

**THOMAS,** Nelson & **HILL,** Susan d/o Richard HILL who is also surety 25 Aug 1826 (OB)

**THOMAS,** Reuben & **SPENCER,** Ann d/o Joseph SPENCER 24 Dec 1787 surety James BROCKMAN (OB)

**THOMAS,** Richard & **TAYLOR,** Milley 24 Aug 1753 (Orange Fee Book)

**THOMAS,** Robert & **BRADFORD,** Sarah Jemima d/o Alexander BRADFORD 29 Oct 1831 surety Joseph BRADFORD (OB)

**THOMAS,** Robert & **MOORE,** Anne; 9 Apr 1757 both of St. Thomas Parish (Orange Fee Book)

**THOMAS,** Robert & **SMITH,** Polly d/o Joseph SMITH; 7 Aug 1793 surety William SMITH (OB)

**THOMAS,** Rowland & **THURSTON,** Jane; 5 Apr 1757 both of St. Thomas Parish (Orange Fee Book)

**THOMAS,** William & **WOOLFOLK,** Elizabeth d/o Joseph WOOLFOLK; 7 Apr 1778 surety Robert THOMAS (OB)

**THOMASSON,** Thomas C. & **SMITH,** Catharine d/o Gaspar SMITH who is also surety 10 Feb 1831 (OB)

**THOMPSON,** Clifton L. & **MARSHALL,** P.E. d/o Coleman MARSHALL who is also surety 3 Nov 1845 (OB)

**THOMPSON,** David & **BROCKMAN,** Elizabeth d/o Samuel BROCKMAN Jr.; 19 Aug 1784 surety James BROCKMAN (OB)

**THOMPSON,** David & **ELLIS,** Maria ward of John ELLIS who is also surety 22 May 1820 (OB)

**THOMPSON,** Henry POC age 70 w POB Fauquier POR Orange s/o Oscar THOMPSON and Kitty _____ wood cutter & **CARTER,** Lydia POC age 40 s POB POR Orange 29 Aug 1880 POM Orange (OMR)

**THOMPSON,** James POC age 21 s POB POR Orange s/o Hannah THOMPSON laborer & **COLEMAN,** Laura POC age 19 POB POR Orange d/o Hampton COLEMAN and Susan MCINTOSH 23 Feb 1873 POM Orange by Thomas R. HAWKINS (OMR)

**THOMPSON,** Joel & **THOMPSON,** Sarah d/o Elizabeth THOMPSON; 8 Jan 1798 surety Walker RAINES (OB)

**THOMPSON,** John & **PIERCE,** Julia 18 Sep 1809 surety Cypress HENSLEY (OB) 24 Sep 1809 by Jacob WATTS (OM)

**THOMPSON,** John G. age 31 s POB POR Orange s/o Reuben L. THOMPSON and Marina QUISENBERRY mechanic & **BRIDWELL,** Ella G. age 22 POB Culpeper POR Orange d/o William H. BRIDWELL and Amanda F. HAWLEY 29 Nov 1870 POM Orange by H.E. HATCHER (OM)

**THOMPSON,** John H. age 23 s blacksmith POB POR Madison s/o William H. THOMPSON and Sarah E. TATUM & **POINDEXTER,** Sallie Ann age 22 s POB Greene POR Orange d/o Joseph D. POINDEXTER and Clarissa J. MITCHELL POM Orange 20 Dec 1877 (OMR)

**THOMPSON,** John P. s/o Philip THOMPSON and Sarah C. MOSELEY age 33 s lawyer POB POR Owensboro, Kentucky & **CAVE,** Maria C. d/o William P. and Isabella CAVE age 23 s POB New York City POR Orange; POM Montebello, Orange 19 Dec 1865 (OMR) (OML)

**THOMPSON**, Joseph & **MOUBRAY**, Clarissa 11 Dec 1838 surety Rice DARNOLD (OB) 15 Dec 1838 by E.G. SHIP (OM)

**THOMPSON**, Rawsaw M. s/o Samuel S. THOMPSON and Lucy A.M. SNELL age 31 s carpenter POB Rutherford Co, Tennessee POR Orange & **BLEDSOE**, Roberta E. d/o S.W. BLEDSOE and Jane WHITE age 24 s POB Madison Co POR Orange; POM Orange 10 Oct 1867 (OMR) 7 Oct 1867 (OML)

**THOMPSON**, Reuben & **QUISENBERRY**, Marina S. 22 Dec 1828 surety Charles B. QUISENBERRY (OB)

**THOMPSON**, Reuben L . s/o Samuel THOMPSON and Sally LINDSAY age 62 w farmer POB POR Orange & **SORRELL**, Ann d/o Edmund DUNAWAY and Sally KNIGHT age 25 w POB POR Orange; POM Orange 30 Apr 1865 (OMR) 29 Apr 1865 (OML)

**THOMPSON**, Samuel & **LINDSAY**, Salley 29 Oct 1801 surety Reubin LINDSAY (OB)

**THOMPSON**, Samuel s/o William THOMPSON & **SNELL**, Lucy Ann Mitchell d/o Joseph SNELL who is also surety 25 Apr 1831 (OB) 26 Apr 1831 by J. GOSS (OM)

**THOMPSON**, Thomas & **ROBINSON**, Frances d/o Francis ROBINSON; 7 Nov 1809 surety Reubin TERRILL (OB) (Nov 1809 by Jeremiah CHANDLER (OM)

**THOMPSON**, William & **BREEDING**, Acquilia; 13 Apr 1785 surety John WARREN (OB)

**THOMPSON**, William & **SINKER**, Catey 20 Nov 1805 surety Brooks SINKER (OB)

**THOMPSON**, William L. & **GRASTY**, Susan L. 8 Nov 1841 surety John H. GRASTY (OB) 9 Nov 1841 by Joseph A. MANSFIELD (OM)

**THOMPSON**, William Theodocius & **MCNEAL**, Jane 30 Jun 1795 by Nathaniel SANDERS (OM)

**THOMSON**, John & **ELLIS**, Sally d/o Thomas ELLIS 10 Nov 1812 surety James H. ELLIS (OB)

**THOMSON**, Rhodes & **VIVION**, Sally d/o John VIVION surety Nathaniel MILLS both of St. Thomas Parish 13 Oct 1778 (Deed Book 17)

**THOMSON**, Rodes & **VIVION**, Sally d/o John VIVION 13 Oct 1778 surety Nathaniel MILLS (OB)

**THOMSON**, William Jr. s/o William THOMSON & **ELLIS**, Rebecca N. d/o Thomas ELLIS 18 Nov 1805 surety John W. SALE (OB)

**THORN**, Silas POC age 35 s labourer POB Rappahannock POR Orange s/o John THORN and Dicey THORN & **WATSON**, Annie age 26 s POB POR Orange POM Orange 25 Dec 1877 (OMR)

**THORNTON,** Anthony & **TWYMAN,** Nancy d/o Samuel TWYMAN surety William BUCKNER 26 Oct 1816 (OB) by Jacob WATSS 27 Oct 1816 (OM)

**THORNTON,** Caleb & **FORD,** Patsy surety James SLEET 20 Dec 1791 (OB) by Nathaniel SANDERS 22 Dec 1791 (OM)

**THORNTON,** Charles & **OGG,** Martha d/o Alexander OGG surety John OGG 22 Dec 1807 by George BINGHAM (OB) (OM)

**THORNTON,** Daniel M.F. & **TALIAFERRO,** Susan F. d/o Hay TALIAFERRO surety Robert A. MAYO 7 Sep 1825 (OB) 8 Sep 1825 by James GARNETT (OM)

**THORNTON,** Daniel & **WRIGHT,** Malinda d/o William WRIGHT surety John SLEET 25 Dec 1826 (OB)

**THORNTON,** George & **WEBB,** Nancy; 31 Dec 1800 surety Reuben WEBB (OB)

**THORNTON,** George s/o Thomas S. THORNTON & **SAMUEL,** Sarah E. surety Thomas J. HUMPHRIES by E.G. SHIP 10 Dec 1839 (OB) (OM)

**THORNTON,** Henry age 30 s POB POR Orange s/o Solomon THORNTON and Nellie WILLIS farm laborer & **MCDANIEL,** Georgianna age 20 s POB POR Orange Samuel MCDANIEL 28 Dec 1869 POM Orange by T.M. CARSON (OMR)

**THORNTON,** James & **JOHNSON,** Eliza A. ward of Henry CLARKE who is also surety 12 Dec 1825 (OB)

**THORNTON,** Jesse & **BOHEN,** Ann d/o Benjamin and Ann BOHEN both of St. Thomas Parish 22 Jul 1784 (OB)

**THORNTON,** John & **HANEY,** Elizabeth d/o Benjamin HANEY who is also surety 24 Dec 1832 (OB)

**THORNTON,** Luke & **SLEET,** Sarah; 24 Jun 1799 surety James SLEET (OB)

**THORNTON,** Peter & **MILLER,** Mary d/o Robert MILLER surety Thomas MILLER 18 Jan 1802 (OB)

**THORNTON,** Thomas age 21 s POB POR Orange s/o Jonathan WALKER and Frances THORNTON laborer & **POWELL,** Martha age 21 s POB POR Orange d/o William POWELL and Malvina _____ 6 Sep 1870 POM Orange by John S. HANSBOROUGH (OMR)

**THORNTON,** Thomas POC age 21 s POB POR Orange s/o Thomas THORNTON, and Martha WHITE laborer & **TYLER,** Charlotte age 20 s d/o Jane TYLER 14 Jan 1872 POM Orange by F.L. GIPSON (OMR)

**THORNTON,** Thomas & **WRIGHT,** Elizabeth d/o William WRIGHT who is also surety 26 Dec 1808 (OB)

**THRIFT,** George N. & **EARLY,** Elisa Jane d/o James EARLY who is also surety 10 Feb 1838 (OB)

**THRIFT**, Robert & **BURTON**, Margaret surety Braxton OZBORNE 1 Mar 1815 (OB)

**THURMAN**, Benjamin F. & **ROUTT**, Martha E.; POM Orange 28 Sep 1852 (OMR) 6 Sep 1852 (OML)

**THURMAN**, Nathan & **LOWRY**, Tabitha; 4 Sep 1796 by George BINGHAM (OM)

**THURSTON**, James Herrn POC age 20 s laborer POB POR Orange s/o Herrn THURSTON and Jane LEWIS & **WHITE**, Clara POC age 21 s POB POR Orange d/o Edmond WHITE and Nelly FRY POM Orange 28 May 1876 (OMR)

**THURSTON**, Samuel POC age 21 s labourer POB POR Orange s/o Dick THURSTON and Bettie LUCAS & **MORRIS**, Mary POC age 22 s POB POR Orange d/o Gabriel and Frances MORRIS POM Orange 27 Dec 1879 (OMR)

**THURSTON**, Thornton POC age 23 s laborer POB POR Orange s/o Richard THURSTON and Betsy LUCAS & **ELLIS**, Sarah POC age 22 w POB POR Orange d/o Tom ELLIS and Martha JACKSON POM Orange 22 Oct 1876 by E. R. PERRY (OMR)

**THURSTON**, William Plumer & **TALIAFERRO**, Lucy Mary both of St. Thomas Parish 11 Jun 1770 (Deed Book 17)

**TIBBS**, George W. POC age 22 s POB POR Orange s/o George TIBBS and Frances WILLIAMS laborer & **WASHINGTON**, Eliza A. age 22 s POB POM Orange d/o Horace WASHINGTON and Martha JOHNSON 8 Dec 1868 POM Orange by Philip JOHNSON (OMR)

**TIMBERLAKE**, James L. s/o George TIMBERLAKE and Elizabeth A. TURNER age 24 s merchant POB Louisa Co POR Richmond, VA & **ESTES**, Juliett M. d/o James ESTES and Sarah MINOR age 22 s POB POR Orange; POM Orange 9 Nov 1865 (OMR) 31 Oct 1865 (OML)

**TIMBERLAKE**, Philip & **ESTES**, Mildred d/o Thomas ESTES who is also surety 17 Dec 1849 (OB)

**TINDAR**, James & **SHADRACK**, Molly d/o Jobe SHADRACK surety John SHADRACK 29 Jan 1785 (OB) 3 Feb 1785 by Nathaniel SANDERS (OM)

**TINDER**, Amos E. s/o George W. TINDER & Sarah QUISENBERRY age 24 s farmer POB POR Orange & **CANADAY**, Caroline F. d/o James CANADAY & Ann TINDER age 22 s POB POR Orange; POM Orange 28 Jan 1866 (OMR) 23 Jan 1866 (OML)

**TINDER**, Anthony Jr. s/o Anthony TINDER Sr. who is also surety and ward of Huldah & **FOSTER**, Huldah 28 Feb 1831 (OB)

**TINDER**, Anthony & **ROBINSON**, Lucy d/o John ROBINSON surety William ROBINSON 18 Dec 1797 (OB)

**TINDER**, Arthur R. & **BLEDSOE**, Hannah M. surety Thomas GRAVES 11 Nov 1848 (OB)

**TINDER**, Benjamin & **TERRILL**, Nancy 16 Dec 1802 by Nathl. SANDERS (Misc Min Ret)

**TINDER**, Edgar A. s/o John A. TINDER and Frances SHADRACK age 22 s farmer POR POB Orange & **BROOKING**, Cassandra B. d/o Charles R. BROOKING and Susan M. SANDERS age 21 s POB POR Orange; POM Orange 26 Oct 1865 (OMR) 23 Oct 1865 (OML)

**TINDER**, George W. & **QUISENBERRY**, Sarah d/o George QUISENBERRY who is also surety 28 Oct 1833 (OB) by Joseph A. MANSFIELD 6 Nov 1833 (OM)

**TINDER**, George T. & **HERNDON**, Susan d/o John Herndon Jr. POM Orange 20 Jan 1853 (OMR) 18 Jan 1853 (OML)

**TINDER**, James permission from Anthony TINDER POR Culpeper Co. & **SHADRACK**, Elizabeth d/o Sarah SHADRACK 7 Jan 1820 (OB) by J.C. GORDON 9 Jan 1820 (OM)

**TINDER**, James R. & **SAUNDERS**, Emily; 12 Oct 1852 (OML)

**TINDER**, James R. s/o James R. TINDER Sr. & **TINDER**, Sarah M.; 22 Dec 1851 (OMR) (OML)

**TINDER**, Jesse & **ABELL**, Aleaper; 11 Dec 1786 surety Richard ABELL (OB)

**TINDER**, John & **SHADRACK**, Frances M. surety Robert SANDERS 25 Mar 1823 (OB)

**TINDER**, John F. age 21 s farmer POB Culpeper POR Orange s/o Thomas R. TINDER and Elizabeth TINDER & **WELLS**, Mauda A. age 17 s POB POR Orange d/o David WELLS and Lucie A. TINDER POM Orange 30 Jul 1876 by Sanders MASON (OMR)

**TINDER**, John S. age 23 s POB POR Orange s/o John T. TINDER and Mary A. JACOBS farmer & **COOK**, Ella H. age 18 s POB POR Orange d/o Noah COOK and Hettie R. ROACH 30 Jan 1872 POM Orange by John C. WILLIS (OMR)

**TINDER**, John T. & **JACOBS**, Margaret A. d/o Benjamin JACOBS surety James R. TINDER 3 Mar 1846 (OB)

**TINDER**, Richard & **QUISENBERRY**, Nancy ward of Richard TINDER surety George W. TINDER 28 Sep 1840 (OB)

**TINDER**, Robinson C. & **MASON**, Ann G. surety George E. MORTON 16 Dec 1843 (OB) by Herndon FRAZER 19 Dec 1843 (OM)

**TINDER**, Talmon D. age 20 s farmer POB POR Orange s/o James TINDER and Emily SANDERS & **DAVIS**, Mary E. age 19 s POB POR Orange d/o William J. DAVIS and Sally A. REYNOLDS POM Orange 12 Dec 1878 by Melzi S. CHANCELLOR (OMR)

**TINDER**, Thomas & **MASON**, Nancy surety Sanders MASON 24 Dec 1824 (OB)

**TINDER**, Thomas R. & **TINDER**, Elizabeth J. d/o Thomas TINDER; POM Orange 16 Mar 1852 (OMR) 13 Mar 1852 (OML)

**TINDER**, Thomas T. age 26 s farmer POB POR Orange s/o Robinson C. TINDER and Ann G. MASON & **FAULCONER**, Alice M. age 27 s POB POR Orange d/o William FAULCONER and Catharine A. CHEWNING POM Orange 20 Dec 1876 (OMR)

**TINDER**, William M. (aka Waller M.) & **LANCASTER**, Sarah E. d/o Sarah LANCASTER; 21 Feb 1852 (OML)

**TINDER**, Zabdal B. age 22 s farmer POB POR Orange s/o James TINDER and Emily SANDERS & **DAVIS**, Lucy T. age 23 s POB POR Orange d/o William J. DAVIS and Sally A. REYNOLDS POM Orange 12 Dec 1878 by Melzi S. CHANCELLOR (OMR)

**TINSLEY**, Edward ward of Thomas ROBINSON & **ROACH**, Lucy Ann d/o Mary ROACH surety William ROACH 4 Jan 18334 (OB)

**TINSLEY**, James W. age 31 s POB POR Orange s/o Edward TINSLEY and Lucy Ann ROACH wheelwright & **APPERSON**, Mary E. age 24 s POB POR Orange d/o Alfred APPERSON and Malinda JONES 24 Mar 1870 POM Orange by John C. WILLIS (OMR)

**TISDALE**, Lemuel age about 28 laborer POR Louisa Co & **ROBERSON**, Elizabeth age about 22 POR Orange; POM Orange 22 Dec 1853 (OMR)

**TODD**, William & **WINSLOW**, Catharine P. surety Joseph CHEW 11 Apr 1804 (OB)

**TODD**, William H. & **MITCHELL**, Jane M.N. d/o Andrew MITCHELL surety William S. MITCHELL 17 Nov 1829 (OB)

**TOLES**, Nelson POC age 21 s POB POR Orange s/o Benjamin TOLES and Matilda WILLIAMS laborer on farm & **TIBBS**, Sarah POC age 21 s POB POR Orange d/o Frank TIBBS 1 Jan 1868 POM Orange by Philip JOHNSON (OMR)

**TOMLINSON**, George & **WHITE**, Elizabeth d/o Henry WHITE; 24 Nov 1785 surety David CAVE (OB)

**TOMLINSON**, John & **WHITE**, Mildred; 20 Jun 1780 both of St. Thomas Parish (OB)

**TOMPKINS**, James M. s/o William TOMPKINS POR Fluvanna & **RUCKER**, Kitty d/o Robert RUCKER surety Robert CAVE 25 Oct 1827 (OB)

**TOWLES**, Albert POC age 23 s saw miller POB POR Orange s/o Nelson TOWLES and Jane SMITH & **JACKSON**, Lucy POC age 17 s POB POR Orange d/o Martha GREEN POM Orange 27 Jul 1879 by L.A. CUTLER (OMR)

**TOWLES**, Henry POC age 21 s labourer POB POR Orange s/o Nelson TOWLES and Jane SMITH & **BARKS**, Sarah A. POC age 18 s POB POR Orange d/o James BARKS and Nancy ROBERTSON POM Mt. Pleasant Church, Orange 27 Apr 1879 by C.T. JOHNSON (OMR)

**TOWLES**, Richard POC age 23 s POB POR Orange s/o Benjamin TOWLES and Matilda WILLIAMS laborer & **LONG**, Jane POC age 21 s POB POR Orange d/o Austin LONG and Evelina PORTER 8 Nov 1873 POM Orange by F.L. GIPSON (OMR)

**TOWNS**, Pannill POC age 24 s merchant POB POR Orange s/o Isreal TOWNS and Charlotte WILLIS & **JONES**, Ida age 22 s POB POR Orange d/o Sarah JONES POM Orange 3 Jan 1878 by Robert R. WOODSON (OMR)

**TOWNS**, William POC age 26 s farmer POB POR Orange s/o Absalom TOWNS and Betty POGE & **LUCAS**, Harriet POC age 22 s POB POR Orange d/o Eliza LUCAS POM Orange 6 Dec 1877 (OMR)

**TREVILIAN**, Charles G. & **COLLINS**, Elizabeth L. d/o Lewis D. COLLINS who is also surety 24 Jul 1837 (OB)

**TRICE** Monroe s/o Joe and Ann TRICE age 23 s farm laborer POB Louisa Co POR Orange POC & **JACKSON**, Ann d/o Jacob and Cassandra JACKSON age 28 s POB Louisa Co POR Orange POC; POM Orange 14 Nov 1867 (OMR) (OML)

**TRICE**, Jesse & **ARNETT**, Liddia d/o William ARNETT who is also surety 22 Nov 1813 (OB)

**TRIPLETT**, Philip POC age 25 s POB POR Orange s/o Dick TRIPLETT and Betsey ___ farm laborer & **JONES**, Mary Lee POC age 18 s POB Madison Co POR Orange d/o Neville PINKARD and Rachel GRAHAM 26 Dec 1873 POM Orange by Frank TIBBS (OMR)

**TRIPLETT**, Robert C. s/o William H. TRIPLETT and Ellen HANSBROUGH age 33 w mechanic POB POR Culpeper Co & **TOWLES**, Mary C. d/o Thomas TOWLES and Catharine STUBBLEFIELD age 40 (?) s POB Spotsylvania POR Orange; POM St. Thomas Church Orange C.H. 28 Jul 1864 (OMR) (OML)

**TROWER**, Solomon & **SMITH**, Nancy d/o John SMITH who is also surety 23 Sep 1805 (OB)

**TRUE**, Thomas & **MURPHY**, Susanna surety Nathaniel MIDDLEBROOK 6 Apr 1802 (OB)

**TUCKER**, Jacob POC age 29 s farm labourer POB Spotsylvania POR Orange s/o George TUCKER and Betsy MARSHALL & **LINDSAY**, Charlotte POC age 26 s POB POR Orange d/o A. LINDSAY and Nancy PRESLEY POM Orange 22 Jul 1877 (OMR)

**TUCKER**, Thornton & **BIGGERS**, Betsy d/o Mason BIGGERS surety Hamlet SANFORD 29 Dec 1808 (OB) by Robert JONES 30 Dec 1808 (OM)

**TUEL**, Isaac s/o Thomas and Mary TUEL age 24 s miller POB Orange POR Madison Co & **FERNEYHOUGH**, Sarah J. d/o John and Elizabeth FERNEYHOUGH age 21 s POB POR Orange; POM Orange 3 Mar 1857 (OMR) 2 Mar 1857 (OML)

**TUEL,** Socrates s/o Thomas TUEL & Mary A. LEE (or SEE)age 28 s carpenter POB POR Orange & **HUGHES,** Sarah F. age 25 s POB POR Orange; POM Orange 17 May 1866 (OMR) (OML)

**TUELL,** Thomas J. & **LEE,** Mary Ann surety Thomas WOOD 25 Dec 1830 (OB)

**TULLOCH,** William & **WHITELAW,** Nancy d/o Thomas WHITELAW surety Nicholas WHITELAW by William DOUGLASS 18 Feb 1806 (OB) (OM)

**TULLUS,** Joseph D. s/o Rhodam and Elizabeth TULLUS age 33 s merchant/farmer POB POR Fauquier Co & **CLARK,** Mary Jane d/o William D. and Jane M. CLARK age 25 s POB POR Orange; POM Orange 3 Mar 1857 (OMR) 2 Mar 1857 (OML)

**TURNELY,** Francis & **WATTS,** Susannah 2 Feb 1791 surety Robert ALCOCK (OB)

**TURNER,** Elisha & **GOODALL,** Polly surety Parke GOODALL 3 Feb 1824 (OB)

**TURNER,** Anderson POC age 22 s farm labourer POB POR Orange s/o Robert TURNER and Mary BANKS & **GALLERY,** Nannie POC age 18 POB POR Orange d/o George GALLERY and Sally BURK POM Orange 16 Feb 1878 by W.J. BARNETT (OMR)

**TURNER,** Elijah & **SEAL,** Mary Newman FAULCONER surety 14 Jan 1811 (OB)

**TURNER,** Ezekiel & **CHISSAM,** Sally d/o Thomas CHISSAM surety Joseph CROXTON 17 Nov 1802 (OB)

**TURNER,** Fleming & **CLARK,** Jane d/o John CLARK surety Thomas WELLS Jr. by George BINGHAM 12 Apr 1808 (OB) (OM)

**TURNER,** George s/o Nelson TURNER and Mary GREEN age 21 s working at saw mill POB POR Orange POC & **LINDSAY,** Mildred d/o Lewis LINDSAY and Ellen DANIEL age 19 s POB POR Orange POC; POM Orange 26 Dec 1867 (OMR) 23 Dec 1867 (OML)

**TURNER,** J. Waller & **RHOADES,** Eliza; 22 Dec 1856 (OML)

**TURNER,** James & **LOYD,** Sarah d/o William LOYD who is also surety 2 Nov 1803 (OB)

**TURNER,** James H. s/o Catlett TURNER & **VASS,** Emily 10 Apr 1845 surety Robert P. CAVE by Herndon FRAZER (OB) (OM)

**TURNER,** John & **BROWN,** Elizabeth 3 Oct 1801 surety James WHITE (OB)

**TURNER,** John & **FITZGARRELL,** Sarah 29 Jul 1790 surety _____ FITZGARRELL (this bond is torn) (OB)

**TURNER,** Nelson POC age 25 s farm labourer POB POR Orange s/o Nelson TURNER and Sally THORNTON & **ELLIS,** Mollie POC age 18 s POB POR Orange d/o Hannah ELLIS POM Orange 14 Jul 1877 (OMR)

**TURNER**, Nelson s/o Nelson TURNER and Mary GREEN age 22 s working at sawmill POB POR Orange POC & **LINDSAY**, Charlotte d/o Lewis LINDSAY and Ellen DANIEL age 18 s POB POR Orange POC; POM Orange 26 Dec 1867 (OMR) 23 Dec 1867 (OML)

**TURNER**, Thomas & **BROWN**, Catey; 31 Jan 1787 surety James BROWN (OB)

**TURNLEY**, Edwin s/o Edmund TURNLEY & **TANDY**, Emma d/o Henry TANDY who is also surety 30 Jul 1827 (OB)

**TURNLEY**, John & **POUND**, Patsy w 23 Dec 1811 surety Nicholas FAULCONER (OB) by Robert JONES 25 Dec 1811 (OM)

**TWENTYMAN**, Bononi & **NUTTY**, Elizabeth w surety James TAYLOR 28 Jan 1790 (OB)

**TWYMAN**, Alfred & **CARPENTER**, Louisa d/o P. CARPENTER 30 Mar 1829 surety John F. CARPENTER (OB)

**TWYMAN**, Anthony & **DAVIS**, Sarah d/o Isaac DAVIS who is also surety by Jacob WATTS 16 Feb 1807 (OB) (OM)

**TWYMAN**, John & **WAYT**, Peggy d/o William WAYT surety Reuben TWYMAN by Jacob WATTS 29 Jul 1809 (OB) (OM)

**TWYMAN**, Jonathan & **RUCKER**, Lucy permission from William RUCKER surety John SHEARMAN 17 Jan 1824 (OB)

**TWYMAN**, Mordecai & **DUKE**, Ellen B. surety Daniel WHITE 21 Oct 1833 (OB)

**TWYMAN**, Paschal & **MELONE**, Elizabeth surety Ely MELONE 3 Dec 1822 (OB)

**TWYMAN**, Reuben & **COWHERD**, Drucilla 2 Jun 1802 by William CALHOON (Misc Min Ret)

**TWYMAN**, Reuben POC age 22 s POB POR Orange s/o Smith TWYMAN and Amelia LINDSAY laborer & **BANKS**, Matilda POC age 15 s POB POR Orange d/o Sampson BANKS and Caroline GREEN 17 Apr 1880 POM Orange by W.H. CAMPER (OMR)

**TWYMAN**, Scott POC age 23 s rail road hand POB POR Greene Co. s/o Robert TWYMAN and Nelly HARRIS & **TERRILL**, Emma POC age 20 s POB POR Orange d/o Robin TERRILL and Betty JOHNSON 1 Jan 1876 POM Orange by E.R. PERRY (OMR)

**TWYMAN**, Thornel & **COLEMAN**, Sarah K. d/o Thomas COLEMAN surety James H. COLEMAN 18 Sep 1820 (OB) by John A. BILLINGSLEY 20 Sep 1820 (OM)

**TWYMAN**, Travis J. age 23 s farmer POB POR Madison s/o Isaac S. TWYMAN and Eliza HILL & **WILLIS**, Emma J. age 24 s POB POR Orange d/o James S. WILLIS and Elizabeth GORDON POM Orange 26 Dec 1876 (OMR)

**TYLER,** James E. age 26 s tinner POB Amherst POR Orange s/o William
H. TYLER and Sarah J. THOMAS & **HALEY,** Mollie W. age 23 s
POB POR Orange d/o William HALEY and Priscilla STEPHENS
POM Orange 7 Mar 1877 (OMR)

**TYLER,** James s/o Byrd TYLER and Lucy BRANDEN age 31 w plasterer
POB Henrico Co. POR Richmond POC & **MADISON,** Mary age 21 s
POB POR Orange POC; POM Orange 17 Apr 1866 (OMR) 16 Apr
1866 (OML)

**TYLER,** John B. age 28 s POB N.Y. State POR Orange s/o John TYLER
and Rebecca WILLIAMS engineer & **SKINNER,** Mary B. age 22 s
POB POR Orange d/o M.B. SKINNER (mother) 26 Oct 1873 POM
Orange by Thomas R. HAWKINS (OMR)

**TYLER,** Absalom & **SMITH,** Frances d/o Jeremiah and Elizabeth SMITH
surety John SMITH 25 May 1796 (OB)

**TYLER,** Richard & **SCOTT,** _____ (illegible) surety John SCOTT 29
Oct 1817 (OB)

**TYLER,** Washington POC age 43 w POB Albemarle Co POR Orange s/o
Major TYLER and Martha ____ blacksmith & **CAVE,** Nelly POC age
26 w POB POR Orange d/o Abraham WHITE & Mary _____ 21 Feb
1869 POM Orange by James A. MANSFIELD (OMR)

**TYLER,** William & **HERNDON,** Mary Ann 21 Jan 1803 POM Orange by
Robert JONES (Misc Min Ret)

**TYREE,** John & **LINDSAY,** Nancy d/o Larkin and Sarah LINDSAY
surety Robert LINDSAY 24 Dec 1819 (OB)

**UNDERWOOD,** Gideon & **DOHONEY,** Mary surety Rhodes
DOHONEY 4 Jan 1791 (OB)

**UNDERWOOD,** Jacoons & **HAMS,** Milly ward of Jacoons
UNDERWOOD surety Littleton ESTES 6 Aug 1820 (OB)

**VASS,** Henry S. age 31 s POB POR Orange s/o Walker VASS and Frances
LEE farmer & **TALLEY,** Mary F. age 32 w POB Louisa Co POR
Orange d/o Joseph BOND and Mildred WHITLOCK 18 Oct 1868
POM Orange by M.S. CHANCELLOR (OMR)

**VASS,** Vincent & Elizabeth **MANNING** w; 24 Aug 1783 surety Richard
DICKINSON both of St. Thomas Parish (OB)

**VASS,** Walker & **LEE,** Frances d/o William LEE 11 Nov 1815 surety
Thomas VASS (OB) by John A. BILLINGSLEY 12 Nov 1815 (OM)

**VAUGHAN,** Bluford Edward age 21 s POB Greene Co POR Orange s/o
Cornelius VAUGHAN and Louisa DUFF farmer & **DEWESE,** Mollie
E. age 24 w POB Rockingham Co POR Orange d/o Arnold DULANEY
and ___ BURK 24 Dec 1873 POM Orange by Thomas R. HAWKINS
(OMR)

**VAUGHAN,** Charles & **CLAYTOR,** Elizabeth 28 Jun 1819 surety John
MALLORY (OB) 30 Jun 1819 by J.C. GORDON (OM)

**VAUGHAN**, Cornelius G. s/o Paschal VAUGHAN and Henrietta DOWELL age 25 s farmer POB Madison Co POR Orange & **YOWELL**, Cornelia Alpha d/o Abraham YOWELL and Susan UTZ age 20 s POB Madison Co POR Orange; POM Orange 29 Mar 1866 (OMR) (OML)

**VAUGHAN**, Edwin age 24 farmer POR Hanover Co & **TURNER**, Lucretia M. d/o William (dec) & Mary (dec) TURNER; POM Louisa Co 7 Feb 1854 (OMR)

**VAUGHAN**, Joseph & **DEANE**, Eliza 26 Dec 1817 surety Archibald BARCUS (OB) 28 Dec 1817 by J. GOSS (OM)

**VAUGHAN**, Joseph & **TURNER**, Nancy d/o Ann TURNER 23 Aug 1798 surety James TURNER (OB)

**VAUGHAN**, Joseph P. s/o Robert VAUGHAN and Martha PRITCHETT age 21 s farmer POB POR Grayson Co. & **JACOBS**, Bettie d/o Daniel JACOBS and Elmira DEMPSEY age 19 s POB POR Orange; POM Orange 4 Feb 1864 (OMR) 1 Feb 1864 (OML)

**VAUGHAN**, Paschal & **DOWELL**, Henrietta d/o William DOWELL who is also surety 29 Jul 1829 (OB)

**VAUGHN**, Horace POC age 23 s POB Madison Co. POR Orange s/o Thomas VAUGHN and Fanny VAUGHN laborer & **JACKSON**, Abby POC age 21 s POB POR Orange d/o Matt JACKSON and Abby JACKSON 13 Jun 1868 POM Orange by T.M. CARSON (OMR)

**VAWTER**, Benjamin & **BELL**, Elizabeth 24 Jan 1822 surety Boswell BELL (OB)

**VAWTER**, William & **BALLARD**, Anne; 16 Jan 1774 by banns both of St. Thomas Parish (Deed Book 17)

**VAWTER**, William & **RUCKER**, Mary d/o Mary RUCKER; 19 Jun 1784 surety James STAPP (OB)

**VAWTER**, William H. age 22 s farmer POB Orange POR Louisa s/o William VAWTER and Mary J. ESTES & **TERRILL**, Ella S. age 23 s POB POR Orange d/o William H. TERRILL and Ann BOSTON POM Orange 10 Oct 1878 by J.T. MASTIN (OMR)

**VEACH**, John & **COOPER**, Nancy 30 Dec 1808 by Robert JONES (OM)

**VEACH**, Lander & **THORPE**, Peggy; 5 Jan 1787 surety James TAYLOR (OB)

**VEALCH**, John & **COOPER**, Nancy 30 Dec 1808 by Robert JONES (OMR)

**VERDIER**, Paul & **MOORE**, Elizabeth widow 4 Dec 1827 surety P.S. FRY (OB)

**VERDIER**, Van N.M. & **MOORE**, Frances C. 5 Sep 1837 surety William S. FRAZER (OB)

**VERNON**, Isaac & **PATTERSON**, Nancy 4 Sep 1804 by George BINGHAM (OM)

**VIA,** Jonathan & **VIA,** Mary Elizabeth 18 Dec 1821 by George BINGHAM (OM)

**VIA,** Reuben & **GARRISON,** Levinia d/o John GARRISON by George BINGHAM 20 Dec 1821 (OM)

**VINNIARD,** Alexander & **HENSLEY,** Polly 16 Mar 1811 John HENSLEY surety (OB)

**VOSS,** Nicholas & **SPOTSWOOD,** Mary d/o John SPOTSWOOD; 30 Apr 1794 surety William BANKS (OB)

**WADDELL,** James Gordon & **GORDON,** Lucy; 22 May 1797 (OM)

**WADDY,** Thomas C. & **GRAVES,** Sarah A. d/o Isaac GRAVES surety Temple GRAVES 3 Jan 1849 (OB)

**WAGGONER,** William G. & **HANSFORD,** Lucinda 23 Jul 1806 by James GARNETT (OM)

**WALDEN,** George A. & **LLOYD,** Lucy surety William WEBSTER 23 Dec 1830 (OB)

**WALKER,** John & **PORTER,** Frances w 2 Feb 1814 surety William TINSLEY (OB) by William MASON 3 Feb 1814 (OM)

**WALKER,** Joseph W. & **TALIAFERRO,** Henrietta d/o Baldwin TALIAFERRO surety James W. WALKER 14 Feb 1825 (OB)

**WALKER,** Andrew POC age 21 s POB POR Orange s/o Dangerfield WALKER and Phoebe Jane SCOTT farm laborer & **JACKSON,** Silva POC age 19 s POB POR Orange d/o Andrew JACKSON and Sally WALKER 18 Apr 1874 POM Orange (OMR)

**WALKER,** Benjamin & **HENSHAW,** Elizabeth V. d/o John HENSHAW 29 Nov 1817 surety Thomas COTT (OB) by J. GOSS 2 Dec 1817 (OM)

**WALKER,** Benjamin & **SIMS,** Polly; 9 Nov 1795 (OM)

**WALKER,** Frank POC age 33 s carpenter POB Albemarle POR Orange s/o William WALKER and Nancy LEWIS & **BRANHAM,** Milly POC age 18 s POB POR Orange d/o Bushrod BRANHAM and Matelda ____ POM Little Zion Baptist Church, Orange 14 Mar 1878 by Willis ROBINSON (OMR)

**WALKER,** Green s/o Zekiel and Eliza WALKER age 21 s laborer at sawmill POB Brunswick Co POR Orange POC & **LINDSAY,** Mary Susan d/o Monroe LINDSAY and Mary TURNER age 17 s POB POR Orange POC; POM Orange 16 Jun 1867 (OMR) 10 Jun 1867 (OML)

**WALKER,** James & **POWELL,** Joice d/o Lewis G. POWELL surety James POWELL brother of Joice 24 Jan 1814 (OB) by George BINGHAM 27 Jan 1814 (OM)

**WALKER,** James W. Jr. s/o Col. James WALKER w farmer POB POR Madison Co & **PORTER,** Mary Jane d/o Col. John and Mary PORTER s POB POR Orange; POM Orange 27 Aug 1856 (OMR) 26 Aug 1856 (OML)

**WALKER,** Jeremiah & **SHEELOR,** Rachel 3 May 1833 surety William
S. WALKER (OB)

**WALKER,** John age 23 s POB POR Culpeper Co s/o John WALKER and
Martha E. GIBSON farmer & **GRAVES,** Annie E. age 18 POB POR
Orange d/o William GRAVES and Ellinor F. FOUSHEE 27 Sep 1870
POM Orange by A.H. BENNETT (OMR)

**WALKER,** Lewis & **HARRIS,** Polly 19 Sep 1797 surety Lindsay
HARRIS (OB)

**WALKER,** Moses s/o George WALKER age 21 s farm laborer POB POR
Orange POC & **REED,** Mary Ann age 19 s POB POR Orange POC;
POM Orange 28 Dec 1867 (OMR) (OML)

**WALKER,** Nepkin POC age 21 s labourer POB POR Orange s/o Michael
WALKER and Sarah GRYMES & **MADISON,** Maria POC age 17 s
POB POR Orange d/o Walker MADISON and Eliza LINDSAY POM
Orange 27 Dec 1877 (OMR)

**WALKER,** Peter s/o Peter WALKER and Fanny CROCK age 51 w farmer
POB POR Orange POC & **ALEXANDER,** Hannah age 46 w POB
Albemarle Co POR Orange POC; POM Orange 7 Apr 1866 (OMR) 29
Mar 1866 (OML)

**WALKER,** Reuben POC age 45 w labourer POB POR Orange s/o Reuben
and Charlotte WALKER & **CARTER,** Martha POC age 30 s POB
Louisa POR Orange d/o William and Ann CARTER POM Blue Run,
Orange 25 Dec 1878 by William ROBINSON (OMR)

**WALKER,** Reuben T. age 27 s POB POR Madison s/o James W.
WALKER and Ann E. ELEASON farmer & **SANFORD,** Mary S. age
23 s POB POR Orange d/o Lawrence SANFORD and Lucy WALKER
20 Dec 1870 POM Orange by R.W. WATTS (OM)

**WALKER,** Robert S. age 33 s POB Madison Co POR Louisville, KY s/o
John D. WALKER and Susan D. STRINGFELLOW merchant &
**GOSS,** Nannie C. age 25 s POB POR Orange d/o Ebenezer GOSS and
Ann NALLE 20 Jan 1874 POM Orange (OMR)

**WALKER,** Thomas & **ANDERSON,** Frances d/o Jacob ANDERSON
surety St. Clair CAVE 3 Dec 1816 (OB)

**WALKER,** Thomas & **POWELL,** Meseniah d/o Mary POWELL 18 Aug
1783 (OB)

**WALKER,** Thomas & **POWELL,** Misiniah (d/o Mary POWELL); 18
Aug 1783 by George EVE (OM)

**WALKER,** William H. & **SPOTSWOOD,** Ann E. W. d/o William L.M.
SPOTSWOOD 7 Sep 1846 surety Ferdinand JONES (OB)

**WALKER,** William J. age 25 s POB Westmoreland POR Orange s/o Rev.
J.W. WALKER and Martha L. JEFFERY farmer & **NEWMAN,**
Nannie B. age 19 s POB POR Orange d/o John F. NEWMAN and Ann

M. BLAKEY 30 Aug 1880 POM Orange by John T. HANSBROUGH of the Protestant Episcopal Church (OMR)

**WALKER**, William POC age 22 farm laborer POB POR Orange s/o Dangerfield WALKER and Phoebe Jane WALKER & **RAGLAND**, Letitia POC age 21 POB POR Orange d/o Alec and Mary TAYLOR POM Orange 16 Apr 1876 (OMR)

**WALKER**, William POC age 22 s POB POR Orange s/o George WALKER and Nancy _____ laborer & **TAYLOR**, Sarah Eliz. POC age 18 S POB POR Orange d/o Spencer TAYLOR and Sally _____ 26 Dec 1872 POM Orange by Philip JOHNSON (OMR)

**WALLACE**, Caesar POC age 50 s farmer POB Spotsylvania POR Orange s/o Harry WALLACE and Cloe _____ & **PERRE**, Julia POC age 22 s POB POR Orange d/o Anderson PERRE and Mary Ann _____ POM Orange 26 Dec 1878 by W.J. BARNETT (OMR)

**WALLACE**, Frank s/o Toby and Amy WALLACE age 74 w laborer POB Culpeper Co POR Orange POC & **TURNER**, Lavinia d/o Johnson and Lucy TURNER age 60 w POB POR Orange POC; POM Orange 16 Sep 1866 (OMR) 1 Sep 1866 (OML)

**WALLACE**, James & **DAY**, Elizabeth (undated filed with returns of 1802) POM Orange by Robert JONES (Misc Min Ret)

**WALLACE**, John & **OAKS**, Mourning d/o Major OAKS who is also surety 26 Feb 1816 (OB) by J.C. GORDON 28 Feb 1816 (OM)

**WALLER**, Ed. POC age 27 w farm labourer POB POR Orange s/o Washington WALLER and Phoebe LINDSAY & **HOLLIDAY**, Maria POC age 25 s POB POR Orange d/o Garrett HOLLIDAY and Barbara GALLERY POM Orange 22 Jul 1877 (OMR)

**WALLER**, Edwin & **LARMAND**, Lucy Ann d/o Francis LARMAND; POM Orange 5 Sep 1852 (OMR) 3 Sep 1852 (OML)

**WALLER**, James & **ATKINS**, Elizabeth Y. d/o Spencer I. ATKINS 1 Jun 1815 surety Elijah DICKENSON (OB)

**WALLER**, Ned POC age 21 s POB POR Orange s/o Washington WALLER and Phoebe HENDERSON laborer & **JACKSON**, Lucy POC age 21 POB POR Orange d/o Gabel JACKSON and Rachel _____ 27 Jun 1869 POM Orange by Herndon FRAZER (OMR)

**WALLER**, Sidney age 40 w POB POR Orange POC & **ARMISTEAD**, Harriet d/o Samuel and Hannah ARMISTEAD age 26 w POB POR Orange POC; POM St. Thomas Ch, Orange 1 Nov 1866 (OMR) (OML)

**WALLER**, Sidney POC age 55 w farm labourer POB POR Orange s/o Louisa FULKERSON & **ROBINSON**, Georgianna POC age 49 w POB POR Orange POM Orange Courthouse 22 Jul 1879 (OMR)

**WALLIS**, Benjamin H. & **BROCKMAN**, Julia A. permission from Sims BROCKMAN 13 Sep 1836 surety G.L. WILLIAMS (OB) by J. GOSS 13 Dec 1836 (OM)

**WALLIS,** George & **HILMAN,** Susan d/o Uriel HILMAN surety Richard ABELL 21 Dec 1816 (OB) by John C. GORDON 24 Dec 1816 (OM)

**WALLIS,** John & **RANDEL,** Nancy d/o William RANDEL who is also surety by Robert JONES 21 Aug 1807 (OB) (OM)

**WALTER,** James & **ATKINS,** Elizabeth Y. d/o Spencer J. ATKINS 1 Jun 1815 (OM)

**WALTERS,** George & **HARVEY,** Nancy surety John HARVEY 30 Oct 1800 (OB)

**WALTERS,** George C. s/o Isaac WALTERS and Ann TALIAFERRO age 30 s farmer POB POR Madison Co & **WILHOIT,** Pamelia Ann d/o Curtis WILHOIT and Louisa HARRISON age 26 s POB POR Orange; POM Orange 24 Dec 1867 (OMR) 19 Dec 1867 (OML)

**WALTERS,** Isaac & **PENCE,** Elizabeth d/o John PENCE who is also surety 27 Apr 1807 (OB) by Robert JONES 29 Apr 1807 (OM)

**WALTERS,** John & **HAMBLETON,** Margaret w 6 May 1807 surety John COLEMAN (OB) by Robert JONES 8 May 1807 (OM)

**WALTERS,** Michael & **MCFARLAND,** Sally surety Robert MANNAN 24 Oct 1812 (OB) 27 Oct 1812 by J. GOSS (OM)

**WALTON,** E. Payson & **SKINKER,** Jeannette C. d/o Samuel T. SKINKER; POM Orange 28 Oct 1852 (OMR) 26 Oct 1852 (OML)

**WALTON,** Edmund P. & **WATSON,** Letice by George BINGHAM 13 Feb 1816 (OM)

**WALTON,** Francis & **SPEERS,** Elizabeth; 22 Dec 1799 by George BINGHAM (OM)

**WALTON,** John & **DAVIS,** Rhoda 26 Nov 1812 by George BINGHAM (OM)

**WALTON,** John & **SNOW,** Agnes 28 Jan 1808 by George BINGHAM (OM)

**WAMBUSIE,** John E. age 42 s farmer POB Baltimore, MD POR Orange s/o E.C. WAMBUSIE and Jane N. _____ & **PARKER,** Alice age 20 s POB POR Orange d/o William PARKER and Mary A. ROLLINS POM Orange 21 Mar 1878by John S. HANSBROUGH minister of the P.E. Church (OMR)

**WARNER,** John & **WALKER,** Ann 26 May 1775 both of St. Thomas Parish by banns (Deed Book 17)

**WARREN,** Charles & **THOMAS,** Mary Ann surety Fountain THOMAS 22 Oct 1833 (OB)

**WARREN,** Edward T.H. s/o Jehu and Harriet WARREN age 26 s lawyer POB Rockingham, POR Harrisonburg & **MAGRUDER,** Virginia Watson d/o James and Louisa MAGRUDER age 18 s POB Fluvanna POR Orange; POM Orange 5 Dec 1855 (OMR) 3 Dec 1855 (OML)

**WASHINGTON,** Alfred POC age 23 s laborer POB POR Orange s/o Milton WASHINGTON and Emily ELLIS & **PRYOR,** Mary E. POC

age 20 s POB POR Orange d/o William PRYOR and Mary A.
STRANGE POM Orange 29 Dec 1876 (OMR)

**WASHINGTON,** Edward POC age 23 s labourer POB POR Orange s/o
Horace WASHINGTON and Martha JOHNSON & **JACKSON,**
Daphne POC age 23 s POB POR Orange POM Orange 5 Aug 1877
(OMR)

**WASHINGTON,** Fielding POC age 21 s POB POR Orange s/o Horace
WASHINGTON, and Martha JOHNSON laborer & **JOHNSON,** Maria
POC age 21 w POB Madison Co POR Orange d/o Jane JOHNSON 21
Aug 1870 POM Orange by Philip JOHNSON (OMR)

**WASHINGTON,** George POC age 22 s chair maker POB POR Orange s/o
Lewis WASHINGTON and Frances MCINTOSH & **JOHNSON,**
Martha age 21 s POB POR Orange d/o John JOHNSON and Sallie
_____ POM Orange 15 Mar 1877 (OMR)

**WASHINGTON,** George POC age 22 s POB POR Orange s/o Lewis
WASHINGTON and Julia HENDERSON farm laborer &
**GWATHMEY,** Alice POC age 19 s POB POR Orange d/o Philip
GWATHMEY 19 Nov 1871 POM Orange by Philip JOHNSON
(OMR)

**WASHINGTON,** George POC age 23 s POB Greene Co POR Orange s/o
Robert _____ and Alpha Jane _____ laborer & **WILLIAMS,** Louisa
POC age 15 s POB POR Orange d/o Spencer WILLIAMS and Keziah
_____ 18 Apr 1870 POM Orange by Philip JOHNSON (OMR)

**WASHINGTON,** George s/o Dudley WASHINGTON and Rose BELL
age 33 s blacksmith POB Albemarle Co POC & **HESTER,** Lucy age
28 s POB Hanover POC; POM Gordonsville, Orange 1 Sep 1866
(OMR) 27 Aug 1866 (OML)

**WASHINGTON,** Isaac POC age 24 w POB Albemarle POR Orange s/o
George & Eliza WASHINGTON laborer & **LEWIS,** Betsy A. POC age
20 s POB POR Orange d/o James LEWIS and Pamlia WALKER 21
Feb 1880 POM Orange (OMR)

**WASHINGTON,** Isaac POC age 25 s saw mill hand POB Albemarle POR
Orange s/o George WASHINGTON and Eliza _____ & **DADE,** Hannah
age 18 s POB POR Orange d/o John DADE and Lucy MCINTOSH
POM Orange 20 May 1877 (OMR)

**WASHINGTON,** James POC age 21 s labourer POB Fauquier POR
Orange s/o James WASHINGTON and Martha VASS & **BROADUS,**
Alice POC age 21 s POB Louisa POR Orange d/o Andrew BROADUS
and Milly WEST POM Orange 18 Aug 1878 by Sanders MASON
(OMR)

**WASHINGTON,** James POC age 35 s farm labourer POB POR Orange
s/o George SCHOOLER and Melvina _____ & **WILLIAMS,** Mary
POC age 35 s POB POR Orange d/o Ellen TALIAFERRO POM Mt.

Calvary Baptist Church, Orange 15 Sep 1878 by W.J. BARNETT (OMR)

**WASHINGTON**, Lewis POC age 42 w POB POR Orange laborer on farm & **ROLLS**, Martha POC age 23 w POB POR Orange 4 Jan 1868 POM Orange by Philip JOHNSON (OMR)

**WASHINGTON,** Littleton POC age 24 s labourer POB POR Orange s/o George WASHINGTON and Lucy MCINTOSH & **POINDEXTER,** Hannah POC age 22 w POB POR Orange d/o Nelson RIVES and Jane MILLS POM Orange 29 Nov 1879 (OMR)

**WASHINGTON**, Moses s/o Henry George WASHINGTON and Eliza WILLIS age 21 s laborer on farm POB POR Madison Co POC & **JONES**, Ann d/o Sam JONES age 21 s POB Green Co POR Orange POC; POM Orange 28 Jul 1867 (OMR) 26 Jul 1867 (OML)

**WASHINGTON**, Ralph POC age 26 s POB Madison Co POR Orange s/o George WASHINGTON and Eliza _____ farm laborer & **HOLMES**, Catherine POC age 26 s POB POR Orange d/o Paul HOLMES and Vinna _____ 7 Jan 1872 POM Orange by Frank TIBBS (OMR)

**WASHINGTON,** Robert POC age 28 s labourer POB Louisa POR Orange s/o Samuel WASHINGTON and Mildred KINNEY & **SHEPHERD,** Hattie M. POC age 21 s POB Louisa POR Orange d/o Robert SHEPHERD and Mary Kent ROBINSON POM Orange 29 Dec 1879 (OMR)

**WASHINGTON**, Tate age 22 s farm laborer POB Louisa Co POR Orange POC & **LEWIS**, Caroline age 22 POR Orange POC; POM Orange 28 Dec 1867 (OMR) 27 Dec 1867 (OML)

**WATKINS**, Robert S. & **DANIEL**, Elizabeth M. surety John P.A. JOHNSON 10 Nov 1842 (OB)

**WATKINS**, Thomas & **MOSLEY**, Frances 5 Jan 1802 POM Orange by Robert JONES (Misc Min Ret)

**WATSON**, Abner & **DEAR,** Elizabeth (d/o Catherine DEAR); 11 Oct 1786 surety Robert LANCASTER (OB)

**WATSON**, Abner & **LONG,** Nancy 1 Jan 1801 surety John LONG (OB)

**WATSON**, Benjamin & **JACOBS,** Frances; 23 Aug 1824 surety George SMITH (OB) 10 Sep 1824 by Jeremiah CHANDLER (OM)

**WATSON**, Benjamin F. age 27 s POB POR Orange s/o Benj. WATSON and Frances JACOBS farmer & **SANDERS**, Lucy A. age 37 s POB POR Orange d/o Hansford F. SANDERS and Polly RHODES 28 Jan 1868 POM Orange by John C. WILLIS (OMR)

**WATSON**, Isaac & **ROBBARDS,** Susanna 4 Apr 1799 by George BINGHAM (OM)

**WATSON**, James & **LAMB,** Catey; 3 Jul 1800 by George BINGHAM (OM)

**WATSON,** Jesse & **BALLARD,** Milly permission from Philip BALLARD 10 Aug 1789 surety Francis COLLINS (OB)

**WATSON,** John & **LAMB,** Mary d/o John LAMB surety Nathan GEAR 17 Sep 1837 (OB)

**WATSON,** Larkin & **SHELTON,** Lurenna M. d/o Thomas SHELTON surety William SHELTON 7 Sep 1834 (OB)

**WATSON,** Meredith POC age 21 s labourer POB Louisa POR Orange s/o Thomas WATSON and Maria RYAN & **PARKER,** Catherine POC age 24 s POB Madison POR Orange POM Gordonsville, Orange 24 Apr 1878 by C.G. WALDEN(OMR)

**WATSON,** Thomas POC age 24 s rail road hand POB POR Orange s/o Thomas WATSON and Polly ___ & **TYLER,** Emma Jane POC age 21 s POB Spotsylvania POR Orange POM Gordonsville 16 Sep 1878 (OMR)

**WATTERS,** Jacob & **BROOKING,** Belinda permission from Robert BROOKING 23 Oct 1820 surety James BROOKING (OB) 31 Oct 1820 by J. GOSS (OM)

**WATTLES,** Andrew J. age 24 s POB POR Orange s/o William H. WATTLES and Jane HANCOCK sawyer & **SMITH,** Mary Eliza age 21 s POB POR Orange d/o James O. SMITH and Clara GUINN 15 Nov 1871 POM Orange by L.A. CUTLER (OMR)

**WATTLES,** William H. & **HANCOCK,** Jane C. ward of William BROWN who is also surety 20 Feb 1834 (OB)

**WATTS,** Charles E. age 25 s POB POR Albemarle Co. s/o James D. WATTS and Lucy A. SIMMS minister & **HUME,** Harriet S. age 25 s POB POR Orange d/o David HUME and Fanny DADE 1 Dec 1868 POM Orange by R.W. WATTS (OMR)

**WATTS,** Elijah D. & **SAMPSON,** Margaret surety Benson HENRY 27 Nov 1823 (OB)

**WATTS,** Johnson & **DAVIS,** Suckey aka Susanna d/o Joseph DAVIS surety James TAYLOR 20 Jul 1785 (OB)

**WATTS,** Joseph William & **FOSTER,** Rachel both of St. Thomas Parish 23 Sep 1773 (Deed Book 17)

**WATTS,** Julius & **EVE,** Mary d/o Ann EVE 22 Dec 1785 surety Prettyman MERRY (OB)

**WATTS,** Thomas & **HEAD,** Sarah 14 May 1809 by George BINGHAM (OM)

**WATTS,** William & **BEAZLEY,** Elizabeth d/o James and Ann BEAZLEY 4 Jun 1778 surety John BEAZLEY both of St. Thomas Parish (Deed Book 17)

**WATTS,** William B. & **BLAKEY,** Sarah B. permission from Benjamin BURTON who is also surety 22 May 1826 (OB)

WAUGH, Alexander & **NEWMAN,** Elizabeth surety Henry NEWMAN 8
Oct 1834 (OB)

WAUGH, Charles A. age 26 s farmer POB POR Orange s/o Charles S.
WAUGH and Fannie FAULCONER & **JONES,** Sallie W. age 19 s
POB POR Orange d/o Montgomery A. JONES and Fannie
TALIAFERRO POM Orange 27 Dec 1877 (OMR)

WAUGH, Charles S. & **FAULCONER,** Mary F. surety Lawrence T.D.
FAULCONER 14 Jan 1847 (OB)

WAUGH, George & **BOSTON,** Elizabeth 19 Mar 1793 surety Pierce
SANFORD (OB)

WAUGH, George L. & **HERRING,** Sarah E. d/o Benjamin HERRING
surety William J. HERRING 22 Dec 1847 (OB) by Joseph S.
JACKSON 23 Dec 1847 (OM)

WAUGH, Goury & **WRIGHT,** Susan permission from William WRIGHT
13 Sep 1813 surety John SLEET (OB) by J. GOSS 23 Sep 1813 (OM)

WAUGH, Goury L. & **CLARK,** Jane D.L. d/o S.F. CLARK; POM Orange
23 Dec 1852 (OMR) 21 Dec 1852 (OML)

WAUGH, Goury R. s/o Goury WAUGH and Susan WRIGHT age 39 w
farmer POB POR Orange & **COLE,** Ellen d/o John COLE (and Lucy
WATKINS written in at a later date) age 26 s POB POR Orange; POM
Orange 28 Feb 1867 (OMR) 25 Feb 1867 (OML)

WAUGH, Napolean B. age 22 s farmer POB POR Orange s/o Charles S.
WAUGH and Fanny FAULCONER & **BLEDSOE,** Bettie S. age 18 s
POB POR Orange d/o William J. BLEDSOE and Jane F.
SUMMERVILLE POM Orange 15 Oct 1879 by J.J. MASTIN (OMR)

WAUGH, Richard & **BROWN,** Elizabeth; 11 Nov 1782 surety Andrew
SHEPHERD (OB)

WAYLAND, Clement & **LONG,** Martha surety Joshua LONG 8 Jan 1828
(OB)

WAYLAND, Fountain & **SNELL,** Amanda Melvina d/o Joseph SNELL
surety Joseph A. MANSFIELD 31 Jul 1827 (OB)

WAYLAND, Henry Jr. s/o Henry WAYLAND Sr. & **MELONE,** Ara d/o
John MELONE 1 Apr 1811 William MELONE surety by George
BINGHAM (OB) (OM)

WAYLAND, Martin V. age 30 s POB POR Orange s/o William
WAYLAND and Frances W. MILLER druggist & **PARROTT,** Mattie
H. age 25 s POB POR Orange d/o Thomas PARROTT and Martha
HOUSEWORTH 10 Jan 1872 POM Orange by R.C. CAVE (OMR)

WAYLAND, William & **MILLER,** Frances permission from Thomas
MILLER surety James MILLER 16 Dec 1823 (OB)

WEAVER, Samuel L. & **LAMB,** Anne d/o Richard LAMD who is also
surety by Edward G. SHIP 6 Jan 1824 (OM) (OB)

**WEBB,** Ellis & **BADGER,** Margaret 28 Aug 1822 surety Richard RICHARDS and William WRIGHT (OB)

**WEBB,** James & **CRASH,** Nancy 1 Jun 1807 surety Daniel HARNER (OB)

**WEBB,** James M. & **JOHNSON,** Rosamond 18 Dec 1834 surety Benjamin P. JOHNSON (OB)

**WEBB,** Jesse B. & **COOPER,** Mary w surety Jesse M. WEBB 7 Oct 1830 by Jeremiah CHANDLER (OB)(OMR)

**WEBB,** Jesse Bennet & **MASON,** Sarah 25 Jan 1790 surety Charles MASON (OB)

**WEBB,** John & **BLAKEY,** Judith 12 Nov 1822 surety John COLLINS (OB)

**WEBB,** John & **JONES,** Judah 12 Oct 1789 surety Thomas JONES (OB)

**WEBB,** John Jr. & **LANTON,** Mildred 15 Jan 1790 surety Jacob LANTON (OB)

**WEBB,** John Jr. & **LANTOR,** Mildred 20 Jan 1790 by John LELAND (OMR)

**WEBB,** John L. & **JOHNSON,** Lucy Ann 9 Jan 1841 surety Edwin MASON (OB)

**WEBB,** John L. s/o William B. WEBB and Martha LANCASTER age 56 w farmer POB POR Orange & **MASON,** Ann C. d/o Charles MASON and Lucy JONES age 44 s POB POR Orange; POM Orange 27 Aug 1867 (OMR) 26 Aug 1867 (OMR)

**WEBB,** John M. & **JONES,** Ricey E.; 21 Dec 1857 (OML)

**WEBB,** Lewis & **WALLER,** Elizabeth 2 May 1821 surety James WALLER (OB) 3 May 1821 by James GARNETT Jr. (OMR)

**WEBB,** Martin & **MARSHALL,** Sarah d/o William MARSHALL 28 Jan 1797 surety Philomen RICHARDS ( OB)

**WEBB,** Richard B. age 20 s POB Madison Co POR Culpeper Co s/o Wyatt B. WEBB and Eliza JOHNSON farmer & **SCHOOLER,** Sarah age 25 POB POR Orange d/o William SCHOOLER and Mary ____ 29 Dec 1868 POM Orange by Thos. R. HAWKINS (OMR)

**WEBB,** Richard C. & **LANCASTER,** Mary S. d/o Edmund LANCASTER who is also the surety 24 Nov 1834 (OB) 17 Dec 1834 by Joseph A. MANSFIELD (OMR)

**WEBB,** Spencer s/o Spencer WEBB and Lila GRAY age 24 s laborer on farm POB Culpeper POR Orange POC & **GRASTY,** Alverta age 18 s POB POR Orange POC; POM Orange 25 Apr 1867 (OMR) (OML)

**WEBB,** Vivion & **WOODWARD,** Lucy 28 Jun 1790 surety Henry LEE (OB)

**WEBB,** William & **ATKINS,** Margaret 27 Jan 1798 surety Caleb WEBB (OB)

**WEBB**, William & **LEATHERS**, Sarah (d/o John LEATHERS) 13 Jan 1785 surety John ATKINS POM St. Thomas Parish (OB) (OM)

**WEBB**, William & **SAMPSON**, Mary 12 Mar 1822 surety Simeon JOLLETT (OB)

**WEBB**, William Bennett & **LANCASTER**, Martha d/o John and Susannah LANCASTER 22 Sep 1806 by Nathaniel SANDERS (OM)

**WEBB**, William Crittendon & **BUCKNER**, Jane 8 Jul 1783 surety W. BUCKNER (OB)

**WEBB**, William J. age 23 s POB POR Orange s/o John L. WEBB and Lucy JOHNSON farmer & **BROWN**, Eliza L. age 21 s POB POR Orange d/o James O. BROWN and Sarah M. COOPER 14 Dec 1871 POM Orange by Charles QUARLES (OMR)

**WEBB**, William Jr. & **SMITH**, Patsy; 23 Jan 1797 surety William C. WEBB (OB)

**WEBB**, Wyatt B. & **JOHNSON**, Ann Eliza d/o Richard JOHNSON who is also surety 15 Dec 1847 (OB)

**WEBB**, Wyatt B. age 54 s carpenter POB POR Orange s/o Richard B. WEBB and Martha LANCASTER & **BLEDSOE**, Harriet V. age 35 s POB POR Orange d/o John DAWS POM Orange 1 Jan 1879 (OMR)

**WEBB**, Wyatt B. age 54 w POB POR Orange s/o Richard B. WEBB and Martha LANCASTER & **BLEDSOE**, Harriet E. age 35 w POB North Carolina POR Orange d/o John DAVIS 2 Jan 1879 POM Orange by Richard STEPHENS (OMR)

**WEBSTER**, Andrew & **SMITH**, Ursilla 28 Jul 1788 surety James GAINES (OB)

**WEBSTER**, George & **HIGHLANDER**, Mary 18 Jun 1793 surety Charles HIGHLANDER (OB)

**WEBSTER**, Vivion & **WEBB**, Elizabeth 12 Oct 1826 surety John R. ATKINS (OB)

**WEBSTER**, William B. & **LOYD**, Susan 11 Aug 1830 surety George A. WALDEN (OB)

**WEEDON**, Thomas W. s/o Thomas W. and M.B. WEEDON age 25 s merchant POB Fauquier Co POR Culpeper C.H. & **STEPHENS**, Mary F. d/o Joseph and Mary STEPHENS age 25 s POB POR Orange; POM Orange 14 Jul 1858 (OMR) 13 Jul 1858 (OML)

**WELCH**, Benjamin & **CAMPBELL**, Ann 8 Jan 1841 surety Frederick W. CAMBELL (OB)

**WELCH**, John age 39 s POB POR Madison Co s/o N.J. WELCH and Viranda NEWMAN farmer & **NEWMAN**, Laura age 32 s POB POR Orange d/o James B. NEWMAN and Sallie B. FITZHUGH 28 Apr 1868 POM Orange by E. BOYDEN (OMR)

**WELCH**, Nathaniel & **MALLORY**, Mary 28 Aug 1812 surety William MALLORY (OB) 2 Sep 1812 by Harry FRY (OM)

265

**WELCH,** Nathaniel J. & **NEWMAN,** Virandy d/o Thomas NEWMAN surety William MORTON Jr. 5 Jun 1818 (OB) by James GARNETT 9 Jun 1818 (OM)

**WELCH,** Oliver s/o Nathaniel WELCH & **MALLORY,** Betsy d/o Uriel MALLORY who is also surety 13 Sep 1810 (OB)

**WELLS,** Davis s/o Henry and Charity WELLS age 45 w minister POB Kentucky POR Alabama & **TINDER,** Lucy Ann d/o Thomas and Lucy TINDER age 35 s POB Culpeper POR Orange; POM Orange 3 Dec 1857 (OMR) 30 Nov 1857 (OML)

**WELLS,** James & **REYNOLDS,** Fennetta d/o Joseph REYNOLDS 5 Dec 1793 surety William Wise REYNOLDS (OB)

**WELLS,** Levi & **MARSHALL,** Charlotte 24 Dec 1805 by George BINGHAM (OM)

**WELLS,** Martin & **MARSHALL,** Sarah 28 Jan 1797 (OM)

**WELLS,** Thomas & **CLARK,** Mary d/o John CLARK Sr. who is also surety 6 Dec 1793 (OB)

**WELLS,** William & **SAMS,** Nancy d/o John SAMS 31 Nov 1801 surety Bledsoe BROCKMAN (OB)

**WEST,** James T. & **FAULCONER,** Sarah M. d/o Edward S. FAULCONER who is also surety 27 Jul 1846 (OB)

**WETZEL,** Lewis A. age 45 w POB Lewisburg, WV POR Spotsylvania s/o William WETZEL and Sarah SPOTTS carpenter & **HEAD,** Mattie J. age 27 s POB Albemarle Co POR Orange d/o Valentine HEAD and Lucy J. KINSOLVING 8 Feb 1872 POM Orange by Jos. A, MANSFIELD (OMR)

**WHARTON,** Charles E. age 24 s farmer POB Culpeper POR Orange s/o Samuel WHARTON and Lucy SIMCO & **TIPTON,** Mary Davis age 19 s POB Howard POR Orange d/o John T. TIPTON and Mary Ann OLIVER POM Orange 21 Sep 1879 by E.R. PERRY (OMR)

**WHARTON,** John S. age 34 s POB Orange POR Orange s/o Samuel WHARTON and Lucy M. SIMES farmer & **CARVER,** Sarah Ann age 24 s POB Louisa POR Orange d/o Franklin CARVER and Elizabeth SPROUSE 28 Oct 1880 POM Orange by E.R. PERRY (OMR)

**WHARTON,** Joseph & **GEORGE,** Catharine surety Robert MOORE 5 Jan 1815 (OB) 6 Jan 1815 by William MASON (OM)

**WHARTON,** Robert & **THORNTON,** Nancy d/o Lizbeth THORNTON surety Luke THORNTON by John CLARK 24 Dec 1832 (OB) (OM)

**WHARTON,** Samuel & **SIMCOE,** Lucy Mary surety John B. SIMCOE 2 Feb 1842 (OB) by J. EARNEST 10 Feb 1842 (OM)

**WHARTON,** Samuel & **WAUGH,** Sarah surety George WAUGH 5 Dec 1815 (OB)

**WHARTON,** Zacheus & **YOUNG,** Sally single surety James TINDER 19 Jan 1790 (OB)

266

**WHEELER**, Jesse & **CASH**, Catey 24 May 1803 POM Orange by Robert JONES (Misc Min Ret)

**WHITE**, Alfred POC age 24 s POB POR Orange s/o Lewis WHITE and Lucy ____ farmer & **WILLIS**, Mary POC age 20 s POB Louisa Co POR Orange d/o Thornton WILLIS and Louisa GRANVILLE 31 Dec 1872 POM Orange by Thomas R. HAWKINS (OMR)

**WHITE**, Anderson & **HUCKSTEP**, Lucinda d/o John HUCKSTEP surety Josias BINGHAM 27 Nov 1818 (OB) by Jacob WATTS 15 Dec 1818 (OM)

**WHITE**, Armistead POC age 30 farm laborer POB Spotsylvania POR Orange s/o Moses WHITE and Eliza COLEMAN & **GORDON**, Fenella POC age 25 POB POR Orange d/o Hardin GORDON POM Mt. Pleasant, Orange 18 Mar 1876 by C.T. JOHNSON (OMR)

**WHITE**, Austin POC age 23 s farm labourer POB POR Orange s/o Isaac WHITE and Julia TAYLOR & **CAMPBELL**, Ann POC age 18 s POB POR Orange d/o John CAMPBELL and Martha ____ POM Orange 5 May 1877 (OMR)

**WHITE**, Beck POC age 21 s farm labourer POB POR Orange s/o Ed. WHITE and Ann STERN & **NEUMAN**, Emma POC age 17 s POB POR Orange d/o Temple NEUMAN and Sarah BURRUSS POM Orange 2 Jun 1877 (OMR)

**WHITE**, Benjamin & **TWYMAN**, Judah or Judith d/o Samuel TWYMAN surety James WHITE 4 Jun 1813 (OB) by Jacob WATTS 6 Jun 1813 (OM)

**WHITE**, Benjamin POC age 22 s POB POR Orange s/o Willis WHITE and Juno MANSFIELD farm laborer & **WHITE**, Malinda POC age 18 s POB POR Orange d/o Jim WHITE and Martha DAWSON 28 Dec 1872 POM Orange by C. GILLUM (OMR)

**WHITE**, Cornelius POC age 22 s POB Louisa Co POR Orange farm laborer s/o Willis WHITE and Louisa _____ & **TALIAFERRO**, Lucy age 21 s POB POR Orange d/o Tom TALIAFERRO and Ellen SPOTSWOOD POM Orange 28 Feb 1877 (OMR)

**WHITE**, Garrett & **MARR**, Martha surety Madison MARR 8 Nov 1831 (OB)

**WHITE**, George W. & **SIMS**, Agnes d/o Mildred SIMS sister of James SIMS who is also surety 22 Dec 1828 (OB)

**WHITE**, Henry P. & **BEADLEY**, Martha B. surety William WHITE 26 Feb 1827 (OB) by J. GOSS 1 Mar 1827 (OM)

**WHITE**, Isaac POC age 21 s POB POR Orange s/o Thomas WHITE and Sarah ELLIS laborer & **RICHARDSON**, Aggy POC age 23 s POB POR Orange d/o Harry RICHARDSON and Nelly JOHNSON 24 Apr 1880 POM Shady Grove Church, Orange by C.T. JOHNSON (OMR)

WHITE, Jacob s/o Willis WHITE age 23 s farm laborer POB POR Orange POC & **RICHARDS**, Emma D. d/o Dick RICHARDS age 22 s POB POR Orange POC; POM Orange 25 Dec 1867 (OMR) 23 Dec 1867 (OML)

WHITE, James & **PLUNKETT**, Frances surety Willis WHITE 17 Dec 1816 (OB)

WHITE, James & **WOOD**, Lucy d/o James WOOD surety James SEBREE by George EVE 26 Nov 1787 (OB) (OM)

WHITE, Jesse & **MARTIN**, Elizabeth surety Robert MARTIN 2 Apr 1792 (OB)

WHITE, Jonathan & **TOWNSEND**, Elizabeth; 16 Nov 1786 (OM)

WHITE, Joel & **RUCKER**, Frankey d/o John RUCKER surety George TOMLINSON 28 Jul 1785 (OB)

WHITE, John & **ADAMS**, Lucy surety William CLARK 20 Aug 1817 (OB) by J.C. GORDON 22 Aug 1817 (OM)

WHITE, John & **GRAVES**, Virginia surety Claibourne GRAVES 22 Nov 1830 (OB)

WHITE, John W. & **YAGER**, Mary Ellen d/o Thomas YAGER who is also surety 25 Aug 1834 (OB)

WHITE, Jonathan & **TOWNSEND**, Elizabeth surety George BROOKE 15 Nov 1786 (OB) by George EVE 16 Nov 1786 (OM)

WHITE, Jonathan POR Fredericksville Parish & **MARTIN**, Nanny of St. Thomas Parish 8 Aug 1776 by banns (Deed Book 17)

WHITE, Pendleton T. & **OFFIELD**, Diannah d/o Agness OFFIELD surety William G. HUCKSTEP 30 Nov 1835 (OB)

WHITE, Richard & **OLIVER**, Catey d/o Tabitha OLIVER surety Bellfield CAVE both of St. Thomas Parish 20 Feb 1783 (OB)

WHITE, Richard & **WAYT**, Anney surety James WAYT 8 Feb 1810 (OB) 11 Feb 1810 by Jacob WATTS (OM)

WHITE, Thomas & **CLARK**, Elizabeth d/o Joseph CLARK who is also surety 4 Jun 1807 (OB)

WHITE, Thomas & **LONG**, Elizabeth surety Zachary BURNLEY 27 Mar 1788 (OB) 3 Apr 1788 by George EVE (OM)

WHITE, Thomas s/o Ben & Fanny WHITE age 38 w laborer at steam mill POB POR Orange POC & **MURRAY**, Phillis age 26 w POB POR Orange POC; POM Orange 9 Nov 1867 (OMR) 4 Nov 1867 (OML)

WHITE, William & **BROCKMAN**, Mary d/o Samuel BROCKMAN surety John HENDERSON 10 Sep 1782 (OB)

WHITE, William & **SCRIVER**, Susan d/o Samuel SCRIVER who is also surety 27 Mar 1820 (OB)

WHITE, William T. POC age 20 s laborer POB POR Orange s/o William WHITE and Susan JOHNSON & **WALLER**, Mary POC age 18 s POB

POR Orange d/o Washington WALLER and Sally JOHNSON POM
Orange 31 March 1877 (OMR)

WHITE, Willis s/o Richard WHITE & **WAYT,** Nancy d/o William
WAYT surety James WHITE by Jacob WATTS 27 Jan 1812 (OB)
(OM)

WHITE, Winston & **HARRIS,** Elizabeth surety William WHITE 16 Oct
1824 by J. GOSS (OB) (OM)

WHITEHEAD, William & **COX,** Malinda surety Charles HAGISH 19
Feb 1831 (OB)

WHITELAW, Alexander & **CHEWNING,** Lucy d/o Robert CHEWNING
who is also surety by Jacob WATTS 3 Feb 1812 (OB)

WHITELAW, David & **DAVIS,** Mary d/o Isaac DAVIS who is also
surety 28 May 1814 (OB) by Jacob WATTS 11 Aug 1814 (OM)

WHITELAW, Nicholas & **BEAZLEY,** Elizabeth d/o James BEAZLEY
Sr. surety Sanford BEAZLEY 17 Jan 1809 (OB) by Jacob WATTS 19
Jan 1809 (OM)

WHITLOCK, George & **EVANS,** Jane d/o John W. EVANS surety
Joseph TRIBBLE 23 Oct 1849 (OB)

WHITLOCK, John Thomas s/o Bartholomew H. WHITLOCK and Mary
E. HOPKINS age 28 s section master on O.& A. railroad POB Louisa
Co POR Orange & **BROWN,** Sallie M. d/o James O. BROWN and
Sarah COOPER age 18 s POB POR Orange; POM Orange 25 Jan 1866
(OMR) 24 Jan 1866 (OML)

WHITLOCK, Robert J. age 22 s POB Louisa Co POR Orange s/o George
WHITLOCK and Jane C. EVANS farmer & **ATKINS,** Lucy M. age 20
s POB POR Orange d/o Charles D. ATKINS and Mary EVANS 26 Dec
1871 POM Orange by Thomas R. HAWKINS (OMR)

WIATT, James M. s/o Francis J. and Elizabeth WIATT age 30 s farmer
POB Fredericksburg & **RICHARDS,** Marie Ann d/o Richard
RICHARDS Jr. and Nancy RICHARDS age 20 s POB Orange; POM
Orange 23 Mar 1854 (OMR)

WIATT, Thomas POR Essex County & **EDMONSON,** Suky d/o John
EDMONDSON, dec'd. of Essex Co. 25 Nov 1747 (Deed Book 11 page
79)

WIGGLESWORTH, Claiborne & **REYNOLDS,** Eliza; 26 Sep 1853
(OML)

WIGGLESWORTH, William J. s/o Joseph WIGGLESWORTH &
**REYNOLDS,** Mary d/o Joseph REYNOLDS surety William
PITCHER 1 Oct 1813 (OB) by John A. BILLINGSLEY 4 Oct 1813
(OM)

WILHOIT, Curtis & **CAVE,** Harriett surety Robert CAVE 14 Mar 1831
(OB) by J. GOSS 17 Mar 1831 (OM)

**WILHOIT,** Milton & **SIMS,** Elizabeth d/o John SIMS surety James P. SIMS 22 Nov 1836 (OB)

**WILHOIT,** Samuel POC age 24 s POB Culpeper Co POR Orange s/o Samuel WILHOIT and Dicey _____ laborer & **SNEED,** Helen POC age 19 POB POR Orange d/o Winston SNEED and Lucy CARTER 30 Dec 1868 POM Orange by Philip JOHNSON (OMR)

**WILLARD,** G.W. age 58 w POB New Hampshire POR Louisa s/o Antonio WILLARD and Betsy WEATHERBY farmer & **HUGHSON,** Elizabeth age 57 w POB Louisa POR Orange Nathaniel SERGEANT and Martha _____ 4 Dec 1870 POM Orange by J.W. MCCOWN (OM)

**WILLET,** David & **BAUGHON,** Polly d/o Thomas BAUGHON who consents surety Joseph BAUGHON 21 Mar 1799 (OB)

**WILLIAM,** Burnett & **CORREL,** Eliza; 1771 (OB)

**WILLIAMS,** Daniel & **MCCULLY,** Jane surety William FINNELL who states Jane is over 21 years 22 May 1807 (OB) 24 May 1807 by Robert JONES (OM)

**WILLIAMS,** John & **ROW,** Hetty d/o Thomas ROW who is also surety 24 Dec 1814 (OB) 25 Dec 1814 by John A. BILLINGSLEY (OM)

**WILLIAMS,** Albert POC age 24 w POB POR Orange s/o Thornton WILLIAMS and Ellen BARBOUR farmer & **GREEN,** Harriet POC age 18 s POB POR Orange d/o Towles GREEN and Chestina HOPKINS 24 Jul 1880 POM Orange by C.T. VAUGHAN (OMR)

**WILLIAMS,** Benjamin age 34 w POB Madison Co POR Orange s/o Charlotte _____ farm laborer & **LEWIS,** Eliza age 30 w POB POR Orange d/o Thomas GRYMES 3 Mar 1870 by Jos. A. MANSFIELD (OMR)[death records for their son indicate that this couple is of color]

**WILLIAMS,** Bluford S. & **WINSLOW,** Mary Bell ward of Blueford S. _____ surety Joseph WILLIAMS 25 Feb 1831 (OB)

**WILLIAMS,** David & **ROW,** Elizabeth d/o Thomas ROW surety Elkanon ROW 24 Sep 1817 (OB) by J.C. GORDON 25 Sep 1817 (OM)

**WILLIAMS,** Douglas POC age 21 s POB POR Orange s/o Reuben WILLIAMS and Grace _____ railroading & **MURRAY,** Rachel POC age 21 s POB POR Orange d/o William MURRAY and Phillis _____ 23 Aug 1873 POM Orange by F.L. GIPSON (OMR)

**WILLIAMS,** Edmund POC age 21 s POB Albemarle Co POR Orange s/o George WILLIAMS and Nettie COLEMAN laborer & **PORTER,** Susan POC age 25 w POB POR Orange d/o John REVELEY (?) and Lucinda BRADLEY 17 Apr 1870 POM Orange by Frank TIBBS (OMR)

**WILLIAMS,** Edward & **POTTS,** Ann Lavinia d/o Ann M. POTTS surety James L. TALIAFERRO 22 Oct 1842 (OB)

**WILLIAMS**, Edward W. s/o Blueford and Mary WILLIAMS age 27 s farmer POB POR Orange & **BEADLES**, Georgianna d/o James and Elizabeth BEADLES age 24 s POB POR Orange; POM Orange 13 Jul 1858 (OMR) 12 Jul 1858 (OML)

**WILLIAMS**, Felix & **HAM**, Franky H. granddaughter of Franky HERRING surety Thomas SHIFFLET 8 Jan 1820 (OB)

**WILLIAMS**, Francis & **HARVIE**, Nanny both of St. Thomas Parish 5 May 1776 (Deed Book 17)

**WILLIAMS**, Francis & **ROGERS**, Sally surety Samuel HAM 23 Mar 1795 (OB)

**WILLIAMS**, Harrison POC age 23 s farm labourer POB POR Orange s/o Thornton WILLIAMS and Ellen BARBOUR & **BOWLER**, Aggy POC age 22 s POB POR Orange d/o Addison BOWLER and Winny _____ POM Orange 13 Apr 1878 by Robert WOODSON (OMR)

**WILLIAMS**, Henry POC age 21 s POB Culpeper Co. POR Orange s/o Henry WILLIAMS and Sarah WILLIAMS laborer & **EVANS**, Mary J. POC age 21 s POB Albemarle Co POR Orange d/o Tom EVANS and Cary Ann EVANS 11 Sep 1869 POM Orange by Frank TIBBS (OMR)

**WILLIAMS**, Henry POC age 23 s POB POR Orange s/o Billy WILLIAMS and Mary _____ laborer & **DAWSON**, Kitty POC age 20 s POB POR Orange d/o Bar DAWSON and Fanny _____ 9 Oct 1869 POM Orange by Philip JOHNSON (OMR)

**WILLIAMS**, Henry T. POC age 23 s farm labourer POB POR Orange s/o Armistead WILIAMS and Harriet THURSTON & **PONDEXTER**, Cordelia POC age 21 s POB POR Orange d/o Daniel POINDEXTER and Patty ROBINSON POM Orange 13 Feb 1879 (OMR)

**WILLIAMS**, Jacob & **DELANEY**, Mary surety John ATKINS 25 Mar 1786 (OB)

**WILLIAMS**, James & **BRUCE**, Elizabeth surety Thomas FARISH 3 Jun 1795 (OB)

**WILLIAMS**, James & **THOMPSON**, Sally d/o John THOMPSON surety Richard CAVE 5 Aug 1800 (OB)

**WILLIAMS**, James POC age 22 s POB POR Orange s/o Edmind WILLIAMS and Mary Ann HOWARD laborer & **GRAVES**, Virginia POC age 20 s POB POR Orange d/o Gilbert GRAVES and Juda GRAVES 16 Apr 1870 POM Orange by Philip JOHNSON (OMR)

**WILLIAMS**, John & **RUMSEY**, Elizabeth both of St. Thomas Parish 5 Mar 1778 by banns (Deed Book 17)

**WILLIAMS**, John P. & **DAY**, Susan R. d/o John DAY who is also surety 26 Mar 1842 (OB)

**WILLIAMS**, John POC age 24 s POB POR Orange s/o Reuben WILLIAMS and Florence JACKSON laborer & **STEARNS**, Laura

POC age 21 s POB POR Orange d/o Richard STEARNS and Julia
LINDSAY 6 May 1880 POM Orange (OMR)

**WILLIAMS**, Joseph & **CATTERTON**, Mary by George BINGHAM 30
Nov 1819 (OM)

**WILLIAMS**, Lewis B. & **BLAIR**, Charlotte J.; POM Orange 7 Dec 1852
(OMR) 6 Dec 1852 (OML)

**WILLIAMS**, Randall POC age 23 s POB POR Orange s/o Garnett and
Matilda WILLIAMS laborer & **FRY**, Martha POC age 21 s POB
Albemarle Co POR Orange d/o Clara FRY 28 Dec 1868 POM Orange
by Jos. A. MANSFIELD (OMR)

**WILLIAMS**, Richard & **BEAZLEY**, Sarah d/o Mildred WILLIAMS
stepdaughter of John WILLIAMS surety James BEAZLEY 30 Dec
1797 (OB) by Hamilton GOSS 2 Jan 1798 (OM)

**WILLIAMS**, Richard & **ROGERS**, Nancy surety James EARLY by
George EVE 7 Jan 1788 (OB) (OM)

**WILLIAMS**, Richard W. & **BELL**, Lucinda surety Francis K. BELL 9
Jan 1835 (OB)

**WILLIAMS**, Robert POC age 21 s laborer POB POR Orange s/o William
H. WILLIAMS and Margaret WHITE & **JONES**, Rosa POC age 22 s
POB Madison POR Orange d/o Frances JONES POM Orange 11 Apr
1877 (OMR)

**WILLIAMS**, Sinclear & **COLYER**, Lucindia d/o Martin COLYER Sr.
surety Martin COLYER Jr. 27 May 1818 (OB)

**WILLIAMS**, Smith POC age 35 s POB POR Orange s/o William
WILLIAMS and Mary _____ carriage driver & **CAMPBELL**, Sally
POC age 25 w POB POR Orange d/o Ellen CHANDLER 29 Apr 1873
POM Orange by F.L. GIPSON (OMR)

**WILLIAMS**, Stewart POC age 24 s POB POR Orange s/o Anderson
WILLIAMS and Daphne PORTER farm laborer & **REDD**, Adelaide
POC age 19 s POB POR Orange d/o Henry REDD and Fanny _____ 31
Dec 1872 POM Orange by N.H. ANDERSON (OMR)

**WILLIAMS**, Thomas s/o Thomas and Hannah WILLIAMS age 22 s
carpenter POB POR Fredericksburg & **JOHNSON**, Jane Frances d/o
R. and P. JOHNSON age 20 s POB POR Orange; POM Orange 14 Feb
1856 (OMR) 12 Feb 1856 (OML)

**WILLIAMS**, Walker POC age 22 s farm laborer POB POR Orange s/o
Thornton WILLIAMS and Ellen BARBOUR & **GREEN**, Nancy POC
age 21 s POB POR Orange d/o Towles GREEN and Christine
HOPKINS POM Orange 25 Nov 1876 (OMR)

**WILLIAMS**, William & **POWELL**, Fanny surety David PANNILL 1 Mar
1850 (OB)

**WILLIAMS**, William & **STUBBLEFIELD**, Mary Ann d/o George
STUBBLEFIELD surety James FARISH 2 Mar 1813 (OB)

**WILLIAMS**, William G. s/o Lewis B. and Mary C. WILLIAMS age 27 s attorney POB POR Orange & **HANSBROUGH**, Roberta B. d/o Alexander H. and Elizabeth C.HANSBROUGH age 19 s POB Culpeper POR Orange; POM Orange 10 Sep 1857 (OMR) (OML)

**WILLIAMS**, William POC age 27 s labourer POB Greene POR Orange s/o Lewis WILLIAMS and Sally BLAKEY & **SIMMS**, Harriet POC age 24 s POB Louisa POR Orange d/o Austin SIMMS and Martha _____ POM Gordonsville 16 Nov 1877 (OMR)

**WILLIAMSON**, John & **WILHOIT**, Elizabeth d/o Ezekiel WILHOIT who is also surety 23 Nov 1829 (OB) by Philip ANDERSON 1 Dec 1829 (OM)

**WILLIAMSON**, Thomas & **BLEDSOE**, Milly d/o Aaron BLEDSOE surety Joseph BLEDSOE 29 Mar 1796 (OB)

**WILLIBY**, Tandy & **CHILES**, Polly d/o James CHILES; sister of Walter CHILES 29 Apr 1815 (OM)

**WILLIS**, Alexander POC age 24 s labourer POB Rappahannock POR Orange s/o Walter and Ann WILLIS & **WILLIS**, Fanny POC age 28 s POB POR Orange d/o Armistead WILLIS and Georgianna JOHNSON POM Mt. Calvary Baptist Church, Orange 21 Apr 1878 by F.L. GIBSON (OMR)

**WILLIS**, Benjamin & **TERRILL**, Rebecca d/o Edmond TERRILL who is also surety 16 Dec 1833 (OB)

**WILLIS**, Daniel POC age 35 w labourer POB POR Orange s/o Henry WILLIS and Nancy _____ & **ELLIS**, Lizzie POC age 29 s POB POR Orange d/o Patience ELLIS POM Orange 30 Dec 1878 by Willis ROBINSON (OMR)

**WILLIS**, H. Lee age 33 s POB POR Orange s/o Robert T. WILLIS and Fanny LEE county treasurer & **BULL**, Nellie B. age 29 s POB POR Orange d/o Marcus BULL and Sarah T. DADE 4 Nov 1880 POM St. Thomas Church, Orange by John S. HANSBROUGH (OMR)

**WILLIS**, Jack POC age 29 w POB POR Orange s/o John F. WILLIS and Fanny HALL brick mason & **VERDIER**, Elizabeth POC age 21 w POB POR Orange d/o Joe VERDIER and Betsy VERDIER 27 Dec 1869 POM Orange by Franklin TIBBS (OMR)

**WILLIS**, James A. & **LEWIS**, Virginia A. aka Virginia H. WILLIS; POM Orange 12 May 1853 (OMR) 10 May 1853 (OML)

**WILLIS**, James age 23 s POB POR Orange s/o James WILLIS and Mary GIBSON laborer & **DAVIS**, Ellen age 21 s POB Spotsylvania Co POR Orange d/o Pleasant DAVIS and Betsy _____ 13 Feb 1870 POM Orange by John C. WILLIS (OMR)

**WILLIS**, James s/o Isaac WILLIS who is also surety & **GORDON**, Elizabeth d/o John C. GORDON who is also surety 7 Aug 1827 (OB)

**WILLIS,** James T. POC age 22 s farmer POB Louisa POR Orange s/o
Thornton WILLIS and Louisa POWELL & **WHITE,** Fanny POC age
18 s POB POR Orange d/o William WHITE and Susan JOHNSON
POM Shady Grove Church, Orange 29 Aug 1878 by C.T. JOHNSON
(OMR)

**WILLIS,** John & **MADISON,** Lucy 1 Jul 1839 Ambrose MADISON
surety (OB)

**WILLIS,** John & **MADISON,** Nelly C. surety Paul VEDIER 12 Nov 1804
(OB)

**WILLIS,** John & **THOMAS,** Sally; both of St. Thomas Parish 27 Apr
1772 (Orange Fee Book)

**WILLIS,** John Jr. s/o John WILLIS and Lucy MADISON age 21 s farmer
POB POR Orange & **ROBINSON,** Lucy S. d/o Thomas A.
ROBINSON and Maria SHEPHERD age 21 s POB POR Orange; POM
Orange 21 Jun 1866 (OMR) (OML)

**WILLIS,** Larkin & **GORDON,** Mary d/o John C. GORDON 12 Jul 1823
surety Alexander BICKERS (OB)

**WILLIS,** Larkin & **LANCASTER,** Rebecca 15 Dec 1834 by Joseph A.
MANSFIELD (OMR)

**WILLIS,** Moses & **THOMAS,** Elizabeth d/o Joseph THOMAS Sr 20 Apr
1781 (OM)

**WILLIS,** Reuben POR St. Thomas Parish & **GARNETT,** Ann POR St.
Mark's Parish 17 Sep 1776 by banns (Deed Book 17)

**WILLIS,** Richard age 21 s POB Powhatan (there may be an error in his
birth place.) POR Orange s/o Lewis WILLIS and Rhody GALLERY
laborer & **ROBINSON,** Amelia age 21 s 29 May 1880 POM Orange
(OMR)

**WILLIS,** Southerland & **LANCASTER,** Rebecca d/o Larkin
LANCASTER who is also surety 3 Dec 1834 (OB)

**WILLIS,** William B. age 42 s farmer POB POR Orange s/o R.H. WILLIS
and Mary NALLE & **WILLIS,** Nellie C. age 29 s POB POR Orange
d/o John WILLIS and Lucy MADISON POM Fairfield, Clarke Co 1
May 1878 by T.F. MARTIN (OMR)

**WILLOUGHBY,** William & **STEVENS,** Lucy 15 Jan 1824 surety
Maurice C. WEBB (OB)

**WILLS,** William & **HARVEY,** Mary surety Samuel SCRIVENER 5 Jan
1790 (OB)

**WILSON,** Franklin N. s/o Ephraim WILSON and Anna SMITH age 21 s
farmer POB POR Fairfield District, S.C. & **POINDEXTER,** Frances
age 24 s POB Louisa Co POR Orange; POM Orange 5 Apr 1864
(OMR) (OML)

**WILSON,** William age 25 s POB Ireland POR Orange s/o John WILSON
and Susan HUDSON & **THACKER,** Lucy O. age 22 s POB Caroline

Co. POR Orange d/o Benjamin THACKER and Lucy G. LOWREY 1
Sep 1868 POM Orange by Melzi S. CHANCELLOR (OMR)

**WILTSHIRE,** Albert & **CLARKE,** Julia surety Augustine PRIEST 11
May 1846 (OB)

**WILTSHIRE,** Alfred & **FAULCONER,** Sarah Ann d/o William and
Elizabeth FAULCONER surety George FAULCONER 21 Dec 1849
(OB)

**WILTSHIRE,** Benjamin & **THORNTON,** Elizabeth Ann d/o Luke
THORNTON who is also surety 20 Nov 1833 (OB)

**WILTSHIRE,** John & **WILTSHIRE,** Elizabeth d/o John WILTSHIRE
who is also surety 19 Dec 1832 (OB)

**WILTSHIRE,** John B. s/o Benjamin WILTSHIRE & **JACOBS,** Angeline
d/o William JACOBS 23 Feb 1839 (OB)

**WILTSHIRE,** Peyton s/o William WILTSHIRE and Catherine
STRATTON age 44 s wheelwright POB POR Orange & **CAMMACK,**
Catherine A.V. d/o William E. CAMMACK and Rebecca MASON age
26 s POB POR Orange; POM Orange 7 Feb 1867 (OMR) 4 Feb 1867
(OML)

**WILTSHIRE,** Robert L. age 24 s POB POR Orange s/o Alfred
WILTSHIRE and Sarah FAULCONER farmer & **MASON,** Azalea D.
age 22 s d/o James L. MASON and Sarah C. POUND 20 Jun 1880
POM Orange by Melzi S. CHANCELLOR (OMR)

**WILTSHIRE,** Weedon & **FAULCONER,** Malinda d/o Elizabeth
FAULCONER surety George FAULCONER 19 Dec 1845 (OB)

**WINE,** John & **EHART,** Rachel 3 Feb 1803 (Misc Min Ret)

**WINFIELD,** John s/o Alex. and Sally WINFIELD age 40 w laborer on
farm POB Stafford POR Orange POC & **COFFMAN,** Celia d/o Ben
and Rhoda COFFMAN age 21 s POB POR Orange POC; POM Orange
28 Sep 1867 (OMR) 23 Sep 1867 (OML)

**WINSLOW,** Henry B. & **GOODALL,** Drucilla A.F. d/o Isaac
GOODALL surety James R. SIMS 19 Nov 1832 (OB)

**WINSLOW,** Moses & **LONG,** Lucy A. d/o Robert B. LONG surety James
NEWMAN 21 Sep 1822 (OB)

**WINSLOW,** Richard P. & **TAYLOR,** Eliza Jane surety Valentine M.
HOUSEWORTH 24 Aug 1836 (OB)

**WINSLOW,** Thomas s/o Moses and Lucy WINSLOW age 30 s farmer
POB POR Orange & **WILLIAMS,** Elizabeth N. d/o S. Bluford and
Mary WILLIAMS age 24 s POB POR Orange; POM Orange 21 May
1858 (OMR) 18 May 1858 (OML)

**WINSLOW,** Valentine & **BEADLES,** Ann [d/o John BEADLES Sr.] 12
Feb 1804 by George BINGHAM (Misc Min Ret)(permission) 8 Feb
1804 surety John BEADLES Jr. (OB)

**WINSTON**, Bickerton, s/o Philip and Sarah M. WINSTON age 41 w farmer POB POR Hanover Co & **BANKHEAD**, Eliza M. d/o William and Dorothea BANKHEAD age 23 s POB Caroline Co POR Orange; POM Orange 1 Jan 1858 (OMR) 31 May 1858 (OML)

**WINSTON**, Frederick age 28 s section hand POB Louisa POR Orange s/o Winston SHARP and Charity HINES & **DANIELS**, Cornelia age 23 s POB POR Orange d/o John DANIEL and Winney _____ POM Orange 18 Apr 1879 by F. TIBBS (OMR)

**WINSTON**, John POC age 23 s farm labourer POB POR Orange s/o _____ WINSTON and Nancy _____ & **SMITH**, Alberta POC age 17 s POB POR Orange d/o Barbara SMITH POM Mt. Pleasant Church, Orange 26 Dec 1878 by C.T. JOHNSON (OMR)

**WINSTON**, Richard M. s/o Philip and Jane D. WINSTON age 23 s farmer POB POR Hanover Co. & **BANKHEAD**, Rosalie S. d/o William and Dorothea BANKHEAD age 21 s POB Caroline Co. POR Orange; POM Orange 10 Nov 1857 (OMR) 9 Nov 1857 (OML)

**WINSTON**, William POC age 22 s POB POR Orange s/o John WINSTON and Nancy HILL laborer & **JOHNSON**, Betty POC age 21 s POB POR Orange d/o Isaac JOHNSON and Mary ELLIS 8 Feb 1873 POM Orange by Philip JOHNSON (OMR)

**WINTERS**, Benjamin & **POTTS**, Mary N. d/o Timothy POTTS surety Jacob CLINEDINST 22 Dec 1840 (OB)

**WISDOM**, Joseph & **GARDNER**, Sarah both of St. Thomas Parish 13 Aug 1773 (Deed Book 17)

**WISEMAN**, Henry A. age 27 s POB POR Danville s/o John WISEMAN and Mary A. WISEMAN druggist & **YAGER**, Willie Anna age 21 s POB POR Orange d/o William B. YAGER and Elizabeth C. YAGER 13 Oct 1870 POM Orange by J.W. MCCOWN (OM)

**WITHERSPOON**, John & **BOSTON**, Mary both of St. Thomas Parish by banns 20 Dec 1774 (Deed Book 17)

**WOIRHAYE**, Francis & **HANCOCK**, Nancy d/o William HANCOCK 22 Feb 1817 by Robert JONES (OM)

**WOLF**, Joseph F. age 20 s farmer POB Dauphin Co., PA POR Orange s/o Samuel WOLF and Catharine BUFFINGTON & **MILLER**, Catherine age 21 s POB Dauphin Co., PA POR Orange d/o Jacob MILLER and Aby SNYDER POM Orange 11 Mar 1877 (OMR)

**WOLFREY**, George B. age 29 s shoe maker POB POR Orange s/o Richard WOLFREY and Betsy BATTAILE & **WOLFREY**, Mary Jane age 23 s POB Spotsylvania POR Orange d/o Richard WOLFREY and Eveline SULLIVAN POM Orange 8 Mar 1877 (OMR)

**WOMRLEY**, Lewis s/o Reuben WOMRLEY and Johanna SCOTT age 21 s laborer POB POR Orange POC & **RAWLINGS**, Louisa d/o Henry

RAWLINGS and Milly MANSFIELD age 18 s POB POR Orange POC; POM Orange 12 May 1867 (OMR) 11 May 1867 (OML)

**WOOD,** William & **AUSTIN,** Mildred by George BINGHAM 12 Dec 1822 (OM)

**WOOD,** Absolum s/o Margaret WOOD age 40 s miller POB Orange & **MARTIN,** Mary E. age 22 s POR Orange; 26 Jan 1857 (OML)

**WOOD,** Blakey POC age 25 s farm labourer POB POR Orange s/o Nat WOOD and Mary BEALE & **TALIAFERRO,** Ella POC age 21 s POB Greene POR Orange d/o Charles TALIAFERRO and Rhoda HARRIS POM Orange 14 May 1879 by F. TIBBS (OMR)

**WOOD,** David POC age 22 s POB POR Orange s/o George WOOD and Ann HOLLIVER [sic] laborer & **HENDERSON,** Caroline POC age 21 w POB POR Orange d/o Jake HENDERSON 26 Dec 1872 POM Orange by John C. WILLIS (OMR)

**WOOD,** Ellet & **CONNER,** Mary both of St. Thomas Parish by banns 19 Oct 1775 (Deed Book 17)

**WOOD,** Garland & **MITCHELL,** Catharine A.C. d/o Isabella M. OSBOURNE; 22 Dec 1852 (OML)

**WOOD,** George POC age 31 w POB POR Orange s/o George WOOD and Ann ____ farm laborer & **TURNER,** Mary POC age 22 s POB POR Orange d/o Nelson TURNER and Mary Ann ____ 1 May 1872 POM Orange by Philip JOHNSON (OMR)

**WOOD,** George s/o George WOOD and Ann JOHNSON age 22 S laborer on farm POB POR Orange POC & **LINDSAY,** Clara d/o Abraham and Milly LINDSAY age 17 s POB POR Orange POC; POM Orange 30 Mar 1867 (OMR) 25 Mar 1867 (OML)

**WOOD,** Henry & **WEATHERSPOON,** Mary w both of St. Thomas Parish surety James TAYLOR Jr. 16 May 1780 (OB)

**WOOD,** Henry O. age 21 s POB Albemarle Co POR Louisa Co s/o Ezekial WOOD and Martha THOMAS railroading & **MILLS,** Bettie M. age 18 POB POR Orange d/o Thomas M. MILLS and Mary S. GRAVES 25 Sep 1873 POM Orange by E.P. HAWKINS (OMR)

**WOOD,** Hezekiah & **BRADLEY,** Sally d/o William BRADLEY who consents 2 May 1802 by Hamilton GOSS (Misc Min Ret) (permission paper)

**WOOD,** Hillory & **SNOW,** Rutha 30 Oct 1827 (permission paper)

**WOOD,** Hopewell & **TERMAN,** Milly by George BINGHAM 22 Apr 1793 (OM)

**WOOD,** James & **MILLS,** Ann surety William S. FRAZER 4 Aug 1817 (OB) by William G. HITER 6 Aug 1817 (OM)

**WOOD,** James & **WHITE,** Sarah d/o Jeremiah WHITE surety John FARNEYHOUGH 3 Jan 1807 (OB) by Jacob WATTS 4 Jan 1807 (OM)

**WOOD,** James H. age 31 s POB Albemarle POR Gordonsville, Orange s/o William H. WOOD and Mary E. ROBERTSON engineer & **TURNER,** Virginia S. age 20 s POB Louisa POR Gordonsville, Orange d/o William H. TURNER and Barbara A. RICHARDSON 27 Oct 1880 POM Exchange Hotel, Gordonsville, Orange by J.A. FRENCH (OMR)

**WOOD,** Jesse & **GOLDING,** Elizabeth Ann d/o Reuben GOLDING 18 Jun 1827 (OB) by George BINGHAM 28 Jun 1827 (OM)

**WOOD,** Jesse & **PAGE,** Nancy surety Jonathan D. GOODALL by William DOUGLASS 19 May 1806 (OB) (OM)

**WOOD,** John & **THOMPSON,** Sarah by George BINGHAM 20 Nov 1821 (OM)

**WOOD,** John F. age 52 s POB POR Orange s/o Adam WOOD and Mary CLARK carpenter & **BERRY,** Lucy Ann age 24 s POB Culpeper POR Orange 11 Jan 1868 POM Orange by E.R. PERRY (OMR)

**WOOD,** John T. s/o Absalom WOOD and Mary CLARK age 52 s carpenter POB POR Orange & **BERRY,** Lucy Ann age 24 s POB Culpeper Co. POR Orange; POM Orange 11 Jan 1868 (OMR) 30 Nov 1867 (OML)

**WOOD,** Joseph & **BELL,** Margaret d/o Mary BELL both of St. Thomas parish surety James TAYLOR 22 Mar 1781 (OB)

**WOOD,** Joseph T. & **WOOD,** Martha Ann; 4 Jan 1858 (OML)

**WOOD,** Leroy & **ESTES,** Susan d/o William ESTES 19 Oct 1811 Peter HARRIS surety (OB)

**WOOD,** Millard age 24 s mail agent POB Culpeper POR Charlotte, NC s/o James WOOD and C.V. CHAMBERS & **WOODVILLE,** Mary S. age 24 s POB POR Orange d/o E.S. WOODVILLE and M.J. SISSON POM Orange 8 Oct 1879 (OMR)

**WOOD,** Monroe POC age 23 s POB Louisa POR Orange s/o Nat WOOD and Elizabeth JACKSON laborer & **TAYLOR,** Arena POC age 20 s POB POR Orange d/o Edmund TAYLOR and Eloise TAYLOR 9 Dec 1880 POM Nazareth Baptist Church, Orange by William ROBINSON (OMR)

**WOOD,** Nicholas L. & **KEY,** Nancy by William DOUGLASS 15 Jan 1807 (OM)

**WOOD,** Richard & **COX,** Tabitha d/o Thomas COX who is also surety by George BINGHAM 27 Oct 1806 (OB) (OM)

**WOOD,** Richard W. s/o William T. WOOD and Sally RHOADES age 22 s blacksmith POB Orange POR Albemarle Co. & **CLARK,** Sarah H. d/o

William CLARK and Frances ESTES age 15 s POB POR Orange; POM Orange 5 Mar 1867 (OMR) 4 Mar 1867 (OML)

**WOOD,** Thomas & **BERRY,** Sarah Frances ward of Weedon SLEET who is also surety 11 Nov 1833 (OB)

**WOOD,** Thomas & **PORTER,** Rebecka d/o Samuel and Rebeckah PORTER consent given by Sarah PORTER surety Pierce SANFORD 30 Mar 1792 (OB) (permission paper)

**WOOD,** William B. s/o Elzy and Lucinda WOOD age 21 s POB POR Orange farmer & **THOMAS,** Frances E. d/o David THOMAS and Frances GARDNER age 18 s POB Albemarle Co POR Orange; POM Orange 28 Dec 1863 (OMR) 21 Dec 1863 (OML)

**WOOD,** William T. & **MITCHELL,** America d/o John MITCHELL who is also surety 3 Oct 1832 (OB)

**WOOD,** Willis POC age 32 s POB North Carolina POR Orange s/o Miles COPELAND and Milly _____ laborer & **MASON,** Flora POC age 29 w POB POR Orange d/o Reuben REID and Mary BROWN 22 Dec 1870 POM Orange by Philip JOHNSON (OM)

**WOOD,** Zachariah & **CLARKE,** Peggy surety Baylor MASON 10 May 1813 (OB) by J. GOSS 18 May 1813 (OB)

**WOOD,** Zachariah & **ESTIS,** Nancy surety John ESTIS 28 Dec 1815 (OB) by George BINGHAM 2 Jan 1816 (OM)

**WOOD,** Zachary s/o Zachary and Margaret WOOD age 40 s miller POB POR Orange & **HUGHES,** Nancy d/o Alexander and Elizabeth HUGHES age 50 s POB POR Orange; POM Orange 5 Oct 1854 (OMR) (OML)

**WOODHEAD,** William & **MAYO,** Lettisa by George BINGHAM 5 Oct 1821 (OM)

**WOODVILLE,** Edward S. (aka Edmund S. WOODVILLE) & **SISSON,** Miranda J.; POM Orange 15 Jul 1852 (OMR) 12 Jul 1852 (OML)

**WOODVILLE,** George C. age 23 s POB Culpeper Co POR Orange s/o John W. WOODVILLE and Mary E. CAMMACK carpenter & **SISSON,** Mary B. age 17 s POB POR Orange d/o Benjamin SISSON and Susan ROACH 15 Dec 1870 POM Orange by C.Y. STEPTOE (OM)

**WOODVILLE,** Horace C. age 24 s POB Culpeper POR Orange s/o John W. WOODVILLE and Mary E. CAMMACK farmer & **DUERSON,** Lizzie Chew age 21 s POB Spotsylvania POR Orange d/o Robert C. DUERSON and Caroline M. CAMMACK 15 Jan 1874 POM Orange (OMR)

**WOODWARD,** Warner M. age 25 s POB Albemarle Co POR Richmond, s/o J.P.L. WOODWARD and Mary M. MINOR merchant & **STEWART,** Mary E.K. age 22 s POB Connellsville, PA POR Orange d/o Kensey J. STEWART and Hannah LEE 28 Oct 1869 POM Orange by Kensey J. STEWART (OMR)

**WOOLDRIDGE**, Albert B. s/o D.S. WOOLDRIDGE and M.A. COX age 21 s student POB POR Richmond & **HANSBROUGH**, Maria S. d/o A.H. HANSBROUGH and E.C. STROTHER age 21 s POB Culpeper Co POR Orange; POM Orange C.H. 28 Oct 1863 (OMR) 27 Oct 1863 (OML)

**WOOLFOLK**, Augustine & **THOMAS**, Frankie both of St. Thomas Parish 28 Aug 1777 (Deed Book 17)

**WOOLFOLK**, James T. s/o Thomas and Frances WOOLFOLK age 22 s farmer POB Louisa Co POR Orange & **MOORE**, Sarah M. d/o William and Mary MOORE age 22 s POB POR Orange; POM Orange 2 Sep 1857 (OMR) 24 Aug 1857 (OML)

**WOOLFOLK**, John & **STANARD**, Mary Champe permission from William H. STANARD surety P.S. FRY 23 Nov 1826 (OB)

**WOOLFOLK**, John S. physician & **MORTON**, Sarah C. d/o George W. MORTON surety John W. GOODWIN 20 Mar 1848 (OB) by Herndon FRAZER 23 Mar 1848 (OM)

**WOOLFOLK**, Robert W. ward of William E. WOOLFOLK & **MORTON**, Mary E. d/o George W. MORTON; 16 Aug 1852 (OML)

**WOOLFOLK**, Thomas & **ELLIS**, Elizabeth w surety John HENDERSON 11 Aug 1828 (OB)

**WOOLFOLK**, William & **ELLIS**, Clarissa W. ward of James H. ELLIS who is also surety 25 Nov 1816 (OB)

**WOOLFOLK**, William & **WOOLFOLK**, Susan d/o Thomas WOOLFOLK surety William WOOLFOLK 30 May 1812 (OB)

**WOOLFOLK**, William T. physician & **GOODWIN**, Sally M. d/o John M. GOODWIN; 18 Jan 1853 (OML)

**WOOLFRY**, Benjamin O. s/o Henry WOOLFRY and Lucy OAKES age 44 w shoemaker POB POR Orange & **WOOLFRY**, Sarah Frances d/o Richard WOOLFRY and Emily SULLIVAN age 21 s POB POR Orange; POM Orange 28 Apr 1867 (OMR) 27 Apr 1867 (OML)

**WOOLFRY**, James W. & **SCOTT**, Eliza d/o George SCOTT surety John SCOTT 16 Dec 1845 (OB)

**WOOLFRY**, Richard & **BATTAILE**, Elizabeth d/o Alfred BATTAILE who is also surety 20 Oct 1820 (OB)

**WOOLFRY**, William S. age 22 s POB Spotsylvania Co. POR Orange s/o Richard WOOLFRY and Emiline SULLIVAN farmer & **MINNICK**, Minerva age 17 s POB POR Orange d/o Daniel MINNICK and Marg. WOOLFRY 10 May 1868 POM Orange by Sanders MASON (OMR)

**WORD**, Quin M. age 23 s rail road employee POB Buckingham POR Fredericksburg s/o William C. WORD and F. A. SNODDY &

**CHEWNING,** Madora E. age 20 s POB POR Orange d/o William B. CHEWNING and Susan OVERTON POM Orange 23 Oct 1878 by Melzi S. CHANCELLOR (OMR)

**WORMLEY**, Frank POC age 42 w POB Culpeper Co POR Orange s/o George WORMLEY and Maria _____ farm laborer & **WASHINGTON**, Ellen POC age 30 w POB Madison Co POR Orange d/o Daniel MEDLEY 4 Jan 1872 POM Orange by Frank TIBBS (OMR)

**WORMLEY,** George POC age 21 s farm labourer POB POR Orange s/o William WORMLEY and Fanny GORDON & **LINDSAY,** Phillis POC age 24 s POB POR Orange d/o Ambrose LINDSAY and Mahala STROTHER POM Mt. Calvery Baptist Church, Orange 15 Sep 1878 by W.J. BARNETT (OMR)

**WORMLEY,** Spotswood POC age 21 s labourer POB POR Orange s/o Reuben and Eliza WORMLEY & **DARNER,** Julia POC age 22 s POB POR Orange POM Shady Grove Church, Orange 24 May 1879 by C.T. JOHNSON (OMR)

**WREN,** Edward & **LOYD,** Lucy d/o Robert LOYD who is also surety 23 Aug 1819 (OB) 2 Sep 1819 by Leeroy CANADAY (OM)

**WRENN**, Albert s/o James WRENN and Lucinda MITCHELL age 27 s POB POR Fairfax Co. & **FOX**, Lucy d/o John FOX and A.M. BARKER age 21 s POB Fairfax Co POR Orange; POM Orange 15 Feb 1866 (OMR) 14 Feb 1866 (OML)

**WRENN,** Charles A. age 25 s miner POB Spotsylvania POR Orange s/o P.M. WRENN and Elizabeth BRUMMER & **JONES,** Martha A.W. age 17 POB POR Orange d/o James JONES and Martha A.W. PATES POM Orange 25 Dec 1877 (OMR)

**WRENN,** John & **LOYD,** Ester permission from Robert LOYD surety Ezekial LOYD 1 Jan 1819 (OB) (permission paper)

**WRIGHT,** Alexander & **BOSTON,** Malinda surety Thomas THORNTON 7 Mar 1816 (OB)

**WRIGHT,** Alexander & **JONES,** Betsy ward of Benjamin FICKLEN of Frederick County surety Edward HOLIDAY 9 Feb 1808 (OB) 10 Feb 1808 by Nathaniel SANDERS (OM)

**WRIGHT**, Alexander & **PITCHER,** Lucy; 24 Jan 1820 (OB)

**WRIGHT,** Augustine & **LINDSAY,** Mary d/o Mary LINDSAY surety Malachi ATKINS 21 Dec 1799 (OB)

**WRIGHT,** Benjamin & **QUISENBERRY,** Eliza d/o George QUISENBERRY who is also surety 22 Oct 1821 (OB)

**WRIGHT,** Benjamin Jr. age 31 s POB POR Orange s/o Benj. WRIGHT Sr. and Eliza QUISENBERRY farmer & **YOUNG,** Columbia age 26 s POB POR Orange d/o Charles W. YOUNG and Ann BROCKMAN 9 Jan 1868 POM Orange by Herndon FRAZER (OMR)

**WRIGHT,** Benjamin s/o Alexander WRIGHT dec'd and Frankey YOUNG stepson of Edwin YOUNG & **HERNDON,** Ann surety James HERNDON 5 Jun 1792 (OB)

**WRIGHT,** Bledsoe & **BEASLEY,** Sarah d/o Augustine BEASLEY surety Daniel WEBSTER 26 Dec 1791 (OB) by Nathaniel SANDERS 5 Jan 1792 (OM)

**WRIGHT,** Booker W. ward of Alex PEACHER who is also surety & **BLEDSOE,** Mary Ann ward of George BLEDSOE who is also surety 25 Jul 1831 (OB)

**WRIGHT,** Dabney & **BELL,** Sally ward of Brockman BELL 26 Aug 1809 surety Joseph WRIGHT (OB)

**WRIGHT,** Dabney s/o Dabney WRIGHT and Sarah E. BELL age 50 w farmer POB POR Orange & **RINER,** Sarah A.E. d/o Jacob RINER and Matilda ESTES age 34 s POB POR Orange; POM Orange 4 Apr 1865 (OMR) 1 Apr 1865 (OML)

**WRIGHT,** Edam J. age 32 w carpenter POB POR Orange s/o William WRIGHT and Susan CHEWNING & **YOUNG,** Laura V. age 21 s POB POR Orange d/o Charles YOUNG and Ann BROCKMAN POM Orange 19 Jun 1877 (OMR)

**WRIGHT,** Edward & **POWELL,** Frankey d/o John POWELL 24 Jan 1787 (OB)

**WRIGHT,** George W. & **COSBY,** Martha J.; 28 Nov 1854 (OML)

**WRIGHT,** Henry POC age 27 s POB Albemarle Co POR Orange s/o Mack WRIGHT and Sydney ____ sawmill hand & **ARMISTEAD,** Lucy POC age 22 s POB POR Orange d/o Hilliard ARMISTEAD and Kitty MCDANIEL 6 Apr 1872 POM Orange by J.S. HANSBROUGH (OMR)

**WRIGHT,** Isaac & **SMITH,** Agnes surety John FISHER 27 Dec 1813 (OB)

**WRIGHT,** James & **ROUSER,** Sarah; 28 Feb 1785 (OB)

**WRIGHT,** James & **SWEENEY,** Mary E. 1 Nov 1828 surety Thomas M. SWEENEY (OB)

**WRIGHT,** James POC age 27 w POB POR Orange s/o Peter WRIGHT and Agnes TAMEWOOD laborer & **HITE,** Roxa POC age 23 s POB POR Orange d/o Major HITE and Harriet COANTY 17 Aug 1870 POM Orange by Frank TIBBS (OMR)

**WRIGHT,** Jefferson & **WRIGHT,** Salley d/o William WRIGHT Jr. who is also surety 5 Dec 1828 (OB) by Jeremiah CHANDLER 10 Dec 1828 (OM)

**WRIGHT,** John & **GRASTY,** Susan Grant d/o Ann GRASTY 25 Sep 1789 surety William EDWARD (OB) by John LELAND the minister's return is dated 20 Sep 1788 (OM)

**WRIGHT**, John & **JONES,** Margaret surety John JONES 5 Nov 1783 (OB)

**WRIGHT**, John & **SEBREE,** Elizabeth surety Valentine JOHNSON 23 Jan 1797 (OB)

**WRIGHT**, John & **SHAVERS,** Polly 17 Nov 1801 by Nath. SANDERS (Misc Min Ret)

**WRIGHT**, John H. s/o Alexander WRIGHT who is also surety & **QUISENBERRY,** Lucy d/o George QUISENBERRY surety William WRIGHT 25 Feb 1828 (OB)

**WRIGHT**, John Jr. & **FAULCONER**, Catey 4 Aug 1801 by Nath. SANDERS (Misc Min Ret) surety John FAULCONER 27 Jul 1801 (OB)

**WRIGHT**, John Jr. & **WRIGHT,** Nancy d/o John WRIGHT who is also surety 25 Aug 1806 (OB) by Nathaniel SANDERS 28 Aug 1806 (OM)

**WRIGHT**, John P.R. s/o Booker and Mary A. WRIGHT age 25 mechanic POB POR Orange & **JONES,** Isabella d/o James and Elizabeth JONES age 21 POB POR Orange; POM Orange 9 May 1858 (OMR) 3 May 1858 (OML)

**WRIGHT**, John s/o James and Sarah WRIGHT age 37 w farmer POB POR Spotsylvania & **MASSEY,** Maria L. d/o James O. and Elizabeth MASSEY age 21 POB POR Orange; POM Orange 23 Aug 1857 (OMR) 17 Aug 1857 (OML)

**WRIGHT**, Larkin & **JAMES,** Lucy surety George JAMES 26 Oct 1799 (OB)

**WRIGHT**, Larkin s/o William WRIGHT Jr. & **HERNDON,** Elizabeth d/o John HERNDON who is also surety 23 Sep 1830 (OB)

**WRIGHT**, Lewis POC age 21 s POB POR Orange s/o Daniel WRIGHT and Tamar DICKERSON laborer & **TAYLOR,** Kitty POC age 20 s POB Albemarle Co POR Orange d/o Daniel TAYLOR and Ann LANDRUM 31 Dec 1868 POM Orange by Frank NICHOLAS (OMR)

**WRIGHT**, Lewis s/o Wade WRIGHT and Rebecca YORK age 27 s gentleman at large POB Bridgeport, Connecticut POR Early Co, Ga & **WHARTON,** Virginia A. d/o Samuel WHARTON and Lucy M. SIMES age 21 s POB POR Orange; POM Orange 16 Nov 1865 (OMR) (OML)

**WRIGHT**, Robert & **FAULCONER,** Lucy d/o John FAULCONER surety John RHOADES 21 Dec 1821 (OB)

**WRIGHT**, Robert s/o James M. WRIGHT and Martha ESTES age 36 w farmer POB POR Louisa Co. & **KING,** Virginia A. d/o Absalom KING and Sarah ELAM age 23 s POB Louisa Co. POR Orange; POM Gordonsville 25 Jan 1866 (OMR) 19 Jan 1866 (OML)

**WRIGHT**, Samuel & **HUGHS,** Susan surety Goury WAUGH 21 Jan 1834 (OB)

**WRIGHT**, Thomas R. s/o John WRIGHT & **FAULCONER**, Mary Ann d/o Ann FAULCONER surety Thaddeus S. WRIGHT 9 Dec 1833 (OB)

**WRIGHT**, William A. age 26 s POB Nelson Co POR Orange s/o Robert WRIGHT and Catharine WILTSHIRE r.r. hand & **AMOS**, Lucy C. age 25 s POB POR Orange d/o William M. AMOS and Intemperance DANIEL 3 Jul 1870 POM Orange by Charles QUARLES (OMR)

**WRIGHT**, William M. & **SLEET**, Lucy A. ward of James WILLIS surety Thomas RHOADES 21 Sep 1840 (OB)

**WRIGHT**, William POC age 31 s POB Culpeper Co POR Orange blacksmith & **PARKER**, Sarah POC age 21 s POB POR Orange d/o Henderson PARKER and Susan WILLIAMS 29 Dec 1868 POM Orange by H. BLAIR (OMR)

**WYANT**, John & **BAUGHKER**, Elizabeth by George BINGHAM 11 Mar 1818 (OM)

**YAGER**, James A. age 21 s POB Albemarle POR Orange clerk s/o Joseph A. YAGER and Martha N. FRAY & **STONESIFFER**, Josie age 18 s POB Shenandoah POR Orange d/o F.H. STONESIFFER and Virginia SEBERT 9 Jan 1877 POM Orange (OMR)

**YAGER**, Thomas & **CAUTHIN**, Fanny surety Noah WATTS 13 Jan 1816 (OB)

**YAGER**, William & **CHANCELLOR**, Jane d/o John dec'd. and Betsy CHANCELLOR John CHANCELLOR, her brother is surety 11 Jan 1809 (OB)

**YAGER**, William B. s/o Eli YAGER & **WHITELAW**, Elizabeth C. d/o Mary WHITELAW 20 Nov 1840 (OB)

**YAGER**, William M. age 21 s POB Albemarle Co POR Orange s/o Joseph H. YAGER and Martha A. FRAY merchant & **CARPENTER**, Virginia F. age 17 POB Greene Co POR Orange d/o James D. CARPENTER and Sally D. BROCK 15 May 1873 POM Orange by J.W. MCCOWEN (OMR)

**YANCEY**, Alexander & **LEE**, Elizabeth Jane d/o Sarah LEE surety William H. LEE 24 Dec 1840 (OB)

**YANCEY**, Edmund POC age 21 s labourer POB Louisa POR Orange s/o Edmund YANCEY and Malinda LEWIS & **TYLER**, Amanda age 20 s POB POR Orange d/o James TYLER and Polly JOHNSON POM Orange 22 Feb 1879 by W.J. BARNETT (OMR)

**YANCEY**, John W. & **TERRILL**, Sarah M. surety George M. MALLORY 6 Jan 1832 (OB)

**YANCEY**, John W. s/o Thomas and Sarah YANCEY age 51 w farmer POB Culpeper Co POR Rappahannock Co. & **TERRILL**, Jane d/o Urial and Jane TERRILL age 35 s POB POR Orange; POM Orange 19 Oct 1854 (OMR) 18 Oct 1854 (OML)

**YANCEY,** William POC age 23 s farm labourer POB Louisa POR Orange s/o Edwin YANCEY and Malinda ___ & **BELL,** Lucy POC age 18 s POB POR Orange d/o Jeff. BELL and Nancy _____ POM Orange 2 Jun 1879 (OMR)

**YANCY,** James E. & **WALLER,** Mary Eliza surety David STITZER 11 May 1843 (OB) by J. EARNEST 12 May 1843 (OM)

**YANCY,** Layton & **MOYERS,** Lurina d/o Michaeal MOYERS surety William H. MOYERS 21 Dec 1820 (OB)

**YARBOROUGH,** George POC age 21 s labourer POB Culpeper POR Orange s/o George YARBOROUGH and Julia SCOTT & **DAWSON,** Nancy POC age 21 s POB POR Orange d/o Strother DAWSON and Dicey _____ POM Hopewell Church, Orange 10 Sep 1879 by W.H. CAMPER (OMR)

**YATES,** Charles & **LOYD,** Betsy d/o William LOYD who is also surety 12 Mar 1810 (OB) by Jeremiah CHANDLER 15 Mar 1810 (OM)

**YATES,** James & **SANFORD,** Sally d/o Pierce SANFORD surety Abner NEWMAN 29 Jan 1799 (OB)

**YATES,** Snowden s/o Joseph and Sarah YATES age about 24 s saddler POB Fauquier Co POR Orange & **CULLEN,** Margaret age about 24 s POB Winchester POR Orange; POM Orange 21 Nov 1854 (OMR)

**YERBY,** John P. & **CLAYTON,** Mary Ella d/o Margaret CLAYTON who is also surety 16 May 1849 (OB)

**YORK,** Armistead & **HILMAN,** Joanna age 21 years 12 May 1801 by Nath SANDERS (Misc Min Ret) surety Uriel HILMAN 27 Apr 1801 (OB)

**YOUNG,** Charles s/o Mary YOUNG & **BROCKMAN,** Ann d/o Curtis L. BROCKMAN who is also surety 27 Jul 1840 (OB)

**YOUNG,** Columbus & **TERRILL,** Nancy D. surety John MORTON 6 Jun 1850 (OB)

**YOUNG,** Daniel & **RICHARDS,** Ann; POM Orange 2 Mar 1853 (OMR) 24 Jan 1853 (OML)

**YOUNG,** Daniel ward of Jeremiah MCKAY & **RHOADES,** Elizabeth d/o George RHOADES 17 Jul 1812 surety Vivion QUISENBERRY (OB)

**YOUNG,** Edward age 49 w POB POR Orange s/o John YOUNG and Mary REYNOLDS farmer & **GOOCH,** Mary E. age 45 w POB POR Orange d/o Elijah MORTON and Mary WEBB 16 Dec 1868 POM Orange by Richard STEPHENS (OMR)

**YOUNG,** Edwin & **WRIGHT,** Frances w surety Benjamin HEALY 19 Dec 1785 (OB)

**YOUNG,** James & **BROCKMAN,** Sarah E. d/o Curtis BROCKMAN who is also surety 14 Oct 1833 (OB)

**YOUNG,** John & **GRADY,** Frankey d/o Samuel GRADY 17 Oct 1795 surety William GRADY Jr. (OB)

**YOUNG,** John & **REYNOLDS,** Mary d/o William REYNOLDS and Nancy [NIXON] surety George QUISENBERRY 8 Dec 1803 (OB)

**YOUNG,** John & **ROGERS,** Sarah d/o Ann ROGERS surety Samuel YOUNG 11 Feb 1788 (OB) 14 Feb 1788 by George EVE (OM)

**YOUNG,** Laurence & **MARTIN,** Catherine; 7 Jul 1800 surety John MARTIN (OB)

**YOUNG,** Samuel M. age 22 POB POR Louisa Co s/o John YOUNG and Sarah EUBANK brick layer & **MAHANES,** Cornelia E. age 23 s POB Albemarle Co POR Orange d/o William C. MAHANES and Mary B. HARRIS 28 Oct 1873 POM Orange by P.H. CUTLER (OMR)

**YOUNG,** William & **DOUGLASS,** Mildred both of St. Thomas Parish surety Edmund MASSEY 29 Nov 1781 (OB)

**YOWELL,** Albert G. & **GUINN,** Lucy J. 19 Dec 1838 surety William WHITE (OB)

**YOWELL,** Ephraim & **EDDINS,** Polly 26 Oct 1812 surety Abraham EDDINS by John GARNETT (OB) (OMR)

**YOWELL,** James N. age 35 s carpenter POB POR Orange s/o A.G. YOWELL and Jane QUINIS (?) & **SMITH,** Louisa S. age 26 s POB POR Orange d/o James O. SMITH and Frances S. TUEL POM Orange 26 Nov 1879 (OMR)

**YOWELL,** John & **DAVIS,** Jane 22 Sep 1813 surety Cudden DAVIS (OB) 30 Sep 1813 by James GARNETT (OMR)

**YOWELL,** John T. age 27 s farmer POB Greene POR Orange s/o A. G. YOWELL and Lucy J. QUIN & **THOMPSON,** Susan F. age 29 s POB Tennessee POR Orange d/o Samuel S. THOMPSON and Lucy M. SNELL POM Orange 22 Mar 1876 (OMR)

**YOWELL,** Robert C. age 23 s POB Greene Co POR Orange s/o Albert YOWELL and Jane GWIN farmer & **CLARK,** Susan F. age 17 s POB POR Orange d/o William CLARK and Frances ESTES 14 Jan 1873 POM Orange by J.W. MCCOWN (OMR)

**YOWELL,** William L. age 25 s POB POR Culpeper Co s/o William N. YOWELL and Amanda THOMAS farmer & **PRIEST,** Mary E. age 18 s POB POR Orange d/o Augustine G. PRIEST and Cordelia CLARK 16 Feb 1869 POM Orange by John CLARK (OMR)

**ZACHARY,** Benjamin POR Brumfield Parish & **WHITE,** Frankie POR St. Thomas Parish 10 Dec 1775 by banns (Deed Book 17)

**ZERBY,** Robert POC age 22 s ostler POB Madison POR Orange s/o George ZERBY and Fanny BLACK & **BROOKS,** Susan POC age 21 s POB Rockingham POR Orange POM Gordonsville 24 Dec 1876 (OMR)

**ZERKLE,** Jacob & **SCROGHAM,** Lucy surety Robert HOLBERT 26 Jun 1837 (OB)

# INDEX

287

ALLEN, (continued)
David W. 3 Fanny 4 George 3
Isreal 3 J. Tanner 3 James 3
John 3 60 John F. 3 John T. 3
134 Julius 3-4 Lizzie 60
Louisa 153 Maria L. 155
Nancy 90 Peachy 134 Polly
227 Pounce 3 Thomas 3
William 3-4
ALLENS, Leana 181 Sally 39
William 39
ALLISON, John W. 4 Lelia 230
Lucy E. 225 Maria 4 Mariah
225 Mary F. 101 Robert 4 101
225
ALMOND, Jefferson 157 John F.
4 Lewis 4 Margaret L. 55
Martha Jane M. 160 Mason B.
55 William 55
ALSOP, Fanny 161 William P. 4
ALVIS, Henry 4
AMES, Alice J. 176
AMFIELD, John 4
AMOS, Charles 4 Charles H. 157
Emily L. 31 Estes 4 Estes W.
86 George A. 31 Jackson 4
Joseph 4 Lucy C. 284 William
M. 4 284 Wirter 4
AMUS, Benjamin 5
ANCEL, Robert 154
ANCELL, Elizabeth 141 Henry 5
James 5 Michael 5 Nancy 154
Robert 5 141
ANDERSON, Albert 56 168 Ann
Eliza 163 Augustine 5
Bathsheba 48 Benjamin 5
Charles W. 5 Charlotte N. 186
Elizabeth 6 Emily 70 Fanny
209 Frances 257 George 5
Harriet Ann 132 Henry 5 Jack
5-6 Jacob 5-6 21 179 257
James B. 5 James M. 5 James
W. 5 Joel 5-6 6 70 132 236
John v 6 John T. 5 John W. 5
Joseph 6 186 Lucy 185
Margaret 5 Mary 21 186 Mary
Jackson 236 Milly 123 N. H.
272 Nancy 209 Nanna 240
Nathan D. 6 Obediah 5 6
Pamelia M. 83 Philip 273
Rachel 236 Sally 111 Sarah
Ann 164 Sary 41 Theodoshia
139 Uriah 10 Washington 6
William 6 163 William M. 163

ANDREWS, Elizabeth Ann 36
Elmira E. 212 Emily S. 49
John L. 58 Lewis 36 49 58
Mary 58
APPERSON, Alfred 6 250
Cincinnatus 6 Evelina 76
Frances 80 Jos. 6 Joseph 6 111
Lucy D. 19 Lucy P. 111
Malvina 141 Mary E. 250
Peter 6 Richard 80 Thomas 6
19 76 141
APPISON, Richard 6
ARANZY, Zanny 202
ARCHER, Amanda M. 25 Ann
38 Emily 204 James 23 25 204
ARGEBRIGHT, George 151
ARHART, Jacob 7
ARMCOL, Mary S. 214
ARMISTEAD, Ellen 124 G. 63
Hannah 7 214 258 Harriet 258
Hilliard 124 282 Lewis 7 Louis
133 Louisa G. 210 Lucy 133
282 Samuel 7 258
ARMSTRONG, Agnes 4 Sarah
F. 199 William J. 13
ARNALL, William B. 7
ARNETT, Jane Ellen 136 Liddia
251 William 136 205 251
ARNHOLD, Willis 231
ARNOLD, Anna 212 Benjamin
212 James 7 Joanna 105 Mary
150 Mary A. 92 Nicholas 114
Sally 212 Sarah 114 Susannah
36 Thomas 7 211 William B. 7
Willis 7 105 139 212
ARRINGTON, Emily 134
ASHBY, Alice S. 16
ASHTON, Henry 7
ATKINS, Achilles 7 99 Ann 8
Ann Maria 37 Annie 81 B. F. 7
Betty 233 Charles D. 7 9 143
269 Davis 7 152 156
Dickinson 7 71 Edward 7 9
Eliza F. 3 Elizabeth 7 147
Elizabeth Y. 258-259 Fanny 8
Gentry 7 Helen G. 121
Hennitta 143 Henry C. 7-8
Hezekiah 8 161 J. 85 James 7-
8 75 173 John 8 16-17 265 271
John R. 265 Jonathan 8 192
Joseph 3 7-8 37 76 85 127 147
204 Lucy 173 Lucy M. 269
Malachi 281 Mallachi 8
Margaret 7 264 Martha J. 76

288

ATKINS, (continued)
Mary 3 76 Mildred 176 Nancy
9 Patsy 155 Rhoda 16 Rhody
81 Robert 8 Robert H. 8
Rosanna 17 Sally 8 Samuel
140 Samuel G. 233 Sarah 71
Sarah M. 37 Silence 8 Spencer
129 Spencer I. 258 Spencer J.
31 37 259 Susannah 16 Waller
8 Walter 8 William 8-9
William C. 8 William G. 9 121
Wisdom 9 Wisdon 7-8
ATKINSON, Bernard 9 Thomas
9 William R. v
AUGUST, P. F. 147 R. F. v
AULT, Sevilla 236
AUSBUM, Robert 9
AUSTIN, Ann 41 David 9 John 9
Mildred 277 Nancy 9 Richard
9 Richard D. 9 Sallie B. 117
Samuel G. 9 William 9 213
William C. 117 Willis 9
AWL, Sarah J. 166
AYHEART, Felicia 149
BABER, Amanda 231 Robert 9
BACK, Lucy 194 Rachel 194
BACON, Delphia 207
BADGER, Lucy 147 Margaret
264 Philadelphia 83
BAGLEY, Fanny 93
BAILES, John T. 231 Joseph 9
Lillie H. 231
BAILEY, Edward D. 9 Jacob 12
Lewis 10 Samuel 9-10 William
P. 10
BAILY, James 10
BAKER, Clementina V. 185
Clementine V. 13 John M. 14
Joseph M. 10 Linneaus M. 10
Lucinda 10 Thomas S. 10
William 10
BALL, Annie H. 195 Eliza Ann
231 Jesse 231 Marcus 195
BALLARD, Anne 255 Charles
B. 93 Curtis 10 David C. 10
Edward 10 Edwin 10 221 Elias
W. 10 Elizabeth 189 Garland
33 103 142 Georgiana 142
Georgianna 103 Helen Peyton
142 John M. 200 Larkin 10
Lora A. 10 Lucy J. 93 Martha
189 Mary 23 Mary E. 103
Medley 10 Milly 262
Moreman 189 Nanny 7

BALLARD, (continued)
Philip 262 Susannah 188
Thomas 10 Virginia C. 221
Washing 10 William 10
William S. 10
BALLS, Malinda 155
BALMAINE, Alexander 10
BALTIMORE, Mary Jane 204
BALY, John 101
BANK, Sally 191
BANKHEAD, Charles L. 10
Charles S. 10 Dorothea 10 163
276 Dorothea B. 167 Eliza M.
276 Ellen 163 Georgianna
Cary 167 Mary Ann 10 Mary
C. 10 Rosalie S. 276 William
10 163 167 276
BANKS, Adam 41 Amanda 186
Betsey 197 Celia 165 Dicey
178 Emma 136 Ezekiel 69 165
Fanny 182 Gerard James 11
Hannah 214 Henry 182 John
11 136 Lucy 153 Martha 114
Mary 252 Matilda 253 Nellie
33 Sampson 11 186 253 Sarah
214 Sophia 165 Susan 69
William 256 Willie Ann 61
BARBAGE, Betsy 231
BARBER, Mary 56 Thomas 11
BARBOUR, Ambrose 11 Betsy
145 C. Ella 5 Cornelia C. 228
Ellen 270-272 Fanny 168
Frances Cornelia 51 Gabriel
240 Hannah 30 32 J. W. 174
James 11 Kitty 40 Lucy 176
Maria 236 Martha 12 Mary
Price 56 Mary T. 33 Nelly 174
Phil 5 Philip C. S. 11 Philip D.
11 Philip P. 11 Philip
Pendleton 11 Philippi 79
Quintus 228 Richard 11 Sarah
96 Thomas 11 33 96 Walker
145
BARCUS, Archibald 255
BARDEN, Alverta Ellsworth 187
Lewis H. 187
BARK, Sally 191
BARKER, A. M. 281 James 11
Leonard 11 Lucinda 175
BARKHART, Margaret E. 237
BARKS, James 250 Sallie 122
Sarah A. 250
BARKSDALE, A. M. 104
Nathaniel 11

289

BELL, (continued)
Frances 143 Francis 60 162
Francis K. 14 272 Grace 7
Granville 14 H. C. 15 Hannah
130 Harriet 122 Henry 14 224
Henry C. 14-15 177 239 Ida F.
74 Jacob 15 James R. 15 Jeff
130 Jeff. 285 Jeffrey 122 John
15-16 55 61 91 143 188 John
B. 14-15 167 John H. 15
Joseph 86 Joseph H. 15 Joshua
G. 15 Larkin G. 15 Lucinda
272 Lucy 285 Mahaloa 224
Margaret 278 Mary 2 60 162
278 Mary Ann 177 Mary
Margaret 60 Milley 6 Minerva
C. 239 Nancy 85 Nannie R. 44
Nelson H. 15 Orville 44 74
Patrick 15 Polly 40 Ralph 16
Rebecca 46 173 Robert A. 15
Robert S. 15 Robert W. 15
Roger 8 15 46 86 143 204
Rose 260 Sally 46 57 60 282
Sally B. 85 204 Sarah E. 282
Susanna 151 Susannah 20
Thomas 6 15-16 20 46 104 144
223-224 Thomas D. 15
Virginia A. 167 William 14 16
85 151 William B. 16
BELLAMY, James 16
BELLOMY, Ambrose F. 16
James W. 16
BELZER, Edw. A. 16 William F.
16
BENNETT, A. H. 44 76 257 B.
22 198 Bartlett v Brittania 232
Howard 131 Nancy 131
BENSON, G. 216 Judith 216
BENT, Daniel 16 133
BENTLEY, Mary E. 122
BERKELEY, Nelly 153 Was 16
Winston 16
BERKLEY, Jane 190
BERNARD, D. M. 99 Mary Ann
99
BERRY, Anthony 16 Eliza 17
Gibbs 16 Lucy A. 144 Lucy
Ann 278 Mary 174 Sarah F. 79
83 Sarah Frances 279 William
P. 16 William S. 16
BESME, Margaret 67
BESS, Sally 223
BETTERMAN, S. M. v
BETTERMANN, S. M. 90

BETTS, Rosa A. 56
BIBB, Maria 123 Thomas 16
William 16
BICKERS, Abner 17 32
Alexander 17 274 Benjamin 17
Benjamin C. 154 Bettie A. 55
Caleb 17 Elizabeth 55 149
George 17 70 Henrietta S. 5
Jairus 17 Joanna 154 Joel 17
John 17 23 Joseph 17 134 149
225 Judy 17 Julia M. 103 170
Lucy 103 160 170 Lucy M. 29
Margaret 85 Mary F. 74 94
Matilda 225 Nancy 32
Nicholas 106 154 Polley 106
Polly 106 Proctor 17 103 160
170 Samuel 17 Selina Anna 70
Serena 103 Susan 32 134
Susan A. 160 Thomas 17
William 17 29 55 William H. 5
BIGGERS, Betsy 251 Huldah
138 Macon 138 211 Mason
251 Phebe 211 William 138
BIGGS, William 17
BILLINGSLEY, John A. v 65
112 190 253-254 269-270 Jos.
A. 230
BINGHAM, George v 2 4-6 9-12
14 17-18 21 23 25 27 32-35
40-43 46 49-52 55 60-62 67-69
71 74 80 83-84 87-89 91 98
100-106 108 110-111 123 126
133 135-136 139-142 144 148-
149 151-152 154 158-160 162-
164 166 169-172 174 177-180
185-186 188-191 193 195 197-
198 201 203 205-206 210-211
214-217 219-221 226-228 231
235-236 241 247-248 252 255-
256 259 261 261-263 266 272
275 277-279 284 John 74 198
Josias 17 267 Maria 74 Milly
198 Polly 105 Rebecca 17
Wyatt 17
BINS, Jane 98
BIRCHETT, George K. 17
BIRD, Harrison 17 Nelson 17
BIRT, Moses 172 Ruthy 172
BISCOE, William E. 17
BISHOP, Ann 60 Joseph 17-18
234 Samuel 18
BLACK, Fanny 286 Jacob 18
Joshua 18 William 18 235
BLACKERBY, Thaddeus 18

BOTHIGHEIMER, Elias 22
BOTT, John 22
BOTTIGHEIMER, Emanuel 22
BOUGHAN, John 22 Nathaniel
    J. 22 Sarah F. 24
BOULLING, Susan 157
BOULWARE, Richard S. 22 71
BOURN, Andrew 22 Jenny 79
    John 22
BOURNE, Ambrose 22
    Elizabeth 80 Henry 80 Jane L.
    119 John 187
BOUSE, James 22 Simon 22
BOUTWRIGHT, John H. 22
    John L. 22
BOWCOCK, Elvira M. 104
    Madeline 76 Susan 62 Tandy
    22 62
BOWEN, Ann 54 Elizabeth 80
    Ephraim 22 Francis 23 Henry
    80 John 23 54
BOWER, Thomas 23
BOWLER, Addison 24 171 271
    Aggy 271 Anderson 230
    Charles 132 David 67 104
    Davis 67 Elizabeth G. 67
    Elizabeth M. 189 Ellen 24
    George W. 23 Harriet A. 66
    Maria 230 Mary E. 31 Mary F.
    104 Mary Frances 104 Robert
    31 66 117 189 Sarah 189 Silah
    171 Winney 23
BOWLING, Caroline V. 66
    Charles 23 John 23
BOWMAN, Abraham 23 N. W.
    23 Rebecca 23
BOXALL, Sophia 181 200
BOXLEY, Drusilla 156 George
    23 Joseph 95
BOYDEN, E. 265
BOYER, Thomas 23
BOYKIN, Robert M. 23 Robert
    Virginius 23
BRACKEN, Edward 85
BRADEN, Joseph 23
BRADFORD, Alexander 19 23
    234 245 John E. 53 Joseph 245
    Joseph B. 234 Lucy Ann 234
    Mollie M. 53 S. Slaughter 23
    Samuel K. 23 Sarah Jemima
    245
BRADLEY, Almeda W. 68 Ann
    E. 39 D. S. 68 Demarcus L. 23
    Elizabeth 48

BRADLEY, (continued)
    George 23 41 48 126 James 24
    James H. 24 Jennie M. 5 John
    24 John H. 5 Lafayette 224
    Lucinda 270 Lucy 41 48 Maria
    F. 142 Mary B. 111 Nancy 86
    126 Pollard 111 Richard 24
    Sally 277 Susan E. 224
    William 24 81 105 142 277
    William N. 24
BRADLY, Nancy 178
BRADY, Sarah 23
BRAGG, Benjamin 24 Joseph 21
    24 Joseph M. 24 Mary Y. 21
    Moore 24 William A. 24
BRAHAM, Millie 220
BRAMHAM, Giles 3 Laura 3
BRAMMER, Elizabeth 127
BRANCH, Nelson 24 Walker 24
BRANDEN, Lucy 254
BRANHAM, Andrew 24-25
    Bashnor 146 Bushrod 256
    Dora 146 John H. 25
    Marmaduke 25 80 118 166 208
    Matilda 146 Milly 220 256
    Nancy 18 Polly 19 Robert 18-
    19 Tavner 25 William 25
BRAWNER, Martha L. 41
BRAXTON, Carter M. 25
    Cornelius 25 Emmanuel 25
    Hannah 178 Jack 25 Nat 25
    Ony 25 Simon 25
BRAY, Patrick 25 Susan 84
BREADWELL, Liddy 35
BREEDING, Acquilia 246
    Berryman 216 Ephraim 25
    Ephriam 25 Ezekial 140
    Ezekiel 25 James 25 Job 82
    Richard 25 82 Sarah 216
    Susannah 82
BREEDLOVE, Broadus 25
    Churchill 25 Edward 26
    Madison 26 Martin 4 26
    Nathaniel 26
BREEDON, Rhoda A. 27
BREEDWELL, Anky 51 Thomas
    26
BREMER, John F. 26
BRENT, Aaron 26 Eliza F. 60
    George Lee 26 George P. 57
    117 Harriet 117 Harriet M. 117
    Jacob 26 Joseph 26 Judith A.
    183 Kendal C. 26 Sarah A. 57
    William 26

293

BREWER, Ellis 204 Violet L.
204
BRIAN, John O. 58
BRIANT, Jeremiah 64 227
Martha 227 Wintifred 8
BRIDEHART, Mary 102
BRIDENHEART, Susan 53
BRIDGES, Matthew 26 125
William 26
BRIDWELL, 11 Ella G. 245
John 26 O. H. 26 William H.
26 245
BRIGGS, W. S. v 71 123
BRIGHTWELL, Absalom 26
John D. 27 Malicia 162
Malissa 162 Sarah 132
BRIMMER, Sallie 97 Sally 97
BRINKER, Mary S. 94
BRISCOE, John Henry 27
William E. 27
BRITT, Charles G. 27 Mary 188
Sally 188
BRITTON, Emma F. 45 Joseph
F. 27 S. F. 45 William A. 27
BROADDASS, William F. v
BROADUS, Addie 108 Alice
260 Andrew 108 260 Betsy
160
BROCK, Alex. 51 Alice 116
Ann 182 Ansalem 27
Archibald 27 Benjamin 27
Courtney 51 Elizabeth 27 183
Harvey 27 Jack 27 Jacob 27
Jemima 102 John C. 27 Mary
14 Phoebe 200 Robert 183
Robert S. 27 Sally D. 284
Winfield 27
BROCKENBROUGH, William
H. 137
BROCKMAN, Adaline 49 Agnes
71 Albert T. 27 Ambrose 25-
26 76 108 111 208 Amelia 27
Andrew 27 Ann 85 281-282
285 Ann E. 44 Asa 27-29 54
107 Belfield 28 177 Bettie 74
242 Bledsoe 28 266 Christo.
229 Curtis 28 95 285 Curtis L.
15 28 212 285 Elijah 28 Elisa
C. 95 Eliza 74 104 200 Eliza
E. 96 Elizabeth 29 107 151
245 Elizabeth C. 29 Elizabeth
F. M. 177 F. D. 207 Fannie 61
Harriet C. 207 Harry 200 Ira S.
58 James 28 244-245

BROCKMAN, (continued)
John 14 28-29 56 152 John H.
28 Joseph 28 Joshua L. 28-29
Julia 227 Julia A. 223 258
Julia F. 176 Lou 96 Lucian T.
28 Lucy 212 234 Lucy B. 134
Lucy I. 211 Major 28 Maria E.
58 Martha 147 Mary 15 139
268 Mary Ann 138 167 Moses
28 Nancy 110 150 Nelly 28 56
Polly 152 Rebecca 14 Sam 28
Samuel 16 27-28 96 184 242
245 268 Sarah 16 Sarah E. 54
285 Sims 207 258 Suckey 86
Susa 184 Susanna 86 Virginia
A. 137 William 27-29 147
150-151 William A. 29
William Joel 29 William L.
28-29 61 138
BRONAUGH, Charles 29
Charles B. 29
BRONOUGH, Martha L. 121
BROODUS, John 97
BROOK, George 240
BROOKE, George 29 268
BROOKING, Amanda 221
Belinda 57 262 Cassandra B.
249 Charles 221 Charles R. 2
29 139 210-211 249 James 262
Jane 139 Jane M. 123 Jennie
E. 221 Lucy J. 2 Mary Ann
210 Mary R. 57 Robert 29 262
Robert U. 29 74 Robert W.
105 123 Samuel 29 William 29
William F. 29 79
BROOKMAN, Courtenay 57
Courtney 57 Courtney F. 57
James 29 Julia 226 Martha 147
Pleasant 148 Sarah 5 Thomas
217
BROOKS, Anthony 29 170
Barwell 30 Catharine 2 135
Ellen 166 170 Fanny 31
Frederick 30 166 George 30
James 30 Jane 160 John 160
Louanna 197 Lucy 37 43
Rachel 160 Sarah 128 135
Susan 286 Susanna 160
Virginia 143
BROUGHAN, Sarah F. 21
BROUGHTON, Thomas 30
BROWN, A. E. 233 Adam 31-32
150 Albert 118 Alice 119 235
Allen 30 Alverta S. 118

294

BROWN, (continued)
Ann 114 Armistead 31 111
Ben 119 Bernis 30 Bettie 122
Bezabel 30 Bushrod W. 30
Carrie C. 237 Catey 253
Charles B. 30 58 Charlotte 66
Daniel v 30 130 Edgar 30 32
Eliza L. 265 Elizabeth 38 169
181 252 263 Emily 19 George
3 Hamet 30 Harriet 11 125
Harry 30 Henry 30-31 Henry J.
30 32 Horace 30 Jake 122
James 30-31 241 253 James E.
31 James O. 30-31 69 139 265
269 James R. 31 James S. 237
James W. 31 Jim 54 John 23
31-32 40 155 157 169 John G.
31 72 156 Joseph F. 31 Julia
54 Lewis 31 Linny 170 Lucy
Ann 155 Maggie B. 237
Margaret 241 Martha 155
Martha A. 49 Martha C. 157
Martha F. 156 Mary 52 140
184 279 Mary D. 60 Mary P.
184 Matthew B. 31 Mollie G.
139 Opian 31 Page 31 Patsey
150 Philippa J. 72 Preston 31
Roberta E. 69 Robinson 60
Sallie M. 269 Sanderson 32
Sarah 47 Sarah F. 52 156 Seth
C. 32 Susan 3 23 68 Susan A.
224 Thomas H. 32 Walker 30
William 32 52 65 262 Wilson
32
BROWNING, Cornelius R. 32
Elizabeth 32 John A. 32
Joshua 32 Julia A. 53 Willis 32
BROZWELL, Mary N. 239
BRUCE, Catherine 80 Elizabeth
271 Loudoun B. 32 Mary 2
Mordecai 32 Sarah 54 74 103
Silas v
BRUMMER, Elizabeth 281
BRUNER, Peter 32
BRUSCH, John 32 John J. 32
BRUSH, Anna 81 John 81
BRYAN, Daniel 33 Edith 80
Edward 13 33 James 33 81
Jeremiah 13 33 63 81 Mary 13
Pauline 81
BRYANT, Charles 33 Jeremiah
135 John 33 Lewis 33 Norris
33 Rebecca 33 Thomas 33
William 33

BRYSON, Mary 55
BUCHANAN, Cornelia 52 John
238 John M. 33 William S. 33
BUCK, Anthony 33 Virginia 134
BUCKHANNON, John 33
BUCKNER, Baldwin 33
Elizabeth B. 27 Jane 265 Judy
26 W. 265 William 247
BUFFINGTON, Catharine 276
BULL, Fanny D. 181 Marcus 33
181 222 273 Mary S. 222
Nellie B. 273
BULLOCK, Oswald 33 Robert
N. 33 Sophia 14 33 Walter 33
William K. 34 William R. 33
BULLS, Alfred 34
BUMPASS, Joseph 34
BUNDY, William 34
BUNNELL, Hardenia 101
BURDINE, Sally 131
BURDON, Willis 34
BURGES, Edmund 78 May 78
BURK, 254 Sally 252
BURKE, Isaac 34 Polly 68
BURKES, Ella 131 Eve 43
James 131
BURKET, Elizabeth R. 155
BURKHART, Margaret E. 237
BURKS, Sarah Ann 43
BURN, James 34
BURNAM, Charles 34
BURNLEY, Frances 2 Garland
34 James 34 215 John 34 Jonas
34 Judith 2 15 Mary 215
Reuben 15 Richard 34 Sally 15
Sarah G. 241 Zachary 215 268
BURNS, James 34
BURRASS, Ann 8 Edmund 8
BURROUGHS, Mourning 96
BURROWS, Jane 192 Mary 184
Suzanna 62
BURRUS, Alfred 34 Ann 83
Anna 3 Anne 147 Edmund 98
183 Elizabeth 183 Frances 55
96 Jane 50 Joseph 2 34 55
Justina 9 Martha Ann 2 Mary
194 208 Roger 34 Rosanna
208 Sam 34 Samuel 34 Sukey
172 Thomas 34 Thomas F. 55
William T. 83
BURRUSS, Alice 27 Ann 82 243
Catharine S. F. 55 Daniel 29
Emily 192 Fannie 121 Frances
192 Hariett 168 Joseph 35 192

295

BURRUSS, (continued)
Kate H. 10 Lancelot 35 Louisa
A. 163 Minor 35 Robert B. 10
27 35 Sally 125 Sam 35 Sarah
267 Thomas 121 192 Thomas
F. 55 William T. 8 28 35 109
168 192
BURTON, A. S. 193-194 Albert
G. 30 Arminta V. 193 Aylett
35 Benjamin 23 55 70 218 262
Betsy 35 Bezabel 35 Clarasa
180 Elizabeth 18 233 Fanny 33
92 Fleming 35 Frankie 163
Hannah 23 James 26 30 35 233
Jesse 35 John 35 John M. 30
35 Joseph 198 208 Judith 19
Lucinda 101 Lucy 50 Margaret
67 248 Maria 70 Martha 218
Mary 70 Mary P. 208 Matilda
1 May 19 23 35 50 70 163 182
218 Nancy 18 30 Polly 26
Robert 18 101 158 Sarah 18
182 Virginia 158 William 18
26 35 101 158
BUSH, Caleb 35 Edmund 35
Francis 26 35 James 188
Thomas 35
BUSICK, Anna 238 Annie R. 27
James 27 Martha Ann 8
Nathan S. 36 Samuel 8
William 36
BUTLER, Alexander F. 36 Bettie
J. 238 David F. 36 Elijah 36
George W. 36 John J. 86 238
Malinda C. 86 Matthew 36 89
Robert E. 36 Robert L. 36
William R. 36
BYERS, David H. 36
BYRUM, Annie E. 98 John 36
98
BÄECKMAN, John 9
CAHOE, Nancy 36 Patrick 36
Richard 36
CALDWELL, B. R. 36 J. T. 36
Porter D. 36
CALHOON, William 253
CALHOUN, William v 12 105
CALVERT, Manifred 138
CAMBELL, Frederick W. 265
CAMIKE, Polly 209
CAMMACK, Caroline M. 279
Catherine A.V. 275 Mary E.
279 William E. 275
CAMP, James 36 William 36

CAMPBELL, Absalom 37
Alexander 36 Amy 37 Ann
265 267 Archibald 36
Benjamin 37 Catharine H. 68
Celas 67 Edmund 19 Edward
37 Emma T. 151 George 195
Isaac 37 Isabella 195 James A.
37 James S. 37 159 Jane A.
127 John 37 67 205 219 228
267 Joseph D. 37 Larkin 37
Milly 19 Ned 37 Peggy 8
Philip 151 Priscilla 151 Robert
37 97 Sally 272 Susan 95 213
Ursulia 159 Virginia M. 158
W. H. v 15 143 W.S. 72
Wesley 151 William 158 165
178 William J. 37 Willis 37
Wythe P. 17
CAMPER, John 37 W. F. 140 W.
H. v 8 24 34 44 51 53 74 125
130 182 189 201 235 244 253
285 William H. 37
CANADAY, Ann 157 Caroline
F. 248 Edward 14 Edward N.
144 James 37-38 248 James D.
37 Leeroy 112 164 185 281
Sarah 14 75
CANADY, Ann C. 157 James
157 Leroy vii
CANNADAY, Bettie D. 77
James 77 James D. 38
CANNON, Edward 231
CANTERBERRY, Joseph 79
182 Mary Ann 242
CARBERRY, Margaret 38
Patrick 38 William 38
CARD, Abraham 38
CAREY, Albert 38 George 38
Wilson 38
CARLETON, Martha 178
CARNEEL, James 38 John 38
CARNS, Martha 178
CARPENTER, Ellen 133
Fountain 38 Henry 38 165
James 38 James D. 284
James W. 38 Jo. 133 John F.
38 253 Jonas 38 Louisa 253
Martha F. 38 Mary 161 165
Mary E. 55 Mildred 65 P. 253
P. M. 180 Philip M. 38
Pleasant 38 65 Reuben 38
Virginia F. 284 William 23
228 William B. 38 William Jr.
v Willis H. 38

296

CARR, Albert 39 David 39 Dick
39 Fanny 39 Matilda 236
Sarah 69
CARRER, Elizabeth 11
CARRIES, Malinda 72
CARROL, Jacob 39
CARROLL, William 39
CARRUTHERS, William H. 39
CARSON, T. M. 34 36 62 135
194 214 233 237 247 255 Theo
M. v 35 138 170 Theo. M. 181
CARTEE, Dorothy 152
CARTER, Aaron 79 Adcock 39
Ann 257 Ben 132 Benjamin 39
Burwell 39 146 Burwwell 39
Cassius 39 Catherine 187 Celie
40 Charles R. 39 Cyrus 39
Daniel H. 224 Dinah 115
Dorothy 152 Edmund 39-40
239 Elizabeth 62 Elizabeth
Lucy 39 Ellen 79 166 Frank S.
224 George 39 Harry W. 39
Howard P. 39 James 40 Jane
A. 210 Jinny 122 John 40
Joseph 40 Judith 44 Lewis 40
Lucinda 146 Lucy 61 270
Lydia 245 Maria 42 Martha
257 Mary A. 190 Milly 131
Miranda 31 Nannie 42 Patsy 3
Patty 3 Rena 237 Reuben 42
Robert 40 Thomas 39 Thomas
W. 40 Tom 31 39 William 40
257 William C. 40 William
Fitzhugh 39
CARTY, Betsey 89
CARVER, Franklin 266 Sarah
Ann 266
CARY, Barney 40
CASEBOLT, Andrew M. 40
CASEY, William 40
CASH, Catey 267 James 40 65
Joseph B. 40 Matilda A. 65
CASON, Benjamin 40 61
Edward 180 236 Elizabath 61
M. H. 40 Mary B. 236 Sallie
M. 61 William 40-41
CASSEN, Elizabeth 14
CATE, Martha 158
CATES, David H. 41 David S.
41
CATLETT, Catharine R. 99 N.
P. 99

CATTERTON, Benjamin W. 41
Elizabeth 180 Francis 41 Mary
272 Nancy 219
CAUTHIN, Fanny 284
CAVE, Abner 41 162 226
Amanda 80 Ann 162 Bartlett
41-42 Belfield 42 132 Bellfield
268 Benjamin 16 41 89 121
David 250 Elizabeth 121 132
Emily A. 39 Frances 140
Frances B. 50 Hannah 180 243
Hannah Jane 15 Harriett 269
Horace 80 I. Delacey 223 Irena
80 Isaac 41 Isabella 245 John
42 L. W. 72 229 Lavinia 71
Lavinia B. 71 Maria 15 Maria
C. 245 Mary A. 188 Mary Lou
193 Nancy 18 Nathan 41 Nelly
254 Philip C. 39 50 215 Polly
226 R. Lin 168 R. C. 94-95
206 226 243 263 Richard 15
41-42 132 236 271 Robert 41
71 153 250 269 Robert C. v 41
124 Robert P. 41 188 232 252
S. F. 188 Sinclair 41 St. Clair
257 Thomas 41 Thomas B. 42
W. E. 212 Walker 193 William
18 41-42 140 180 234 William
P. 223 245
CAZA, William 42
CHAMBERLAIN, Alice 107
CHAMBERLANE, Alice 107
CHAMBERS, Abraham 42 C. V.
278 Caty 195 Elizabeth 80
Mary 1 Rachel 220 Rebecca 80
Thomas 1 42 220 Willis 42
CHAMHART, Henry 42
CHAMP, Philip 42 Robert 42
CHAMPE, Lewis 42 Mary 42
Nannie 42 Robert 42
CHANCELLOR, Betsy 284
Elizabeth 136 Jane 284
Jeremiah 206 John 206 284 M.
S. 200 254 Melzi 141 158
Melzi S. v 6 21 31 45 49 64 97
101 104 111 113 135 156 161
181 186 194 211 249-250 275
281 Penelope 206 Sarah 93
CHANDLER, Edmund 222 Ellen
272 Fred. 40 Frederick 42
James 43 Jane 178 Jeremiah v
6 11 14 28 66 68-69 75 78 80
95 98 101 106 120 125-126
136 145-146 150 167 171

CLARK, William (continued)
211 268 279 286 William D.
102 252 William O. 46
William S. 89
CLARKE, Ann 179 Ann H. 39
Armistead 186 Barsheba 21
Catey 156 Cordelia G. 190
Elizabeth 39 Eunice H. 161
Frances 178 Henry 46 144 247
Henry James 46 Henry T. 176
James 176 John 46 156 John J.
46 Julia 275 Mary Ann 193
Mary Jane 176 Nancy 158
Peggy 279 Richard S. 46
Robert 178 Stokely 175
Stokely T. 46 190 Thomas 46
193 Virginia 174 Walker 46
William 21 39 46 174 William
D. 39
CLARKSON, Anselm 46 Nancy
41
CLASBY, Courtney 67
CLATTERBUCK, Mary 167
William 167
CLAXTON, Benjamin 47 Harriet
240 Reuben 47
CLAY, Henry 47
CLAYTON, Ella Margaret 285
Hannah 2 Mary 285 Philip 47
CLAYTOR, Elizabeth 254
CLEAVE, Sarah 215
CLEE, Elizabeth 149 John 149
CLEGHORN, Elisha B. v
CLEMENS, Henry 174 Polly
174
CLEMENT, Julia E. 222
CLEMMER, David F. B. 47
George L. 47
CLEMMONS, Henry 172
Mildred 172
CLEVELAND, Patty 224
CLEVELY, Agnes 233
CLINEDINST, Jacob 276
CLITHERALL, Fannie 23
CLOPTON, N. V. 47 Nathaniel
A. 47
CLORE, Charles 47 Silas F. 47
William 47
COANTY, Harriet 282
COATES, John 47
COATS, Jeremiah 47
COBB, Mary 21

COBBS, Courtney 86 Lucetta N.
181 Mary Ann 86 Peter N. 47
86 181
COCHRAN, Ellen 3 Patrick 61
COCKBURN, Robert 47
COCKE, Alexander 47
COCKERELL, Sarah 47
COCKERILL, James A. 47
Margaret 44 Thompson 44
COCKERILLE, Eleanor 175
COCKRANE, Patrick 47
COCKRELL, John 47 Martha
199 235
COCKRELLE, Martha 117
COCKRILL, Sarah E. 134
COFER, James 114 Joel 242
Judah 114
COFFERY, Amey 143 Anny 143
COFFMAN, Ben 275 Celia 275
David C. 48 Rhoda 275
William S. 48
COGWELL, Ralph 48
COKELY, Daniel 161
COLE, Ann E. 110 Catharine A.
205 Ellen 263 John v 79 148
263 John W. 48 Josephine C.
80 Louisa 123 Mary F. 110
Philip 80 Susan 23 43 167
Wesley 48 William 2 43 110
William J. 48
COLEMAN, Addison S. 49
Ambrose 48 48-49 193 Betsy
106 Bettie 28 49 Burrell 48
Camomile 42 Catharine 209
Charlotte 131 David P. 48
Edmand M. 48 Eliz. 171 Eliza
267 Eliza J. 62 Elizabeth 49
171 Elizabeth F. 210 Elizabeth
S. 243 Fanny 186 Frances M.
49 Francis 48 George W. 48-
49 Hampton 245 James 48 50
75-76 106 170-171 186-187
James H. 253 James L. 48 62
Jim 49 John 48-49 81 102 259
John M. 31 John P. 49 John T.
49 Laura 243 245 Littleton L.
49 Margaret 102 Mary 116 230
243 Matildah 140 Milly 1
Mollie E. 76 Molly 170 Nancy
76 Nettie 270 R. L. 50 R. L. v
119 128 Reuben L. 49 Robert
49 Samuel 49 Sarah 49 Sarah
K. 253 Susanna 185 Sylvia
187 Thomas 49 94 171 253

299

300

COVINGTON, Abraham 54 Ben
54 109 Lucy 231 Polly 173
Rebecca 109
COWGILL, Daniel 54 George 54
Isaac 54
COWHERD, Ann 213 Coleby 54
94 213 Drucilla 253 E. F. 214
Edwin F. 102 Eliza 94 Francis
54 110 212 Francis K. 54
Harriet 212 James 19 John S.
54 212 Jonathan 19 Mary Jane
54 Reuben 54 S. Lelia 102
Sarah 19 110 Susan E. 213
William 54 213
COX, Abner 54 Amanda 104
Ann 215 Benjamin F. 54
Francis S. 55 202 Franky 91
George 80 Joab 55 Joan 69
John 55 Leah 55 M. A. 280
Malinda 269 Sally 80 Sally W.
74 Sarah 69 74 Tabitha 278
Thomas 5 55 215 278 Warner
55 74 William 55 74 William
D. 55
CRACKER, Mary Jane 63
CRAIG, Elijah v 55 James 55
John v Julia 75 199 Lidia 94
Samuel 55
CRANE, Jonas 55 Thomas J. 55
CRASH, Nancy 264
CRASK, James 55
CRATON, Sarah 194
CRAWFORD, Archelan 55
Charles Y. 55 Ezekial 189
Janey 55 Jemima 208 Jeremiah
55 Martin 55 P. v 153 Peter 48
Reuben 55 Zachariah 55
CRAYTON, Lucinda 194
CREBBS, Hannah 55 John 55
John C. 55
CREEL, Benjamin v 55 74 110
225 232 Benjamin F. 55
CRENSHAW, Spotswood
Dabney 56 Thomas 56
William G. 56
CREW, Jacob 56 Tabitha 142
CRIGLER, Christopher 88 Peter
56 William 88
CRITCHFIELD, Anna 168
CROCK, Fanny 257
CROCKETT, Thomas J. 56
Thomas R. 56
CROCKFORD, John 56 108
Rosa E. 108 William H. 56

CROOKS, Catherine 107 Elvira
S. 107 Joseph B. 56 103 133
Mary E. 159 Mary F. 133
Winney B. 103 Winney P. 102
Winnifred P. 103
CROSS, Charles H. 56 George
56 Joshua 56
CROSSWHITE, Elizabeth 173
John 173 Milly 173
CROSTHWAIT, Aaron 56
Elizabeth 173 John 173 Joseph
173
CROW, Elizabeth 168
CROXTON, Joseph 56 252
CRUMP, Benjamin 56 John 168
187 Lucy 131 Mary 115 174
187 Susan 168
CRUTCHFIELD, Albert G. 56
Thomas 56
CUDDEN, Milly 9
CUDDING, Peggy 181
CULLEN, Barbara 56 Barbara
Ann 161 Emma 200 George 56
161 200 Margaret 285 Marietta
161
CUNNINGHAM, Bob 57 Ellen
152 Henry 57 Henry F. 57
Henry H. 57 James H. 57
Peyton 57 William F. 57
CURRY, Albert B. v
CURTIS, Elijah 57 Margaret 172
CUTLER, L. A. v 10 12-13 16
23 48 104 156 167 188 250
262 P. H. 286
DABNEY, Alexander 57
Emmely A. 96 John 42 Robert
L. vi Susan 42
DADE, Adam 131 Agnes 7
Albert 109 Albert G. 25 57
Alice 128 Amy 128 Ann W. 25
Benjamin 131 137 Emma J.
137 Fannie 25 Fanny 262
Frances E. 120 Francis 25 57
80 236 Hannah 260 Harriett 99
Harriett S. Grymes 120 Jack
128 John 260 Langhorn 57
Lawrence T. 159 Lewis 57
Mary 109 131 Mary O. 138
Milly 218 Nancy 72 122 Patsy
7 Richard 57 Sarah 57 195
Sarah I. 33 181 222 273
Sarcossan T. 138 Spencer 57
Townsend 57 William 57 236

DAHONEY, Peggy 50 Rhodes
57
DAILEY, Alexander 57
DAILY, Charles Riggs 57
Samuel 57
DALEY, Alexander 58 John 58
DALTON, John 58
DANCE, Beverley 58
DANIEL, Abel M. 58 Albert 58
Ann 244 Ann L. 167 Beverly
58 Beverly R. 58 Cornelius O.
58 Elizabeth 39 Elizabeth M.
203 261 Ellen 252-253 Esther
159 Eveline 167 Fannie S. 41
Frances 42 Frances A. 67 91
195 207 Frankey 109 Henrietta
146 Intemperance 284 James
58 232 James B. 56 67 Jane
192 Jenny 193 John 58 276
John F. 175 John M. 58 58-59
188 244 John T. 59 Joseph S.
59 Laura 167 Louisa 116
Lucinda 35 Lucy 52 Lucy W.
54 Maria 42 74 Martha 138
Mary 29 Mary C. 67 Mary E.
244 Mildred A. 188 Minerva
146 Nancy 56-57 Nancy R.
123 Phil 58 Polly 39 Reuben
59 Reuben R. 59 Reubin 52 74
Robert 59 189 Sally 28 Samuel
A. 59 Tempy 4 Thomas 59
Travis 116 Virginia 139
Vivion 192 William 59
William F. 41 139 William M.
59 William Travers 59
DANIELS, Cornelia 276
DANSON, William 118
DARBY, Adam 59
DARGAN, Edwin C. 59
DARGON, J. O. B. 59
DARLINGTON, Henry 59 John
T. 59
DARNALL, Jennie 31
DARNELL, Abraham 59 Ancell
59 Anna 195 Annie 231
Elizabeth 59 127 Fielding 4
Frances 4 Harriet 231 James
D. 79 Jincy 79 Lucy 206 Mary
4 219 Mary Ann 206 Nelson
60 Rice 4 60 86 105 127 216
219 Susanna 121 Thomas 60
William 231 Zachariah 60 67
DARNER, Julia 281
DARNOLD, Rice 246

DAUNEY, Alexnader 60
DAVENPORT, Evelina B. 132
John H. 60 John Tanner 60
Lewis 60 Martha 60 Mary J.
71 Peter 60 William 60
DAVIS, William J. 249 Abraham
60 Absolem 60 Aggie 88
Albert 186 Alexander 60
Andrew J. 60 Ann 11 Asa 60
Bartlett 60 Benjamin 60 62
Betsy 61 Bettie 165 Bettie W.
92 Betty 48 Carthagena 40
Cudden 286 Edna 136 Edward
61 Edward A. 60 Edy 197
Elijah 18 61 Elizabeth 10 19
27 48 69 91 111 229 Elizabeth
M. 222 Elizabeth P. F. 48
Elizabeth W. 170 Ellen 273
Evan 61 Evers 107 Frances 69
126 229 Frank 61 Frederick D.
61 George W. 61 Gillie Ann
132 Harriet 60 Harriot 107
Henry 61 Horace 61 Ida 97
Isaac 18 69 154 253 269 James
61 88 92 166 James M. 61 210
Jane 286 Jenkinias 61 Jerusha
60 158 Joe 62 John 61-62 91
151 171 265 John A. G. 62
Jonathan 91 186 Joseph 48 62
70 88 91 262 Julia 151 Justian
216 Kesiah 165 Leman 62
Leonard 62 Lewis 62 Lizzie 38
Lucinda M. 158 Lucy 35 58 91
126 222 Lucy B. 58 Lucy M.
104 Lucy T. 250 M. S. 166
Margaret R. 27 Maria Jane 10
Martha E. 186 Martha H. 110
Mary 70 115 119 168 185 269
Mary E. 100 249 Mary L. 150
Mary M. 94 210 Milly 186
Mitchell 62 Nancy 70 Nelly 62
Parke B. 61 Parker B. 134
Philemon 111 229 Philomen
126 Pleasant 139 165 273 Poly
12 Rachel 176 Ransom 62
Rebecca 139 Reuben 62 Rhoda
259 Richard T. 62 Robert 61
Sally 91 206 Sally Ann 170
Sarah 149 253 Sarah E. 92
Suckey 262 Susan 61 Susan A.
T. 171 Susanna 216 262
Susannah 101 Susannah
Winston 18 Thomas 48 61-62
114 210 Thomas J. 62

DAVIS, (continued)
Thornton 62 Walker 229
Washington 62 William 63
219 William I. 104 150
William J. 10 27 63 92 100
170 250 William P. 62 Willis
61
DAVISON, D. G. 63 Percey G.
63
DAWS, John 265
DAWSON, Amandy 2 Bar 271
Fanny 42 110 Frances 149
Isaac C. 63 James 63 John 42
48 63 85 149 171 220 Kitty
271 Laughter 110 Leroy 2
Lewis 63 Martha 267 Mary 42
Musgrave 63 Nancy 171 285
Polly Stevenson 220 Sally 80
Strother 285 William 42 78
118 171 196 William H. 2
DAY, Alice 131 Charles 63
Elizabeth 258 Henry C. 63
James F. 63 Jemima 227 John
227 271 Phebe 60 Susan R.
271 Susanna 168
DEALE, Ann 225
DEAN, Charles 118 Frankey 218
Nancy 235 Rebecca 136
William 148
DEANE, Charles 63 Eliza 255
Elizabeth 102 George 63
George W. 64 John 64 221
Mary 64 Reuben 64 William
63-64 64 102
DEAR, Catherine 261 Elizabeth
261 Frankey 218 John 64 152
Polly 19 Sally 61 Thomas 19
64
DEDMAN, Frances 161 John
149 Mary 118 Nancy 149
Philip 149
DEER, Betty 91
DEERING, James 64 Mary 209
Robert 82 136 209 Sarah 136
Susannah 82 Thomas 64 136
DEHONEY, Hannah 10 Jane 10
Thomas 10 50
DELACY, Isabella 223
DELANEY, Dise 99 Lisza 198
Mary 271 Sarah 96
DELANY, John 64
DEMAINE, Charles W. 64
William 64

DEMPSEY, Almira 125 Daniel
160 238 Elmira 255 Isabella
210 James 64 James A. 64 64-
65 John 64 John L. 210 Joseph
D. 64 Katharine 238 Lewis 64-
65 120 Lucy E. 174 Mary C.
31 Phebe 160 Pleasant 64 64
238 Pleasant R. 64 Robert 65
Robert D. 64 Thomas A. 12
125 Thomas J. 65 Virginia A.
120 Wellford 65 William A.
65
DEMSEY, Allen 26 Polly 26
DENNISON, James 65
DEREY, Lavey 65
DEVENNEY, C. 66 Cornelius
139 Mary M. 66
DEWESE, Mollie E. 254
DICKENSON, Allen 65 Bennett
65 Douglass 65 Elijah 258
DICKERSON, Irene 201 Tamar
283 Thomas 65 166
DICKEY, Elizabeth B. 160
James 160 Joanna 160
DICKIE, William L. 65
DICKIN, Christopher 96
DICKINSON, Charles 65 Flora
J. 75 Hugh M. 37 James 65
Nelly 17 Ralph 65 Richard 254
Robert 65 199 Robert W. 75
William 65
DIGGES, Boswell 65 Brice 65
Cole C. 65
DIGGS, Cole C. 66 89 Eliza 13
Mary 44 William H. 18
DILLARD, Clementine 76 Nicey
218 Sarah 48 Susan 76
DILLY, Richard 66
DINWIDDIE, J. C. 81 214 John
C. vi 150
DIXON, John 66 Samuel 66
DOANE, John 66
DOBBINS, Clementina 165
DOD, John 66 William 66
DODD, Anna 144 Henry 120
James 66 120 John 66 Joseph
H. 66 Margaret 120 William
66 167
DODSON, Amanda 25
DOHERTY, John vi 136
DOHONEY, Elizabeth 190
Hanner 190 Mary 254 Rhodes
66 254
DOHONY, James 66

303

DOLAND, Thomas 66
DOLBY, Clementine 159
DOLEN, Julia P. 28
DOLIN, Elizabeth 204 Frances
    176 John 22 176 204 Julia F.
    28 177 Patsy 22
DOLING, Elizabeth 86 Nancy 86
DOLLINS, John 189 Martha 56
    Reuben 66 Sucky 170 William
    28 56 170
DOLSON, John 126
DONALD, William 66
DONALDSON, Mary 146
DONATHAN, John 66
DONDIE, Sallie 68
DONOHOE, P. 5 Patrick 227
DONOVER, John 66
DONSTON, Mary 147
DOOLEY, Harden B. 66 Harriet
    A. 117 Susan 66 Thomas 66
DOOLING, Thomas 66
DORAND, Nancy 166
DORSCH, Sophia 188
DOTSON, John 44
DOUGHERTY, James 79
DOUGLAS, Anne 11 Charles 66
    Robert G. 62 Sarah A. 89
    William 89 105 154 227
DOUGLASS, Carter 67 Delia E.
    214 Delphia 67 Dorcas 226 E.
    T. 70 Edwin T. 67 F. E. 214
    Frances 189 James M. 67
    James P. 67 John 22 67 220
    John B. 67 Judith 22 Lewis
    Porterfield 67 Mary E. 195
    Mildred 286 Rice J. 67 Sallie
    122 William vi 19 40 60 195
    227 252 278 Wm 142
DOVELL, Elizabeth 105 Nancy
    25
DOWELL, Atwell 47 Berryman
    67 Elizabeth Atwell 185
    Harriet 185 Henrietta 44 255
    Jane 186 John 67 Lucy 47
    Madison 67 Maj. M. 67 Mary
    M. 67 Nathan 67 Pleasant 51
    217 Richard 67 William 255
DOWIN, Casey 199
DOWLING, John 67
DOWNER, Ann E. 190 Lucy F.
    42 Maria E. 91 Mildred A. 195
    Phoebe G. 207 Reuben C. 67
    Robert 42 Robert E. 195

DOWNER, (continued)
    Robert G. 67 91 207 William
    C. 190 William W. 67
DOWNEY, John 67 Mary J. 67
    Mildred C. 141 Sanders 141
DOWNIN, S. S. 67 Virgil 67
DRAPER, Chiswell G. 67
    Richard 67
DREWRY, Giles B. 68 Isaac N.
    68
DUDLEY, Julia A. 230
DUERSON, Lizzie Chew 279
    Robert C. 279
DUFF, Louisa 254 Louisa R. 189
DUKE, Amanda 26 145
    Elizabeth 235 Ellen 11 Ellen
    B. 253 Eveline 163 Isaac 11
    Lee 145 Mary A. 11 William
    68 149 163
DULANEY, Arnold 68 254
    George 68 Mary E. 80 Sarah
    G. 38 William 38 68 80 193
    William J. 80
DULANY, Sarah N. 177
DULIN, Burruss 71
DUNAVANT, George 68
DUNAWAY, Admond 228 Ann
    228 Edmund 111 158 246
    George 68 Jane 111 John 68
    Margaret 158 Martha 94
    Mildred 111 Nannie 182
    Richard 68 Susannah 93
    Thomas 68 93-94 William 93-
    94
DUNCAN, Joseph 68 Robert 37
    Winney 230
DUNCOME, Elizabeth 84
DUNN, Benjamin F. 68
    Elizabeth 58 Fountain D. 68
    Garland 68 John 68 M. A. 39
    118 Martin A. 68 T. R. 68
    William 68 William G. 68
DUNNIVEN, Elizabeth 69
DUNOVAN, William 68
DURRETT, Achilles 68 Betsy
    118 Davis 69 Dawson 69 Joel
    28 118 147 192 John D. 69
    Killian 69 Milly 192 Nancy 28
    William 69
DUVALL, Albzerah 217
    Altizerah 217 Ann H. 146
    Clabourn 69 Comfort 92 217
    John P. 69 Sally 232 Sarah E.
    92 William L. 92 217

EMMANUEL, Preston B. 73 W.
P. 73
EMMERSON, James 73
EMMONS, Ann 73 James 73
James S. 73
ENGLAND, George W. 73
Georgie 89 John 73 R. H. 89
William S. 73
ERMON, Elizabeth 100
ERNEST, J. 4
ESKEW, Annie C. 94 Willaim J.
94
ESQUE, William 74
ESSEX, William 74
ESTES, 15 Abraham 74 Andrew
F. 74 Betsy 55 Caroline F. 54
Edmund 163 Elisha 74 159
Eliza M. 103 Elizabeth 203
Fannie L. 96 Fanny 88 104
Frances 53 116 203 279 286
Garrett 55 74 Isaac L. 74
James 203 248 James R. 74 96
James W. 59 241 Jane M. 14-
15 28 32 68 74 Jenny 159 John
74 137 John H. 74 Juliett M.
248 Littleton 74 254 Lizzie K.
241 Lucinda C. 200 Lucy 55
105 Maria Ellen 59 Martha
283 Martha D. 54 Martha P. 29
Mary E. 74 Mary F. 44 Mary
H. 29 Mary J. 255 Mary
Stanfield 104 Mary T. 74
Matilda 282 Mildred 248
Mildred A. 203 Mildred T. 32
Milly 32 Nancy F. 201 Robert
74 Sallie 36 Sally 104 Samuel
17 Sarah 104 Sarah R. 129
Susan 278 Thomas 74 129 200
248 Thomas B. 74 Triplett H.
104 Willaim 104 William 32
55 74 88 104 129 278 William
B. 29 54 74 103 William T. 74
ESTIS, Barbara 206 Edmund 5
Frances 5 John 279 Nancy 279
ESTREGE, Stephen 173
ETHERTON, Anderson 75
Thomas E. 75
EUBANK, Elias D. 75 George
W. 75 Sarah 286
EUREN, Eliza 224
EVANS, Cary Ann 271 Frances
224 Frances A. 224 George
165 Harriet 50 James A. 147
Jane 269 Jane C. 269

EVANS, (continued)
John 75 224 John W. 7 47 103
269 Margaret C. 47 Mary 7 9
143 269 Mary J. 271 Nancy
224 238 Rebecca 228 Septener
165 Tom 271 Virginia Taylor
147
EVE, Ann 262 Elizabeth 202
George vi 2 11 13 28 30 33-34
40-42 48 50 55 81-82 86 91 98
110-111 126 131 138 140-141
151 154 158-160 162 164 167
174 176-178 181 188 193 200
203 208 210-211 215 217 220
227 230 236 240 257 268 272
286 Joseph 75 Mary 55 262
Sarah 55 202
EVES, Thomas 75
EWING, Daniel B. vi 60 96 138
FABER, John G. 75 Lewis J. 75
FACKLER, Henry 75
FAIRFAX, Edward 75 Flora 199
Minor 75
FALLIN, H. H. 75 John A. 75
FALLIS, Thomas 75
FAMEWOOD, Agnes 234
FANDREE, Joseph 75
FANT, John T. 75
FARGUSON, Elizabeth 206
John 75 150 Vivion 75
FARISH, Elizabeth 136 George
B. 76 James 149 272 John 234
John D. 76 Mary Stevens 149
Thomas 149 196 271 William
H. 76 William P. T. 76
FARMER, Maria 101
FARNEYHOUGH, John 278
FARRAR, David S. 76 Garland
76 Mary L. 76
FARROW, Mary S. 16
FAUDREE, Jane C. 217 Joseph
172 217 Lucy M. 172 Susan
172
FAULCONER, Alfred 76 147
Alfred M. 76 76-77 232 Alfred
N. 77 Alice M. 250 Alma E.
153 Ambrose 76 Ann 77-78
125 284 Benjamin 76-77 104
Carter B. 31 76 78 137 152
185 Catey 283 Catherine J.
142 David 69 76 184 Dolly M.
147 E. J. 153 155 E. N. 76
Edward 32 166 Edward S. 76
266 Elias 76 156

306

307

GAINES, (continued)
George 84 Gilford 161
Guilford 84 James 20 265
Jenny 84 John 84 210 Martha
5 Mary 59 106 Mary Ann 123
Patsy 25 Percilia 71 Reuben 84
Reubin 168 Richard 84 107
Robert 243 Rosa 213 Sally 10
Thomas 84 231 Urcilla 71
GALASBY, John 84
GALISPIE, John N. 84 Jonathan
84
GALLARY, George 85 Sam 85
GALLERY, Annie 195 Barbara
258 Fanny 122 George 122
191 252 Nannie 252 Rhody
274 Rosa 165 Urslie 191
GAMBAL, William 222
GAMBLE, Matthew 85
GAMBOE, Samuel 85 182
GAMBREL, Walter 85
GAMBRILL, Julia 214
GAMBUL, Walter 85
GAOR, E. C. 218
GARBER, Levi 88
GARDE, William 85 141 151
GARDEN, Lydia 241
GARDENER, Alexander Z. 85
Daniel 85 James M. 85
GARDNER, Daniel 85 David 85
Dowell L. 85 Frances 115 279
Mary C. 153 Minerva 173
Nathan 85 Sarah 276
Zachariah 85
GARITSON, Elizabeth 67
GARNER, E. W. 85 Jinnette 174
William A. 85
GARNET, Thomas 85
GARNETT, Andrew 85 Ann 274
Elizabeth 86 Fanny 19 James
vi 18-19 22 29 52 54 56 63 65
85-86 93 101 137-138 138 175
193 195 205 207 209 223 226
228 230 235 247 256 264 266
286 James J. 86 Jeremiah 70
Joel 86 John 42 158 286 John
O. 86 Larkin 86 Lucy M. 235
Mary E. 115 Milton 86 Sarah
244 Thomas 86 Ursula 138
GARR, Willis 86
GARREL, James 86
GARRELL, Demey 86 Elisha 86
GARRETT, Benjamin F. 86
Jackson 86 John vi M. A. 85

GARRISON, Catherine W. 104
John 256 Levinia 256
GARTH, D. C. 86 Susan 89
GARTON, Charles 86 Churchill
H. 85 Frances S. 89 Jemima A.
66 John 86 Martha 216 Mary
66 137 201 Mary J. 89 Mary
Jane 230 Reuben 53 Spencer
86 Susannah 53 Truesy 85
Uriah 53 William 230 Zachary
86
GATES, Charles 86
GATEWOOD, Henry 86
GAY, Bettie F. 166 Everett 232
Sally 232 William 166
William E. 86
GAYDEN, John 87
GEAR, Joshua 87 Nathan 262
William 87
GEE, Joseph C. 87 Lucy 1
Samuel M. 87
GEER, Elizabeth 169 John 87
Jonathan 87 Nathaniel 87
Ransom 87
GENTRY, 85 Aaron 87 Charles
H. 87 Fanny 88 George A. 125
James 87 John R. 87 Mary 36
Robert H. 87 Sarah 136 Susan
A. 75 136 Susan Jane 125
GEORGE, Catharine 266
Cumberland vi Edward 87
Isaac 87 John 87 William 87
Wintifred 229
GERRELL, Susanna 242
GIBBENS, Ann 149 Rachel 25
Thomas 149
GIBBS, Alex. L. 87 James 87
John 87 John H. 68 Julius 88
Lini 68 Pinkston A. 87
William 88 William C. 88
Zachariah 88
GIBERNE, William vi
GIBSON, 119 Albert 84
Amarilous 114 Angelina 36 B.
F. 88 Ben 148 Burwell 88 E.
Dorsey 88 Edwin E. 89
Elizabeth 243 Elizabeth E. 243
F. L. 25 273 Fanny 25 Ida 148
Jesse 88 John 88 152 223
Joseph H. 88 Joseph M. 88
Joshua 88 Levina 84 Margaret
84 Martha E. 257 Mary 50 118
152 273 Mary E. 36 239 Mary
Jane 88 Merriman 241

309

GOOLSBY, G. R. 92 William E.
92
GORDALL, Andrew 92
GORDEN, Charles 92 Henry 92
GORDON, Abraham 43 Amanda
43 Ann S. 18 Austin 241 Betsy
242 Ceasar 63 Edmund 92
Edward 93 Eliza 34 Elizabeth
202 253 273 Eve 237 Eveline
193 Fanny 43 191 237 281
Fanny F. 93 Fenella 267
Hannah 13 Hardin 267 J. C. 1
21 46 61 67 77-78 84 86 107
125 133-135 197 199 205 207
211 213 215 249 254 258 268
270 Jack 237 James 13 92 144
Jane 88 93 Jere 191 John 13
John A. 93 230 John A. B. 93
John C. 77 93 vi 107 169 200
222 259 273-274 John
Churchill 86 John H. 93
Joseph H. 93 Judy 99 Lucy 30
256 Lucy H. 86 230 Mary 13
93 115 274 Mildred 30 Nathan
13 Nathaniel 93 Priscilla 70
Priscilla C. 139 Reuben L. 13
Samuel 70 Sarah 144 Susan 29
63 Susan V. 13 Thomas C. 93
William 93 William A. 93
GORE, John 93
GOSNEY, Reubin 93
GOSS, Ebenezer 93 257
Hamilton vi 1 5 11 23-24 35
58-60 70-71 79 84 86 93 96
102 105 112 121 126 135 143
149-150 150-151 157 163 188-
189 193 203 218 229 233-235
240-241 272 277 J. 3-4 14-15
26 33 39 46-47 50 54 59 65-66
71 78 89 95 98 103 110 137
148 153 156 158 169-170 173
173-174 179 179-180 186 192
194 202 213 217 220 224 242
246 255-256 258-259 262-263
267 269 279 J. H. 93 James 15
vi James W. 134 173 Jesse H.
93 John vi John W. 93 Mary
93 Nannie C. 257
GRACE, George 21 91 93
Gracey 91 93 Polly 21
GRADY, Alexander 62 183
Andrew 93 Ann 40 96
Benjamin 94 Fanny 190
Frankey 285 John 94 190

GRADY, (continued)
Joseph 36 Lincfield 96 Louisa
Kate 186 Lucy 62 Margaret 81
Mary 19 Mary E. 186 Mary W.
36 Richmond 94 Sallie J. 44
Samuel 94 285 Sarah 76
Walker 81 William 19 62 76
81 94 96 190 285
GRAHAM, David 94 Martha
109 Rachel 251
GRAMMER, Jim 94 Rolley 94
Rose 94
GRANT, Jesse 94 John N. 94
John R. 94 Samuel 94
GRANVILLE, Louisa 267
GRASTY, Alverta 264 Ann 282
Eliza 93 Elizabeth L. 65 G. I.
45-46 G. S. 243 George 94
George G. 94 Goodrich L. 171
Goodrich Lightfoot 94 Isaac B.
94 John 48 94 119 John H. 246
John Thomas 94 L. B. 91 Mary
Ann 48 Nancy 46 Nanney 45
Peachy 61 Susan 94 Susan A.
243 Susan Grant 282 Susan L.
246 Thomas 45
GRAVATT, Anada 94 Ellis W.
94 John C. 94 Mary T. 129
GRAVES, 256 A. W. 73 218
Abner 68 Absolem 95 Amanda
M. 95 Ann 27 84 Ann E. 10 28
35 Annie E. 257 Benjamin 95
Benton V. 95 C. E. L. 95
Catharine Single 213 Charles
T. 95-96 213 Claibourne 28-29
268 Coalby 56 Colby 95 Dick
129 Drucilla 23 Eddie W. 13
Elijah 19 Elizabeth 28 45
Elizabeth C. 29 61 Elizabeth
W. 95 Ester 123 Esther 146
Eudora C. 212 Fanny E. H. 56
Frances 27-28 219-220 240
Frances A. 96 242 Frances
Ann 109 Gilbert 271 Hattie F.
68 Isaac 23 56 95 256 Isaac F.
95 Isaac L. 95 Isaac W. 74 95-
96 104 Jacob 95-96 109 James
W. 13 95 212 Joanna 177 Joel
95 John 82 Jonathan 23 40 56
168 Joseph 73 95 Juda 271
Julia A. 74 Kate F. 97 Layton
G. 240 Lewis 35 95-96 98
Lucinda 129 Lucy A. 59 Lucy
F. 96 Lyddia 157 Maria L. 240

311

GRAVES, (continued)
Martha 109 Mary 165 Mary S.
33 277 Nancy 40 82 Nannie B.
103 Pamela A. 213 Pamilia A.
100 Paschal 95 Peter 130
Phillipa 43 Rachel 133 Richard
82 96 169 Richard P. 56 95-96
96 Robert 43 221 Roda 96
Rufus E. 96 Sallie 73 Sally 115
Sarah 69 95 212 Sarah J. 13
Sarah Jane 95 Susan 14 130
Susan B. 134 Susanna 14
Susannah 169 Temple 256
Thomas 14 82 96 115 157 177
248 Thomas E. 96 Thornhill
73 Virginia 268 271 Waller 96
William 96 106-107 116 134
257 William C. 59 96 213
Winifred 56
GRAY, Courtenay 142 Elisa Ann
224 Gabriel 96 Gibbon 243
John 142 Lila 264 Mary Page
3 Puryfee 88 Thomas 136
Thomas W. 88
GRAYSON, Mary 79
GREEN, A. G. 97 Adam 97
Aggy 97 Anderson 109 128
Ann 97 Betsy 39 Betty Ann
109 Bolling 97 Caroline 97
186 253 Elijah 97 Eliza 57
Ellen 37 83 Emily 79 Frank
168 George 97 Hannah 96 177
Harriet 270 Harrison 97 Irison
229 Jere 231 Jim 57 97 John
31 50 97 Judy 124 Littleton 97
Lucy 93 Margaret 231 Martha
250 Mary 37 128-129 252-253
Mary A. 191 Milly 130 204
Nancy 272 Nicholas 97 Otho
97 Overson 97 Pelina 128
Pleas 97 Polly 229 Rachel 123
Richard 97 Robert 97 Sam 96
Spotswood 97 Stephen 97
Stephen G. 97 Susan 168
Towles 270 272 Viney 131
William 37 William N. 97
Willis 96 128 Winney 31-32
GREENING, Nehemiah 98
GREGORY, Isaac 98 Obediah
98
GRESHAM, Sally 149
GRESSOM, Betsey 121
GREVIERS, Fountain 98 Henry
98

GREY, Rebecca 143
GRIFFE, Harris 98 John 98
GRIFFETH, Mary 236
GRIFFEY, Abell 98 Joseph 98
GRIFFIE, Catharine 174
GRIFFIN, David 236 Edmund
215 James 98 James H. 98
Joseph W. 98 Lucy 58 207
Phillipa A. 215 Richard I. 98
William E. 98
GRIFFITH, Benjamin 39 David
69 Edmund 236 Sarah 69
GRIGRY, Ann 232 John 232
GRIGSBY, Elisha 98 Reuben 98
GRIMES, Mary L. 10
GRIMSLEY, George 98 John 98
Pollie 98 Richard 98 Thomas
F. 48
GRINNAN, Daniel 59 Emily 132
William S. 99
GRINNELS, Rebecca 165 Sarah
165
GRISSIM, M. P. 102
GROOM, Elizabeth 7 James 99
John 99 John Z. 99 Major 192
Mourning 16 Sally B. 192
Solomon 7 99 Solomon R. 16
Virginia Ann 20
GRUBBS, Albert S. 101 Alfred
S. 101 Betti 240 Catharine 238
Martha S. 101 Mary Ann 101
Sarah F. 98 Sarah S. 98
Thomas 101
GRUNTER, Jemima 169
GRYMES, Abraham 99 Abram
99 Alberta 117 Alice Beale
105 Amy 84 Benjamin A. 99
105 Betty Johnson 168 Clara
92 Eliza 145 Ellen 133 Hannah
212 Hariett S. 153 Jacob 99
Jane 124 Jim 92 John R. 82
Judith Robinson 54 Lucy N.
236 Lucy Nelson 237 Ludwell
168 212 Mary 117 Peter 99
Peyton 99 Sarah 3 257
Spotswood 117 Susan 145
Thomas 270 Thomas M. 99
William S. 99
GUARD, Elizabeth 26 John 26
GUINN, Clara 262 Lucy J. 286
GULLEY, Enoch 99 John 99
GUNDERSHEIMER, Amelia 22
Bettie 22 Henrietta 20 Jacob
20 22

312

GUNNELLS, James 99 Patrick
  99
GUNNER, Patrick 181
GUNNERS, Bettie 181
GWATHMEY, Alfred 86 Alice
  260 Lucinda 86 Philip 99-100
  260 Robinette 128 Sally 86
  Stork 99 William 100 128
  Wortham 100
GWATHWAY, Eleanor 65
GWIN, Jane 286
GWYNN, Henry B. 100
GWYNNN, Charles R. 100
HACKETT, Lucy 172 Lucy
  Mary 1 Reuben 1 100 128
HACKLEY, Mary Ann 213
  Robert 213 Sarah F. 213
HACKNEY, Jane S. 176 Nancy
  176
HAGISH, Charles 269
HAINES, Jacob 100
HAINEY, James 68 May 100
  Peggy 68
HALE, Daniel W. 100 Ermon C.
  100 Jacob 100
HALES, John 39 100 119 218
HALEY, Louisa 118 Mollie W.
  254 William 254 William S.
  100
HALL, 148 Alice M. 233
  Ambrose 100 Andrew 100
  Ann 148 211 Bazel 100 Ben
  100 Catharine 187 Dudley 100
  Fanny 273 Ferrill 101 Hasten
  101 Henry 65 173 187 James
  101 Joseph 101 Lucy 101 109
  Lucy M. 148 Margaret 134
  Maria 148 Mary A. 40 Mary
  Knight 71 Matilda 65 Melvina
  226 Millicent 75 Nancy 46
  Peter A. 101 Ralph 239
  Richard 101 Richard P. 101
  Susan 173 Thomas 101
  Timothy A. 101 William 101
  William J. 101 William L. 233
HALSEY, Annie A. 3 Joseph J. 3
HAM, Bennett 101 Betsy 50
  Dashia 62 Franky H. 271
  Joseph 50 101 206 Judith 149
  Lurinna 101 Mary 206 Milly
  197 Sally 87 Sam 87 Samuel
  101 197 203 206 271
  Theodocius 62 Vernon 101

HAMBLETON, Edward 33 101-
  102 Elige 101 Ellis 202 John
  101 Leroy 101 Margaret 259
  Polly 33 Sarah 178 Theophilus
  101 Thomas 102
HAMILTON, Alexander 56-57
  103 James 4 John 102 Louisa
  J. 87 Margaret D. 4 Mary Jane
  161 William 102
HAMM, Eliza 206
HAMPER, W. H. vi 143-145
HAMS, John 102 Milly 254
HAMSBROUGH, J. S. 47
HANCOCK, Elender 102 James
  102 Jane 262 Jane C. 262
  Mary 32 Munroe B. 102
  Nancy 276 Polly 86 Rebecca 9
  14 Sally 24 Susan 231 William
  9 14 24 36 86 102 276 William
  B. 102
HAND, Absalom 100
HANDY, Frederick A. G. 102 I.
  W. K. 7 59 102 137 175 213
  Isaac W. K. vi Isaac W. K. 102
  J. W. K. 16
HANELSON, Elizabeth J. 202
HANES, Sarah 219
HANEY, Ann 64 181 200 Ann
  T. 128 Bazel 25 Bazle 102
  Benjamin 247 Betsy 25 Buly
  E. 130 Elizabeth 247 Emily
  126 Fanny 25 Jacob 126 James
  25 31 64 87 102 128 130 140
  John I. 102 John J. 102 125
  200 Lucinda 64 Luraney 140
  Mary 73 Mary Ann 31 May
  170 Nancy 25 140 William J.
  102
HANKINS, D. R. 102 Martha D.
  187 Matthew C. 102 Thomas
  R. 187
HANLEY, Benjamin 102
HANSBOROUGH, J. S. 73 99
  229 John S. 63 247
HANSBRAUGH, John S. 181
HANSBROUGH, A. H. 280
  Alexander H. 273 Elizabeth 57
  103 Elizabeth C. 273 Ellen 251
  Georgie G. 103 J. S. vi 24 49
  52 133-134 223 282 John S. 3
  103 161 167 194 204 222 259
  273 John T. 258 Maria S. 280
  Martha S. 56 Peter A. 103
  Roberta B. 273

HANSDEN, Susan 140
HANSFORD, Benjamin 187
   Benoni 178 John 56 103
   Lucinda 256 Mary G. 56 Sallie
   J. 76
HANY, John 103 Peggy 68
HARDIMAN, James E. 103
HARDING, Mildred 225
HARDY, Charles W. 103
   William J. 103
HARE, Caroline E. 214
HARLEY, Batt 103
HARLOW, James G. 103 John
   W. 103 Joseph C. 103 Julius B.
   102-103 Lucian M. 103 Lucy
   Mary 102 Rebecca 103
   Richard 103 Richard F. 103
HARNER, Daniel 264
HARPER, Dudley 78 Patsey 1
HARRELL, Richard 103
   Theodore 103
HARRING, Thomas 18
HARRIS, Ally 177 Annie 239
   Calvin D. 104 Catherine 91
   Caty 179 Charles M. 104
   Elizabeth 99 269 Frances 46
   161 Frank 104 Gilbert 104
   James 104 Jane 121 John 104
   John C. 104 Joseph 85 Lewis
   104 Lindsay 121 257 Littleton
   91 104 Lora Ann 10 Lucy 161
   Mary A. 50 Mary B. 16 286
   Matilda 85 Moses T. 104 Nelly
   253 Overton 99 Peter 104 278
   Philip 104 Polly 257 R. M. C.
   104 Rhoda 277 Richard H. 104
   Sabina 149 Sam 44 Samuel 78
   Samuel J. 104 Samuel M. 105
   Sarah 96 141 177 Sarah E. 152
   Thomas 46 149 W. V. 153
   William 105 239 William D.
   105 William M. 105
HARRISON, Ann 57 Burr 205
   Clara 65 Harriett 16 Jabez 105
   Jane Lewis 16 John C. 105
   John R. 105 Lewis 105 Louisa
   259 Lucy 201 Mary H. 205
   Nancy 105 Pamelia 123
   Thomas B. 105 Thomas Botts
   105 William 105 Zachariah F.
   105
HARROD, Benjamin 105 John
   30 Nancy 30 Richard 105

HART, John 105 Rose 213
   Susan 168
HARTSOOK, Ann M. 146
   Elizabeth 180 James W. 105
   John B. 108 180 Mary 19 168
   180
HARVEY, Anthony 74 105
   Benjamin 105 Elizabeth 62 88
   149 Frances 74 Haney 26
   James 162 Jenny 228 John 105
   259 Layton 26 105 Lewis 200
   Lucinda 26 Mary 274 Nancy
   259 Polly 74 119 Sally 91 154
   Susanna 105 Thomas 105-106
   154 William 106 149
HARVIE, John 50 Nanny St. 271
   Sarah 50
HARVY, Jonathan 106
HARWOOD, Moses 106
HASEY, Michael 106
HATCH, Ann E. 169 198 Ann
   Eliza 197 Anna E. 170 Henry
   153 197 Mabel Estelle 153
HATCHER, H. E. vi 7 31 39-40
   53 58 75 79 85 87 103 122 128
   138 144 153 167 173 200 211
   236 238 245 H. W. 184 Hilary
   E. 106 Mary 241 Uriel 106
HAUS, John 207
HAUSE, Conrad 106 John 181
HAWK, Mary 199 Mary Ann
   121 Mary R. 199
HAWKINS, Alex 200 Alexander
   106 Alice E. 223 Ann 198 234
   Ann M. 115 Arculus 159
   Areulues 106 Ben J. 115
   Benjamin 17 63 106 106 168
   198 Benjamin F. 106 Benjamin
   J. 106 Betsy 106 Buly Ann 184
   Columbia 115 E. P. vi 177 277
   Elijah 106 184 Elisha 223
   Elizabeth 5 17 29 172
   Elizabeth J. 106 115 Ellick 1
   Henry 218 Henry S. 106 James
   106 James H. 107 Jehu 106
   John 106 John B. 106 John D.
   190 John T. 107 Julia 218
   Louisa 218 Lucy 6 87 127 167
   Lucy May 6 M. Mary 201
   Margaret 106 200 Margaret M.
   199 Margaret N. 200 Martha
   D. 187 Mary K. 36 Moses 107
   175 Nicholas 107 Phebe 20
   Rachel 85 Reuben 107

HAWKINS, (continued)
Reubin 6 Roddy 107 Sarah 21
33 224 Sarah A. 48 Susannah
49 Tabitha 82 Thomas 107
Thomas R. vi 7 16 34 36 44
88-89 97 114 128 183 186 199
201 221 224 241 244-245 254
267 269 Thos. R. 7 9 109 244
264 William 107
HAWLEY, Abram 107 Amanda
F. 245 Amanda T. 26
Benjamin 107 George W. 107
L. A. 51 Lucy M. 51 Mary A.
107 Thomas 51 William vi 42
HAWS, John 107
HAXALL, R. Barton 176 Rosalie
176
HAYES, Lucy C. 74 Moses 48
107 Richard 40 Thomas 74
107
HAYNA, Eliza 52
HAYNES, Jasper 13 John 119
Lucinda 13 Sarah N. 119
HAZELHURST, Robert 108
HAZLEHURST, William 108
HEAD, Amanda 86 Benjamin
108 Emily A. 45 Fanny 163 G.
Edgar 108 George M. 208
George Marshall 108 Harriett
208 Henry 108 James 65 81
108 John 45 86 108 208
Marshall 108 Mattie J. 266
Sally 81 Sara 191 Sarah 3 35
262 Selma 214 Tavenah 108
Valentine 108 266 William
108 Wilton 108
HEALY, Benjamin 285
HEAREN, Francis 101 Sarah
101
HEASTINE, Monroe N. 108
HEASTON, Lewis 108
HEATWELL, David 135 Eliza
135 Mary 221
HEFLIN, Ella V. 174 George W.
174
HEIDEN, Joseph 151 Lucy M.
151
HELM, William 108
HENDERSAN, Betsy 95
HENDERSON, Alexander 69
Alfred 165 Ambrose 108 Ann
116 Betsy 130 Bettie 5 Billy 5
Caroline 277 Ceasar 108
Daniel 108 Dick 109

HENDERSON, (continued)
Dinah 145 Doc 123 Eliza 130
Elizabeth 69 77 195 197
Elizabeth M. 196 Fanny 145
Hannah 123 Henrietta J. 202
Henry 109 Huldy 148 Jacob
108 110 116 Jake 145 277
John 27 67 94 109-110 192
196 268 280 John H. 109 Jos.
109 Joseph M. 109 167 Julia
236 260 Julianna 188 Lewis
109 169 Louisa 108 169
Lucinda 131 Lucy M. 164
Minor 108-109 Nancy 149 237
Nelson 109 Phoebe 258 Sadie
L. 166 Sally 110 Samuel 130
Sarah 109 Susan 109 128
William 109-110 202
HENDON, John 198
HENELY, Mary Ann 82 Pleasant
82
HENING, James R. 216 Joice
216 William 216
HENISON, Abram 110 Neptune
110
HENKLE, Rebecca C. 228
HENLEY, Osborn 110
HENNESEY, Kitty M. 56
HENNESSY, Peter 110
HENRY, Agatha 158 Belfield
110 Benjamin 110 Benson 110
158 262 Dulley 159 Frances
203 J. M. 82 Jeremiah 42
William 110 159 203 Zachary
110
HENSHAW, Ann 40 Anna 40
Cortney A. 47 Edmund 47 110
188 213 Edward 111 Elizabeth
146 Elizabeth V. 256 George
T. 110 Jane 111 John 54 110
176 180 256 John S. 110 Lucy
Walker 180 Malinda 232 Mary
Newman 188 Mary V. 228
Philip T. 110-111 Sarah A. 54
110 T. P. G. 228 Thomas P. G.
111 Virginia 228 Virginia O.
213 William 232
HENSLEY, Cypress 111 192
245 Elizabeth 66 Hannah 192
Hanner 229 James 111 Jeder
111 John 111 229 256 Lewis
66 111 Polly 256 William 66
HERMAN, Frederick 111

315

HERNDON, Andrew J. 111 Ann
198 282 Ann V. 189 B. P. 70
Benjamin 67 111 113 189
Davis C. 111 E. Frazer 111
Edward 111-112 123 219
Edward F. 97 111-112 Eliz.
192 Eliza J. 219 Elizabeth 82
112 192-193 196 283 Ella S.
142 Emanual 113 Emma J. 48
Esther 112 Ezekiel 112 Fanny
93 Fielding 112 167 185
George 112-113 161 242
Harrison 112 Henry 112 220 J.
H. 112 James 112-113 141-142
205 282 James C. 112 James
F. 232 Jane 90 93 119 141-142
230 Jane L. 93 Jane S. 93 Joel
112 John 70 112-113 172 207
249 283 John B. 113 John D.
113 129 John W. 113 Joseph
113 142 Larkin 90 113 Leah F.
84 Linnia 129 Lucy 207 Lucy
D. 70 Mahala 112 Margaret
194 Martha Ann 185 Mary 113
123 135 141-142 Mary A. 37
119 161 Mary Ann 254
Mildred 185 Nancy 167 Nelly
4 Pamelia 145 Polly 123 190
R. D. vi 128 R. I. 48 Richard
T. 113 136 Robert N. 113
Sally 187 233 Sarah 57 Sarah
F. 97 Sarah S. 118 Susan 188
249 Susan A. 136 Tandy 113
Thomas 111 113 209 Virginia
L. 119 W. P. 112 William 113
192 William G. 84 William T.
57 Wyatt 113
HERNER, Sarah 81
HERNSON, Edward 113 James
112 Richard A. 113
HERRIN, Milly 216
HERRING, Benjamin 82 263
Elizabeth 18 78 141 Elizabeth
M. 76 Franklin T. 114 Franky
271 George 114 140
Georgianna 140 James 114
Jane 81 Lucy 114 82 Sally 216
Sarah E. 263 Sarah Holbert
140 Thomas 81 William
Daniel 82 William J. 24 263
William R. 216
HESTAND, John 114
HESTER, Lucy 260

HESTIN, Lewis 108 Monroe N.
108
HETER, William Y. 210
HEUSTEN, John 114
HIATT, Benjamin 58 Elizabeth
191 Jane 58 Jonathan 114
Susannah 62
HICKERSON, Lucy 73
HICKS, 72 155 Ann 217 Charles
M. 114 Elizabeth 158 Fanny
119 John 118 John R. 114
Mary 147 Peter W. 114 Rachel
217 Robert 114 Sarah F. 119
Sarah Frances 118
HIDEN, Joseph 45 96 Lucy M.
83 Martha A. 59 96
HIEATT, John 114 Lewis 114
HIGDON, Elizabeth 71 John 71
HIGGASON, Richard 19
HIGGENBOTHAM, Mildred 37
HIGGERSON, Benjamin 31 229
James 25 Mary E. 229
HIGGINS, Lannie J. 233 Martha
A. 236 Michael D. 236 Robert
M. 135 233
HIGHLANDER, Ann H. 200
Charles 265 George 69
Madison 114 200 Mary 265
Nancy 69 Sarah 200 Thomas
114
HILDERBRAND, Rebecca 212
HILL, Benjamin F. 114 Betsy
117 Eliza 253 Elizabeth 153
Ellen 174 Henry 208 228
Horace 114 John 67 Laura 62
Lucetta 143 147 Lucy 100
Margaret 67 Martha 137 Mary
115 Mary C. 75 Mary L. 210
Nancy 276 Parthenia 147 Polly
52 Rebecca 124 242 Richard
52 115 137 169 244 Robert 62
Sady 71 Samuel 53 114-115
Sucky 114 Susan 244 William
A. vi 48 118 190
HILLE, William A. 27
HILLMAN, Fanny 48 Frances 49
HILMAN, Betsy 96 Delilah 43
Diadema 215 Fanny 48
Frances 193 Joanna 285
Joannah 213 Joseph 1 43 48 61
116 198 Lucy 183 Martha 150
Mary 95 Polly 61 Sally 116
Sarah A. 1 Susan 198 259

JACKSON, (continued)
Lewis 122-124 Lottie 230
Louisa 170 173 Lucy 40 122
250 258 Major 124 Maria 84
Marshall M. 124 Martha 110
248 Mary 3 122 124 232 Mary
E. 62 Matt 255 Mildred 58 244
Mildred A. 58-59 Milly 30-31
100 Mollie 194 Monroe 90 124
Moses 84 124 173 232
Nathaniel 6 Ned 194 Oscar
124 Patrick 123 Polk 124
Randal 122 Robert 123 146
159 Sally 240 Sarah 6 92 Silva
256 Tabitha 92 Tandy 124
Thomas 122 124 Vinie 232
William 125 William E. 125
Wilson 125
JACOB, William 125
JACOBS, Absalom E. 126
Angeline 275 Annie E. 150
Bejamin 154 Benjamin 78 125
249 Betsy 225 Bettie 255
Catharine 152 222 Catherine
126 Daniel 125 255 Elizabeth
78 102 125 223 Frances 261
George 125-126 150 165 222-
223 Huldah 102 James 125
James B. 77 James M. 71 125
223 Joel 125 Margaret A. 249
Mary A. 249 Mary F. 159
Nancy 223 Nancy H. 126
Nathan 125 195 Nathaniel 126
222 Richard F. 125 Robert 223
Sarah 77 Solomon 125 Susan
195 Thomas 125 William 126
275 William P. 126
JAMAR, Richard 126
JAMASON, Mary 111
JAMES, Anney 210 Daniel vi
126 Elijah 43 Fanny 75 George
283 Isaac 37 Joseph 75 Lucy
75 283 Maria 37 Milly 8
Nancy 168 Polly 75 Richard
126 Spencer 126 Thomas 46
Willie Ann 43
JAMESON, Catharine R. 46
Dolly A. 225 Joseph 126
Thomas R. 126 William 24
126
JARRALD, James 126 Jeremiah
126
JARRALL, John 193 Patsy 193

JARRELL, Abraham 240 Adam
126 Anderson 126 Ann 205
Elisha 126 Frances 35 James
126 126-127 240 Jefferson 127
205 Jeremiah 200 John 205
240 Joseph 127 Mary 21 55
240 Mildred 35 44 Nancy 131
Reuben 127 Tabitha 205
William 127 Zachariah 127
JASPER, William 237
JEFFERY, Martha L. 257
JENKINS, David 127 Fanny 75
George 223 John 127 Lucy
143 Mary F. 115 Quire 127
Sarah 228 Sarah J. 236
Thomas 127 William 75
William S. 127 228 William T.
127 236
JENNINGS, Ann 164 Ann
Chapman 164 Berryman 164
Charles C. 224 Eliza 79
Frances 8 James J. 127 John 8
127 Lucy 136 Luke 8 201
Mary Ida 115 R. S. 127
William A. 115 136 William
C. 127 164
JERDONE, Francis 37 127 John
127 Mary C. 37
JOHNS, Ann Maria 166 James F.
127 Jamese F. 127 Mary A. 77
Mason 78 127 166 Sarah 78
William C. 127
JOHNSON, Aaron 128 Abner
128 Abram 128 Adeline 181
Allen 128 Amanda 223 Amos
130 Amy 1 Ann 87 277 Ann
Eliza 265 B. T. 65 Baylor 129
148 Belfield 65 Belfield C.
177 Belle 110 Benjamin P. 73
264 Benjamin V. 26 Betsy 243
Betsy S. 26 Bettie 237 Betty
253 276 C. I. 123 C. J. 116 146
C. T. vi 5 26 40 49 82 97 123
130 146 159 173 178 191 201
236 250 267 274 276 281
Carter 129 Celia 112 Charles
84 128 Charlotte 201 Clara
132 Colin 128 Davy 130
Edmund 130 Edward R. 128
130 Edwin R. 200 Eliphalet 46
51 119 131 133 Eliphalett 132
Elisabeth 73 Eliza 129 264
Eliza A. 247 Eliza K. 227
Elizabeth 45

JOHNSON, (continued)
Elizabeth Cave 16 Ellen 30
182 200 212 Emma 148 Fanny
100 Frances T. 11 Frank 128
Franklin 128 Frederick 128
Frimednzas 130 Garrett 153
Garrick 132 George 105 129
George T. 129 Georgianna 273
Harriet 129 Horace 129 Ira 128
Irma 124 Isaac 80 90 129-131
133 212 276 Isaac L. 129 J. P.
132 Jacob 131 James 129
James B. 129 James S. 129
Jane 37 260 Jane Frances 272
Jeffrey 132 Jesse 128 Jo. 237
Joe 130 John 129 201 219 260
John B. 129-130 229 John P.
A. 129 John P. A. 261 John T.
130 Jonathan 188 Jones 130
Joseph 100 130-131 176
Joseph Bain 130 Joseph H. 212
Joseph W. 130 L. B. 105 Lelia
212 Lewis 110 129-130 Lewis
B. vi Lucie A. M. 177 Lucinda
131 Lucy 11 37 128 145 154
159 265 Lucy Ann 264 Lydia
84 Major 131 Malissa 151
Malvina 128 Maria 260
Marietta 120 Martha 248 260
Martha A. 38 Martin 157 Mary
30 61 99 130 133 195 204 219
229 May 30 Mildred Ann 128
Mildred C. 50 Milly 154
Minerva 37 67 Nancy 73 183
Nelly 199-200 239 267 Ninna
183 Ophelia 151 Peggy 128
Peter 130 Peter R. 11 130 Peter
T. 130 132 Peyton 130 Phil
234 Philip vi 1 5 26 30 37 42
54 62 73 83-84 97 100 104 109
118 120-121 123 128 130 145
148 151 161 176 187 190 193
195 204 225-227 230 234 239
248 250 258 260-261 270-271
276-277 279 Phillis 90 Polly
284 R. P. 272 Randall 131
Reuben 124 131 Rhoady 98
Richard 112 120 129 131 154
265 Richard P. U. 130 Robert
131 Robert C. 50 Rosa 200
Rosamond 264 Ryland 64 181
Salley Ann 65 Sally 66 214
269 Sally Ann 65 Samuel 131
Sarah 129 176 183 242

JOHNSON, (continued)
Sarah J. 105 Solomon 129
Stephen 129 131 182 Susan 38
204 230 268 274 Susan F. 38
Susannah 69 220 Thomas 131-
132 159 Thomas H. 131 Tom 3
Valentine 50 65 131-132 283
Verlinday J. 51 Virginia 181
Wilhelmina 112 William 30 73
128 130 132 William G. 132
William H. 132 William Henry
132 William M. 132 William
W. 132 Wyatt 132 Zalinda L.
129
JOHNSTON, Elizabeth 30
Hannah B. 32 James 133 Mary
30 William W. 33
JOLLET, James 138
JOLLETT, Clarissa 210 Drada
210 Elizabeth 138 Fielding
210 James 40 42 133 154 177
210 240 Judy 42 Lucy Walker
154 Malindey 154 Mary 42
Sally 210 Simeon 138 154 265
Simson 133 Sophia 177
JOLLETTE, James 154
JONES, A. S. 214 Amanda S. 46
Ambrose 135 Ann E. 129
Angelina 46 Ann 152 157 261
Ann E. 33 Ann Eliza 24 Ann
R. 157 Annie E. 2 B. F. 159
Barbara 12 Benj. R. 134
Benjamin 133 Benjamin F. 133
Benjamin H. 133 Benjamin P.
133 Benjamin R. 133 Betsy
281 Bettie S. 52 Burkett 133
Catharine 105 Catherine 157
Caty 158 Cavy 134 Charles
133 Charles E. 134 Churchill
46 133 144 Douglass G. 133
Edmonia H. 181 Edmund 133
Eli 135 Elijah 229 Eliza Swan
34 Elizabeth 32 61 78 78-79
107 117 155 219 239 283
Elliott 112 Evelina 86 Fannie
W. 88 Fanny 205 229
Ferdinand 257 Fielding 12 120
133 135 157-158 170 182 198
229 Frances 82 181 272
Frances A. 32 Francis 102 107
210 George S. 133 Gillard 134
Gillie 17 Gillie Frances 106
Grace 51 Hannah 195 209
Harrison 133 Henry W. 134

KENNEDY, Albert 2 Edmund N.
76 Fannie 78 Fountain 137
Hiram P. 78 137 156 Isaac 137
John 27 Leroy vii Littleton 137
Livingston 137 Louisa W. S.
119 Lucy M. 156 Mary 121
156 Nannie 78 Reuben 29 35
84 137 Sarah 14 Sarah A. 32
Teressa 27
KENNEY, America A. 137
Mickleberry 137 William H.
137 Winston 137
KENNIDAY, Newman 137
KENNON, Ira 137 Jos D. 137
Philip 138 Richard 137-138
KENNY, Ben 12 Charity 139
Rachel 72 Susan 12
KERSEY, William 138
KEY, Nancy 278 Walter 138 145
KEYSEAR, Jacob 198
KEYSER, Elizabeth 98 Sarah
198
KEYTT, Peyton 138
KEZEL, William 27
KHEEN, Sarah 160
KIBLINGER, Barbary 81 Catey
32 Daniel 32 Jacob 81
KILSH, Sally 115
KINCHELOE, Daniel 138 Paul
138 Remand S. 138 Robert E.
138
KINDALL, Robert 138
KINDELL, Betsy 148 Robert 14
Thomas G. 138
KINDLE, Mary 63
KING, Absalom 283 Azariah
138 Fanny 241 Gabriel 138
Holcombe R. 138 John 138
John F. 138-139 John S. 8
Julian 75 138 Julien 7 Maria
61 Maria F. 134 Miles Edward
138 Music D. 136 Nancy 75
Reuben 138 Rhoda 191 Robert
139 Sadrut 139 Sally 1 Sarah
56 103 Virginia A. 283
Virginius B. 139 William 138
KINGER, Virginia W. 21
KINNEY, Louisa 169 Lucy 99
Marshall 123 170 Massey 123
Mildred 261 Shelton 99
William 139
KINNY, Dudley 139 Ella 72
Shelton 139
KINSER, Susan 75

KINSOLVING, Lucy 108 Lucy
J. 266
KINZER, C.f. 8 147 Christian F.
47 139 232 Christian T. 139
Elizabeth 8 George C. 139
John 12 139 John H. 139
Mildred C. 12 Mildred Jane 47
Philip F. 139 Philip S. 139
Rachel 147 Steurman 139
Virginia 114
KINZOR, Elizabeth K. 103
Steurman 103
KIRK, Judith 2
KIRTLEY, Elizabeth 14 50 110
Elizabeth Jannet 108 Jonathan
139 Joseph 139 178 Lucy 110
Sinclear 139 St. Clair 139 188
Willis 139
KISHPAUGH, Mary F. 104
KITE, Eliza J. 48 Emma 140
George 140 Henry 140 Siram
140 William H. 48 140
KLEE/CLEE, John 140
KNIGHT, Agnes 203 Ann E. 208
Eliza Ann 154 Elizabeth 34
206 Ephriam 154 Fanny 68
James 34 Lewis 140 208 Mary
154 Mathew 203 Matthew 68
140 Sally 246 Sarah 158
William 68 140 William B. 34
62 William Butcher 140
KNIGHTEN, Benjamin F. 140 E.
Watkins 140 Frances 140
Mordecai 140 R. T. 140 Robert
A. 140 Roderick H. 140
Taliaferro 140 William 140
William J. 140
KNIGHTING, Taliaferro 48
KNIGHTON, Maggie L. 120
Roderick T. 140 William 120
KNORR, Catherine 96
KNOWLES, Lydia 194
KNOX, John 140
KORBLAR, Frederick 119
KRISE, Elizabeth 36 Jacob 141
Martha J. 36 88 114 Mary Ann
36
KUBA, William 141
KUBE, Bettie 197 Catharine
Elizabeth 197 Cornelius W.
141 Fredericka 197 Henry 141
193 John 141 197 John B. 141
Katherine 141 Mary 141

322

LEE, (continued)
Frances 84 171 254 George 15
144 155 Hannah 280 Henry 58
144 264 James 143-144 Jane
16 45 118 145 Jeny 125 John
144 John H. 24 144-145 John
Henry 144 Joseph 137 144
Kendall 144 Lafayette 144 154
Lewis H. 144 Lititia R. 151
Lizzie M. 24 Lucy 46 Luther
144 Malinda 15 Martha 58
Mary A. 252 Mary Ann 252
Milly 58 171 Moses 144
Nathaniel 16 Polly 144
Richard 144 Sally 143 Samuel
143 Sarah 154 284 Sarah I. 15
Sidney 137 Susanna 66
Sylvester S. 144 Timothy 144
William 85 144-145 254
William B. vii 145 148 171
William H. 145 284 Winifred
B. 26 Zachariah 153 Zachary
145
LEEF, Henry 214 William F. 214
LEFOE, Danel 180 Judah 180
LELAND, John vii 89 102 144
150 178 209 215 220 264 282
LEMOINE, John E. 145
LENOX, Thomas W. 159
LEONARD, Grace 135
LEWIS, Adam 145 Betsy 84
Betsy A. 260 Buller 145
Caroline 261 Cato 84 Ed 145
Eliza 270 Ellen 116 George 17
145 175 Huldah 115 James 39
145 260 Jane 248 Jim 145
John Wesley 146 Johnson 145
Kemp 145 Lizzie 165 Lucinda
73 Madison 145 Malinda 231
284 Martha 38 116 Mary 233
Mary Ann 232 Mat 39 Milly
39 145 Nancy 84 256 Philip P.
145 Putner 145 Rebecca 121
Sally 39 Thomas 145 Thomas
M. 145 Thornton 145 Virginia
A. 273 Warner 146 William
146 William B. 38 William L.
146 Willis 146
LILE, Abner 158
LILLARD, Martha 181
LIMMANDS, Elijah 146
LINDSAY, A. 251 Abby 73
Abraham 277 Absalom 26 72
Adam 86 138 182

LINDSAY, (continued)
Ambrose 281 Amelia 253
Betsy 202 Billy 147 Caleb 29
56 109 146 202 225 Charlotte
125 251 253 Clara 277
Courtena 97 Daniel 146 Eliza
257 Eveline A. 175 Harriet
227 Henry 146 James 146
James G. 9 41 153 175 197
John 146 John S. 146 Julia 272
Julia V. 232 Lancelot 146
Landon 123 146 Larkin 254
Lewis 83 252-253 Maria 26
Mary 37 43 281 Mary Susan
256 Mildred 252 Milly 277
Minor 146 Monroe 256 Moses
146 Nancy 254 Phillis 281
Phoebe 258 Reuben 146
Reubin 124 246 Rhoady 54
Robert 146 254 Salley 246
Sally 246 Sarah 254 Sarah F.
41 Squire 73 Sucky 182 Susan
26 Susan Ann 153 Susan M.
218 William 43 147 224
LINDSEY, Matilda 72 Moses
147
LINNEY, H. M. vii 11 21 31 36
39 77 175 190 198 Henry B.
147 Henry M. 147 William
147
LINTON, Moses 147
LINTOR, Peggy 178
LIPSCOMB, Arthur B. 147
Fitzhugh 121 Fleming 138 147
M. B. 59 Martha 121 Martha
F. 121 Mary Ella 59 Miles B.
30 William J. 147 Willie Ann
138
LLOYD, Belfield 147 Berlinda
36 Calvin 147 Comora F. 143
Eliz. 36 Eliza 147 235
Elizabeth 112 Ellen 17 Fanny
148 George 148 George H.
147 Henry 148 164 James 147
John 147 Lucy 256 Lucy M.
86 Mary 164 Reuben 147
Robert 112 143 147 164
Robert A. 147 Robert H. 147
Sarah 24 121 164 Thompson
148 William 148
LOBAN, James 148
LOBB, Frances 6
LOCHNER, Lewis vii Louis 115
LOCKER, Dabney 194

MELONE, (continued)
Rebeckah 204 Susan 172 204
William 163 263
MELTON, J. H. 163 Jenetta 209
Jenette 163 Samuel N. 163
MENEFEE, Spencer 163
MENSER, Mary 124
MEREDITH, Elizabeth 138 158
Jaquelin M. 163 Mary 163
Reuben 163
MERIWETHER, Charles H. 163
MERIWITHER, Garrett M. 163
MERRIWETHER, Charles 163
MERRY, Elizabeth 59 Mary 209
Prettyman 229 262
MERRYMAN, William 163 232
MICHALBACHER, M. J. 22
MICHEL, Mary E. 27
MICHENS, Caroline 63
MICHIE, James 163 James H.
163 James M. 163 John 163
Lewis 163
MIDDLEBROOK, Archibald 46
153 164 Elizabeth 179 Lucy C.
113 Martha 22 Mary Ann 153
Nathaniel 22 173 251 Susan
242
MILBURN, Sarah 15
MILLER, Adiliza 126 Alexander
vii Alonzo 150 Amanda J. 70
Andrew J. 164 Ann 125 174
Anna 164 Aylett 164 Betsy
153 Catharine 206 Catherine
276 Caty 242 Christian 164
Cornelia R. 150 Daniel 164
Elizabeth 161 227 Elizabeth
M. 54 Emma 41 Frances 103
263 Frances W. 263 George
Henry 164 Henry 164 J. H. 57
Jacob 276 James 103 164 263
James K. 164 Jane 34 220
Jesse 126 164 John 5 37 68
161 164 John A. 164 John E.
164 Judith 161 Julia S. 57
Lurenna 13 Mary 5 164 247
Raweana 68 Robert 34 164
174 180 227 247 Sally 158
Sarah 68 Thomas 13 143 158
164 172 247 263 William 13
158 220
MILLS, Alice 124 Ann 157 172
184 277 Bettie M. 277 Cely
146 Cynthia 34 Edgar 124
George 165 Hannah 16

MILLS, (continued)
Jackson 75 James 164 Jane
261 Jennie C. 33 Lucilla 124
Lucinda D. 171 Margaret 232
Mary A. 75 Milly 123 Mitchell
164 Nathanial 232 Nathaniel
34 75 124 146 191 246 Polly
99 Sarah 124 Sophia 198-199
Thomas M. 33 165 277
William 165
MILTON, James C. 165
MING, R. F. 73
MINGER, Sallie 128
MINICH, Daniel 165
MINION, John M. 165
MINNICK, Daniel 165 280 John
C. 165 Minerva 280
MINOR, Aaron 165 Addison 165
Ann 163 Ann M. 212 Dabney
90 163 Daniel 165 George 165
Hannah 123 Henry 165 Jane
151 John 123 165 Lucius 165
Lucy 212 Martha 173 Mary
172 Mary Ann 163 Mary M.
279 Sandy 165 Sarah 90 146
248 Susannah 177 Thomas 165
Thornton 146 Watson 123
MINTON, Fanny 15 John 15
MITCHEL, William 165
MITCHELL, America 279
Andrew 250 Benjamin 166
Benjamin L. 179 Catharine A.
164 Catharine A. C. 277
Clarissa 206 Clarissa J. 245
Clearissy Jane 187 Elender 26
Elijah 233 Elisabeth 4
Elizabeth 50 118 Griffin 187
Henry 143 166 I. N. 127 Isaac
N. 166 Isabella M. 179 Jane
143 Jane M. N. 250 John 166
169 187 279 Lucinda 281 Lucy
143 Mary 143 201 Mary J. 231
Nancy Ann 127 Newton 166
Polly 233 Robert 166 208
Sarah 107 Thomas 125 166
West 118 William 4 26 50 166
233 William F. 166 William S.
250 William T. 143
MODENA, Benjamin J. 166
Thomas H. 166
MODISET, Ann 61 Mary 61
MOFFETT, Anderson vii
MONCURE, Charles P. 167
Henry 166 Henry W. 166

NEWMAN, (continued)
James F. 175 235 Jane 22 39
146 Jane E. 12 24 John 46 77
146 175-176 176 John F. 257
John R. 126 175 Julia 93 Laura
265 Lucetta A. 47 Lucetta T.
150 Lucy 12 142 175 Malinda
75 206 Maria 24 78 Martha
238 Mary 110 176 Mary Ann
40 Mary E. 235 Mary F. 77
Mary Frances 63 Mildred E. 7
Morris D. 12 235 Nannie B.
257 Patsy 187 Patty 110 Polley
76 Polly 76 Reuben 7 9 12 94
176 233 Reubin 195 Robert G.
176 S. B. 93 Sarah 175 184
Sarah A. B. 87 Susan 46
Thomas 22 47 63 78 87 89 110
175-176 176 184 238 266
Viranda 265 Virandy 266 W.
E. 150 Wilhelmia 160 Willi
Anna 185 William 110 176
187 William S. 175
NEWTON, Sarah A. 89 223
NICHOLAS, Bettie 8 Frank 8 97
166 283 James 176 Ned 176
NICHOLS, Edwin 176 Frank vii
142 John 176 Sarah 100
NICKENS, Sarah 221
NICKINGS, Elizabeth 160
Nathaniel 160
NIPPER, Jacob 176
NIXON, Harrison 176 Nancy
196 286
NOLAN, Thomas 176
NOLAND, Cuthbert P. 176 R. P.
176
NOLLE, Sara E. 213
NOOMES, Joseph 176
NORFORD, Elizabeth 176 James
M. 82 176-177 James T. 177
Mary F. 82 Matthew 177
Thomas G. 177
NORMAN, Cuthbert 177
Cuthburt 240 Daniel 16 177
July Ann 240 Lucy Cary 45
NORRIS, Caleb 177 Celie 79
Henry H. 177 William 177
NORVILL, Anna M. 147
NORWELL, Ester 222
NOWELL, Tanlipy 114
NUCKOLLS, Maria 238
NUN, Sam 177 Willis 177
NUSLOW, Frances S. 108

NUTTY, Elizabeth 253
O'NEAL, Alice 191 Bridget 65
O'NEIL, Charles vii
O'SULLIVAN, Jeremiah 177
John 177 Mary 177
OAKES, Delphia 140 Lucy 280
Mainyard 177 Mary C. 142
Reubin 127 Sarah A. T. 96
Thomas 140
OAKS, Elizabeth A. 140 John 96
177 Lucy 244 Major 177 258
Mary F. 141 Mourning 258
Nancy 157 244 Polly 141
Reuben 177 Sarah 221 Thomas
A. 96 Weltha 177
OATS, Rachel 61
OFFALL, Elizabeth 102 John
102
OFFIELD, Agness 268 Diannah
268 Sarah 207
OGG, 209 Alexander 247 James
74 Jane 74 John 177 247 Laura
163 Martha 247 Peggy 87
Sarah A. 92 150 Thomas 163
William 177
OGLESBY, Ann 98
OLIVE, Elizabeth 102 James 177
Jensy 102
OLIVER, Caleb 178 Catey 268
Ealey 178 Elizabeth 111 Fanny
203 Francis 71 111 173 James
178 Killis 178 183 Lydia 71
Mary Ann 266 Nancy 173 208
Tabitha 208 268
OLLIVER, Cency 9 David 9
Frances 9 Milley 55 Tabitha 55
OLVIN, Lena 239
OMOHUNDRO, Ann 134
ORANT, John 90 178
OSBORN, Nancy 70 Robert 70
OSBORNE, Fielding 178
OSBOURNE, Isabella M. 277
OTT, Michael 178
OVERPACK, George 178
OVERTON, Beverly 178
Catherine 199 Elizabeth 157
175 Fanny 201 John 178
Joshua 178 Lucinda 117 Lucy
17 Mary 119 Mary J. 214
Nancy 118 Obediah 168 201
Peggy 135 Sidney 102 Susan
135 281 Willis 6 81 119 135
157 178 180 240

332

PAYNE, (continued)
Robert 181-182 203 Sally 12
45 Sarahn 195 Susan Ann 204
Thomas 143 152 182-183
Thornton 182 W. E. 210
William 121 181-182 William
G. 23 182 William H. 218
William W. 16 Willie S. 16
PEACHER, Alex 282 Alexander
112 Edmund 76 183 James 183
Jonathan 157 Joseph W. 183
Mary Ann D. 138 Mary F. 112
Nicy 112 Peter M. 183 Reuben
183 Sarah W. 183 William 138
183
PEARCE, John 8 Phillippa 8
PEARL, Lewis 183 Ned 183
Sally 101
PEARSON, Elizabeth 240 Joel
183 John 183 Mary 82 Peggy 2
Robert 2 198 Tabitha 198
William H. 183
PECK, Jacob 183
PENCE, Catharine 178 Elizabeth
259 John 113 183 259 Mary
113
PENDLETON, Agnes A. 148
Benjamin 183 Frances R. 107
John 183 220 John S. 183
Philip 39 Rice 183 Robert 183
PENNY, John H. 183
PENYMAN, Eliza 187
PERCEY, Charles 184
PERCY, Charles 81
PEREGORY, Moses 176
PEREGOY, Eli M. 184 John W.
184 Moses 184
PERESON, Frances 5
PERRE, Anderson 258 Julia 258
PERRY, Abraham 184 Ann 20
Benjamin 20 184 210
Benjamin R. 184 Benjamin S.
106 E. R. 37 45 90 109 119
128 144 150 155 159 173 179
182 184 209 226 229 231 237
248 253 266 278 Edmund A.
184 Elijah 184 Elijah R. 184
Elijah Richard vii Elizabeth 77
George 184 George L. 184
James 184 James Lewis 184
Jane 184 Levi L. 184 Lewis
184 Lucinda 6 111 Margaret
19 Mary 107 Moses 184
Nancy 210 Peggy 6 159

PERRY, (continued)
Peter 19-20 77 107 158 184
Rachel 20 Sally 158 Sukey 113
167 William 185 William F.
185 William W. 185
PETIT, Isaac 20
PETITT, Columbia F. 77
Fountain P. 185 Ira W. 185
PETROS, Mathew 102 Nancy
102
PETTESS, John 127
PETTETT, Fountain 57 Martha
A. 57
PETTIS, Eliza S. 29 Sally 127
Sarah 114
PETTIT, Fountain P. 77
PETTITT, Corbin Lee 185
Samuel 185
PETTY, Abner 46 Ann 222
Betsy 231 Ellen 167 Frankey
21 George 21 46 137 185 222
John 222 231 John S. 227
Lizey 46 Patrick 169 Patsy 222
Polly 169 Rebecca 222 Sally
137-138 Sarah 107 Zachary
185
PETTYS, Edmund B. 127
PEYTON, Catherine 73 Eliza P.
137 F. Bradley 185 Garnett 10
Georgianna 204 James 185
John S. 185 Peachey 185
William 34 William S. 185
PHILIPS, Catharine 185 Conyers
185 David 185-186 H. Thomas
186 Hughey 185 John W. 185
Reuben G. 185 Richard 186
229 Thomas 186 William 13
PHILLIPS, Emily 82 Thomas 82
Zachariah 185
PHIPS, Thomas 186
PIATT, William 186
PICKER, Catey 160
PICKET, Elizabeth 101
PICKETT, Charles 186 Esther
188 Mace 174 188 215
PIERCE, Amanda M. 59 Delphia
A. 97 Eliza H. 98 Frances 186
Henry M. 186 Jeremiah 105
John 59 97 186 John W. 98
186 Julia 245 Oscar J. 186
Patsy 161 Sarah 214-215
PIGG, Anny 8
PIGLEN, Margaret 164
PILCHER, Laura N. 244

POWELL, (continued)
William 21 156 189 247
William L. 14 21 209 William
Lewis 189 200 209 Willis 189
Winney 45 Winny 210 Yancey
5 189
POWERS, Jesse 221 Mildred
163
PRATT, Fanny 56 J. H. 189
Jonathan 56 Julia 108 William
189
PRESLEY, Courtenay 49 Emily
72 130 George 130 Nancy 72
251 Susan 130 Thornton 49
PRESSLEY, J. H. vii
PRESTIGE, Campbell 189
Wilson M. 189
PREWETT, Sarah 234
PRICE, Agalon 167 Catey 167
Catharine 167 Catherine 140
Elizabeth 30 41 81 97 George
30 90 George W. 189 217 J. 81
192 Jeffrey 190 Jeremiah 190
John vii 24 90 188 190 240
Joshua 190 Mary Barber 56
Mary Jane 217 Milly 104 Polly
90 Robert 190 Thomas 190
PRIEST, Albert T. 190
Augustine 190 275 Augustine
G. 190 286 Eliza A. 73
Fellows 73 Henry C. 190 Mary
E. 286
PRINDLE, Bill 115
PRITCHETT, Benjamin 190
Elizabeth 166 Harriett 208
Lucinda 69 Martha 255 Mary
F. 219 P. B. 190 Robert 18 69
176 Sarah 176
PROCTER, Oscar 190 Thomas
137 183 190
PROCTOR, Abraham 190 Betsy
187 Elisabeth 144 Elizabeth
143 Frances 19 George 94 187
190 Gracie E. 35 Hezikiah 190
Jane 148 John 94 Lucy Ann
144 Madaline 19 Mary 191
Olander 191 Sarah 94 Susan
129 206 244 Thomas 1 19 191
222 Uriah 191 William 191
PROELER, Jane 148
PRYOR, Alice 72 Louisa 223
Mary E. 259 Pleasant 191
William 72 191 223 260
PUFFER, Laura W. 39

PULLIAM, Absalom 191 David
191 Drucilla 27 James 54 John
E. 191 Mary E. 241 William
149
PURCEL, Eliza A. 155
PURKS, Martha 10
PURNELL, Mary I. R. 102
PURTON, May 191
QUAN, Daniel 65
QUANE, Mary J. 65
QUANN, Daniel 191 John D.
191
QUARLES, Ann 243 Bartlett 97
179 Charles vii 28-29 32 51 54
68 91 127 134 139 168 171
173 207 211 227 238 243 265
284 Duncan M. 191 Fleet 191
Hawkins 191 Henrietta 137
John T. 191 Julia 151 Lucy 97
Martin 26 191 Mary 191 Ona
P. 179 Patsy 187 Ralph 191
William 191 Winnie 26
QUICK, George 191
QUIN, Lucy J. 286
QUINIS, Jane 286
QUINN, Clarissa 224 Garland 66
192 Jane 203 John 66 Lucinda
66 Lucy J. 112 Mary 105
Richard 192
QUISENBERRY, Aaron 171 192
Albert 77 192 196 Amy 86
Ann 65 197 Ann F. 33
Benjamin 113 192 Bevin 192
Charles B. 246 Daniel 192
Dolly 212 Eliza 281 Elizabeth
112 142 174 183 Emily 33
George 8 77 112 183 192-193
196 232 249 281 283 286
Henry 192 212 Hezakiah 33
Hezekiah 50 192 James 54 192
Jane 196 Jannie 198 John 48
183 192 Joice 107 196 225
Lucy 28-29 283 Lucy E. 27
Lydia 68 Marina 26 245
Marina S. 246 Mary 54 65 129
Mary Ann 77 Mildred 175
Milly 8 Moses 54 68 86 107
192 Nancy 28 129 197 249
Polly 15 Salley 109 Sally 51
196 Sarah 48 193 248-249
Sidnah 175 Vivian 193 Vivion
48 192-193 197-198 285
William 183 193 225
Winneyfret 171

336

QUISENBERY, George 175
RABESKY, Anna 193 Henry
193 Philip 193
RAFFLE, Sylvia 100
RAGLAND, Letitia 258 Matilda
16 Philip W. 193 Pleasant 193
Winston 193
RAINER, Anderson 193 Frances
217
RAINES, Catherine 45 Merry
193 Polly 126 217 Walker 245
RAINS, Alpha 18 Cibba 55
Fielding 193 Mildred 191
Reubin 191 Richard 193
William 193
RALLS, Betty 50 Eliza 193 John
50 193 Minor 193 Robinson
193
RAMSDELL, Lyman 193 Oliver
193
RANDAL, Richard 194
RANDALL, Elizabeth 208
RANDEL, Nancy 259 William
259
RANDOLPH, James 4 194 John
194 Letitia 224 Margaret 4
William 194
RANSDELL, Betsy 211 John
211 Molly 81 Sanford 81 188
RANSDELL, Patty 188
RANSON, James 194
RATLIFF, Eliza W. 168
RAWLINGS, Edward T. 194
Elizabeth 20 Hannah G. 194
Henry 218 276-277 James M.
vii John L. 194 Liddy 218
Louisa 276 Lucy S. 58 Mary
Lucetta 82 Richard 58 82
Sarah J. 58
RAWLINS, Benj. 194 William
194
RAWLS, Betty 130 Ed 194 Sam
194
RAWSON, Sarah 201
RAY, Ellen 191
RAYLAND, Mary 239
READ, Albert 194 Carvel H. 194
John 194 Reuben 194 Teal 195
William 194
READER, Isaac 194
REAGAN, Malinda 80
RECTOR, Elizabeth 106 Martha
97
RED, Henry 195

REDD, Adelaide 132 272 Ann
Maria 49 Ellen 26 Henry 132
272
REDDIS, Ann V. 143
REDDISH, Lucy May 6
REED, Benjamin 195 Dicey 242
Dyannah 195 Mary Ann 257
Nancy 147
REESE, Catharine 218 John 195
REEVES, Betsy 195 Stafford
195 Timothy 195
REID, Ann 234 J. Dorsey 195
James A. 195 Reuben 279
REIDI, Margaret 81
REINS, William 195
RENNOLDS, John T. 63 179
Sarah Ann 63 William 195
REVELEY, John 270 Thomas
195 Thomas C. 195
REYNOLDS, Aaron 195 Ann
197 Benjamin F. 195 Catharine
232 234 D. G. 46 Daniel G. 44
195 Eliza 161 269 Elizabeth 15
59 149 196 Emily G. 44
Fennetta 266 Henrietta 192
James D. 197 James S. 195
John 195 John D. 195 John N.
M. 196 John T. 15 John W.
195 Joseph 196 266 269
Joseph D. 67 77 196 Laura H.
44 Lewis H. 44 196 Lillie E.
77 Lucy 15 Lucy Ann 67 Lucy
F. 225 Lucy Mary 67 Margaret
192 Mary 269 285-286 Mary
E. 53 Mary F. 46 Mary T. 15
Octavia C. 141 Philip S. 192
196 R. H. 46 Rachel 39
Richard 196 207 221 234
Robert E. 53 67 196 Sally A.
249-250 Sarah 48 192 Tabitha
39 Tobias 197 Washington 196
William 15 146 192 196 232
286 William A. 196 William
G. 197 William H. 197
William J. 197 William S. 197
William W. 196-197 William
Wise 266
RHINE, John 197
RHOADES, Achilles 197 Catlett
197 Charity 197 Clifton 178
197 Eliza 252 Elizabeth 285
Ella R. 170 George 192 197
285 John 169 197-198 212 283
John R. 170 Lillian M. 169

337

RHOADES, (continued)
Lucy 44 196 Lucy F. 196
Martha 178 Mary 99 192 Mary
Ann 70 Mary V. 212 Nancy
197 Nicholas 197 P. S. vii 21
Richard 212 Richard B. 197
Sally 278 Sarah J. 5 Susan 197
Thomas 197 197-198 284
Thomas N. 99 William 197
William H. 198
RHOADS, Catlett 192 Elizabeth
192 Epaphroditus 81 Frankey
81
RHODES, Catlett 198 Clifton
198 George 198 John 198
Nancy 198 P. S. 83 88 112
Polly 261 Richard 198 Robert
198 Theodosia 200 Thomas
198 William 225
RIADON, John H. 161
RIALL, Edward 228 Mary 228
RICE, Henry 198 Lucy 23
RICHARD, Frances 102 William
102
RICHARDS, Amanda J. 209
Ambrose 182 Ann 285
Diannah 131 Dick 268 Dinah
129 Emma D. 268 Ezekiah 173
Ezekial 85 188 194 198-199
Ferdinand 198 Fountain 198-
199 George W. 198 Hezekiah
198 Ike 64 157 198 Ikey 106
180 James 198 James P. 199
John 120 199 219 John S. 199
John W. 129 199 Lucy 157
Marie Ann 269 Mary 214
Mary A. 211 Mary E. W. 9
Minerva 85 Morgan 199
Nancy 129 269 Patty 178
Philemon 199 Philomen 131
264 Richard 5 118 141 168
174 198-199 264 269 Richard
L. 68 Robert 185 199
Robinson C. 9 199 Sallie M.
51 Sarah 188 Susan 199
Weedon 199 William 51 131
178 178 199 William W. 199
RICHARDSON, Aggy 267 Ann
Eliz. 106 Barbara A. 278
Charles 199 Charles S. 181
200 E. E. 199 Emma J. 181
George 199 Harry 199-200
267 Henry 200 John A. 106-
107 199-200 Josiah 126 200

RICHARDSON, (continued)
Mary A. 132 Quarles 200
Robert A. 200 Robert M. 200
Sarah 107 126 Sarah F. 126
Senora 97 Susan 107 William
200 William Henry 200
RICKER, Angelina 202
RICKETTS, H. 200 William H.
200
RIDDELL, James 200 Joyce 200
William 200
RIDDLE, Charles 200 Fanny 51
Fielding 200 Frances 189
Hazelworth 200 James 51 178
John 91 189 200 Lewis 200
Lucy 91 Sarah 200 Tavener
201 Tavner 201 Thompson
201 Valentine 51 178 201
William 200 Winney 178
RIDLEY, Emanuel 201 Henrietta
168 Uriel 201
RIEVES, Moses 201 William
201
RIFE, Henry 198
RIGHT, Edward 201 James 201
RILES, Alex 79 Missouri 79
RILEY, Alexander 225 227
Dorothea V. 155 Jacob 147
155 Jacob Frederick 201 John
201 Mary A. 225 Sarah A. 226
RINER, Aaron 201 Daniel 201
Jacob 101 201 282 Jacob E.
201 John 201 Mary E. 101
Matilda 101 Sarah A. E. 282
RIORDAN, George F. 201
Lafayette W. 201
RIPLEY, William 202
RIPPETO, Ann G. 185 Peter 202
Thomas P. 67 202
RIPPETOE, Sarah W. 102
RIPPITO, Elizabeth 101 John
101 William 101 202
RIVES, Louis 202 Moses 202
Nelson 261 Phil 202 Willis
202
RIXEY, John 202
ROACH, Ann 182 196 Christian
F. 157 Emanuel B. 202 Henry
D. 202 Hettie R. 53 249 Hetty
53 James 202 205 John 202
205 220 Lucy A. 12 49 215
Lucy Ann 6 250 Martha A. 77
185 Mary 157 250 Mary J. 49
Mary K. 76 Michael 202

338

ROACH, (continued)
Molly 171 Nancy 162 205
Nancy Jane 76 Robert 182 202
Sallie 57 Susan 220 279 Susan
M. 197 Thomas J. 76 William
53 202 250
ROADS, Horace 202 Samuel P.
202
ROBBARDS, Susanna 261
ROBBINS, Thomas 203 Wilber
Fiske 203
ROBERSON, Elizabeth 250
William 71 William S. 203
ROBERTS, Amos 203 Andrew
S. 203 Curtis 203 George 203
Hugh 110 203 J. P. 203 James
203 James D. vii 146 John 203
Mary 52 Nancy 110 Robert W.
203 Thomas 110 203 240
Waller 203 William 203
William H. 203
ROBERTSON, C. C. 204 John
117 203 John H. vii 37 39 94
110 130 237 Joseph H. 204
Mackenzie B. 204 Mary E. 278
Nancy 250 Octavia H. 22 103
Richard 204 Robert Randolph
204 W. E. vii Willis 204
ROBINS, John S. 203 W. F. 172
ROBINSON, Achilles D. 204
Adeline 4 Agnes 231 Amelia
274 Ann 132 Ann E. 193
Artemis 80 Artimus 42
Benjamin W. 205 Betsy 234
Beverley 132 Caroline 43 Caty
134 Charles 11 Edmund 204
Elijah 195 203 Eliza 239 Eliza
A. 164 Elizabeth 80 198
Elizabeth T. 193 Frances 148
246 Francis 11 204 246
Garland 204 George 204
Georgianna 258 Hannah 11
Hugh 204 J. L. 221 James 201
204 James E. 204 James R.
204 Jane 51 181 Jane J. 51
John 121 134 198 204 231 248
John H. 25 70 127 John J. 204
Joseph 204 Keturah 11 Lewis
D. 204 Lillie E. 127 Lucinda
56 209 Lucy 187 205 248
Lucy S. 274 Margaret 56
Maria 137 Martha E. 158
Martha J. 201 Martha P. 203
Mary 165 182 195 235

ROBINSON, (continued)
Mary Ann 4 Mary J. 140 Mary
Kent 261 Michael 205 Milly
42 Moses 17 80 96 205
Octavia 176 Patty 271 Philip
148 Phoebe 80 Richard G. 59
Richard H. 182 205 240
Richard J. 205 Richard James
203 Sarah 190 Sarah A. 162
235 Sarah E. 162 Sarah J. 59
Scylla 137 Siler 121 Sukey 43
Thomas 4 59 193 205 250
Thomas A. 205 274 Violet 97
William 38 53 61 84 121 131
151 198 205 248 257 278
William R. 158 Willis vii 1 4
24 38 41 47 84 96 117 122
130-131 145 165 174 181 216
256 273
ROBUKS, Hugh 205
RODGERS, Joseph 175 Malinda
175 Margaret R. 175
ROGERS, Achilles 228
Alexander 210 Amy 210 Ann
286 Auley 63 Benjamin 205
Charles P. 205 Chesley 205
Eliza 228 Elizabeth 140
Elizabeth F. 75 Isaac N. 205
James 205 Jermenius 206 John
63 87 206 210 Jonathan 206
Jos. 206 Joseph 75 126 206
230 Kelles 206 Maria N. 126
Nancy 272 Polly 87 Rachel A.
97 Reuben 206 Robert H. 206
Sally 271 Samuel 206 Sarah
286 Thomas 206 William 206
ROHR, John 206 John F. 206
Robert M. 206
ROLL, Roberson 207
ROLLINS, Mary 7 Mary A. 259
Richard 207
ROLLS, Eliza 61 Frank 207 John
61 207 Martha 261 Ophelia
Ann 34 William 34
ROOT, George 207 Herbert A.
207
ROSE, Allen 207 Henry 207
James 207 Nancy 5 Robert H.
130 207 Robert N. 207
ROSEMBAUM, Theresa 90
ROSS, Jennie 226 Judy 215
Lewis 216 Margaret 106 Patsy
179
ROSSER, Ephraim 101

ROSSON, Archelaus 207
ROSZELL, Delphea 233
ROTHROCK, George 207
ROTHWELL, Benjamin C. 207
  John 207
ROUSER, Sarah 282
ROUTT, Ancel P. 207 Dorenda
  A. 159 Elbert 47 Lucy 75 Lucy
  S. 104 Martha E. 248 Mary F.
  47 William P. 47 56 Winney
  110 151
ROW, Abner 138 Ann 26 Biddy
  92 Cynthia 138 Edmund 14 26
  138 Elhanon 45 192 196 202
  207 221 Elizabeth 270
  Elizabeth K. 196 Elkanon 270
  Hetty 270 Mary 26 Mary E.
  192 Mildred C. 215 221 Milley
  84 Rachel 16 Sarah J. 221
  Sarah Jane 221 Thomas 16 26
  84 191 202 207 270 Tincey
  202 William 84
ROWE, James W. 208 John S.
  208 Keeling 208
ROWLAND, Isaac 208 William
  H. 208
ROWZIE, Frances 104
ROYSTER, Jane 111
RUBY, Cathrin 193
RUCKER, Albert 208 Albert G.
  186 Allen 208 Belfield 208
  Catey 34 Columbia 115 Elliot
  208 Ellzy 208 Ephriam 208
  Frances 153 Frankey 268
  James 208 Jane 186 Joel 108
  208 208 John 108 208 268
  Kitty 250 Larkin 166 Legrand
  115 227 Lucy 253 Margaret
  227 Margaret S. 215 Mary 96
  108 255 Milly 108 Minor 208
  Peter 114 208 Polly 96 Robert
  250 Sarah 153 Sarah A. 164
  Thornton 208 215 William 35
  50 69 96 153 208 215 253
  Wisdom 208
RUFFIN, Silva 100
RUFFLES, Silvia 99
RUMBAUGH, Jacob 208
RUMBOUGH, Jacob 65 216
RUMSEY, Dysa 194 Elijah 208
  Elizabeth 271 James 209
  Lianna 137 Lucy 66 Mary 64
  Nancy 166 Peggy 196

RUMSEY, (continued)
  Thomas 166 196 209 Walker
  209 William 11 66 209
RUNKEL, George 209
RUNKLE, Emanuel 209 George
  209 George M. 209 George W.
  85 Jacob 100 Mary Macklin
  100 St. Clair 209 Susan M. 85
  William H. 209
RUNNOLDS, William 209
RUSSELL, Nehemiah 209
  Patsey 29 Patsy 91 William
  209
RYAN, Maria 262 Nancy 201
SACEY, Allie 113
SACRA, Charles R. 209 Sarah
  A. 56 Thomas J. 56
SACRE, Beverley 209 Thomas J.
  209
SALE, Catharine E. 61 Eliz. S.
  229 John W. 61 209 246
  Mollie E. 94 Robert C. 94 168
  210 Virginia M. 168 William
  B. 210
SALMER, Eveline 76
SAMAR, John 210 John H. 210
SAMPSON, Elijah 210 Elizabeth
  16 Frances 189 George 210
  James 210 John 40 98 210
  Louisa 40 Lucy 98 Margaret
  262 Mary 265 Sally 210
  Thomas 210 Virginia Ann 101
  William 101 189 210
SAMS, John 210 266 Nancy 266
SAMUAL, Amanda 3
SAMUEL, Adaline C. 28
  Amanda 60 134 Andrew 225
  Andrew C. 210 Arkansas C.v.
  222 Carrie V. 49 Henry 126
  Lucy Catharine 222 Maria 222
  Meshach 210 Philemon 46 222
  Polly 126 Sarah E. 247
  Thornton V. 49 Trenton E. 28
  210 Trenton V. 49
SANDAGE, Lucy 146 219
SANDERS, Ann 22 211 Ann J.
  234 Benj. 210 Benjamin 6 29
  84 210 Benjamin T. 210 Cora
  J. 198 Dudley T. 210 Elizabeth
  215 Emily 103 249-250
  Francis J. 29 211 234 Hansford
  F. 261 Hansford T. 4 196 211
  Harriet 61 James 199 211 233
  Joanna 84 John 84 207

SEBREE, (continued)
Nancy 18 235 Richard 214
William 214
SEE, Almyra A. 35 Charles S.
M. viii Dallas 214 Delilah 88
141 Jacob 214 James 35 John
H. 20 214 Lucy Ellen 20 Mary
A. 252 Willis 214
SEEDS, Benjamin 214 George
W. 214
SEEF, Henry 214 William F. 214
SEEVERS, Christopher 214
SEIDELL, Elizabeth A. 195
Mary 195
SEKLE, Peter 81
SELDEN, Samuel M. 214
Samuel M. 214
SELF, Mary 80 Matthew 214
Samuel 215
SEPIN, Joseph Q. 215
SEPON, George W. 215
SERGEANT, Nathaniel 270
SEWERS, Christopher 215
SHACKELFORD, Dabney O.
207 Uriel 215 Zachariah 215
SHACKLEFORD, Edmund 215
SHADRACH, John 215 Lucy
190 S. 207
SHADRACK, Elizabeth 249
Frances 249 Frances M. 249
Jobe 248 John 248 Molly 248
Nelly 213 Sarah 249 Thomas
215
SHADRICK, John 213
SHAPE, Mary A. 72
SHARMAN, George 44
SHARMARARD, Elisha 215
SHARP, David 215 Winston 276
SHARPE, Dany 173 Esther 173
SHAVERS, Polly 283
SHAW, Thomas J. 215
SHA__, Dennis 236
SHEARMAN, Alice 127 George
127 George W. 180 John 253
John H. 127 215
SHEELOR, Nancy 188 Rachel
257
SHEFLET, Waller C. 217
SHELAR, Caty 133 James 188
John 133
SHELLER, John 215
SHELLY, Resin 128

SHELTON, Frances D. 162 Lucy
41 Lurenna M. 262 Thomas
162 215 262 William 162 262
SHENK, Anne T. 15
SHEPHERD, Abraham 225
Abram 215 Alexander 18 215
Andrew 33-34 59 101 198 263
Andrew T. 216 C. R. 12
Catherine 59 Edward 114
Elizabeth Bell 101 Elizabeth
M. I. 12 Emma J. 225 George
99 215 Harriet 99 Hattie M.
261 Helen 18 James 105 205
215-216 216 James V. 216
John M. 216 Lucy 52 Maria
274 Maria L. 205 Mary 33
Mary Miller 99 Mollie 83
Nancy 147 Robert 261 Robert
W. 216 Wash 84 Wash. 52
William 101 216
SHER, Robert 216
SHERICK, Philip B. 216
SHERMAN, Jesse 216
SHIEER, Jane 202
SHIFFLET, Absalom 189
Bennett 216 Edmund 216
Edward 216 Felix 216 James
216 John 216 Nancy 189
Overton 216 Phebe 216 Polly
216 Rhoda 216 Slaton 216
Thomas 271 Vina 216
SHIFFLETT, Archibald 216-217
James 217 John 217 Merry 217
Mordecai 217 Pickett 217
Pleasant 217 Polly 217 Powell
217 Richard 217 Sarah F. 82
Slaten 217 Trice 217
SHIFLET, John 217
SHIFLETT, Archer 217
Archibald 44 Bluford P. 217
Elizabeth 2 179 215 Fanny 170
Frances 215 James 57 John
214 Malinda 217 Mordecai 24
170 Patsy 169 Sarah 81 170
Stephen 217 Sukey 170 Waller
C. 217 Wilhelma 44 William
169-170 Winny 179
SHIP, E.g. 27 50 70 86 96 120
164 177 194 200 204 216 220
246-247 Edward 234 Edward
G. viii 38 263 James T. 217
Martha 55 Robert M. 218
SHIPP, Edward G. 218 John M.
218

342

SLEET, (continued)
Sarah Carter 80 Weedon 22
222 279 William C. 64
SLOVAM, Elizabeth 79
SMATTS, Betsy 81
SMILEY, William 222
SMILLET, Jane W. 5
SMITH, Absalem 133 Absalom
222 Absolem 222 Agnes 205
282 Albert 40 123 Alberta 276
Ambrose 222 Ambrose A. 152
Amy 39 146 Angelina 53 Ann
149 Ann E. 33 Anna 274
Annie 100 Archie 116
Arianner 164 Barbara 276
Barnett 163 Benjamin 179
Benjamin M. viii Betsy 117
Bradford 223 Caleb 53 223
Caleb A. 223 225 Caroline 182
Catharine 64 125 150 245 Caty
224 Charles 223 Charles E.
223 Christiana 226 Coalby 121
Colby 223 D. T. 223 Daniel
225 Daniel M. 223 David H.
225 Dealen 192 Delia 1
Delpha 242 Downing 223
Edmund 223 Edward 223 Eliz.
223 Eliza 67 Elizabeth 10 53
64 133 168 238 254 Elizabeth
W. 65 Ellen 98 Ellen H. 30
Elzy 223 Emily 52 Ernest C.
223 Fayette 52 Frances 104
109 238 254 Frances S. 152
Francis M. 223 Gaspar 245
Gasper 98 George 28 104 125
212 222 224 226 261 George
A. viii Georgie E. 223 Harison
98 Harriet 236 Harris 4 225
Henry 33 Ida I. 191 Isaac 100
227 James 1 48 53 174 213
224 James O. 224 262 286
James W. 223-225 Jane 4 189
224 250 Jane E. 184 Jere 225
Jeremiah 238 254 John 8 67 75
98 164 185 224 251 254 John
C. 191 John R. 224 John W.
224-225 Joseph 226 245 Judith
179 Laura 37 Lena 43 Lewis
225 Louisa S. 286 Lucinda 226
Lucy 69 185 204 Lucy Ann
224 Marcellus W. 225
Margaret 182 Maria 109 237
Marion M. 225 Martha 104
Martha A. 134 Mary 28 33 212

SMITH, (continued)
Mary A. 40 98 223 225 Mary
E. M. B. 225 Mary Eliza 262
Mathias 225 Mildred 53 Nancy
116 208 251 Noah 225 Origen
226 Oswald 225 Owen 225
Pamelia 226 Patience 98 Patsy
116 265 Patty 75 Peter C. 223
Philip 225 Polly 75 245
Presley 225 Presley N. 79 Raif
75 Raife 224 Rebecca Hite 168
Reuben 225-226 Rice 226
Richard A. 225 Robert 225-
226 Robert A. 225 Robert J.
225 Sallie J. 238 Samuel 48 86
126 208 225-226 Sarah 60 98
174 233 Sarah Ann Elizabeth
212 Sarah E. 235 Sarah J. 40
Sarah L. 48 Serrepta A. 185 St.
Clair 226 Stephen 226 Sukey
224 Susan 4 98 127 184 225
Susannah 242 Tabby 122
Tartan 226 Thomas 223-224
226 Timoleon 226 Ursilla 265
William 33 98 224 226-227
227 245 William B. 226
William F. 224 William Henry
226 William J. 226 William M.
225-227 William S. 40
William T. 30 223 226-227
Wilson 225 Zachary 227
SMITHERS, Howard S. 227
John S. 227
SMITHSON, Amanda 19
SMOOT, Caleb 91 101 159 227
James T. 227 Jenifer 227 John
227 Nancy 101 W. H. 227
SMOUTS, John 227
SNEED, Alice 61 Helen 270
Henry A. 38 L. W. 227 Milly
61 Sarah E. 162 William 61
William T. 227 Winston 61
270
SNELL, Amanda Melvina 263
Caty 82 Caty A. 229 Eastham
111 Eastman 150 John 156 211
Joseph 227-228 246 263 Lucy
A. M. 20 Lucy A. M. 246 Lucy
Ann Mitchell 246 Lucy M. 286
Margaret 156 Mildred 71 Patty
51 Philadelphia 204 Robert
204 229 Sally Garnett 150
SNELSON, Mary 12 Polly 22
SNODDY, F. A. 280

SNODGRASS, Ann S. 162 Paul
V. 228
SNORR, Wiatt 228
SNOW, Agnes 259 Augustine
228 Berd 228 Bird 60 Early
228 Henry 203 Holand 228 Icy
217 James 119 228 Jenny 41
John 217 228 Mary 9-10 60
Polly 33 Raney 217 Rutha 277
Saluda 49 Sarah 42
SNYDER, Aby 276 William 228
SNYDOR, Patsy 208
SOMERVILLE, James 228 Mary
E. 228
SOMMERS, Edgar F. 228
George A. 228
SOMMERVILLE, Harrison 228
Jane E. 20
SOREL, Mary E. 22
SORRELL, Ann 246 Lucy J. 114
Mary Ann 114 140 221
SORRILLE, Elizabeth 164 John
228 John N. 228 Joseph C. 228
Maria Ann 18 Nancy 166
Sarah Ophelia 158 Thomas 18
74 158 164 166 203 220 228
Virginia 220
SORVELL, Jos. 182
SOUDER, Charles M. 228
SOUTHARD, Elias 229
SOUTHARDS, Mildred 41
SOUTHERLAND, Alex 132
Catharine 186 Eliza 5 James 5
James L. 229 John 5 229 Julia
225 Julia A. 79 Mary E. 132
Mildred 36 98 Nancy 208
Robert 36 Sarah Jane 169
William 229 William P. 208
SOUTHERLIN, Alexander 229
Diana 229 William 229
SOUTHWORTH, Martha 200
SOVIELL, Mary 244
SOVILL, Mary A. 10
SOVRELL, Laura E. 182
SOWDER, Elias 228
SPALDING, Robertson 229
SPANGLER, Mary E. 117
SPEERS, Elizabeth 259
SPENCER, Ann 116 244
Caroline 122 Catharine 87
Edward 229 Elizabeth Gaines
168 Fanny 130 Francis 229
George 229 James 229 Jane
109 Joseph 168 234 244

SPENCER, (continued)
Laura 130 Martha Ann 229
Sarah J. 153 Seth 229 William
130 Winifred 47
SPERRY, Peter viii
SPICER, Benjamin 229 David
229 George S. 229 John S. 229
Rawser 229
SPILMAN, Alex H. 164 Maria
235 Mary 164 Robert B. 164
SPINDLE, Jefferson 229 John E.
229 Lucy J. 144 150
SPOTSWOOD, Albert 230
Alexander D. 230 Ann E. W.
257 Catharine H. 191 Edmonia
94 Ellen 267 Jack 230 John
145 230 256 John R. 230 Juda
190 Lewis 230 Martha P. 191
Mary 256 Mary B. 145 Mary
S. 210 Phil A. 210 Robert 22
Robert G. W. 145 Susannah C.
22 William L. M. 191 257
Winnie 70
SPOTTS, Sarah 266
SPRADLIN, John 230
SPRADLING, David 9 Nancy 9
SPRAGLE, Mary E. 117
SPRIGGS, Ebenezer 230
SPROUSE, Alexander 66
Angelina 66 Elizabeth 266
William 230 William H. 230
SPROWER, Charles 230
STAGE, David R. 230
STANARD, Adam 129 Beverley
194 Beverly 230 Cassie 129
Charles 230 Elizabeth Janeiro
120 Ellen B. 215 Fanny P. 215
Harriet 135 Julia 71 91 Mary
Champe 280 Mary E. 43 129
Mildred C. 194 Robert B. 230
Robert Beverley 215 Sarah
Ann Ophelia 228 William H.
120 190 228 280
STANTON, Ann 240 Betty 230
Beverly 230 Charity 240
Christy 86 Elizabeth 241
Jemimah 230 Sally 86 Spencer
230
STAPLES, Elizabeth 89 Sarah F.
201 William 230 William E.
89 201
STAPP, Achilles 231 James 255
Thomas 231
STARKEY, Frances E. 194

345

STUBBLEFIELD, Bettie Ellen
96 Catharine 251 Elizabeth
Hackley 47 Frances 223
George 47 223 234 272 James
234 Mary 243 Mary Ann 272
Sarah 243 Smith 136 Susan 95
Thomas 95 107 243
STUBBLING, Susanna 81
STUBBS, Jacob 209 Jesse H.
234 Virginia 99
STUNZ, Fredericka 141
STYERS, Leonard 235
SUDDUTH, George A. 235
Thomas J. 235
SUGGET, Elizabeth 224
SUGGETT, Elizabeth 224
SULIVAN, John 147
SULLIVAN, Ann 136 Dawson
235 Delilah 81 Emiline 280
Emily 280 Eveline 276 Everet
235 Everit 64 George 155
Laura Jane 155 Margaret 118
R. B. 159 Richard B. 235
William 81
SUMMERVILLE, Jane F. 263
SUPTON, Daniel N. 134 Kate E.
134
SURRY, Caty 80
SUTHAND, Mary 28
SUTHERLAND, Alex 226
Alexander 68 Betsy 202
Catherine 226 Joseph 202 Julia
227 Kennith 235 Mary 73
Polly 68 Richard W. 235 Sarah
J. 197 William 235
SUTHERLIN, Sarah J. 170
SUTHERLING, Eliza M. 141
William 141
SUTPHIN, Mary F. 227
SUTTON, Catherine 98
Elizabeth 52 106 Mildred 139
Nancy 224 William 98 106
224 235
SWAIN, James H. 235 William
E. 235
SWAN, Alexander 207 Catharine
196 Ellen A. 207 Frank 235
Robert G. 235 Robert S. 235
Samuel 196
SWANN, Annie W. 148 Charles
W. 148 George W. 235 Hatch
196
SWARTSWELDER, William
235

SWARTZ, Frederick 235 George
235
SWATS, Jacob F. 235
SWEENEY, Mary E. 282
Thomas M. 282
SWENEY, Daniel 236
SWIFT, Calvin 236 Harlan J.
236 Jane 236 Sally A. 49
William T. 236
SWINDELL, Joel S. 236 Joseph
236
SWISER, David 236
SWITZER, Lawrence 236
SYDE, Jane F. 59
SYLVA, George 236
SYLVEY, Lucy 224 William
224
SYLVIE, Sally 9
TAIT, Moses 236 Nelson 236
TALIAFERO, Baldwin 42
Jackson 236 Scott 236
TALIAFERRO, 122 Ann 15 80
179 237 259 Ann Hay 12
Annie P. 22 Baldwin 256
Caroline 237 Charles 39 277
Charles C. 63 210 Dick 237
Edmund P. 103 Edmund T. 22
Elizabeth 80 116 119 Ella 277
Ellen 260 Ellen B. 194 230
Fannie 263 Fanny 239 Francis
108 237 George G. 1-2 90 236
Hay 57 108 159 236 247
Henrietta 256 Horace D. 236-
237 Horace G. 237 Isaac 237 J.
P. 237 Jackson 237 James L.
270 Jane A. 39 Jaq. P. 237
John 179 236-237 John F. 158
John Henry 237 John S. 236
John T. 236 Julia Ann 90
Lawrence 57 80 237 Lawrence
H. 237 Lewis 80 237 Louisa
G. 39 Lucy 267 Lucy Mary
248 Maria 131 Martha H. 15
Martha M. 229-230 Mary M.
1-2 Mary V. 158 Matilda 108
Nicholas 237 Richard H. 236
Sarah 57 Sarah D. 159 Susan
F. 247 Thomas Garland 237
Tom 267 Verlinda 52 Victoria
103 William 119 237 William
Q. 237 Willis 237
TALLEY, Anderson 238 Delilah
134 Ida I. 190 James S. 238
Jane E. 79 Lucy M. 155

347

TALLEY, (continued)
Lucy V. 140 Mary F. 254
Mary J. 133 Meriwether 133-
134 Merriweather 238 Nathan
238 Nathan M. 238 Peyton 190
Peyton G. 238 Prudence W.
238 Richard 140 William E.
155 William N. 238
TAMEWOOD, Agnes 282
TAMPLIN, Amanda 8 186
Edward 186 Frances 59 97
Frances W. 186 Sarah 136 239
TANDY, Amanda 171 Ann 157
Emma 253 Frances 34 192
Henry 157 171-172 184 238
253 Jackson 183 Mary 172
Nancy 184 Roger 34 184 238
Will 157
TANNER, Eunice 107 James
107 Mollie T. 107
TANSEL, Malinda 75
TANSIMON, Lewis 238 Thomas
238
TAPP, Wincent 238
TARRY, Fountain 122 Lila 122
TATE, A. L. 238 Elizabeth 244
John W. 238 Malvina 6 Nancy
115 Nelson 6 Uriah 115
TATHAM, Jane 219
TATTUM, Elizabeth 169
TATUM, Alexander G. 238
Isham viii 46 179 238 Joseph
H. 238 Mary 238 Mary A. 12
235 Rachel A. 29 Sarah E. 245
Thomas 238 William 8
TAYLOE, George E. 238 George
P. 238
TAYLOR, Absolem 238 Adeline
97 Aggy 232 Agnes 40 138
Albert 63 239 241 Alec 258
Alexander 239 Andrew 239
Andrew J. 239 Ann M. 65 Ann
Pendleton 56 Arrena 278
Barbour 72 Ben 82 Benjamin
W. 239 Bennet 47 Betsey 3
Betsy Hord 69 Bettie T. 204
Billy 57 Catherine 47
Chapman 29 Charles 40 52 80
127 138 163 239 241 Charles
W. 239 Conway 239 Daniel
239 283 Dinah 25 Dorothy 30
Edmund 240 278 Edmund P.
230 Edward 239 Eleanor 175
Eli 240 Elijah 240

TAYLOR, (continued)
Eliza Jane 275 Elizabeth 90
105 183 Elizabeth G. 127
Ellen 239 Eloise 278 Erasmus
10 Eugenie 221 Evelina M.
171 Frances 34 Francis 10 35
48 118 240 Frank 240
Gabriella 32 124 Garland B.
127 240 George 240 George B.
240 George G. 241 George W.
239 Georgianna 204 Harriet 52
Jacob 25 165 James 2 11-12 17
35 48-49 54 56 86 89 110 125
183 212 220 233 240-241 244
253 255 262 277-278 James H.
240 Jane 118 191 Jane F. 105
Jeanne 47 John 240-241
Jonathan 241 Joseph 239 241
Judy 122 Julia 267 Kitty 283
Larkin 241 Levi G. 241
Lucinda 35 216 Lucretia 210
Lucy 10 72 Lurenna 162
Margaret 220 Margaret Ann E.
147 Maria 63 Martha 202
Mary 11 29 125 165 244 258
Mary Conway 241 Matilda
129 243 Matilda R. 169 Milley
244 Milly 99 172 Mollie 165
Nancy 47 116 214 Nelson 241-
242 Nettie 99 Pascal 210
Patrick D. 241 Rebecca 82
Reuben 241 Richard 241
Richard S. 65 Robert 34 171
175 204 221 241 Robinette
195 Robinette F. 195
Samantha 70 Sarah 48 86 126
163 Sarah Eliz. 258 Spencer
97 239 258 St. Clair 214
Stclair 35 Stanton 241 Thomas
N. 239 Virginia 123
Washington 241 William 105
202 241 William B. 2 103
Wilson 241-242 Zachariah 126
208 210 241-242 Zachary 242
TEALE, Henry 112 Sarah 112
TEASDALE, Martin C. 242
TEASEDALE, Thomas 242
TEEL, Henry 194 242 John 242
Samuel 242
TEMPLE, John 242
TERMAN, Milly 277
TERRELL, 204 Edmund 242
Elizabeth 43 Henry C. 242
Jane 18 John 242 Julia 139

348

THORNTON, (continued)
Daniel 247 Daniel M. F. 247
Elizabeth Ann 275 Frances
247 Frankie 33 George 69 139
208 227 247 Henry 247 James
222 247 Jesse 247 John 247
John C. 73 John S. 54 Leanna
90 Lizbeth 266 Lucy Buckner
227 Luke 247 266 275 Mary
Ella 73 Mary Presley 139
Moses 116 Nancy 240 266
Peter 139 247 Rebecca 116
Sally 252 Seamia 128
Solomon 247 Sydney 222
Taliaferro 208 Thomas 247
281 Thomas S. 247 William 73
81
THORPE, Peggy 255
THRACKWELL, Sarah 87
THRIFT, George N. 217 247
Robert 248
THRUSTON, Lucy Mary 236
William Plummer 236
THURMAN, Benjamin F. 248
Nathan 248
THURSTON, Albert 35 223
Anthony 117 238 Dick 248
Harriet 271 Herrn 248 James
Herrn 248 Jane 245 Maria 116
Mary 31 31-32 Nellie 109
Richard 248 Sally 238 Samuel
248 Thornton 248 William 109
William Plumer 248
TIBBS, Aggy 145 Betsy 139
Elliott 33 F. 30 58 63 72 122
241 276-277 Frances 118 132
Frank 3 6 16 27 43 97-99 122-
124 124 133 137 154 197 225
239 241 250-251 261 270-271
281-282 Franklin viii 17 32 79
116 241 273 George 3 118 248
George W. 248 Gray 39
Harriet 132 Jane 118 Mary 118
Rhody 241 Sarah 250 Tabby
181
TILDEN, Barbara 175
TILGHMAN, Barbara 204
TIMBERLAKE, George 248
James L. 248 Margaret 69
Mary A. E. 104 Philip 248
Rachel 58
TINDAR, James 248
TINDER, Adaline Tutt 142
Alepain 73 Amanda L. 113

TINDER, (continued)
Amos E. 248 Ann 37 37-38 77
248 Anthony 37 62 76 248-249
Arthur 160 Arthur R. 19 248
Benjamin 243 249 Catharine
62 Cornelia A. 160 E. J. 133
Edgar A. 249 Elizabeth 9 135
199 249 Elizabeth J. 249
Elizabeth L. 199 Elizabeth R.
188 Ephraim 73 Eugene E. 141
George T. 188 249 George W.
248-249 James 215 249-250
266 James R. 19 103 199 249
Jane 19 Jane Ann Frances 19
Jemimah 73 Jesse 73 249 John
114 249 John A. 249 John F.
249 John S. 249 John T. 249
Lucie A. 249 Lucy 76 266
Lucy Ann 266 Lucy R. 160
Lydia J. 44 Margaret 1 6 134
Mary E. 135 Mildred 135
Mildred A. 133 Mildred S. 135
Nancy 142 Nannie J. 133
Priscilla 77 142 Richard 157
249 Robinson 37 62 76
Robinson C. 249-250
Robinson G. 44 Sarah E. 198
Sarah M. 249 Susan Ann 103
Talmon D. 249 Thomas 2 113
135 141-142 249 266 Thomas
R. 133 135 249 Thomas T. 250
Waller M. 250 William M. 250
Zabdal B. 250
TINSLEY, Abraham 166 Betty
208 Edw. 12 Edward 6 49 215
250 Harriet 237 James W. 250
John 208 Mary F. 49 Milly
S.v. 215 Sarah B. 12 Susan A.
6 William 151 256
TIPPETT, Luvina 203 Samuel
203
TIPTON, John T. 266 Mary
Davis 266
TISDALE, Jane Q. 204 Lemuel
250
TODD, William 250 William H.
250
TOLES, Bejamin 250 Nelson
250
TOMLINSON, George 250 268
John 250 Sally 28 William 28
69 214
TOMPKINS, James M. 250
William 250

350

TOWLES, Albert 250 Ann 243
Benjamin 251 Bettie C. 88
Fanny 99 Frances 136 Henry
250 Mary C. 251 Nelson 250
Richard 251 Thomas 251
Thomas T. 195
TOWNS, Absalom 38 213 251
Charlotte 128 Isreal 251
Malinda 213 Mary Ella 38
Pannill 251 William 251
TOWNSEND, Elizabeth 268
Jerusa 2
TREASEY, Mary 64
TREVILIAN, Charles G. 251
TRIBBLE, Joseph 269
TRIBLINGS, Pallas 5
TRICE, Ann 251 Jesse 251 Joe
251 Mary F. 50 Monroe 251
Samuel 50
TRIPLETT, Dick 251 Philip 251
Robert C. 251 William H. 251
TROWER, Solomon 251
TRUE, Delila 12 Martin 12
Thomas 251
TRUEBLOOD, Ann 103
TUCKER, George 251 Jacob 251
John W. 108 Thornton 211 251
TUEL, Frances S. 286 Isaac 251
Mary 251 Socrates 252
Thomas 251-252
TUELL, James 83 Thomas J. 252
TULLOCH, William 252
TULLUS, Elizabeth 252 Joseph
D. 252 Rhodam 252
TURNELY, Francis 252
TURNER, Anderson 252 Ann 53
159 255 Ann M. 3-4 Anna M.
4 Cary 159 Catlett 252
Charlotte 83 Clary 159 Delphy
56 Elijah 252 Elisha 252 Eliza
F. 237 Elizabeth A. 248
Ezekiel 56 252 Fleming 252
George 252 Grace 187 J.
Waller 252 James 159 252 255
James H. 252 John 99 252
Johnson 258 Lavinia 258
Lucretia M. 255 Lucy 258
Mary 187 255-256 277 Milly
28 84 Nancy 255 Nelson 252-
253 277 Peggy 166 Polly 53
Robert 187 252 Texana 99
Thomas 253 Virginia S. 278
William 255 William H. 278
Zeph 52

TURNLEY, Edmund 253 Edwin
253 John 190 253
TUTMAN, Elizabeth 175 John
175
TUTT, Mary 47
TWENTYMAN, Bononi 253
TWENTYMEN, Betsy 90
Jonathan 166 Polly 24
TWIMAN, George viii
TWYMAN, Alfred 166 253
Alice 186 Anthony 253
Frances 206 Isaac S. 253 John
253 Jonathan 164 253 Judah
267 Judith 267 Martha A. 128
Mordecai 253 Nancy 247
Paschal 253 Reuben 253
Reubin 65 Robert 253 Robert
D. 60 Samuel 247 267 Scott
253 Smith 253 Thornel 253
Travis J. 253
TWYMN, Judith 267
TYLER, Absalom 224 254
Amanda 284 Byrd 254
Charlotte 247 Emma Jane 262
Fanny 188 James 254 284
James E. 254 Jane 247 John
254 John B. 254 Major 254
Richard 254 Tamer 62 Violet
188 Washington 254 William
254 William H. 254
TYREE, Betty 176 John 254
Lettie 100
UNDERWOOD, Gideon 254
Jacoons 254
URQUET, Charles 188
URQUHART, Elizabeth 11
Samuel L. 17
UTZ, Susan 255
VASS, Emily 252 Henry S. 254
Martha 260 Thomas 254
Vincent 208 254 Walker 254
VAUGHAN, Bluford Edward
254 C. T. 8 270 Charles 254
Cornelius 189 254 Cornelius
G. 255 Edwin 255 Elmellia
189 Harriet E. 44 Henrietta 58
Joseph 255 Joseph P. 255
Pascal 44 Paschal 255 Robert
255
VAUGHN, Ada 207 Barlinda 44
Birlinda 217 C. T. viii 31 109
148 Elizabeth 21 Fanny 255
Horace 255 James 12

353

354

355

Heritage Books by Therese Fisher:

*CD: Heritage Books Archives: Virginia Marriage Records*

*Marriage Records of the City of Fredericksburg, and of
Orange, Spotsylvania, and Stafford Counties, Virginia, 1722–1850*

*Marriage Records of the City of Fredericksburg,
and the County of Stafford, Virginia, 1851–1900*

*Marriages in the New River Valley, Virginia:
Montgomery, Floyd, Pulaski, and Giles Counties*

*Marriages in Virginia: Spotsylvania County, 1851–1900
and Orange County, 1851–1867*

*Marriages of Caroline County, Virginia, 1777–1853*

*Marriages of Orange County, Virginia, 1747–1880*

*Marriages of Orange County, Virginia, 1757–1880*

*Skeletons in the Closet: 200 Years of Murders in Old Virginia*

*Vital Records of Three Burned Counties: Births, Marriages, and Deaths of
King and Queen, King William, and New Kent Counties, Virginia, 1680–1860*